P9-EEP-655

WILSON:

Campaigns for Progressivism and Peace, 1916-1917

BY THE SAME AUTHOR

Wilson: The Road to the White House
Wilson: The New Freedom
Wilson: The Struggle for Neutrality, 1914-1915
Wilson: Confusions and Crises, 1915-1916

WILSON

CAMPAIGNS FOR

PROGRESSIVISM AND PEACE

1916-1917

By ARTHUR S. LINK

PRINCETON, NEW JERSEY

PRINCETON UNIVERSITY PRESS

1965

Printed in the United States of America
by Princeton University Press
Princeton, New Jersey

FOR

JOHN W. LINK, JR.

AND

JOHN M. DOUGLAS, M.D.

THIS fifth volume in my study of the life and times of Woodrow Wilson begins with the immediate background of the presidential campaign of 1916, following the happy settlement of the *Sussex* crisis, and concludes with the adoption of the war resolution against Germany in April 1917. This period was crowded with events of momentous significance for Wilson, the American people, and the entire world. Wilson's apprenticeship in statecraft, particularly in diplomacy, had long since ended by the time that events in this volume begin, and we now see him at full maturity as a masterful leader driving his party and Congress and as a diplomatist of increasing deftness and skill, constantly probing and deploying. During this same period Wilson also grew markedly in powers of leadership and in understanding of the European war and the role that he thought America should play in the unfolding tragedy of mankind.

This volume has two great themes. One is Wilson's orientation toward advanced progressivism and his success in creating a new coalition to carry him to victory in the presidential election of 1916. The other is the President's campaign for mediation, which he began early in 1916 and carried to culmination later in that year and early in 1917. It marked the first American thrust into European affairs since the founding of the United States. This volume describes Wilson's emergence as a world leader just beginning to voice mankind's hopes for a different international order, along with the varying European reactions to the President's efforts.

There is no need to repeat what I said in the preceding volume in this series, *Wilson: Confusions and Crises, 1915-1916*, about the sources for the study of this period of American history. But I am obliged to repeat the following statement:

Thanks to the kindness of certain individuals who must remain anonymous, I was given access to an important French diplomatic archive that contains voluminous materials relating to Anglo-French, Franco-American, and Anglo-American relations during the period of American neutrality. The sole condition imposed was that I should neither quote directly from the documents nor cite them. This accounts for the absence of footnotes in many instances. I must ask my readers to believe that I have taken extraordinary care in copying, translating, and using documents in this collection.

Completion of this fifth volume brings to an end my story of American reactions to the European war and Wilson's policies toward the belligerents during the period of American neutrality, 1914-1917. Perhaps this is a good place to make some general remarks about what the evidence in my third, fourth, and fifth volumes seems to say on these subjects:

1. The evidence, especially Wilson's correspondence with Secretaries Bryan and Lansing now in the archives of the State Department, shows clearly that Wilson played the dominant role in the conduct of foreign policies, wrote much of the important diplomatic correspondence, and made all vital decisions, often contrary to the advice of Bryan, Lansing, and House.

2. The evidence, particularly in the fourth and fifth volumes, also sheds much new light on House's and Lansing's conduct of diplomacy and their relations with President Wilson. Among other things, it will surely raise grave doubts about Lansing's and House's loyalty to their superior and reveal for the first time some of the difficulties that plagued Wilson, without his knowing it, in his conduct of foreign relations.

3. The older view of Wilson's reactions to and policies toward the German submarine war must now be considerably revised in light of the evidence presented in these volumes. Wilson never pursued a single policy toward Germany, to begin with. His opposition to the submarine campaign was never as great as it has formerly been said to have been. He constantly sought to find compromises that would protect American lives on passenger ships and American merchant vessels without wresting the submarine weapon from German hands.

4. Wilson's policies toward submarine attacks against armed Allied merchant ships has been grossly misunderstood by earlier writers, including the present author. Contrary to the earlier view, Wilson refused to follow a rigid policy toward submarines and armed ships. The armed ship issue was never a source of significant international controversy.

5. If any single conclusion comes out of the evidence, it is that Wilson tried sincerely to pursue policies of rigid neutrality toward the Entente Allies. The record of the period 1914-1917 shows that any emotional bias he may have felt in their favor had no significant impact on his policies. The evidence also shows an important hardening of Wilson's

attitudes toward the Allies between the late spring of 1916 and the early winter of 1917.

6. Wilson's overriding objective after the first months of 1916 was a negotiated peace through his own mediation. Evidence on the American side clearly reveals his determination to press for peace. Evidence on the British side shows conclusively that he had the power to force the Allies to go to the peace table. Evidence on the German side shows that the leaders of Imperial Germany did not believe either assertion, and that they made the fateful decision to extend hostilities on the assumption that a negotiated peace was impossible, that they would lose the war if they did not win it quickly, and that an all-out submarine campaign offered a good chance of decisive victory.

7. It is now possible to say a fairly confident word about the reasons for Wilson's decision to go to war in 1917. He was not influenced by considerations of immediate national security. That is, he did not accept belligerency because he thought that the Allies were about to lose and a German victory would imperil American security. But Wilson was profoundly affected by considerations of the long-range interest. He stubbornly resisted the decision for war because he believed that American interests, to say nothing of the interests of mankind, would be best protected and served by a negotiated peace without victory. Wilson accepted belligerent status for two reasons, mainly: because he could see no other way to protect American national rights and shipping on the high seas in the face of repeated German assaults, and because he believed that the war was in its final stages and American participation would hasten its end.

I have profited more than most authors from help rendered in various ways since I began research on this book in about 1948, and I take this opportunity to make grateful acknowledgment of what institutions, scholars, and other friends have done for me. A fellowship from the John Simon Guggenheim Foundation, supplemented by a grant from the College of Liberal Arts of Northwestern University, enabled me to do my first long stint of research in 1950-1951. The Rockefeller Foundation underwrote work in British archives in 1958-1959. The University Research Committee of Princeton University provided funds for research in Paris and additional work in Great Britain in the summer of 1962. Finally, the Rockefeller Foundation and Princeton University cooperated to make it possible for me to have the academic year 1962-1963 free to write this volume. I thank these institutions from the bottom of my heart. I thank particularly Dean Simeon E. Leland of Northwestern University, Dr. Henry Allen Moe, former Secretary of the Guggenheim Foundation, President Robert F. Goheen and Dean J. Douglas Brown of Princeton University, and Dr. Kenneth W. Thompson, Dr. John P. Harrison, and Dr. Gerald Freund of the Rockefeller Foundation. They all gave generously in support and indispensable encouragement.

Librarians, both in the United States and Europe, have been, as always, unstinting in assistance, and it would be invidious to mention some and not all. But I cannot fail to acknowledge the help of the former Curator of the Wilson Papers in the Library of Congress, Miss Katharine E. Brand. I thank Professors Pierre Renouvin and J. B. Duroselle of the Sorbonne and Professor Max Beloff of Oxford University for their hospitality and assistance. Mrs. Maria P. Alter, Dr. Kenneth Negus, and Messrs. Nicholas Niles, Konrad Mueller, and Bert Thurber worked patiently with me through German newspapers, memoirs, and documents. Mrs. Donna Gunderson typed various drafts of this manuscript, and Mrs. Helen Spiro helped to check footnotes, quotations, and bibliography. Mr. Herbert S. Bailey, Jr., Miss R. Miriam Brokaw, and Mrs. Marjorie Putney of Princeton University Press have guided this book to publication. The late President-emeritus Charles Seymour of Yale University gave generous permission to use the House Papers and Diary.

Finally, I must mention the contribution of friends who read this manuscript with meticulous care: my wife, Mrs. Margaret Douglas Link; my old colleague at Northwestern, Professor Richard Leopold; my present colleague at Princeton, Professor Arno J. Mayer; my former student, Professor William H. Harbaugh of Bucknell University; Professor Gerhard Ritter and Dr. Klaus Schwabe of the University of Freiburg im Breisgau; Dr. David W. Hirst, Associate Editor of the Papers of Woodrow Wilson; Professor Ernest R. May of Harvard University; and Dr. T. H. Vail Motter. I am sure that it goes without saying that they are not responsible for whatever errors remain in this book. The dedication is a small token of my affection for my brother and brother-in-law.

A.S.L.

Princeton, New Jersey
December 14, 1964

CONTENTS

W| ILLUSTRATIONS |W

Following page 178

CHAPTER I

Preludes to the Presidential Campaign

THERE was no surcease of slaughter in Europe in the middle of May 1916. French and German blood was still flowing at Verdun, and the British were completing grim preparations for their own onslaught against German trenches along the Somme. But in the United States events wore a happier visage. It was still touch and go in Mexico, to be sure, and the crisis caused by General John J. Pershing's prolonged stay in that country would not reach its climax for another six weeks. But America's relations with Germany were almost serene following the crisis over the *Sussex* that had brought the two nations to the brink of war. And Democratic leaders in Congress, under President Woodrow Wilson's goad, had broken the impasse over preparedness legislation and were pressing steadily for completion of defense and other measures.[1]

The sudden relaxation of high tension with Germany greatly stimulated a presidential campaign fever that had been rising since Elihu Root of New York and Senator Henry Cabot Lodge of Massachusetts had opened the preconvention campaign in February and March with heavy blasts against Wilson's alleged failures at home and abroad.[2] These speeches stirred great excitement in the Republican camp and much talk about a presidential nominee. Earlier minor booms in Wall Street and big business circles for Root and Myron T. Herrick of Ohio had fizzled completely by the end of 1915, as even the most optimistic Republicans had to admit that these two eminent conservatives could not possibly win the presidency in 1916. But agreement that an avowed conservative should not be nominated left the major questions of the Republican preconvention campaign still unresolved.

The biggest enigma of all was Theodore Roosevelt. He had long since shed his advanced progressivism and was now wooing big businessmen and attempting to effect a union between the decimated Progressive party and the G.O.P. He announced on March 9 that he would

---

[1] For events immediately preceding those discussed in this volume, see A. S. Link, *Wilson: Confusions and Crises, 1915-1916.*

[2] For which, see *ibid.*, p. 319.

Another Punitive Expedition

Marcus in the *New York Times*

not campaign for the Republican nomination, but he changed his mind and embarked in May upon an intense tour through the Middle West, calling frankly (and, in the circumstances, bravely) for universal military service, "Americanism," and aggressive defense of American rights.[3] Actually, Roosevelt had no chance. For one thing, he was swimming against strong tides of public sentiment; for another, the men who controlled the Republican party had no intention of nominating the bolter who had wrecked their hopes in 1912.

There were, besides, too many signs in the spring of 1916 that it would be sheer suicide to take the forward stand on preparedness and foreign policy that Roosevelt, Root, and Lodge were demanding. Former President William Howard Taft, who still had much influence with powerful Republican state leaders, had said all along that Roosevelt and company were leading the party down the road to defeat. "The only hope of the Republican party," Taft wrote as early as January 3, 1916, "is to be conservative in the matter of war, and to rebut the idea of a jingo policy as opposed to the present Administration's action. . . . Now these facts are not circumstances hid in a cave—they are known of all men."[4] If Root should commit the G.O.P. to the views of his speech, Taft wrote somewhat later, "it would be a dangerous thing for the Republican party and for the country, and, on the whole, instead of helping the party, I think the reaction from it will have a tendency to hurt it."[5]

Evidence that Taft was right about grass roots sentiment came in the spring, with the success of the eccentric pacifist and automobile manufacturer, Henry Ford, in the Republican presidential primaries in Michigan and Nebraska on April 5 and 18, even though Ford was not a candidate.[6] German-American spokesmen of a constituency that was largely Republican announced quite frankly in March and again in May that they would enter the campaign against any candidate who followed the Roosevelt-Root line.[7] The defeat of the openly pro-Allied Robert Bacon for the Republican senatorial nomination in New York on September 19 by William M. Calder, who had German-American

---

[3] George E. Mowry, *Theodore Roosevelt and the Progressive Movement*, pp. 320-344; William H. Harbaugh, *Power and Responsibility, The Life and Times of Theodore Roosevelt*, pp. 484-486.

[4] W. H. Taft to G. J. Karger, January 3, 1916, the Papers of William Howard Taft, Library of Congress; hereinafter cited as the Taft Papers.

[5] W. H. Taft to G. J. Karger, February 20, 1916, *ibid.*

[6] *New York Times*, April 6, 7, 19, 20, and 21, 1916.

[7] *ibid.*, March 8 and May 30, 1916.

and antiwar support, was belated testimony to the fact that Republicans were not in a heroic mood even in Roosevelt's and Root's own state.[8]

All signs pointed inexorably by the late spring of 1916 to Charles Evans Hughes, Associate Justice of the Supreme Court, as the only possible Republican candidate. He greatly resembled Wilson in integrity, independence, powers of leadership, and intellect—indeed, in almost every respect except physical appearance. Hughes wore a full beard. He had come first into public view in 1905 as an investigator of New York utilities and insurance companies. Elected Governor of New York in 1906 and again in 1908, he, very much like Wilson a few years later, electrified the country by defying bosses and fighting for reform legislation. Hughes went on the Supreme Court in 1910 and soon won leadership of the liberal minority on that tribunal. He could have had the Republican nomination in 1912 but had flatly refused to run.[9]

Many of the party leaders, particularly in the powerful New York machine, liked Hughes not much more than Roosevelt.[10] But, as Taft pointed out in March 1916, the Justice was the only Republican who could win.[11] A regular, who had not participated in events that had caused the rupture in 1912, he was also a progressive who might reunite the party. Most important of all, he had said not a word about public issues because of his position on the bench. As Roosevelt complained, even while saying that he might support Hughes if he was nominated, "No human being knows how he stands on Preparedness, whether he is prepared for really bold action on the subject of Americanism, or whether he has real and effective convictions about International Affairs."[12]

The drift to Hughes was so strong by the opening of the Republican national convention in Chicago on June 7, 1916, that the only question to be answered was whether Roosevelt would succeed in forcing Hughes and the convention to come out squarely for bold preparedness and foreign policies as the price of his, Roosevelt's, support of the Republican ticket. Roosevelt had earlier arranged to have a convention of the remnant of Progressive leaders meet in Chicago at the same

[8] *ibid.*, September 20 and 21, 1916.

[9] Merlo J. Pusey, *Charles Evans Hughes* (2 vols.), I, 132-324.

[10] e. g., H. C. Lodge to T. Roosevelt, December 4, 1916, the Papers of Theodore Roosevelt, Library of Congress; hereinafter cited as the Roosevelt Papers.

[11] W. H. Taft to D. Baird, March 6, 1916, Taft Papers.

[12] T. Roosevelt to W. Noble, May 2, 1916, Roosevelt Papers.

time as the Republican convention. Most Progressives did not know it, but Roosevelt had hoped to use them in bludgeoning Republicans into nominating himself. That, Roosevelt now knew, was virtually impossible; he would, however, try to force Republicans to adopt a strong platform by threatening to run again on the Progressive ticket if they refused.

It looked briefly as if Roosevelt might have his way simply through good luck. His intimate friend, Senator Lodge, was chairman of the resolutions committee, and he and Senator William E. Borah of Idaho, another friend of Roosevelt, prepared a platform before they went to Chicago. It demanded, among other things, universal military service, a Regular Army of 250,000 men, and a navy second to none. George W. Perkins, chairman of the Progressive National Committee and Roosevelt's spokesman, approved.

The heroic mood did not survive for long once all the members of the resolutions committee gathered in Chicago. They knew the temper of the American people, particularly in the Middle West, and they forced Lodge to write a new preparedness plank calling only for "adequate but thorough and complete national defence"—a "sufficient and effective Regular Army" and a "strong and . . . well proportioned" navy. The platform was equally ambiguous on policy toward the European belligerents. It denounced Wilson's "shifty expedients" and "phrase-making" but demanded "a strict and honest neutrality" and (to please German Americans) insistence "upon all our rights as neutrals without fear and without favor." Only on Mexico was the platform at all belligerent. It condemned Wilson's recognition of Carranza and promised American "aid in restoring order and maintaining peace in Mexico."[13] "I did what I could," Lodge wrote afterward to Roosevelt. But it was all too obvious that the Republican platform measured up to Roosevelt's demands, as one of his friends put it, "to about the same degree the Kaiser's answers did to Wilson's notes."[14]

There was also much maneuvering in Chicago just before the Republican convention met over the presidential nomination. Roosevelt, through his spokesmen in the city, suggested the joint nomination of Henry Cabot Lodge. The Republicans, ignoring all overtures,

---

[13] The Republican platform went on to denounce the Underwood tariff, demand creation of a tariff commission and an "effective system of Rural Credits," federal subsidies to shipping lines, and continued supervision of the political development of the Philippines. Kirk H. Porter and D. B. Johnson (eds.), *National Party Platforms, 1840-1956,* pp. 204-207.

[14] W. H. Harbaugh, *Power and Responsibility,* p. 487.

nominated Hughes on the third ballot on June 10. Roosevelt, surrendering even before the third Republican ballot was completed, urged his followers to ratify Hughes's nomination. They replied in disgust and defiance by naming Roosevelt himself.[15] "The result at Chicago," Taft observed with much pleasure, "is very satisfactory. Roosevelt got what

"This hurts me worse than it does you?"
Morris in the New York *Independent*

was coming to him. His arrogance received a proper rebuke. Hughes will, in my judgment, be elected because Roosevelt will not run on a third party ticket, whatever else happens, and the Bull Moose vote, without Roosevelt at the head of it, will be negligible."[16]

Taft was right, at least about Roosevelt's intentions. He would do nothing to risk another four years of alleged national infamy and cowardice under Wilson. Thus he declined the Progressive nomination politely and then, on June 26, persuaded a majority of the Progressive National Committee to join him in full support of the Republican ticket.[17] "There is only one thing we can do," Roosevelt admitted, "and

[15] *New York Times*, June 11, 1916.
[16] W. H. Taft to C. H. Kelsey, June 12, 1916, Taft Papers.
[17] *New York Times*, June 27, 1916.

that is support Hughes, but I do wish the bearded iceberg had acted a little differently during the last six months so as to enable us to put more heart into the campaign for him."[18] He had earlier lamented to his sister, "Well, the country wasn't in heroic mood! We are passing through a thick streak of yellow in our national life."[19]

Hughes meanwhile had sent a telegram to the Republican convention on June 10 accepting the nomination and a curt note to the White House announcing his resignation, as follows:

> To the President:
> I hereby resign the office of Associate Justice of the Supreme Court of the United States.
> I am, sir, respectfully yours,
>
> Charles E. Hughes

Wilson dictated the following reply at once:

> Dear Mr. Justice Hughes:
> I am in receipt of your letter of resignation and feel constrained to yield to your desire.
> I, therefore, accept your resignation as Justice of the Supreme Court of the United States to take effect at once.
>
> Sincerely yours,
Woodrow Wilson[20]

[18] T. Roosevelt to W. A. Wadsworth, June 23, 1916, Elting E. Morison *et al.* (eds.), *The Letters of Theodore Roosevelt* (8 vols.), VIII, 1078.

[19] T. Roosevelt to Anna R. Cowles, June 16, 1916, *ibid.*, p. 1063.

[20] As printed in the *New York Times*, June 11, 1916. Hughes later recorded and also told his authorized biographer, Merlo J. Pusey, a remarkable story. He said that Secretary Lane had intimated to him before the Republican convention that he would be appointed Chief Justice if he remained on the Court. Hughes also said that Chief Justice Edward D. White had come to him just before the Republican convention, saying that he, White, intended to retire and intimating strongly that Wilson planned to appoint Hughes to succeed him. Hughes and Pusey believed that Lane and White were in fact emissaries of the President. See M. J. Pusey, *Charles Evans Hughes*, I, 324.
The suggestion that Woodrow Wilson would promise the Chief Justiceship to Hughes in return for his refusal to run for the presidency, and Pusey's further insinuation that Wilson made such an offer because he feared Hughes as the strongest possible opponent, are, it must be said in all candor, two of the gravest charges ever brought against Wilson. It is, of course, possible that Lane and White did say exactly what Hughes remembered their saying. We have only Hughes's own testimony, given long after the alleged event, to support his story. Circumstantial evidence does not seem to support Hughes's recollection. White had been Chief Justice only six years in 1916 and was still in full vigor. There was no reason, therefore, why he should have thought of retiring. More important, the Chief Justice had assured William Howard Taft, "not once but many times . . . that he was holding on to turn over the place to me." W. H. Taft to J. D. Dickinson, April 25, 1921, Taft Papers (by courtesy of Professor

The situation in the Democratic camp was altogether serene by the late spring of 1916. There had, indeed, been only minor flurries of excitement and no serious challenges to a second term for the President during all the early months of 1916. A group of German Americans in New York City formed a "Champ Clark Presidential Campaign Committee" in January, but the Speaker of the House of Representatives indignantly repudiated them and declared that he would of course support the President if he desired to run again.[21] There seemed to be a possibility in February and early March that William J. Bryan's resentment at Wilson's preparedness and foreign policies might culminate in a fatal rupture.[22] This threat, which caused Wilson some concern,[23] had passed entirely by early May. At no time during the preconvention period did any Democrat challenge the President's right to seek vindication in November.[24]

Wilson's biggest political problem at this point was finding some unobtrusive but effective way of disposing of William F. McCombs, chairman of the Democratic National Committee. The alienation between the two men was now complete, and Wilson had grimly resolved that McCombs had to go. Unhappily, the National Chairman was determined to stay in his post and even wrote to Wilson in April saying that he would like to come to the White House to talk about plans for the campaign.[25] It was a delicate situation, for McCombs might well wash much dirty Democratic linen in public if he was dismissed. Wilson let his intimate adviser, Colonel Edward M. House, handle the negotiations, and House called on Bernard M. Baruch, a Wall Street broker who knew McCombs well, to extract the resignation. Baruch obtained the letter on April 20 after wrestling with the neurotic National Chairman for two days.[26] He was, McCombs wrote to Wil-

A. T. Mason). To this writer's knowledge there is not a shred of evidence, direct or circumstantial, even to suggest that Wilson ever thought of getting Hughes out of the way by offering to make him Chief Justice. The insinuation that he was privy to the alleged intrigue must be dismissed as unworthy of serious consideration.

[21] *New York Times*, January 26, 1916.

[22] See the article by David Lawrence in the *New York Evening Post*, February 15, 1916.

[23] The Diary of Edward M. House, March 7, 1916, Yale University Library; hereinafter cited as the House Diary.

[24] Wilson entered the preconvention race technically on February 14, 1916, by giving formal permission to Ohio Democrats to put his name on the ballot in the Ohio presidential primary. *New York Times*, February 15, 1916.

[25] W. F. McCombs to W. W., April 13, 1916, the Papers of Woodrow Wilson, Library of Congress; hereinafter cited as the Wilson Papers.

[26] E. M. House to W. W., April 21, 1916, *ibid.*

son, forming a new law partnership and would have to curtail his political activities. "I am writing you at the earliest moment," he went on, "to let you know that I could not, under any circumstances, assume the leadership of the coming Democratic campaign. I am happy in the thought, however, that there are hosts of able and true men who can very readily take my place."[27] Wilson replied as House and Baruch had suggested, as follows:

"I have your letter of April 20, apprising me of your inability to retain the Chairmanship of the Democratic National Committee for the approaching campaign.

"I fully appreciate the necessity you feel yourself to be under to resign after the convention shall have been held in June; I know that you would not have reached such a decision had not your new business obligations made it unavoidable. I do not feel at liberty, therefore, to urge you to make the sacrifice that a retention of the Chairmanship would be in the circumstances involved.

"You have made many and great sacrifices already for the party, and I know that I am speaking the sentiment of all loyal Democrats when I express the very deep appreciation I have felt of the great services you have rendered. I am sure that the greatest regret will be felt at your retirement and that a host of friends will join me in the hope that your new business connections will bring you continued abundant success."[28]

Wilson sent his letter to Colonel House by special delivery on April 22 and gave the correspondence to the press two days later. And that, as House said, got "rid of an ugly situation and eliminate[d] McCombs for all time." House and other leaders suggested Vance McCormick, a newspaper publisher of Harrisburg and leader in the progressive wing of the party in Pennsylvania, as McCombs's successor. "I want reassurance on this doubt," Wilson replied, "whether he is aggressive enough and whether he is not too 'high brow' and intolerant of the rougher elements that have to be handled and dealt with."[29] House continued to press McCormick, but Wilson preferred Homer S. Cummings of Connecticut and was not at first persuaded that McCormick was enough of a "warhorse" to inspire the party faithful.[30] Perhaps, the

[27] W. F. McCombs to W. W., April 20, 1916, *New York Times*, April 25, 1916.
[28] W. W. to W. F. McCombs, April 22, 1916, printed in *ibid.*
[29] E. M. House to W. W., May 19, 1916, Wilson Papers; W. W. to E. M. House, May 22, 1916, the Papers of Edward M. House, Yale University Library; hereinafter cited as the House Papers.
[30] W. W. to E. M. House, June 6, 1916, *ibid.*

President suggested, House would accept the appointment. House refused, and Wilson named McCormick on June 15 because there seemed to be no one else available.[31]

It is easy to forget but important to remember that Wilson had to plan for the coming campaign in a context the shape of which was profoundly influenced by events abroad. The controversy with Mexico over the Punitive Expedition was roaring to its frightening climax during these very weeks. Tension with Germany subsided rapidly in the wake of the settlement of the *Sussex* affair, but there were abundant signs that American relations with the Allies, particularly Great Britain, were beginning to worsen as a consequence of Anglo-French decision—made, no doubt, in light of House's advice to leaders in Paris[32]—to maintain the blockade in full vigor, indeed, to intensify it in certain particulars. Sir Edward Grey, British Foreign Secretary, signalized this decision in his very belated reply to the American government's important protest of October 21, 1915, against alleged illegal suppression of innocent American trade to European neutrals and the Central Powers. The British note, which the British Ambassador, Cecil Spring Rice, delivered to Secretary of State Robert Lansing in the form of a memorandum on April 24, 1916, was politely phrased; but it repudiated the American accusation that the blockade had injured American trade, and it defended the basic legality of the entire Anglo-French maritime system.[33]

Another dispute between the United States and the Allies was coming to a head in the spring of 1916. The British, at the request of the French government, had begun in December 1915 to remove first-class mail, along with parcel post mail containing contraband, from neutral ships bound between the United States and neutral European ports. British cruisers had even adopted the practice of forcing neutral vessels to come into British ports for search of mail bags. Lansing, after sending several futile protests, dispatched a stern note with Wilson's approval[34] on May 24. "The Government of the United States," it

[31] E. M. House to W. W., June 12, 1916, Wilson Papers; House Diary, June 17, 1916; W. W. to H. S. Cummings, June 15, 1916, Wilson Papers; *New York Times*, June 16, 1916.

[32] A. S. Link, *Wilson: Confusions and Crises*, pp. 123, 126.

[33] The British Ambassador to the Secretary of State, April 24, 1916, *Papers Relating to the Foreign Relations of the United States, 1916, Supplement, The World War*, pp. 368-382; hereinafter cited as *Foreign Relations, 1916, Supplement*.

[34] See R. Lansing to W. W., May 20, 1916, and W. W. to R. Lansing, May 22, 1916, *Papers Relating to the Foreign Relations of the United States, The Lansing Papers, 1914-*

concluded, "in view of the improper methods employed by the British and French authorities in interrupting mails passing between the United States and other neutral countries and between the United States and the enemies of Great Britain, can no longer tolerate the wrongs which citizens of the United States have suffered and continue to suffer through these methods. To submit to a lawless practice of this character would open the door to repeated violations of international law by the belligerent powers on the ground of military necessity of which the violator would be the sole judge. . . . The rights of neutrals are as sacred as the rights of belligerents and must be as strictly observed."[35]

"With regard to the contents of the note I refrained from comment, which under the circumstances would be superfluous," Spring Rice wrote to Grey on May 26, after receiving a copy of the mails note. ". . . You will no doubt bear in mind that from now onward to the moment of the elections every possible subject, including foreign politics and religion, is viewed solely from the standpoint of the personal claims of the contending candidates. The interference with the mails is a matter which greatly affects the German voter. . . . Under these circumstances an interference with the mails would be a serious matter."[36]

"The account of the American note to England in the New York Press is most significant," a distinguished English historian observed. "I have felt for some time past that Wilson would be driven to fight his Presidential campaign on the anti-British line. . . . It is possible that this Presidential contest may be of world-wide significance and consequence. All is very abstruse and complicated in it at present. It reminds me strongly of Jefferson's advocacy of war with England, and an espousing of France, against the opposition of Washington and John Adams."[37]

Other Allied practices nagged American public and official opinion.

1920 (2 vols.), I, 308-309, hereinafter cited as *The Lansing Papers*; also the *New York Times*, May 24, 1916.

[35] R. Lansing to the French Ambassador, May 24, 1916, *Foreign Relations, 1916, Supplement*, pp. 604-608. Lansing addressed this protest to the French Ambassador because the French government, contrary to Ambassador Jusserand's advice, had sent the Anglo-French reply to an earlier protest from the State Department.

[36] C. Spring Rice to E. Grey, No. 477, May 26, 1916, in *Contraband. Confidential, June 5* [1916], printed Cabinet paper.

[37] G. O. Trevelyan to Lord J. Bryce, May 30, 1916, the Papers of James, Viscount Bryce, Bodleian Library, Oxford; hereinafter cited as the Bryce Papers.

The British, for example, had barred the export of hospital supplies from the United States to the Central Powers and refused to permit a group of German Americans headed by Professor Edmund von Mach of Harvard to ship canned milk to German children. Officers from a British cruiser boarded an American ship off the coast of China on February 18, 1916, and forcibly removed thirty-eight passengers who were subjects of the Central Powers. This dispute, in which the British eventually yielded, came to a head in late April and early May.[38]

The most important consequence of this continuing exacerbation was its impact both on British and American opinion. Nerves were already beginning to fray, and continued American notes of protest only intensified the British conviction that Americans were oblivious to the moral issues of the war and glad to profit from Allied misfortunes. "The General Public—both in France and England—," one American correspondent in London reported to Colonel House, ". . . firmly believe—without any qualifications or doubts—all that is told them about their Just Cause. . . . And, of course, neutrality seems shameful to them. The thing they cannot forgive us is that our attitude casts a certain doubt on the justice of their cause."[39] The British, the same correspondent wrote on May 1, wanted Americans to break relations with Germany and stop bothering them about the blockade. "It is widely felt," he added, "that it is we who encourage the small neutrals of Europe to stand up for their rights. If we would join the British to the extent of admitting their right to do as they please at sea, it would have—so they say—'a good effect on the Neutrals.' Holland and Greece, for instance, might submit."[40] American prestige, another American correspondent in London wrote to President Wilson, "has sunk to the lowest depths it ever has reached. . . . Do you know that your picture, thrown on a screen in any music-hall or theatre in London, is more apt than not to provoke hissing and booing?"[41] Ambassador Page summarized British sentiment at this time as follows:

"I hope that I have made it plain that *primarily* English opinion does not show any eagerness for us to come into the war for the help we shd give the Allies. . . . But they feel a deep disappointment in us—that we took a righteous stand in the *Lusitania* controversy

[38] *New York Times*, April 28, 1916; New York *World*, May 14, 1916.

[39] Arthur Bullard to E. M. House, March 31, 1916, the Papers of Arthur Bullard, Princeton University Library; hereinafter cited as the Bullard Papers.

[40] A. Bullard to E. M. House, May 1, 1916, *ibid*.

[41] E. P. Bell to W. W., March 7, 1916, enclosing "Open Letter to Woodrow Wilson," Wilson Papers.

and have (as they see it) been enveigled into inaction for well-nigh a year; that the Germans have caused us to submit to delay so long that delay is equivalent to surrender; . . . in a word, as the English think, we are become a peace-at-any-price conglomeration of folk—no longer a people with the English love of freedom and a willingness to fight for it. They have, therefore, made up their minds that we can be of no use for any virile action—the bringing of peace, or the maintaining of it, because we are so divided and so 'soft' that, when action is required, we do not even keep up our own pledge, made of our own volition. . . . In some minds this feeling takes the form of bitterness. In most minds, it takes the form of disappointment or pity. Instead of regarding us as partners in the furthering of civilization, as they did two years ago, they regard us as having fallen aside."[42]

Strong majority sentiment on the American side, if we may judge by all the accumulation of evidence, continued through the very early months of 1916 to be massively neutralist without becoming more anti-British than it had been since the outbreak of the war. The first severe hardening of American sentiment against Great Britain occurred in April and May.

The jolting catalyst was the British army's ruthless suppression of the nationalist rebellion that broke out in Dublin on April 24, 1916, followed by the trial and execution of the Irish nationalist, Sir Roger Casement, who had come from Germany to Ireland in a German submarine to lead the rebellion. "I doubt if the Germans have ever been as hopelessly stupid in Alsace-Lorraine or Poland," one American wrote in shocked unbelief. ". . . Certainly everything for which British Liberalism has stood, as contrasted to Prussian Junkerism, has been brushed away."[43] Anguished protest came from a distinguished novelist, heretofore a leading Anglophile: "Nothing more lamentable in the course of the war now raging has come to pass than this act of bloody vengeance by the English Government. . . . The shooting of the Irish insurrectionists is too much like the shooting of prisoners of war, too much like taking a leaf from the German classic of Schrecklichkeit; and in giving way to her vengeance, England has roused the moral sense of mankind against her. What a pity, what an infinite pity! She has left us who loved her cause in the war against despotism without another word to say for her until we have first spoken our abhorrence of her inexorable legality in dealing with her Irish prison-

---

[42] W. H. Page to W. W., March 30, 1916, *ibid*.
[43] A. Bullard to E. M. House, May 23, 1916, Bullard Papers.

ers."[44] And the *New Republic* was not far from the mark when it observed: "The Dublin executions have done more to drive America back to isolation than any other event since the war began. . . . The *muddle of Ireland* . . . has made America question the liberalism of Britain and the sincerity of her talk about small nationalities or the good faith of her interest in Poles, Danes, and Alsatians."[45] The impact of the affair on Irish-American sentiment was particularly inflammatory. It fused all Irish-American factions, some of which had heretofore been friendly to the British government, into implacable hatred of Albion.[46]

The British and French Ambassadors of course kept their governments informed about this, for them, catastrophic turn in American sentiment. Spring Rice, for example, sent a long telegram to the Foreign Office on about May 21 describing the growing anti-British sentiment. The French Ambassador, J. J. Jusserand, summarized Spring Rice's dispatch in a telegram to the French Foreign Ministry on May 21, adding that the rigorous measures in Ireland had caused the turn in American opinion. Jusserand, in another telegram on May 25, said that Lansing's mails note had been written to please Irish Americans inflamed against Britain. "The executions in Ireland," Spring Rice wrote in his Telegram No. 477 of May 26 about the mails note, cited above, "have very greatly added to the bitterness of the Irish voters here, and any step taken against British action will be hailed with enthusiasm. As Mr. [Frank L.] Polk [Counselor of the State Department] observed, the language used to Great Britain will appear to these gentlemen to be unduly moderate."

The War Committee of the British Cabinet discussed the matter on May 29. "I was rather painfully impressed," Arthur Balfour, head of the Admiralty, wrote to Grey after the meeting, "by the views expressed this morning by [David] Lloyd George [Munitions Minister] and yourself on the effect which the Irish rebellion has had upon public opinion in the U. S. A. American public opinion—especially when

---

[44] William Dean Howells to the Editor, May 6, 1916, *New York Evening Post*, May 8, 1916.

[45] *New Republic*, vii (July 29, 1916), 321-322. See also "The New Irish Revolt," *Literary Digest*, lii (May 6, 1916), 1263-1265, and S. Brooks to W. Long, June 7, 1916, the Papers of Herbert Asquith, Bodleian Library, Oxford, hereinafter cited as the Asquith Papers, for reviews of American reactions.

[46] C. Spring Rice to E. Grey, May 10 and 30, June 16, 1916, Stephen Gwynn (ed.), *The Letters and Friendships of Sir Cecil Spring Rice* (2 vols.), ii, 331, 335-336; hereinafter cited as *Letters of Spring Rice*. For an excellent analysis of the impact of the affair on Irish-American sentiment, see Carl Wittke, *The Irish in America*, pp. 280-281.

rendered sensitive by the approach of a Presidential Election—sways from side to side in the most disconcerting fashion."[47] There was much discussion afterward about the necessity of getting the truth of the Irish situation before the American public.[48] The correspondent, Sydney Brooks, returning to London after six months in the United States, reported that British policy in Ireland had had a very bad effect. But he was absolutely positive, he added, that the Irish Americans and German Americans would not obtain an arms embargo.[49] There was some comfort in his reassurance. As one member of the Cabinet wrote to Prime Minister Herbert Asquith, Americans would "never sacrifice their pockets to their politics."[50]

Hard on the heels of the news of the Dublin executions came publication of Grey's memorandum of April 24 on the blockade and of Lansing's stern mails note of May 24. It would be an exaggeration to say that there was a violent anti-British hue and cry in the United States. Some newspapers more or less took the British side, more were critical of British policy. But the effect was to emphasize important Anglo-American controversies and to speed the shift in sentiment against Great Britain that was already in progress. The *Milwaukee Sentinel, Springfield Republican, Indianapolis News*, Baltimore *Sun*, and *Brooklyn Eagle*, among others, reacted to the British memorandum of April 24 by demanding that the Washington government move in all earnestness to force Great Britain to respect American neutral rights.[51] Senator Paul Husting of Wisconsin echoed this demand in a letter to the President on May 16.[52] Editorial pages positively bristled with anti-British reaction after publication of Lansing's mails note. "The security of mails is a small thing beside the security of lives, of course," a leading midwestern editor observed, "but at the bottom the English and German causes of difference with the United States have a common root."[53] The case called for an ultimatum, a Pittsburgh editor exclaimed, adding, "Nothing less will be effective in securing satisfactory results.

[47] A. J. Balfour to E. Grey, May 29, 1916, Asquith Papers.
[48] E. Grey to H. H. Asquith, May 30, 1916, *ibid.*
[49] S. Brooks to Walter Long, June 7, 1916, *ibid.*
[50] W. Long to H. H. Asquith, June 8, 1916, *ibid.*
[51] *Milwaukee Sentinel*, May 15, 1916; *Springfield* (Mass.) *Republican*, May 16, 1916; *Indianapolis News*, May 15, 1916; and Baltimore *Sun* and *Brooklyn Eagle*, undated clippings enclosed in J. P. Tumulty to R. Lansing, May 18, 1916, the Papers of Robert Lansing, Library of Congress; hereinafter cited as the Lansing Papers, LC.
[52] P. Husting to W. W., May 16, 1916, Wilson Papers.
[53] *St. Louis Republic*, cited in the *Literary Digest*, LII (June 10, 1916), 1686.

It was so in the case of Germany; no more respect for our rights need be expected from the Allies. Their words and their acts prove this."[54]

Spring Rice studied the portents and frankly warned Sir Edward Grey to be prepared for dangerous times ahead. The Ambassador wrote:

"It will be wise therefore to count on a new phase in our relations with this country. Violent notes will no doubt be sent and violent threats will be used. At the same time we shall be told that the President is ready to help us to make peace. If we refuse, we shall be called bloodthirsty and we shall be made to feel the weight of American displeasure. We shall be told that it is more cruel to starve women and children than to drown them. We shall be told that to exclude Red Cross supplies is a refinement of barbarism before which the impulsive destruction of Louvain sinks into insignificance. Signs of this coming campaign are sufficiently plain. . . . This country is a long way from war with anybody. It is extremely unlikely that America will go to war against the Allies. But it is not at all unlikely that there will be a violent diplomatic campaign against Britain. In the meanwhile feeling in England is also no doubt growing more bitter. We may conclude therefore that our relations are now entering into a difficult and dangerous stage. I hope that every effort will be made to impress on our different departments interested the grave importance which may attach to incidents in which the United States are concerned."[55]

The foregoing section has been written for the main purpose of showing the context of developments and events in which Wilson made one of the most important decisions of his career to this point. It was to move for peace along the lines of the House-Grey Memorandum, the instrument for Anglo-American collaboration that House and Grey had initialed in February 1916.[56] Such action was, from Wilson's point of view, even more urgent after the settlement of the *Sussex* crisis than before. The Germans had left no doubt that they might launch all-out submarine warfare if Wilson failed to open trade routes to the Central Powers; they had also given broad hints that they would welcome an American peace *démarche*.[57] Wilson also knew that he

[54] *Pittsburgh Gazette-Times*, cited in *ibid.*, p. 1687.

[55] C. Spring Rice to E. Grey, May 10, 1916, S. Gwynn (ed.), *Letters of Spring Rice*, II, 332-333.

[56] For the negotiation of this document, see A. S. Link, *Wilson: Confusions and Crises*, pp. 130-135.

[57] See Ambassador Gerard to the Secretary of State, April 25, 1916, quoted in *ibid.*, p. 261, and a later message, J. W. Gerard to E. M. House, May 3, 1916, Wilson

might have to move sternly against the British in the near future, particularly if American opinion should be further aroused. The war, he thought, was already a draw and would end inconclusively while destroying Europe and setting off political and social revolutions if it was permitted to continue.[58] Finally, he could not have been un-influenced by domestic political considerations. A peace move would be enormously popular in any event; a successful peace move would make him irresistible in the presidential campaign. Moreover, he had it in mind to commit the Democratic party in its platform to support American membership in a postwar league of nations and to make such proposal a leading issue in the ensuing campaign. Ambassador Spring Rice emphasized some of these motivations in a letter to Grey on May 10, as follows:

"It is quite plain from the President's language that he has no intention whatever of entering the European arena as a belligerent and that he has every intention of entering it as a mediator. The immense majority of the people wants peace, but as they are rather restive under the accusation of playing a rather ignoble part, they are anxious to gain the eternal glory of the peacemaker who inherits the earth. If the President can appear before the country as the great pacificator before the end of October, his re-election is almost certain. Consequently it is not surprising to see that his mind is turning that way. His standpoint seems to be that the world is mad and can only be saved by the few sane men who are left in it. As one of the madmen, you will form your own opinion, presumably a mad one, as to the claims of our sane Saviour. No one can doubt the President's perfect sincerity in his desire to help in the work of peace. The highest moral principles as well as enlightened interests point that way."[59]

Wilson discussed the way to proceed with Colonel House at the

---

Papers, as follows: "The Chancellor also says that Germany is strong enough & has won enough in war to be able to talk about peace and the hope is that the President will force a peace which Germany is willing to make reasonable. . . . The Chancellor said he hoped you would come over under the President's direction and *make peace*." In the same vein, see also Ambassador Gerard to the Secretary of State, May 11, 1916, *Foreign Relations, 1916, Supplement*, p. 267; also J. W. Gerard to E. M. House, May 17, 1916, House Papers.

[58] As he told a friend on March 8, 1916. A. C. Imbrie, "Memorandum of talk with President Wilson, March 8th, 1916," the Ray Stannard Baker Collection of Wilsoniana Library of Congress; hereinafter cited as the Baker Collection.

[59] C. Spring Rice to E. Grey, May 10, 1916, S. Gwynn (ed.), *Letters of Spring Rice*, II, 331-332.

White House on May 3. Grey had said in earlier correspondence that Britain could not consent to American mediation without a prior firm pledge of cooperation in the postwar world. Very well, Wilson said, he would give that pledge by affirming, in a speech in the near future, America's readiness to join a postwar international organization. He would also "demand the calling of a conference that might end the war, at the same time that he laid down the principles upon which a durable peace must be based."[60]

The first step, House and Wilson agreed, was to appeal to Grey to consent to putting the Memorandum's machinery in motion,[61] and House went home to draft a letter getting negotiations to this end under way. He warned Grey against trying to crush Germany and Austria, said that Germany had now reached the point at which she might be susceptible to American pressure, and promised that the American people would uphold the President if he took leadership for peace. "Delay," House went on, "is dangerous and may defeat our ends. . . . Therefore, England should be immediately responsive to our call. Her statesmen will take a great responsibility upon themselves if they hesitate or delay; and in the event of failure because they refuse to act quickly, history will bring a grave indictment against them."[62]

"I think it will fetch a favorable reply," House wrote as he sent a copy of this letter to Wilson on May 7. "It should be sent without delay in order to get an answer back in time for the purpose you have in mind. Please re-write it in part or in whole as seems to you best. I know Sir Edward's mind in regard to this subject as well as I know your own and have merely outlined what we all three feel."[63] Wilson replied at once: "I hasten to return the enclosed with my approval. You could even heighten the emphasis with which you warn Sir Edward that the sympathy of this country is apt to be alienated from Great Britain in a very significant degree in the immediate future and its peace sentiment become more and more insistent. It is much better for Great Britain that we should initiate the final movement than that the Pope should."[64] The peace intimation contained in the *Sussex* note, Wilson wrote again on the following day, May 9, "seems now to be

[60] Charles Seymour, in *The Intimate Papers of Colonel House* (4 vols.), II, 294.
[61] House Diary, May 3, 1916.
[62] This was sent as E. M. House to E. Grey, May 11, 1916, House Papers.
[63] E. M. House to W. W., May 7, 1916, Wilson Papers.
[64] W. W. to E. M. House, May 8, 1916, House Papers. Wilson was referring here to recent press reports about the Pope's peace activities. *New York Times,* April 24 and 25, 1916.

holding the attention of the country, and it is my prediction that it is going to be increasingly difficult to keep off the insistent demand that I act. Perhaps you will think it best to send a somewhat full cable to Sir Edward."[65]

House on that very day had made arrangements for the President to make his contemplated speech before the League to Enforce Peace, an American group dedicated to creation of a strong postwar agency, in Washington on May 27.[66] "I have had a feeling for some time," he wrote to Wilson on May 10, "that it would be advisable and even necessary for you to act soon whether the Allies desire it or not."[67] But it was now all the more urgent to bring Grey into the discussions, and House, as Wilson had suggested, dispatched the following cablegram to the Foreign Secretary on May 10:

> There is an increasingly insistent demand here that the President take some action towards bringing the war to a close. The impression grows that the Allies are more determined upon the punishment of Germany than upon exacting terms that neutral opinion would consider just. This feeling will increase if Germany discontinues her illegal submarine activities.
>
> I believe the President would now be willing publicly to commit the United States to joining with the other Powers in a convention looking to the maintenance of peace after the war, provided he announced at the same time that if the war continued much longer he purposed calling a conference to discuss peace.
>
> If the President is to serve humanity in a large way, steps should be taken now rather than wait until the opportunity becomes less fortunate. His statement would be along the lines you and I have so often discussed and which you expressed in your letter to me of September 22, 1915; that is, the nations subscribing to this agreement should pledge themselves to side against any Power breaking a treaty. The convention should formulate rules for the purpose of limiting armaments both on land and sea and for the purpose of making warfare more humane to those actually engaged in safeguarding the lives and property of neutrals and noncombatants.
>
> The convention should bind the signatory Powers to side against any nation refusing in case of dispute to adopt some other method of settlement than that of war.
>
> I am sure this is the psychological moment for this statement to be made,

[65] W. W. to E. M. House, May 9, 1916, House Papers.

[66] House Diary, May 9, 1916; E. M. House to W. W., May 9, 1916, Wilson Papers; W. H. Taft to W. W., May 9, 1916, *ibid.*, extending the invitation from the League to Enforce Peace.

[67] E. M. House to W. W., May 10, 1916, *ibid.*

and I would appreciate your cabling me your opinion as to the advisability of such a move. If it is not done now, the opportunity may be forever lost.[68]

House then, on the following day, May 11, sent the letter that he had earlier drafted to Grey.

Grey replied quite bluntly in a telegram on May 12 that he thought that Britain's allies would think that a suggestion of peace from him was premature, and that a public peace appeal by the President unaccompanied by any indication of definite terms would surely be construed as a move favorable to Germany. "I hope," Grey concluded, "you will realize this telegram is a purely personal opinion sent in reply to your request without consulting my colleagues [in the Cabinet], not even the Prime Minister who is now in Ireland, but if you desire it I will consult him on his return."[69]

"I see evidences of the Allies regaining their self-assurance and not being as yielding to our desires as they were when they were in so much trouble," House wrote bitterly to Wilson as he sent him a copy of Grey's telegram and a proposed reply. "We have given them everything and they ever demand more."[70] For two years, the Colonel wrote in his diary, "he [Grey] has been telling me that the solution of the problem of international well-being depended upon the United States being willing to take her part in world affairs. Now that we indicate a willingness to do so, he halts, stammers and questions. I am distinctly disappointed. . . . I can see, too, a distinct feeling of cock-sureness in the Allies since Verdun. This will grow in the event they have any success themselves, and I can foresee trouble with them."[71]

Wilson was disappointed, too, but he was still grimly determined to press Grey as hard as possible. As he explained in a letter to House on May 16:

"I have been giving some very careful thought to your question, how we should deal with Sir Edward and his Government at this turning point,—for it really is that.

"It seems to me that we should get down to hard pan.

"The situation has altered altogether since you had your conferences in London and Paris. The at least temporary removal of the acute German question has concentrated attention here on the altogether in-

[68] E. M. House to E. Grey, May 10, 1916, House Papers.
[69] E. Grey to E. M. House, May 12, 1916, House Papers.
[70] E. M. House to W. W., May 14, 1916, Wilson Papers.
[71] House Diary, May 13, 1916.

defensible course Great Britain is pursuing with regard to trade to and from neutral ports and her quite intolerable interception of mails on the high seas carried by neutral ships. Recently there has been added the great shock opinion in this country has received from the course of the British Government towards some of the Irish rebels.

"We are plainly face to face with this alternative, therefore. The United States must either make a decided move for peace (upon some basis that promises to be permanent), or, if she postpones that, must insist to the limit upon her rights of trade and upon such freedom of the seas as international law already justifies her in insisting on as against Great Britain, with the same plain speaking and firmness that she has used against Germany. And the choice must be made immediately. Which does Great Britain prefer? She cannot escape both. To do nothing is now, for us, impossible.

"If we move for peace, it will be along these lines 1) Such a settlement with regard to their own immediate interests as the belligerents [*sic*] may be able to agree upon. We have nothing material of any kind to ask for ourselves and are quite aware that we are in no sense or degree parties to the quarrel. Our interest is only in peace and its guarantees; 2) a universal alliance to maintain freedom of the seas and to prevent any war begun either a) contrary to treaty covenants or b) without warning and full inquiry,—a virtual guarantee of territorial integrity and political independence.

"It seems to me to be of imperative and pressing importance that Sir Edward should understand all this and that the crisis cannot be postponed; and it can be done with the most evident spirit of friendliness through you. Will you not prepare a full cable putting the whole thing plainly to him? We must act, and act at once, in the one direction or the other."[72]

House drafted a cablegram on May 17 and sent it to the White House for Wilson's approval. Wilson, House noted, did not make "a single change,"[73] and House dispatched it on May 19. It began by explaining that the American government had no desire to force the Allies' hands, "or to urge upon them something for which they are not ready." But it was clear, it went on, that the United States was at a crossroads, "and if we cannot soon inaugurate some sort of peace discussion there will come a demand from our people, in which all neutrals will probably join, that we assert our undeniable rights against the Allies with the

[72] W. W. to E. M. House, May 16, 1916, House Papers.
[73] House Diary, May 18, 1916.

same insistence we have used towards the Central Powers." Friction with the Allies would cause such resentment in the United States that the American people would not sustain the President in "doing those things which they would now welcome." The time was critical, and delay was dangerous. America was ready to join England in fighting for the emancipation of Europe, but England had to recognize the conditions under which Anglo-American cooperation was possible. "It is not the President's thought," House went on, "that a peace conference could be immediately called, and the Allies would have ample time to demonstrate whether or not Germany is indeed in a sinking condition and the deadlock can be broken. I would suggest that you talk with the three of your colleagues with whom we discussed these matters, for it is something that will not bear delay."[74]

"The President and I are getting into deep waters," House wrote in his diary on the day that he drafted this telegram, "and I am not sure we are coming out as we desire. If he will play our hand with all the strength within our power, I believe we can make them do as we wish. But if he does not, we will lose some prestige and perhaps the good will of the Allies."[75]

Wilson and he believed, House wrote again to Grey on May 23 in a letter that went by mail, that the war could be ended on terms that would make the recurrence of militarism impossible. A just settlement would be much easier to achieve now than in the future, for the Allies still had the advantage of a friendly American public opinion. That advantage would lessen day by day if the war continued. England, unfortunately, did not seem to realize this. England and France seemed to prefer the doubtful advantage of a crushing victory to a just settlement with American cooperation. "Your seeming lack of desire to coöperate with us," House concluded, "will chill the enthusiasm here— never, I am afraid, to come again, at least in our day. There is a fortunate conjunction of circumstances which makes it possible to bring about the advancement and maintenance of world-wide peace and security, and it is to be hoped that the advantage may not be lost. If it is, the fault will not lie with us."[76]

Grey replied to House's cablegram of May 19 as soon as he received it, promising to discuss the matter with Prime Minister Asquith at

[74] E. M. House to E. Grey, May 19, 1916, House Papers.
[75] House Diary, May 17, 1916.
[76] E. M. House to E. Grey, May 23, 1916, House Papers.

once.[77] Ambassador Jusserand gave an indication at the same time of the kind of response that might be expected from his government if it was approached. He did not know about House's recent messages to London, but he had been profoundly disturbed by Wilson's strong intimation, in a speech in Charlotte on May 20, that he was contemplating a peace move.[78] Jusserand went to the State Department on his own initiative, without instructions, on the afternoon of May 22 to say that France had to fight on until Germany had been adequately punished, and that "anyone trying at this time to bring about peace would be considered a friend of Germany." He would be grateful, he added, if this message was communicated to the President at the earliest moment.[79] "Signs multiply," Wilson wrote to House, sending him a copy of a memorandum of this conversation, "that The [*sic*] Allies are becoming alarmed at the possibility of our making a move for peace."[80]

Wilson and House had meanwhile begun to discuss what Wilson should say in his address before the League to Enforce Peace. House suggested on May 17 that the President emphasize the need for a strong navy—"If we are going to join with other great powers in a world movement to maintain peace, we ought to immediately inaugurate a big naval programme"—and not to go into specific plans for a postwar security organization.[81] "The more I see of the dealings of governments among themselves," House wrote again on the same day, "the more I am impressed with the utter selfishness of their outlook. Gratitude is a thing unknown and all we have done for the Allies will be forgotten if we antagonize them now. Nevertheless, I am convinced that it is your duty to press for a peace conference with all the power at your command, for whether they like it or whether they do not, I believe you can bring it about."[82]

"I am thinking a great deal about the speech I am to make on the twenty-seventh," Wilson replied, "because I realize that it may be the most important I shall ever be called upon to make, and I greatly value

[77] E. Grey to E. M. House, cablegram, n.d., but c. May 22, 1916, quoted in E. M. House to W. W., May 22, 1916, Wilson Papers.

[78] For this address, see Ray S. Baker, and William E. Dodd (eds.), *The Public Papers of Woodrow Wilson, The New Democracy* (2 vols.), II, 178-183; hereinafter cited as *The New Democracy*.

[79] The Confidential Diary of Frank L. Polk, May 22, 1916, Yale University Library; hereinafter cited as the Polk Confidential Diary; F. L. Polk to W. W., May 22, 1916, Wilson Papers.

[80] W. W. to E. M. House, May 22, 1916, House Papers.

[81] E. M. House to W. W., May 17, 1916, Wilson Papers.

[82] E. M. House to W. W., May 17, 1916, *ibid.*

your suggestion about the navy programme. Would you do me the favour to formulate what you would say, in my place, if you were seeking to make the proposal as nearly what you deem Grey and his colleagues to have agreed upon in principle as it is possible to make it when concretely formulated as a proposal? Your recollection of your conferences is so much more accurate than mine that I would not trust myself to state the proposition without advice from you, though it may be wise to strengthen and heighten the terms a little." He could not understand, Wilson concluded, why House was so confident that it was idle to hope that the European nations would be interested in a postwar peace league. "The only inducement we can hold out to the Allies is one which will actually remove the menace of Militarism."[83]

House replied, explaining that he thought it important to obtain agreement on general principles before discussing means of enforcing them, and sending certain documents that he thought would be helpful to Wilson in preparing his address.[84] Then two days later, on May 21, he sent the outline for the address that the President had requested. It asserted that the war had been caused by hideous misunderstanding among the European powers about each other's intentions, and it called for a universal alliance to maintain freedom of the seas, prevent war, and achieve disarmament. House, significantly, did not include a direct call for a peace conference.[85]

Wilson came to New York on May 24 to attend the wedding of his physician, Cary T. Grayson, and found time for a conference with Colonel House at his apartment. Both men were now utterly discouraged by Grey's recalcitrance and Jusserand's pointed warning. "It is evident," House said, "that unless the United States is willing to sacrifice hundreds of thousands of lives and billions of treasure we are not to be on good terms with the Allies." He and Wilson agreed, House wrote in his diary, that "it would be wise in the circumstances to greatly modify the speech he is to make next Saturday before the League to Enforce Peace. He is to treat the subject as we have outlined it, with the exception that he is not to do more than hint at peace. He asked for a pad and made a memorandum. We divided the subject into four parts, and indicated just how far he should go." Wilson also suggested that House talk to Jusserand, and House said that it would be wise for the President to show his speech to Lansing before he delivered it.[86]

[83] W. W. to E. M. House, May 18, 1916, House Papers.
[84] E. M. House to W. W., May 19, 1916, Wilson Papers.
[85] E. M. House to W. W., May 21, 1916, enclosing "thoughts on the speech," *ibid.*
[86] House Diary, May 24, 1916.

Wilson, relying heavily on House's draft, began composing the address certainly no earlier than the morning of May 25. He obviously decided at the outset to make only a brief statement. He would indicate America's desire for peace without, however, issuing any direct call for immediate peace discussions. Most important, he would make it clear to the whole world that the United States was prepared to do its part. He completed his draft probably during the evening of May 25. Lansing was sick, and Wilson took the draft to the Secretary's home at three o'clock in the afternoon of May 26 and read it to him.[87] They discussed it, and Lansing presumably approved. Then Wilson went to the New Willard Hotel at 7:20 p.m. on May 27 to launch his bolt before some 2,000 listeners and the world.

The desire of the whole world, he began, now turned eagerly toward peace, and it was right that he should speak for the American government and people at this moment. Americans were not interested in the war's "causes and its objects." But Americans had been profoundly affected, and they were not "disconnected lookers-on." We are, he went on, announcing the end of American isolation, "participants, whether we would or not, in the life of the world. The interests of all nations are our own also. We are partners with the rest. What affects mankind is inevitably our affair as well as the affair of the nations of Europe and of Asia." It was surely obvious that the war had grown out of secret counsels and bitter rivalries, and that the peace of the world in the future had to depend upon a "new and more wholesome diplomacy." Nations had become neighbors and had to cooperate in a common cause. He now came to the basic affirmations and the climactic commitment:

"We believe these fundamental things: First, that every people has a right to choose the sovereignty under which they shall live. Like other nations, we have ourselves no doubt once and again offended against that principle when for a little while controlled by selfish passion as our franker historians have been honorable enough to admit; but it has become more and more our rule of life and action. Second, that the small states of the world have a right to enjoy the same respect for their sovereignty and for their territorial integrity that great and powerful nations expect and insist upon. And, third, that the world has a right to be free from every disturbance of its peace that has its origin in aggression and disregard of the rights of peoples and nations.

"So sincerely do we believe in these things that I am sure that I

[87] The Desk Diary of Robert Lansing, May 26, 1916, Library of Congress; hereinafter cited as the Lansing Desk Diary.

speak the mind and wish of the people of America when I say that the United States is willing to become a partner in any feasible association of nations formed in order to realize these objects and make them secure against violation. . . .

"If it should ever be our privilege to suggest or initiate a movement for peace among the nations now at war, I am sure that the people of the United States would wish their Government to move along these lines: First, such a settlement with regard to their own immediate interests as the belligerents may agree upon. We have nothing material of any kind to ask for ourselves, and are quite aware that we are in no sense or degree parties to the present quarrel. Our interest is only in peace and its future guarantees. Second, an universal association of the nations to maintain the inviolate security of the highway of the seas for the common and unhindered use of all the nations of the world, and to prevent any war begun either contrary to treaty covenants or without warning and full submission of the causes to the opinion of the world—a virtual guarantee of territorial integrity and political independence. . . . God grant that the dawn of that day of frank dealing and of settled peace, concord, and co-operation may be near at hand!"[88]

Reverberations began immediately at home. Roosevelt's spokesman and the leading champion of the Allies in the United States professed indignation at the President's refusal to take sides,[89] and some isolationists condemned the proposal for a league of nations out of hand.[90] But most thoughtful Americans approved Wilson's momentous declarations. "Mr. Wilson," as *The New Republic* asserted, "has broken with the tradition of American isolation in the only way which offers any hope to men. Not only has he broken with isolation, he has ended the pernicious doctrine of neutrality, and has declared that in the future we cannot be neutral between the aggressor and the victim. That is one of the greatest advances ever made in the development of international morality."[91] Wilson's utterance, a prominent editor added, would rank in importance with the Declaration of Independence and the Monroe Doctrine.[92] "It directs us and the world in a new path," the president of Williams College added.[93] "I cannot tell you," Colonel

---

[88] *The New Democracy*, II, 184-188.
[89] *The Outlook*, CXIII (June 7, 1916), 303-304; *New York Tribune*, May 29, 1916.
[90] e. g., New York *Sun*, May 29, 1916; *Pittsburgh Gazette-Times*, May 29, 1916.
[91] "Mr. Wilson's Great Utterance," *New Republic*, VII (June 3, 1916), 102-104.
[92] H. Holt to W. W., May 29, 1916, Wilson Papers.
[93] H. A. Garfield to W. W., May 30, 1916, *ibid.*

House wrote, "how pleased I am with your speech last night. It will be a land mark in history."[94]

Few observers in western Europe failed to note the obvious significance of the address. "It brings the United States," the *Westminster Gazette* said in a typical comment, "definitely into world politics and makes her from henceforth one of the nations that must be reckoned with in any scheme of international politics, balance of power, association of nations or whatever it may be."[95] Henceforth, a liberal English weekly agreed, "the States are a 'Great Power' within the European orbit."[96]

But that assertion, particularly insofar as it implied that Wilson had some right to interfere in the present conflict, was not a cheering thought to most European commentators. Editors in Paris generally denied Wilson's right to mediate, although they resorted to sarcasm or innuendo to avoid the censor's blue pencil while expressing their opinions. "What a small affair!" Georges Clemenceau exclaimed, for example. "Wait. If the Creator needed seven days to organize a couple of creatures of which the first born instinctively tore each other apart, Mr. Wilson, in one sovereign word, is going to create men such as have never been seen, whose first need will be love and universal harmony. . . . You [Wilson] offer yourself magnanimously as a mediator. But for simple inhabitants of the earth, what is a mediation that envisages right only beyond the clouds?"[97] President Wilson, added the French Ambassador in London, Paul Cambon, "is surely obeying German instigations when he speaks the word of peace."[98] The right and center of English opinion reacted violently, complaining that Wilson's speech was a mere campaign document for domestic consumption, and that his statement about America not being concerned with the causes or objects of the war was additional proof of his moral blindness. "We think it right," one London editor said, "to state quite clearly that the Allies are not and will not be disposed to allow American internal politics to be intruded into their righteous quarrel. . . . And they will

[94] E. M. House to W. W., May 28, 1916, *ibid.* For comment in the same vein, see C. R. Crane to W. W., May 29, 1916, *ibid.*, and the review of American press opinion in "President Wilson's Peace-Plan," *Literary Digest*, LII (June 10, 1916), 1683-1685.

[95] London *Westminster Gazette*, May 29, 1916.

[96] London *Nation*, XIX (June 3, 1916), 274.

[97] Paris *L'Homme Enchaîné*, May 31, 1916; also Paris *Journal des Débats*, June 2, 1916; Paris *Le Temps*, May 31, 1916; and A. H. Frazier to E. M. House, June 2, 1916, House Papers.

[98] P. Cambon "à son fils," May 31, 1916, Henri Cambon (ed.), *Paul Cambon, Correspondance, 1870-1924* (3 vols.), III, 108.

listen to proposals for peace only when they come from the beaten foe."[99] Or, as Lord Cromer put it in a letter to *The Times*:

"It is more than doubtful, in spite of the very friendly feelings entertained towards America and the Americans generally, that the people of this country would under any circumstances welcome the idea that President Wilson should assume the role of mediator. As Note has succeeded Note and speech speech, the conviction has been steadily gaining ground that President Wilson has wholly failed to grasp the view entertained by the vast majority of Englishmen on the cause for which we and our Allies are fighting. This opinion will certainly be confirmed by the amazing statement that America is 'not concerned with the causes and objects of the war.' Confidence in President Wilson's statesmanship has been rudely shaken, neither for the moment does it appear likely to be restored to the extent of acquiescence in the proposal that he should be in any way vested with the power of exercising any decisive influence on the terms of peace upon which the future destinies of this country and of the civilized world will greatly depend."[100]

Wilson was of course more interested in reactions in foreign offices and chancelleries. "I am immensely pleased," he wrote to Colonel House on May 29, "that you approved and liked the speech. I was handling critical matter and was trying to put it in a way that it would be hard for the Allies to reject, as well as for Germany."[101] He did not succeed. Rejections came quickly and so emphatically as to affect the President's fundamental thinking about America's relation to the belligerents.

Lukewarm, if not unfavorable, response came quickly from the one quarter, Berlin, in which Wilson expected to find sympathetic hearing. Colonel House had been careful to let the German Ambassador in Washington, Count Johann von Bernstorff, know that the President was not interested in specific terms, and that the Allies viewed an American peace *démarche* coldly. Thus the Ambassador wrote to the Foreign Office immediately after Wilson's speech:

"The peace programme of President Wilson becomes plainer every day. The only question is whether he will have enough influence to

[99] London *Times*, May 29, 1916; in the same vein, London *Daily Mail*, May 30, 1916; London *Morning Post*, May 30, 1916; Liverpool *Post*, cited in the *New York Times*, May 30, 1916.

[100] Lord Cromer to the Editor, May 30, 1916, in the London *Times*, May 31, 1916.

[101] W. W. to E. M. House, May 29, 1916, House Papers.

compel our enemies to accept his mediation. Col. House is convinced that Mr. Wilson will succeed. The President has ever before his eyes the summoning of a Congress at the Hague in which only neutrals are to take part in so far as the freedom of the seas is concerned. If he succeeds in this Col. House will probably take part in the Congress, though he is not likely to be the official American representative. His influence could, however, be very great as no other person stands in such intimate relations with the President. The latter is still of opinion that the U.S.A. cannot interfere in respect of the conditions of peace. He and his 'alter ego' are very positive that our enemies will remain recalcitrant, because the latter think, or endeavor to make others think, that the President is acting on behalf of Germany in undertaking peace interventions. On the part of England, this latter notion is being continually pressed. At one time we are informed that a person is coming in order to bring Mr. Wilson German peace proposals; at another time, that Germany is in the throes of starvation and therefore must demand peace. We must counteract as far as possible these efforts of the enemy. In any case they will not do any great harm, as the peace tendencies of the American people are continually increasing, and Mr. Wilson can now apparently count upon re-election should he be able to bring about a Peace Congress. We shall in consequence gain here in popularity in so far as we can let it be understood that we are ready to accept his interventions, whereas our enemies are cold shouldering him."[102]

However, events at this very time were causing the Imperial Chancellor, Theobald von Bethmann Hollweg, and the Foreign Office to have second thoughts about the desirability of Wilsonian action. General Erich von Falkenhayn, Chief of the German General Staff, in a conversation with the Chancellor on May 28, was fairly optimistic about the military outlook and even indicated that Germany might win the war in 1916-1917 without resorting to all-out submarine warfare. Prospects for the coming harvest had greatly improved. Bethmann also had some hopes for a separate peace with France.[103] More important, most German editors either viewed Wilson's address before the League to Enforce Peace as a campaign speech aimed only at the American electorate, or else repudiated the very suggestion of Wilson as a mediator.[104] Gustav Stresemann, speaking for the National Liberal

[102] Ambassador von Bernstorff to the Foreign Office, May 28, 1916, "Bernstorff Wireless Despatches—1916," MSS. in the Papers of Walter H. Page, Houghton Library, Harvard University; hereinafter cited as "Bernstorff Wireless Despatches—1916."

[103] Fritz Fischer, *Griff nach der Weltmacht*, pp. 274-277.

[104] Ambassador Gerard to the Secretary of State, May 30, 1916, *Foreign Relations,*

Party, and Count Kuno von Westarp, speaking for the Conservative Party, echoed the latter opinion in the Reichstag on June 2 and June 6.[105]

Consequently, the Foreign Secretary, Gottlieb von Jagow, sent new definitive instructions to Bernstorff on June 7. His dispatch, after commenting on Wilson's failure to take action against the British blockade, went on:

"Doubtless your Excellency has already realized from the news which has arrived over there that our concession in the submarine question with regard to the United States is regarded as impracticable in many broad and influential circles in Germany. Should President Wilson continue his inactive course with regard to England, it is greatly to be feared that even that portion of German public opinion which has up to this time supported the attitude of the Government will join those who are opposed to the Government's policies, and that the entire public opinion of Germany will insistently demand the resumption of submarine warfare in its earlier forms. The Imperial Government would then be still less in a position to forestall this demand for any length of time because of the fact that all the military authorities regard and recommend, as they did before, unrestricted U-boat warfare as the only really effective war measure which could bring about the complete defeat of England. And, moreover, I must add that, as we have been informed from absolutely confidential sources, the Entente has determined upon a marked severity of blockade measures, and at the same time has decided to reject the protests of the neutral Powers in the future, particularly those of the United States, relying upon the argument that it is only in this way that a termination of the war can be brought about in such a manner as to conform to the interests of the neutral Powers. Your Excellency will therefore call President Wilson's attention through Colonel House to the serious dangers lurking in his attitude of inaction, so far as England is concerned.

"Regarding Mr. Wilson's purpose to bring about peace by mediation, this is from time to time meeting with the most lively opposition in England. From our point of view, it would be very desirable for England to be the one to reject these overtures, for the fact is that we entertain but little hope for the result of the exercise of good offices by one

1916, Supplement, p. 32; also the review of German press opinion in Neutral Conference for Continuous Mediation, *President Wilson and the Peace of Europe*.
[105] Karl E. Birnbaum, *Peace Moves and U-Boat Warfare*, pp. 105-106.

whose instincts are all favorable to the English point of view, and who, in addition to this, is so naive a statesman as President Wilson.[106] And we are impelled to this attitude by the consideration that the President would from the outset exert himself to bring about a peace based in the main on the *status quo ante*, particularly with regard to Belgium. Difficult as it is to state at this time to what extent we would be in a position to bring about a solution of the Belgian question which would be in accord with our interests (a question which has become a vital one as the result of the war), we can at least say this much today, that if the progress of the war were to continue favorable for us, a peace founded on the absolute *status quo ante* would be unacceptable to us. As the President interprets his rôle, to wit, that of a Lord Protector designated to uphold everything which, in his opinion, constitutes right and justice, there is reason to fear that our refusal to conclude peace on these terms might induce him to go over openly into the camp of our enemies. It is not, however, impossible that public opinion in England might, in the course of time, turn again to Mr. Wilson and his desire to mediate. As soon as Mr. Wilson's mediation plans threaten to assume a more concrete form and an inclination on the part of England to meet him begins to manifest itself, it will be your Excellency's duty to prevent President Wilson from approaching us with a positive proposal of mediation. The choice of the means of reaching this result without endangering our relations with the United States I venture to leave to your Excellency's ability as a diplomat, since I am not able to form a complete estimation of the situation in the United States from here."[107]

As Jagow and Bernstorff both knew, it would be infinitely preferable to avoid giving the appearance of being uninterested in peace, and to let the British bear all the onus for repelling Wilson's mediation. Thus the Foreign Secretary told the American Ambassador in Berlin, James W. Gerard, on June 14 that the President and Colonel House should not think that the recent debates in the Reichstag meant that Germany no longer welcomed Wilson's mediation.[108] And Bernstorff did not have to use his instructions during subsequent weeks because an Ameri-

---

[106] In an earlier draft this sentence read as follows: "Your [Excellency] will please bear in mind that we must endeavor *to avoid at all costs* the mediation of a man so naive in his English-oriented point of view as President Wilson." Quoted in *ibid.*, pp. 106-107. My translation.

[107] Foreign Secretary von Jagow to Ambassador von Bernstorff, June 7, 1916, *Official German Documents Relating to the World War* (2 vols.), ii, 977-978; hereinafter cited as *Official German Documents*. I have altered the translation slightly.

[108] J. W. Gerard to E. M. House, June 14, 1916, House Papers.

can peace move did not materialize on account of British and French opposition. Bernstorff, in his correspondence with House, could, therefore, take the high ground that nothing could be done with the Allies and emphasize the urgency of some American move against the British.[109]

It was not so easy for the British to evade the question. For one thing, the French leaders, who believed that Wilson was interested in mediation mainly as a means of assuring his re-election, were implacably opposed to any equivocation. Ambassador Jusserand, now supported by instructions from his government, saw Colonel House in New York on May 31. The war, House said, could not last much longer without irreparable consequences. The Allies had lost their best chance to end the war by force. The United States would exercise its influence, perhaps even to the point of war, to see that Belgium was restored and France recovered Alsace-Lorraine. Jusserand replied that peace at this time could only serve German interests. France would persevere in spite of losses in blood and treasure. America had nearly as much stake in the outcome as France. "He believes," House reported to the President, "that the salvation of France depends upon her courage and he believes that any peace talk at this time will have a tendency to encourage her enemies and break the spirit of her people."[110] Jusserand, repeating this warning to Frank Polk on June 3, made it clear that the French government desperately feared that Great Britain might respond to an American peace overture.[111] "I cannot quite understand," House said, "why they are so set against peace for if it should come, it would probably come only upon terms that would be satisfactory."[112]

British leaders were themselves becoming acutely worried about what seemed to be the imminent threat of Wilsonian intervention. The chief task just before and after Wilson's speech to the League to Enforce Peace was composition of a reply to House's telegram of May 19.[113] The

[109] e. g., J. von Bernstorff to E. M. House, July 14, 1916, House Papers.

[110] A. Briand to Ambassador Jusserand, May 28, 1916, cited in Erwin Hoelzle, "Das Experiment des Friedens im Ersten Weltkrieg," *Geschichte in Wissenschaft und Unterricht*, 13th Year (August 1962), p. 475; Ambassador Jusserand to the Foreign Ministry, June 2, 1916, cited in *ibid.*; E. M. House to W. W., June 1, 1916, Wilson Papers.

[111] F. L. Polk to W. W., June 6, 1916, *ibid.*; F. L. Polk to E. M. House, June 6, 1916, House Papers.

[112] E. M. House to F. L. Polk, June 8, 1916, *ibid.*

[113] House sent a supplementary enticing message on May 27, 1916: "There is one thing to which I wish to call your attention, and that is the German Chancellor's

Foreign Secretary discussed the matter at least with Asquith and Balfour on May 22 or 23. They were no more willing than French leaders to consent to a mediation that would be highly risky at best, fatal at worst. German armies occupied Europe from the North Sea to the Adriatic and from the Marne to beyond the Vistula. Peace at this time could mean only German victory—unless the United States was really prepared to use the threat of war to compel German withdrawal. But American diplomatic intervention, British leaders knew, could at best achieve no more than a peace based on the *status quo ante bellum*, with German power actually strengthened *vis-à-vis* France and Russia. There was of course the possibility of American military intervention. But who could guarantee it? Not Colonel House, the British statesmen undoubtedly knew. Not even President Wilson. It was doubtful that he was seriously contemplating actual participation.[114] But who could guarantee that he could bring the American Congress and people into the war if he tried?[115] And he would probably insist upon a peace of reconciliation even if he succeeded!

Grey took the position at this time, as he did several times later, that the British government should not consider proposals for mediation, even Wilsonian mediation, so long as there was a chance of an Allied victory. Wilson would be useful as a mediator only in the event that the Allies were about to lose the war. Allied military fortunes seemed far from desperate in the late spring of 1916. The German assault on Verdun had failed. The new British army on the Somme had some hopes of striking a decisive blow. The Foreign Office's efforts to bring Rumania into the war and hit Austria-Hungary on her Achilles' heel were on the verge of success.

---

statement that Germany would make peace on the basis of the map as it stands to-day. This cannot mean anything except a victorious peace for Germany. If England and France, under our invitation, should go into a peace conference now, it would probably lead either to Germany's abandonment of this position or war with us. I thought I would call your attention to this, although I take it you have considered it." E. M. House to E. Grey, May 27, 1916, House Papers. This was sent by mail and arrived *after* Grey had sent his reply.

[114] Grey, for example, told Lord Bertie, British Ambassador to France, on April 10, at the height of the *Sussex* crisis, that he did not believe that Wilson would do more than continue to write notes to Germany. Balfour said on April 14 that he did not believe that the United States would enter the war, for "Wilson wants votes and the country does not want war." Lady Algernon G. Lennox (ed.), *The Diary of Lord Bertie of Thame* (2 vols.), I, 334-336.

[115] As Spring Rice pointed out very trenchantly in a letter to Grey on May 30, 1916, S. Gwynn (ed.), *Letters of Spring Rice*, II, 334-335.

Balfour, at Grey's request, drafted a reply to House's telegram on May 24. It revealed the thinking of the inner circle of the British government so much more clearly than the reply that Grey soon sent that it is printed in full:

"Two questions are raised by your telegram, different though closely connected. The first relates to the territorial arrangements to be made at the conclusion of the war. The second relates to the methods by which a lasting peace may thereafter be secured.

"As regards the first of these, we are evidently bound to our Allies. Separate negotiations are impossible: and even a separate interchange of ideas with a friendly neutral is not easy. But this much may perhaps be said. While no British statesman desires to wage a bloody and costly war in order either to 'destroy' Germany or to be 'revenged' on her, it seems impossible to believe that a peace satisfactory to the Allies can be secured unless Belgium be restored, Alsace and Lorraine given back to France, Poland relieved from German domination, the status of Turkey profoundly modified—*not* in the interests of the Central Powers —and some other changes made in the map of Europe in accordance with the principle of nationality.

"Probably enlightened opinion in America would be favourable to such a consummation. But unless the United States is prepared actively to promote it either by war or the threat of war, it is not easy to see how she can effectively carry out the plans she cherishes for organising an international machinery for the future maintenance of peace. No such plans would be looked at by a Germany which either was in fact successful in the great struggle, or which could persuade itself that it was successful. Britain would be their chief friend, and the friend who could most be trusted to stand by them in the hour of stress. But if they come up for international debate in connection with an unsatisfactory peace, at a moment when perhaps America, by diplomatic pressure, may have whittled down to the utmost the value of that sea power (her own and ours) by which alone the proposed peace machinery can be made effective—then it seems that she would stand but a poor chance of impressing her ideals on the world. Germany will certainly lack the will to help: Britain might lack the power.

"The *best* chance for the great scheme is that it should be proposed by the United States in connection with a peace favourable to the Allies, obtained by American aid.

"The *worst* chance would be that it should be proposed in connection with an inconclusive or disastrous peace accompanied, perhaps promoted, by diplomatic friction between the Allies and the United States over maritime affairs.

"Between these extremes there are endless intermediate possibilities. But evidently a premature announcement of intervention by the President might be dangerous to the cause we have at heart, because it would be interpreted as meaning that he desired peace on the basis of the *status quo ante*, and for the reasons above stated, no such peace could lead to an international organisation of the kind he contemplates."[116]

Grey rewrote Balfour's telegram, omitting its statement of British war objectives and adding the suggestion that House might approach the French government directly about the possibility of peace. He dispatched his message to House on May 29.[117]

House and Grey extended this interchange in a futile correspondence that lasted until nearly the end of August. House wrote on June 8 in reply to Grey's cablegram of May 29, saying that he had already discovered that one got nowhere talking to the French about peace. France, he went on, could *probably* get a peace based on the *status quo ante*, with perhaps Alsace-Lorraine added and Germany given compensation elsewhere. The Allied military position, he warned, could worsen, and the Allied position in the United States could materially change after November. "As far as I can see," he concluded, "there is nothing to add or to do for the moment and if the Allies are willing to take the gamble which the future may hold, we must rest content."[118] No Englishman could urge the French to make peace after their heroic sacrifices at Verdun, Grey replied on June 28; moreover, the British army was determined to make its own effort on the western front.[119] House came back on July 15, warning that forces were at work to drive Britain and America apart.[120] Grey replied petulantly on August 28 in a letter that ended the interchange. It was obvious, he wrote, that the American people were determined to avoid war and it was doubtful that American membership in a league of nations would mean anything. England would not contemplate peace until all the Allies agreed that the right moment had come. None of the Allies was likely to

[116] *SECRET. SUGGESTED DRAFT IN REPLY TO PRIVATE TELEGRAM SENT TO SIR E. GREY* (printed at the Foreign Office, May 25, 1916), copy in the Asquith Papers.
[117] E. Grey to E. M. House, May 29, 1916, House Papers.
[118] E. M. House to E. Grey, June 8, 1916, copy in the Wilson Papers.
[119] E. Grey to E. M. House, June 28, 1916, copy in *ibid*.
[120] E. M. House to E. Grey, July 15, 1916, copy in *ibid*.

consider peace as long as there was a possibility of military victory.[121]

It was hard to accept the unpleasant truth that the Allies did not want Wilson's help. The French had tried to make this clear to House as early as February 1916 and had failed. Grey might have misled House in their conversations during the same month, but he had never made any commitment, not even in the House-Grey Memorandum, to consent to Wilson's mediation. House had believed what he wanted to believe. He had, moreover, led the President to share his fantasies. Awakening had to come, and, when it came rudely in May and June 1916, Wilson and House were both deeply wounded by what they thought was Grey's rejection of their hand of friendship. The conviction grew, as they read Grey's cablegrams and letters in May and June, that the Allies did not want a just peace through American cooperation but were determined to destroy Germany and impose their own peace even at the risk of destroying Europe. Wilson expressed his irritation, for example, in the following letter to Colonel House on June 22:

"The letters and the glimpses of opinion (official opinion) from the other side of the water are not encouraging, to say the least, and indicate a constantly narrowing, instead of a broad and comprehending, view of the situation. They are in danger of forgetting the rest of the world, and of waking up some surprising morning to discover that it has a positive right to be heard about the peace of the world. I conclude that it will be up to us to judge for ourselves when the time has arrived for us to make an imperative suggestion. I mean a suggestion which they will have no choice but to heed, because the opinion of the nonofficial world and the desire of all peoples will be behind it."[122]

---

[121] E. Grey to E. M. House, August 28, 1916, House Papers. Grey, in his aspersion against American unwillingness to use force in a league of nations, was echoing the following comments by Spring Rice: "It is quite evident that the country does not desire war, even when United States territory has been actually invaded [by Mexicans] and Americans killed in their own houses. We may draw the conclusion that this country is by no means ready to assume obligations in the future in Europe in connection with the Peace Treaty, however laudable be the objects. I am sure we would make a mistake if we counted on the active intervention of America as one of the guardians of a world peace. Every indication points in the opposite direction." C. Spring Rice to E. Grey, July 14, 1916, S. Gwynn (ed.), *Letters of Spring Rice*, II, 339. "I must also remind you again that this country is radically and inalterably opposed to intervention in extra-American affairs, except by word, and then only when words cost nothing," Spring Rice wrote again two weeks later. "The American people will not accept liability which entails intervention abroad." C. Spring Rice to E. Grey, July 31, 1916, *ibid.*, pp. 342-343.

[122] W. W. to E. M. House, June 22, 1916, House Papers.

House vented his own feelings, among other times, in his diary and in a letter to Wilson as follows:

"I believe the French and English are prolonging the war unnecessarily. It is stupid to refuse our proffered intervention on the terms I proposed in Paris and London. I made it clear to both Governments that in the event of intervention we would not countenance a peace that did not bring with it a plan which would make for permanent peace, as far as human foresight could do so. If Germany refused to acquiesce in such a settlement, I promised we would take the part of the Allies and try to force it. It would mean the end of militarism, but it would also mean an end of navalism, and that perhaps is where the shoe pinches. Great Britain desires to destroy militarism and at the same time perpetuate navalism, when the war has shown that of the two, navalism might be made the more oppressive of the two branches of military service. . . ."[123]

"When Noel Buxton [an English liberal] was here I told him how impossible it was to satisfy the Allies. It is always something more. . . . It was tiresome, I told Buxton, to hear the English declare they were fighting for Belgium, and that they entered the war for that purpose. I asked if in his opinion Great Britain would have entered the war against France if she had violated Belgium or, indeed, whether Great Britain would not have gone into the war on the side of the Allies even if France had violated Belgium. In my opinion, the purpose of Great Britain's entrance into the war was quite different from that. The stress of the situation compelled her to side with France and Russia and against the Central Powers. Primarily it was because Germany insisted upon having a dominant army and a dominant navy, something Great Britain could not tolerate in safety to herself."[124]

"The conservative or reactionary forces in England are getting a firm grip upon the Cabinet and Asquith is not strong enough to withstand them. They will not want the United States to be a party either to a peace conference or a settlement afterward.

"It is this force in the British Cabinet that has prevented a settlement of the Irish question. Lloyd George, acting under the advice of Asquith, made a proposal to both Nationalists and Ulsterites which was accepted, but when it was placed before the British Cabinet as a whole, the Conservatives refused to ratify it and Asquith did not have the courage to force it through.

[123] House Diary, June 23, 1916.
[124] *ibid.*, June 29, 1916.

"I am afraid we will have the same difficulty in mediation. It may be necessary to arouse the latent feeling of the people in both England and France in such a way that they will compell [*sic*] their governments to act."[125]

It was a crushing disillusionment which, as we will see in a later chapter, had direct consequences both for Anglo-American relations and Wilson's conduct of the presidential campaign.

Meanwhile, preparations for the Democratic national convention that would open in St. Louis in mid-June consumed most of Wilson's energy and attention during the two weeks following delivery of his address before the League to Enforce Peace. Wilson and House had already chosen former Governor Martin H. Glynn of New York to give the keynote speech,[126] and House had been hard at work with Glynn on a draft. The Colonel sent a copy to Wilson on June 1. "Mr. House," the President wrote to Glynn on that same day, "sent me the speech and I have read it with real approval and gratification. I congratulate you. I asked Mr. Tumulty to read it also and between us we have made several minor suggestions."[127] Wilson had also asked his old friend, Judge John W. Wescott of New Jersey, who had nominated him at the Baltimore convention in 1912, to do him the honor of nominating him again at St. Louis.[128]

The platform was the President's main concern during the first days of June. He first appealed through his Postmaster General, Albert S. Burleson, to Democratic leaders in Congress for suggestions, and most of these were in his hands by June 7. Senator William J. Stone of Missouri, chairman of the foreign relations committee, wanted to emphasize Wilson's success in keeping the country out of war and preserving honorable neutrality, and to say that the United States would keep troops in Mexico until order had been restored. Senator

[125] E. M. House to W. W., July 30, 1916, Wilson Papers.

[126] House Diary, May 3, 1916. Glynn had been chosen because he delivered what Wilson and House thought was a particularly effective reply to Root before the Democratic state convention at Syracuse on March 1, 1916. For Glynn's address, see the *New York Times*, March 2, 1916. Wilson was eager to have Speaker Clark as permanent chairman of the convention and turned to Senator Ollie M. James of Kentucky after Clark declined. See W. W. to W. G. McAdoo, May 29, 1916, the Papers of William G. McAdoo, Library of Congress; hereinafter cited as the McAdoo Papers. W. G. McAdoo to W. W., May 29, 1916, *ibid.*

[127] W. W. to M. H. Glynn, June 1, 1916, Wilson Papers.

[128] *New York Times*, May 16, 1916.

Furnifold M. Simmons of North Carolina also put a peace plank at the head of his list. Senator Oscar W. Underwood of Alabama submitted a tariff plank that merely approved the Tariff Act of 1913. Senator Thomas J. Walsh of Montana emphasized the peace theme and maintenance of troops in Mexico.[129]

These were rather obvious points, as were other suggestions for highlighting the administration's record of constructive legislation since 1913. The one big question was how far the party should go in endorsing the federal social legislation that various groups, particularly the National Child Labor Committee and American Association for Labor Legislation, had been pressing upon Congress since the beginning of the Sixty-fourth Congress. It included, among other things, a federal child labor bill, a model workmen's compensation bill for federal employees, and national assistance to the states for vocational education. Wilson and congressional leaders had not included these measures on the list of bills to be passed, much less supported them,[130] and they seemed doomed by early June.

Senator Robert L. Owen of Oklahoma, in a letter to Wilson on June 3, first suggested appropriating the social justice plank of the Progressive platform of 1912 and committing the Democratic party to support of measures now interred in committee. This would be right, Owen said; it would also draw many former Progressives into the Democratic party.[131] "I have your letter of June second [third]," Wilson replied, "and realize the importance of the suggestion you make. Many of the Progressive principles set forth in the Progressive platform of 1912, however, were merely in thesis, because they affected matters controlled by the state and not by the national government. I would be very glad if you would let me have a memorandum as to those which you think we could all agree upon."[132]

The constitutional issue—that is, how far the federal government could invade the police powers of the states in attempting to regulate social and economic relationships—was the great unanswered question of the day. Owen solved the problem by drafting a plank approving everything that every social justice worker had ever proposed and

---

[129] A. S. Burleson to W. W., June 7, 1916, Wilson Papers.

[130] *The Survey*, xxxv (February 26 and March 11, 1916), 623, 693; *ibid.*, xxxvi (April 1, 1916), 38-40.

[131] R. L. Owen to W. W., June 3, 1916, Wilson Papers. Senator Henry F. Hollis of New Hampshire, in the suggested planks that Burleson gathered and sent to Wilson on June 7, seconded Owen's suggestion.

[132] W. W. to R. L. Owen, June 5, 1916, *ibid.*

rather neatly evading the constitutional question. After recounting the struggle of the Democratic party for advanced political democracy, it continued:

"With the triumph of these principles, the people both in the Nation and in the States, can carry out the spirit of Progressive Democracy in the conservation of human resources through enlightened measures of social and industrial justice; for the prevention of industrial accidents, occupational diseases and overwork; involuntary unemployment and other injurious effects incident to modern industry; the fixing of minimum safety and health standards for the various occupations, and the harmonious exercise of the public authority of State and Nation in maintaining such standards; the prohibition of child labor; the establishment of minimum wage standards for working men, women, and children, and a living wage scale in industrial occupations; the establishment of an eight hour day for women and young persons, and one day's rest in seven for all wage workers; improved methods of dealing with delinquent citizens in prison and out of it; the preservation of the rights of human beings to the opportunity of labor, self support and development, and the establishment of such social and industrial reforms as will increase to the highest point the efficiency, the self respect, and the happiness of the American people."

Such commitment, Owen urged in a covering letter to Wilson on June 8, "would be of special value as a plank to attract the progessive elements in the country who ought to be with us, and not dividing their forces as an independent party, much less in the impossible relations of supporting Barnes, Penrose, Cannon and Root, who are absolutely hostile to the progressive program."[133] Wilson replied four days later: "Your letter of June eighth, with its enclosure reached me, and I think you will find in the suggestions I have made to the Resolutions Committee by their kind invitation the substance of a greater part of what you so opportunely suggest."[134]

Wilson had assembled a preliminary draft of the platform by June 9 and read it to the Cabinet on that date. He apparently gave a revised copy of this draft to Senator Stone,[135] chairman of the convention's resolutions committee, before Stone left for St. Louis on June

[133] R. L. Owen to W. W., June 8, 1916, *ibid.*

[134] W. W. to R. L. Owen, June 12, 1916, *ibid.*

[135] Revised after receipt of a long letter from Secretary of the Treasury William G. McAdoo suggesting changes. See W. G. McAdoo to W. W., June 10, 1916, McAdoo Papers.

11.[136] The President, on the following day, sent a further revised draft to St. Louis by Secretary of War Newton D. Baker and a special tariff plank by A. Mitchell Palmer, Democratic politician from Pennsylvania.[137] Wilson was in frequent communication by telephone with members of the resolutions committee until they completed their work. On June 14, for example, he helped to prepare a new plank condemning so-called disloyal hyphenates and vetoed a proposed plank criticizing Hughes for leaving the Supreme Court to run for the presidency.[138] There were some fierce struggles in the resolutions committee, but the President had his way on all major planks, yielding only to the degree of permitting incorporation of a declaration in favor of keeping American troops in Mexico until the border was secure. The platform, approved at the end of the convention on June 16, was, therefore, Wilson's own creation.

It was also one of the most important documents in the history of modern American democracy. The opening sections, proudly reviewing Democratic achievements since 1913, were, to be sure, unremarkable, as were the planks endorsing an "adequate" army, a navy "worthy to support the great naval traditions of the United States and fully equal to the international tasks which this Nation hopes and expects to take a part in performing," neutrality in foreign policy, Pan-American concord, and friendship with Mexico. What was remarkable— and determinative in the long run—was the platform's open, unreserved, and unabashed espousal of internationalism abroad and bold nationalistic progressivism at home, and its vision of a powerful government busy building the peace of the world and protecting the welfare and security of its own citizens.

"The circumstances of the last two years," the plank on foreign policy read, in Wilson's words, "have revealed necessities of international action which no former generation can have foreseen. We hold that it is the duty of the United States to use its power, not only to make itself safe at home, but also to make secure its just interests throughout the world, and, both for this end and in the interest of humanity, to assist the world in securing settled peace and justice." Here followed a reaffirmation of the international ideals that Wilson had stated in his address of May 27. "We believe," the plank continued "that the time has

---

[136] *New York Times,* June 10 and 12, 1916.

[137] N. D. Baker to R. S. Baker, April 30, 1932, Baker Collection; *New York Times,* June 14, 1916.

[138] *ibid.,* June 15, 1916.

come when it is the duty of the United States to join the other nations of the world in any feasible association that will effectively serve those principles, to maintain inviolate the complete security of the highway of the seas for the common and unhindered use of all nations."[139]

The affirmation of nationalistic progressivism was equally forthright. The tariff plank reaffirmed allegiance to the principle of tariff for revenue only, but it said in the same breath that tariff rates were of course subject to changing world conditions, and it endorsed a non-partisan Tariff Commission. The platform also called for strong federal action to restore the American flag to the seas, endorsed federal rural credits and aid to highway construction, pledged the federal governments to provide a living wage and workmen's compensation protection to its own employees, demanded adoption of a federal child labor bill and other social justice measures, and commended the cause of woman suffrage to the states. The plank on Americanism was a clear call to different nationalities and races to be "welded into a mighty and splendid Nation," followed by a warning to subversives and political parties that catered to them.[140]

Democrats had meanwhile gathered at the huge flag-draped Coliseum in St. Louis at noon on June 14 for the opening session of their national convention. Wilson, determined that his followers should outdo Republicans in their display of patriotism, had sent personal instructions that "Americanism" should be the keynote of the Democratic conclave. The convention would open by singing verses of "America" and "The Star-Spangled Banner," to be followed at other sessions by "The Red, White, and Blue" and other patriotic songs. "Dixie" might be sung in moderation, but not as often as "The Star-Spangled Banner." Loud cheers should follow mention of America and the flag, and the sergeant at arms should bring the convention to its feet at appropriate climaxes.[141]

The delegates sang verses of "America" and "The Star-Spangled Banner" without any enthusiasm, stood uncomfortably during a long prayer, and applauded dutifully when William F. McCombs, retiring chairman of the National Committee, made the somewhat obscure observation in his address opening the convention that the Demo-

---

[139] The resolutions committee struck out, whether with Wilson's approval we do not know, the conclusion of this sentence as the President had written it, as follows: "and to prevent any war begun either contrary to treaty covenants or without warning and frank submission of the provocation and causes to the opinion of mankind."

[140] K. H. Porter and D. B. Johnson (eds.), *National Party Platforms*, pp. 194-200.

[141] *New York Times*, June 15, 1916.

cratic party's "chief tenet of faith is that America is Americanism, and Americans are American." Then former Governor Glynn began his keynote address. He, too, began by playing upon the patriotic theme. Democrats, he said, stood for "the Americanism of the Fathers . . . which under the magic spell of citizenship and the mystic influence of the Stars and Stripes converts men of every country into men of one country, and that country our country." The great audience responded indifferently until Glynn declared that the paramount issue of the campaign was President Wilson's foreign policy. Delegates thundered applause when Glynn shouted the "self-evident truths" that the United States should stay out of the war, maintain strict neutrality, and defend its neutral rights against *every* belligerent.

Glynn then began a long and matter-of-fact recital of precedents to prove that neutrality, patience, and refusal to go to war under provocation had places of honor in American annals. When he reached the settlement of the *Alabama* claims, he indicated that he would pass over the rest of his historical account. "And so goes our history," he said. "I don't want to take too much time to enumerate it all, but the—" The entire convention rose to its feet in protest. There were loud cries of "Go on, go on," "Hit him again," "Hit him again," "Give it to them." Glynn, thinking that the delegates were merely being kind, responded with a deprecating smile. He suddenly realized as he studied the sea of faces before him that his listeners were passionately eager to hear further proof that all great leaders in American history had been against war, and that neutrality had been the cornerstone of American foreign policy.

"All right," he said, "I'll hit them again, and I'll hit them fair, and I'll hit them hard."

"Eat 'em up," some one shouted.

"Now you want some more of it, do you," Glynn said.

"Yes." "Yes." "Yes." "Yes," voices replied.

"All right," Glynn said.

Glynn went on citing precedents, backtracking to Washington, Adams, and Jefferson. Then he came to the *Chesapeake* affair. He hesitated, wondering how the audience would react to this most humiliating assault on American sovereignty and Jefferson's refusal to seek redress by appeal to arms. The delegates approved with a great roar. As Glynn cited one case after another in which the United States had refused under provocation to go to war, the throng would chant,

"What did we do? What did we do?" And Glynn would shout back, "We didn't go to war."

Bryan, who had been defeated for election as a delegate in Nebraska, was sitting in the press box as a correspondent. He wept with emotion. Other Democratic leaders were not so happy. Senator John Walter Smith of Maryland came running to the platform in wild agitation to tell McCombs that something had to be done to stop the stampede. Otherwise, he said, it would appear that Democrats were for peace at any price. McCombs wrote "But we are willing to fight if necessary" on a slip of paper and passed it to Glynn. The speaker nodded and called back, "I'll take care of that." But the crowd would not let him stop his paean of peace. He went on:

"This policy does not satisfy those who revel in destruction and find pleasure in despair. It may not satisfy the fire-eater or the swashbuckler. [Laughter and applause.] But it does satisfy those who worship at the altar of the God of Peace. It does satisfy the mothers of the land [applause], for whom [great applause]—But, my friends, this policy does satisfy the mothers of the land, at whose hearth and fireside no jingoistic war has placed an empty chair. It does satisfy the daughters of this land, from whom brag and bluster have sent no husband, no sweetheart and no brother to the mouldering dissolution of the grave. It does satisfy the fathers of this land, and the sons of this land, who will fight for our flag, and die for our flag, when Reason primes the rifle—[Long continued applause.]

"A VOICE: 'Say it again.' 'Repeat it.' Cries of 'Repeat it.' 'Repeat it.' 'Say it again.' 'Say it again.'

"MR. GLYNN: All right. Give me a chance. I shall repeat. You want me to repeat it. All right. (Repeating): But this policy does satisfy the mothers of the land, at whose hearth and fireside no jingoistic war has placed an empty chair. It does satisfy the mothers of this land, from whom brag and bluster have sent no husband, no sweetheart and no brother to the mouldering dissolution of the grave. It does satisfy the fathers of this land, and the sons of this land, who will fight for our flag, and die for our flag, when Reason primes the rifle—[Great applause.]

"[Cries of 'Say it again.']

"MR. GLYNN (Continuing):—when Reason primes the rifle, when Honor draws the sword, when Justice breathes a blessing on the standards they uphold. [Great applause. Cries of 'Say it again.']

"MR. FRANK DAVIS, of Texas: And, Mr. Speaker, don't forget that this policy also satisfies William Jennings Bryan."

The delegates were finally exhausted, and Glynn passed on to preparedness and other domestic issues. The storm had passed; the mood of exaltation was gone. Glynn droned on until the end; then he tried to revive enthusiasm with a climactic tribute to Wilson. The weary delegates cheered for one minute; then there was dead silence. Alfred E. Smith of New York read the President's Flag Day proclamation, and Glynn and others on the platform tried to start a demonstration. They failed, and the convention adjourned.[142]

A dramatic, unexpected event, which occurred soon after the second session was called to order at a few minutes before noon on June 15 revealed that the delegates were entirely and permanently out of control. The convention rose and cheered with obvious affection when Bryan entered the press box. The credentials committee made its long report, and Senator Ollie M. James of Kentucky then began his address as permanent chairman. He was a huge man, with a face like a prize fighter, but his gestures were supple, and his strong voice had the virtuosity of a fine pipe organ. He was also a veteran campaigner who knew how to handle a crowd. Thus he did not begin with his climax, as Glynn had done accidentally, but with a careful review of the Democratic party's achievements under Woodrow Wilson. The delegates were friendly but restrained, and James knew that they were waiting for the only subject that excited them. He tested reactions by a brief excursion into foreign problems. "There are happily two kinds of courage," he suddenly roared, "the courage of the man who is willing to undertake the danger himself, and the courage of the man that sends others to the conflict. The courage of the man who wishes himself to enter the conflict may be rash, for he alone is to suffer, but the courage to take a nation into war, where millions of lives may be sacrificed, is another kind of courage. [Applause.] It is a courage that must be able to stand bitter abuse; a courage that moves slowly, acts coolly, and strikes no blow as long as diplomacy may be employed, the honor of the country upheld, the flag respected and the lives of Americans protected. [Applause.]"

---

[142] The quotations from McComb's and Glynn's speeches are from J. Bruce Kremer (comp.), *Official Report of the Proceedings of the Democratic National Convention . . . 1916*, pp. 11-41. I have relied heavily on the *New York Times*, June 15, 1916, for my account of the scene in the convention. The square brackets are in the text in the *Official Report*.

The convention roared approval, and James, not yet ready for the climax, changed the subject and talked about Mexico, the shipping bill, and other matters equally unexciting. Suddenly he changed from conversational tone to crescendo as he began to tell about Wilson's diplomatic triumphs. "Without orphaning a single American child," he said, "without widowing a single American mother, without firing a single gun, without the shedding of a single drop of blood, he wrung from the most militant spirit that ever brooded above a battlefield an acknowledgement of American rights and an agreement to American demands." Most delegates did not hear the last part of this sentence, although James bellowed it at the top of his voice, for a sound like the rush of a storm began in the Coliseum before he uttered the word "spirit," and a crashing wave of sound broke over the platform as he finished the sentence. Then the crowd checked itself, and there were cries of "Repeat it!" "Repeat it!" James was stunned and stood at the podium with mouth open, lips motionless. "Repeat it!" "Repeat it!" they shouted again, and James stepped to the edge of the platform and sent the sentence rolling over the heads of the great audience. The delegates listened in intense silence to every syllable. Then they leaped to their feet, waving hats, fans, and flags, and cheered. The Virginia delegation began a procession through the aisles. They were joined by the delegations from Indiana, Tennessee, Texas, and many other states. The roar and pandemonium were mounting all the time.

The demonstration subsided after twenty-one minutes, and James resumed his tribute. Republicans, he said, accused the President of being "evil and vacillating" because he had not gone to war when Belgium was invaded. Democrats were willing to submit that issue to the American people. "When the last great day shall come," he went on, building to another climax, "and before the Court of God the nations of this earth shall march in judgment review, the monarchs of the Old World shall have to answer for this awful carnage ..., and on that last day I can see our President holding in his hand the accusing picture of Henri Danger, of Christ upon the battlefield, with the dead and dying all about him, with the roar of cannon, the screaming of shrapnel, the wail of the dying, and above his head written these words; 'And He said unto them, love one another.' [Applause.] When that day shall come, who is it that would have our President exchange places with the blood-spattered monarchs of the Old World? [Applause.] I can see him with the white light streaming upon his head and hear the Master say, 'Blessed are the peacemakers, for they shall be called the children of God.' [Applause.]" Delegates cheered this intended climax lustily, but they were too exhausted to demonstrate for long, and the convention adjourned at 1:28 p.m. in order not to miss the hospitality being offered by the city of St. Louis.[143]

They came back that evening at nine o'clock feeling much enlivened. There were shouts of "Bryan!" "Bryan!" soon after James called the convention to order, and the rules were suspended to permit the Commoner to speak. It was, next to the occasion of his Cross of Gold speech in 1896, the greatest moment in his life. He had been rejected, scorned, and despised since his resignation as Secretary of State. Now he stood before *his* Democracy, vindicated and rewarded, once more the cornerstone of his party. All doubt, resentment, and bitterness were gone from his capacious heart and mind. He reviewed the reform legislation of the past three years, giving unstinted credit to the leader who had made it possible. He saved his warmest praise for Wilson's labors for peace. "My friends," he said, "I have differed with our President on some of the methods employed, but I join with the American people in thanking God that we have a President who does not want this nation plunged into this war."[144]

James called for nominations for a candidate for the office of President of the United States at 10:14 p.m. Alabama, the first state called, yielded to New Jersey, and Judge Wescott went ponderously to the podium. "Prophecy is fulfilled," he began, ". . . The nation is at work. The nation is at peace. The nation is accomplishing the destiny of Democracy." He went on for thirty minutes apotheosizing the man of peace, not mentioning his name until the grand conclusion: "Therefore, my fellow-countrymen, not I, but his deeds and achievements; not I, but the spirit and purposes of America; not I, but civilization itself, nominates to succeed himself to the Presidency of the United States, to the Presidency of one hundred million free people, bound in impregnable union, the scholar, the statesman, the financier, the emancipator, the pacificator, the moral leader of Democracy, Woodrow Wilson." The crowd, breaking into its first heart-felt demonstration for the President, marched, sang, and shouted for forty-five minutes. Seconding speeches followed, and Wilson was nominated by acclama-

[143] *New York Times,* June 16, 1916; *Official Report of the Proceedings of the Democratic National Convention . . . 1916,* pp. 79-91, for the text of James's speech.
[144] *ibid.,* pp. 94-99; *New York Times,* June 16, 1916.

tion (by a vote of 1092 to 1) at 11:53. Vice President Thomas R. Marshall was nominated by acclamation two minutes later.[145]

Delegates met the next day, June 16, to consider the platform. It had been changed significantly following Glynn's address, by whom and whether with Wilson's approval we do not know. To the sentence commending Wilson and Marshall for faithful performance of duties had been added the words: "In particular, we commend to the American people the splendid diplomatic victories of our great President, who has preserved the vital interests of our Government and its citizens, and kept us out of war." It was the first time that the phrase "He kept us out war" had been used. It would not be the last. As soon as the platform was read, Martin M. Lomasney of Massachusetts moved adoption of a plank affirming the Democratic party's "profound sympathy with the aspirations of the people of Ireland for the complete independence of their country." His resolution was discreetly and quickly referred to the resolutions committee. Then Governor James E. Ferguson of Texas, speaking for a minority of the resolutions committee, moved to strike the plank recommending the cause of woman suffrage to the states. It was defeated by an overwhelming majority, and the convention approved the unamended platform by voice and adjourned *sine die* a few minutes later.[146]

It was the eve of battle, and it found the Democracy strong and confident and united by passion for peace. Wilson left no record of his immediate reactions to the remarkable events that had produced their unexpected culmination at St. Louis. Would he yield to the tide, perhaps even seize leadership of the pacifistic movement? He gave some indication of intention in the letters that he wrote to Glynn, James, and Wescott on June 22 and June 23, thanking them for their "wonderful" speeches. "The extraordinary and deserved success of your remarkable speech at the convention," he wrote, for example, to Glynn, "has already received the most unusual acknowledgment from the convention itself and from the Press of the country, but I want to add my word of appreciation and gratitude. It was and I am sure will remain one of the most notable things of a campaign which, before we get through with it, should stir to the very bottom the conscience and thought of the United States."[147]

[145] *ibid.; Official Report of the Proceedings of the Democratic National Convention . . . 1916*, pp. 100-107.
[146] *ibid.*, pp. 114-148; *New York Times*, June 17, 1916.
[147] W. W. to M. H. Glynn, June 22, 1916; W. W. to O. M. James, June 22, 1916; W. W. to J. W. Wescott, June 23, 1916, all in the Wilson Papers.

CHAPTER II

Summer Interlude

ONSET of summer found Democratic leaders hard at work in New York building a campaign organization and Wilson in Washington more engrossed in affairs of state than at any time since the *Sussex* crisis. Congress had completed only the Army Reorganization and rural credits bills. The other measures in the President's legislative program—the naval appropriation, shipping, Philippine, and revenue bills—were making steady progress but still needed a strong presidential hand to guide them to completion. Storm clouds were also gathering and breaking on the diplomatic horizon. It was no time for a part-time President.

Of course it was not possible to ignore Democrats and friends who were now rallying throughout the country in preparation for the great battle. Wilson encouraged them as best he could by correspondence.[1] He sent special greetings to independents and former Progressives who were organizing in his behalf. "Your telegram of July second," he wrote, for example, on July 4 to Francis J. Heney, Progressive of San Francisco, who had just come out in his support, "I need hardly say gives me sincere satisfaction, not only because of the support it so generously promises, but also because of the added emphasis it contributes to the real issues of the campaign and the objects which all true friends of popular government should keep prominently in mind."[2] To another Progressive, Wilson wrote: "I sincerely desire and have tried to deserve the support of all progressive, forward-looking men."[3] He was particularly pleased when Representative William Kent of California accepted the chairmanship of the newly-formed Woodrow Wilson Independent League,[4] and when Bainbridge Colby, Matthew Hale, and other former leaders of the Progressive party came to the White House to tell him that they planned to organize former Progres-

[1] e. g., W. W. to Mrs. D. S. McKenna, June 23, 1916, Wilson Papers; W. W. to J. L. Sullivan, July 18, 1916, *ibid.*; W. W. to M. L. Gorey, July 24, 1916, *ibid.*

[2] W. W. to F. J. Heney, July 4, 1916, *ibid.*

[3] W. W. to J. C. Parker, July 14, 1916, *ibid.*

[4] W. W. to W. Kent, July 18, 1916, published in the *New York Times*, July 20, 1916.

sives behind the Democratic standard.[5] Wilson also prepared a long letter to Representative A. F. Lever of South Carolina, reviewing Democratic legislation since 1913 to benefit farmers.[6] It was distributed widely as a campaign document.[7]

But crushing burdens in Washington made it impossible to think about playing an active role at this time. "I found the President embarrassed by the thought that he ought not to turn to politics until the business of the Congressional session was over," Vance McCormick told reporters on July 17 after talking with Wilson about his notification speech. ". . . He feels it to be his duty to postpone the notification ceremony until the adjournment of Congress."[8] It seemed, besides, to be the safe as well as the right thing to do once Hughes made his speech of acceptance on July 31, for reaction to the Republican candidate's captious criticism and utter lack of constructive alternatives was extremely hostile except in regular Republican circles.[9] Wilson, wrote Homer S. Cummings, secretary of the Democratic National Committee, in a memorandum of a meeting at the White House on August 7, "was apparently in a cheerful mood. He seemed in good health and greeted us [Cummings and McCormick] affably. We talked over matters of the campaign. Anyone who believes that the President is not a practical man or an astute politician is making a profound mistake. . . . He has an abiding faith that despite all false issues and the misrepresentations and the confusion of an active campaign, somehow the people will judge aright and will understand what he has done and is trying to do. He is not disposed to take the stump. He believes he is making better progress by attending to his duties than he could hope to make in a political tour. He is quite willing, as he says, to let Mr. Hughes 'blow himself off' in his tour across the country."[10] As Wilson put it, "I am inclined to follow the course suggested by a friend of mine who says that he has always followed the rule never

[5] New York *World*, August 18, 1916. For other letters to independents and Progressives during this early stage of the campaign, see W. W. to R. S. Baker, June 23, 1916, Wilson Papers; W. W. to Mayor Ole Hanson of Seattle, July 18, 1916, *ibid.*; and W. W. to W. L. Hall, secretary, Railway Workers' Non-Partisan Association, August 17, 1916, *ibid.*

[6] *New York Times*, August 21, 1916.

[7] Democratic National Committee, *How Wilson Has Kept Faith with the Farmer.*

[8] *New York Times*, July 18, 1916.

[9] e. g., *Denver Post, New York Times, Springfield* (Mass.) *Republican, New York Evening Post, New York World*, all dated August 1, 1916; *New York Nation*, CIII (August 3, 1916), 96; and *New Republic*, VIII (August 5, 1916), 4-5.

[10] H. S. Cummings, memorandum dated August 7, 1916, Baker Collection.

to murder a man who is committing suicide, and clearly this mis-directed gentleman [Hughes] is committing suicide slowly but surely."[11]

The Mexican crisis following the engagement at Carrizal was the matter that consumed most of the President's thought and time during the two weeks following the St. Louis Convention. It would not be possible to withdraw the Punitive Expedition without giving Republicans a powerful issue and, incidentally, violating the Democratic platform even before the campaign had begun. And yet some *modus vivendi* had to be found to permit the troops to remain and avert war at the same time. Only in this way could Mexico be neutralized as a campaign issue.

Wilson led the way in his address before the New York Press Club on June 30.[12] Reaction proved beyond doubt that the great mass of Americans did not want war with Mexico any more than with Germany. It also evoked a friendly response in Mexico City, where newspapers used large type in printing Wilson's statements that the American people did not want war and he was not the servant of Americans with investments in Mexico. Mexicans also mistakenly interpreted Pershing's action in pulling his forward troops from Namiquipa toward Colonia Dublan to mean that a general withdrawal had begun. Venustiano Carranza, Mexican First Chief, had been playing a dangerous game in the belief that Wilson would not make the choice for war by permitting Pershing to flout his, Carranza's, limitations on the movement of the Punitive Expedition. The First Chief had kept his nerve all through the tense days following Carrizal, yielding the minor point of the release of the prisoners while standing firm on the major point of the containment of the American troops. He, no more than Wilson, had ever wanted war, and Wilson's New York speech afforded the opportunity to renew diplomatic negotiations without loss of face.

Hence Cándido Aguilar, Mexican Foreign Secretary, responded on July 3 in a note to pave the way. The Mexican government, it said, sincerely desired to reach a peaceful solution of its difficulties with the United States—the prompt release of the prisoners at Chihuahua was proof enough of peaceful intentions. The real causes of the present controversy, Aguilar went on, were the American government's understandable desire to protect the border and the Mexican government's resentment against American violation of its sovereignty. The Mexican

---

[11] W. W. to B. M. Baruch, August 19, 1916, Wilson Papers.
[12] For which, see A. S. Link, *Wilson: Confusions and Crises*, pp. 316-317.

government was prepared to negotiate for a solution that would eliminate both causes of discord. It was also willing to accept the mediation of certain Latin American governments and would leave the choice between direct negotiation and mediation to the Washington government.[13] "When you transmit the above to the Department of State," Aguilar instructed Eliseo Arredondo, Carranza's representative in Washington, "I request of you very specially, in behalf of the First Chief, to do all you can to impress on that Department the conviction of the Mexican Government's sincerity in all its pursuits and our eager wishes to find a peaceful solution to the present difficulties between countries which must needs maintain good relations."[14]

Arredondo delivered the note to Lansing in the morning of July 5. The Secretary of State was so pleased that he, or his spokesman in the Department, told reporters that it was the wisest and most restrained communication that the American government had ever received from the *de facto* authorities.[15] Wilson had already asked Lansing, on July 3, to suggest a plan, and Lansing had proposed a joint high commission[16] to consider causes of Mexican-American discord and their alleviation.[17] "I believe from the tone of this note," he wrote to Wilson on July 5, as he sent an English translation of Aguilar's communication, "that the suggestion in my letter of the 3rd instant may possibly be worked out. Just how we should approach the Mexican Government on the subject I am not quite sure. Would you think it advisable for me to talk the matter over with Mr. Arredondo informally?"[18]

[13] E. Arredondo to the Secretary of State, July 4, 1916, *Papers Relating to the Foreign Relations of the United States, 1916*, p. 599; hereinafter cited as *Foreign Relations, 1916*.

[14] C. Aguilar to E. Arredondo, July 3, 1916, Mexican Foreign Office, *Diplomatic Dealings of the Constitutionalist Revolution in Mexico*, p. 265; hereinafter cited as *Mexican White Paper*.

[15] *New York Times*, July 6, 1916.

[16] Creation of such a commission had in fact already been suggested by Willard E. Simpson, a friend of the publisher, Oswald Garrison Villard, and by a group representing the Executive Council of the American Federation of Labor and the labor movement of Mexico. See W. E. Simpson to O. G. Villard, June 25, 1916; J. P. Gavit to J. P. Tumulty, June 27, 1916, enclosing Simpson's letter; W. W. to J. P. Tumulty, c. June 29, 1916, commenting on Simpson's letter; report of the Executive Council of the American Federation of Labor and representatives of organized labor in Mexico, dated July 3, 1916, all in the Wilson Papers.

[17] "If the Carrizal incident was a clear case of Mexican aggression," Lansing explained, "I doubt if I would be favorable to this policy, but it appears to me that Captain Boyd was possibly to blame. At least there is sufficient contradiction in the statements of those present to put us on inquiry as to the facts before taking drastic action." R. Lansing to W. W., July 3, 1916, *The Lansing Papers*, II, 560-562.

[18] R. Lansing to W. W., July 5, 1916, Papers of the Department of State, National Archives; hereinafter cited as the State Department Papers.

Wilson was so delighted by Aguilar's note that he called Lansing by telephone as soon as he had read it, asking the Secretary to talk to Arredondo and meanwhile to prepare a reply suggesting appointment of a joint high commission.[19] Arredondo thought well of the plan, and Lansing, after further discussion with the President in the morning of July 6 (during which the two men decided that it would be well to let the suggestion of a commission come from the Mexicans), completed his draft that afternoon. "Will you kindly indicate any changes you would desire," he wrote as he sent the draft to Wilson, "and I would be very much pleased if you could send this note to my house tonight, or else have it at the Department very early in the morning."[20] Wilson made, as he said on returning the note that same evening, "a few verbal alterations which . . . clarify the expression a little."[21] Delivered to Arredondo on July 7, it expressed profound gratitude for Aguilar's "frank statement," along with the American government's desire for continued friendly relations with Mexico and readiness to exchange views about a practical plan to remove causes of conflict between the two countries.[22]

Carranza responded eagerly on July 12, suggesting appointment of a joint high commission composed of three representatives of each government to arrange for evacuation of the Punitive Expedition and settle other differences.[23] It seemed momentarily that agreement might fail, in spite of the obvious good will on both sides, because Wilson and Counselor Polk, who was managing the negotiations, proposed that the commission be empowered to discuss internal Mexican problems as well as more immediate matters.[24] Carranza, correctly suspecting that the American government still desired a large voice in determination of Mexican social and economic policies, at first flatly refused to listen to the American suggestion.[25] "The Mexicans," Polk wrote on July 22, "are as unsatisfactory as usual and are not playing fair. . . . My difficulty is that I have no confidence in any promise or agreement they may make. I keep in close touch with the President in this matter,

---

[19] Lansing Desk Diary, July 5, 1916.

[20] R. Lansing to W. W., July 6, 1916, State Department Papers.

[21] W. W. to R. Lansing, July 6, 1916, enclosing R. Lansing to E. Arredondo, July 6, 1916, with Wilson's emendations, *ibid*.

[22] The Secretary of State to E. Arredondo, July 7, 1916, *Foreign Relations, 1916*, p. 600.

[23] E. Arredondo to the Secretary of State, July 12, 1916, *ibid*., p. 601.

[24] F. L. Polk, memorandum dated July 14, 1916, the Papers of Frank L. Polk, Yale University Library; hereinafter cited as the Polk Papers.

[25] F. L. Polk, memorandum dated July 18, 1916, *ibid*.

as I feel that it is his particular problem."[26] In the end both sides resorted to ambiguity to break the impasse. Polk, at Wilson's direction,[27] replied to the Mexican note of July 12 on July 28, suggesting only that the commission be authorized to "consider such other matters the friendly arrangement of which would tend to improve the relations of the two countries; it being understood that such recommendations as the Commission may make shall not be binding upon the respective Governments until formally accepted by them."[28] Carranza agreed at once, insisting only that the commission give preference in its discussions to withdrawal of the Punitive Expedition and Mexican-American efforts to protect the border. In the same note the First Chief announced appointment of the Mexican commissioners.[29] Wilson announced his own appointees on August 22: Secretary of the Interior Franklin K. Lane, Judge George Gray of Delaware, and John R. Mott, the Y.M.C.A. leader.[30]

Some officials in Washington were not optimistic about the chances of Mexican-American understanding and cooperation. "Personally," Polk wrote to Lansing on August 3, "I have a feeling that nothing is going to come of this conference. Carranza is acting with even more stupidity than usual, if that is possible, and I think when the Commission meets his Commissioners will decline to discuss anything until the evacuation of Mexican territory by American troops is disposed of. Arredondo seemed very suspicious of any suggestion to widen the scope of the Commission and has told people in confidence that he sees nothing for them to consider beyond the border difficulties. This also seems to be the opinion of many in Mexico City. They certainly are discouraging people to try to help."[31]

Even so, the President, who made every single important decision on Mexican policy during these weeks, had succeeded by mid-summer both in blunting the Republican attack and in putting himself in a position from which he could launch his own counterattack. He had done this by making three fundamental decisions:

[26] F. L. Polk to E. M. House, July 22, 1916, House Papers.

[27] See C. L. Swem to F. L. Polk, n. d., but July 28, 1916, State Department Papers, on which Polk wrote: "President telephoned me at Metropolitan Club July 27 – 1916 that this met with his approval, to polish it up & give it to Arredondo. He repeated these instructions at Cabinet today. F. L. P. July 28 – 1916."

[28] The Acting Secretary of State to E. Arredondo, July 28, 1916, *Foreign Relations, 1916*, p. 604.

[29] E. Arredondo to the Secretary of State, August 4, 1916, *ibid.*, p. 606.

[30] *New York Times*, August 23, 1916.

[31] F. L. Polk to R. Lansing, August 3, 1916, Lansing Papers, LC.

First, to accept the proposal for a Joint High Commission. This enabled him, as well as Carranza, to postpone decision on the really vital issues, such as withdrawal of the Punitive Expedition, until after the presidential election.

Second, to avoid war with Mexico, unless, of course, the Mexicans themselves opened hostilities. Mutual acceptance of the plan for a Joint High Commission averted this danger.

Third, to keep Pershing's troops in Mexico, in spite of advice from General Frederick Funston, American commander in the Southwest, that Villa's bands had been destroyed and difficulties of supply made withdrawal all the more advisable.[32] The political risks of following sound advice were simply too great, and Wilson announced on August 20 that the troops would stay a while longer, until the American members of the Joint High Commission were convinced that the *de facto* authorities were able to maintain order and protect the border.[33]

Polk explained American policy at this time, and surely spoke for the President, in discussion with the British Ambassador on August 4. "I told him frankly," Polk wrote in a memorandum of this conversation, "the situation, to my mind, was something like this: That Carranza was the leader of his country, such as he was. That we had two courses open to us, either to deal patiently with Carranza or to break off relations and go into Mexico; that if we went into Mexico it would mean a matter of years and that no government could be established now, which would stand. It would also mean that our attention would be directed, and our army and navy would be busy, with Mexico at the most critical time of the European war. That our entrance into Mexico would also, as he should know, seriously affect certain British interests (oil supplies, although I did not say so).

"He said he fully realized that it would be most unfortunate if we were drawn into a war with Mexico at the present moment. I said the alternative would be to be as patient with Mexico as we could, but loss of prestige was not to be seriously considered, for we were confident of the fact that we had the power and strength to assert ourselves when the time came and we should not allow pride to dictate the policy with a smaller power. That therefore if we were to be patient with Carranza, we should be patient as long as we possibly could."[34]

[32] F. Funston to the Adjutant General, received August 17, 1916, State Department Papers.

[33] New York *World*, August 21, 1916.

[34] F. L. Polk, memorandum of a conversation with the British Ambassador, August 4, 1916, Polk Papers.

Other unforeseen legislative and diplomatic problems prolonged the interlude between the conventions and the beginning of Wilson's campaign. Secretary of the Navy Josephus Daniels and A. J. McKelway, secretary of the National Child Labor Committee, pointed out the first problem—the necessity of obtaining action on the child labor and federal workmen's compensation bills—on July 17. A child labor bill sponsored by Representative Edward Keating of Colorado and Senator Owen had passed the House of Representatives by the thumping majority of 337 to 46 on February 2, 1916. It forbade the shipment in

He Doesn't See Them

Richards in the Philadelphia *North American*

interstate commerce of products manufactured in whole or in part by children under fourteen, of the output of mines and quarries in which the labor of children under sixteen was involved, and of any products by children under sixteen working at night or more than eight hours a day.[35] It was reported favorably by the Senate interstate commerce committee in April and then sidetracked, mainly because the National Association of Manufacturers and state rights southern senators opposed it as signaling the beginning of a broad federal regulation of hours and wages under the commerce clause of the Constitution. As a spokesman of the N.A.M. explained:

"The measure has been opposed by industrial organizations throughout the country, not because they object to any reasonable regulation of child labor, which, in fact, nearly all these associations have approved and participated in making, but because they feel that it takes from all industry local self-government of conditions of manufacture essentially local in nature.

"It is frankly stated by the proponents of the legislation that if the principle is recognized by the enactment of this proposal, which gathers strength from the sentimental appeal which it carries, they will then urge further legislation prohibiting the shipment in interstate commerce of any commodity produced in whole or part by the labor of men or women who work more than eight hours, receive less than a minimum wage, or have not certain educational qualifications. The whole effect of this and still further measures will be to reduce the police power of the state with respect to purely internal and domestic affairs to one of legislative impotence."[36]

That, indeed, was the prospect that frightened many conservatives. But such worries seemed unfounded. The Democratic senatorial caucus met on July 15 and agreed at the insistence of Southerners not to consider the child labor bill during the present session.[37]

Prospects for the federal workmen's compensation bill, sponsored by Senator John W. Kern of Indiana and Representative Daniel J. McGillicuddy of Maine, did not seem much brighter. Labor leaders and lobbyists for the American Association for Labor Legislation had finally obtained passage of the Kern-McGillicuddy bill by the House of Representatives on July 12, by a majority of 287 to 3.[38] There was no active opposition in the Senate; Democrats, after all, had approved a federal compensation bill in their platform of 1912, as well as in the

---

[35] *New York Times*, February 3, 1916; *Congressional Record*, 64th Cong., 1st sess., p. 2035.

[36] J. A. Emery to W. H. Taft, April 4, 1916, Taft Papers.

[37] *The Survey*, xxxvi (July 22, 1916), 424-425.

[38] *New York Times*, July 13, 1916; *Congressional Record*, 64th Cong., 1st sess., p. 10916.

one just adopted in St. Louis. It simply seemed that senators were too busy to consider it.

This, then, was the situation when McKelway and Daniels appealed to Wilson. Failure of the child labor and federal compensation bills, the former warned, would cost the Democrats heavily before the campaign was over. "I understand," he went on in a more pointed warning, "that Mr. Hughes is to hold a conference next week with social workers and has already agreed to swallow the social justice programme whole. In spite of the progressive record of the Democratic Party, I fear that the action on the child labor bill will be regarded as a test of genuine interest in humane measures opposed by commercial interests."[39] The situation, Daniels added in his letter, was really alarming, for Senator Jacob H. Gallinger of New Hampshire, Republican minority leader, had announced on July 14 that Republicans in the upper house were eager to vote on the two measures. "In view of the closeness of the vote in many of the states and that women will vote in a large number of states," the Secretary of the Navy continued, "I feel that it would be a grave mistake if the Senate does not pass the child-labor bill as well as the workmen's compensation bill before it adjourns. I know that many Southern Senators oppose it but I believe that the failure to pass that bill [the child labor bill] will lose us more votes in the close states than our Southern Senators appreciate. Besides, I strongly feel that it is essential to protect child labor and that such protection is the very basis of the social legislation which gave the Progressives hold on the conscience of that portion of their party that cannot be controlled by [George W.] Perkins."[40]

Wilson had never actively opposed the child labor bill. He had simply refused earlier to support it, presumably because he doubted its constitutionality and did not want to imperil other legislation by giving right of way to a measure that might provoke a long filibuster. He had shown no interest, either, in the Kern-McGillicuddy bill, apparently because he did not think that Congress would have time to put it through. But he had already crossed his constitutional Rubicon when he included a demand for a federal child labor law in the St. Louis platform. Daniels and McKelway, he concluded after reading their letters, were obviously right; Democratic victory might well depend upon the votes of social-justice progressives. "Thank you sincerely

[39] A. J. McKelway to W. W., July 17, 1916, Wilson Papers.
[40] J. Daniels to W. W., July 17, 1916, *ibid.*

for your memorandum . . . about Gallinger's speech," he wrote to Daniels on July 18. "I am going to try to see some of the Senators at once and see if we cannot assist to get them out of the hole that the old fox has put them in."[41]

He went unannounced and accompanied only by two Secret Service men on that same day to the President's Room in the Capitol and summoned members of the Democratic senatorial steering committee. The child labor and workmen's compensation bill, he told them, had to be put through. Democrats had to honor their platform pledges— that was simple political expediency.[42] "I . . . am encouraged to believe that the situation has changed considerably," the President reported to McKelway on the following day, July 19.[43] It had, indeed, or at least it soon would change. Democratic senators promised Wilson on July 18 to put the Kern-McGillicuddy bill through quickly, and the Democratic senatorial caucus voted on July 25 to push the child labor bill as well.[44] The Kern-McGillicuddy bill passed without difficulty on August 19.[45] Southerners fought the child labor bill fiercely in debate but did not filibuster, and it passed the Senate on August 8 by a vote of fifty-two to twelve.[46] "I want to say with what real emotion I sign this bill," Wilson said to a group of social justice leaders as he affixed his signature on September 1, "because I know how long the struggle has been to secure legislation of this sort and what it is going to mean to the health and to the vigor of the country, and also to the happiness of those whom it affects. It is with genuine pride that I play my part in completing this legislation. I congratulate the country and felicitate myself."[47]

Everyone knew who was responsible, and reactions proved that rewards for political virtue are not always deferred to the next world. The congregation of one church in Tacoma, Washington, gave Wilson a rising vote of thanks at its service on July 23.[48] Social workers and labor leaders were unstinting in praise—and, later, in vital support. "The step," McKelway wrote, thanking Wilson for going to the Capitol on July 18, "was taken just at the right time and in just the right

[41] W. W. to J. Daniels, July 18, 1916, *ibid.*
[42] *New York Times*, July 19, 1916.
[43] W. W. to A. J. McKelway, July 19, 1916, Wilson Papers.
[44] *New York Times*, July 26, 1916.
[45] *ibid.*, August 20, 1916; *Congressional Record*, 64th Cong., 1st sess., p. 12902.
[46] *ibid.*, p. 12313.
[47] *New York Times*, September 2, 1916.
[48] R. C. Sargent to W. W., July 24, 1916, Wilson Papers.

way."[49] The Denver reformer, Ben B. Lindsey, added significantly to the President: "Your splendid attitude on this question and willingness to change from your former position with the states rights Democrats to Federal or National control when it becomes clearly apparent that it is the best method to put an end to certain evils or advance certain rights should be sufficient proof to wavering Progressives that the Democratic Party is as willing as the Republican Party in proper cases to put the National welfare above state considerations."[50] And from the organ of the main American labor movement came honeyed words of approval: "Nothing that the President of the United States has done has met with such general approval as his laying aside the critical affairs of state to go to the Capitol to make personal protest against the program which omitted the Keating-Owen bill from the list of legislation to be enacted at this session of Congress."[51]

The major piece of unfinished and unreported legislation in the early summer of 1916 was the revenue bill, which, as we have seen, was destined to include Wilson's own provisions for a Tariff Commission and protection for the American chemical industry.[52] It was also destined to reap a rich harvest of votes for the Democratic ticket in November, not so much on account of its concessions to the business community as because of its emphatic embodiment of progressive, almost radical, demands for a more democratic tax policy.

This latter consequence was not among Wilson's plans for 1916, at least not in the beginning. The President had followed Secretary McAdoo's advice in recommending, in his Annual Message of December 7, 1915, measures to raise an additional $300,000,000 revenues to pay for the preparedness program. Their burdens would have fallen much more heavily on the middle and lower classes than upon the rich who paid, relative to their wealth, scarcely any tax at all.[53]

[49] A. J. McKelway to W. W., July 20, 1916, *ibid.*

[50] B. B. Lindsey to W. W., August 9, 1916, *ibid.*

[51] *American Federationist*, XXIII (September 1916), 843. In the same vein, see also F. L. Siddons to W. W., July 19, 1916; O. F. Carpenter to W. W., July 20, 1916; C. S. Jackson to W. W., July 21, 1916; J. H. Holloway to W. W., July 22, 1916; G. C. Epps to W. W., July 29, 1916; Mrs. J. M. Lee to W. W., August 8, 1916; Mrs. W. M. Stone to W. W., August 15, 1916; Colorado State Federation of Labor to W. W., August 15, 1916; A. Lewisohn to W. W., September 2, 1916, all in the Wilson Papers.

[52] A. S. Link, *Wilson: Confusions and Crises*, pp. 341-345.

[53] "The federal tax structure in 1914 [it was not very different in 1915] was so constructed as to throw the major share of the tax burden on the lower and middle classes. Almost $300 million of the government's total revenues of $734,673,167, ex-

Bitter protests from radicals and progressives followed, as well as from nervous Democratic politicians with eyes on the coming campaign, especially after Congress approved and the President signed a bill on December 17 extending the emergency war taxes of 1914 for another year.[54] The groundswell of discontent and demands for heavy increases in taxes on large incomes grew enormously during the early months of 1916.[55] Representative Warren Worth Bailey, Pennsylvania radical Democrat, introduced a bill on February 1 to levy an additional tax on incomes ranging from 5 to 50 per cent. "If the forces of big business are to plunge this country into a saturnalia of extravagance for war purposes in a time of peace," Bailey exclaimed, "it is my notion that the forces of big business should put up the money."[56] Antipre-

clusive of postal receipts, came from customs receipts, which were paid by the mass of consumers. Another $300 million were paid by the rank and file in the form of taxes on tobacco, liquor, wine, and beer. Individuals and corporations paid $71 million in income taxes, while the balance was derived from surplus postal receipts, the sale of public lands, and miscellaneous sources. The wealthy, obviously, enjoyed relative immunity from taxation." A. S. Link, *Woodrow Wilson and the Progressive Era*, pp. 192-193.

McAdoo had suggested, specifically, and Wilson had endorsed, provisions to (1) retain the emergency war taxes voted in the autumn of 1914 (they were mainly stamp and excise taxes); (2) retain the duty of one cent a pound on sugar, instead of permitting sugar to go on the free list in 1916, as the Underwood Tariff Act provided; (3) reduce the income tax exemption from $4,000 to $3,000 for married persons and from $3,000 to $2,000 for single persons; (4) begin application of the surtax on incomes at $10,000 or $15,000, instead of at $20,000, without, however, increasing the surtax; (5) double the normal income tax of 1 per cent; and (6) levy new taxes on gasoline, crude and refined oil, and automobile horsepower. W. G. McAdoo to W. W., October 6 and November 23, 1915, Wilson Papers; *New York Times*, November 26, 1915.

[54] See R. B. Glenn to C. Kitchin, December 30, 1915, the Papers of Claude Kitchin, University of North Carolina Library; hereinafter cited as the Kitchin Papers; W. J. Bryan, "President's Message Analyzed," *The Commoner*, xv (December 1915), 1; identical resolutions adopted by the Central Labor Union of Seattle; Local No. 5, Amalgamated Sheet Metal Workers' Alliance, Youngstown, Ohio; and Local No. 24, International Association of Machinists, Topeka, Kan., Wilson Papers, demanding that Congress authorize the War Department to seize all personal and corporate liquid assets worth more than $5,000 in order to pay for the war that capitalists wanted and the common people would have to fight.

[55] Partly in response to the organization of the Association for an Equitable Income Tax by a group of eastern radicals and progressives that included John Dewey, George L. Record, and Frederic C. Howe. The Association's secretary, Benjamin C. Marsh, made a speaking tour of the Middle West in January 1916 and reported strong sentiment in that section in favor of massive increases in surtaxes on large incomes. B. C. Marsh to W. W. Bailey, February 3, 1916, the Papers of Warren Worth Bailey, Princeton University Library; hereinafter cited as the Bailey Papers.

[56] *Johnstown Democrat*, February 2, 1916.

paredness Democrats in the House of Representatives, equally aroused, deluged Representative Claude Kitchin of North Carolina, chairman of the ways and means committee, with letters in late January and early February warning that they would not support the administration's tax program even if the House Democratic caucus ordered them to do so. They all demanded large increases in the income tax, an inheritance tax, and a special levy on munitions manufacturers.[57] Kitchin, one of the leaders in the fight against preparedness, was not displeased. "I am persuaded to think," he wrote to Bryan, "that when the New York people are thoroughly convinced that the income tax will have to pay for the increase in the army and navy, they will not be one-half so frightened over the future invasion by Germany and that preparedness will not be so popular with them as it now is."[58]

The ways and means committee reported a special bill to repeal the free sugar clause of the Underwood Tariff Act, and the House and Senate approved the measure on March 16 and April 11, 1916, respectively. The committee took no further action during the spring but waited to see what the government's needs would be under the defense legislation then being worked out. Wilson all this time apparently said no word either to defend his own recommendations or to comment on the now obviously strong movement for a more progressive tax program.[59] There was one indication in an exchange in late June that he, too, was shifting policies radically. Old Senator "Pitchfork Ben" Tillman of South Carolina wrote to Wilson on June 23, as follows:

"The more I think about it, the more I am convinced that a trump card which ought to be played by the Democratic Party at this time is to raise the graduated income tax to the limit. Preparedness is demanded by wealth for its protection, as much as from patriotic motives,

[57] See the following letters to Kitchin from Democratic congressmen, all in the Kitchin Papers: R. L. Doughton, January 25, 1916; O. Callaway, January 26, 1916; C. C. Van Dyke, January 27, 1916; C. H. Tavenner, January 27, 1916; I. R. Sherwood, January 27, 1916; W. L. Hinsley, January 27, 1916; W. Gordon, January 27, 1916; W. W. Bailey, January 27, 1916; T. J. Steele, January 28, 1916; W. W. Hastings, January 29, 1916; J. McClintic, January 29, 1916; J. H. Mays, January 29, 1916; J. S. Davenport, January 29, 1916; D. V. Stephens, January 29, 1916; W. A. Ayres, January 29, 1916; J. Shouse, January 31, 1916; C. Hayden, January 31, 1916; W. H. Murray, January 31, 1916; S. Ferris, February 1, 1916; D. S. Church, February 1, 1916; and J. R. Connelly, February 1, 1916.

[58] C. Kitchin to W. J. Bryan, January 31, 1916, *ibid.*

[59] I use the adjective "progressive" here to characterize the program calling for a heavier tax on wealth without meaning to imply that it was either good or bad, and only because the great body of men, both in and out of Congress, who advocated it were generally called progressives at this time.

and the poor people throughout the country who have votes are watching us to see if the Party is going to call on these millionaires to pay for this preparation for the defense of the country, or even their just share of it.

"Therefore, I take the liberty of urging you to press this view. I have talked with many men from all parts of the country, and they all entertain the same ideas that I do. Let us see to it that the millionaires and multi-millionaires contribute very very liberally to this condition in which we find ourselves."[60]

Wilson replied:

"[Your letter] . . . certainly expresses a view which can be pressed home with very strong arguments. I have been rather leaving the matter to the Committee on Ways and Means of the House. I would appreciate it very much if you would tell the Secretary of the Treasury what you have told me in this letter, for I know the Committee is constantly seeking his advice."[61]

Wilson was mistaken in his reference to McAdoo's relation to the ways and means committee. Kitchin reported the committee's own, not McAdoo's, bill on July 1. It doubled the normal income tax, from 1 to 2 per cent, without lowering exemptions, and raised the surtax on incomes over $40,000 from the old maximum of 6 per cent to a new maximum of 10 per cent. It included a new federal estate tax ranging from 1 per cent on net estates of more than $50,000 to 5 per cent on net estates worth more than $450,000. It also imposed a new levy of from 5 to 8 per cent on the gross income of munitions manufacturers. Finally, the bill repealed the much-condemned stamp taxes of the emergency war tax of 1914, created a Tariff Commission, and provided special protection for chemical products. The measure, Kitchin said in introducing it, would raise additional revenues of $250,000,000—enough to pay for the military and naval increases that Congress contemplated.[62]

Conservatives were aghast. "The bill," the *New York Times* exclaimed, "has been frankly fashioned to secure the enthusiastic approval of those who have been taught to believe that the rich can and should be made to pay all the costs of government."[63] Secretary of Agriculture David F. Houston and McAdoo urged the President to

---

[60] B. R. Tillman to W. W., June 23, 1916, Wilson Papers.
[61] W. W. to B. R. Tillman, June 27, 1916, *ibid*.
[62] *New York Times*, July 2, 1916.
[63] *ibid.*, July 3, 1916.

appeal to congressional leaders to lower the income tax exemptions. "I think I know the thought in the minds of the members of Congress who framed the bill," Houston wrote, saying that McAdoo agreed, "and I think it is largely a political thought."[64] But Wilson did not have a word to say while bitter debate proceeded in the House from July 6 to July 8, with Republican members charging that Southerners and Westerners had combined in a gigantic raid on northern wealth.[65] The House approved the bill with a few minor amendments on July 10 by a vote of 238 to 142.[66]

The President did not, moreover, interfere in the angry debates in the Democratic senatorial caucus when it discussed the revenue bill from August 11 to August 15. The Democratic members of the finance committee had voted to retain the stamp taxes of the emergency war tax, increase the maximum surtax on incomes and the tax on estates to 14 and 10 per cent, respectively, and also to lower income tax exemptions as McAdoo had earlier suggested.[67] Democratic senators approved the increases, struck the new provision to lower exemptions, retained only a few of the stamp taxes, and added a new levy on surplus funds of corporations.[68] The Senate approved the revenue bill in this form with a few unimportant amendments on September 6. The conference committee quickly agreed to eliminate all the controverted stamp taxes and to accept the Senate's increases in the income and inheritance taxes and its provision for the new undivided profits tax. In addition, it increased the tax on munitions manufacturers to a maximum of $12\frac{1}{2}$ per cent. Both houses approved the conference report during the night of September 7, and Wilson signed the bill on the following day.[69]

It was a landmark in American history, the first really important victory of the movement, begun by Populists in the 1890's and carried on by progressives in the early 1900's, for a federal tax policy based upon ability to pay. It was, admittedly, a sectional and class measure intended to appeal to farmers, workers, and the lower middle classes. No nation in modern times, not even Great Britain in David Lloyd

[64] D. F. Houston to W. W., July 7, 1916, the Papers of David F. Houston, Houghton Library, Harvard University.

[65] e. g., Representative Martin B. Madden's speech on July 8, *New York Times*, July 9, 1916.

[66] *ibid.*, July 11, 1916; *Congressional Record*, 64th Cong., 1st sess., p. 10768.

[67] *New York Times*, August 6 and 8, 1916.

[68] *ibid.*, August 12-15, 1916.

[69] *ibid.*, September 6, 8, and 9, 1916.

George's "Tax on Wealth" of 1909, had imposed such heavy burdens on incomes and inheritances during peacetime.[70] Wilson, insofar as we know, had had no part in this, one of the most significant achievements of the progressive movement.

The President was, on the other hand, very much responsible for certain provisions inserted in the revenue bill during the last days of the discussions about the measure. Hereon hangs a tale about developments that almost seemed to threaten a severe crisis in Anglo-American relations during the summer interlude.

Two events were specially responsible for the excitement and alarm. The first was the British government's publication on July 18, 1916, of a blacklist of eighty-seven American and some 350 Latin American firms accused or suspected of trading with the Central Powers. British subjects were forbidden to have any dealings, direct or indirect, with the blacklisted firms.[71] The second was the British Foreign Office's delivery to Ambassador Walter H. Page on July 22 of a completely unresponsive preliminary reply to Lansing's mails protest of May 24.[72]

An angry, thundering wave of protest swept over the country.[73] It seems curious at first glance that Americans should have been so agitated by two measures that affected them relatively slightly, when they had endured more or less patiently much more serious infringements of their neutral rights by British blockade measures. Two things made mail seizures and the blacklist particularly exacerbating at this time. One was their uncomplicated character. They seemed to be flagrant violations of American sovereignty—in contrast to the blockade, the legal issues of which were infinitely complicated.[74] The other was the fact that controversy over these two measures occurred in a context of growing Anglo-American estrangement. Wilson, as we have seen, was being alienated by Grey's refusal to implement the House-Grey Memorandum. His estrangement—and that of many other Americans, particularly Irish Americans—was intensified by the British govern-

[70] For a superb analysis, see the *New Republic*, VIII (August 26, 1916), 81-82.

[71] The blacklist was published in the British press on July 18 and in the American press on the following day. *New York Times*, July 19, 1916.

[72] Ambassador Page to the Secretary of State, July 22, 1916, *Foreign Relations, 1916, Supplement*, pp. 613-614; *New York Times*, July 24, 1916; New York *World*, July 25, 1916.

[73] See the review of press opinion in "Britain's Black List of Firms in America," *Literary Digest*, LIII (July 29, 1916), 235-236.

[74] As the British Ambassador pointed out in C. Spring Rice to E. Grey, July 31, 1916, S. Gwynn (ed.), *Letters of Spring Rice*, II, 343.

ment's failure to agree upon any settlement of the Irish question and the hanging of Sir Roger Casement after the Senate, on July 29, adopted a resolution appealing for clemency.

"This blacklisting order of the English," Frank Polk, who was Acting Secretary of State while Lansing was on vacation, reported to Colonel

Here's Your Mail!

Cesare in the New York *Evening Post*

House on July 22, ". . . is causing tremendous irritation and we will have to do something."[75] "This week has been absolutely hideous," Polk wrote shortly afterward to Lansing, describing the scene in Washington. ". . . The blacklist has caused an awful row. The innocent and the guilty have come down here together, wildly protesting. It was an extraordinarily stupid move on the part of the British and both

[75] F. L. Polk to E. M. House, July 22, 1916, House Papers.

Jusserand and Spring Rice threw up their hands over it. . . . I should have written you before and kept you posted of what is going on, but I really have not had a moment as the place has been filled with Senators, Representatives, and prominent politicians bringing in victims of the blacklist."[76]

The loudest explosion went off in the White House. "I am, I must admit," Wilson wrote to House on July 23, "about at the end of my patience with Great Britain and the Allies. This black list business is the last straw. I have told Spring Rice so, and he sees the reasons very clearly. Both he and Jusserand think it a stupid blunder. I am seriously considering asking Congress to authorize me to prohibit loans and restrict exportations to the Allies. It is becoming clear to me that there lies latent in this policy the wish to prevent our merchants getting a foothold in markets which Great Britain has hitherto controlled and all but dominated. Polk and I are compounding a very sharp note. I may feel obliged to make it as sharp and final as the one to Germany on the submarines. What is your own judgment? Can we any longer endure their intolerable course?"[77] Wilson told reporters on the following day, July 24, that the blacklist had "got on his nerves,"[78] while Polk or some other spokesman at the State Department said on the same day that the British memorandum on the mails question, which had just been received, was "both insolent and imprudent."[79]

Cone Johnson, Solicitor of the State Department, and Assistant Secretary of State William Phillips completed a draft of a protest against the blacklist on July 24, and Polk sent it to the White House on that day.[80] Wilson virtually rewrote it ("You will have no difficulty in recognizing the style," Polk wrote as he sent a copy to Lansing), only slightly softening its harsh phrases, and it was sent to London late in the evening of July 26, following a conference between the President and the Acting Secretary of State at two o'clock in the afternoon. The American government, the note said, had received news of the blacklist with "the most painful surprise." The blacklist would have "harsh and even disastrous" effects upon American trade. The British government had said that the measure had been aimed only at the enemies of Great Britain, the note continued, but it was evident that it would very

[76] F. L. Polk to R. Lansing, July 28, 1916, Lansing Papers, LC; also F. L. Polk to F. R. Coudert, July 27, 1916, Polk Papers.
[77] W. W. to E. M. House, July 23, 1916, House Papers.
[78] *New York Times*, July 25, 1916.
[79] New York *World*, July 25, 1916.
[80] F. L. Polk to W. W., July 24, 1916, Wilson Papers.

directly affect all neutral commerce. American citizens had a right to trade with whom they pleased, subject only to restraints permitted by international law. The blacklist brushed all such restraints aside. Whatever might be said about the legality of the British action, the American government felt bound to say that it was inconsistent with "that true justice, sincere amity, and impartial fairness which should characterize the dealings of friendly governments with one another."[81]

"Here is a note we yesterday sent to Great Britain," Wilson wrote to Colonel House on July 27. "I hope that you will approve both its substance and its method. Polk had already intimated to Spring Rice that I would probably be obliged to go to Congress and ask for retaliatory powers, though he had not specified what powers I would ask for. . . . It was evident to Polk when he last saw Spring Rice[82] that the British Government was not a little disturbed (and surprised, poor boobs!)"[83] Wilson had, in fact, already discussed retaliatory legislation with Polk and Senator Stone on July 26.[84] Whether the President and Congress put threats into statutes would depend largely upon what the men in Whitehall did during the following month.

Unfortunately for Anglo-American relations, they did not act as if a crisis was possible. Spring Rice left a memorandum at the State Department on July 29 that seemed to indicate that his government might make some concessions in enforcing the blacklist.[85] But Lord Robert Cecil, Minister of Blockade (acting no doubt, on Spring Rice's advice that American politicians were responding to Irish-American and German-American pressure, and that the only effective deterrent to "awful" American action was fear of unpleasant consequences[86]), dashed these hopes in an interview with American correspondents on August 11. "Personally," he said, "I cannot see any way by which we can forego our undoubted right to prevent our subjects from providing resources of trade to our enemies. There is not likely to be any change in the policy of the Allies as a result of neutral protests."[87] The British

[81] The Acting Secretary of State to Ambassador Page, July 26, 1916, *Foreign Relations, 1916, Supplement*, pp. 421-422.

[82] On July 25. See F. L. Polk to W. W., July 25, 1916, Wilson Papers.

[83] W. W. to E. M. House, July 27, 1916, House Papers.

[84] "Saw Pres. at White House. . . . Discussed Black List. He said that Stone had discussed legislation to forbid clearance of ships & loans." The Diary of Frank L. Polk, July 26, 1916, Yale University Library; hereinafter cited as the Polk Diary.

[85] *New York Times*, July 30, 1916.

[86] C. Spring Rice to E. Grey, July 31, 1916, S. Gwynn (ed.), *Letters of Spring Rice*, II, 339-342.

[87] *New York Times*, August 12, 1916.

and French governments did not even deign all through August and September to reply to the American note of July 26, much less to do anything substantially to satisfy American discontent. The British Ambassador in Paris no doubt expressed a common Anglo-French point of view when he wrote in his diary on August 2 after reading the American blacklist note: "The present conduct of the American Government is disgusting. For electoral purposes the President is trying to twist the lion's tail. If that animal showed his teeth the President would collapse."[88]

Relations were, in fact, further embittered by a nagging quarrel over the visit of the German commercial submarine, *Deutschland*, to Baltimore with a cargo of dyestuffs on July 9. The State Department decided after careful investigation that the vessel was an ordinary merchantman. This drew a sharp warning from the British and French, and, later, all the other Allied governments, that neutral submarines ran grave risks in navigating regions frequented by belligerent submarines, and an even sharper reply from Lansing saying that the United States needed no advice from other governments on the rules of neutrality.[89]

This incident had a particularly dangerous aftermath. The French Naval Minister, in consequence of *Deutschland's* visit, instructed French cruisers in the western Atlantic to open fire immediately on all submarines seen outside the territorial limits of neutral powers. The United States Navy Department announced that the Atlantic Fleet would hold extensive maneuvers in the region north of Cape Hatteras from August 20 to September 1, thus raising the possibility of actual collision between a French cruiser and an American submarine. Ambassador Jusserand finally persuaded the French Naval Minister to rescind his order, but only by warning that the most dreadful consequences, equivalent to a German victory, would ensue if a French cruiser destroyed an American submarine and killed American seamen.

A final Anglo-French action added to American irritation. The British had heretofore permitted export of American tobacco to neutral European consignees for re-export to the Central Powers. The British Ministry of Blockade, under pressure from the French government, announced on June 29 that it would no longer give free transit to tobacco.[90] The Foreign Office did, after protest from the State Department, promise immunity for all American tobacco bought and paid for

---

[88] Lady Algernon G. Lennox (ed.), *The Diary of Lord Bertie of Thame*, II, 9.
[89] See the documents printed in *Foreign Relations, 1916, Supplement*, pp. 765-771.
[90] Ambassador Page to the Secretary of State, June 29, 1916, *ibid.*, p. 510.

before August 4.[91] This concession did not assuage angry southern farmers who only now were harvesting a crop that had been planted in expectation of a free European market. Their spokesmen hastened to Washington to appeal to the State Department for redress, and to warn that their representatives and senators would obtain effective relief if the Department did not act at once.[92]

This affair simply gave the final impetus to the growing movement in Washington for retaliatory legislation. Lansing (who had since returned from vacation) prepared—undoubtedly at Wilson's request—a joint resolution empowering the President to retaliate against nations denying shipping privileges to blacklisted firms. "Mr. Burleson," Lansing wrote as he sent a copy of the resolution to the President on August 26, "telephoned me early this morning that he had seen Senator Kern, Senator Stone, and Senator [Charles S.] Thomas [of Colorado], and they were decidedly in favor of some legislation of this sort. That in order to have it passed they felt it should be in their hands this morning. I am therefore sending you the draft of a Resolution for your consideration and hope that it may reach Mr. Burleson before noon if possible. He was very anxious, apparently, that it should be in his hands by that time."[93] Wilson conferred with senatorial leaders at the Capitol that same afternoon; he probably delivered the resolution himself. It was incorporated in the shipping bill then in conference committee.[94]

Senator James and Senator Claude A. Swanson of Virginia, along with Representative Harry Flood of Virginia, called at the State Department on August 29, the day after spokesmen of tobacco growers gathered in Washington, to discuss means of forcing the Allies to lift their ban against tobacco.[95] Lansing then drafted a resolution empowering the President to prohibit the import of any or all products from any country that discriminated against the products of American soil or industry, or prevented them from going to other countries in contra-

[91] The Acting Secretary of State to Ambassador Page, July 20 and 21, 1916; Chargé I. Laughlin to the Secretary of State, August 22, 1916, *ibid.*, pp. 510-513.

[92] The Conference of Tobacco Growers of the United States to the Secretary of State, August 29, 1916, *ibid.*, pp. 514-516.

[93] R. Lansing to W. W., August 26, 1916, the Papers of Albert S. Burleson, Library of Congress; hereinafter cited as the Burleson Papers. The Papers of Lester H. Woolsey, Library of Congress, contain various drafts of this and other retaliatory provisions and reveal the part that Lansing and other officials in the State Department played in framing this legislation.

[94] *New York Times*, September 1, 1916.

[95] Lansing Desk Diary, August 29, 1916.

vention of international law. It was introduced by Senator James and adopted as an amendment to the revenue bill on August 31.[96] The Senate adopted three additional amendments on September 5. The first, offered by Senator Thomas, authorized the President, during a war in which the United States was not engaged, to deny use of American ports to ships of nations that denied ordinary privileges to American vessels. It also empowered the President to use the armed forces to enforce its terms and imposed heavy penalties for violation. The second, offered by Senator James D. Phelan of California, empowered the President to deny use of American mails and communications services to citizens of countries that interfered with American mails or communications. The third, submitted by Senator George E. Chamberlain of Oregon, was aimed at Canadian discrimination against American fish products.[97]

The conference committee, while preparing the final draft of the revenue bill, gave the President and Secretary of State exactly what they wanted. The committee retained the James and Thomas amendments, which Wilson had approved. The President wavered on the Phelan amendment, indicating on September 6 that he favored it, then saying on the following day that he did not want it included. The conference committee struck it out, along with the Chamberlain amendment, which the State Department strongly disapproved, at its final session on September 7.[98] It will be recalled that legislation aimed specifically at the blacklist had also been incorporated in the shipping bill.

Walter Page, who came to Washington from his post in London on about August 17 ("for a vacation in which it is our hope," Wilson said, "that he may get back a little way at least to the American point of view about things"[99]), has left revealing if somewhat jaundiced testimony about the mood in Washington during the period just before and after adoption of the revenue bill. "Nobody ever takes me seriously about anything," he wrote to his wife on August 26. "The Cabinet are jocular. No member of Congress has a serious word. Yet something

[96] *New York Times*, September 1, 1916; *Congressional Record*, 64th Cong., 1st sess., pp. 13485, 13488.

[97] *New York Times*, September 6, 1916; *Congressional Record*, 64th Cong., 1st sess., pp. 13792-13794.

[98] Lansing Desk Diary, September 6, 1916; New York *World*, September 7 and 8, 1916.

[99] W. W. to E. M. House, July 23, 1916, House Papers.

could be done. Sen. Owen was filled with anti-British wrath and was talking reprisals and to hint of war."[100]

"I am greatly alarmed and distressed," Page wrote in his diary at about the same time, "at the mood that I find in governmental circles in Washington towards Great Britain—a mood of suspicion based on a total misunderstanding of British aims and actions. I find only complaint about commercial 'cases'—nowhere a constructive policy, nowhere a willingness to put all the facts about any 'case' on the table, nowhere an appreciation of the desirability or value of British good will. I have tried in vain to inform the Secretary of the larger view of the subject: he changes the topic of conversation and discusses some technicality or some 'case.' He has not informed me why I was summoned home."[101] "A mere routine-clerk, law-book-precedent man," Page wrote of the Secretary of State; "no grasp, no imagination, no constructive tendency or ability—measuring Armageddon, if he tries to measure it at all—with a 6-inch rule. . . . Oh, God! What a crime and what a shame to have this manikin in that place now. . . . He cared nothing about our relations with Great Britain. It was hopeless—utterly hopeless. If England were blotted out, the world would be the same to him, except that he would have another historical fact, parallel in his mind to the theft of Bosnia."[102] "It would be hard to forget these 2 weeks in Wash^ton and their grave depressions," he wrote again in his diary at the end of his visit.[103]

The President had Page to luncheon twice while he was in the capital, but the presence of other guests prevented private conversation. The only word about foreign relations was spoken at the second meal, when Ambassador William G. Sharp, who had just returned from Paris, said that the French people and government were wholly satisfied with the President's policies. Wilson, Page wrote, looked as if he believed it.[104]

Page finally obtained a private interview with the President at "Shadow Lawn," in Long Branch, New Jersey, on September 22. It was not a pleasant experience for the Ambassador. "The President said to me," he wrote in his diary, "that when the war began he and all the men he met were in hearty sympathy with the Allies; but that now the

[100] W. H. Page to Mrs. Page, August 26, 1916, the Papers of Walter H. Page, Houghton Library, Harvard University.

[101] The Diary of Walter H. Page, n.d., Houghton Library, Harvard University; hereinafter cited as the Page Diary.

[102] *ibid.*, August 30, 1916.

[103] *ibid.*

[104] *ibid.*, n.d.

sentiment toward England had greatly changed. He saw no one who was not vexed and irritated by the arbitrary English course. . . . The President said, 'Tell those gentlemen for me'—and then followed a homily to the effect that a damage done to any American citizen is a damage to him, etc. He described the war as a result of many causes, some of long origin. He spoke of England's having the earth and of Germany wanting it. Of course, he said, the German system is directly opposed to everything American. But I do not gather that he thought that this carried any very great moral reprehensibility. . . . He added that one of the worst provocations was the long English delay in answering our Notes. Was this delay due to fear or shame? He evidently felt that such a delay showed contempt. He spoke of the Bryan treaty [for conciliation of Anglo-American disputes, signed in 1914]. But on no question had the British 'locked horns' with us—on no question had they come to a clear issue so that the matter might be referred to the Commission."[105] "To him it [the war] seemed a quarrel to settle economic rivalries between Germany and England," Page afterward wrote about this conversation. "He showed a great degree of toleration for Germany; and he was, during the whole morning that I talked with him, complaining of England."[106]

News of the retaliatory legislation jolted leaders in London and Paris, particularly because it was immediately followed by signs that the Washington government was seriously contemplating putting the new provisions into force. Lansing told Ambassador Jusserand on about September 9 that American patience had worn thin, and that the President and he had had to go to great effort to persuade congressional

---

[105] *ibid.*, quoted in Burton J. Hendrick, *The Life and Letters of Walter H. Page* (3 vols.), II, 185-186.

[106] Page Diary, April 1, 1917. Wilson made some interesting observations about the complexity and obscureness of the causes of the war and America's interest in its outcome in a speech to members of the American Neutral Conference at the White House on August 30, as follows: "The U.S. has nothing to gain and nothing to lose in one sense in respect of this war. She has a great deal to gain, of course, if permanent peace can be brought out of it in some way, but directly she has very little to gain or to lose and she certainly has nothing to fear. . . . [He went on to say that the one part of his speech before the League to Enforce Peace that had been widely quoted was the sentence to the effect that the United States was not interested in the causes or objects of the war.] Now, in one sense we don't care, for what the quarrel is, because we don't know, partly because nobody knows what the quarrel is. It is just a fight . . . to see who is strong enough to prevent the other from fighting better. I don't see anything else that is involved." Manuscript in the Charles L. Swem Collection of Wilsoniana, Princeton University Library; hereinafter cited as the Swem Collection.

leaders to refrain from making the retaliatory measures mandatory.[107] Lansing told Jusserand, somewhat cryptically, to wait and see what use Wilson would make of his new powers. It was not impossible, the Ambassador wrote in a telegram to the Foreign Ministry, that the President had concluded that the Allies had forced his hand. This report was followed by a public statement by Lansing on September 11 that he was making a close study of the retaliatory provisions of the revenue bill with a view to determining their application as a means of protecting American rights.[108]

Spring Rice sent nothing but alarming news and forecasts during the week after approval of the revenue bill. "I think it my duty to make it as clear as I can that from now on until the election," he warned Lord Grey[109] on September 15, "the interest of both political parties, certainly of the political party now in power, is to have trouble with England. . . . I think we should exercise the greatest care. We should also be prepared for the worst, because a serious crisis might possibly occur. It seems to me that as the President is empowered to use the armed forces of the Republic against the Allies in certain circumstances, we should if the case arose, make an appeal to the Bryan treaty, and ask that the matter should be referred to a commission."[110]

"Of course these powers have not been used by the President," Spring Rice wrote to the Canadian Prime Minister two days later, repeating what he was saying to the Foreign Office. "But the mere fact that Congress has passed them has excited public opinion very greatly and pressure may be brought to bear on the President to use the power conferred on him. If he does so the result will be that if a British ship in conformity with British law (which is also the law of nations) refuses to carry enemy's goods, with an American destination, the President can employ the armed forces of the U S against that ship. . . . The situation here is that the President is losing ground and may very probably be beaten. His advisers may tell him that the only thing which can save him is an appeal to American patriotism against the British. The Republicans would be obliged to follow his lead, or be stamped with the mark of un-Americanism & disloyalty. Therefore the next

[107] Lansing told Page the same thing. Page Diary, n.d.

[108] New York *World*, September 12, 1916; *New York Times*, September 12, 1916.

[109] Sir Edward Grey had been ennobled as Viscount Grey of Fallodon in July.

[110] C. Spring Rice to E. Grey, September 15, 1916, S. Gwynn (ed.), *Letters of Spring Rice*, II, 348-349.

two months are a dangerous period during which a crisis may occur of a serious nature."[111]

Leaders in Whitehall did not underestimate the dangerous possibilities. Lord Robert Cecil sent a message to Colonel House by the American correspondent, Frederick Dixon, that Britain would break off diplomatic relations and end all trade with America if the President used his retaliatory powers.[112] This was both pique and, as House thought, bluff. Grey sent an informal protest to Washington on about September 16. The Germans, it said, had resumed large-scale submarine operations and were taking a heavy toll of ships. Now the American government was threatening to force the Allies to carry enemy trade. "Such action by the United States," it went on, "will present an inconceivably invidious contrast to that of refraining from action, or even (as has been the case for the last four or five months) protest, regarding German submarine warfare against merchantmen, which is being allowed to proceed all the time."[113]

The War Committee of the British Cabinet had a long discussion of Anglo-American relations on September 20. "The War Committee," the minutes of this meeting read, "inclined to the view that, having regard to the imminence of the American elections, the possibility of a serious controversy with the United States of America at an early date could not be excluded." The Committee directed the Foreign Office, among other things, to "prepare, for use if and when required, a complete exposition and vindication of our action and attitude in regard to all the questions at issue between the Government of the United States and the Allies."[114] The Foreign Office not long afterward asked various

[111] C. Spring Rice to R. L. Borden, September 17, 1916, the Papers of Sir Robert L. Borden, Canadian Public Archives, Ottawa; hereinafter cited as the Borden Papers.

[112] House Diary, September 20, 1916.

[113] Memorandum left with the Secretary of State by the British Ambassador, September 17, 1916, *Foreign Relations, 1916, Supplement*, pp. 445-446.

[114] "Very Secret. Extract from the Proceedings of the War Committee—Wednesday September 20, 1916," MS. in the Papers of John Maynard Keynes, Economics Library, Cambridge University; hereinafter cited as the Keynes Papers.

The Foreign Office, on about October 1, drafted a statement to be sent as an Anglo-French declaration to the American government. It asserted that the Allies were fighting for the liberty of mankind and could not neglect any legitimate means of shortening the war. The Allies would continue to wage economic warfare—incomparably the most humane method of modern warfare—against Germany, but only in ways permitted by international law and indispensable to appropriate execution of lawful acts of war. They would at the same time do as little as possible to interrupt ordinary American commerce. The French Foreign Ministry sent a copy of this declaration to Jusserand on

departments to submit memoranda on the subject "How far this country is dependent commercially and financially on the United States and to what extent measures of reprisal by the United States could effectively be met by commercial or other forms of retaliation at the disposal of His Majesty's Government."[115]

Apprehension in London waned rapidly as reports arrived from Washington between September 22 and September 27. Spring Rice telegraphed on September 22 that the Associated Press had just issued a statement to the effect that responsible officials in Washington were beginning to have misgivings about the legality and possible effect of the reprisal clauses of the Revenue Act.[116] Much more comforting was the telegram that Spring Rice sent on the same day, transmitting a report by Sir Richard Crawford, Trade Adviser in the British Embassy, of a conversation with Secretary Lansing on September 21. Crawford said that he had commented on the unfortunate impression that the reprisal clauses had made in the United Kingdom, particularly the one giving the President summary powers to use force if necessary to prevent the departure from American ports of British vessels refusing to carry goods for blacklisted firms. Crawford went on:

"Secretary of State replied that President would never exercise those powers except in the last resort. That it should be remembered that this legislation was the outcome of political situation on the eve of the Presidential Election. Public opinion in the United States had been much irritated by Black List and by operation of Censorship and President was so pressed to take retaliatory action that reprisal clauses had been drafted to forestall proposals of a more drastic and mandatory character. I felt that Secretary of State desired to convey to me impression that there was no intention to utilize power of reprisals but I observed that their announcement and enactment would unfortunately embitter public opinion in United Kingdom and increase difficulties of His Majesty's Government in making concessions to the United States. . . .

"Secretary of State then observed that publication of Black List had

---

October 5, 1916, with instructions that he and Spring Rice should deliver it to the Secretary of State when they thought that the time was ripe. They apparently never delivered it.

[115] E. Percy to J. M. Keynes, September 30, 1916, *ibid.* See below, pp. 178-184, for the outcome of this inquiry.

[116] Ambassador Spring Rice to the Foreign Office, Telegram No. 2884, September 22, 1916, Keynes Papers.

seriously interfered with United States trade particularly with South American centres and had generally aroused much resentment in the United States. He thought that it was a grave mistake. . . . Secretary of State felt that in certain cases our action had been vindictive and hardly justifiable. . . .

"He next observed that our exercise of Censorship had caused much annoyance to American public. I told him that we were ready to consider any cases of unreasonable delay or interference. . . . Finally he referred to our recent restrictions on shipments of tobacco to Scandinavia and Netherlands. He said that on the strength of understanding of last year American growers had sown larger area of dark tobacco for sale in Germany and that our restrictions imposed before this crop could be marketed exposed them to serious loss. Our action had aroused the greatest irritation and would have led to strong demand for retaliation had not German prohibition of import luckily stemmed for the time feeling of resentment against us. . . ."[117]

Finally, Spring Rice telegraphed on September 27 that he had heard from a good source—perhaps Colonel House—that the President had considerable doubt as to whether the retaliatory provisions of the Revenue Act could be put into effect without bringing on a financial and commercial crisis in America.[118]

These and other similar reports seemed to confirm what Grey, Cecil, and others in the Foreign Office had suspected—that the retaliatory legislation was a play to German-American and Irish-American galleries, and that the President would not dare to take forceful measures because such action would irreparably damage the American economy.[119] As the British Ambassador in Paris put it, "I hope that we shall be very firm with our American cousins. They don't mean fighting. They prefer making vast sums of money individually and doing a roaring trade with us. If we show hesitation in regard to the new American retaliatory law we shall encourage the President to do some electoral bluff."[120]

---

[117] Ambassador Spring Rice to the Foreign Office, Telegram No. 2883, September 22, 1916, *ibid*. Lansing was referring to a German decree of about August 28 (received in Washington on September 5), forbidding the import of any but Turkish tobacco. *New York Times*, September 6, 1916.

[118] Ambassador Spring Rice to the Foreign Office, Telegram No. 2936, September 27, 1916, Keynes Papers.

[119] See below, pp. 180-181.

[120] Lady Algernon G. Lennox, *The Diary of Lord Bertie of Thame*, II, 28-29; entry for September 16, 1916.

We have no evidence whatever to indicate that Lansing ever told Wilson what he had said to Sir Richard Crawford. But we can be certain that the Secretary of State did not accurately represent Wilson's point of view. "He said," Walter Page wrote after his talk with Wilson on September 22, "that he wouldn't do anything with the retaliatory act till after election lest it might seem that he was playing politics. But he hinted that if there were continued provocation afterward (in case he were elected) he would."[121] Or, as Wilson put it in a letter: "Of course, my position with regard to the action of the British Government in the matter of the so-called black list has not altered, and if it will be of any public advantage, I will say so, but the fact is, as you no doubt realize, that until the election is over there is no use saying anything, because upon the election will turn the question whether foreign governments are to believe the American people to be back of the present administration or not. If they are back of it, many things will be simplified."[122]

Wilson gave additional proof of his unwillingness to play politics with foreign policy in an interesting exchange with the Secretary of State in late September. Lansing had concluded by some strange reasoning that the administration could satisfy public opinion and avoid radical measures against Great Britain only by maintaining a steady flow of notes to London. This, he thought, would also avert the danger of impulsive presidential action. "The real danger, the one which I fear," Lansing wrote in a memorandum at this time, "is that the President's resentment at British invasion of our rights will continue to increase. It is already very bitter and he even discussed bringing that Government 'to book.' . . . I am almost unhappy over the situation, because on no account must we range ourselves even indirectly on the side of Germany, no matter how great the provocation may be. The amazing thing to me is that the President does not see this. In fact he does not seem to grasp the full significance of this war or the principles at issue. I have talked it over with him, but the violation of American rights by both sides seem [*sic*] to interest him more than the vital interests as I see them. That German imperialistic ambitions threaten free institutions everywhere apparently has not sunk very deeply into his mind. For six months I have talked about the struggle

[121] Page Diary, quoted in B. J. Hendrick, *The Life and Letters of Walter H. Page*, II, 186.
[122] W. W. to M. B. Blumenthal, October 30, 1916, Wilson Papers.

between Autocracy and Democracy, but do not see that I have made any great impression."[123]

Lansing wrote to Wilson on September 22, suggesting that he be permitted to send a telegram (the draft of which he enclosed) which the American Chargé in London should show unofficially to Lord Grey. "It has seemed to me that it might be advisable to pursue this method at the present time in bringing home to the British Government the growing irritation in this country . . . ," Lansing went on. "I am afraid that London does not appreciate that the tide of resentment is rising very high in this country, and that there is a tendency to demand drastic action by this Government."[124] Lansing's telegram reviewed Anglo-American difficulties and said that the British government had never once admitted the soundness of a single American argument over principle. Moreover, it answered Grey's informal protest by reminding him that the American government was concerned with submarine warfare only insofar as it affected American interests. "If the British Government," it went on, "is expecting an attitude of 'benevolent neutrality' on our part—a position which is not neutral and which is not governed by the principles of neutrality—they should know that nothing is further from our intention." The telegram went on to emphasize the growing American resentment against British practices and refusal to meet reasonable American protests. Much of this resentment, it said, was in fact justified. The situation was becoming really dangerous to continuance of good relations, and the British government ought to know.[125]

Wilson replied on September 29:

"I think it would be quite unjustifiable to do anything for the sake of public opinion which might change the whole face of our foreign relations. Therefore I think it would be most unwise to send a message like this.

"I had a talk with Walter Page of the most explicit kind, and am sure that he will be able to convey to the powers that be in London a very clear impression of the lamentable and dangerous mistakes they are making. I covered the whole subject matter here dealt with in a way which I am sure left nothing to be desired in the way of ex-

---

[123] "The President's Attitude toward Great Britain and Its Dangers," the Diary of Robert Lansing, September 1916, Library of Congress; hereinafter cited as the Lansing Diary.

[124] R. Lansing to W. W., September 22, 1916, *The Lansing Papers*, I, 314.

[125] "Draft Telegram . . . ," *ibid.*, pp. 315-318.

plicitness or firmness of tone; and I think that our method had better stop with that for the time being. Let us forget the campaign so far as matters of this sort are concerned."[126]

Wilson wrote a second letter to Lansing on September 29 in response to other suggestions:

"I think the matter of protesting against the invasion of Belgium has been made sufficiently plain to our public.

"As for the other matter, it might be well to take up a settlement of the *Lusitania* outrage with Bernstorff if he thinks it can be settled now without soon widening into the ancient difficulty. . . .

"Please keep me informed of any conversations you may have with him, and take no step without my advice.

"At present I hope that the Department will confine itself as much as possible to routine matters. We should ourselves no doubt be unconsciously influenced by political considerations [otherwise] and that would be most unfair to the country."[127]

There was an interesting dénouement. Ambassador Jusserand finally delivered the Anglo-French reply to Lansing's mails protest of May 24 on October 13. It promised that the French and British governments would do everything possible to avoid delay and inconvenience to American citizens; but it also asserted that England and France were entirely within their rights in censoring ocean-borne mail, and that they had no intention of desisting from exercise of that right.[128] Grey at about the same time handed his reply to the American protest against the blacklist to Ambassador Page. It was a forthright defense of the legality of the policy and, moreover, a firm reaffirmation of determination not to permit British subjects to furnish facilities for enemy trade.[129] This story is not without its ironical twist. It was undoubtedly Lansing's own conversation with Crawford that had led Grey to conclude that he could return such replies safely.

Culmination of protracted negotiations with the Danish government for purchase of the Danish West Indies, or Virgin Islands, consisting of St. Thomas, St. John, and St. Croix, was another diplomatic diversion, albeit a minor one, for leaders in Washington during the

---

[126] W. W. to R. Lansing, September 29, 1916, *ibid.*, p. 319.

[127] W. W. to R. Lansing, September 29, 1916, *ibid.*, pp. 570-571.

[128] Ambassador Jusserand to the Secretary of State, October 12, 1916, *Foreign Relations, 1916, Supplement*, pp. 624-628.

[129] Ambassador Page to the Secretary of State, October 12, 1916, *ibid.*, pp. 461-465.

summer interlude. An earlier treaty, signed in 1902, had failed on account of Danish refusal to ratify, and the American Minister in Copenhagen, Maurice Francis Egan, had kept the project alive by quiet discussions since his appointment in 1907. He proposed renewal of negotiations in March 1915 in a dispatch to the State Department emphasizing the possibility that Germany might absorb Denmark, and the Virgin Islands along with her, if she won the war.[130] He wrote again in May 1915, reporting that the Danish Foreign Minister, Erik de Scavenius, had just said that a sale might be possible.

Fears of German acquisition of the islands had prompted the American government to try to purchase them in 1902. These fears were even stronger in 1915. "I have read these papers through with close attention, and thank you for handing them to me," Wilson wrote to Lansing on June 16, 1915, returning Egan's dispatches. "As I said to you yesterday, I am, and have long been, deeply interested in the purchase of the Danish West Indies. I hope that you will take the matter up very seriously and that it may be possible to have a concrete proposal, if possible in the form of a treaty, to lay before the Senate at its next session."[131]

Lansing and Egan now pushed negotiations as rapidly as Danish leaders would permit. The first breakthrough came after a conversation between the Secretary of State and the Danish Minister in Washington, Constantine Brun, on November 15, 1915. Brun, in considerable embarrassment, asked Lansing whether the United States would seize the Virgin Islands if his government refused to sell them. Lansing replied that he certainly had no such action in mind but that he could conceive of circumstances that might require American seizure. They were Denmark's absorption by a great power, or Denmark's decision to transfer title to the islands to another European power.[132] This shot hit home in Copenhagen, and de Scavenius replied at once that Lansing's statement left Denmark no alternative but to consider a proposition from the United States.[133] "I am glad," Wilson wrote to Lansing after the Secretary of State had brought him up to date, "the Danish Minister gave you an opportunity to be so frank with

[130] Minister Egan to the Secretary of State, March 8, 1915, *Papers Relating to the Foreign Relations of the United States, 1917*, pp. 588-590; hereinafter cited as *Foreign Relations, 1917.*

[131] W. W. to R. Lansing, June 16, 1915, *The Lansing Papers*, II, 501.

[132] "Memorandum by the Secretary of State . . . ," November 15, 1916, *ibid.*, pp. 501-502.

[133] The Danish Minister to the Secretary of State, c. November 25, 1915, *ibid.*, p. 502.

him, and I hope he realizes how entirely friendly to Denmark the frankness was. It would appear from the enclosed message from the Danish Minister of Foreign Affairs that he does. I hope that you will . . . proceed at once to the negotiation of a treaty for the purchase of the Danish West Indies. The opportunity has apparently come, and we may be able to relieve the Danish Government of a considerable embarrassment."[134]

Negotiations now went forward rapidly. The Danes asked the huge sum of $27,000,000 for what was admitted to be run down real estate (they had asked only $5,000,000 in 1902), but Wilson was not inclined to haggle, particularly after the General Board of the Navy advised on December 10, 1915, that the Virgin Islands had harbors that would make good naval bases, and that the United States could not safely permit a potential enemy to acquire the islands.[135] "I think," Wilson wrote to Lansing on January 7, 1916, "it would be a mistake to break off at this evidently opportune time on a question of money, within reasonable bounds."[136] The Danes reduced their price to $25,000,000, and Lansing and Brun signed a purchase treaty, drafted by Lester H. Woolsey, Assistant Solicitor of the State Department, in New York on August 4. There were minor differences at the end over concessions enjoyed by Danish firms and individuals in the islands, and over Denmark's insistence that the United States reaffirm Danish claim to the whole of Greenland. Lansing wanted to haggle, but Wilson insisted on yielding all minor points in order not to jeopardize Danish ratification.[137]

Wilson sent the treaty to the Senate on August 8, and Lansing bluntly warned the foreign relations committee on August 18 that Denmark might sell the islands to some other power if the United States did not pay the price demanded. That, he added, would be a direct challenge to the Monroe Doctrine.[138] The Senate, after a favorable report by the foreign relations committee on September 5, debated the treaty in executive session for only two hours on September

[134] W. W. to R. Lansing, December 5, 1915, *ibid.*, pp. 504-505.

[135] G. Dewey to J. Daniels, December 10, 1915, quoted in Charles C. Tansill, *The Purchase of the Danish West Indies*, pp. 481-483.

[136] W. W. to R. Lansing, January 7, 1916, *The Lansing Papers*, II, 507.

[137] F. L. Polk to R. Lansing, July 28, 1916, Lansing Papers, LC, relating Wilson's comments on the suggestions that Lansing, then on vacation, had made in correspondence. For the text of the treaty as signed, see *Foreign Relations, 1917*, pp. 694-700.

[138] New York *World*, August 19, 1916.

7 and consented to ratification by a huge majority.[139] The Danish parliament approved ratification in December 1916, after a national plebiscite; ratifications were exchanged on January 17, 1917; and Commander Edwin T. Pollock accepted transfer of the islands from the Danish Governor in St. Thomas on March 31, 1917.

Meanwhile, Wilson's leadership had been tested as never before as the country had staggered through one of the severest domestic crises since the Civil War, the threat of a nationwide strike of railway workers. The crisis began when the presidents of the four brotherhoods and spokesmen of the railroads came to an utter impasse in early June over the brotherhoods' demands for an eight-hour day, without reduction in wages then being paid for a ten-hour day, and time and a half for overtime work.[140] Twenty railroad presidents and managers flatly rejected these demands and appealed for federal arbitration on June 15.[141] "This is indeed the most ominous cloud on the horizon," Wilson wrote, "but Secretary [of Labor] Wilson seems confident that the matter is going to be submitted to mediation and that a solution can be worked out. I have at no time lost sight of the matter."[142]

The bargaining conference met again in New York on August 8 under the aegis of the United States Board of Mediation and Conciliation. The brotherhood leaders announced at the first session that 94 per cent of their members had voted to strike if they did not get the eight-hour day. "Now, gentlemen," A. B. Garretson, chairman of the brotherhoods' committee, said to the railroad men, "it's up to you." Elisha Lee, speaking for the managers, replied that the demands were utterly impossible and again appealed for federal arbitration. The brotherhood leaders refused, and Judge William L. Chambers, chairman of the Mediation Board, announced on August 12 that agreement was nowhere in sight.[143]

The President sent his secretary, Joseph P. Tumulty, to New York on the four o'clock train on that same afternoon with identical letters to the brotherhood presidents and representatives of the railroads.[144]

[139] *New York Times*, September 8, 1917.
[140] *ibid.*, June 3, 1916.
[141] *ibid.*, June 16, 1916.
[142] W. W. to W. G. McAdoo, July 27, 1916, Wilson Papers.
[143] *New York Times*, August 9, 10, 12, and 13, 1916.
[144] W. W. to W. L. Chambers, August 12, 1916, Wilson Papers. See also W. L. Chambers to W. W., August 13 [12], *ibid.*, suggesting that the President send the invitations by special messenger.

"I have learned with surprise and with keen disappointment that an agreement concerning the settlement of the matters in controversy between the railroads and their employees has proved impossible," each letter read. "A general strike on the railways would at any time have a most far-reaching and injurious effect upon the country. At this time the effect might be disastrous. I feel that I have the right, therefore, to request, and I do hereby request, as the head of the Government, that before any final decision is arrived at I may have a personal conference with you here. I shall hold myself ready to meet you at any time you may be able to reach Washington."[145]

Garretson led some thirty brotherhood officials to the Green Room of the White House at 10 a.m. on August 14. Wilson, standing under a portrait of Andrew Jackson, listened while Garretson explained that railroad workers had been preparing for this final battle for thirty years. Wilson interrupted from time to time to ask for specific information. He said, when Garretson had finished, that he would not attempt to judge the merits of the case. But he described the effects of a nationwide railroad paralysis and appealed to his listeners to weigh carefully every move for the sake of the national welfare.

Elisha Lee ushered seventeen railway presidents, members of the National Conference Committee of the Railways, to the White House at three o'clock that same afternoon. The eight-hour day, Lee said, alone would cost the railroads $100,000,000 a year; the eight-hour day with time and a half for overtime work would simply bankrupt them unless the Interstate Commerce Commission permitted them to raise rates. Even so, Lee went on, the railroads were still willing to accept arbitration. Wilson replied, describing the disastrous consequences of a strike and reminding his listeners that they had to consider the national welfare above the interests of their stockholders. They should make settlement possible by agreeing to accept the eight-hour day in principle, leaving overtime pay and other matters to arbitration. He would be grateful, Wilson concluded, if the gentlemen would bring their answer at nine o'clock the next morning. "I have met both sides and have gone over the case with the utmost frankness," the President told reporters after the two meetings. "I shall not be able to judge until tomorrow, whether we have found a feasible basis for settlement."[146]

[145] W. W. to W. S. Carter, W. S. Stone, A. B. Garretson, W. B. Lee, and E. Lee, all dated August 13, 1916, *ibid*.

[146] *New York Times*, August 15, 1916.

Neither side would budge when Wilson saw the railroad managers in the morning and brotherhood officials in the afternoon of August 15. It was too much, the President told reporters. He would work out his own compromise and ask Congress to impose it if it was not accepted.[147] He typed out a memorandum embodying his terms on the following day, as follows:

"Proposal. R. R. Conference

"Concession of the eight-hour day.

"Postponement of the other demand, as to payment for overtime, and of the counter suggestions of the Railway managers until experience actually discloses the consequences of the eight-hour day.

"In the meantime, the constitution, by the authority of Congress, of a commission or body of men, appointed by the President, to observe, investigate and report upon those consequences, without recommendation.

"Then such action upon the facts as the parties to the present controversy may think best."[148]

Wilson sent his proposal to Lee that same day, August 16, probably in the afternoon. The railroad presidents, breaking the silence that Wilson had asked them to observe, talked bitterly to reporters. They believed in and would fight to the last ditch for arbitration, they said. The President was playing politics, and they did not intend to help him win. He was asking the railroads to commit suicide and threatening to murder them if they did not. Lee took the managers' refusal to the White House that same evening.[149]

Wilson read it as soon as he went to his office the next morning. Refusing to see the Railway Conference Committee, he sent telegrams summoning the presidents of all large railroads to Washington. Then in the afternoon he received some six hundred chairmen of divisions of the brotherhoods, whom he had earlier summoned. He explained the settlement that he had proposed to the railway managers, adding that he had decided to demand the eight-hour day, not to prevent a strike, but because it was right. He then talked passionately about what it would mean to one hundred million Americans if trains stopped running. Great cities would be without food within a few days; industry and business would suffer a gigantic shock. His proposal, Wilson went on, was fair. Railroad workers would get the eight-hour day if

[147] *ibid.*, August 16, 1916.
[148] Undated MS. in the Wilson Papers.
[149] *New York Times*, August 17, 1916.

his plan went through, and he was prepared to stand or fall with it.[150] The division chairmen voted after fierce discussion on August 18 to accept the compromise, even though it meant yielding the one provision—time and a half for overtime work—that would force the railroads to institute the eight-hour day in actual practice.[151]

Wilson received thirty-one presidents of major railroad lines in the Green Room on that same afternoon and pleaded for acceptance of his plan, warning at the end that refusal would only encourage the movement for nationalization.[152] The railroad heads returned on the following day, and Hale Holden, president of the Burlington, read their reply. They, Holden said, were fighting for the principle of arbitration. The workers' inflexible demand that the eight-hour day should not be honestly debated raised this question "above and beyond the lesser contentions of hours of service, or payment of wages." Submission to the President's demands would "place in peril all that has been accomplished in the peaceful adjustment of labor controversies by methods of arbitration." Wilson replied that he faced a condition, not a principle. He had to save the nation's life. He was willing, if the railroad presidents would only cooperate, to do everything within his power to influence the Interstate Commerce Commission to grant an increase in rates if the eight-hour day should add heavy new financial burdens. Concluding, he walked up to his listeners, pointed his finger at them, and said, "If a strike comes, the public will know where the responsibility rests. It will not be upon me."[153]

The railroad presidents withdrew, still refusing, and Wilson sent telegrams to the presidents of all railroads not already in Washington, inviting them to come to the capital at once. He then drafted and issued an appeal to the country. "I have recommended the concession of the eight-hour day—that is, the substitution of an eight-hour day for the present ten-hour day in all the existing practices and agreements," it began. "I made this recommendation because I believed the concession right. The eight-hour day now, undoubtedly, has the sanction of the judgment of society in its favor and should be adopted as a basis for wages, even where the actual work to be done cannot be completed within eight hours." Only experience would show whether

[150] *ibid.*, August 18, 1916.

[151] W. S. Stone *et al.* to W. W., August 18, 1916, Wilson Papers; *New York Times*, August 19, 1916.

[152] *New York Times*, August 19, 1916.

[153] *ibid.*, August 20, 1916.

the eight-hour day would throw undue burdens on the railroads. Meanwhile, he would seek authority from Congress to appoint a commission to ascertain the facts and make appropriate recommendations. "This seems to me," the statement concluded, "a thoroughly practical and entirely fair program, and I think that the public has the right to expect its acceptance."[154]

The augmented group of fifty railroad presidents met Wilson again in the East Room in the afternoon of August 21. The temperature was 101 degrees in the shade, but the President seemed to be unaffected. He talked earnestly, sometimes passionately, for nearly an hour, adding to his earlier comments observations about the necessity of being prepared, not merely for defense, but for "the extraordinary situation that will immediately emerge out of the European war." The United States had to be prepared, he went on, to play its role as one of the dominant influences in world affairs. Then he concluded:

"I will not allow passion to come into my thought in this solemn matter. We are both acting as trustees of great interests.

"I am willing to allow this matter to go to the great American jury and let them assess the responsibility. The responsibility of failure will not rest with me.

"I wish you to consider the consequence as affecting the people in the cities and countrysides, of a failure to agree. The country cannot live without railroad service and the fortunes of 100,000,000 men, women and little ones—many of whom may die—depend upon what may be done in this room.

"I appeal to you as one American citizen to another to avert this disaster."[155]

The railroad presidents retired to the New Willard Hotel and issued a long statement denouncing the President's plan.[156] They remained in Washington another week, apparently in the hope that an irate public opinion would force the brotherhoods and Wilson to yield, and finally delivered their formal reply to the President on August 28.[157] It contained certain concessions, but acceptance of the basic principle of the eight-hour day was not among them; and the brother-

[154] *ibid.*

[155] *ibid.*, August 22, 1916.

[156] *ibid.*

[157] Actually, Wilson asked them, when they brought it to the White House on August 28, to defer formal delivery until he had talked to congressional leaders. The railroad presidents brought the reply back on the following day, August 29. For its text, see the New York *World*, August 30, 1916.

hood presidents at once published an order, which they had issued on August 14, calling a nationwide strike of 400,000 workers on September 4.

Wilson had already gone twice to the Capitol in recent days to confer with Democratic leaders. He went again that afternoon, as soon as he heard news of the strike order, and talked for two and a half hours with members of the Democratic steering committee of the Senate. He won their approval for legislation that he said he would propose to Congress on the following day. That same evening he called the brotherhood heads to the White House and asked them whether the strike order had actually been issued. They admitted that it had; Wilson said that he was shocked and begged them to recall the order. They replied that it was beyond recall and a strike was inevitable.[158]

The President went before a joint session of Congress at two-thirty in the afternoon of August 29 dressed in a blue coat, white flannel trousers, and white shoes. It was, observers said, the first time that a President had ever appeared in the Capitol in informal dress. He began by reviewing the background of the controversy and relating the part that he had played. It had seemed to him, he said, that the foundation of a settlement was acceptance of the principle of the eight-hour day. "It has been adjudged by the thought and experience of recent years," he went on, "a thing upon which society is justified in insisting as in the interest of health, efficiency, contentment, and a general increase of economic vigor. The whole presumption of modern experience would, it seemed to me, be in its favor, whether there was arbitration or not, and the debatable points to settle were those which arose out of the acceptance of the eight-hour day rather than those which affected its establishment." He had submitted a plan of settlement. The brotherhoods had accepted it; the railroad presidents had refused, not caring to rely upon the friendly assurances of Congress or the President. Then the brotherhoods had called a strike for September 4. Thus he "earnestly" recommended legislation to provide the following:

First, immediate enlargement of the Interstate Commerce Commission.

Second, establishment of the eight-hour day "as the legal basis alike of work and of wages in the employment of all railway employees who

[158] *New York Times,* August 29, 1916.

are actually engaged in the work of operating trains in interstate transportation."

Third, appointment of a commission to study the practical effects of the application of the eight-hour day.

Fourth, approval by Congress of the Interstate Commerce Commission's consideration of increased freight rates should institution of the eight-hour day increase operating costs.

Fifth, amendment of existing legislation to require arbitration of railroad labor disputes before a strike or lockout could occur.

Sixth, power for the President to take control of the railroads and draft into the military service of the United States such crews and management officials as might be required for safe and efficient operation.

This, Wilson said in conclusion, was a program designed not to meet an emergency, but to satisfy imperative national needs in the future. "We need . . . [such laws] now and we shall continue to need them."[159]

Congress roared its approval, but Democratic leaders were soon saying that the President had asked for too much, and that it simply would not be possible to adopt all his legislation in time to prevent the strike.[160] This report—along with another to the effect that House leaders were offended because the President had not consulted them—brought Wilson back to the Capitol for a conference that evening (August 29) with Speaker Champ Clark, Majority Leader Kitchin, Representative William C. Adamson of Georgia, chairman of the interstate commerce committee, and ranking Republican members. They all told the President that he could get approval of a measure that included provisions only to establish the eight-hour day and a commission of inquiry. More than this, they said, would probably not pass the Senate before September 4. Congress could consider the balance of the President's program at its next session. Wilson agreed to consider the suggestion.[161]

Kitchin and Adamson drafted a truncated measure on the following day. It said that, beginning January 1, 1917, eight hours should constitute a day's work for railway workers engaged in interstate transportation, and that overtime should be paid at the rate of time and a half. It also authorized the President to appoint a commission of three mem-

[159] *The New Democracy*, II, 267-274.
[160] *New York Times*, August 30, 1916.
[161] *ibid.*

bers to investigate. "These two pages enclosed," Adamson wrote to all Democratic members of the House, sending them a copy of the bill, "contain the propositions which the President made to the Brotherhoods and to the Carriers and Mr. Kitchin and I have canvassed the subject to-day with those members of the House who are in touch with the Brotherhoods and we have become satisfied that the enactment of these provisions at this time and nothing more will avert a strike, and at the next session of Congress we can legislate on the entire subject."[162]

Wilson, accompanied by Burleson, returned to the Capitol in the morning of August 31 for a full-dress conference with Democratic representatives and senators. He said that he was now persuaded that only a brief bill could pass, and he would approve it. However, he went on, the brotherhood spokesmen had agreed to accept pro rata pay instead of time and a half for overtime work, and he would prefer to stand by his original proposal concerning overtime. Congressional leaders agreed to change the bill to meet his wishes.[163] Wilson called the brotherhood chieftains to the White House and again pleaded with them to rescind the strike order. They replied that they were helpless.[164]

Adamson introduced the eight-hour bill in the House at five o'clock in the afternoon of August 31. The interstate commerce committee submitted a favorable report the next morning, and the House approved the measure by a vote of 239 to fifty-six in the late afternoon.[165] The Senate agreed that evening to vote on the bill not later than six p.m. on the following day. Wild debate ensued as Republicans, seeking to make as much political capital as possible, hurled charges of political expediency and cowardice at their opponents. But the Senate approved the Adamson bill by a vote of forty-three to twenty-eight at 6:04 p.m. on September 2.[166] It was signed, sealed, and delivered at the White House at 7:10 p.m. The presidents of the brotherhoods sent messages at 8:35 p.m. to division chairmen rescinding the strike

---

[162] W. C. Adamson, circular letter to Democratic members of the House of Representatives, August 30, 1916, copy in the Kitchin Papers.

[163] Adamson later wrote that he made this concession reluctantly. He and other members of the interstate commerce committee had, he added, wanted to impose the eight-hour day in fact. W. C. Adamson to R. S. Baker, February 9, 1927, Baker Collection.

[164] *New York Times*, September 1, 1916.

[165] *Congressional Record*, 64th Cong., 1st sess., p. 13608.

[166] *ibid.*, p. 13655.

order, after Secretary of Labor William B. Wilson had given them the President's personal promise that he would sign the bill. "It is the climax of a very happy day," President Wilson, then in Long Branch, New Jersey, said.[167] He signed it at 9:11 on the following morning in his private car "Federal" at Union Station. An engineer passing in a yard engine celebrated the event with several long blasts of his whistle.[168]

It was, Wilson thought, not the best solution, but it was the only one possible. "I felt," he wrote a few days later, "that it was inevitable and right that the eight-hour day should be accepted, but there is a great deal more to do in connection with the matter which Congress has been obliged, because of the pressure for an early adjournment, to postpone until another session."[169] Kitchin was even franker in saying that the President and Congress had had no choice. As he put it:

"Of course, after the President took the matter in hand and failed to avert the strike by personal negotiations and then threw the matter into Congress, it was up to both the President and Congress to pass some legislation that would avert the strike. All here recognized that the strike would be the greatest catastrophe that ever befell our country and that it would have almost culminated into a Civil War. Another thing, if the strike had not been averted, the present Administration would have been destroyed. Under the circumstances, we all thought the wisest thing to do was to pass the legislation which we did. At the next, or following session, it is then incumbent upon the Administration and Congress to give their best thought to the question and evolve some wise legislation which is just to both the Railroads and the operatives alike, which will hereafter prevent such calamity as was threatened a few weeks ago."[170]

The presidential campaign had now begun in full vigor, and it was already obvious that the Adamson Act would be a leading, perhaps the chief, domestic issue. Comment depended, therefore, in the main on political alignment, and Republicans denounced Wilson's and Congress' alleged humiliating surrender to labor bosses.[171] It was significant that

---

[167] *New York Times*, September 3, 1916.

[168] *ibid.*, September 4, 1916.

[169] W. W. to C. R. Holcomb, September 6, 1916, Wilson Papers.

[170] C. Kitchin to W. R. Capehart, September 5, 1916, Kitchin Papers.

[171] e. g. (on the Republican side), *New York Tribune, Albany Knickerbocker Press,* and *Indianapolis Star,* all dated, September 1, 1916; J. T. Morse, Jr., to H. C. Lodge, September 4, 1916, copy in author's possession furnished by Professor H. K. Beale; T. Roosevelt to L. Abbott, September 2, 1916, Roosevelt Papers; *Collier's,*

independent progressives came out more quickly in defense of the law than Democrats.[172]

Only a few contemporaries saw the long-range significance of these events. Wilson had demonstrated the possibilities of national, unifying, and transforming leadership in the presidency more dramatically and effectively than he had ever done before. As *The New Republic* put it, "Mr. Wilson has done what high statesmanship in a democracy must do: he has interpreted the demands, principles, and interests of group interests, and lifted them up into a national program. In a very real and accurate sense the President has made himself the spokesman of a whole people. He has not treated the demands of special groups as something to be ignored or stamped upon as the mere demagogue or tory would. He has integrated those demands with the larger and more persistent interests of the nation. He has shown how to turn an emergency to constructive purposes."[173] Equally important, the Adamson Act was another milestone in the inexorable movement toward expansion of the authority and activity of the federal government. As one observer across the Atlantic wisely said, "The imposition of an eight-hour day for adult skilled male workers, and this by federal (as distinct from State) legislation, is an almost revolutionary departure for America. Mr. Wilson started his period of office as a rather old-fashioned believer in *laissez faire*, very jealous of State rights. He has evolved, with four years' administrative experience, towards an active and constructive Liberalism."[174]

LVIII (September 23, 1916), 14-15; W. H. Taft to J. B. Holton, November 7, 1916, Taft Papers. The following independent or Democratic commentators were strongly condemnatory: *New York Times*, Baltimore *Sun* and *St. Louis Republic*, all dated September 1, 1916; Dallas *Baptist Standard*, XXVIII (September 7, 1916), 3; New York *Nation*, CIII (September 7, 1916), 213; and *The Independent*, LXXXVII (September 18, 1916), 399-400.

[172] e. g., R. M. La Follette, "Another Step toward Industrial Justice," *La Follette's Magazine*, VIII (September 1916), 1-2; *The Public*, XIX (September 8, 1916), 841; *Des Moines Register*, September 1, 1916; *New Republic*, VIII (September 9, 1916), 130-131.

[173] *ibid.*, September 2, 1916, p. 100.

[174] London *Nation*, XIX (September 9, 1916), 711.

The Campaign of 1916 Begins

PRESIDENTIAL campaigns were launched in the good old days with elaborate ceremony. The permanent chairman of the national convention, accompanied by a great throng of the party faithful, would meet the nominee at some designated place, usually his home town, and break the news to him that he had been nominated for the highest office in the land. This was called being "notified." The nominee would then accept (none ever refused) with due thanks and promises to lead the party to great and glorious victory in November and the country to new heights afterward.

This was still the way it was done in 1916, and through the hot weeks of July and August Wilson worked on his acceptance speech when he could find the time. Senator Hollis, at the President's request, sent a memorandum on the rural credits bill and its benefits to farmers.[1] Tumulty gathered a large package of campaign pamphlets, memoranda on legislation, and the like on August 4, and Wilson, accompanied only by Mrs. Wilson and Charles L. Swem, his stenographer, boarded the *Mayflower* that same evening for a cruise down Chesapeake Bay. He returned to Washington in the morning of August 7 with a first draft. He reworked it during the next weeks in response to new suggestions and events. For example, Walter Lippmann, an editor of *The New Republic*, offered interesting advice through Secretary Baker.[2] "You can assure Mr. Lippmann," Wilson replied, "that that is one of the matters which I have, as a matter of fact, had most vividly in mind, and I hope sincerely that as his ideas clarify he will let me have the benefit of them, either directly or in an editorial expression."[3] Harold Laski, the English political scientist, wrote to Norman Hapgood soon afterward, asking him to urge the President to "come out strong." As Hapgood later explained, after sending Laski's letter to Wilson, Laski hoped

[1] M. B. Griffin to J. P. Tumulty, July 6, 1916, Wilson Papers.

[2] W. Lippmann to N. D. Baker, August 2, 1916, referred to in a White House memorandum dated August 7, 1916, *ibid*. Wilson returned the letter to Baker, but it is not to be found in the Papers of Newton D. Baker, Library of Congress; hereinafter cited as the N. D. Baker Papers.

[3] W. W. to N. D. Baker, August 7, 1916, Wilson Papers.

that Wilson would "come out strong" for liberal doctrines. It would affect independent voters very much, Hapgood added, if Wilson would make his progressivism as clear in public speeches as he did in private conversation.[4] "I have no doubt that in the course of the campaign," Wilson replied, "I can find an opportunity for letting my underlying philosophy come out plainly enough."[5]

Wilson and his campaign managers, after postponing the notification ceremonies to be held at "Shadow Lawn," Wilson's new summer home in Long Branch, on the New Jersey shore, finally set the date for September 2, even though they knew that Congress would still be in session. The President and Mrs. Wilson arrived at Long Branch in the evening of September 1 to be greeted by a huge crowd and two brass bands and escorted to "Shadow Lawn" by a procession of automobiles with blaring horns. They entertained some three hundred party workers at a buffet luncheon on the following day. The ceremonies, held on a platform erected in front of the house, began with Senator James's notification speech at 2:30 in the afternoon. A brass band, led by Wilson's old foe from Newark, James R. Nugent, marched across the lawn playing "The Wearing of the Green" just as James was warming up. "On behalf of the Democrats of the whole Republic, who are proud of your great administration," the Kentuckian intoned in conclusion, "we pledge you their enthusiastic and united support, and our prayer is that God, who blesses the peacemaker, may guide you to a glorious victory in November."[6]

Wilson spoke almost in a conversational tone, but his voice carried well, and there was frequent applause and laughter from the throng of fifteen thousand persons on the lawn. He began with appropriate thanks to the Democratic party for its nomination and loyalty. Then he reviewed the record of Democratic achievement, emphasizing its variety and benefits to businessmen as well as to workers, farmers, and children. "This record," he went on in a direct word for independents and former Progressives, "must equally astonish those who feared that the Democratic party had not opened its heart to comprehend the demands of social justice. We have in four years come very near to carrying out the platform of the Progressive party, as well as our own; for we are also progressives."

[4] W. W. to N. Hapgood, August 9, 1916, *ibid.*; N. Hapgood to W. W., August 10, 1916, *ibid.*

[5] W. W. to N. Hapgood, August 12, 1916, *ibid.*

[6] *New York Times*, September 3, 1916; *Official Report of the Proceedings of the Democratic National Convention . . . 1916*, pp. 149-151.

Passing to foreign affairs, he said that the United States had been neutral, not only because neutrality was the nation's settled policy and the United States had had no part in bringing on the war, but also because it was manifestly America's duty to prevent the spread of hostilities and save her strength "for the anxious and difficult days of restoration and healing which must follow when peace will have to build its house anew." He had based his policies toward the belligerents, he continued, on the fundamental principle that property rights could be vindicated by damages after the war, and that loss of life was irreparable. However, he said in obvious reference to recent British measures, "direct violations of a nation's sovereignty" would be met immediately and "called to account by direct challenge and resistance." Then followed severe condemnation of hyphenate groups. "I am," Wilson said, "the candidate of a party, but I am above all things else an American citizen. I neither seek the favor nor fear the displeasure of that small alien element amongst us which puts loyalty to any foreign power before loyalty to the United States."

Mexican policy, Wilson continued, was the test of American sincerity, and all Latin America was watching to see how the United States dealt with her weaker neighbor. He had sent troops into Mexico only in order to protect American lives along the border. There had been no other remedy. But he would do nothing to impair the struggle for freedom of the enslaved Mexican people, "15,000,000 oppressed men, overburdened women and pitiful children in virtual bondage in their own home." Some of the leaders of the Mexican Revolution had been selfish and mistaken, but "the revolution itself was inevitable and is right."

There were difficult days ahead. America, no longer isolated and provincial, had to help build strong foundations for peace in the postwar world. But America had to be strong and vital at home before she could lead abroad. She had to marshal her resources and protect her laboring men and women. "We are," he concluded, "Americans for Big America, and rejoice to look forward to the days in which America shall strive to stir the world without irritating it or drawing it on to new antagonisms, when the nations with which we deal shall at last come to see upon what deep foundations of humanity and justice our passion for peace rests. . . . Upon this record and in the faith of this purpose we go to the country."[7]

There was another reception after the speech, followed by a quiet

[7] *ibid.*, pp. 151-161.

dinner with relatives and Vance McCormick. The President and Mrs. Wilson left for Washington later in the evening. Wilson's first act upon arriving in the city on September 3 was, as we have seen, to sign the Adamson bill. He and Mrs. Wilson went to the White House for half an hour; then they returned to Union Station to board the train to Hodgenville, Kentucky, where Wilson, on the following day, accepted for the nation a memorial encasing Lincoln's birthplace. Wilson's speech was one of the most probing and perceptive reflections on Lincoln that has ever been written. "How eloquent this little house within this shrine is of the vigor of democracy!" he said. "There is nowhere in the land any home so remote, so humble, that it may not contain the power of mind and heart and conscience to which nations yield and history submits its processes. . . . This little hut was the cradle of one of the great sons of men, a man of singular, delightful, vital genius who presently emerged upon the great stage of the nation's history, gaunt, shy, ungainly, but dominant and majestic, a natural ruler of men, himself inevitably the central figure of the great plot. No man can explain this, but every man can see how it demonstrates the vigor of democracy, where every door is open . . . for the ruler to emerge when he will and claim his leadership in the free life. Such are the authentic proofs of the validity and vitality of democracy." Was Wilson thinking of himself when he said:

"I have read many biographies of Lincoln. . . . I nowhere get the impression in any narrative or reminiscence that the writer had in fact penetrated the heart of his mystery, or that any man could penetrate to the heart of it. That brooding spirit had no real familiars. I get the impression that it never spoke out in complete self-revelation, and that it could not reveal itself completely to anyone. . . . There is a very holy and terrible isolation for the conscience of every man who seeks to read the destiny in affairs for others as well as for himself, for a nation as well as for individuals. That privacy no man can intrude upon. That lonely search of the spirit for the right perhaps no man can assist. This strange child of the cabin kept company with invisible things, was born into no intimacy but that of its own silently assembling and deploying thoughts."[8]

The Wilsons returned to Washington on September 5, and the President plunged into work again, particularly on the retaliatory provisions of the revenue bill. He and Mrs. Wilson were finally able to leave for their extended stay at "Shadow Lawn" on September 8. They

[8] *New York Times*, September 5, 1916; *The New Democracy*, II, 292-296.

stopped on their way at Atlantic City, where Wilson spoke that evening to some 4,000 members of the National American Woman Suffrage Association. They stood and cheered when Wilson declared that woman suffrage was inevitable and said that he had come to fight for the cause. "You touched our hearts and won our fealty," Mrs. Carrie Chapman Catt, president of the Association replied.[9]

"Shadow Lawn" was a big, rambling white house with huge porches all around, surrounded by spacious lawns. It was sheer delight to be there after the discomfort and distractions of Washington. Wilson had planned the next two weeks to be as free a vacation as a President of the United States could ever hope to enjoy. There would be only one speech to prepare and deliver, no politicians at the door, nothing but minimum work and golf and leisure.

Tragedy upset these plans almost as soon as the Wilsons arrived. The President received word on September 11 that his sister, Annie W. Howe, was dying from peritonitis in New London, Connecticut. He and Mrs. Wilson went at once to her bedside.[10] It happened that the Mexican-American Joint High Commission was holding its first sessions in New London, and Wilson received the members on the *Mayflower* on September 12.[11] The Wilsons returned to Long Branch on the yacht on the following day, after doctors told the President that there was no hope and Mrs. Howe could not recognize him because of heavy sedation.[12] She died on September 16, and the President, Mrs. Wilson, and Doctor Grayson went to Columbia, South Carolina, for the funeral services at the First Presbyterian Church two days later. After the interment Wilson visited his aged aunt, Mrs. James Woodrow. She greeted him as "Tommy" and said to Mrs. Wilson, "Since he took to writing books he calls himself Woodrow." Wilson next called at the Columbia Theological Seminary, where his father and uncle, James Woodrow, had taught; afterward he walked to the house that his father and mother had built. Then he boarded his special train for the return trip to New Jersey; several thousand persons stood bareheaded and silent as he entered the station.[13]

Wilson had asked Newton D. Baker to take his place in filling his sole speaking engagement during this period—an appearance before the

[9] *New York Times,* September 9, 1916.
[10] *ibid.,* September 12, 1916.
[11] *ibid.,* September 13, 1916.
[12] *ibid.,* September 14, 1916.
[13] *ibid.,* September 19, 1916.

Association of Life Insurance Underwriters in St. Louis on about September 18. "It was my purpose at St. Louis," he wrote to the Secretary of War, "to dwell upon the idea of life insurance and point out the fact that the field of legislation and of policy had shifted in our time to questions of social welfare, the development and vitalization of the life of the nation in all its phases. Hence, such movements as the Progressive. The new circumstances of the world after the war likely to emphasize such questions and put them in a new light, etc."[14]

Vance McCormick, Democratic National Chairman, had meanwhile been at work with other party wheelhorses, particularly Robert W. Woolley, Director of the Mint, building a campaign organization. It was complete by August 10. Daniel C. Roper, former First Assistant Postmaster, was in command at Democratic headquarters on the second floor of the Forty-Second Street Building in New York City. There were perhaps a dozen different departments or bureaus assigned to various duties. Hugh C. Wallace, a close friend of Colonel House, headed a Special Bureau to cultivate foreign-born voters and editors.[15] Robert S. Hudspeth of New Jersey was in charge of a Labor Bureau, Mrs. Charles Dana Gibson, of an Eastern Women's Bureau. But the most important department was Woolley's Publicity Bureau. It prepared and distributed a twelve-page magazine section, sent postpaid to any newspaper that would use it, along with a flood of books, pamphlets, and other campaign materials covering every issue and appealing to every conceivable interest group.[16] McCormick also established a smaller separate western

[14] W. W. to N. D. Baker, September 16, 1916, Wilson Papers.

[15] H. C. Wallace to E. M. House, August 31, October 2 and 3, 1916, House Papers; *New York Times*, October 1, 1916.

[16] e. g., *The Democratic Text Book*; *"Yes" or "No! Mr. Hughes"?*; *Woodrow Wilson and Social Justice*; *The Schoolmaster in the White House* (aimed at teachers); *President Wilson a True Progressive. . . . Issued by a Committee of Progressives Formed to promote the Re-election of President Wilson*; *Record of Hughes as an Enemy of Labor*; *Why Justice Hughes Should Not Be a Candidate, by Justice Charles E. Hughes, Judge William H. Taft, Concurring*; *Cornelius A. Hughes Discusses Wilson and Why Colored Men Should Favor His Re-election*; *Wilson and Labor*; *Charles "E-vasion" Hughes*; *Prosperity Under the Democratic Tariff*; *How Wilson Has Kept Faith with the Farmer*; *Ten Reasons for Voting for Wilson, by Dr. Irving Fisher*; *Sixteen Million Voters Appeal for Light!*; *Labor's Charter of Freedom, Labor Legislation Passed by Congress and approved by President Wilson*; *The Whole Truth About the Eight-hour Law*; *Children's Emancipation Day*; *"Complete Accord with Roosevelt"*; *The So-Called American Truth Society*; *Independents Are for Wilson. WHY?*; *Mexico. Woodrow Wilson Fights for the Just Rights and the Liberty of an Oppressed and Helpless People—Against Billions of Money*, all issued by the Democratic National Committee, New York City, 1916.

headquarters in Chicago in early August, with Senator Walsh of Montana in command. It distributed campaign materials sent from New York and assigned Democratic speakers in midwestern and western states. Its work increased vastly after Democrats shifted the major emphasis of their campaign when the Maine election in early September revealed a strong, perhaps irreversible, Republican tide in the East. Finally, the National Chairman encouraged organization of what appeared to be purely voluntary groups of former Progressives, independents, and businessmen. The most important were the Wilson Business Men's National League, led by Wilson's friend, Charles R. Crane of Chicago, and the Woodrow Wilson Independent League, headed by William Kent of California.

The most difficult tasks of all fell to Wilbur W. Marsh and Henry Morgenthau, treasurer and chairman of the finance committee of the Democratic National Committee, respectively. Morgenthau got off to a flying start in June with the promise of a contribution of $100,000 from Cleveland H. Dodge, Wilson's classmate and dear friend.[17] Contributions came in modestly but well until adoption of the Adamson Act. Then, so Woolley later said, large contributions virtually ceased, and the Committee's treasury was nearly bankrupt, because angry businessmen not only stopped giving to the Democratic fund but turned en masse to Hughes. "The action of Congress has aroused and banded together the business interests of the country against the President," McCormick wrote in alarm on September 11. "Before this they were lukewarm, but now they are fighting mad and are offering freely their support to Hughes both in money and effort."[18] "Every sordid and reactionary interest is more embittered now than ever before against the President and the Democratic party," McAdoo wrote at the same time, "and they are more determined than ever to win the next election by hook or crook, and especially by crook if they can get it no other way."[19] Breckinridge Long, a New York lawyer, was, according to Woolley, the man who kept the New York headquarters running during these dark days. He came into McCormick's office on the day after the Adamson Act was signed, wrote out a check for $5,000, and offered

[17] H. Morgenthau to E. M. House, June 28, 1916, House Papers.

[18] V. McCormick to E. M. House, September 11, 1916, *ibid.*

[19] W. G. McAdoo to W. B. Wilson, September 4, 1916, the Papers of William B. Wilson, Pennsylvania Historical Society. See also E. Sedgwick to E. M. House, September 6, 1916, House Papers.

to lend $100,000 more if it was needed. McCormick had to borrow $30,000 from him to keep the office open.[20]

Marsh organized committees in cities and towns all over the country to raise at least $500,000 in a "dollar" Wilson fund,[21] but Democratic leaders had no illusions about the possibilities of support from the so-called common people. As a circular sent out to newspaper editors who were helping in the drive for funds advised, "Get all the large subscriptions as early as possible. DON'T ALLOW AN IMPRESSION TO BE CREATED THAT YOU WANT ONLY SMALL CONTRI-BUTIONS. It might happen, for instance, that a person able and willing to contribute $10 or $25 will find it easy and convenient to give a smaller sum. DON'T LET HIM."[22] We do not know how well or badly these efforts fared, for Marsh and Morgenthau did not issue a report on campaign contributions and expenditures.

Hughes had meanwhile tried to find an issue and get his own campaign into high gear following his fumbling acceptance speech on July 31. It was not easy for him to escape the dilemmas that had already begun to confound his campaign. He was too upright to be a demagogue and attack that large part of Wilson's achievements which he undoubtedly admired. Hughes was a moderate progressive, but he could not come out in bold support of a progressive program without endorsing the Democratic record and, more important, risking alienation of the conservative and business leaders who had nominated him and were supporting his campaign with generosity unparalleled since 1896. So from the outset he decided to work with and through the regular Republican organization and cut his losses among progressive voters. It is impossible to say where Hughes really stood on foreign policy. He was probably sincere in saying that he stood for an "honest and straightforward neutrality." But he could not criticize Wilson's policies toward the European belligerents too strongly without running the risk of alienating German Americans and offending the peace sentiments of ordinary voters. It was difficult even to find an issue in the Mexican situation, for Hughes could not advocate military intervention without violating his own conscience and producing violent reactions among voters who wanted no war with Mexico.

[20] A. H. Meneely, interview with R. W. Woolley, February 2, 1929, MS. in the Baker Collection.

[21] *New York Times*, August 8, 1916.

[22] *Suggestions to Aid Newspapers in Conducting a Canvass for Popular Contributions to the Woodrow Wilson Campaign Fund*, circular in the Wilson Papers.

These dilemmas, and new ones, plagued Hughes all through the cross-country tour that he began in Detroit on August 7. He talked there mainly about Mexico, but only to condemn Wilson's methods and alleged mismanagement of Mexican policy.[23] "Governor Hughes," one

Vacillation

Rense in the New York *World*

New York editor said, "acts in this affair too much as if he were just an ordinary humdrum Republican orator, striving hard to find an 'issue.' "[24] In Chicago on August 8, he concentrated on Wilson's alleged

[23] *New York Evening Post*, August 8, 1916.
[24] *ibid.*

violations of good civil service principles and practices. He also intimated the line that he would follow in attacking Wilson's policies toward the European belligerents—that the President's weakness and failure to carry out threats had increased the danger of war, and that the best hope of continued peace lay in firm defense of neutral rights against all offenders.[25] Hughes reiterated his attack against Wilson's civil service record in St. Paul on August 9.[26] "I stand," he said in Fargo, North Dakota, on the following day, "for a businesslike administration of the United States."[27] He waved a slightly bloody shirt at Butte, Montana, on August 12, charging that the Democratic party and Wilson administration were dominated by Southerners.[28]

Hughes went on and on, campaigning into the Pacific Northwest and then into California. What he did in that state mattered more than what he said. California Republicans were split into two savagely hostile factions, each more eager to knife the other than to defeat their Democratic opponents. Regular Republicans controlled the party machinery. Their chief objective was to prevent Governor Hiram Johnson, Progressive vice presidential nominee in 1912, from winning the *Republican* nomination for United States senator. Hughes, from the moment that he entered California, permitted himself to be surrounded and sponsored by the regulars, and he said not a single word even intimating sympathy for the Republican progressives. He crossed a picket line to attend a luncheon at the Commercial Club in San Francisco on August 19. He was in the same hotel with Governor Johnson in San Diego on August 21, but Johnson refused to see him.[29] Hughes, one Republican who had been working to reconcile the Johnson faction wrote, "did not make votes by coming to California; and the state would be in much better shape politically if he had never come here."[30] As Wilson wrote to Lansing a short time later, "I even have a sort of sympathy for the man. He is in a hopelessly false position. He dare not have opinions: he would be sure to offend some important section of his following."[31]

Hughes—and other Republican orators—finally found an issue in the

[25] *New York Times*, August 9, 1916.

[26] *ibid.*, August 10, 1916.

[27] *ibid.*, August 11, 1916.

[28] *ibid.*, August 13, 1916.

[29] *ibid.*, August 19, 20, and 21, 1916; New York *World*, August 22, 1916.

[30] P. A. Stanton to W. H. Taft, August 31, 1916, Taft Papers.

[31] W. W. to R. Lansing, October 2, 1916, the Papers of Robert Lansing, Princeton University Library; hereinafter cited as the Lansing Papers, Princeton.

Adamson Act. It was a godsend in view of the paucity of good issues, William R. Willcox, chairman of the Republican National Committee, told reporters somewhat indiscreetly on September 5, after he and Hughes had agreed to go all out in attacking the eight-hour law.[32] "This," Hughes wrote to former President Taft, who had urged him to hit hard, "is the most shameful proceeding that has come to my attention since I have observed public life and it presents, as it seems to me, a fundamental issue. I propose to press it constantly."[33] He opened his assault in Nashville, Tennessee, on September 4, attacking the President and Congress for yielding to railroad workers in order to gain votes and exclaiming, "I would not surrender to anybody in the country."[34] Wilson and Congress, he said at Lexington, Kentucky, on the following day, had endangered priceless freedom by bending their knees to organized labor.[35] The Adamson Act, he cried at Beverly, Massachusetts, on September 7, was the paramount issue of the campaign. "Transcending every other issue," he said, "is the issue that has just presented itself—whether the Government shall yield to force. . . . This country must never know the rule of force. It must never know legislation under oppression."[36]

Wilson, on September 23, delivered the first of a series of "front porch" addresses that he was scheduling for various groups who were to come in sequence about once a week to "Shadow Lawn." He would deal intensively with only one subject at a time, thus gradually covering all the major issues and educating the American people step by step. Hughes's recent massive assault made it inevitable that Wilson should choose the Adamson Act as the subject of his first "front porch" address. Friends and advisers were urging him to counterattack strongly by defending the measure as wise and right as well as necessary to save the country from disaster.[37] He needed no advice on this score; indeed, he had bolder plans of his own.

[32] *New York Times*, September 6, 1916.

[33] C. E. Hughes to W. H. Taft, September 16, 1916, Taft Papers. "I felicitate you most heartily on your courageous stand with reference to the strike," Taft had written to Hughes, "and the outrageous surrender to force and political exigency which Wilson made. It is the most humiliating thing in the recent history of the United States." W. H. Taft to C. E. Hughes, September 13, 1916, *ibid*.

[34] *New York Times*, September 5, 1916.

[35] *ibid*., September 6, 1916.

[36] *ibid*., September 8, 1916.

[37] H. Thompson to W. W., September 20, 1916, Wilson Papers; R. S. Hudspeth to W. W., September 21, 1916, *ibid*.; W. L. Chambers to W. W., September 21, 1916, *ibid*.

He unveiled what he had in mind as he spoke to some 2,000 members of the Wilson Business Men's National League and others on September 23. He began by commenting on the new era that lay ahead for American business, and on the one dark cloud—hostility between management and labor—then on the horizon. He went on to describe his experience during the recent railroad crisis. He had soon concluded, he said, that the one great issue at stake, the eight-hour day, was right and sound, not merely for railroad workers, but for all workers. "We believe in the eight-hour day," Wilson went on with what can only be called incredible boldness, "because a man does better work within eight hours than he does within a more extended day, and the whole theory of it, a theory which is sustained now by abundant experience, is that his efficiency is increased, his spirit in his work is improved, and the whole moral and physical vigor of the man is added to. This is no longer conjectural. Where it has been tried it has been demonstrated. The judgment of society, the vote of every Legislature in America that has voted upon it is a verdict in favor of the eight-hour day."

Wilson continued, saying that he had devised his own program for labor peace on the railroads, asking neither side whether it suited it. He had stood and fought, neither for management nor labor, but for the American people. "The business of government," he added, driving home a basic progressive concept, "is to see that no other organization is as strong as itself; to see that no body or group of men, no matter what their private interest is, may come into competition with the authority of society." It was necessary to find some way to prevent labor disputes from damaging society, and he would be glad to have some constructive suggestions. He had submitted a program, and he hoped that Congress would consider it.[38]

One of the most celebrated incidents of the campaign occurred just a few days later. Wilson, on September 29, received a long telegram from Jeremiah A. O'Leary, president of the American Truth Society, a virulent anti-British, pro-German propaganda organization, saying among other things, "Your foreign policies, your failure to secure compliance with all American rights, your leniency with the British Empire, your approval of war loans, the ammunition traffic are issues in this campaign."[39] "Your telegram received," Wilson shot back. "I would feel deeply mortified to have you or anybody like you vote for me. Since you have access to many disloyal Americans and I have not, I will

[38] New York *World*, September 24, 1916.
[39] J. A. O'Leary to W. W., September 29, 1916, *New York Times*, September 30, 1916.

ask you to convey this message to them."[40] This telegram, published in the newspapers on September 30, struck like a thunderbolt over the country. "How many votes will be turned to Wilson by this episode, we cannot venture to estimate," one editor commented, "but it is certain that it has warmed the blood of many a man who had been cold or hostile, and made him feel like registering at once approval of the President's splendid utterance and disgust at the 'enemies he has made' by casting a vote for a second term for Woodrow Wilson."[41] Colonel House afterward told the French Ambassador that the O'Leary telegram was the turning point in the campaign.

After a nonpolitical speech to the Grain Dealers' National Association in Baltimore on September 25, Wilson spoke again at "Shadow Lawn" on September 30 to members of the Young Men's Democratic League among a larger throng of 3,000 listeners. He had talked with Walter Lippmann about the speech for an hour and a half on September 27, and Lippmann, in a letter written on the following day, had repeated his advice that Wilson come out squarely as a progressive in a bid for the support of Roosevelt's followers in 1912.[42]

Wilson began his address on September 30 somewhat academically, reviewing the history of American political parties like a professor lecturing to a class of students. Four years ago, he said, a great body of progressive Republicans had rebelled against their party's enslavement to special interests. They had formed the great Progressive party—great, not in numbers, but because it had the real red blood of human sympathy in its veins and was ready to work for mankind and forget the interests of a narrow party. "I want," he went on, "to pay my tribute of respect to the purposes and intentions of the men who formed that group in politics." The interesting thing was that Democrats had done what Progressives hoped to do. There were standpatters in the Demo-

[40] W. W. to J. A. O'Leary, September 29, 1916, *ibid.* For O'Leary's reply, see *A Statement issued by the American Truth Society in defense of its President against an unjust attack made upon him by the President of the United States*, and J. A. O'Leary, *Why Woodrow Wilson Should Be Defeated and a Republican Congress Elected*.

[41] New York *Nation*, CIII (October 5, 1916), 312; also *New Republic*, VIII (October 7, 1916), 232-233, and the review of press opinion in "The President and the Hyphen," *Literary Digest*, LIII (October 14, 1916), 935.

[42] I have been unable to find Lippmann's letter. Wilson answered it on September 29 as follows: "Thank you heartily for your letter of September twenty-eight. I shall certainly be guided by it in my speech tomorrow. It was a genuine pleasure to have you down here to have such a delightful talk." W. W. to W. Lippmann, September 29, 1916, Wilson Papers.

cratic party, but they were a minority. "I am a progressive," Wilson continued. "I do not spell it with a capital P, but I think my pace is just as fast as those who do. It does not interfere with the running and I am very much astonished to see the company that some gentlemen who spell their name with a capital are keeping."

Something in the situation—perhaps the sight of so many young men—supercharged the atmosphere for Wilson, and he struck out extemporaneously:

"Unfortunately, however, one thing has become reasonably clear, my fellow citizens, and it is a very serious thing indeed. One thing has become evident, not because it was explicitly stated, for nothing has been explicitly stated, but because it is unmistakably implicit in almost everything that has been said. Am I not right that we must draw the conclusion that, if the Republican Party is put into power at the next election, our foreign policy will be radically changed? I cannot draw any other inference.

"All our present foreign policy is wrong, they say, and if it is wrong and they are men of conscience, they must change it; and if they are going to change it in what direction are they going to change it?

"There is only one choice as against peace, and that is war. Some of the supporters of that party, a very great body of the supporters of that party, outspokenly declare that they want war; so that the certain prospect of the success of the Republican Party is that we shall be drawn in one form or other into the embroilments of the European war, and that to the south of us the force of the United States will be used to produce in Mexico the kind of law and order which some American investors in Mexico consider most to their advantage. . . . The one thing I want to lay emphasis upon in this connection is this—that a great, fundamental, final choice with regard to our foreign relationsships [*sic*] is to be made on the 7th of November. Some young men ought to be interested in that."[43]

It was like a fire bell in the night, and response was so encouraging that Wilson told McCormick on October 2 that he would go to Omaha for an address on October 5 and return to the Middle West for a brief tour later in the month.[44] Large and enthusiastic crowds greeted the

[43] New York *World*, October 1, 1916.

[44] He made this decision also in response to a strong letter from Senator Stone. "I wish you would take my voice to the President," Stone wrote to Tumulty on October 1, "and add it to those who think it *very* important that he should make a speaking tour across the country, especially visiting the doubtful States. He can do more, ten

presidential train along the way in Ohio, Indiana, and Illinois. Railroad workers were especially demonstrative, one brakeman, for example, putting out his hand to Wilson and saying, "Right there, Mr. President. She's dirty, but she's going to hit the rooster hard."[45] Wilson spoke to a crowd of 10,000 cheering listeners in the Auditorium in Omaha on October 5, not about staying out of the war, but about America's duty to help maintain peace once the war had ended. "What disturbs the life of the whole world," he said, "is the concern of the whole world, and it is our duty to lend the full force of this nation, moral and physical, to a league of nations which shall see to it that nobody disturbs the peace of the world without submitting his case first to the opinion of mankind." The crowd cheered most loudly when he said that no man understood the origins and objects of the European war, and that the United States had played no part in bringing it on.[46] "What a rotten speech President Wilson's at Omaha on Thursday!" Lord Bertie wrote in his diary on October 6. "America *was* too proud to fight: *now* the cause must be just and important. . . . He is trimming his sails for any electoral breeze that he may be able to catch."[47]

Wilson took up the peace theme again in a speech before delegates from the Woodrow Wilson College Men's League at "Shadow Lawn" on October 7. "The Republicans," House had advised, "are much concerned over that part of your last Saturday's speech [on September 30] in which you declared that Hughes' election would mean war. I would suggest that you emphasize this again."[48] The advice was probably unnecessary. What would happen, Wilson asked his audience, if the Republican party succeeded on November 7? "The only articulate voice, a very articulate voice," he went on in obvious reference to Theodore Roosevelt, "professes opinions and purposes at which the rest in private shiver and demur. When the whole country is clamoring for definition, it is legitimate to take it where you can get it, and the definitions are backed by certain things that have already happened in our politics. One branch of that party . . . backed as a candidate for the United States Senate in the State of New York a man [Robert Bacon] whose avowed position in respect of international affairs was

---

times over, than anybody else; and don't forget we have a h—— of a fight on." W. J. Stone to J. P. Tumulty, October 1, 1916, Wilson Papers.

[45] *New York Times,* October 5, 1916.

[46] *ibid.,* October 6, 1916.

[47] Lady Algernon G. Lennox (ed.), *The Diary of Lord Bertie of Thame,* ii, 40.

[48] E. M. House to W. W., October 5, 1916, Wilson Papers.

unneutral and whose intention was . . . to promote the interests of one side in the present war in Europe. Therefore, we are warranted in believing that if the Republican party should succeed, one very large branch of it would insist upon what its leader has insisted upon, a complete reversal of policy. And in view of the support that the candidate I have referred to in New York received, that reversal of policy can only be a reversal from peace to war."[49]

For Woodrow Wilson and the Democratic party there were now two, and only two, great battle cries—progressivism and peace. No one could cavil at the choice of the first. The effect of the rupture of the G.O.P. had been to place conservative, business-oriented politicians in undisputed control of that party, and Republicans in 1916 stood squarely for an end to, if not a reversal of, the progressive program. Democrats, by their platform and legislation in 1916, had gone the second mile in bidding for independent, labor, farm, and Progressive votes. Wilson quite frankly wanted to fuse these voters and regular Democrats into a new party. His championship of advanced progressivism was thus inevitable. It was also natural and logical, given the transformation that had occurred in his own political thought.

Circumstances also made it virtually inevitable that Wilson should take open and aggressive leadership of peace sentiment. Progressives and groups to whom progressives appealed were overwhelmingly pacifistic or opposed to participation in the European war, unless there was an overwhelming assault upon American rights and sovereignty. Anti-war progressives were most numerous in the Middle West and Far West, the very regions that the Democrats had to carry if they were to win. These were the obvious facts of political life in 1916. Bryan pointed them out in May, saying that the only hope of Democratic victory lay in winning a substantial part of the peace element in the Republican party.[50] "During my western trip," Morgenthau informed the President early in June, "I met and talked with and at a great many people, and found that they are not as 'heroic' as T. R. wants them to be. They want [you] to keep us out of the war at almost any price."[51] The power of the peace appeal was of course all the more apparent by early October. "The issue is going to be pretty soon 'Peace or War,'" one Democratic leader observed then. "I believe it is a safe issue. . . .

[49] New York *World*, October 8, 1916.
[50] W. J. Bryan, "The President's Opportunity," *The Commoner*, xvi (May 1916), 1.
[51] H. Morgenthau to W. W., June 2, 1916, Wilson Papers.

There is an enormous body of sound-thinking people in the country, normally Republicans, that will unhesitatingly vote the Democratic ticket if they see that that is the issue."[52]

Democratic campaign managers and orators with fingers on the popular pulse had in fact already begun to exploit the peace issue heavily before Wilson took it up. He probably could not have reversed their momentum in any event. Fortunately for the President, conviction also counseled swimming with the tide. He was now more than ever eager to avoid participation in the war, in the hope that he could take the lead for peace in the near future. He was now more than ever detached and neutral in his own attitudes toward the belligerents and convinced that the war, whatever its origins, had degenerated (as he put it in a speech in Cincinnati) into something like a drunken brawl without any worthy ends or purposes. And it *was* true, as Wilson was saying, that virtually all champions of unneutrality *vis-à-vis* the European belligerents and of military intervention in Mexico were Republicans. He sincerely believed that Republican victory would increase the possibilities of involvement. He was not only well aware of peace sentiment in the Middle West but also thought that it was right. People in that section, he wrote as early as June 5, were "doing their own thinking."[53] Conscience could therefore approve the policy that expediency strongly recommended.

Democratic campaign managers and speakers all over the country opened all stops in playing upon the peace theme after Wilson's speech at "Shadow Lawn" on September 30.[54] The response to that address in the Middle West was so immediate and overwhelming that Senator Walsh at once sent instructions to an army of orators in Illinois, Iowa, Nebraska, the Dakotas, Missouri, Kansas, and Colorado to highlight the peace issue in their speeches.[55] They went up and down the prairies and plains thundering the battle cry of peace, "He kept us out of war!" Setting the pace was none other than William J. Bryan, carrying the good news of peace and progressivism to countless throngs.[56] "Bryan's

[52] G. W. Anderson to E. M. House, October 2, 1916, House Papers.

[53] W. W. to H. Morgenthau, June 5, 1916, Wilson Papers.

[54] See especially the superb analysis in the *New York Times*, October 22, 1916, of how Democrats used the peace issue among farmers and women in Ohio.

[55] New York *World*, October 7, 1916. Walsh probably did this with Wilson's knowledge and approval. The two men conferred in Chicago when Wilson passed through that city on October 4 on his way to Omaha. *New York Times*, October 5, 1916.

[56] See W. J. Cochran to J. P. Tumulty, September 23, 1916, Wilson Papers, for Bryan's itinerary during September and early October.

speeches at Pueblo last night and Colorado Springs tonight," a former Governor of Colorado reported to Walsh on October 13, "were masterpieces in argument and power. He never surpassed these efforts. You can place Colorado in the list of sure Wilson states. Halls not large enough for the crowds."[57] A Democratic leader in Wisconsin wrote to Walsh later in the month: "I wish to advise you of the results of Mr. Bryan's trip through our state. He closed his speaking tour in the state at the Auditorium building in this city [Milwaukee] last evening, where he addressed an audience in excess of 10,000. . . . Mr. Bryan spoke at Kenosha, Racine, West Allis, Waukesha, Oshkosh, Appleton, Fond du Lac, and Milwaukee and had a splendid audience at each place. He addressed overflow meetings at both Oshkosh and Milwaukee. He delivered a remarkable speech at all places, and it was very well received."[58]

Wilson watched with grateful approval. "I cannot refrain from dropping you at least a line to express my admiration of the admirable campaign you are conducting," he wrote to the Commoner. "It is, of course, nothing novel to see you show your strength in this way, but I feel so sincerely appreciative of your efforts in the interest of what we all feel to be the people's cause that I must let you know with what deep interest I am looking on."[59] Bryan was glad to be on the stump again, among the people he loved. "I believe I am making a more convincing speech in your behalf," he replied to the President, "than I have ever been able to make in support of my own candidacy, history being more conclusive than promise or prophecy."[60]

The pamphlets and newspaper advertisements streaming from Democratic headquarters also highlighted the peace issue. New York headquarters, for example, distributed five million copies of Glynn's speech at the St. Louis convention and six million copies of Wilson's speech against war with Mexico before the New York Press Club on June 30.[61] The peace issue was always useful, no matter what particular subject was being discussed. A pamphlet entitled *Woodrow Wilson and Social Justice* concluded, for example, "More than all, our country is at peace in a world at war," while another pamphlet, *Children's Emancipation*

[57] A. Adams to T. J. Walsh, October 13, 1916, the Papers of Thomas J. Walsh, Library of Congress; hereinafter cited as the Walsh Papers.

[58] J. Martin to T. J. Walsh, October 27, 1916, the Papers of William Jennings Bryan, Library of Congress; hereinafter cited as the Bryan Papers, LC.

[59] W. W. to W. J. Bryan, September 27, 1916, Wilson Papers.

[60] W. J. Bryan to W. W., October 8, 1916, *ibid.*

[61] *New York Times*, July 23, 1916.

Day, reminded mothers that Wilson had saved their children from mines, mills, and sweatshops just as he had "saved their sons and their husbands from unrighteous battlefields!" Democratic pamphleteers had a field day when Roosevelt took the stump on Hughes's behalf with speeches in Maine and Michigan, and Hughes sent a telegram congratulating Roosevelt on a bellicose speech in Lewiston, Maine.[62] Democratic headquarters in New York hit back in a devastatingly effective pamphlet *"Complete Accord with Roosevelt,"* addressed as much to German Americans as to the antiwar rank and file. After quoting Hughes as saying that he was in "complete accord with Roosevelt," it accused the Republican candidate of being pro-British and anti-German and said: "If Mr. Hughes is elected President on this issue, it is notice to all the world that America repudiates her policy of peace for the Roosevelt-Hughes policy of war. Let the issue not be misunderstood. . . . A vote for Hughes is a potential vote for war."

The climax of the Democratic counterattack was the following full-page advertisement, published in leading newspapers on November 4 by the Wilson Business Men's National League:

> You Are Working—*Not Fighting!*
> Alive and Happy;—*Not Cannon Fodder!*
> Wilson and Peace with Honor?
> or
> Hughes with Roosevelt and War?
> Roosevelt says we should hang our heads in shame because
> we are not at *war* with Germany in behalf of Belgium!
> Roosevelt says that following the sinking of the Lusitania
> he would have foregone diplomacy and seized every ship in our
> ports flying the German Flag. That would have meant *war!*
> Hughes Says He and Roosevelt are in Complete Accord!
>
> .   .   .   .
>
> The Lesson is Plain:
> If You want WAR, vote for HUGHES!
> If You Want Peace with Honor
> VOTE FOR WILSON!
> And Continued Prosperity

Democrats also maintained unrelenting pressure on the Republican candidate. They published full-page advertisements in newspapers in cities where he was scheduled to speak, demanding that he say what *he*

---

[62] *The Outlook,* cxiv (September 13, 1916), 63; *Boston Post,* October 1, 1916.

would have done when Belgium was invaded and the *Lusitania* was sunk. Then they heckled him at meetings, shouting, "What would you have done, Mr. Hughes?" He finally shot back in Louisville on October 12 that he would have broken diplomatic relations with Germany after

His Master's Hand

Macauley, for the Democratic National Committee, in the *New York Times*

the sinking of the *Lusitania*, although he hastened to add that the ship would never have been torpedoed if the Germans had believed what Wilson had said about holding them to "strict accountability" for loss of American lives.[63]

[63] *New York Times*, October 13, 1916.

Wilson's and the public's attention from
·d at this point. It was the *U53* affair,
·rican shores and threatened momentarily
United States and the Allies.

·art of its preparations for a new cruiser-
·cided to test the capacities of its new
·ing one of them on a mission to Amer-
·ınder Hans Rose, was selected for the
·eptember 17 with orders to sail to the
·und and attack any Allied warships in
·to Newport, Rhode Island, and, after
·erican coast and sink as many merchant-
Rose arrived at Newport on October 7
·rican naval officers and ordinary visitors
·bout fifty miles off Nantucket on the
sank four English, one Norwegian, and
·can destroyer flotilla stood nearby and
·passengers from their lifeboats. One
·*ham*, moved at Commander Rose's re-
···· that the *U53* could sink one of the English merchantmen.
Rose sank three more ships on the following morning and sailed for
home.[65]

Panic hit the stock market, marine insurance rates jumped from 100
to 500 per cent, and a wave of excitement swept through the press on
October 9 and 10.[66] Wilson, watching events from "Shadow Lawn,"
issued a calming statement on October 9. "The Government," he said,
"will, of course, first inform itself as to all the facts, that there may be
no doubt or mistakes as far as they are concerned, and the country may
rest assured that the German Government will be held to the complete
fulfillment of its promises to the Government of the United States.
I have no right now to question their willingness to fulfill them."[67]

This statement masked considerable apprehension. Wilson received
Ambassador von Bernstorff at "Shadow Lawn" on October 9 for a
conference on possible American relief work in Poland. "Concerning

[64] Arno Spindler, *La Guerre Sous-Marine* (3 vols.), III, 314-315.

[65] *ibid.*, pp. 316-319; *New York Times*, October 9, 1916; the Secretary of State to
Chargé Grew, October 10, 1916, *Foreign Relations, 1916, Supplement*, p. 772; Lansing
Desk Diary, October 15, 1916.

[66] *New York Times*, October 10, 1916; "Bringing the War to Our Doors," *Literary
Digest*, LIII (October 21, 1916), 1015-1017.

[67] *New York Times*, October 10, 1916.

the war on commerce which our U-boats are carrying on along the American coast," the Ambassador reported to the Foreign Office, "Wilson is naturally very anxious, because his entire hope of being re-elected depends exclusively on this, that up to this time he, according to the opinion on this side of the water, has not allowed the United States to be drawn into war, and on top of this, has put an end to our so-called illegal attacks upon American lives. This whole structure will fall in ruins if Americans come to grief, or if strong manifestations of feeling are apparent against a U-boat war along the American coast. . . . It was for this reason that Wilson spoke expressly with regard to continuation of U-boat warfare on the American coast. He found the circumstance particularly serious that two neutral ships had been sunk and also one Canadian passenger ship which was on its way to the United States. Such occurrences, he said, were inconceivable from the standpoint of the American public. Wilson gave his remarks a particular weight through referring to the fact that the leaders of the opposition, Roosevelt, Lodge, *et al.*, wanted war with Germany, a desire which he could not understand. He stated that he had but the one wish, to remain neutral and to help bring the war to an end, since in his opinion a decision could not be reached by force of arms. Neither of the two belligerent parties could bring about a decisive victory. For this reason, he said, it was better to make peace today than tomorrow, but he added that every opportunity of ending the war would vanish if the United States were drawn into the conflict."[68] Wilson must have seen Bernstorff a second time on October 9 or 10, for the Ambassador sent a telegram to Berlin on the latter date, as follows: "On the occasion of a further interview Wilson impressed upon me very earnestly that he feared that a carrying on of the U-boat war along the American coast would bring such excitement of public opinion on this side with regard to the election that he would not be able to control it."[69]

Lansing, at the President's invitation, hurried to "Shadow Lawn" on October 10, and the two men discussed the *U53* incident and its implications during the evening. One of them told reporters on the following day that the evidence showed that Commander Rose had not violated German pledges to the United States and that the American government would not protest against hostile submarine operations so close to

<hr/>

[68] Ambassador von Bernstorff to the Foreign Office, received October 14, 1916, *Official German Documents*, II, 988.

[69] Ambassador von Bernstorff to the Foreign Office, October 10, 1916, *ibid.*, p. 989.

its shores. The *U53* affair would pass into history insofar as the United States was concerned, unless new facts revealed wrongdoing.[70]

There seemed to be no danger from the German side, as the Imperial Foreign Office hastened to send assurances that U-boats would not violate the *Sussex* pledge.[71] In fact, German authorities heeded Wilson's warning, without ever officially acknowledging it, and sent no more submarines to American waters during the balance of the period of the neutrality of the United States. The most serious diplomatic consequence of the *U53* affair was its exacerbation of bitterness against the United States in Great Britain, particularly in official circles. Lord Grey, in a conversation with Ambassador Page on October 11, seemed to intimate that the American government shared some responsibility for the raid because it had insisted that British cruisers on blockade patrol stand off at some distance from the American coast and objected to British merchantmen carrying defensive armament when they visited American ports.[72] The Foreign Secretary, in another private conversation with Page a week later, commented on the "almost fierce public feeling" in Great Britain against the American government for permitting the *U53* to visit Newport and failing to send a strong protest against its depredations.[73] Meanwhile, Ambassador Jusserand had seen the President at "Shadow Lawn" on October 11 and urged him to use the *U53* incident as the excuse for prohibiting all belligerent submarines to enter American waters.

Acting Secretary of State Polk sent what was perhaps the only possible reply. The State Department, he said in an informal message to Page on October 22, could not understand why the British government should expect an official communication on the *U53* affair from the American government. The United States had sent no report to the German government on the activity of British and French warships in American waters. British and French cruisers had withdrawn only slightly and still hovered off the American coast.[74] Not long afterward, perhaps at the same time, someone in the State Department informed the British Ambassador about the President's conversation with Bernstorff on

[70] *New York Times*, October 12, 1916.

[71] Chargé Grew to the Secretary of State, October 11, 1916, *Foreign Relations, 1916, Supplement*, p. 774, in response to the Acting Secretary of State to Chargé Grew, October 10, 1916, *ibid.*, p. 772, warning that American opinion had been much aroused.

[72] Ambassador Page to the Secretary of State, October 11, 1916, *ibid.*, pp. 773-774.

[73] Ambassador Page to the Secretary of State, October 18, 1916, *ibid.*, p. 779.

[74] The Acting Secretary of State to Ambassador Page, October 22, 1916, *ibid.*, pp. 780-781.

October 9. That, in addition to the absence of any German submarines off the American coast during the following weeks, satisfied the British and French and ended the discussions.

Wilson had meanwhile begun greatly to accelerate the tempo of his campaign. He went to Indianapolis for a rousing reception by 150,000 Indianans and several speeches on October 12.[75] He spoke two days later at "Shadow Lawn" to some five thousand Pennsylvanians. He talked on this occasion mainly about domestic politics, charging that vested interests controlled the G. O. P. and affirming that the Democratic party was committed heart and soul to forward-looking government. But he did not fail to intimate once more that a vote for Hughes might be a vote for war. As he put it, "America knows that it is faced with this choice: Peace, the continuance of the development of business along the lines which it has now established and developed and the maintenance of well known progressive lines of action, on the one hand or, on the other, a disturbance of policy all along the line—new conditions, new adjustments, undefined alterations of policy, and back of it all invisible government."[76] He pressed this attack in a speech to a group of Wilson Volunteers led by Amos Pinchot and Rabbi Stephen S. Wise two days later, October 16. Reactionary business interests, he said, wanted to get control of the Federal Reserve System and use the armed forces to protect their investments in Mexico and throughout the world.[77] "May I not express to you," he wrote on the following day in public greetings to New York shoe manufacturers who had just instituted the eight-hour day, "my interest in the action you have taken in the eight-hour day and the admiration I feel for men who act at once with such public spirit and such genuine business wisdom."[78]

Wilson also spoke to the American people in a statement on Mexico published in the October issue of *Ladies' Home Journal*,[79] and more intimately in interviews with Ray Stannard Baker and Ida M. Tarbell published in *Collier's* on October 7 and October 28, 1916.[80] He trusted

[75] *New York Times*, October 13, 1916; New York *World*, October 13, 1916.

[76] *New York Times*, October 15, 1916; New York *World*, October 15, 1916.

[77] *New York Times*, October 17, 1916.

[78] W. W. to Messrs. Endicott and Johnson, October 17, 1916, Wilson Papers.

[79] It is reprinted in *The New Democracy*, II, 339-343, and reiterated what he had said many times before.

[80] R. S. Baker, "Wilson," *Collier's*, LVIII (October 7, 1916), 5-6, and I. M. Tarbell, "A Talk with the President of the United States," *ibid.*, October 28, 1916, pp. 5-6, 40. Wilson read, approved, and made some changes in the text of Miss Tarbell's article. See W. W. to Ida M. Tarbell, October 3, 1916, Wilson Papers.

these two journalists and opened his mind and heart to them; they in turn portrayed him as a warm and fascinating human being who conformed not at all to the popular stereotype. Miss Tarbell wrote, for example:

"Would that every man and woman in the country could sit with him for an afternoon as I recently had the privilege of doing, and read the man Wilson. He is open as a book. I have in a rather long journalistic career talked with many men of high position, both in this country and Europe, with every president since and including Mr. Cleveland, with scores of our captains of industry, with great statesmen and scientists and writers, but never have I talked with any man who showed himself more direct, less engaged with himself and more engaged with the affairs committed to him, more just and more gentle in his estimate of people, less bitter, emotional, prejudiced, and yet never for an instant fooled. Mr. Wilson is a fine, humorous, cultivated American gentleman. He and Mrs. Wilson receive you into the temporary White House at Shadow Lawn with the simplicity and cordiality of gentlefolk the world over. A president, yes, every instant; but also a gentleman, who, having invited you to his table, treats you as a fellow human being, interested in the things he is interested in and frankly willing to talk them over *with* you, not *at* you. The sight of him moving so quietly yet energetically through his exacting daily program, treating the grave matters which so dominate him gravely, yet able to turn gayly and with full sense of human values to the lighter matters which are equally a part of his business, humanizes and endears him. The common things of life *interest* him, and this fact somehow strengthens enormously the estimate which any candid examination of his career forces, and that is that here at last we have a president whose real interest in life centers around the common man, and on whom we can count to serve that man so far as his ability goes."

The campaign, Wilson told Miss Tarbell, was a really fundamental struggle between two opposing forces for control of the government. As he put it:

"The philosophy of the situation, as I see it, is this: The Democratic party is offering a program of principles based on a belief of the control of the people. The policy of the other side is and will be determined by those who have the largest stake. They are not interested in policies; to them policy is neither here nor there if they can control. For instance, they are not opposed to the Federal Reserve Bank, but they don't want the people to control it. They will consent to almost any policy if you will allow them to manage it. . . . Who shall control? That is the issue to-day. What the other side is trying to do is to bring Mark Hanna back, that is, return to the day of vested rights. . . . I have lived with this group for fourteen years. They have no other ambition or desire but to control men's thoughts and lives. We are up against the very essence of privilege to-day. Nobody can predict the profundity of change in this country after the war; nobody can predict the hold on the country that privilege is going to take again if this class is put in power.

"One can't sit by and see this done without protest. In my old days at Princeton one of my friends used to say to me: 'Can't you let anything alone?' and I always answered: 'If you will hold anything where it is without deterioration I will let it alone, but you can't do that.'"

The campaign was now running in high gear, and Wilson's friends called for more hard-hitting attacks. "I also talked with Lippmann and [Walter] Weyl on the tone of the President's speech," Norman Hapgood reported to Colonel House at this time. "They thought it would be extremely dangerous to go back to the gentle abstract or remote tone. . . . The recent speeches of the President, we all agreed, have been ideal, including the one yesterday."[81]

There were more to come in the immediate future. Wilson set out for Chicago on October 18 aboard a special train that took him through Poughkeepsie, Albany, and cities along the main line of the New York Central through up-state New York. There were cheering crowds everywhere. "I am a very poor hand, my friends," he said in Albany, "at commending myself. You all know just exactly what has been done by the present Administration, and you know just as well as I do how to judge it; so that I am perfectly content to leave myself in the hands of the jury."[82]

The reception in Chicago was almost suffocating, and police had great difficulty in restraining the crowds that swarmed around the President's automobile along the route from La Salle Street Station to the Blackstone Hotel. Wilson spoke first to three hundred newspapermen at a luncheon at the Press Club. "One of the things that has struck me recently," he said, "is that so many men have said to me, when I have asked: 'What is all this about?' that they want to stop all this 'Progressive Business.' The thing has amazed me, because what they call this 'Progressive Business' is the inevitable process of life. It is a process of

[81] N. Hapgood to E. M. House, October 17, 1916, House Papers.
[82] *New York Times*, October 19, 1916.

adjustment. Things will not stand still, and if things will not stand still, laws cannot stand still."

Wilson then went to the Chicago Auditorium for an address to some 4,000 women. Miss Jane Addams sat with Mrs. Wilson and Helen Bones while he enunciated his progressivism more clearly than he had ever done before in public discourse. "Society," he said, "is now organizing its whole power in order that it may understand itself, in order that it may have a new organization and instrument of civilization, and I am ambitious that America should show the way in this great enterprise." If employers would not voluntarily establish proper working conditions, then society should oblige them to conform to right standards. He went on in a special word to women:

"The whole spirit of the law has been to give leave to the strong, to give opportunity to those who could dominate, but it seems to me that the function of society now has another element in it, and I believe that it is the element which women are going to supply. It is the element of mediation, of comprehending and drawing the elements together. It is the power of sympathy, as contrasted with the power of contests."

There was a final speech that evening, under the auspices of the New Citizens' Alliance, to some 18,000 persons in the International Amphitheater in the stock yards. They cheered wildly for ten minutes when the President entered. Wilson spoke mainly to new citizens in the audience, reminding them that they had an obligation to "put their new allegiance above every other allegiance." But he also talked about the part that the United States should claim in the settlement ending the European war, exclaiming at the end, "Let us show that we want no boundaries to the rights of mankind."[83]

Large and friendly crowds stood in pouring rain to greet the presidential train along the main line of the Pennsylvania Railroad through Ohio and Pennsylvania on the following day, October 20. The train stopped for an hour and a half in Pittsburgh, and the President and Mrs. Wilson drove with Bryan through the city. Fifth Avenue was so dense with people that the automobile had to stop once. There were whistle stops in Harrisburg and Lancaster, and a huge crowd with red fire and torches greeted the President in Philadelphia.[84]

October 21 was "Farmers' Day" at "Shadow Lawn," and Wilson recounted the benefits of the Democratic farm program to some three thousand visitors, some of whom presumably tilled the soil. It was, he

[83] *ibid.*, October 20, 1916; New York *World*, October 20, 1916.
[84] *New York Times*, October 21, 1916.

said, simply part of a coordinated effort at national reconstruction and cooperation. He came back once again to the peace issue in words that clearly implied that if re-elected he would keep the country out of war: "I am not expecting this country to get into war. I know that the way in which we have preserved peace is objected to, and that certain gentlemen say they would have taken some other way that would inevitably have resulted in war, but I am not expecting this country to get into war, partly because I am not expecting these gentlemen to have a chance to make a mess of it." He was, he said, glad that the campaign was nearly over. "I am in a hurry to get down to business again. There is a great deal of irresponsible talk being indulged in. Men are saying lots of things that they know perfectly well they cannot make good on, and it disturbs the national counsel."[85]

The Mexican problem was always in the background, not merely as an issue, but as a more or less urgent matter of state demanding Wilson's attention throughout the entire period of the presidential campaign. The outcome of the election might well depend on the President's success or failure in preventing events from catapulting the issue to the forefront. This in turn would depend on vital decisions respecting dramatic events in Mexico and discussions of the Joint High Commission which, as we have seen, had been appointed to consider alleviation of Mexican-American tension and discord.

That Commission began its work at the Hotel Griswold in New London, Connecticut, on September 6, following a preliminary meeting at the Hotel Biltmore in New York City two days before. Wilson sent warm greetings on September 7,[86] and discussions seemed to get off to a good beginning, particularly after Wilson received the Commission aboard the *Mayflower* on September 12[87] and assured the Mexican members that he understood and thoroughly sympathized with the high objective of their country's struggle for liberty.[88]

The Mexicans, however, began to stiffen just as soon as the American design became apparent. It was to persuade the Mexican commissioners to engage in a searching inquiry into the general causes and alleviation of Mexican social and economic unrest, and especially measures

[85] *ibid.*, October 22, 1916.

[86] W. W. to the American and Mexican Joint Commission, September 7, 1916, Wilson Papers.

[87] It will be recalled that he had gone to New London to be at the bedside of his sister, Mrs. Howe.

[88] *New York Times*, September 13, 1916.

for protection of foreign lives and property in Mexico, *before* the Joint High Commission turned to protection of the border and withdrawal of the Punitive Expedition. Luis Cabrera, chairman of the Mexican commissioners, tried to call a halt to general talk about Mexican rehabilitation on September 15, saying that he and his colleagues had come to New London to discuss removal of American soldiers from Mexican territory first of all.[89] Cabrera was even more emphatic on September 18.[90] As Secretary Lane, chairman of the American delegation, reported to the Secretary of State:

"This morning's session devoted exclusively to the question of protection of the person and property of foreigners in Mexico. We strongly impressed upon Mexican Commissioners vital importance of definite provisions for adequate protection as an integral part of the International situation.

"At the afternoon session the question of a program of the labors of the Commission arose and gave rise to protracted discussion. Mexican Commissioners urged very strongly the importance of reaching definite agreement on withdrawal of troops and border patrol before proceeding to other questions. Their contention was that their instructions required them to do this and that these two questions were so acute that Mexican public opinion demanded their early solution. They furthermore attempted to justify this procedure by citing the terms of the notes exchanged between the American and Mexican governments. They stated that after reaching definite agreements on these two questions they would be willing to proceed to the discussion of other matters. American Commissioners urged upon them the fact that border raids were simply symposium [symptomatic] of anarchic domestic conditions and that the elimination of this cause is a necessity prerequisite to the proper safeguarding of the border. We used very plain language in informing them of the insistent demand of American people that an early and satisfactory solution be found for all questions now pending with Mexico. Commission adjourned at six o'clock this evening without reaching definite agreement on this vital point."[91]

Jolting news from northern Mexico at this very moment threatened to provoke violent American action that would have wrecked the Joint High Commission and probably plunged Mexico and the United

[89] *ibid.*, September 16, 1916.
[90] J. B. Rojo to C. Aguilar, September [1]9, 1916, *Mexican White Paper*, p. 276.
[91] F. K. Lane to the Secretary of State, September 18, 1916, State Department Papers.

States into war. Dispatches from American agents brought indisputable proof that a greatly reinforced Villa was on the rampage once again. His forces boldly raided Chihuahua City on September 16, seizing governmental buildings, liberating *Villistas* in the state penitentiary, and capturing quantities of ammunition before withdrawing.[92] George C. Carothers, the State Department's Special Agent in northern Mexico, reported on September 19 that Pancho now had 4,000 well-armed men in the State of Chihuahua not far from Pershing's lines.[93]

Receipt of a report from General George Bell, Jr., at El Paso confirming the news of Villa's raid on Chihuahua City[94] caused new excitement and discussions both in Washington and New London of the possibility of a quick thrust by Pershing to apprehend and destroy Villa and his force.[95] It was a decision that only the President could make, because it carried the risk of war with *Carrancistas* as well as *Villistas*, and Secretary Baker discussed the matter with Wilson, then at "Shadow Lawn," probably by telephone. Wilson was emphatic in saying that he would not permit any action that might conceivably lead to conflict. As Baker explained in a telegram to Lane at New London:

> General [Tasker H.] Bliss and I have talked over the suggestion that General Pershing be authorized to take up the pursuit of Villa with the consent of the Mexican authorities. After discussing the matter with General Bliss, I took up the question with the President. He feels that before he could consider authorizing such activity on the part of General Pershing's command, he ought to have the most complete assurances that such an expedition had the full approval and concurrence of those in control of the de facto Government of Mexico and that even then very definite understandings ought to be had as to the character, task and purpose of the expedition. For instance, it would not do to have General Pershing start a fresh pursuit and then either have a change in sentiment on the part of the Mexican officials leading to the interposition of obstacles or the withdrawal of the consent of the Mexican authorities; nor ought such an expedition, if considered, assume the task of the general pacification of northern Mexico which might be involved if recent disturbances in

[92] Z. L. Cobb to the Secretary of State, September 18, 19, and 20, 1916, *ibid.*; Consul T. D. Edwards to the Secretary of State, September 18, 1916, *ibid.*; *New York Times*, September 22, 1916.

[93] G. C. Carothers to the Secretary of State, September 19, 1916, State Department Papers.

[94] It was transmitted in General F. Funston to the Secretary of War, September 20, 1916, *Foreign Relations, 1916*, pp. 609-610.

[95] Based on the *New York Times*, September 24, 1916, and the document cited in the next footnote.

Chihuahua turn out to be serious. The President directed me to ask that you would lay before him any proposal looking to the use of General Pershing's force in Mexico before assenting to the same, and if any such proposal is made, to have it indicate the character of assurances proposed with regard to the consent and sympathy of the de facto Government of Mexico in the expedition throughout its entire course.[96]

This averted even the possibility of new military complications, but Wilson gave no guidance whatsoever to lead his spokesmen at New London out of the impasse created by their insistence upon discussing Mexican internal problems. Perhaps he had no time, now that the campaign was in full swing, for careful thought. Or, as seems more likely, since Villa's revival made Pershing's withdrawal too hazardous to undertake, he preferred to have futile talks continue until the election was over and new decisions could be made with comparative safety.

That, at any rate, is what happened. On September 22 the American commissioners formally requested their Mexican colleagues to join them in systematic discussion of protection of foreign life and property and religious toleration in Mexico and establishment of a claims commission, "while the military details of a plan of border control formulated by us are under consideration at Washington."[97] The Mexicans said that they could not give an answer until they had received instructions from the First Chief, and the Commission adjourned to meet later in Atlantic City. The irritation and frustration of the American commissioners mounted as the days passed without any word from Mexico City, and Lane spent a good part of the interim writing long letters filled with classical and literary allusions, accompanied by complaints about Mexican ingratitude and semi-barbarity.[98]

Even so, no untoward disturbance erupted to give Republicans additional ammunition. It was, from Wilson's point of view, the best possible momentary outcome.

[96] Transmitted in R. Lansing to F. K. Lane, September 25, 1916, State Department Papers.

[97] F. K. Lane *et al.* to L. Cabrera *et al.*, September 22, 1916, quoted in F. K. Lane to W. W., October 6, 1916, Wilson Papers. The American commissioners were referring to a plan for a Mexican-American border patrol that they and General Bliss had drafted and submitted to the War Department for its opinion. F. K. Lane to the Secretary of State, September 22, 1916, State Department Papers; L. S. Rowe to the Secretary of State, September 22, 1916, enclosing a copy of the draft agreement, *ibid.*

[98] e. g., the twenty-two-page typed letter, F. K. Lane to R. Lansing, September 29, 1916, *ibid.*

CHAPTER IV

Alignments, Cross-Currents, and Campaign Climax

NOT since 1896 had the United States seen such a clear-cut political alignment as occurred in 1916; not until 1936 would it see such division again. Wilson's aggressive championing of the eight-hour day and various measures of social and economic justice, and his rapid movement toward the incipient welfare state, stood in vivid contrast to Hughes's failure to make his own progressivism clear. Uniting all the various interest groups to whom Wilson's progressive program appealed was the one great common obsession for peace. It built the platform upon which virtually all elements of the new Wilsonian coalition could stand. The President's commitment to peace if possible stood again in vivid contrast to Hughes's intimations of bellicose intentions toward Mexico, demands for a strong if ill-defined foreign policy, and, above all, affirmation of accord with Roosevelt.

Independent progressives—social workers, sociologists, and intellectuals—moved en masse into the Wilson column. To name them is to list virtually the entire leadership of the advanced wing of the progressive movement in the United States: Lincoln Steffens, George Creel, William Kent, Frederic C. Howe, A. J. McKelway, Ben B. Lindsey, Jane Addams, John Dewey, Amos Pinchot, Norman Thomas, Bishop Francis J. McConnell, Norman Hapgood, George Foster Peabody, and countless others. Raymond Robins of Chicago seems to have been the only important social justice leader who supported Hughes. "Within the last few weeks . . . ," the editor of *Pearson's Magazine* wrote, "I have found my mind coming around slowly but surely to the feeling that the President ought to be returned for a second term. . . . During the past ten days when he publicly took his stand for the eight hour day for the railroad employees and braved the wrath of Wall Street, my passive approval took the form of enthusiastically active approval."[1] Norman Hapgood put it more succinctly, "It seems

---

[1] A. W. Little to E. M. House, August 23, 1916, House Papers.

to me that the whole question comes down as to whether one is a Liberal or a Tory."[2]

Even leaders in the extreme left wing of the reform movement, including Socialists, single taxers, and assorted radicals, were pulled toward the Democratic column by the twin magnets of progressivism and peace. "Many of us have no enthusiasm for Wilson," a single tax editor explained. "He has made serious mistakes and shown weakness or opportunism where strength and greater courage had been expected of him. But, as things stand now, and with the Hughes and Republican statements before us, it is not easy to see how independent radicals and anti-militarists can hesitate for a moment. They must support Wilson."[3] Max Eastman, Socialist editor of *The Masses*, added on October 13: "I would rather see Woodrow Wilson elected than Charles E. Hughes because Wilson aggressively believes not only in keeping out of war, but in organizing the nations of the world to prevent war. . . . His announcement that the best judgment of mankind accepts the principle of the eight-hour day is another proof that he has vision and sympathy with human progress. Hughes has given proof to the contrary by his petty and indiscriminate scolding."[4] William English Walling, another Socialist intellectual, endorsed Wilson a few days later, adding that from 100,000 to 200,000 Socialists would support the Democratic ticket.[5]

Perhaps the strongest proof that Wilson was succeeding in his efforts to re-create and transform the Democratic party was the movement of former leaders of the Progressive party into the Democracy. Men and women who had supported Roosevelt in 1912 to fight for principles and causes rather than to follow a hero came out for Wilson one by one—Francis J. Heney of California, John M. Parker of Louisiana, Edgar S. Snyder of the State of Washington, Bainbridge Colby of New York, Victor Murdock of Kansas, Edward P. Costigan of Colorado, Matthew Hale of Massachusetts, and others. Eleven out of the nineteen members of the committee that wrote the memorable Progressive platform of 1912 issued an appeal for Wilson on October 31, saying that the President and his party had embodied twenty-two

[2] N. Hapgood to C. H. Davis, September 13, 1916, copy in the Papers of Louis D. Brandeis, University of Louisville Law School Library; hereinafter cited as the Brandeis Papers.

[3] V. S. Yarros in *The Public*, xix (June 16, 1916), 560. See also L. F. Post, "A Campaign Talk to Old Friends," *ibid.*, October 20 and 27, 1916, pp. 992-994, 1016-1019.

[4] *New York Times*, October 14, 1916.

[5] New York *World*, October 20, 1916.

of the thirty-three planks in the Progressive platform of 1912 wholly or partially in legislation.[6] Some former Progressive leaders who supported Hughes did so with no enthusiasm. William Allen White of Emporia, Kansas, spoke for many of them when he wrote:

"Of only two things am I at all sure in my mind. The first is that whatever course I take nothing will bring me to speak unkindly of President Wilson. . . . The truth is that I see no very great reason why he should be defeated; and—woe is me—no considerable preponderance of evidence in favor of his election. All my life I have been able to take fairly definite stands; to see my side white and the other side at least fairly dark. But now it is all gray and I have no clear guidance as to what I shall do. Mrs. White is frankly and militantly for the President. But I am a political jelly fish."[7]

Spokesmen and leaders of organized labor were drawn irresistibly into the Democratic column by the President's espousal of their cherished goals, and Hughes's attacks on the Adamson Act simply accelerated the movement. The *Literary Digest* sent out questionnaires to officials of various labor unions in late September. Three hundred and thirty-two of the 457 who replied said that their members favored Wilson; forty-seven, that their members favored Allan Benson, Socialist presidential candidate; forty-three, that their members supported Hughes; and thirty-four, that sentiment among their members was either noncommittal or evenly divided.[8] One *Republican* survey made at about the same time showed 90 per cent of the members of the brotherhoods disposed to vote Democratic.[9] The chiefs of the four brotherhoods sent a personal appeal to their members on October 26 urging them to vote for Wilson.[10] The *Locomotive Firemen's and Engineers' Magazine* issued another clarion call in its November issue.[11] (Hughes and other Republicans dropped their "paramount" issue in early October, as soon as they saw this trend.[12]) Samuel Gompers, president of the American Federation of Labor, and the *American Federationist*, organ of the union, came out strongly for Wilson early

[6] *New York Times*, November 1, 1916.

[7] W. A. White to N. Hapgood, July 29, 1916, Wilson Papers.

[8] "A Presidential 'Straw Vote' of Union Labor," *Literary Digest*, LIII (October 7, 1916), 871-874.

[9] *New York Times*, October 5, 1916.

[10] *ibid.*, October 27, 1916.

[11] Quoted in *ibid.*, November 2, 1916.

[12] D. Baird to W. H. Taft, October 7, 1916, Taft Papers; *New York Times*, October 5, 1916.

in the campaign.[13] The Executive Committee of the A. F. of L., abandoning all pretense of neutrality, appealed on October 14 to all officers of the union to get members to the polls. "Never at any time within the last fifty years," the committee's message read, "have the workers had more at stake in any political campaign than in the one that is to be decided in the election November 7th. . . . The issue is represented in the campaign by the conflicting interests represented by Labor and Wall Street."[14] Polls taken by Republicans among workers in Michigan at the end of October showed Wilson running ahead of Hughes by three and four to one.[15] Another Republican poll in Illinois in late October indicated that from 75 to 80 per cent of the union labor vote would go to Wilson.[16]

Farm leaders and voters, particularly in the crucial midwestern and Plains states, were not far behind. The newly-organized Non-Partisan League, which was spreading like wildfire in the northern Plains states, announced in August that it would work with all its might for Wilson's re-election.[17] The farm editor, Herbert Quick, traveled with the Federal Farm Loan Board through the Middle West in early September. "That great non-partisan equity league of farmers," he reported to McAdoo, "in my opinion will vote almost solidly for Wilson, and it numbers about 45,000 farmers in North Dakota. I feel sure that Wisconsin, Minnesota, and North Dakota will cast their votes for the President this Fall. So many men have said in our meetings: We are Republicans but we think the present Administration has done more for the farmers than all past Administrations combined."[18] David Lubin, father of the rural credits movement in America, endorsed Wilson on September 16.[19] A poll taken by *Farm Journal* in October yielded returns of two to one for the President.[20]

[13] S. Gompers to T. H. Nichols, n. d., published in *ibid.*, August 10, 1916; S. Gompers, *Wilson and Labor*, printed statement dated August 25, 1916, copy in the Wilson Papers; S. Gompers, "Promises and Performances," *American Federationist*, XXIII (July 1916), 539-542; S. Gompers, "On Which Side Are You?" *ibid.*, November 1916, pp. 1067-1068.

[14] S. Gompers *et al.*, "To the Officers of All Organized Labor," October 14, 1916, copy in the Wilson Papers, also published in part in the New York *World*, October 22, 1916.

[15] W. H. Taft to H. D. Taft, October 29, 1916, Taft Papers.

[16] See the detailed analysis in the *New York Times*, October 25, 1916, of the impact of the campaign on labor voters in Illinois; also *ibid.*, October 19, 1916, for reactions and alignments among labor voters in Toledo, Ohio.

[17] *Farmer's Open Forum*, I (August 1916), 8.

[18] H. Quick to W. G. McAdoo, September 2, 1916, Wilson Papers.

[19] *New York Times*, September 17, 1916.   [20] *ibid.*, October 21, 1916.

Most impressive, and perhaps most decisive for the final outcome, was the massive movement of independent newspapers and magazines into the Wilson ranks as the campaign progressed. This was in part a reaction against Hughes's campaign. He began with the good will if not the open endorsement of most independent editors. He ended it having alienated and driven most of them to Wilson's side. The New York *Nation* and *The New Republic*, the two leading independent journals of comment, for example, hailed Hughes's nomination. "There is no man in American public life," the latter said, "who combines so much character with so much ability."[21] They were both badly shaken by Hughes's acceptance speech,[22] and disillusionment followed rapidly in the wake of his campaign. "That it has been a woeful disappointment to his friends and admirers," the *Nation* said, "there can be no manner of doubt. . . . No one could in advance have believed it possible. In the presence of the fact, now undeniable, people are bewildered. . . . It is as if one of our most assured national assets had melted away under our eyes. The failure of Hughes is, indeed, something like a calamity. We feel intellectually poorer."[23] Wilson had certain disqualifications, *The New Republic* added, "but formidable as they had once seemed, they began to look negligible in the light of the issue which Mr. Hughes had allowed President Wilson to establish. The utterances of the Republican candidate, so far from redeeming the reactionary record of his party, had served as its partial confirmation."[24] The *Nation*, at least, ended by supporting Wilson mainly because it was disgusted with Hughes.[25] As its owner explained in a revealing letter:

"I never remember a more difficult . . . [election], though the campaign of 1900 came very close to it. Personally, I have a feeling of real distrust of Mr. Wilson's intellectual integrity and I really do not wish to see him or have anything to do with him again; and, as you know, I have been his great admirer and cooperated with him very warmly. I could not bring myself to vote for him, though I could not vote for Hughes. . . . But the bulk of the staff felt, as I had to, too, that between the two, . . . it was better that Mr. Wilson should be reelected. Even that decision we took with great reluctance, but Hughes drove

[21] *New Republic*, VII (June 17, 1916), 158; also the New York *Nation*, CII (June 15, 1916), 635.

[22] *ibid.*, CIII (August 3, 1916), 96; *New Republic*, VIII (August 5, 1916), 4-5.

[23] New York *Nation*, CIII (October 19, 1916), 367.

[24] *New Republic*, VIII (October 28, 1916), 312.

[25] New York *Nation*, CIII (November 2, 1916), 411.

us to it with his utterly stupid campaign, which defeated himself. In my judgment . . . had the election been held in July or August, I believe that Hughes would have been triumphantly elected. Everywhere he went he lost votes."[26]

Herbert Croly and Walter Lippmann, editors of the chief oracle of progressivism, *The New Republic*, were more typical of the large group of independent editors who supported Wilson with growing enthusiasm.[27] Croly and Lippmann had not been among the President's early admirers. They were convinced in the early months of 1916 that Wilson could neither unite nor lead the country and were searching for someone to support in the coming campaign. As late as June 24 they said that they were honestly on the fence and that, if a choice had to be made then, they would vote for the Democratic party *and* Hughes.[28] They began to change, almost grudgingly, in reaction mainly to Wilson's legislative achievements during the summer of 1916.[29] They liked parts of the President's acceptance speech but were not yet fully converted. As Croly put it, "Mr. Wilson is manifestly in a transitional state of mind. The old individualist partisan Democrat, with a political philosophy derived from the Virginia Bill of Rights, is developing into a modern social Democrat, but the transition is incomplete, and Mr. Wilson expresses himself either in the old language or the new, according to the needs of the occasion."[30]

They crossed their Rubicon in mid-October. "Not Mr. Wilson's eloquence," Lippmann wrote in announcing his decision, "but his extraordinary growth has made the case for him. I shall vote not for the Wilson who has uttered a few too many noble sentiments, but for the Wilson who is evolving under experience and is remaking his philosophy in the light of it, for the Wilson who is temporarily at least creating, out of the reactionary, parochial fragments of the Democracy, the only party which at this moment is national in scope, liberal in

[26] O. G. Villard to E. B. Morris, November 10, 1916, the Papers of Oswald Garrison Villard, Houghton Library, Harvard University; hereinafter cited as the Villard Papers.

[27] Including, in addition, the editors of the *New York Times*, the *Springfield* (Mass.) *Republican*, the Scripps newspapers, the *Philadelphia Record*, the New York *Nation*, the *New York Evening Post*, and *Pearson's Magazine*, besides the left-wing, labor, and farm journals already mentioned.

[28] *New Republic*, vii (June 24, 1916), 181-182.

[29] See, particularly, "The Democrats as Legislators," *ibid.*, viii (September 2, 1916), 103-104.

[30] "The Two Mr. Wilsons," *ibid.*, September 9, 1916, p. 129.

purpose, and effective in action."[31] Croly said a week later: "I shall vote for the reëlection of President Wilson on November 7th, chiefly for a reason which if its decisive effect had been predicted a few years ago would have seemed to me incredible. I shall vote for him chiefly because he has succeeded, at least for the time being, in transforming the Democracy into the more promising of the two major party organizations. . . . In order to resurrect the Democratic party Mr. Wilson has been modifying the Democratic creed. Had he remained faithful to the group of party dogmas with which he started his presidential career, had not the Democratic party itself developed an unexpected self-control, adaptability and competence, his enterprise would certainly have been a failure. . . . The New Freedom has been discarded. . . . The party program no longer seeks the restoration of a régime of incoherent, indiscriminate, competitive, localistic individualism. It foreshadows rather a continuing process of purposive national reorganization determined in method by the realities of the task but dedicated to the ultimate enhancement of individual and associated life within and without the American commonwealth. For the first time in several generations the party has the chance of becoming the embodiment of a genuinely national democracy."[32]

Wilson could not please everyone, least of all those Roman Catholic leaders, already disaffected by the President's Mexican policies, were now more than ever alienated by his support of the Clarke amendment to the Philippine bill and appointment of John R. Mott, the Y.M.C.A. leader, to the Mexican-American Joint High Commission.

There was a subterranean whispering campaign among Catholics so covert that no one in Democratic headquarters ever knew who was stimulating it. There were stories to the effect that Wilson had called James Cardinal Gibbons "Mr. Gibbons," treated Archbishop John Ireland discourteously, refused on religious grounds to attend the traditional Pan-American Thanksgiving Day Mass in Washington in 1914 and 1915, and declined to receive Monsignor Bonzano, Apostolic Delegate, who had come to the White House with a message from the Pope. Some Roman Catholic priests circulated stories about Wilson's alleged infidelities to his first wife. There were also rumors that Cardinals Gibbons and William O'Connell, indeed the entire hierarchy, were doing all they could to bring about the President's defeat, and that

[31] W. Lippmann, "The Case for Wilson," *ibid.*, October 14, 1916, p. 263.
[32] H. Croly, "The Two Parties in 1916," *ibid.*, October 21, 1916, p. 286.

Cardinal Gibbons had said, "Any Catholic who votes for Wilson, should be damned."

These tales spread like wildfire across the country. "Some of my most intimate friends are Jesuit priests," a Republican in Seattle wrote to Taft, for example. "One called on me yesterday & told me that Bishop O'Connell of Va. formerly private secretary to Cardinal Gibbons told him that when the Cardinal called on President Wilson the latter met him standing[,] greeted him with 'how do you do Mr. Gibbons' and did not ask him to be seated, and also did the same thing with Monsignor Bonzano."[33] A Democratic leader in Wisconsin reported, to cite another example, that he had just talked with a priest who told him that the President had been charged with a personal matter. "I find," he wrote, "that this thing seems to be general among Catholic Priests. I am a Catholic myself but I think this matter is a slander on Mr. Wilson."[34]

There were, in addition, new Catholic assaults on Wilson for his recognition and support of Carranza. "The Knights of Columbus as well as the A[ncient]. O[rder]. [of] H[ibernians].," one Democrat reported from Worcester, Massachusetts, "have a very strong feeling against President Wilson, the cause of which as far as I can discover, is that they blame him for the outrages committed on the Catholic churches and buildings, and sacred vestments, and also upon the priests and nuns in Mexico. . . . I know that many priests have denounced President Wilson from the altar and this has probably added to the feeling against him."[35] The most violent printed attack on Wilson's Mexican policies, *The Book of Red and Yellow*, by Father Francis C. Kelley, president of the Catholic Church Extension Society, was widely distributed among Catholic societies and editors, along with another tract, "The Story of Mexico from Alpha to Omega," published in the October issue of the *Catholic News Bulletin*.[36] "The appointment of Mott," one priest in Connecticut wrote to Tumulty, voicing another grievance, "I consider a challenge and an insult in the light of what I

[33] E. Brainerd to W. H. Taft, July 11, 1916, Taft Papers.
[34] W. B. Ackerman to V. McCormick, September 13, 1916, Wilson Papers. In the same vein, see also J. B. Berteling to T. J. Walsh, September 22, 1916, Walsh Papers; N. W. Mullen to J. P. Tumulty, October 4, 1916, Wilson Papers; E. E. Pierson to J. P. Tumulty, October 7, 1916, *ibid.*; F. Gaudin, Supreme President, Catholic Knights of America, to the Editor, October 21, 1916, *New Orleans States*, October 22, 1916; J. C. Hammond to E. M. House, n. d., House Papers.
[35] J. A. Thayer to J. P. Tumulty, August 10, 1916, Wilson Papers.
[36] "The Story of Mexico from Alpha to Omega," *Catholic News Bulletin* (Washington), October 1916.

wrote you recently. . . . I will give you five days to explain if you can and at the end I shall advise every Irish Catholic in State of Connecticut to vote against your ticket. I shall also use all the newspaper control I command to defeat this anti-Catholic administration."[37]

Many Catholic priests and politicians joined the anti-Wilson campaign because they were of recent German and Irish origin and thought that Wilson was pro-British. "Of course you realize by this time," one Irish American wrote to Tumulty in late September, "what I have told you so often before that the great bulk of Catholics and those of Irish descent are opposing the President."[38] A Democratic leader in New York City, Norman Hapgood informed House in October, "spent last night with a bunch of leaders very close to [Charles F.] Murphy [head of Tammany Hall] and found most of them for Hughes. He thinks we shall lose 25% of the Tammany Catholic vote in New York City, and a considerable percentage in the West, unless we can find some way before election of changing the situation."[39]

Finally, it did the Democratic cause no good among Catholic voters when an organization dedicated to combating Roman Catholic influence in public life came out in mid-October with a pamphlet urging Wilson's re-election on the grounds that he had courageously resisted Catholic demands on Mexico and appointed few Roman Catholics to office.[40]

It was, of course, all grist for the Republican campaign mill. Louis Seibold described the Republican campaign among Catholic voters in one state, Indiana, as follows:

The Republican plan of campaign has been predicated on the theory that with the assistance of the voters of Teutonic origin and those of the Catholic faith and sympathies, and with the union of the regular and Progressive factions of their party, they are sure of victory in spite of the heavy handicaps imposed by Mr. Hughes and Colonel Roosevelt.

It is assumed by the Republican leaders, who are openly courting the hyphenate and Catholic voters, that the influence to which voters of those classes ordinarily respond will lead them to rebuke the Democratic President for his refusal to surrender to the dictation of either. . . .

The only interest displayed by voters in the relations of the Administration with Mexico has obviously been inspired by a propaganda inaugurated

[37] The Reverend E. Flannery to J. P. Tumulty, August 24, 1916, Wilson Papers.
[38] M. F. Doyle to J. P. Tumulty, September 29, 1916, Lansing Papers, LC.
[39] N. Hapgood to E. M. House, October 9, 1916, House Papers.
[40] Publicity Bureau for the Exposure of Political Romanism, Masonic Hall, New York City, *Stupendous Issues, The Case Stated and Evidence Presented.*

by professional Roman Catholic agitators. It is the view of unprejudiced observers that the leaders and spokesmen of the Catholic Church in Indiana are opposing the President because of his refusal to comply with their demands that he compel obedience by the Carranza regime to the ambitions of the church leaders, even if such insistence requires a resort to force and intervention.

This movement, which is assuming widespread proportions throughout the country, particularly in the West, is being extensively exploited by the Republican managers in Indiana.

An observer is informed that "the church is opposed to Mr. Wilson"; that "every priest in the country is secretly counselling his parishioners to vote for Mr. Hughes," and "that Cardinals Gibbons, Farley and O'Connell are fully aware of the undertaking and are in sympathy with it." . . .

Indiana is being flooded with literature to influence the minds of Catholic voters. A thick volume distributed by "The Catholic Church Extension Society of the United States of America" contains some outrageous attacks on the President, questioning both his personal and official motives in dealing with the Mexican problem.

It is entitled "The Book of Red and Yellow," and the authorship of it is credited to Francis Clement Kelley. It is published in Chicago and several Catholic clergymen are given as sponsors for it. The brochure has this sub-title: "Being a Story of Blood and a Yellow Streak."

There is little question that this publication and others of a similar nature and purpose have exercised considerable influence over the minds of a great many voters.

Henry Lane Wilson, former Ambassador to Mexico, is the chief promoter of the Catholic propaganda against President Wilson. He has established himself here to direct it. Under his instruction literature, moving pictures and cart-tail oratory are being provided by the Republican campaign managers.

The ex-Ambassador is confident that the majority of the Catholic Clergy are antagonistic to the President. He told one of his callers today that twenty-three out of the thirty Catholic clergymen of Indianapolis were using their influence against the President and in the interest of Mr. Hughes.[41]

There were other ways of inflaming Roman Catholic sentiments. A New York studio produced a motion picture called "Watchful Waiting" for the Republican National Committee. It depicted nuns in a Mexican convent being assaulted by *Villistas* while President Wilson slept at his desk. It was heavily edited after members of the National Committee saw it, and then discarded altogether.[42] But Republican

[41] New York *World*, October 16, 1916.   [42] *ibid.*, September 18, 19, and 21, 1916.

campaign advertisements on Mexico did not ignore the one group most sensitive to their thrust. For example, one entitled "Flag or Rag?" included the following sentence: "How many more Americans must be massacred, how many more women violated, how many more miles of property seized before the strange arithmeticians at Washington will be able to count the game of retribution worth the risk of alienating the support of peace-at-any-price adherents?"[43]

Democratic leaders did what they could to blunt the mounting campaign. The National Committee prepared and distributed a pamphlet recounting virulent attacks on the Wilson administration for being pro-Catholic and describing the numerous benefits that had come to Catholics under a Democratic regime.[44] Wilson prepared a memorandum for Tumulty denying that he, Wilson, had called Cardinal Gibbons "Mr. Gibbons," and so on.[45] Tumulty used it at least once, in a public telegram to Democratic leaders in the Bronx.[46] A representative from Democratic headquarters in New York arranged for Cardinal Gibbons to make a public statement to the effect that neither he nor other members of the hierarchy would presume to tell Roman Catholics how to vote.[47] It was distributed among bishops and priests all over the country.[48] The same representative obtained a similar statement from Cardinal O'Connell on October 23, and it was published in the New York *World* on October 29.[49] Archbishop S. G. Messmer of Milwaukee forbade priests in his archdiocese to take any part in the campaign.[50]

[43] *Boston Evening Transcript*, October 10, 1916.

[44] I have not seen a copy of this pamphlet. It is described in *America*, xvi (November 25, 1916), 147-148.

[45] W. W., "Memorandum for Mr. Tumulty," dated August 15, 1916, Wilson Papers.

[46] C. V. Halley, Jr., to J. P. Tumulty, November 5, 1916; J. P. Tumulty to C. V. Halley, Jr., November 6, 1916, both published in the *New York Times*, November 7, 1916.

[47] R. F. Kernan to J. P. Tumulty, October 17, 1916, Wilson Papers; Cardinal Gibbons's statement, published in the New York *World*, October 20, 1916. Compare this, however, with W. H. Taft to G. W. Wickersham, October 20, 1916, Taft Papers: "I heard from General [Felix] Angus [publisher of the Baltimore *American* and a leading Republican] . . . about the Cardinal's attitude which was very strong for Hughes and very much against Wilson, and I think he can be counted upon to help. The truth is I have discovered in a good many different ways the working of that leaven. It works quietly always. It is something that you can not flush."

[48] R. F. Kernan to J. P. Tumulty, October 20, 1916, Wilson Papers.

[49] R. F. Kernan to F. I. Cobb, October 23, 1916; R. F. Kernan to J. P. Tumulty, October 28, 1916, both in *ibid*.

[50] New York *World*, October 27, 1916.

All signs at the beginning of the campaign seemed to indicate that German Americans would be implacably aligned against President Wilson on November 7. Indeed, some Democratic leaders were inclined at the outset to write off the German-American vote as irreparably lost. Prominent German-American leaders—John B. Mayer, publisher of the Philadelphia *Demokrat*, Joseph Frey, president of the German-American Catholic Bund, and Horace L. Brand of Chicago, among others—had formed a German-American Central Alliance for political action in Chicago in May.[51] They began to rally German Americans behind Hughes soon after his nomination and worked furiously all through the campaign.[52] They—and Hughes—had the support of George Sylvester Viereck's *The Fatherland*, the leading weekly defender of the German cause, and of all German-language newspapers except *Der Staats Anzeiger* of Bismarck, North Dakota, which was for Wilson, and of the Chicago *Abend Post*, Milwaukee *Demokrat*, and Buffalo *Demokrat*, which were opposed to Hughes without being openly for Wilson.[53]

There were, however, some evidences by early autumn that the rank and file of German Americans were beginning to have second thoughts on account of Roosevelt's support of Hughes, and that Wilson and Democratic managers had some chance to capture at least the normal Democratic share, about 25 per cent, of the German-American vote.[54] It was probably no accident that Wilson began to temper, almost abate, his attacks against so-called hyphenates, and he certainly must have had German-American voters in mind when he hammered on the peace issue. The Democratic National Committee, as we have already seen, saturated German-American communities with its pamphlet, *"Complete Accord with Roosevelt."* Most important, Senator Stone,

[51] *New York Times*, May 30, 1916; Clifton J. Child, *The German-Americans in Politics, 1914-1917*, pp. 122-128, hereinafter cited as *The German-Americans*.

[52] *New York Times*, June 13 and October 21, 1916; New York *World*, June 13 and 14, 1916; C. J. Child, *The German-Americans*, pp. 131-138.

[53] See the poll of the German-language press in the *New York Times*, October 1, 1916; and, e.g., the *New Yorker Herold, New Yorker Staats-Zeitung*, and Pittsburgh *Volksblatt und Freiheitsfreund*, quoted in the New York *World*, September 16, 1916.

[54] T. J. Walsh to W. W., August 18, 1916, Wilson Papers, relating a conversation with one Mueller, editor of the Chicago *Abend Post*; D. C. Roper, "MEMORANDUM FOR COLONEL HOUSE," sent to E. M. House, October 9, 1916, *ibid.*; A. J. Beveridge to A. T. Wert, October 10, 1916, the Papers of Albert J. Beveridge, Library of Congress; *New York Times*, October 26, 1916, indicating a very considerable division among German Americans in Milwaukee; W. H. Taft to H. D. Taft, October 31, 1916, Taft Papers, saying: "Roosevelt is a liability, not an asset now. Every speech of his drives away votes."

Kent E. Keller, a German-American Democrat from Illinois, Senator James A. Reed of Missouri, and other Democratic leaders made fervent overtures to German Americans in New York, Philadelphia, Chicago, and St. Louis. Stone, for example, met Viereck, Frey, Victor F. Ridder, publisher of the *New Yorker Staats-Zeitung*, and others in New York City on September 16 and warned them that Hughes's election meant war with Germany.[55] "A little more 'punch,' " Stone wrote to Tumulty, telling him about his work among German Americans, "against the interference with our mails, commerce, and free use of the sea by the Allies would help with the Germans, as tending to show that the Administration was observing impartial neutrality, and standing for American rights against all infringement."[56]

Democratic managers and editorialists played the hyphenate game the other way, by hitting Hughes hard because he had the support of those virulent German-American and Irish-American organizations, the American Truth Society and the American Independence Conference. For example, the New York *World*, pre-eminent Wilsonian spokesman in the country, savagely tarred Hughes with the German brush all through the campaign. "The followers of the Kaiser in the United States," it said on June 13, "have set out to destroy President Wilson politically for the crime of being an American President instead of a German President. They have adopted Mr. Hughes as their candidate and made his cause their cause." "With Mr. Hughes crawling on his belly before the Kaiserbund," it exclaimed on September 22, "the German Party has every reason to be proud of its power over the Republican Party."[57]

This was guilt by association, but Hughes had only himself to blame for the worst single blow that hit his campaign, apart from the more prolonged disaster of Roosevelt's participation. The Republican candidate conferred in mid-September, probably in New York City, with O'Leary and other officials of the American Independence Conference and apparently satisfied them that he was truly neutral. Then he

[55] The approximate text of Stone's speech is printed in the *New York Times*, October 13, 1916; see also V. F. Ridder, statement in *ibid.*, October 12, 1916; W. J. Stone, statement in *ibid.*; and Henry Abeles, statement in *ibid.*, October 13, 1916.

[56] W. J. Stone to J. P. Tumulty, September 25, 1916, Wilson Papers. For other evidence on the Democratic campaign to woo German-American leaders, see the *New York Times*, October 12, 1916, reporting Senator Reed's speech to German Americans in St. Louis on October 11, and K. E. Keller, statement in *ibid.*, October 13, 1916.

[57] C. J. Child, *The German-Americans*, pp. 139-141, discusses this aspect of the Democratic campaign in some detail.

Berlin's Candidate
Kirby in the New York *World*

declared in an address at Milwaukee on September 20: "I propose that we shall enforce American rights on land and sea without fear and unflinchingly with respect to American lives, American property, and American commerce."[58] He spoke even more pointedly at Philadelphia on October 9, as follows: "We propose to protect American lives on land and sea. We do not propose to tolerate any improper interference with American commerce or with American mails. We do not propose to tolerate that any American who is exercising any American rights shall be put on any blacklist by any foreign nation."[59]

[58] *New York Times*, September 21, 1916. [59] New York *World*, October 10, 1916.

The Democratic National Committee, unhappily for the luckless Hughes, obtained certain records of the American Independence Conference, including those of the meeting with Hughes, through Representative Robert J. Bulkley of Ohio and published them in the newspapers in late October, after Colonel House had approved.[60] The Democratic National Committee also formally accused Hughes of knuckling under to demands of subversives and cited his Milwaukee and Philadelphia speeches, among others, as proof. Moreover, it charged that the Republican National Committee had come to complete agreement with the American Independence Conference for cooperation in the campaign.[61] One of the documents (obtained and published, actually, by the New York *World*) was particularly embarrassing. It was a form letter sent by Will R. MacDonald, secretary of the American Independence Conference, on October 11, which read in part:

> What follows is a report of the results accomplished by the delegation that left our Chicago conference to confer with certain Republican leaders. Following the conference with this delegation at the Blackstone Hotel a representative went East to endeavor to secure from Mr. Hughes what we have all been anxious to hear, namely, a ringing declaration of Americanism that would make every American citizen who is loyal to the United States . . . feel confident that we could support a man who, if elected, would be a real and big American President.
>
> It is possible for me to notify you that our delegation was accorded the same consideration as has been given to Mr. George Perkins and his followers; and Mr. Hughes very gladly listened to our request that he state just how he stood upon American issues. . . .
>
> Mr. Hughes was told that the bulk of the people did not consider Mr. Wilson's foreign policy to be the best thing for American interests. He was asked to outline his ideas of what he would do as President. . . . In answering these questions, Mr. Hughes declared that he was perfectly willing to tell all the world just how good an American he was, and he was perfectly willing to state his position on any specific instance that might be brought up. He declared that he had no reason to conceal where he stood on the question of mail seizure, etc., and then, to show the people just exactly how he felt, he made his speech in Philadelphia and touched upon these questions.

[60] House Diary, October 20 and 22, 1916.
[61] The Democratic National Committee's statement is printed in the *New York Times*, October 23, 1916, the documents in *ibid.*, October 23, 24, and 25, 1916.

This speech by Mr. Hughes was perfectly satisfactory to all of our leaders in the East, North, West and South. His speech should satisfy every one that in this election we will secure the services of a real American President, and from this time on it is to be understood that organization leaders will instruct all of their section leaders and others to do all that is possible to bring about the election of Mr. Hughes. . . .[62]

"I saw the persons mentioned, at their request, about the middle of September," Hughes declared in a statement on October 22, "just as I have seen all persons and delegations so far as possible who have asked me to receive them. I have said nothing in private that I have not said in public. At the very beginning, in my speech of acceptance, I declared my position, in favor of the absolute protection of American lives and American property and American commerce. This I reiterated to these persons and I have stated it to all others who have asked interviews, as well as in my public speeches. To this maintenance of American rights I adhere and shall continue to adhere."[63] Two days later he said in New York: "I want the support of every true American who believes in the principles for which I stand, whatever his race. I don't want the support of any one to whom the interest of this nation is not supreme."[64] It was undoubtedly sincere, but it looked weak compared to Wilson's telegram to O'Leary.

Every presidential campaign leaves a trail of ironies for the historian to follow. There were two particularly choice ones in the campaign of 1916. First, the German Ambassador preferred Wilson's re-election and was much embarrassed by the activity of organizations like the American Independence Conference. "The future will show whether the German Americans are right in taking sides with Mr. Hughes," Bernstorff wrote to the Foreign Office on October 5. "In any case this cannot be altered, as there is a strong prejudice among the German-Americans against Mr. Wilson. . . . As all pacifists are on the side of Wilson, I would myself prefer to see him elected. It is moreover very doubtful whether Mr. Hughes will succeed in shaking off the influence of Mr. Roosevelt. The fact is that the real situation is complicated by the attitude of the German-Americans, which has resulted in Mr. Hughes being considered as the German candidate, although we have

[62] W. R. MacDonald to "My dear Sir," October 11, 1916, New York *World*, October 24, 1916.

[63] *New York Times*, October 23, 1916.

[64] *ibid.*, October 25, 1916.

no guarantee that he will not be worse than Mr. Wilson."[65] Second, Democrats, at least in Ohio and Wisconsin, were at this very time redoubling their work among German Americans, and with some success.[66]

One fact was as clear as daylight by the time that the campaign reached its climax in late October. Democratic legislation during the spring and summer, particularly the Revenue and Adamson Acts, and Wilson's unequivocal affirmation of advanced progressivism had united the business community and conservative Republicans in deepening hatred of Wilson and all his works. Class lines have never been drawn absolutely in any American presidential contest, and there were mavericks in the business community in 1916. Most of them, like Cleveland H. Dodge, George Foster Peabody, Charles R. Crane, Andrew Carnegie, and Henry Morgenthau, were philanthropists and intimate friends of Wilson. There were a few others—Henry Ford, George E. Johnson and H. B. Endicott, owners of the largest shoe factory in the United States, Robert S. Lovett, president of the Union Pacific Railroad, F. D. Underwood, president of the Erie Railroad, and Samuel Fels, the soap manufacturer, among them[67]—but the great mass of businessmen and bankers closed ranks and poured money into the Republican campaign chest with generosity unparalleled since 1896. The treasurer of the Republican National Committee did not disclose the total of these contributions, but Samuel J. Graham, Assistant Attorney General of the United States, concluded after careful investigation that the Republicans had raised and spent no less than $15,000,000 altogether and $3,000,000 in New York alone.[68] "I believe the whole business and intelligent part of the community," Taft wrote in mid-October, "to be thoroughly roused against Wilson, except may be the Jews, and the college professors who are crazy on the subject of humanity without knowing what humanity means."[69] The point was, one of these "humanitarian" professors wrote from Chicago, "the

[65] Ambassador von Bernstorff to the Foreign Office, October 5, 1916, "Bernstorff Wireless Despatches—1916." Hugo Münsterberg, a leading German propagandist in the United States, was apparently working among German-American groups for Wilson's re-election. See H. Münsterberg to W. W., October 24, 1916, Wilson Papers.

[66] R. A. Taft to W. H. Taft, October 27, 1916, Taft Papers; Representative M. E. Burke to C. Kitchin, November 2, 1916, Kitchin Papers.

[67] New York *World*, May 29, 1916; *New York Times*, September 29, and October 3 and 9, 1916.

[68] S. J. Graham to L. C. Woods, December 13, 1916, the Woods-Graham Correspondence, Princeton University Library.

[69] W. H. Taft to G. W. Wickersham, October 15, 1916, Taft Papers.

Republicans know their whole future as a party is at stake, they have by heredity and recently by active agitation the conservative and reactionary forces with them, the tory element which is always powerful in any country, and these men have the wealth as a rule. They are honest in the view that the country will be ruined if they do not govern it."[70]

Evidences of hatred of Wilson approaching malignity abound in the private papers of Republican leaders of the time. The following must suffice to show its intensity:

William Howard Taft

I feel great embarrassment in the campaign, because no one in the campaign has as much contempt for Wilson as I have. My contempt is based on the fact that I regard him as a ruthless hypocrite, and as an opportunist, who has no convictions that he would not barter at once for votes. He is a man who has a certain kind of tenacity that can not be characterized as firmness, because that is to be regarded as a virtue when it is exhibited in the maintenance of a cause, not in support in pride of opinion or because of personal spite, or for some personal advancement. On the other hand, he surrenders a conviction, previously expressed, without the slightest hesitation, and never even vouchsafes to the public the arguments upon which he was induced to change his mind.[71]

We have never had such an artful demagogue and one so willing to sacrifice all principle to retention of power.[72]

I regard this election as the most critical one during my career. If Wilson becomes President, he will have the appointment of four justices of the Supreme Court. He has disgraced the Supreme Court already by putting Brandeis on it, and he is seeking to break down the guaranties of the Constitution by selecting men who are radical in their views, who have no idea of preserving the rights of property or maintaining the protection of the Constitution, which has enabled us to live and be strong.[73]

Elihu Root

I am so disgusted with the course of this administration towards Latin-America, its hypocrisy and humbug and its destruction of the basis of really friendly relations, that I have become inarticulate. I have declined the invitations of the City Club of Baltimore and I speak only where I am at liberty to be profane.[74]

We discussed the presidential campaign and Mr. Root expressed very

[70] W. E. Dodd to E. M. House, October 26, 1916, House Papers.
[71] W. H. Taft to C. Cobb, July 19, 1916, Taft Papers.
[72] W. H. Taft to H. D. Taft, October 29, 1916, *ibid.*
[73] W. H. Taft to J. Markham, October 21, 1916, *ibid.*
[74] E. Root to C. P. Anderson, October 25, 1916, the Papers of Chandler P. Anderson, Library of Congress; hereinafter cited as the Anderson Papers.

gloomy forebodings as to both our internal and external situation in case of Wilson's election.

He said that we had had weak presidents and wrong-headed presidents, but never until Wilson had we had an unscrupulous and dishonest president, and that it would be a most shocking and disturbing thing if a man who was known by his intimates and a wide number of other people in public life to be both unscrupulous and dishonest, should be continued in that office by the American people.

He again said what he wrote to me the other day that he felt so strongly about it that it was impossible for him to speak of it without profanity, and he certainly was very much in earnest and most emphatic in the expression of his opinion.[75]

Henry Cabot Lodge

My one, overwhelming desire is to beat the Wilson administration. It is, with me, no question of a party victory, because I feel that what is at stake far transcends all party considerations. The Wilson administration has debauched public sentiment, lowered and disintegrated the American spirit; and I shudder to think what four years more of that crowd would mean. This is the dominant question, of course. . . . Four years more of Daniels would ruin the navy; and while this administration remains, we shall get nothing but language, and there will be nothing done either for army or navy.[76]

Theodore Roosevelt

Wilson is a worse and a feebler President than Buchanan. He has done more damage to the future of our national character than any President we have ever had; he is a far more dangerous and mischievous demagogue than poor, silly, emotionally sincere Bryan. He is dangerous precisely because he has such adroit, shifty, elocutionary ability that he deceives large masses of people—apparently as much so in England as here, for he represents a type which your people also have delighted to honor of recent years. . . . Your people really seem to understand Wilson much less than the French; and they appear to regard men like ex-President Eliot as their real friends because they mouth about "peace" and "Anglo-Saxon brotherhood," and yet support Wilson who is himself mainly responsible for the growth and influence of the German propaganda in this country. Our own people have of course behaved even worse; and moreover the fighting part of your people have made a splendid showing, a heroic showing, whereas we—thanks chiefly to Wilson, but also to the peace propaganda of the last fifteen years have never before occupied so abject a position.[77]

[75] The Diary of Chandler P. Anderson, November 6, 1916, Library of Congress; hereinafter cited as the Anderson Diary.

[76] H. C. Lodge to T. Roosevelt, June 14, 1916, Roosevelt Papers.

[77] T. Roosevelt to H. Plunkett, July 9, 1916, the Papers of Sir Horace Plunkett, Plunkett Foundation, London; hereinafter cited as the Plunkett Papers.

It was easy for men to do extraordinary things when so much seemed at stake. Republicans conducted against Woodrow Wilson in 1916 what must have been one of the dirtiest whispering campaigns in American history. There is no evidence that the Republican National Committee or any of its agencies participated in the worst aspects. We have one piece of evidence showing that Theodore Roosevelt perhaps did,[78] but none to implicate other distinguished Republicans. Whispered words are usually spoken in a corner, not put on paper for historians to see. We have extensive and reliable evidence to warrant the following summary:

1. Republicans, as they had done in 1912, widely circulated remarks derogatory of Wilson's character that Grover Cleveland was alleged to have made during the troubled time of Wilson's presidency of Princeton University. One member of Republican headquarters in New York wrote to President John Grier Hibben of Princeton saying that Republican campaign managers were sure that they could defeat Wilson if they could obtain written confirmation of Cleveland's aspersions. "I am sure," he went on, "that I can get authority in Princeton to quote Cleveland's remarks if you will withdraw your opposition to anybody in Princeton being involved in this campaign. . . . *Is the possible danger to Princeton through anything Wilson might say about her, a sufficient excuse for further suppression, at this time of a truth, which might be a decisive factor?*"[79]

Hibben was revolted at the very suggestion. If the Republican National Committee was in such desperate straits that it "must stoop to these measures," he replied, "it will be a confession of weakness before the whole American public. . . . If the Committee is so wanting in resourcefulness that it must use such weapons, their plight is most deplorable."[80]

Hibben's correspondent replied that he agreed but added that Cleveland's remarks were being quoted from Maine to California.[81] It is interesting that a straw vote of the Princeton faculty taken in early November gave Wilson ninety votes to forty-four for Hughes.[82]

2. Republicans whispered far and wide that Wilson had had an illicit affair with Mrs. Mary Allen Hulbert, the former Mrs. Peck; that Ellen Axson Wilson had really died of a broken heart because

[78] See Roosevelt's reference to Wilson's alleged philandering, printed in John A. Garraty, *Right-Hand Man, the Life of George W. Perkins*, p. 347.

[79] R. E. Annin to J. G. Hibben, October 17, 1916, the Papers of John Grier Hibben, Princeton University Library; hereinafter cited as the Hibben Papers.

[80] J. G. Hibben to R. E. Annin, October 20, 1916, *ibid.*

[81] R. E. Annin to J. G. Hibben, October 24, 1916, *ibid.*

[82] New York *World*, November 4, 1916.

of this affair; that Mrs. Hulbert had been prepared to institute breach of promise proceedings against the President; and that Louis D. Brandeis, Wilson's go-between, had purchased Mrs. Hulbert's silence for $75,000. There were numerous variations of this story. "It seems to me strange," a Boston lawyer wrote to a clergyman in Watertown, Massachusetts, repeating all the gory details, "that you as a clergyman urge any man to vote for Mr. Wilson. Half the people in the United States know the general facts regarding his expensive acquaintance with Mrs. Peck of Washington. In fact the matter is so generally known that you ask any man who is Peck's Bad Boy, and, with a smile, you will be told that it is Mr. Wilson."[83] Brandeis called the letter a "vile slander" when the Watertown clergyman sent it to him.[84]

Republican women in cities organized and conducted the whispering campaign on a block basis.[85] "Williams said Chicago was fairly teeming with scandalous stories about the President," Woolley reported in June.[86] "The back stairs, sewer gossips . . . are doing deadly work among the women in states where women vote," he wrote a short time later from Denver.[87]

3. There were other assorted rumors and accusations, for example, that Wilson pushed Ellen Axson Wilson down the stairs of the White House, causing the complications that led to her death; that he was ashamed of his own prematurely born child;[88] and that Ellen Axson Wilson contemplated divorce proceedings, was jealous of Mrs. Galt, and died of a broken heart because of her husband's love for Mrs. Galt.[89]

Wilson and Democratic campaign managers of course heard numerous echoes and were appalled. "I do not know how to deal with the fiendish lies that are being invented and circulated about my personal character," Wilson wrote to his former pastor in Princeton, "other than to invite those who repeat them to consult anybody who

---

[83] F. N. Fay to E. S. Meredith, November 2, 1916, Brandeis Papers. For another *written* version of this same tale, see A. L. Benson to J. P. Tumulty, April 11, 1916, House Papers, enclosing an anonymous communication that Benson had just received.

[84] L. D. Brandeis to E. S. Meredith, November 11, 1916, Brandeis Papers.

[85] R. S. Baker, memorandum of an interview with Vance McCormick, July 15, 1928, Baker Collection; F. P. Stockbridge to R. S. Baker, December 11, 1927, *ibid.*

[86] R. W. Woolley to E. M. House, June 1, 1916, House Papers.

[87] R. W. Woolley to E. M. House, June 10, 1916, *ibid.*

[88] See C. A. Hamilton to L. D. Brandeis, November 6, 1916, Brandeis Papers, asking if these stories were true.

[89] H. M. Price, Marshall, Tex., to J. P. Tumulty, August 16, 1916, Wilson Papers, saying that these stories were being circulated in Texas.

has known me for any length of time. . . . Poison of this sort is hard to find an antidote for."[90] And the President added after the election: "The campaign was indeed one of the most . . . unfair on the part of the Republican opposition that the country has ever seen."[91]

The resourceful Colonel House found one effective way of answering the scandalmongers without giving the impression of dignifying their campaign. It was to ask the President's brother-in-law, Professor Stockton Axson of the Rice Institute, to write an article about Wilson's family life. "It would have a telling effect just now," House added.[92] Axson loved and worshipped Wilson, who had been like a father to him, and he gladly sent back the manuscript of an article entitled "Mr. Wilson as Seen by One of His Family Circle." House edited it, cutting out what he said was "sob stuff."[93] It was published first in the *New York Times Magazine* on October 8 and reprinted in at least twenty newspapers. Democratic headquarters sent out a million copies in pamphlet form.

Tempers and tension were further exacerbated in the last days of the campaign by an ugly contretemps between President Wilson and Senator Lodge. The Senator charged in a speech at Brockton, Massachusetts, on October 26 that Wilson had added a postscript to his *second Lusitania* note, advising the German government not to take seriously the strong language of the first *Lusitania* note and offering to submit the incident to arbitration. This pleased Bryan, Lodge went on, but other members of the Cabinet threatened to resign and expose "the whole thing." Wilson removed the postscript, and Bryan resigned.[94]

Burleson, Secretary of Commerce William C. Redfield, and Attorney General Thomas W. Gregory denied the whole story,[95] whereupon Lodge returned to the attack in a speech at Somerville, Massachusetts, on October 28, by reading a letter from Doctor Charles H. Bailey of the Tufts Medical School saying that Henry Breckinridge, former Assistant Secretary of War, had told him the story. "This," Lodge said,

---

[90] W. W. to S. W. Beach, June 26, 1916, *ibid.*

[91] W. W. to G. Droppers, December 12, 1916, *ibid.*

[92] E. M. House to S. Axson, August 19, 1916, House Papers.

[93] House Diary, September 30, 1916.

[94] The text of this part of Lodge's speech is printed in the *New York Times*, October 31, 1916.

[95] A. S. Burleson to the Editor, *Philadelphia Public Ledger*, October 27, 1916, Burleson Papers; *New York Times*, October 28, 1916.

"simply throws an additional light on the shifty character of this Administration in its foreign policies."[96] Breckinridge retorted that Bailey was a "scoundrel"[97] and a "sneak and a falsifier."[98] Lodge, in a speech at Fitchburg, Massachusetts, on October 30, then read a letter from John T. L. Jeffries of Boston testifying that Breckinridge had also told him the story of the postscript affair.[99]

Wilson was inundated with requests for an explanation. Among them was a telegram from one Walter Lippmann, apparently not the editorialist, saying, "As a Democratic worker I wish to know if the charge made by Senator Lodge, concerning the Lusitania note, is true. Please wire."[100] The President replied at once in a telegram that he gave to the newspapers, as follows:

> In reply to your telegram let me say that the statement made by Senator Lodge is untrue. No postscript or amendment of the Lusitania note was ever written or contemplated by me except such changes as I myself inserted which strengthened and emphasized the protest. It was suggested, after the note was ready for transmission, that an intimation be conveyed to the German Government that a proposal for arbitration would be acceptable and one member of the Cabinet spoke to me about it, but it was never discussed in Cabinet meeting, and no threat of any resignation was ever made, for the very good reason that I rejected the suggestion after giving it such consideration as I thought every proposal deserved which touched so grave a matter. It was inconsistent with the purpose of the note. The public is in possession of everything that was said to the German Government.[101]

It was a case of using language that was generally accurate insofar as it went to hide the whole truth. Wilson had not written any postscript or amendment to the first (not the second) *Lusitania* note. He had written, at Bryan's urgent request, a press release, to be issued when the note was given to the newspapers, intimating that the American government might be willing to submit the *Lusitania* incident to German-American inquiry and negotiation under the rubric of the Bryan conciliation treaties. Wilson was inaccurate in saying that "one

[96] Bailey's letter, C. H. Bailey to G. D. Cushing, n. d., and portions of Lodge's speech at Somerville are printed in *ibid.*, October 29, 1916.

[97] H. Breckinridge to the Editor, October 28, 1916, *ibid.*, October 30, 1916.

[98] H. Breckinridge to the Editor, October 30, 1916, *ibid.*, October 31, 1916.

[99] *ibid.*, October 31, 1916.

[100] W. Lippmann to W. W., October 30, 1916, Wilson Papers.

[101] W. W. to W. Lippmann, October 30, 1916, *ibid.*, published in the *New York Times*, October 31, 1916.

member of the Cabinet" had proposed *arbitration*.[102] No Cabinet member had threatened to resign, but there had been heated discussion among a group consisting of Tumulty, Burleson, and Lindley M. Garrison, and Wilson had decided not to issue the press release mainly because of their objections.[103]

Something approximating the exact truth came out on the same day that Wilson's telegram appeared in the press. George C. Warren, Jr., of Jersey City gave out a detailed account of the controversy over the press release and the part that Tumulty, Burleson, and Garrison had played in killing it. He had the story, Warren said, from a member of President Wilson's official family.[104]

Lodge had the final word. "The President of the United States," he said at North Adams, Massachusetts, on October 31, "has denied that there was any postscript to the Lusitania note, and we are all bound, of course, to accept the President's denial just as he makes it." However, the Senator went on, it was Henry Breckinridge, not he, who had said that there had been a postscript. The President's own statement, and Warren's as well, Lodge added, proved that administration leaders had at least discussed arbitrating the loss of American lives on the *Lusitania*.[105]

The affair inevitably worsened the bad feeling between Wilson and Lodge. Wilson's own hostility came out not long afterward, when the Reverend Doctor Roland C. Smith, rector of St. John's Episcopal Church of Washington, invited the President to speak at an anniversary service to be held on January 13, 1917. Wilson said that he would come even if he could not speak. Then he saw, on reading the formal invitation, that Lodge was to be one of the speakers at the affair. He wrote at once to Doctor Smith, reviewing the background and adding:

"Senator Lodge's conduct during the recent campaign makes it impossible for me with self-respect to join in any exercise in which he takes part or to associate myself with him in any way.

"I would not refer to this matter if I did not feel that I owed you

[102] As Bryan pointed out in W. J. Bryan to J. P. Tumulty, October 31, 1916, Wilson Papers.

[103] For this episode, see A. S. Link, *Wilson: The Struggle for Neutrality, 1914-1915*, pp. 385-389.

[104] *New York Times*, October 31, 1916. Tumulty, when questioned by reporters, said that he did not remember ever meeting Warren. Garrison was probably Warren's source.

[105] *ibid.*, November 1, 1916. For another account of this episode, see John A. Garraty, *Henry Cabot Lodge, a Biography*, pp. 329-332.

the most candid statement of my quandary, and I want to beg that you will make no change in your arrangements. It would not be possible for me in any case to speak and I should be very much distressed if I felt that I had in any way interfered with arrangements already consummated.

"I say all this, my dear Doctor Smith, in the greatest simplicity and sincerity and beg that you will take me exactly at my word and excuse me without anything said one way or the other outside our own confidence."[106]

Smith said that he understood and asked whether Secretary Lane might not be permitted to represent the administration. "I must frankly say ...," Wilson replied, "that I should personally prefer that no official member of the administration should appear upon the programme with the gentleman I have mentioned."[107]

As luck would have it, reporters got wind of the President's letters (not, apparently, from Smith) and gleefully broke the news in the Washington press.[108] Then Wilson gave a dinner in honor of the Allied diplomatic corps and failed to invite the Massachusetts Senator while inviting another Republican member of the Senate foreign relations committee and the ranking Republican member of the House foreign affairs committee. There could be no doubt now, reporters said, that Wilson was snubbing Lodge on account of the *Lusitania* postscript affair.[109]

The campaign was now at its climax, and Wilson was going at a frantic pace. He was in Cincinnati on October 26 for a tremendous civic welcome and four speeches in one day. One of them, a luncheon address at the Women's City Club, contained the following significant passage:

"Have you ever heard what started the present war? If you have, I wish you would publish it, because nobody else has, so far as I can gather. Nothing in particular started it, but everything in general. There had been growing up in Europe a mutual suspicion, an interchange of conjectures about what this Government and that Government was going to do, an interlacing of alliances and understandings, a complex web of intrigue and spying, that presently was sure to

---

[106] W. W. to R. C. Smith, December 29, 1916, Wilson Papers.
[107] R. C. Smith to W. W., January 2, 1917; W. W. to R. C. Smith, January 5, 1917, both in *ibid.*
[108] *Washington Post*, January 13, 1917.
[109] *Boston Evening Transcript*, January 13, 1917.

entangle the whole of the family of mankind on that side of the water in its meshes.

"Now, revive that after this war is over and sooner or later you will have just such another war, and this is the last war of the kind or of any kind that involves the world that the United States can keep out of.

"I say this because I believe that the business of neutrality is over; not because I want it to be over, but I mean this, that war now has such a scale that the position of neutrals sooner or later becomes intolerable. . . .

"We must have a society of nations, not suddenly, not by insistence, not by any hostile emphasis upon the demand, but by the demonstration of the needs of the time. The nations of the world must get together and say, 'Nobody can hereafter be neutral as respects the disturbance of the world's peace for an object which the world's opinion cannot sanction.' . . . America must hereafter be ready as a member of the family of nations to exert her whole force, moral and physical, to the assertion of . . . [human rights] throughout the round globe."[110]

It was his most forthright call for a postwar league of nations during the presidential campaign of 1916.

Wilson was back at "Shadow Lawn" to greet 15,000 visitors on "Woodrow Wilson Day" and "New York Day," October 28.[111] Three days later he sent a letter to a correspondent in North Dakota that was blazoned in the newspapers. "Thank you warmly for your letter of October twenty-third," it read. "The reason you give for supporting me touches me very deeply, that you should feel when you see 'the boys and mother' together in your home circle that I have preserved the peace and happiness of the home. Such a feeling on the part of my fellow-citizens is a sufficient reward for everything that I have done."[112] On the same day that he wrote this letter he gave a long interview to a reporter, Henry N. Hall, reviewing once again what he thought hung on the outcome of the battle. It was printed in the New York *World* on November 5, but it did not include the following two off-the-record comments:

"I hope to God we will win without New York . . . so as to put it in a normal relation to the rest of the Union. . . .

[110] *New York Times*, October 27, 1916.
[111] *ibid.*, October 29, 1916.
[112] W. W. to J. W. Wasson, October 31, 1916, Wilson Papers.

"Just between you and me, I have such an utter contempt for Mr. Hughes now that I don't want to pay him the compliment of referring to him, he has sunk so low."[113]

November 1 found Wilson on his way to Buffalo. Large crowds stood in cold rain to greet the train as it sped through up-state New York, and ten thousand persons, most of them employees of Endicott, Johnson and Company, were at the station in Johnson City when Wilson's train stopped. "I am not making speeches, my fellow-citizens," he said from the rear platform, "but I want to express my regret that I was not able to be here last Saturday to celebrate what I think was a very significant thing, the action of the firm of Endicott, Johnson & Co. in giving their employes eight hours, not only for the reasons that are generally given, but also for better reasons: because they regard the men and all their employes as members of the same business family with them. If that sort of feeling existed everywhere there would be no question between capital and labor. I want to congratulate you upon living under such auspices and tell you how very much obliged to you I am for this royal welcome."

A large crowd lined the streets in Buffalo to watch the President and Mrs. Wilson drive to the Ellicott Club for luncheon with many of the city's business leaders. The great task ahead, Wilson told them, was to transform law into a compassionate and dynamic instrument of change. "The only way to prevent social revolution," he went on, "is to be beforehand by doing social justice. These are serious matters of perception of sympathy, of knowledge, and the particular thing that stands in their way is anything like the formation of classes." Wilson continued:

"There are things that we ought to see to that we have not been seeing to—the health, the moral opportunity, the just treatment, the neighborly relationships of men of all sorts and classes and conditions. I tell you, my fellow-citizens, until a political party or any other group of men get that thought at their hearts they are unfit for the national confidence.

"That is the sort of question that we have to face in the future. And then there are the most important questions of organization. It is all very well to know what justice is, but it is another thing to know how to make it work. . . . I have no ready made program for this. This is a thing in which one must feel his way."

[113] Transcription dated October 31, 1916, Swem Collection.

Wilson then passed to foreign affairs, saying that he could not regard any man as a patriot who made "play with the loss of the lives of American citizens" for political advantage—an obvious slap at Senator Lodge. He came back more directly to foreign policy in a speech in the Buffalo Auditorium that night, as follows:

"What we want everybody to understand is this, that we are not going to be drawn into quarrels which do not touch the thing that America has set her face to. America is not interested in seeing one nation or one group of nations prevail against another, but she is interested in seeing justice founded upon peace throughout the world.

"We are not only not afraid to fight, but we are not disinclined to fight when we can find something as big as American ideals to fight for."[114]

The grand climax came in New York City on the following day, Friday, November 2. Wilson's train arrived at Grand Central Terminal at nine in the morning, and the President and his party, joined by Vance McCormick and Colonel House, spent the morning on the *Mayflower* in the East River. "We talked to him for an hour and a half," House wrote in his diary on November 2, "and it was the most acrimonious debate I have had with him for a long while. He did not like the New York programme, he did not like the Republican expenditure of money to defeat him, as evidenced by the full-page advertisements in the morning papers. The Republicans had sixteen columns to our one and a half. He thought New York was 'rotten to the core,' and should be wiped off the map. . . . He thought both McCormick and I had 'New Yorkitis,' and that the campaign should be run from elsewhere. He was absolutely certain of the election without New York. . . .

"The President reminds me of a boy whose mother tells him he has ridden long enough on his hobby-horse, and that he must let little Charlie have a turn. If left to the boy it would never be Charlie's turn. . . .

"However, before we left, the President put his arms around us both and expressed appreciation for what we were doing, saying we must not mind his not agreeing as to the advisability of today's program."[115]

House and McCormick left, and Wilson went to the Waldorf-Astoria Hotel to speak to a luncheon meeting of the Wilson Business

[114] *New York Times*, November 2, 1916.
[115] House Diary, November 2, 1916.

Men's National League. It was another hard-hitting warning that only progressive adaptation and change could avert social revolution: "Every age is an age of transition. Everything grows old and has to be renewed; everything gets out of adjustment and has to be adjusted; everything gets out of alignment and has to be reassociated." There was one particularly poignant passage:

"I have seen some things within the last two or three weeks, my fellow-citizens, that have touched me very deeply in the great crowds that one encounters in going about in a season like this. I have seen poorly dressed women, tears streaming down their faces, holding up little children to me, as if they had discovered a friend, when, God knows, all I was trying to do was to be just. I hope I am their friend; I shall always try to be. But why should they pick me out? I can think of only one thing, they have thought that men in prominent places were not giving them any consideration at all, and the minute any one of us who is supposed to have influence shows that our heart beats with theirs and that we regard them as like ourselves in all that touches their welfare, whether of the body or of the mind, they come to us with tears on their faces, and outstretched arms and thank God for a friend."

Wilson went to Democratic headquarters for a brief reception later in the afternoon. He then returned to the *Mayflower* until after dinner, when he drove down Fifth Avenue between lines of cheering Democrats to Madison Square Garden. Some 25,000 persons milled about the building, and the President and Mrs. Wilson had to climb a fire escape to get inside. The 15,000 persons massed in the Garden cheered and demonstrated for thirty minutes when Wilson made his entry. He again spoke, briefly but movingly, of the need for social justice and compassion and forward progress. He went afterward to Cooper Union for a crushing reception and another speech at 1:15 in the morning.[116]

Delegations from Trenton, Princeton, and other cities in New Jersey, and a crowd of Princeton undergraduates singing "Old Nassau," came to "Shadow Lawn" on November 4 for "Old Home Day." A volunteer trio led the crowd of five thousand in singing a new Wilson campaign song that ran as follows:

> We want Wilson in the White House
> Four years more;
> We want Wilson there to guide us
> As he's done before.

[116] *New York Times*, November 3, 1916.

> He is first, last and always for America
> And he's kept us out of war—God bless him.
> We want Wilson in the White House
> Four Years more.

Wilson made his final speech, appealing for the New Jersey Democratic ticket and reviewing all the major issues of the campaign.[117] "The fight is won I fully believe," he said in telegrams to county and state Democratic chairmen throughout the country on the following day, "though I take this means of urging you to renewed exertions and vigilance to see that belated efforts to confuse the public judgment do not succeed."[118]

It was evident by mid-October that Wilson and Hughes were running neck and neck in the closest presidential race since 1896. Wilson obviously had a good chance to win, but he could not be certain about the outcome. As he explained in a letter to his brother on October 16:

"It is hard to answer your question as to how the campaign is going. I hear all sorts of reports, most of them encouraging (except about Maryland), but I never allow myself to form confident expectations of any kind. I believe that the independent vote, the vote of the people who aren't talking and aren't telling politicians how they are going to vote, is going to play a bigger part in this election than it ever played in any previous election, and that makes the result truly incalculable. It is evident, of course, that Mr. Hughes is making very little headway, because he has done so many stupid and so many insincere things, but other influences are at work in his behalf which are undoubtedly very powerful, chiefly the influence of organized business. I can only conjecture and hope."[119]

It was no time, Colonel House thought, for an interim government should Hughes be elected. "It occurred to me yesterday," House wrote in his diary on October 19, "to suggest to the President, in the event of his defeat, to ask both Marshall and Lansing to resign, and then appoint Hughes Secretary of State. He should then resign himself, making Hughes President of the United States. Times are too critical to have an interim of four months between the election and inaugura-

---

[117] *ibid.*, November 5, 1916; New York *World*, November 5, 1916.

[118] *New York Times*, November 6, 1916.

[119] W. W. to J. R. Wilson, October 16, 1916, Wilson Papers. "I think that the election of Mr. Hughes with the motley crowd that is behind him," Wilson wrote a week later to the Secretary of Labor, "would be a national calamity." W. W. to W. B. Wilson, October 23, 1916, *ibid.*

tion of the next President."[120] House made the suggestion in a letter to Wilson on the following day, October 20.[121] He discussed the matter with Attorney General Gregory and Frank Polk soon afterward, and with Lansing on November 3. "Lansing," House recorded in his diary, "was somewhat staggered at first, but recovered himself and finally expressed approval. He said he had worried considerably over the thought of the interim between November 7 and March 4 in the event of the President's defeat, but the way would be immediately cleared if the President would do as I advised."[122]

We do not know precisely when Wilson decided to follow House's advice. It is of course entirely possible that the idea had occurred to him before he received the Colonel's letter of October 20. He had been concerned all his adult life about the rigidities of the American constitutional system and had tried to devise ways of making the President and Congress immediately responsible to the electorate. House's suggestion must, therefore, have evoked a favorable response even if Wilson's own thoughts had been running along the same line. The President said not a word to his associates, not even to House when he saw him in New York on November 2. He sat down at his desk in his study at "Shadow Lawn" on November 5 and began to draft a letter to Lansing in his Graham shorthand.[123] That completed, he next typed the letter on his portable Hammond, transcribing and editing slightly as he went. Never had he been more in earnest. Colonel House saw him on November 15. "I asked him the direct question whether he had made up his mind before the election to follow my suggestion about resigning," House wrote in his diary. "He said he had absolutely decided to do so, and that it was in line with his lifetime views upon the subject, and that he had taken the precaution to write Lansing before the election in order to put himself on record so that he could not be charged with doing something hastily from pique. I asked how soon he would have resigned, and he replied, 'Immediately.' "[124]

The letter ran to three pages on the plainly printed note stationery that Wilson used for his private correspondence. He sealed it with wax; then, probably on the following day, he asked Polk, who had

[120] House Diary, October 19, 1916.

[121] E. M. House to W. W., October 20, 1916, Wilson Papers.

[122] House Diary, November 3, 1916.

[123] For the text of a transcription of this draft, see A. S. Link, "President Wilson's Plan to Resign in 1916," *The Princeton University Library Chronicle*, XXIII (Summer 1962), 169-170.

[124] House Diary, November 19, 1916.

come to "Shadow Lawn" for a conference, to take the letter personally to Lansing. "When I arrived in New York on election day, after voting in Watertown, New York," Lansing writes in his memoirs, "Mr. Frank L. Polk handed me a letter which he brought to me from the President. It was enclosed in a wax-sealed envelope addressed in Mr. Wilson's handwriting and marked 'most confidential' and to be opened by no one except myself."[125] It follows:

> There is a matter which has occupied my thoughts throughout the campaign and which I want to lay before you before the election, while I can discuss it without any touch of feeling as to the result.
>
> Again and again the question has arisen in my mind, What would it be my duty to do were Mr. Hughes to be elected? Four months would elapse before he could take charge of the affairs of the government, and during those four months I would be without such moral backing from the nation as would be necessary to steady and control our relations with other governments. I would be known to be the rejected, not the accredited, spokesman of the country; and yet the accredited spokesman would be without legal authority to speak for the nation. Such a situation would be fraught with the gravest dangers. The direction of the foreign policy of the government would in effect have been taken out of my hands and yet its new definition would be impossible until March.
>
> I feel that it would be my duty to relieve the country of the perils of such a situation at once. The course I have in mind is dependent upon the consent and cooperation of the Vice President; but, if I could gain his consent to the plan, I would ask your permission to invite Mr. Hughes to become Secretary of State and would then join the Vice President in resigning, and thus open to Mr. Hughes the immediate succession to the presidency.
>
> All my life long I have advocated some such responsible government for the United States as other constitutional systems afford as of course, and as such action on my part would inaugurate, at least by example. Responsible government means government by those whom the people trust, and trust at the time of decision and action. The whole country has long perceived, without knowing how to remedy, the extreme disadvantage of having to live for four months after a [sic] election under a party whose guidance had been rejected at the polls. Here is the remedy, at any rate so far as the Executive is concerned. In ordinary times it would perhaps not be necessary to apply it. But it seems to me that in the existing circumstances it would be imperatively necessary. The choice of policy in respect of our foreign relations rests with the Executive. No such

[125] R. Lansing, *War Memoirs*, p. 164.

critical circumstances in regard to our foreign policy have ever before existed. It would be my duty to step aside so that there would be no doubt in any quarter how that policy was to be directed, towards what objects and by what means. I would have no right to risk the peace of the nation by remaining in office after I had lost my authority.

I hope and believe that your own judgment will run with mine in this critical matter.

Cordially and faithfully Yrs.

Woodrow Wilson

P. S. I beg that you will regard this as in the strictest sense confidential until I shall have had an opportunity to discuss it with you in person, should circumstances make it a practical problem of duty.

W. W. [126]

It is interesting that betting odds in New York were ten to seven against Wilson on the day that he wrote this letter, and even by midnight on November 6.[127]

Wilson rose early on Tuesday, November 7, and left "Shadow Lawn" with Mrs. Wilson at 7:30 for the motor trip to Princeton. He voted at about nine o'clock at the firehouse on Chambers Street and returned at once to Long Branch. He worked as usual during the day and had a quiet dinner with Mrs. Wilson, Margaret Wilson, Doctor Grayson, Miss Bones, Mrs. W. H. Bolling, Bertha Bolling, and Francis B. Sayre, his son-in-law. The group played Twenty Questions until about ten o'clock. Then a reporter called to say that the *New York Times* had just conceded the election to Hughes. Grayson telephoned from Asbury Park to say that it was true. The New York *World* conceded soon afterward on the basis of a Hughes tidal wave in the East.

It did look bad, Wilson said. "Well," he went on, "I will not send Mr. Hughes a telegram of congratulation tonight, for things are not settled. . . . There now seems little hope that we shall not be drawn into the War, though I have done everything I can to keep us out; but my defeat will be taken by Germany as a repudiation of my policy. Many of our own people will so construe it, and will try to force war upon the next Administration." He added to Mrs. Wilson, "Well, as we got up so early, what do you say to having a glass of milk and going to bed? . . . I might stay longer but you are all so blue."[128]

[126] W. W. to R. Lansing, November 5, 1916, from the original letter in the Princeton University Library.

[127] *New York Times*, November 7, 1916.

[128] The two preceding paragraphs are based on *ibid.*, November 8, 1916, and Edith B. Wilson, *My Memoir*, p. 115.

Tumulty spent the night in the temporary Executive Offices in Asbury Park scanning returns. McCormick, Woolley, Morgenthau, and other Democratic leaders sat at a gloomy dinner in New York. Hughes went to bed in his suite in the Hotel Astor thinking that he would probably be the next President of the United States. He had carried all the big eastern and midwestern states and had an almost certain 247 electoral votes out of the total of 266 necessary for election.

Then returns from states west of the Mississippi began to filter in at about two o'clock in the morning. They were fragmentary at first, but they showed an unmistakable trend toward Wilson in normally Republican states like Kansas and Utah. Tumulty called Wilson before breakfast with the cheering report that the election was now in doubt and he had a good chance to win. The President and Mrs. Wilson played golf and went for a drive later in the morning. It was obvious by afternoon that Wilson had carried most of the trans-Mississippi states, and that California, Minnesota, North Dakota, and New Mexico were in doubt. Wilson had lunch with Dean Henry B. Fine and another Princeton friend. Then he spent the afternoon in his study following the returns. By midnight he had 251 electoral votes, Hughes, 247. California's thirteen electoral votes, Minnesota's twelve, North Dakota's three, and New Mexico's five were still in doubt. Hughes was leading by 925 votes in North Dakota; Wilson, by 1,499 votes in California, by 595 in Minnesota, and by 170 in New Mexico. But southern California, which was presumably Hughes territory, had not yet sent in complete returns. The chairmen of both Republican and Democratic National Committees retained counsel for possible legal proceedings. McCormick sent the following message to Democratic state and county chairmen: "President Wilson has been re-elected. Our opponents are desperate. You must personally see that the ballot boxes are guarded and the count protected and nothing left undone to safeguard this victory."[129]

The outcome was virtually certain by eleven in the evening of November 9. Returns from isolated rural districts in New Mexico had given Wilson an impressive majority in that state. Hughes was now leading in Minnesota, but North Dakota seemed safe for Wilson, and the result was now in doubt in New Hampshire. Most important, Hughes's majority of 21,000 in southern California had not been enough to offset Wilson's lead in the rest of the state. Wilson was still ahead

[129] The entire preceding paragraph is based on articles in the *New York Times*, November 9, 1916.

by about 3,000 votes. He was on his way to Williamstown, Massachusetts, to attend the baptism of his granddaughter, Eleanor Axson Sayre. His valet brought him a wireless message from Tumulty at 7:30 in the morning of November 10 (it had been sent at midnight) that read: "I am here [Asbury Park] surrounded by the local Democrats of Old Monmouth, and beg leave to send you our greetings and congratulations. The cause you so nobly represented at last triumphed, and we greet you. Our hearts, our thoughts and our affections go to you."[130]

Large crowds greeted the President and his party when they arrived in Williamstown at 1:30 in the afternoon. Wilson stood as godfather when the sacrament of infant baptism was administered at St. John's Episcopal Church at 3:30. President Harry A. Garfield of Williams College and Samuel P. Blagden, chairman of the Town Council, led a crowd of students to the Sayre home at five o'clock. "It is very delightful to meet you here, and especially in this informal way," Wilson said. "It is a real pleasure to come away for a short space from the field of politics. I am glad that the political campaign is over and that we can settle down in soberness and unity of spirit to work for the welfare of the country, without thinking of the advantage of parties." The town began to fill up with rejoicing Democrats later in the evening. Some 5,000 of them paraded with a band and a fife and drum corps to the Sayre home and demanded a speech. Wilson, smiling broadly, came out on the porch and said, "Let us remember, now that the campaign is over, to get together for the common good of all and not merely for the good of parties. Let us be ready to devote ourselves to the common service of our great country, which has given us liberty and peace."[131]

Wilson spent November 11 quietly at the Sayre home, seeing only a few intimate friends and poring over a stack of congratulatory telegrams and letters that warmed his heart. He and Mrs. Wilson took the train in the afternoon to Rhinecliff, New York, where they boarded the *Mayflower* in the evening. The yacht took them to New York City where they boarded a train for Washington the next day. A crowd of 5,000 persons, including Tumulty and members of the Cabinet, greeted them at Union Station at nine in the evening.[132]

The President spent the next few days at work answering letters and sending his own thanks to Democratic leaders. "The first letter I

[130] *ibid.*, November 10, 1916.
[131] *ibid.*, November 11, 1916.
[132] *ibid.*, November 12 and 13, 1916.

"Hold Your Course, Pilot!"
Kirby in the New York *World*

write from my desk here must be to you," he wrote to Vance McCormick, for example, on November 13. "It makes me deeply glad to think how the whole country has seen and appreciated your quality. You have won the admiration and affection of all Democrats not only, but the sincere admiration of all parties. No campaign, I think it can be said, was ever conducted with such a combination of harmony and vigor and system as this one from your headquarters and the headquarters at Chicago, and you were throughout the moving and guiding spirit. It must be a source of deep satisfaction to you that you should have won this admiration by an unselfish service of the first magnitude. May I not say for myself how entirely I have had my trust in you confirmed, and how throughout these trying months my genuine affection for you has grown and strengthened. My own sense of obligation and gratitude to you is immeasurable. Mrs. Wilson and all my household join me in sending you the most affectionate greetings and congratulations."[133]

The election was well settled by the time that the Wilsons returned to Washington. Wilson had carried New Hampshire by a plurality of fifty-six votes; California, by 3,773; New Mexico, by 2,530; and North Dakota, by 1,735. Hughes had carried Minnesota by a plurality of 392. Wilson won 9,129,606 popular and 277 electoral votes; Hughes, 8,538,221 popular and 254 electoral votes. Democrats would control the Senate in the next Congress by a vote of fifty-four to forty-two, but no one knew how the House of Representatives would go. It would contain 213 Democrats, 217 Republicans, two Progressives, one Prohibitionist, one Socialist, and one Independent. Hughes finally sent congratulations on November 22.[134] "It was," Wilson said, referring to his telegram, "a little moth-eaten when it got here but quite legible."[135]

It was as spectacular a personal triumph for Wilson as it was a close contest. Hughes polled some 850,000 more votes in 1916 than Taft had polled in 1908 (comparisons with the Republican vote in 1912 are inconclusive because of the division in the vote in that year). Wilson polled some 2,700,000 more votes in 1916 than Bryan had won in 1908, and some 2,830,000 more votes in 1916 than he had polled in 1912. "It is the most remarkable personal triumph that the politics of this country have produced," a former Republican Governor of New Jersey wrote, perhaps somewhat hyperbolically. "It demonstrates another thing—that the American people are not to be stampeded or driven away from a man who does his duty, and it will establish another thing, that in this country hereafter no one will attempt to win the Presidency by personal attacks which practically amounts to the abuse of a candidate for President."[136]

[133] W. W. to V. C. McCormick, November 13, 1916, Wilson Papers; also e.g., W. W. to T. J. Walsh, November 16, 1916; W. W. to D. C. Roper, November 18, 1916; W. W. to R. F. Wolfe, November 9, 1916, all in *ibid.*

[134] C. E. Hughes to W. W., November 22, 1916, *New York Times*, November 23, 1916.

[135] W. W. to J. R. Wilson, November 27, 1916, Wilson Papers.

[136] J. F. Fort to J. P. Tumulty, November 14, 1916, *ibid.*

Analysts and politicians set to work as soon as the returns were in to discover why it turned out this way, and their scrutiny yielded many surprises and signs for the future of American politics. To begin with, the vaunted German-American bloc had been so riddled by the Democratic peace appeal and Roosevelt's participation that it was not a decisive factor in the outcome.[137] The peace issue apparently also prevented any important defections from normal Democratic allegiance among Irish-American voters,[138] and it was a powerful factor in turning many Scandinavian-American voters to Wilson in the North Central states. Analysts could not find any pronounced alignment among Roman Catholic voters on purely religious grounds. Roman Catholic bishops and priests played a significant role in the outcome—against Wilson—apparently only in Oregon.[139] The labor vote went largely to Wilson and helped him to carry at least New Hampshire, Ohio, California, Washington, Idaho, and New Mexico, although it was apparently decisive only in the latter three states. The woman's vote in the Middle and Far Western states, local observers all agreed, went disproportionately to Wilson on account of the peace issue.[140]

The decisive factor, perhaps, was Wilson's success in winning former

[137] The German-American vote went largely to Hughes in Oregon, Minnesota, and Illinois, and was apparently important in the Republican success in the first two states. On the other hand, German Americans in Maryland voted largely for Wilson and probably swung that state to him. Hamilton County, Ohio (Cincinnati), an important German-American center, returned a plurality of 12,000 for Hughes. On the other hand, Taft carried the county by 18,374 votes in 1908, and the combined vote for Taft and Roosevelt exceeded Wilson's vote by 16,036 in 1912. Ohio, with its large German-American population, gave Wilson a plurality of 89,503 in 1916, although Taft had carried the state by 69,591 in 1908, and Taft and Roosevelt together polled a vote that exceeded Wilson's by 83,341 in 1912. In the six "German" wards of St. Louis, Hughes gained only two tenths of 1 per cent over the combined Republican-Progressive percentage of the total vote four years before. Hughes polled 12,480 votes in twelve "German" counties in Wisconsin, but Wilson carried the most important of them, Milwaukee County, by 7,000 votes, although not another Democrat received a majority in the county. This note is based on the superb analyses in the *New York Times*, November 12, 1916, and the *New York Times Magazine*, November 19, 1916.

[138] C. Wittke, *The Irish in America*, pp. 282-283.

[139] F. S. Myers to A. S. Burleson, November 13, 1916, Burleson Papers; S. White to T. J. Walsh, November 15, 1916, Walsh Papers.

[140] Democratic and Republican leaders in Kansas, for example, estimated that 70,000 women Republicans in the state, out of a total of 625,000 voters, voted for Wilson on the peace issue. Observers in the State of Washington, which Wilson carried by a plurality of 16,594, estimated that 90,000 out of 155,000 registered women voted for Wilson. Women also helped to carry California, Idaho, Utah, and Arizona for the President. See the *New York Times*, November 12, 1916.

Progressives. Generally speaking, he carried those states in which he did well among former Progressives and lost those states in which he did poorly among former Progressives. Statisticians estimated that he received, all told, about 20 per cent of the former Progressive vote, but it varied importantly from state to state, as the following table reveals:

Wilson's gains in 1916 over 1912 as percentages of the Progressive vote in 1912

Utah	109	New Hampshire	45
Wyoming	72	North Dakota	40
Idaho	68	New Mexico	39
Montana	59	Nebraska	34
Colorado	53	Ohio	34
Washington	47	Kansas	30

Finally, approximately three hundred thousand Socialists and independents in the left wing of the progressive movement who had voted for the Socialist candidate in 1912 swung to Wilson in 1916. Their support was also decisive in states like California, Ohio, and Washington.

As for the issues, virtually all observers agreed that Democratic success had come on account of Wilson's and his party's promises of continued peace, prosperity, and progressivism. "The President," Senator La Follette said, "must accept the outcome of this election as a clear mandate from the American people to hold steadfastly to his course against war."[141] Bryan said, "The peace argument evidently had more weight than arguments based upon economic progress . . . the country is against war. It is opposed to intervention in Mexico, and it protests against being drawn into the war in Europe."[142] The British Ambassador in Washington agreed in a post-election report, "The United States does not want to go to war, and the elections have clearly shown that the great mass of the Americans desire nothing so much as to keep out of the war. It is undoubtedly the cause of the President's re-election."[143]

No one missed the striking configuration of the election map in 1916, or what it signified. Contemporaries expressed it as follows:

[141] *La Follette's Magazine*, VIII (November 1916), 1.

[142] *The Commoner*, XVI (November 1916), 1.

[143] C. Spring Rice to E. Grey, November 24, 1916, S. Gwynn (ed.), *Letters of Spring Rice*, II, 354-355. William Allen White was the only important contemporary observer who thought that progressivism had been the sole issue, and that the peace appeal had had no effect. See W. A. White, "Who Killed Cock Robin?" *Collier's*, LVIII (December 16, 1916), 5-6, 26-27.

One other consideration, I venture to call to your attention: the sectional character of the vote. It is the combination which made Jefferson and Jackson. It is the South and the West united; the farmers, small business men and perhaps a large sprinkle of Union labor against the larger industrial, transportation and commercial interests.[144]

The West has indeed spoken, and nothing better has happened in a generation than this shifting of the political balance to a section which still maintains the old ideals of the Republic.[145]

The States of the West, in a new political alliance with the States of the South, decided the election. That is a geographical and political fact of which party managers will necessarily take notice. . . . The South and the West united for a reaffirmation of Jefferson's political philosophy.[146]

More than any election which has taken place since the Civil War, the old American territorial democracy, the democracy of Jackson and Douglas, has reasserted itself. Mr. Wilson has done what Mr. Bryan failed to do. He has recovered for the Democratic party the support of a great majority of the predominantly agricultural states. This support has not the same economic meaning as it had during the pioneer period, when the farmers in the newer parts of the country were in debt and thought themselves oppressed by the money power. The Far West is not aggrieved and rebellious as it was at the time of the "greenback" and "Populist" movements. But it still has a mind of its own, sharply defined from that of the rest of the country. In a combination with the solid South and with one or two other industrial states of the Middle West it is strong enough barely to swing a national victory.[147]

It was, indeed, the South and West united in emphatic mandate for progressivism and peace. Wilson had consummated the union of most of the agricultural states, which Bryan had narrowly failed to do in 1896. He had also added to the Democratic column two eastern states and a large portion of the social justice element who had followed Roosevelt in 1912. He had, in short, made a new coalition. Only the future could show whether he had made a truly new party.

He, at any rate, seemed to understand clearly why the new alliance had come into being. "You may be sure that I draw the same conclusions from the election that you do," he wrote to one progressive, "and that I feel very keenly the fresh obligations the election places upon me to fulfill the expectations of those who have so generously and emphatically stood by me. I am exceedingly proud to have received

[144] W. E. Dodd to E. M. House, November 10, 1916, House Papers.
[145] New York *World*, November 9, 1916.
[146] *New York Times*, November 10, 1916.
[147] *New Republic*, ix (November 11, 1916), 31-32.

support in such measure from such independent quarters, and I feel that the obligation upon me to make good is greater than ever."[148] He did not know whether he could weld a new party during the next four years, but he was sure that he would try to do so. As he wrote to the treasurer of the Progressive party, who had suggested the formation of a new liberal party:

"I do not feel that I am ready yet to express an opinion about the suggestion you make in the letter to Mr. McCormick, of which you send me a copy. I have read so attentively the history of parties in this country, and realize so keenly the rigidity of party association so far as it affects a very large proportion of voters, that one of the most puzzling questions to which one can address his thought is this, How can what has already been accomplished be given unbroken continuity by the use and combination of existing elements? It is by no means easy to figure it out, but I agree with you that this is the fundamental job in the next four years. I gladly open my mind to instruction on the subject."[149]

These were problems for the future. For Democrats and progressives it was joy enough to be alive in mid-November of 1916. The poet Witter Bynner expressed their feeling as follows:

> They pitied us, they thought us disappointed.
> Companions of their stocks and bonds, they turned
> And were at ease again. . . . For us, dark-urned
> In those first tidings lay our best-anointed,
> Our destiny, our star. We tried disjointed
> Efforts at pleasantry; but we had learned
> That in our gates the torch no longer burned,
> No vision gleamed there and no freedom pointed.
>
> The morning-sun arose, the evening star;
> America renewed her light all day
> And stood serene at evening, and from far
> Freedom was visible with lifted ray. . . .
> Wilson!—humanity once more is true—
> The light that shone on Lincoln shines on you.[150]

[148] W. W. to O. R. Holcomb, November 20, 1916, Wilson Papers.

[149] W. W. to J. A. H. Hopkins, November 16, 1916, *ibid*. See also W. W. to N. D. Baker, November 22, 1916, N. D. Baker Papers, saying: "My present feeling is that it is extremely desirable that we should make practically all our important appointments in the immediate future out of the great West which has just been added to the Democratic ranks."

[150] W. Bynner, "Wilson," St. Louis *Reedy's Mirror*, xxv (November 17, 1916), 721.

W CHAPTER V W

The Decision for Independent Mediation

THREE weeks before Wilson's dramatic re-election, Ambassador von Bernstorff wrote to Colonel House enclosing the following note from the German Foreign Office addressed to Ambassador Gerard:

"Your Excellency hinted to His Majesty in your last conversation at Charleville in April that President Wilson possibly would try towards the end of the summer to offer his good services to the belligerents for the promotion of peace.

"The German Government has no information as to whether the President adheres to this idea and as to the eventual date at which this step would take place. Meanwhile the constellation of war has taken such a form that the German Government foresees the time at which it will be forced to regain the freedom of action that it has reserved to itself in the note of May 4th last [the *Sussex* note] and thus the President's steps may be jeopardized. The German Government thinks it its duty to communicate this fact to your Excellency in case you should find that the date of the intended action of the President should be far advanced towards the end of this year."[1]

This, along with the two *Arabic* notes and the *Sussex* note, was the most important communication that the Washington government had received from Berlin since the outbreak of the war. It signified a radical change in German foreign policy and led, as we will see, to even more important action by the President of the United States. Let us go back and review developments that brought the German government to this juncture.

Certain events in the summer of 1916 caused Bethmann and other civilian leaders in Berlin to doubt the wisdom of discouraging Wilson's mediatory efforts, as von Jagow had done, as we have seen, in instructions to Bernstorff on June 7. The most important was the continued agitation of the naval authorities for permission to conduct unrestricted submarine warfare, which, Bethmann knew, would

---

[1] Undated memorandum included in J. von Bernstorff to E. M. House, October 18, 1916, Wilson Papers.

surely lead to war with the United States. This agitation began again, ironically, because Admiral Henning von Holtzendorff, head of the German Admiralty, tried to find a form of submarine operations that would win the approval of both civilian and naval authorities. He suggested a plan in May to proclaim a regular blockade of the British Isles, using submarines to stop *all* commerce to Great Britain in cruiser-type operations. Bethmann vetoed this project on June 13 on the ground that neutral states might retaliate by stopping or limiting their trade with Germany.[2]

Holtzendorff then appealed to the High Seas Fleet and Navy Corps in Flanders to begin a vigorous cruiser-type submarine campaign against merchant shipping, to be accompanied by unrestricted operations against armed merchantmen. Admiral Reinhold Scheer, commander of the High Seas Fleet, and most other naval captains had completely lost confidence in the head of the Admiralty by this time because of his numerous concessions to the civilian branch. They wanted freedom to use submarines where and how they pleased; moreover, they feared that a cruiser war with submarines would prove sufficiently effective to assuage the popular demand for an all-out campaign. Scheer went so far as to blackmail Holtzendorff by asserting on June 21, in a telegram destined also for the eyes of the Emperor, William II, that the only alternative to an unlimited campaign was use of submarines in purely military operations against the British fleet.[3] Conversations with Bethmann, Admiral Georg A. von Müller, the Emperor's naval adviser, and others convinced Holtzendorff that the general military situation was too precarious to permit any risks of hostility with America and other neutral states.[4] He talked to von Müller and had an audience with the Emperor on June 30. Then the Admiralty chieftain replied to Scheer's telegram, saying that the Emperor would not permit unlimited submarine operations at this time, could not understand why Scheer refused to use submarines in a cruiser-type campaign, and had approved the Admiral's plan to employ submarines against the British fleet during the month of July.[5]

[2] A. Spindler, *La Guerre Sous-Marine*, III, 260-266.

[3] *ibid.*, pp. 266-269; R. Scheer to H. von Holtzendorff, June 21, 1916, printed in part in Alfred von Tirpitz, *Politische Dokumente von A. von Tirpitz* (2 vols.), II, 555; hereinafter cited as *Politische Dokumente*.

[4] Walter Görlitz (ed.), *Regierte der Kaiser? Kriegstagebücher, Auf-Zeichnungen und Briefs des Chefs des Marina-Kabinetts Admiral Georg Alexander von Müller, 1914-1918*, p. 190, entries for June 12-13, 1916; hereinafter cited as *Regierte der Kaiser.*

[5] *ibid.*, p. 197, entry for June 30, 1916; A. Spindler, *La Guerre Sous-Marine*, III, 269-273.

The Navy Corps came back in early August at General von Falkenhayn's prompting, requesting permission to sink all merchantmen without warning in the English Channel in order to halt the swollen flow of men and matériel to British armies. Holtzendorff discussed this proposal with the Emperor on August 2 and, at William's direction, with the Imperial Chancellor soon afterward. Bethmann was adamantly opposed. It was futile to hope, he said, that President Wilson would acquiesce, and another *Sussex* incident would lead straight to war with America. The German military situation was so perilous by mid-August that even Falkenhayn concurred when Holtzendorff vetoed the proposal on the ground that Germany could not risk a rupture with the United States.[6]

Bethmann had won these skirmishes easily, but the situation changed gravely when Falkenhayn and Holtzendorff united in a demand for all-out submarine operations on August 27, using as a pretext a recent incorrect report by the Wolff News Bureau that the British Admiralty had announced the arming of all British merchantmen. Holtzendorff rushed to Pless Castle in Silesia, Supreme Headquarters in the East, for another showdown with Bethmann, Falkenhayn, and the Emperor. He found the Imperial camp in great consternation and gloom, for news had come during the evening of August 27 that Rumania had declared war against Austria-Hungary. The following day brought news of a Rumanian declaration of war against Germany. The situation on the western front, where both British and French armies were attacking strongly on the Somme and the French were holding on doggedly to Verdun, was bad enough. Now it seemed that the southeastern part of the eastern front, already weakened by a strong Russian offensive in Galicia, was on the verge of collapse. The Emperor had a virtual breakdown. "That means the end of the war," he said upon receiving news of the Rumanian declaration of war against his ally. "Austria will have to conclude peace, and then we must consider peace in general."[7] The immediate result was the dismissal of Falkenhayn and the appointment on August 29 of Field Marshal Paul von Hindenburg, commander on the eastern front, as chief of the Army General Staff, accompanied by appointment of Hindenburg's alter ego, General Erich Ludendorff, to the new post of Quartermaster

[6] W. Görlitz (ed.), *Regierte der Kaiser*, pp. 210-211, entry for August 14, 1916; A. Spindler, *La Guerre Sous-Marine*, III, 273-276, particularly pp. 275-276, printing the Imperial orders that H. von Holtzendorff sent to the High Seas Fleet and Navy Corps, c. August 14, 1916.

[7] W. Görlitz (ed.), *Regierte der Kaiser*, p. 216, entry for August 27, 1916.

General. Ironically, in view of later developments, Bethmann had a large hand in the shift in command.

The immediate danger, from the Chancellor's point of view, was that the Emperor and his new military chieftains might yield to Holtzendorff's demand for an unlimited submarine campaign in the panic of the moment. There were preliminary discussions on August 29 and 30 in which Admiral von Müller (ominously, in Bethmann's eyes) supported Holtzendorff.[8] The important confrontation occurred on August 31 at a conference in Pless Castle attended by Bethmann, Hindenburg, Ludendorff, Secretary of the Treasury Karl Helfferich, Holtzendorff, Admiral Eduard von Capelle, Naval Secretary, Wild von Hohenborn, Prussian Minister of War, Jagow, and others. The Admiralty head led off by reviewing the general tonnage situation and concluding that an unrestricted submarine campaign would bring England to her knees before the end of 1916. He warned that delay, in view of the threats to Germany's allies, might mean *finis Germaniae*. Jagow replied that an unlimited submarine campaign also meant American belligerency and the hostility of most European neutrals. "Germany," he warned, "will in such case be looked upon as a mad dog against whom the hand of every man will be raised for the purpose of finally bringing about peace." Helfferich added some trenchant observations on the Admiralty's claims, saying that it was very doubtful whether even an effective U-boat war could force the British to sue for peace. It would be fatal, he went on, to underestimate the importance of American participation on the Allied side, "I see," he concluded, "nothing but catastrophe following the application of the U-boat weapon at this time." Admiral von Capelle countered with the assertion that Germany would lose the war unless she took up the submarine campaign boldly. An exchange between Holtzendorff and Helfferich then followed.

This was the point at which Bethmann intervened. Much depended, he said, on the High Command's estimate of the general military situation and outlook. There was no point in talking about a risky submarine venture until one knew whether Turkey and Austria-Hungary would collapse. A lively exchange over various aspects of the question ensued. Then Ludendorff and Hindenburg agreed that the future was too dark to permit any gambles. The danger from a

[8] *ibid.*, p. 217, entries for August 29 and 30, 1916.

break with Holland and Denmark, they said, was simply too great. There was general agreement at the end to postpone decision until the Rumanian situation was clarified.[9]

These discussions and events during the last week of August convinced Bethmann that Germany had no choice but to seek peace, immediately and urgently, through President Wilson's mediation. He was of such a mind even before Rumania's entry into the war. "Our situation is such," he told von Müller on August 25, "that we must make peace as soon as possible. To be sure, we still stand as victors in general. We have to strive for the status quo while protecting our opportunities for development, yes—do not be shocked—even adjustment of the borders with France in the sense of cessions in French Lorraine and upper Alsace in exchange for part of the Briey territory."[10] Bethmann was in an even more desperate mood when he talked to Helfferich and Jagow on August 31. "He said," Helfferich writes in his memoirs, "that we would have to do anything in order to make peace. The only way that he still saw open was through Wilson, and this way would have to be taken, however uncertain the prospects. Only Wilson had the strong position with our enemies which was necessary for an effective peace move. We would have to tell Wilson that we are prepared to restore Belgium on the condition that our relations with Belgium should be set in order by direct negotiations after her restitution." Helfferich observed that Wilson was anti-German and thought the best way out was a separate peace with Russia, even at Austria-Hungary's expense. "The Chancellor, however, believed that there was no longer any hope in this direction. All such attempts had been shattered, even the attempt to get Turkish agreement on the Straits question."[11]

Bethmann, as soon as he had returned to Berlin, went to the Foreign Office and wrote out a personal message to Bernstorff. It briefly reviewed the general military situation and then asked whether the Ambassador thought that Wilson's mediation would be possible and successful if Germany promised to restore Belgium under certain conditions. "Otherwise," the note concluded, "all-out submarine warfare is hardly avoidable." Bethmann then changed this sentence to read:

[9] "Conference with regard to the adoption of the unrestricted U-boat war," *Official German Documents*, II, 1154-1163; A. Spindler, *La Guerre Sous-Marine*, III, 278-285.
[10] W. Görlitz (ed.), *Regierte der Kaiser*, p. 215, entry for August 25, 1916.
[11] K. Helfferich, *Der Weltkrieg* (2 vols.), II, 351-352.

"Otherwise all-out submarine warfare would have to be seriously considered."[12]

Bernstorff had already had a long talk with Colonel House[13] by the time that he received this inquiry. He had also informed the Foreign Office that Wilson could not and would not move for peace while the presidential campaign was in progress, would take steps if he was re-elected, and thought that a draw in Europe would best serve American interests.[14] Thus Bernstorff reported again on September 8, saying that his preceding telegram had answered Bethmann's question. But he added that America was interested mainly in the restoration of Belgium, that American mediation before the end of the year was likely if Wilson was re-elected, and that unrestricted submarine warfare would prolong the war on account of American belligerency.[15]

Bernstorff's telegrams, as well as something that Gerard said at this time, made it clear to Bethmann that Wilson would not move without some prodding. Thus he drafted new instructions to Bernstorff on September 23, after talking with Holtzendorff, and sent them to Pless for the Emperor's approval. This note said that the war was a stalemate and Germany desired peace for many reasons. Naval authorities, it went on, promised to achieve a decision by unrestricted submarine warfare, but there was another way out—a peace appeal by President Wilson. It would have to avoid territorial terms, as these would be the object of peace negotiations. Wilson had to move quickly; otherwise the German government would be compelled to "reach different decisions." It would be too late if the President postponed action until after the presidential election. A peace move in Washington would receive a warm reception in Berlin and guarantee Wilson's re-election.[16]

[12] T. von Bethmann Hollweg to J. von Bernstorff, September 2, 1916, K. E. Birnbaum, *Peace Moves and U-Boat Warfare*, p. 129; J. von Bernstorff, *My Three Years in America*, p. 287. The translation in *Official German Documents*, II, 983, is egregiously incorrect.

[13] On September 3. See the House Diary, September 3, 1916.

[14] Ambassador von Bernstorff to the Foreign Office, Telegram No. 100, September 6, 1916, J. von Bernstorff, *My Three Years in America*, pp. 285-286. "I doubted," House told the Ambassador, "whether this country could live on amicable terms with either the Central Powers or the Entente should one or the other become entirely triumphant. He shared this opinion." House Diary, September 3, 1916.

[15] Ambassador von Bernstorff to the Foreign Office, Telegram No. 101, September 8, 1916, J. von Bernstorff, *My Three Years in America*, pp. 287-288.

[16] Bethmann's draft instructions are printed in German in K. E. Birnbaum, *Peace Moves and U-Boat Warfare*, pp. 355-358.

The Emperor read the proposed dispatch with mounting irritation. His *Reichskanzler* had given the impression that Germany was supplicating desperately. He had been too vague about the probability of an all-out submarine campaign. Worst of all, he had not made it clear what the Germans wanted Wilson's mediation to do. As William wrote at the conclusion of Bethmann's draft, "The mediation must seek to achieve an armistice of limited duration—short as possible—in the course of which a preliminary peace would be agreed on. Without a conference—that is to say, without the neutrals—only between the belligerents alone." The Emperor redrafted the instructions so as to leave no doubt on these vital points.[17] He also discussed the note with Hindenburg and Ludendorff, and the latter revised the Emperor's draft.[18] It was Ludendorff's redraft that was returned with Hindenburg's and William's endorsement to the Foreign Office and sent, perforce (with a few minor changes and a new last paragraph), to Bernstorff on September 26. It follows:

"The enemy's intention of breaking through our fronts has not, so far, succeeded, and will not succeed, any more than his Salonika and Dobrudja offensives. On the other hand, the operations of the Central Powers against Rumania are making encouraging progress. Whether we shall succeed this year in gaining a victory there that will bring the war to an end is still doubtful; therefore, for the present we must be prepared for a further prolongation of the war. Meanwhile, the Imperial navy is confident that by the unrestricted employment of large numbers of submarines they could, in view of England's economic position, meet with a success which within a few months would make our principal enemy, England, more disposed to entertain thoughts of peace. It is therefore essential that G.H.Q. should include a submarine campaign among their other measures to relieve the situation on the Somme Front, by impeding the transport of munitions, and so making clear to the Entente the futility of their efforts in this area.

"The whole situation would change if President Wilson, following the plans he has already indicated, was to make an offer of mediation to the Powers. This would necessarily have to be done without definite proposals of a territorial nature, as these questions should

[17] The Emperor's draft is printed in *ibid*. For his comment, quoted above, see *ibid*., p. 157. The translation is mine.

[18] The note was apparently widely discussed in the Emperor's entourage. See W. Görlitz (ed.), *Regierte der Kaiser*, p. 223, entry for September 25, 1916.

form part of the agenda of the peace negotiations. Such a move, how-ever, would have to be made soon, as otherwise we could not continue to stand calmly aside and watch England, realizing as she does the many difficulties to be reckoned with, exert with impunity increas-ingly strong pressure on the neutrals, with a view to improving her military and economic position at our expense, and we should have to claim the renewed liberty of action which we reserved for our-selves in the Note of the 4th of May of this year. Should Mr. Wilson insist on waiting until immediately before or after the election, he would lose the opportunity for such a step. Also the negotiations should not at first aim at the conclusion of an armistice, but should be carried on solely by the belligerents themselves, and within a short period directly bring about the preliminary peace. A further pro-longation would be unfavorable to Germany's military situation, and would result in further preparations by the Powers to continue the war into next year, so that there would be no further prospect of peace within a reasonable time.

"Your Excellency should discuss the matter cautiously with Colonel House and find out Mr. Wilson's intentions. A peace move on the part of the President which gave the appearance of being spontaneous would be seriously considered by us, and this would also probably have some effect on the result of Mr. Wilson's campaign for election. Gerard has asked for leave as the result of a personal letter from House but has received no answer from the State Department."[19]

Bernstorff, after receiving these instructions, saw House on October 3 and cautiously broached the subject of Wilson's possible mediation—so cautiously, in fact, that House interpreted his inquiry as being merely routine.[20] The Ambassador at once advised the Foreign Office that the President could move only if re-elected.[21]

The Emperor had meanwhile—on the same day that he redrafted the note to Bernstorff—personally written the memorandum to Am-bassador Gerard quoted at the beginning of this chapter. He did this, he said, because the Foreign Office's English was impossible ("das

[19] The Imperial Chancellor to Ambassador von Bernstorff, September 26, 1916, "For Your Excellency's personal information," *Official German Documents*, II, 984-986, and J. von Bernstorff, *My Three Years in America*, pp. 288-290. I have altered the translation slightly.

[20] House Diary, October 3, 1916.

[21] Ambassador von Bernstorff to the Foreign Office, Telegram No. 121, October 5, 1916, *Official German Documents*, II, 986.

Englisch der Wstrasse unmöglich ist").[22] Gerard was returning home for vacation,[23] and William had hit upon the idea of sending this message, which rather obviously threatened an unrestricted submarine campaign if Wilson did not move for peace, by the Ambassador in order to apply direct pressure on the President. That, precisely, was what Bethmann was most eager to avoid. He seized upon Gerard's announcement that he was going only to Copenhagen as an excuse for not giving the message to the Ambassador. Then, when Gerard said that he was going on to America, the Chancellor informed the Emperor that he would send the memorandum to Bernstorff with the request that he give it to Gerard. Gerard, Bethmann went on, was utterly untrustworthy and would strongly underscore the threat of U-boat warfare in handing the message to the President. It would be better to let Bernstorff transmit the message in the light of instructions sent to him on September 26.[24] The Emperor thought that Bethmann was being excessively cautious, but this is the way it was eventually done.

Bethmann waited, however, until he had received Bernstorff Telegram No. 121 of October 5. He then dispatched the memorandum on the following day, October 9, along with the following covering instructions:

"His Majesty the Emperor desires that the enclosed *aide mémoire* should be handed to Ambassador Gerard upon his arrival.

"Your Excellency should do this in strict confidence and say that the *mémoire* is not to be understood as constituting a threat of submarine warfare. I should desire, however, that the Ambassador, before his interview with the President, should be reminded of the hopes that we placed in Wilson in the spring, and that reference should be made to the increasing ruthlessness with which our enemies are conducting the war. I take it for granted that Gerard will consider my *mémoire* as strictly confidential and not publish it.

"Should Your Excellency, however, consider the delivery of the *mémoire* too risky, I ask you to refrain from delivering it.

[22] K. E. Birnbaum, *Peace Moves and U-Boat Warfare,* p. 159.

[23] The German Foreign Office had done everything that it could to speed his departure. See Foreign Office to Ambassador von Bernstorff, August 20, 1916, "Bernstorff Wireless Despatches," and E. M. House to W. W., September 3, 1916, Wilson Papers.

[24] T. von Bethmann Hollweg to William II, September 30, 1916, printed in K. E. Birnbaum, *Peace Moves and U-Boat Warfare,* pp. 160-161.

"For Your Excellency's strictly confidential information:

"1. This *mémoire* was personally written by His Majesty.

"2. Unrestricted submarine warfare will not be carried on for the present."[25]

Bethmann followed this a few days later with an even more urgent message, asking Bernstorff to appeal to Wilson to intervene to stop the European slaughter. "If he cannot make up his mind to act alone," the dispatch continued, "he should get into communication with [the] Pope, King of Spain and European neutrals. Such joint action, since it cannot be rejected by Entente, would insure him re-election and historical fame."[26]

Meanwhile, Gerard had given such an indiscreet interview to the reporter Herbert Bayard Swope even before landing at New York[27] that Bernstorff decided to send the memorandum only to House. This he did on October 18, taking care to add in his covering letter: "Of course the memorandum is strictly confidential and is not intended as a threat with more drastic U-boat warfare on our part. In view, however, of the methods of our enemies, which become more ruthless every day—Greece, blockade, illegal pressure on neutrals—my Government wishes to remind Mr. Gerard of the confidential negotiations which were carried on last spring." He would leave it up to House, Bernstorff concluded, to decide whether to show the memorandum to Gerard.[28]

House showed the memorandum to Gerard on October 20.[29] On that same day he sent Bernstorff's letter and the memorandum to Wilson with the following comment: "The German memorandum is clearly a threat, their idea being to force you before election to act, knowing if you are defeated nothing can be done by anyone for many months to come. They do not want to take the chance."[30] Gerard

[25] The Imperial Chancellor to Ambassador von Bernstorff, October 9, 1916, *Official German Documents*, II, 986-987; J. von Bernstorff, *My Three Years in America*, pp. 293-294.

[26] T. von Bethmann Hollweg to Ambassador von Bernstorff, October 14, 1916, *ibid.*, p. 298.

[27] Gerard told Swope on October 9 that he was not bringing any peace message to the President and that he would tell Wilson that Germany would launch unrestricted submarine warfare soon after the American election unless the unexpected happened and peace intervened. This was blazoned in the American press, e. g., the New York *World*, October 10, 1916.

[28] J. von Bernstorff to E. M. House, October 18, 1916, Wilson Papers.

[29] House Diary, October 20, 1916.

[30] E. M. House to W. W., October 20, 1916, Wilson Papers.

saw Wilson at "Shadow Lawn" on October 24. He presumably told the President what he had told Swope, and perhaps even more. Wilson did not swerve from his resolution to make no peace move until his re-election. But he had obviously been greatly excited by the German memorandum and was beginning to think very seriously about future action should the American people invest him with their sovereignty for another four years.[31]

It had become evident to Wilson, long before House sent the German memorandum, that the British and French feared an American peace move as strongly as they resented its implication of the right to interfere. Irwin Laughlin, Counselor of the American Embassy in London, after talking with Lord Hardinge at the Foreign Office on August 27, informed Page that Hardinge had said that the British government would "snub" Wilson if he supported an anticipated German *démarche*.[32] Page conveyed the warning, in diluted form, to be sure, to Wilson during their conference at "Shadow Lawn" on September 22.[33]

Ambassador Spring Rice told Chandler Anderson in Washington on September 15 that the British government had information indicating that the President was about to propose an armistice, preliminary to a peace conference, and that the London authorities would never agree to cooperate. Anderson suggested that the simplest way to forestall presidential action would be to have a member of the government make a public statement of the official British attitude. Spring Rice said that he would cable such a recommendation to London.[34]

"There have been reports," Sidney Brooks wrote to Colonel House from London on the same day, "that Mr. Wilson was meditating an offer of mediation. I can't believe he is contemplating anything so hopeless & so inopportune. The mere suggestion of it would make our people wild with fury."[35] A member of the British government wrote on September 17, "It seems possible that, if the Allied offensive can be maintained on its present scale for another six weeks, an armistice will be proposed. President Wilson, whose recent action shows how deeply he is obsessed by electioneering ambition, will be quite

[31] J. W. Gerard, *My Four Years in Germany*, pp. 349-350.
[32] I. Laughlin to W. H. Page, August 30, 1916, Page Papers.
[33] B. J. Hendrick, *The Life and Letters of Walter H. Page*, II, 186.
[34] Anderson Diary, September 15, 1916.
[35] S. Brooks to E. M. House, September 15, 1916. House Papers.

ready to make such an offer, even though he anticipates a refusal, provided his party can profit thereby."[36]

Fears came sharply to a head in London after receipt of the cablegram that Spring Rice sent following his conversation with Chandler Anderson. The Ambassador warned that Wilson's hand had been forced by the Irish Americans and German Americans, and that he would soon make a peace move unless someone in high authority in London headed him off.[37] Lloyd George (now War Minister), without consulting the Prime Minister or Foreign Secretary, called in the American reporter, Roy W. Howard, on September 28 to do some plain talking to the American public and President. England, the War Minister said, would view any peace move by the United States, the Vatican, or any neutral as pro-German. There was a general suspicion in Great Britain that President Wilson might "butt in" and try to stop the war. "The fight must be to the finish—to a knockout." The whole world, Lloyd George went on, "including neutrals of the highest purposes and humanitarians with the best motives, must know that there can be no outside interference at this stage. Britain asked no intervention when she was not prepared to fight. She will tolerate none now that she is prepared until Prussian military despotism is broken beyond repair." The war had to go on until Germany was completely beaten. "Peace now or at any time before the final and complete elimination of this menace is unthinkable."[38] This was soon popularly interpreted as the policy of the knock-out blow.

It drew from Grey one of the sharpest letters that he ever penned. The warning to Wilson, he wrote to Lloyd George on September 29, had been unnecessary, would turn the President and Americans generally toward the German side, and had forever closed the door on Wilson's mediation, which the Allies might desperately need some day. "I may be wrong in my view," he concluded, "but a public warning to the President of the United States is an important step, and I wish I had had an opportunity of putting these considerations before you and discussing them with you."[39]

[36] C & B, memorandum dated September 17, 1916, in *Printed for the Committee of Imperial Defence. October 1916. SECRET. CONDITIONS OF AN ARMISTICE,* copy in the Asquith Papers.

[37] It was Telegram No. 2943, partially summarized in D. Lloyd George, *War Memoirs* (2 vols.), I, 511-512.

[38] *New York Times,* September 29, 1916. Premier Aristide Briand of France had said much the same thing in an impassioned speech in the Chamber of Deputies on September 19. *ibid.,* September 20, 1916.

[39] Grey of Fallodon to D. Lloyd George, September 29, 1916, D. Lloyd George, *War Memoirs,* I, 511.

Lloyd George's interview also prompted the Prime Minister to ask the members of the War Committee of the Cabinet to express their views on possibilities of a peace settlement. The request drew some interesting replies. Balfour submitted a long, detailed exposition of moderate British terms and objectives.[40] Lord Lansdowne, Minister without Portfolio, argued that the war was a stalemate, its prolongation could only bleed Europe cruelly to no purpose, and the British government should be prepared to meet President Wilson and even the Germans half way. Lansdowne continued: "The interview given by the Secretary of State for War in September to an American correspondent has produced an impression which it will not be easy to efface. There may have been circumstances of which I am unaware, connected, perhaps with the Presidential election, which made it necessary to announce that at the particular moment any intervention, however well meant, would be distasteful to us or inopportune. . . . Surely it cannot be our intention, no matter how long the war lasts, no matter what the strain on our resources, to maintain this attitude. . . ."[41]

General Sir William R. Robertson, Chief of the Imperial General Staff, retorted that of course the Allies could deliver the knock-out blow, and that "As for ourselves, there are amongst us, as in all communities, a certain number of cranks, cowards, and philosophers, some of whom are afraid of their own skins being hurt, whilst others are capable of proving to those sufficiently weak-minded to listen to them that we stand to gain more by losing the war than by winning it."[42]

The two chief figures at the Foreign Office had the final word. Lord Robert Cecil, warning that a peace settlement made at the present time would be disastrous, concluded that the Allies had no choice but to fight on for another year in the hope that the Central Powers would collapse. Lord Grey observed that it all depended on what the military and naval authorities said about the general outlook, particularly about the submarine menace. If the Allies had good

[40] A. J. Balfour, memorandum dated October 4, 1916, *Printed for the use of the Cabinet. October 1916. CONFIDENTIAL. THE PEACE SETTLEMENT IN EUROPE*, copy in the Papers of Austen Chamberlain, University of Birmingham Library; hereinafter cited as the Chamberlain Papers.

[41] The Marquis of Lansdowne, memorandum dated November 13, 1916. *Printed for the use of the Cabinet. November 1916. CONFIDENTIAL*, copy in *ibid.*

[42] W. R. Robertson, printed memorandum dated November 24, 1916, copy in *ibid.* This evoked from Lansdowne the observation that Robertson's paper was surely not a very helpful contribution to the discussion. Lord Lansdowne, memorandum dated November 27, 1916, *Printed for the use of the Cabinet. November 1916*, copy in *ibid.*

chances of winning, then the war should proceed. If military authorities believed that Allied fortunes would not improve in 1917, then it would be better to end the war now on the best terms available. "If the time arrived when either the military or the naval authorities considered the chances to be that the situation would change in the course of the next few months to the disadvantage of the Allies and would progressively deteriorate, then it would be incumbent on the Governments of the Allies to wind up the war at once on the best terms obtainable, presumably through the medium of not unsympathetic mediation; and, if they did not do so, they would be responsible for future disaster to their countries."[43]

There were, obviously, cracks in the hitherto solid British wall. And what if Wilson set out to force the Allies to the peace table? How far could the British government go in resisting him? And how long could the London government continue returning negative or partially unresponsive answers to American protests? These two questions were really components of the larger question that the Foreign Office put to an interdepartmental committee on about September 30, 1916: How far is Great Britain dependent commercially and financially upon the United States, and to what extent can Britain meet American commercial and other retaliation? Upon the answer to this question would depend the British—and Allied—response to a Wilsonian peace call.

The data had been assembled by mid-October. The Ministry of Munitions reported on October 11 that its recent efforts to expand home production of armament and munitions had made the United Kingdom largely self-sustaining in small arms. However, Britain still depended upon the United States for a large proportion of howitzers, shells, and shell components,[44] and it was more or less totally dependent upon American suppliers for the metal raw materials essential to the manufacture of munitions[45] and explosives like Acetone, nitrocellulose powder, and T.N.T. The War Office warned that it

[43] R. Cecil, memorandum dated November 27, 1916, *Printed for the use of the Cabinet. November 1916*, copy in *ibid.*; Grey of Fallodon, memorandum dated November 27, 1916, *Printed for the use of the Cabinet and War Committee. November 1916*, copy in *ibid.*

[44] e. g., for 50 per cent of 9.2-inch howitzers, 20 per cent of 8-inch howitzers, 30 per cent of 15-inch, 12-inch, 9.2-inch, 8-inch, and 6-inch shells, 30 per cent of fuses, and 25 per cent of 12-inch shell forgings.

[45] e. g., British munitions plants received 66 per cent of their aluminum and 75 per cent of their copper from America in 1916.

Wilson and His Cabinet in 1916
From left to right, front row: W. C. Redfield, R. Lansing, D. F. Houston, the President, W. G. McAdoo, A. S. Burleson; back row: J. Daniels, W. B. Wilson, N. D. Baker, T. W. Gregory, F. K. Lane

Wilson Accepts the Democratic Presidential Nomination at "Shadow Lawn"

Charles Evans Hughes on the Campaign Trail in 1916

The President Signs the Jones Bill for Philippine Self-Government, August 29, 1916

William II with the New Military Masters of Germany
From left to right: P. von Hindenburg, William II, Erich von Ludendorff

A Prince of Diplomatic Bunglers
Arthur Zimmermann

The President and Mrs. Wilson after the Second Inaugural

William J. Stone

Robert M. La Follette

James K. Vardaman

George W. Norris

FOUR "WILLFUL MEN"

Brown Brothers

Wilson Reading His War Message to Congress

could not meet its requirements without American cotton, lubricating oils, and leather. The Board of Trade was even more emphatic: "To sum up, it is quite evident that any failure to obtain imports from the United States would at once affect this country irremediably from the point of view of our food supplies, of military necessities, and of raw materials for industry. For numerous articles important from one or other of these points of view, America is an absolutely irreplaceable source of supply."[46]

J. M. Keynes, speaking for the Treasury on October 10, returned the gloomiest report of all. The British Treasury, he said, now derived two fifths of its funds for prosecution of the war from North America. The Treasury had raised three fifths of its money in the United States during recent months by the sale of gold and securities, two fifths by loans. However, British gold and dollar resources were diminishing at a fearful rate, and the Treasury would soon have to raise four fifths of its money in the United States by unsecured public loans. Keynes went on:

"A statement from the United States Executive deprecating or disapproving of such loans would render their flotation in sufficient volume a practical impossibility, and thus lead to a situation of the utmost gravity.

"It is not necessary, however, that matters should go so far as an overt act of the executive, in order that the financial arrangements of the Allies should be prejudiced. Any feeling of irritation or lack of sympathy with this country or with its policy in the minds of the American public (and equally any lack of confidence in the military situation as interpreted by this public) would render it exceedingly difficult, if not impossible, to carry through financial operations on a scale adequate to our needs. The sums which this country will require to borrow in the U.S.A. in the next six or nine months are so enormous, amounting to several times the entire national debt of that country, that it will be necessary to appeal to every class and section of the investing public.

"It is hardly an exaggeration to say that in a few months' time the American executive and the American public will be in a position

[46] "The satisfactory element in the consideration," this report continued, "is that, if America is necessary to us, we are also of immense advantage to America, and it appears almost inconceivable that, unless diplomatic relations become strained to breaking point, she would be so foolish as to imperil her hold on this most valuable market for her goods."

to dictate to this country on matters that affect us more nearly than them.

"It is, therefore, the view of the Treasury, having regard to their special responsibilities, that the policy of this country towards the U.S.A. should be so directed as not only to avoid any form of reprisal or active irritation, but also to conciliate and to please."[47]

The interdepartmental committee concluded in view of all these reports that the United Kingdom was at present and would continue to be "dependent upon the United States for a large proportion of the supplies essential to the conduct of the war" and even more dependent upon American financial resources. "It is obvious, therefore," the committee concluded, "that in any negotiations with the United States our present position is extremely weak, and must continue to be so unless, and except in so far as, our dependence upon the United States for supplies can be reduced in every way compatible with the efficient conduct of the war."[48]

This evoked from Grey, on October 20, the following analysis of Anglo-American relations:

1. The enclosed record of the views arrived at by the Interdepartmental Committee appointed to consider the dependence of the British Empire on the United States raises certain questions on which it is right that the Foreign Office should express an opinion.

2. We have certain controversies with the United States, notably regarding the censorship of mails, on which we cannot yield to the United States Government. We have also imposed certain far-reaching restrictions on American trade, and especially on the importation into the United States of raw materials from British sources, which, although not the subject of any immediate controversy except on points of pure detail, are so vital to the maintenance of the blockade that it is of the first importance that they should not be disturbed.

3. The Foreign Office believes that we do not need to yield on any of these points so far as our relations with the United States *Government* are concerned, since the latter do not wish to proceed to extremes, and their only weapons against us are too big for them to use. Even the imposition of embargoes on certain classes of goods, our demand for which threatens to inconvenience important interests in the United States, and might

[47] These memoranda are printed in *Secret. Printed for the use of the War Committee of the Cabinet. November 1916*, copy in the Asquith Papers.

[48] "Considered Views of Interdepartmental Committee to consider Dependence of the British Empire on the United States," undated memorandum in *Printed for the use of the Cabinet. October 1916. CONFIDENTIAL*, copy in *ibid.*

therefore furnish a reasonable ground for prohibiting their export from the United States (for instance, wheat and steel), would raise the whole question of commercial relations between the United States and this country. The United States is so dependent upon the British Empire, both as a market for American goods, on which, in present conditions, American prosperity depends, and also as a source of raw materials indispensable to American industries, that it would be, to say the least of it, highly inexpedient for any Government at Washington to raise that question.

4. Consequently, our real danger is irritation of American opinion operating against our loans. This is not a question of our relations with the Government of the United States, but of the feeling of American financial and business interests and of the whole lending public towards us. Irritation in these circles is especially liable to be produced by our censorship and our black list, and above all by apprehensions as to our economic policy after the war. It is true that the more this country borrows from the United States, the more does the latter become our partner in the war, and the less likely is it that Americans will do anything to compromise our success; but, on the other hand, as a purely commercial calculation, Americans might well estimate that speedy peace would offer better security for the money they have already invested, than a prolonged war conducted on further American loans.

5. In these circumstances, the Foreign Office makes the following recommendations:—

(1.) No concession should be made to the Government of the United States on any matter of principle. We can, and must, maintain our belligerent measures. If the situation should change for the worse, we might conceivably have to reconsider this position, but at present the best way to prevent such a danger arising is to show a bold front.

(2.) At the same time, the greatest possible consideration, compatible with solid military requirements, should be given to American interests individually in such matters as—
   (a.) The censorship, and especially the cable censorship;
   (b.) The black list;
   (c.) Our coal policy;
   (d.) The operation of our trade agreements and guarantees in the United States.

Any standard form of communication that any Department may have for replying to enquiries, such as enquiries relating to missing cables, should be revised where necessary in the direction of greater civility. It is probable that not very much can be done in this direction, but the Foreign Office will closely examine its own procedure, and would be glad if other Departments could do the same.

(3.) A very early decision should be taken on the extent to which we contemplate applying the principles of the Paris Economic Conference, other principles on which we have acted during the war, against the United States, at least as far as is necessary to make it possible to give satisfactory assurances, not indeed to the United States Government, but to American business interests."[49]

The ink was scarcely dry on this document before new reports came describing the desperate Allied financial situation more clearly and shockingly than Keynes had earlier done. One was a report of the British members of a Joint Anglo-French Financial Committee which had met with Henry P. Davison, J. Pierpont Morgan, Jr., and other members of the House of Morgan from October 3 to October 10. The French delegates, the document said, had reported that their government's gold and dollar resources were totally exhausted, and that France would need £40,000,000 to £50,000,000, in addition to money already promised by the British Treasury, in order to meet her dollar payments to the United States during the next six months. Expenditures in America, they said, were showing "une augmentation constante et sensible," filling "Monsieur Ribot with sentiments of the gravest despondency and alarm."

It was almost impossible, the British delegates had replied, for Britain to help. The British Treasury had spent $1,038,000,000 in America from May to September 1916. This outlay had been met three fifths by sale of gold and securities, two fifths by loans. British expenditures in America, not allowing for any new outlays, would run to a total of $1,500,000,000 during the six months from October 1916 to March 1917. British-owned American securities (which had yielded $300,000,000 in the last five months) were virtually exhausted. The British Treasury had built up a secret gold reserve of £100,000,000. Perhaps half, or $250,000,000, could be spent during the next six months. Thus $1,250,000,000, or five sixths of British expenditures in the United States, would have to be raised by unsecured American loans during the next half year, as compared to $400,000,000 during the past five months. Perhaps Canada could furnish $100,000,000. If

[49] Grey of Fallodon, memorandum dated October 20, 1916, in *ibid*. Grey was referring in the last paragraph to the so-called Paris Economic Conference of April 1916. This conference of Allied governments had adopted certain provisions for Allied economic cooperation, particularly against Germany, in the postwar era. For comment on the fears that it had raised in the United States, see Lord E. Percy, "Memorandum respecting Commercial Relations with the United States after the War," dated October 21, 1916, printed in *ibid*.

so, $1,150,000,000 would remain to be raised by American loans. The members of the Joint Committee had asked Morgan and Davison whether American banks could supply $1,500,000,000 by March 31, 1917. "They did not conceal their dismay." Morgan said that he did not see any way to answer that "awful question." Perhaps it would be possible to meet the crisis by temporary bank overdrafts and short-term credits. They both thought that it was too risky to try to float a large unsecured public loan in the United States.

The main problem, the British delegates advised, was the pace of the borrowing necessary. Their report continued:

"14. We considered the suggestion that the industrial and financial world of America is now so deeply committed to the Allied cause, that it cannot afford to let us fall into difficulties. There is force in this contention. But it must not be pushed too far. We believe that this factor will enable us to obtain *some* supplies, and will prevent us from being left entirely and absolutely without resources, even when we cannot find means of immediate payment. But if pushed beyond this point it is fraught with the gravest danger. We cannot expect that these influences will induce the United States to finance anything approaching the total requirements of ourselves and our Allies.

"Our financial requirements have got far beyond any total which can be met by the great capitalist interests, whose liquid resources are much less than in this country, and who are not all of them good friends of ours. We have to look beyond these interests to the great investing public, not only on the Atlantic seaboard, but in the Middle and Far Western States, where the European War is a distant and un-realised adventure. Those upon whose money we must depend are not only or even chiefly the same as those with whom we place our orders. The New York capitalists can provide only a fraction of what we require. The problem is whether the general public can be induced to subscribe to our loans at a *pace* equal to our expenditure. To raise the interest payable would not serve us, as such action, by provoking suspicion of our credit, might diminish the proceeds of our loans and could not materially increase them. . . .

"16. In short, desperate expedients may always keep us supplied with *some* resources. But they certainly will not yield to us or our Allies all we want.

"Without venturing to prophesy the exact term for which we can hope to meet the present rate of expenditure, we believe that the problem of how long our immediately available resources will hold out, and consequently of how they can be utilised most wisely, is now one of pressing, practical importance.

"The seriousness of the situation as it is now developing cannot be more vividly illustrated than by the statement that, out of the 5,000,000 £ which the Treasury have to find daily for the prosecution of the war, nearly 2,000,000 £ has to be found in America."[50]

Reginald McKenna, Chancellor of the Exchequer, submitted this report to the Cabinet on October 24 along with some dire warnings of his own. He had, he said, already spent £20,000,000 of the £100,000,000 secret gold reserve during the past fortnight as a consequence of a temporary break in the American exchange. At all times, he went on, the British government had been dependent upon American good will. "But up to now I have always been able, if necessary, to last out financially any temporary wave of adverse sentiment or unfriendly executive action. If the President had deprecated publicly the issue of loans to belligerents, I should have been disconcerted but not helpless, because of our considerable liquid resources in the form of gold and securities. I am still to some extent in this position. Our stock of American securities is much depleted, but our gold would enable us to last three months *if necessary* without a public issue in America. After the end of this year we shall never be in that position again. At the same time, the degree of our dependency makes a great deal of difference. We ought never to be so placed that only a public issue in America within a fortnight stands between us and insolvency. Yet we are quickly drifting in this direction. . . . If things go on as at present, I venture to say with certainty that by next June or earlier, the President of the American Republic will be in a position, if he wishes, to dictate his own terms to us."[51]

It seemed momentarily during the early weeks of November that an eruption of the German-American submarine controversy might prevent so much as contemplation of a peace move in Washington.

The decision of the Pless Conference, that Hindenburg and Ludendorff should decide when the time was ripe to reopen the question of all-out submarine warfare, only spurred naval leaders to intensify

[50] "EXTRACT FROM THE REPORT OF THE BRITISH MEMBERS OF THE JOINT ANGLO-FRENCH FINANCIAL COMMITTEE," memorandum dated October 18, 1916, in *Printed for the use of the Cabinet. October* [25] *1916. CONFIDENTIAL. OUR FINANCIAL POSITION IN AMERICA*, copy in the Asquith Papers.
[51] R. McKenna, memorandum dated October 24, 1916, in *ibid.*

their pressure on the Army High Command. Holtzendorff and the Chief of Staff of the High Seas Fleet, Captain Adolf von Trotha, appealed to Ludendorff in early September, although the Admiralty head was also willing and eager to use submarines in cruiser-type operations if he could not obtain permission for an all-out effort.[52] Ludendorff was unresponsive at first, but the smashing success of the German campaign against Rumania caused him and others to turn receptive ears to the U-boat champions in late October. Reports from Pless led Holtzendorff to believe that the Army High Command had approved launching an all-out submarine campaign around the middle of October, and he so informed Bethmann on October 1. The Imperial Chancellor dispatched an angry telegram to Hindenburg, saying that he could not believe that the military authorities would presume to make such an important decision, involving war with Holland and Denmark as well as with America, without the Emperor's and Chancellor's endorsement.[53] Richard von Kühlmann, who had just come from The Hague and was on his way to Turkey as German Ambassador, was in Pless at this very moment. He warned that Holland, with her 700,000-man militia, would surely declare war in retaliation against a declaration of unrestricted submarine warfare. This warning was apparently decisive with Hindenburg and Ludendorff.[54] The former replied to Bethmann on October 2 that he had discussed only the *possibility* of a new submarine move, and that in any event he would make his decision only in loyal cooperation with the Imperial Chancellor.[55]

The matter was settled, at least for the near future, when Holtzendorff, in audience with the Emperor during the evening of October 4, presented an order for an unlimited submarine campaign. William interrupted the Admiralty chieftain to say that the general situation was now running in Germany's favor and it would be foolish to divert the current with ruthless submarine warfare. It would, besides, wreck plans for a German peace offer. Holtzendorff, changing pace quickly, suggested, among other things, immediate inauguration of a submarine campaign against merchant shipping according to the rules

---

[52] K. E. Birnbaum, *Peace Moves and U-Boat Warfare*, pp. 170-173.

[53] T. von Bethmann Hollweg to Kurt von Grünau (representative of the Chancellor and Foreign Office at Supreme Headquarters), October 1, 1916, *Official German Documents*, II, 1168-1170.

[54] W. Görlitz (ed.), *Regierte der Kaiser*, p. 225, entry for October 1, 1916.

[55] K. von Grünau to T. von Bethmann Hollweg, two telegrams, October 2, 1916, *Official German Documents*, II, 1170-1171.

of cruiser warfare.[56] The Emperor approved, and Holtzendorff sent an Imperial Order to the High Seas Fleet and Navy Corps on October 6. It commanded them to begin a vigorous war against merchant shipping not later than October 15, observing scrupulously the rules of cruiser warfare even against armed ships and special care in dealing with American, Spanish, Swedish, and Danish ships.[57]

The new campaign, launched on schedule, soon proved devastatingly effective, much, apparently, to Admiral Scheer's chagrin. German submarines, raiders, and mines sank an average of about 350,000 tons a month from October 1916 through January 1917, in spite of the difficulties of operating during winter months. They had taken a toll of 185,800 tons in August 1915 and 191,600 tons in April 1916.[58] Submarine commanders tried hard to follow instructions, but there were borderline cases, and incidents involving Americans inevitably occurred. They in turn set off a new submarine scare in the United States.

News of the first incidents came to Washington on October 30 in a report from Wesley Frost, American Consul at Queenstown, Ireland. It told of the torpedoing without warning in heavy seas of the armed British steamer *Marina* on October 28, with the loss of six Americans among the crew; and of the apparently excessive shelling of another British freighter, *Rowanmore*.[59] Lansing wired at once to Chargé Grew in Berlin for information.[60] He also told reporters on November 1 that the President was particularly concerned about the *Marina* incident and determined to hold Germany strictly to the *Sussex* pledge. Newspapermen naturally concluded that a break in relations was possible.[61] There was a second potentially dangerous in-

---

[56] W. Görlitz (ed.), *Regierte der Kaiser*, p. 226, entry for October 4, 1916; A. Spindler, *La Guerre Sous-Marine*, III, 320-321.

[57] A. von Tirpitz, *Politische Dokumente*, II, 584. A supplementary Imperial Order of October 10 instructed submarine commanders to make provision for the safety of passengers and crews aboard armed ships even when such vessels had fired on a submarine after being warned. A new Imperial Order of October 17 amended the preceding order by permitting submarines to torpedo merchantmen (except passenger liners) at once when they opened fire after being warned. *ibid.*

[58] See the tables in R. H. Gibson and M. Prendergast, *The German Submarine War, 1914-1918*, pp. 380-381. A. Spindler, *La Guerre Sous-Marine*, III, 457-458, gives a total of 1,230,537 tons of neutral and belligerent shipping sunk by submarines and mines in all theaters from October 1, 1916, through January 31, 1917.

[59] *New York Times*, October 31 and November 1, 1916.

[60] The Secretary of State to Chargé Grew, October 30 and 31, 1916, *Foreign Relations, 1916, Supplement*, pp. 298-299.

[61] *New York Times*, November 2, 1916.

cident on November 6—the torpedoing without warning of the Penin-
sula and Oriental armed liner *Arabia* in the eastern Mediterranean,
with the loss, apparently, of about fifty-seven lives, none American.[62]
Lansing again wired for information, adding that the American government was unable "to square this disaster with the German assurance of May 4, 1916."[63]

Lansing, at least, was not averse to pressing the German government
hard on the *Marina* and *Arabia* cases, perhaps to the point of rupture
in relations if investigation proved that the ships had been destroyed
in violation of the *Sussex* pledge. Wilson, too, was profoundly disturbed, but he had no intention of being pushed into conflict. He did
not say so, but it seems altogether likely that he was extremely re-
luctant to make an issue over *armed* ships like the *Marina* and *Arabia*.
He also had deep doubts whether American public opinion would
sustain a strong policy. Colonel House mentioned the *Marina* case
in the conversation that he and Vance McCormick had with the President on November 2. "Just as we were leaving," House wrote in his
diary, "I told him I was glad the Marina incident had not come sooner
because a decision could now be deferred until after the election. . . .
His reply astonished both McCormick and me. He said: 'I do not
believe the American people would wish to go to war no matter
how many Americans were lost at sea.' He said he was sorry that this
was true, but nevertheless it was his opinion. He also stated it was a
merchantman and not a passenger ship, and that our understanding
with Germany was as to passenger boats. I was surprised at this and
argued the point for a moment, for our demand and Germany's
promise clearly covers all merchantmen and their crews."[64] Lansing
was much alarmed when House repeated this remark to him on the
following day.[65]

The most important cause of Wilson's reluctance to make an issue
over isolated sinkings was his deep desire to move for peace at the
earliest possible date. Colonel House went to the White House at
Wilson's request on November 14. "The President," House wrote in his
diary on that date, "desires to write a note to the belligerents, demand-

[62] Ambassador W. H. Page to the Secretary of State, November 7 and 14, 1916,
Foreign Relations, 1916, Supplement, pp. 308-309; *New York Times*, November 15,
1916.

[63] The Secretary of State to Chargé Grew, November 18, 1916, *Foreign Relations,
1916, Supplement*, p. 310.

[64] House Diary, November 2, 1916.

[65] *ibid.*, November 3, 1916.

ing that the war cease, and he desired my opinion. His argument is that, unless we do this now, we must inevitably drift into war with Germany upon the submarine issue. He believes Germany has already violated her promise of May 4, and that in order to maintain our position we must break off diplomatic relations. Before doing this he would like to make a move for peace, hoping there is sufficient peace sentiment in the Allied countries to make them consent." House observed that the Allies would regard a peace move as an unfriendly act and understand that Wilson was trying to avoid controversy with Germany. They then discussed the possibility of House's going to Europe and dismissed it on the ground that the time was too short. House advised Wilson to "sit tight and await further developments." Wilson replied that there was no time for delay. House went on:

"He wondered whether we could not have a separate understanding with the Allies by which we would agree to throw our weight in their favor in any peace settlement brought about by their consent to mediation.

"In reply to this I thought the Allies would begin by asking for our views as to peace terms, and we would soon get into a hopeless tangle. It would be easy as far as the evacuation of France and Belgium, but what would he say about Alsace and Lorraine? What would he say about Poland, Serbia, the Balkans, Constantinople, etc. etc.? It would be like sitting in a peace conference in advance to determine what the best terms should be.

"It was eleven o'clock before he proposed going to bed and I could see he was deeply disturbed."[66]

Wilson did not sleep much that night, and long thought produced new resolution to proceed in spite of obvious hazards. He revealed his mind to House in conversation the following morning. It is here reproduced for the first time as House recorded it:

"The President said we should never get anywhere in the discussion unless he wrote his views in concrete form, and he had made up his mind to write his message and then write a note to the belligerents. That after he had written it and made his points clear, we could go over it again and discuss it with more intelligence.

"I did not yield a point in my opinion that he would make a mistake if he finally sent it, nor did he yield in his argument that it might be effective. We dropped this subject, for the moment, and discussed his message to Congress. . . .

[66] *ibid.*, November 14, 1916.

"Before we parted for the morning, he suggested I see the German Ambassador, and I suggested that I also see Lansing and Polk. . . .

"This morning in discussing these matters with the President, he went so far as to say if the Allies wanted war with us we would not shrink from it. This was in reply to my contention that a proposal of peace would be accepted by Germany and refused by the Allies, and that Germany would then feel that she could begin an unrestricted U-boat warfare. This would lead him to try to break with Germany, but our people would not follow him for the reason that Germany having consented to peace parleys, would be thought more or less justified in employing unrestricted submarine warfare.

"I also told the President that in the event Germany did not do this, and did not violate international law further, we would inevitably drift into a sympathetic alliance with her, and if this came about, England and France might, under provocation, declare war against us. He thought they would not dare resort to this and if they did, they could do this country no serious hurt. I disagreed with him again. I thought Great Britain might conceivably destroy our fleet and land troops from Japan in sufficient numbers to hold certain parts of the United States. He replied they might get a good distance but would have to stop somewhere, to which I agreed.

"In repeating this conversation to Polk, he thought the probable stopping place would be the Gulf of Mexico. Polk thought I should talk to Lansing, so we went to the Secretary's office. He put off his other engagements in order that we might talk over this serious situation uninterruptedly.

"Lansing was as emphatic as Polk in believing that our people would resent such a policy. He thought the immediate result of the President's note demanding peace would be received favorably in this country, but when the real outcome began to be understood, a storm of indignation would be aroused against him.

"I suggested to Lansing that he 'soft pedal' on the U-boat activities and not press the President to action on the Marina, the Stephano, the P & O liner or any of the recent bad cases. I thought if this were done we could drift for awhile until we could get our bearings. We were unanimous in our belief that it would be stupendous folly to wage war against the Allies. If war must come, we thought it should be on their side and not against them. . . .

"When I reached the White House the President and I were met by Tumulty who told us he had been talking with Maurice Low, Washington correspondent for the London Post, and that Low had said he had reason to believe that peace proposals would not be badly received in either England or France. I regretted this, because the President immediately stiffened in his attitude and asked me to see Low. ... When the President and I walked away I insisted there was nothing in it and that Tumulty was mistaken. The President, however, was insistent that I should probe it to the bottom.

"There was no one at dinner except the family. After dinner the President and I talked until half past ten o'clock. I had told him that Lansing, Polk and others did not see any crisis in the U-boat controversy, and asked him to forget the entire matter for the present. This quieted him appreciably and put him in better spirits. He had been depressed. I believe, as a matter of fact, Lansing had been urging him to break off diplomatic relations with Germany, when he sent the telegram for me to come to Washington. I also have a notion, though not confirmed, that Tumulty is doing his best to persuade him to call a peace conference."[67]

House saw Bernstorff in New York on November 20. "I told the Ambassador," the Colonel recorded, "that we were on the ragged edge and brought to his mind the fact that no more notes could be exchanged: that the next move was to break diplomatic relations."[68] House also told Bernstorff that the President would move for peace at the first opportunity. As the Ambassador reported to the Foreign Office:

"Wilson of his own accord commissioned House to tell me in strict confidence that he is eager to take steps toward mediation as soon as possible, probably between now and the New Year. He makes it a condition, however, that until then mediation should be spoken and written of as little as possible, and, further, that we should conduct the submarine war in strictest conformity to our promises and not allow any fresh controversies to arise.

"Wilson's reasons for the above conditions are as follows: He believes that he can resort to mediation only if public opinion over here remains as favorable to us as it has been during the last few months. ... Any new submarine controversy would again arouse public feeling against us, whereas resentment against England will increase if this question can be eliminated. The British answer dealing with the black

[67] *ibid.*, November 15, 1916.
[68] "Memorandum by Colonel E. M. House . . . , November 20, 1916," *The Lansing Papers*, I, 573.

lists, together with the comments of the English press on Wilson's election, have put governmental circles on this side very much out of humor. But unfriendly glances are again and again cast in our direction as a result of the U-boat question. . . .

"If Your Excellency still desires Wilson to intervene it is necessary, in view of the above, to settle the *Marina* and *Arabia* incidents as soon as possible without further controversy. . . . I think that, with House's help, I can bury these two incidents without attracting much attention, as this is Wilson's own wish. As House stated, the reason why the President viewed this case as having such a tragic aspect was because, after the *Sussex* note, he could not possibly write another, and there is nothing left but to end diplomatic negotiations should it be impossible to settle the matter privately and confidentially with me."[69]

The arrival of this telegram in Berlin on November 25 found Bethmann in the midst of preparations for a peace *démarche* of his own and still eager for Wilson's peace move. He consequently was also eager to avoid any possibility of controversy with the United States over the submarine question. But it was not easy for the Imperial Chancellor to steer a safe course. The British had recently begun to arm as many mechantmen as they could find guns and gun crews for,[70] and Lord Crewe, in a speech in the House of Lords on November 15, had admitted that it was now British policy to "regard a German submarine as the kind of enemy which it is permissible and proper to destroy, if you can, at sight."[71] Moreover, a German submarine commander had found a copy of the French Naval Ministry's instructions to French armed merchantmen. They clearly ordered offensive action in case of contact with German submarines.[72] The German Admiralty and naval captains were, consequently, clamoring for permission to attack all armed merchantmen without warning.

Bernstorff's telegram of November 21 made it clear to Bethmann what he had to do. He had already conferred with Holtzendorff on

[69] Ambassador von Bernstorff to the Foreign Office, November 21, 1916, *Official German Documents*, II, 993-994; J. von Bernstorff, *My Three Years in America*, pp. 305-306.

[70] A. J. Balfour, *Report on Recent Naval Affairs, October 1916*, memorandum dated October 14, 1916, copy in the Asquith Papers; "Defensively Armed Merchant Ships," mimeographed memorandum, n.d., but c. November 15, 1916, *ibid.*; A. J. Balfour, *Guns for Merchant Ships*, Cabinet paper dated November 22, 1916, *ibid.*

[71] *Parliamentary Debates, House of Lords*, Fifth Series, XXIII, column 523.

[72] The Foreign Office to the German Embassy, Washington, December 1, 1916, *Official German Documents*, II, 996.

November 24 and won his approval of a note about the *Marina*. It said that the submarine commander had been convinced that he was torpedoing a naval transport and the German government would not hesitate to make full reparation if investigation proved that the commander had violated his instructions.[73] Count Adolf Montgelas, head of the American section at the Foreign Office, handed this note to Grew on November 25. Then, on the following day, Bethmann dispatched a second note (drafted by Count Montgelas and revised by Arthur Zimmermann, the new Foreign Secretary[74]) to Bernstorff. It said that the German government would be pleased to let Wilson take the initiative for peace. "At the same time," the note continued, "it is our urgent wish that Wilson will decide to take early steps in the matter; if possible, by the time Congress opens or, in any event, soon thereafter. Should this be put off until the New Year or later, the lull in military operations during the winter campaign would moderate an inclination to peace on the part of public opinion in hostile countries and, on the other hand, would make essential further military preparations for the spring offensive, the carrying out of which would presumably strengthen existing military opposition to the peace move. Please urge these points cautiously and without *empressement* [eagerness], and as representing your personal opinion in your talks with House, and keep me continuously informed by telegraph with regard to the situation."[75]

Bethmann then moved decisively to obtain new guarantees against further submarine incidents that would, he knew, probably turn Wilson from the path of peace. Holtzendorff was uncooperative, and Bethmann went personally to the Emperor on December 2 and won his approval for an Imperial Order instructing submarine commanders, "on account of the *Marina* and *Arabia* incidents," to avoid any action that might lead to complications with America.[76] Bethmann, Admiral von Müller recorded in his diary on that day, "stressed once again that he must avoid a conflict with America at all costs until the peace move, which both we and America are planning, had come off." The Chancellor, von Müller noted on the following day, "tormented him-

[73] Chargé Grew to the Secretary of State, November 27, 1916, *Foreign Relations, 1916, Supplement*, pp. 312-313.

[74] Von Jagow had resigned on November 24, 1916.

[75] A. Zimmermann to Ambassador von Bernstorff, November 26, 1916, sent over the American diplomatic cable, *Official German Documents*, II, 994-995; J. von Bernstorff, *My Three Years in America*, p. 307.

[76] A. Spindler, *La Guerre Sous-Marine*, III, 422.

self with doubt whether he must not demand even stronger limitations on underwater torpedoings in order to avoid further chances of conflict with America, at least until the outcome of his peace action . . . was decided."[77]

The Imperial Order of December 2 must have made some impression. There were numerous sinkings of merchantmen (but none of passenger liners) with Americans on board during the following weeks. But submarine commanders acted well within the rules of cruiser warfare in each instance, and they evoked only requests for information, not protests, from the State Department.[78] This fact, together with receipt of a note about the *Arabia* from the German Foreign Office reaffirming Germany's loyalty to the *Sussex* pledge,[79] eased all of Wilson's apprehensions. He did not even acknowledge Lansing's letter when the Secretary of State wrote on December 8 saying that the *Marina* and *Arabia* notes made it clear that there was nothing to do but sever relations with Germany.[80]

We have no evidence that Bernstorff conveyed the message in Zimmermann's telegram of November 26 to Colonel House. He probably thought that he had made German eagerness for peace plain enough in his conversation with the Colonel on November 20. As House recorded that conversation, the Ambassador "said that peace was on the floor waiting to be picked up. He does not believe a belligerent government could refuse to parley, particularly since Germany is willing to evacuate both France and Belgium and any refusal to negotiate would be an admission that they would continue the war for conquest."[81]

House at once repeated these remarks in a letter to Wilson. They

[77] W. Görlitz (ed.), *Regierte der Kaiser*, pp. 238-239, entries for December 2 and 3, 1916.

[78] For a complete list of these sinkings to January 12, 1917, see "Memorandum. Vessels Sunk by German and Austrian Submarines, November 13, 1916," and "List of December 8, 1916, amended to January 12, 1917," Wilson Papers.

[79] Chargé Grew to the Secretary of State, December 4, 1916, *Foreign Relations, 1916, Supplement*, p. 319. See also Secretary Zimmermann's statement reaffirming Germany's intention to honor pledges to the United States, in the *New York Times*, December 14, 1916.

[80] It was R. Lansing to W. W., December 8, 1916, *The Lansing Papers*, I, 575-576. For evidence that Wilson did not answer it, see R. Lansing to W. W., December 21, 1916, Wilson Papers.

[81] "Memorandum by Colonel E. M. House . . . , November 20, 1916," *The Lansing Papers*, I, 573.

were not the only hopeful signs to come within the President's purview. Bethmann had told the Budget Committee of the Reichstag on November 9 that Germany was fighting only a defensive war, would join a postwar league of nations to help guard the peace, and would not continue the war in order to annex Belgium.[82] The American Chargé in Berlin, Joseph C. Grew, wired a week later that the Chancellor's recent interview with the American reporter, William Bayard Hale (in which Bethmann once again affirmed Germany's eagerness for peace), had been "in the nature of an informal suggestion to the President, whose response is awaited with eagerness."[83] In addition, someone writing under the pen name of Cosmos—he was Nicholas Murray Butler, president of Columbia University—had begun a series in the *New York Times* calling for a negotiated peace.[84] Lord Derby told a reporter in London on November 22 that the Allies would give any German peace proposal all the consideration it deserved.[85] J. Howard Whitehouse had come as spokesman of a group of antiwar members of Parliament to urge House to persuade the President to move immediately for a negotiated peace on liberal lines. He had already had his first conversations with House.[86]

Wilson was much encouraged. "Your letter about your interviews with Whitehouse, Carver, Bernstorff et al," he wrote to House on November 21, "has given me a great deal to think about and has brought at least a ray of light, corroborating in some degree the impression I expressed to you, that this is very nearly the time, if not the time itself, for our move for peace. . . . I have completed my message to Congress and am just about to sketch the paper I spoke of when you were here. Just so soon as I can give it enough elaboration to make it a real proposal and programme I am going to beg you to come down and we will get at the business in real earnest. I will make the best haste I can consistent with my desire to make it the strongest and most convincing thing I ever penned."[87]

There was the danger at this very time that another unhappy in-

[82] Chargé Grew to the Secretary of State, November 10, 1916, *Foreign Relations, 1916, Supplement*, p. 64.

[83] Chargé Grew to the Secretary of State, November 17, 1916, *ibid.*, pp. 64-65.

[84] *New York Times*, November 18, 20, and 21, 1916.

[85] *ibid.*, November 23, 1916.

[86] "The House Report, 14 November 1916 to 14 April 1917" (entry for November 14, 1916), MS. in the Papers of J. Howard Whitehouse, Bembridge School, Bembridge, Isle of Wight; hereinafter cited as "The House Report," Whitehouse Papers.

[87] W. W. to E. M. House, November 21, 1916, House Papers.

cident would stay Wilson's hand. The German government in mid-October had begun the practice of deporting Belgian workers to Germany for labor service. Reports of the deportations, first published in the American press in mid-November, set off a wave of indignation that equaled if it did not exceed American anger at the invasion of Belgium.[88] Lansing dispatched a protest to Berlin on behalf of the Belgian government on November 2,[89] and the President permitted the Secretary to send a solemn protest on behalf of the United States Government to the Imperial German Chancellor on November 29.[90] The immediate point, aside from moral considerations, was, as Wilson himself wrote in a confidential message accompanying the protest, "the very serious unfavorable reaction in the public opinion of this country caused by the Belgian deportations at a time when that opinion was more nearly approaching a balance of judgments as to the issues of the war than ever before; and also, and more particularly, the great embarrassment which that reaction has caused the President in regard to taking steps looking towards peace. You [Wilson went on in his instructions to Grew] are authorized to say that the President is watching the whole situation with the utmost solicitude, having the desire and definite purpose to be of service in that great matter at the earliest possible moment, and has been repeatedly distressed to have his hopes frustrated and his occasion destroyed by such unhappy incidents as the sinking of the *Marina* and the *Arabia* and the Belgian deportations. You are also authorized to say that the President has noted with the deepest interest your report in a

[88] e. g., R. U. Johnson to W. W., November 19, 1916, Wilson Papers; W. W. Keen to R. Lansing, November 20, 1916, Lansing Papers, LC; C. W. Eliot to W. W., November 21, 1916, Burleson Papers; *New Republic*, IX (November 25, 1916), 78-79; E. Root *et al.* to W. W., November 25, 1916, Wilson Papers; report of a protest meeting in Tremont Temple, Boston, November 28, 1916, in the *Boston Herald*, November 29, 1916; report of a protest meeting in Carnegie Hall, New York City, December 15, 1916, in the *New York Times*, December 16, 1916; *The Living Church*, LVI (December 16, 1916), 219.

[89] The newspapers incorrectly reported (e. g., the *New York Times*, November 15, 1916) that Lansing had sent a protest on behalf of the American government. Wilson was furious when he read this report and called the Secretary of State by telephone to reprimand him. It was ridiculous, Wilson told Colonel House, who was with him at the time, for the American government to protest against the deportation of Belgians when it had not objected to the German invasion of Belgium. House Diary, November 15, 1916. For Lansing's explanation, see R. Lansing to W. W., November 15, 1916, *The Lansing Papers*, I, 40-42.

[90] R. Lansing to W. W., November 21, 1916, *ibid.*, pp. 42-44; W. W. to R. Lansing, November 26, 1916, Baker Collection.

recent despatch of the evident distress and disappointment of the Chancellor that nothing had come of his intimations about peace, and that what the President is now earnestly desiring is practical co-operation on the part of the German authorities in creating a favorable opportunity for some affirmative action by him in the interest of an early restoration of peace."[91]

House, indeed, had already given a similar warning in his conversation with Bernstorff on November 20, and the Ambassador had passed it on in his telegram of November 21.[92]

Wilson, actually, had no intention of permitting the Belgian deportations to interrupt his plans. He explained the reasons for delay and made some interesting observations in a letter to Colonel House on November 24. "I have had a really overwhelming cold during nearly the whole of the week, and it has sadly thrown my plans out," he began. "The paper I had intended to write needed the clearest thinking I could do, and not until to-night have I ventured to begin it. Even now I have gone no further than a skeleton outline. I wanted to make these suggestions:

"First, that you convey to Kuhn, Loeb & Co. through Mr. [Jacob H.] Schiff, who would be sure of my personal friendship, the intimation that our relations with Germany are now in a very unsatisfactory and doubtful state, and that it would be most unwise at this time to risk a loan.

"Second, that you write to Lord Grey in the strongest terms to the effect that he could be sure that the United States would go any length in promoting and lending her full might to a League for Peace, and that her people were growing more and more impatient with the intolerable conditions of neutrality, their feeling as hot against Great Britain as it was at first against Germany and likely to grow hotter still against an indefinite continuation of the war if no greater progress could be shown than now appears, either for the Allies or the Central Powers.

[91] The Secretary of State to Chargé Grew, November 29, 1916, *Foreign Relations, 1916, Supplement*, pp. 70-71; Wilson's text is in W. W. to R. Lansing, November 28, 1916, Lansing Papers, Princeton. Grew was not able to deliver this message until December 5 (Chargé Grew to the Secretary of State, December 5, 1916, *ibid.*, p. 868), hence it had no effect on Bethmann's actions in late November and early December settling the *Marina* and *Arabia* incidents and putting new restraints on submarine commanders.

[92] Ambassador von Bernstorff to the Foreign Office, November 21, 1916, *Official German Documents*, II, 993.

"It might be well to intimate to him that Page no longer represents the feeling or point of view of the United States any more than do the Americans resident in London.

"I hope that these suggestions commend themselves to you. I do not think that he ought to be left in any degree in ignorance of the real state of our opinion. It might even be well to intimate that we, in common with the other neutral nations, look upon the continuation of the war through another winter with the utmost distaste and misgiving.

"I am so sorry I am not to see you to-morrow, but it would be folly for me to risk the exposure at the present stage of my cold."[93]

Wilson worked in his study all through the afternoon and evening of Friday, November 24, and completed a first draft of his peace note just before lunch on Saturday, November 25. It began by stating the reasons why he had a right to speak. The war had disturbed life in every quarter of the world, and the position of neutrals had been rendered all but intolerable. "Their commerce is interrupted, their industries are checked and diverted, the lives of their people are put in constant jeopardy, they are virtually forbidden the accustomed highways of the sea, their energies are drawn off into temporary and novel channels, they suffer at every turn though disengaged and disposed to none but friendly and impartial offices." And yet the world still did not know what the war was all about. "If any other nation now neutral should be drawn in, it would know only that it was drawn in by some force it could not resist, because it had been hurt and saw no remedy but to risk still greater, it might be even irreparable, injury, in order to make the weight in the one scale or the other decisive; and even as a participant it would not know how far the scales must tip before the end would come or what was being weighed in the balance!"

Leaders on both sides, the note went on, had declared very earnestly that they did not wish to crush their enemies, wage a war of conquest, or oppress weak nations. They had all affirmed desire for a lasting peace. The American government had been struck by the similarity of the general war aims that belligerent leaders had announced. The people and government of the United States would eagerly support

[93] W. W. to E. M. House, November 24, 1916, House Papers. House wrote to Grey on the same day, November 24, that he received Wilson's letter. The Colonel's message (E. M. House to Lord Grey, November 24, 1916, *ibid.*) was by no means as strongly phrased as Wilson had suggested that it be.

such objectives, indeed, would join a postwar league of nations to help attain and guarantee them. But they could not help Europe if Europe insisted on prolonging the useless carnage and the rival belligerents attempted to impose a settlement by force. The note now came to the point:

"In such circumstances and moved by such considerations, I deem myself to be clearly within my right as the representative of a great neutral nation whose interests are being daily affected and as the friend of all the nations engaged in the present struggle, and speaking with the utmost respect for the rights of all concerned, in urging, as I do most earnestly urge, that some means be immediately taken, whether by conference or by a separate formulation of demands and conditions, to define the terms upon which a settlement of the issues of the war may be expected. It has become necessary that the nations that are now neutral should have some certain and definite guide for their future policy. It is necessary that they should have some certain means of determining what part they shall henceforth play should the terms defined be impossible of realization and the end of the war be indefinitely postponed.

"The simplest means of arriving at this end would be a conference of representatives of the belligerent governments and of the governments not now engaged in the war whose interests may be thought to be most directly involved, and it is such a conference that I take the liberty of urging, whatever its outcome may be. If that be not feasible, it is possible that other means may be found which will in effect accomplish the same result."

His sole purpose, Wilson's note went on, was to bring the war to an end before it was too late to repair the damage it had done. "I am doing a very simple, a very practical, and a very different thing," the note concluded. "I am asking, and assuming that I have the right to ask, for a concrete definition of the guarantees which the belligerents on the one side and the other deem it their duty to demand as a practical satisfaction of the objects they are aiming at in this contest of force, in addition to the very great and substantial guarantee which will, I feel perfectly confident, be supplied by a league of nations formed to unite their force in active cooperation for the preservation of the world's peace when this war is over. To answer these questions need not commit any belligerent to peace at this time; but until they are answered no influential nation of the world not yet involved in the struggle can intelligently determine its future course of action. The United States feels that it can no longer delay to determine its own."[94]

Wilson, as soon as he had finished typing the note, sent a telegram asking House to come to Washington. "I think," he added, "things are thickening and we should choose our course at once, if we have data enough to form a judgment on."[95] House arrived in the late afternoon on Monday, November 27, and he and Wilson worked over the draft after dinner. House objected strongly to Wilson's statement that the causes and objects of the war were obscure. This, he warned, would enrage the Allies, who were quite certain that they knew why they were fighting. Could not the President substitute a clause to make the Allies believe that he sympathized with them, and do this without offending Germany? And would not Wilson insert a sentence to the effect that he was not seeking to mediate or demand peace? Wilson rejected the first suggestion and accepted the second. He also said that it would be well if House was in England when his note was delivered there. House said that this would cause a crisis with Page; Wilson replied that he did not care if Page resigned. House then said that the President should delay dispatch of the note until he had prepared the way for its reception in the Allied countries. "My whole idea," he wrote in his diary, "is to delay until the time seems propitious. It is too important a matter to bungle, and if he is not careful, that is what he will do."[96]

House repeated this advice to Lansing on the following day, November 28; and the Secretary of State, when Wilson read his draft to him in the afternoon, said that he agreed entirely with House. "I am convinced," Lansing wrote in his diary a few days later, "that the President's hope of making peace can not possibly be realized. I am not sure that it would be a good thing for the world if it could be. If it is not realized, we are certain to be drawn into this war. Our present position is becoming impossible. We are very near the edge of the precipice. When we do go into this war, and we might as well make up our minds that we are going in, we *must* go in on the side of the Allies, for we are a democracy. Suppose, however, Germany listens to the President and the Allies decline to do so, what will be our situa-

[94] MS. in the Wilson Papers, printed in full in R. S. Baker, *Woodrow Wilson: Life and Letters* (8 vols.), VI, 380-386.
[95] W. W. to E. M. House, November 25, 1916, House Papers.
[96] House Diary, November 27, 1916.

tion? How can we turn then to the Allies? This is causing me the gravest concern. It will be most serious and regrettable."[97]

Wilson had, in fact, already given new evidence of determination, not only to proceed, but also to use all his power to force Britain and France to the peace table if German policy seemed to recommend such strong diplomacy. As Spring Rice put it a short time later, "The President can always take action about our credit and about armed merchantmen. He is fully conscious of his power. And he is prepared to use it."[98] This came out in one of the most significant and revealing incidents of the late period of American neutrality.

Henry P. Davison had come home following the Joint Anglo-French Financial Conference in early October to search for an answer to the impending exchange crisis. He and other members of the House of Morgan found what would be at least a temporary expedient—purchase by American banks of short-term British and French treasury notes that might be renewed over and over. To prepare the way, Davison went to Washington on November 18 and presented the plan to members of the Federal Reserve Board. They did not think much of the proposal, mainly because they had been growing worried about American dependence upon the war trade and had been discussing ways to keep it within reasonable bounds. One member of the Board wrote not long after this meeting:

"Governor [W. P. G.] Harding (who had taken the precaution during these last weeks to place himself in touch with the leading authorities in questions of foreign policy in order to be sure that we were acting in fullest accord with what generally would be considered the best interest of the country) pointed out to Mr. Davison that there was some danger of a creditor becoming so much involved with one debtor that finally, no matter whether the creditor wanted to or not, he would have to go in deeper and deeper. In other words, while you thought you had the bull by the tail, as a matter of fact, the bull had you by the tail. In this case, it is *John Bull* who would have us by the tail.

"England has now outstanding in short loans an amount which must be as large as between one and two billions of pounds. How these are to be funded, nobody knows. England's per capita debt

<hr />

[97] "What Will the President do?" Lansing Diary, December 3, 1916.

[98] C. Spring Rice to E. Grey, December 15, 1916, S. Gwynn (ed.), *Letters of Spring Rice*, II, 360-361.

next year will have multiplied by seven as against the beginning of the war. The continuation of the war, therefore, appears madness, and as long as nobody knows how long this madness will last, there is no saying in what condition Europe will be when the war ceases. The feeling generally appears to be breaking through here at Washington (and I think also amongst a substantial part of the cooler elements of the country) that the end of this war will be a draw; that the sooner it ends the better, and that continuing the war means only a needless and fruitless sacrifice of life and treasure. To think that this war must go on to keep our trade going is an abomination. To think that it ought to be the duty of the Government or the Federal Reserve Board to prevent disastrous economic consequences by prolonging it is unjustifiable. And we said to Mr. Davison that it was the general feeling that we had grown enough and that we should be in a position of contemplating the 'breaking out' of peace without a thought of alarm; that to our mind it was better to let this extraordinary trade gradually go down to more nearly normal proportions than to have it stop with a vengeance."[99]

Davison then conferred with the President at the White House in the late afternoon. He presumably told Wilson something about the Allied financial situation, and Wilson asked for information about Britain's and France's external debts.[100] The President was apparently cordial but gave no sign that he would approve "easy future financing."[101]

Harding discussed the Davison plan with Lansing on November 19, and the Secretary of State observed that the Board should go slowly in approving unliquid securities with no collateral.[102] Then Harding drafted a statement cautioning American banks against investing too heavily in renewable short-term Allied treasury notes. The Federal Reserve Board revised the statement on November 25, and Harding took it to the White House in the early afternoon. We may be sure that he explained to the President the Board's grave doubts about the

[99] P. M. Warburg to B. Strong, Jr., November 23, 1916, Senate Special Committee on Investigation of the Munitions Industry, *Munitions Industry*, 74th Cong., 2d sess., Senate Report No. 944, Part 5, pp. 196-198 (the quotation is from p. 197); hereinafter cited as Senate Special Committee, *Munitions Industry*, Pt. 5.

[100] H. P. Davison to W. W., November 25, 1916, *ibid.*, pp. 205-206, sending the information that Wilson had requested.

[101] H. P. Davison to J. P. Morgan, Jr., November 20, 1916, quoted in R. S. Baker, *Woodrow Wilson*, VI, 376.

[102] The Diary of Charles S. Hamlin, November 19, 1916, Senate Special Committee, *Munitions Industry*, Pt. 5, p. 206.

soundness of the war trade and its larger implications. Wilson said that he had hoped that the Board would issue some such statement, but that he had not felt like suggesting it himself. There were, he added, important considerations of foreign policy involved. Relations with England were more strained than with Germany. He would, he added, send his comments as soon as possible.[103] He gave his opinion in a letter on the following day:

"I am taking the liberty of using my own pen (for so I regard this typewriter) to make reply to the question you put to me yesterday about the enclosed statement.

"I like it. I am glad that the Board has determined that it is its duty to make it. Such advice to the banks seems to me very timely and indeed very necessary. My only suggestion is that the statement be made a little stronger and more pointed and be made to carry rather explicit advice against these investments, as against the whole policy and purpose of the Federal Reserve Act, rather than convey a mere caution. The securities spoken of, though nominally liquid, will in the event, I should say, certainly not be so, and our domestic transactions might be seriously embarrassed and impeded should the national banks tie up their resources in them.

"Thank you very much for consulting me on this extremely important matter, which might at any time be radically affected by a change in the foreign policy of our government."[104]

Harding, on November 27, sent Wilson a copy of a strengthened statement that the Board had just approved.[105] "The addition," Wilson replied, "seems to meet very adequately what I had in mind."[106]

The "addition" was, indeed, the very heart of the warning that the Federal Reserve Board issued to member banks in the Federal Reserve System on November 27. It read:

"The Board deems it, therefore, its duty to caution the member banks that it does not regard it in the interest of the country at this time that they invest in foreign Treasury bills of this character.

"The Board does not consider that it is called upon to advise private investors, but as the United States is fast becoming the banker of foreign countries in all parts of the world, it takes occasion to suggest that the investor should receive full and authoritative data—

[103] The Diary of Charles S. Hamlin, November 25 and 30, 1916, *ibid.*, pp. 206-207.
[104] W. W. to W. P. G. Harding, November 26, 1916, copy in the House Papers.
[105] W. P. G. Harding to W. W., November 27, 1916, Wilson Papers.
[106] W. W. to W. P. G. Harding, November 27, 1916, *ibid.*

particularly in the case of unsecured loans—in order that he may judge the future intelligently in the light of present conditions and in conjunction with the economic developments of the past."[107]

It sent the price of Allied bonds and American war stocks tumbling on November 28, and the Morgan firm had to buy nearly $20,000,000 of sterling to maintain the exchange rate.[108] Panic almost ensued in London in the wake of the news. The Exchange Committee of the Treasury advised the Cabinet that there was no choice but to go off the gold standard, even though this would cause complete disruption of exchange and trade. The Cabinet decided to go as long as possible without resorting to this drastic measure.[109] J. Pierpont Morgan, Jr., was defiant at first, saying that his firm intended to proceed with plans to offer short-term British and French treasury notes on December 1.[110] He changed his mind—and his public statement—after communicating with Reginald McKenna, Chancellor of the Exchequer. "We have been instructed by the British and French Governments," Morgan & Company said on December 1, "to withdraw their Treasury bills from sale. . . . This action is taken because, as explained by the British Chancellor of the Exchequer and by the French Minister of Finance, these Governments desire to show every regard to the Federal Reserve Board, a governmental body of which the Secretary of the Treasury and the Controller of the Currency are ex-officio members."[111]

A minor incident soon afterward gave further evidence that Wilson was very deliberately tightening the vise in preparation for his peace move. John Skelton Williams, Comptroller of the Currency, was apparently upset by the Board's statement (perhaps because he thought that it reflected on the solvency of American banks) and prepared one of his own saying that the holdings of foreign securities of American national banks were actually quite small in view of the enormous resources of those institutions. "We had it held up by Lansing's

[107] *New York Times,* November 28, 1916.

[108] J. P. Morgan & Co. to Morgan Grenfell & Co., November 28, 1916, Senate Special Committee on Investigation of the Munitions Industry, *Munitions Industry,* 74th Cong., 2d sess., Senate Report No. 944, Part 6, p. 132.

[109] *Printed for the Imperial War Cabinet. April 1917. MR. BONAR LAW'S STATEMENT ON FINANCE AT THE SEVENTH MEETING OF THE IMPERIAL WAR CABINET HELD AT 10 DOWNING STREET, S.W., ON THE 3RD OF APRIL, 1917,* copy in the Chamberlain Papers.

[110] *New York Times,* November 29, 1916.

[111] *ibid.,* December 2, 1916.

help," one member of the Board wrote in his diary on December 4.[112] Williams then appealed to the President, enclosing a copy of his statement with the explanation that national banks held a total of only $239,566,000 of foreign governmental and other foreign securities on September 12, 1916, and that this figure was less than was generally thought.[113] Wilson replied on December 8, asking Williams to do nothing about the statement until he had heard from him.[114] "I appreciate your withholding the statement of the national bank investments for the present," he added on December 11. "I am not sure what indirect effect the publication might have on some of our foreign relations."[115]

The sword now hung more perilously over the heads of the British and French governments. They had enough gold and dollar assets to continue purchases to about April 1. Disaster loomed after that date unless some way was found to maintain exchange.

Worse news, if possible, came to the Foreign Office in London in a long telegram from Spring Rice on December 5. It was quite certain, the Ambassador wrote, that the Secretary of State had either promoted or approved the Federal Reserve Board's warning. "It is, of course," Spring Rice went on, "very important to know how far the action of the Federal Reserve Board, which was certainly imposed on it from without, was the work of the President himself. I know it was not the work of the Cabinet." The State Department, he continued, was now warning that it would be difficult to prevent Congress, when it met, from insisting on retaliatory measures against England. He went on:

"In many departments of the State Department I understand that the common talk is anti-British. . . . I think we should conclude that at least in small matters the attitude of the State Department will be hostile, and that their influence in Congress will not be friendly. Threats are openly conveyed to us. We expect that some consul or other official will be accused of some infraction of diplomatic propriety, especially in relation to the statutory list, and that he will be summarily dismissed. It is of course notorious that if I had done one-thousandth part of what Bernstorff has done, I should have been

[112] The Diary of Charles S. Hamlin, December 4, 1916, Senate Special Committee, *Munitions Industry*, Pt. 5, p. 207.

[113] J. S. Williams to W. W., December 6, 1916, Wilson Papers.

[114] We do not have a copy of this letter, which Wilson apparently wrote on his own typewriter. It is referred to in J. S. Williams to W. W., December 9, 1916, *ibid.*

[115] W. W. to J. S. Williams, December 11, 1916, *ibid.*

given my passports long ago. The slightest slip would be visited with an immediate penalty. Of this, I have little doubt. . . .

"We must also expect some unfriendly action against our shipping. . . . Measures should be taken accordingly. The general result is that the question of supplies from this country is one which we cannot regard as settled. We cannot count with certainty upon this country as a source of supplies or of money. We must have the possibility before our eyes of a crisis of greater or less magnitude. In any case we must not count among our assets a cheque drawn on the United States which may not be honoured when delivered. . . . The upshot of it all is, do not be too confident in American goodwill or too much afraid of American hostility. . . .

"The question which presents itself in a serious form is this: It is much to the advantage of the President to play the rôle of peacemaker in Europe, because this would relieve him of the reproach that he has done nothing for humanity. The obvious way to be mediator is to force the Allies to accept mediation by cutting off supplies and to conciliate Germany by conniving within certain limits in Germany's submarine warfare. Would the President adopt this policy, which is being pressed upon him by many of his advisers and, above all, by his financial supporters? It is possible he might. On the other hand is the danger of war with Germany, which is always imminent if Germany chooses to sink an American passenger ship. Because it is to be presumed there is some limit to American patience. A war with Germany may have unforeseen consequences of the most serious character, and it would be the breakdown of his peace policy. On the other hand, it is not thought that there is any danger of war with the Allies. They will not resent an injury, certainly not by force of arms; to insult or wrong them is safe. And they would be quarrelling with their victuals if they resented the manners of their grocer. Therefore, great caution should be taken with Germany. None is necessary with the Allies. . . .

"We must not forget what this country could do to us if she really intended mischief. . . . If we regard ourselves as fighting for a cause bound up with the existence of America, and as a people of the same blood and language and principles as the people of the United States, we might be filled with rage at the thought of their attitude. If we regard them as a foreign nation who happen to speak our language, but who by history have been estranged from us, we could only be thankful that their attitude is more satisfactory to us than that, for instance, of Sweden. They could do us much more harm than they are doing, and, in fact, their power of mischief is incalculable. And we had better not count too much on their goodwill."[116]

House returned to New York in the afternoon of November 28. Second thinking strengthened his conviction that the Allies would reject the President's proposed peace note, and that only the Germans could profit from action at this time. He voiced these apprehensions in an urgent letter to the President on November 30.[117] Wilson, after reading this letter, talked to Lansing on the following day. He had decided, he said, that it was best not to act hastily. He would work further on his note and decide later when and how it was to be sent. He also agreed when Lansing suggested that it would be unfair to ask House to go abroad at this time. House noted that he was very much relieved after Polk telephoned a report of this conversation.[118]

Events, however, were moving too rapidly for statesmen anywhere to stand still. "The situation," Wilson wrote to House on December 3, "is developing very fast and if we are going to do the proposed thing effectively we must do it very soon." One reason for early action, he went on, was Bryan. The Commoner had told Gerard that he intended to go to Berlin for personal peace discussions with the Emperor and Foreign Secretary. "Gerard," Wilson concluded, "hopes that I will do what we discussed, and do it at once, and thinks, with us, that it is not what Germany wishes and not what either side could object to or decently decline if done in the terms I suggested,—as a neutral demand."[119]

Events intruded at this very moment to distract and delay. News came on December 4 that the Asquith Cabinet had resigned and Lloyd George was in process of forming a new government. Nothing, surely, could be done until this crisis was resolved. Wilson's thoughts were also momentarily diverted by other events at this particular moment. He went to New York on December 2 to deliver an address at ceremonies inaugurating the illumination of the Statue of Liberty.[120] He conferred on December 3 with Speaker Clark and Majority Leader Kitchin about a legislative program for the lame-duck session of the

---

[116] C. Spring Rice to Viscount Grey, December 5, 1916, *Printed for the use of the Cabinet. December 1916.*

[117] E. M. House to W. W., November 30, 1916, Wilson Papers.

[118] Lansing Desk Diary, December 1, 1916; House Diary, December 2, 1916.

[119] W. W. to E. M. House, December 3, 1916, House Papers.

[120] *New York Times*, December 3, 1916.

Sixty-fourth Congress that was to open on the following day.[121] A delegation from the American Federation of Labor came to the White House on December 4 to ask the President to do something to halt the increase in food prices caused by short wheat and corn crops, and to urge Congress to approve a bill to encourage vocational and industrial education.[122] Then Wilson went to the Capitol on December 5 to deliver his Annual Message. The Democrats gave him an unusually warm reception when he entered the chamber of the House of Representatives at one o'clock in the afternoon.

He began by reminding the lawmakers that they still had things to do before their terms expired. Most important was the program for labor peace on the railroads that he had recommended some months before. Congress had enacted only part of this program. "The other suggestions—," he went on, "the increase in the Interstate Commerce Commission's membership . . . , the provision for full public investigation and assessment of industrial disputes, and the grant to the Executive of the power to control and operate the railways when necessary in time of war or other like public necessity—I now very earnestly renew." Something had to be done, he added, to guarantee uninterrupted operation of the railroads. He was not suggesting forcing men to work against their will, but there should be some way to prevent "organized bodies of men" from paralyzing the nation's economic life "until a public investigation shall have been instituted which shall make the whole question at issue plain for the judgment of the opinion of the Nation."[123]

There were, Wilson went on, other items in the administration's still uncompleted program—bills to permit American manufacturers to combine in order to carry on export trade, expand the self-government of Puerto Rico, and provide more systematic regulation of expend-

[121] *ibid.*, December 4, 1916.

[122] *ibid.*, December 5, 1916.

[123] There were good reasons for Wilson's concern at this time. He had, on October 5, appointed a commission of inquiry headed by Major General George W. Goethals to study the impact of the Adamson Act when it went into operation on January 1, 1917. *ibid.*, October 6, 1916. The railroads, however, were unwilling to give the measure a fair trial and had filed suits in federal district courts in mid-November praying for injunctions forbidding execution of the law on the grounds of unconstitutionality. *ibid.*, November 16, 1916. Judge William C. Hook of the Federal District Court of Kansas City had ruled on November 22 that the Adamson Act was unconstitutional in order to make possible a speedy appeal to the Supreme Court. *ibid.*, November 23, 1916. Hence by the time that Wilson spoke to Congress the nation once again faced the prospect of a nationwide railroad strike if the Supreme Court should nullify the Adamson Act.

iture of money in elections. They had, in fact, already been approved by the House of Representatives and awaited only the endorsement of the Senate. In addition, there was a measure providing federal support for vocational education. The Senate had approved it at the last session, and the House should complete its passage. "Inasmuch," Wilson concluded, "as this is, gentlemen, probably the last occasion I shall have to address the Sixty-fourth Congress, I hope that you will permit me to say with what genuine pleasure and satisfaction I have cooperated with you in the many measures of constructive policy with which you have enriched the legislative annals of the country. It has been a privilege to labor in such company. I take the liberty of congratulating you upon the completion of a record of rare serviceableness and distinction."[124]

There were other nagging distractions and duties at this particular time. "Members of Congress," the President wrote to Colonel House on December 8, "have been sucking the life out of me, about appointments and other matters affecting the destiny of the world, and I have been prevented from perfecting the document [the peace note]. I shall go out of town (on the MAYFLOWER no doubt) for the purpose, if it can be done in no other way."[125] He had also recently been upset by an unhappy incident. Wilson, yielding to the importunities of his wife and Colonel House, had asked Tumulty to resign and accept another appointment. Tumulty had begged Wilson in a tearful interview not to make him go, and Wilson had relented. The affair had taken a heavy toll of his emotional reserves.[126]

The crush of business attendant upon the opening of Congress had abated by December 8 or 9. More important, the Cabinet crisis in England was over: Lloyd George was the new Prime Minister, Balfour had succeeded Grey as Foreign Secretary, and Conservatives dominated the new Coalition. House followed events in London carefully, fearing at the outset that the triumph of Lloyd George allied with Conservatives would be fatal to peace hopes.[127] The Colonel saw J. Howard Whitehouse on December 5 and asked him how he thought Wilson's peace note would be received in London. Whitehouse replied that a mediation offer would begin such a discussion in Parliament and the

[124] *ibid.*, December 6, 1916; *Foreign Relations, 1916*, pp. ix-xiii, for the text of the message.
[125] W. W. to E. M. House, December 8, 1916, House Papers.
[126] A. S. Link, *Wilson: The New Freedom*, pp. 142-144; John M. Blum, *Joe Tumulty and the Wilson Era*, pp. 120-122.
[127] E. M. House to W. W., December 3, 1916, Wilson Papers.

country that the government would have to acquiesce. "I found House," he wrote in a memorandum of the conversation, "most responsive all the time and unusually excited and animated for him."[128] Whitehouse saw House again on December 7, after news of the completion of the new Cabinet. Whitehouse was even more certain than before that circumstances favored Wilson's peace move.[129] House, remembering that Lloyd George, earlier in the year, had seemed positively eager for Wilson's mediation, now wrote to Wilson, suggesting an effort to revive the House-Grey Memorandum and enclosing a letter to be sent to the new Prime Minister as the first step.[130]

Wilson, too, was ready to move, but along a different route. "The time is near at hand for *something!*" he replied to House on December 8. "But that something is not mediation such as we were proposing when you were last on the other side of the water, and therefore I do not think it would be wise to send the letter you were kind enough to submit to me to Lloyd George. We cannot go back to those old plans. We must shape new ones."[131]

He immediately set about revising his peace note, changing it in a fundamental way by eliminating the suggestion of an early peace conference. Then he sent the second draft to Lansing on December 9, writing, "Here is the demand for definitions. I would be very much obliged if you would give me your detailed criticism of it. . . . I think that the time is at hand for something of this kind to be done with effect. Affairs may disclose it at any moment."[132] Lansing returned the draft on December 10 with a number of stylistic changes and only one important substantive alteration. It was to remove Wilson's commitment to use American force in a postwar league of nations. The note, the Secretary of State said, was an admirable paper and certainly justified by America's increasingly intolerable situation. Perhaps it was the only hope of preventing an open rupture with one side or the other. But Lansing was still profoundly troubled by the prospect of Allied rejection and German acceptance. As he put it:

"Unless the answers of *both* parties are made in the right spirit, will

[128] E. M. House to W. W., December 5, 1916, *ibid.*; "The House Report," White-house Papers, entry dated simply December 1916.

[129] J. H. Whitehouse, memorandum for Colonel House, December 7, 1916, Wilson Papers.

[130] E. M. House to W. W., December 7, 1916, enclosing E. M. House to D. Lloyd George, December 7, 1916, *ibid.*

[131] W. W. to E. M. House, December 8, 1916, House Papers.

[132] W. W. to R. Lansing, December 9, 1916, Wilson Papers.

there be any other course than to declare in favor of the one most acceptable and abandon a neutrality which is becoming more and more difficult? But suppose that the unacceptable answer comes from the belligerents whom we could least afford to see defeated on account of our own national interest and on account of the future domination of the principles of liberty and democracy in the world—then what? Would we not be forced into an even worse state than that in which we are now? I think that we must consider the possibility of such a situation resulting; and if it does result, which seems to me not only possible but very probable, can we avoid the logic of our declarations? And if we act in accordance with that logic, would it not be a calamity for the nation and for all mankind? I have told you how strongly I feel that democracy is the only sure guarantee of peace, so you will understand how these questions are worrying me, and why I think that they should be considered with the greatest deliberation and care before we take a step which cannot be withdrawn once it is taken."[133]

Wilson probably intended to polish the note during the next few days and to send it to the belligerents on about December 15. His plan, if, indeed, this assumption is correct, was again disrupted on December 12, by news from Berlin that the Imperial Chancellor had informed the Reichstag that he had just sent Germany's own peace offer to the Allied governments. Let us review the background of this momentous event.

Bernstorff's reports, particularly the one of October 20 saying positively that Wilson would not and could not make any peace move until after the election,[134] convinced Bethmann that it was too risky to depend upon the American President alone to take the initiative. He, the Chancellor, would have to move as well. The past month had brought great improvement in the immediate military fortunes of the Central Powers. German forces had contained the Anglo-French offensive on the Somme, and the German campaign in Rumania was going well. But the long-range prospect was no better now than it had been at the beginning of the year. There were, besides, more immediate necessities for a peace *démarche*. The Austro-Hungarian Foreign Minister, Baron Burián, was eager to move.[135] Germany faced severe difficulties at home on account of failure of the potato crop.

---

[133] R. Lansing to W. W., December 10, 1916, *ibid.*

[134] Ambassador von Bernstorff to the Foreign Office, October 20, 1916, *Official German Documents*, II, 990.

[135] "Notes in the handwriting of [the] Imperial Chancelor [*sic*] . . . ," October 18, 1916, *ibid.*, pp. 1053-1056.

The German people were obviously war weary and eager for peace. Most important, Bethmann knew that unrestricted submarine warfare and hostilities with America were not only possible but probable at an early date. He feared that the German people would not have the heart and will to go on if America came into the war unless they believed that their government had made sincere efforts for peace. He thought, moreover, that there was at least a chance that the United States would remain neutral after inauguration of an all-out submarine campaign, provided that Germany had proved her good intentions by making a peace offer and the Allies had demonstrated their determination to crush Germany by rejecting it. Hence Bethmann decided to adopt what he called a policy of *zwei Eisen im Feuer*, two irons in the fire. He would continue to encourage a Wilsonian peace move while preparing one of his own.[136]

The immediate stimulus was receipt in Berlin on October 25 of a report of a speech by Viscount Grey in London on October 23, which the Imperial Chancellor interpreted as intimating British readiness for serious peace *pourparlers*.[137] The Emperor was enthusiastic when Bethmann broached the matter of an independent peace move.[138] Hindenburg and Ludendorff insisted only upon prior adoption of a compulsory labor service law, proclamation of Polish autonomy, and a favorable military situation. Bethmann then obtained the Emperor's and High Command's approval of terms. They included, *in the East*, establishment of the Kingdom of Poland and German annexation of the Baltic provinces of Courland and Lithuania; *in the West*, "guarantees in Belgium" or the annexation of Liège "with corresponding areas," annexation of Luxembourg and the French territories of Briey and Longwy, which contained large iron deposits, strategic boundary adjustments in Germany's favor in Alsace-Lorraine, and war indemnities; *overseas*, the return of all German colonies except Kiaochow, the Carolines, and the Marianas, and acquisition of all or part of the Belgian Congo.[139] The Austro-Hungarian government approved these and added terms of its own on November 15, 1916.[140]

[136] T. von Bethmann Hollweg, *Considérations sur la Guerre Mondiale* (2 vols.), II, 263-265; K. Helfferich, *Der Weltkrieg*, II, 349-354.

[137] *ibid.*, pp. 355-356.

[138] William II to T. von Bethmann Hollweg, October 31, 1916, *ibid.*, p. 358.

[139] The Imperial Chancellor to K. von Grünau, November 7, 1916; K. von Grünau to the Foreign Office, November 8, 1916, *Official German Documents*, II, 1064-1065; also Hans W. Gatzke, *Germany's Drive to the West*, pp. 139-144.

[140] The Imperial Chancellor to Ambassador B. von Wedel, November 23, 1916, *Official German Documents*, II, 1065-1068.

Bethmann now had to decide whether to move independently or wait upon the President. Receipt in Berlin on November 25 of Bernstorff's dispatch of November 21, reporting that House had just said that Wilson was eager to take early steps,[141] brought the first authoritative word about the President's intentions. However, Bethmann still had his doubts. As he wrote to Hindenburg on November 27: "Whether he [Wilson] will really carry out his purpose remains wholly uncertain. He is undecided and fearful of a set-back. We must reckon on this, that he will issue his appeal only if he no longer feels certain that the Entente will meet it with a curt rejection, and that means if the Entente finds itself in a situation in which it would not be likely to meet a peace proposal coming from us with a curt refusal. I leave open the question of whether our position at the council table would be more favorable if the negotiations had been brought about as a result of an appeal by Wilson, than if they had resulted in consequence of a peace proposal made by us. However this may be, it is certain that our situation would be better if the Entente rejected the offer to enter into negotiations made by Wilson than if it rejected a proposal coming directly from us. . . . On the other hand, in view of the uncertainty which until the very last moment will characterize Wilson's actions, and in view of the probable growing disinclination on the part of our enemies to enter upon peace negotiations as the winter season passes by, we will not be justified in letting the psychological moment for our own peace proposal escape, irrespective of any hope we may entertain with regard to an appeal by Mr. Wilson."[142]

Other reasons seemed to demand independent German action. The government in Vienna was now insisting upon German approval of Austro-Hungarian terms; only a quick German move could head off the complications that were bound to result from protracted negotiations. Wilson's message on the Belgian deportations, delivered to the Chancellor on December 5, along with a subsequent message from Bernstorff,[143] threatened new delay on the American side. The fall of

141 See above, pp. 190-191.

142 T. von Bethmann Hollweg to P. von Hindenburg, November 27, 1916, *Official German Documents*, II, 1069. I have altered the translation slightly.

143 It was Ambassador von Bernstorff to the Foreign Office, December 4, 1916, received December 7, 1916, J. von Bernstorff, *My Three Years in America*, pp. 308-309, saying in part: "Everything is prepared for a peace move, but with Mr. Wilson still hesitating, it is still doubtful when he will take action. All the authorities here have now been won over to favor such a step. This may then come at any time, especially if it is possible for us to adopt a conciliatory attitude on the Belgian question. Mr. Wilson believes that he is so hated in England that he won't be listened to."

Bucharest on December 6 offered a splendid occasion for a German move. Bethmann therefore went to Pless on December 7 to obtain Hindenburg's and Ludendorff's approval for a peace offer to be sent on December 11 or 12.[144]

The Field Marshal and his alter ego were by this time much less interested than before in any kind of peace move. Germany's military situation, they believed, was now reasonably secure, at least for the immediate future. Success in Rumania meant that they would be able to use reserve troops for defense against an attack from Holland and Denmark. They told the Emperor that they would approve dispatch of a peace offer only provided that it was agreed, among other things, that an unrestricted submarine campaign should be launched no later than the end of January 1917 if the peace move failed.[145] William made no decision and merely passed these demands on to Bethmann when he arrived at Supreme Headquarters on December 8. The Chancellor replied that one would have to wait and see about the all-out U-boat campaign, but that the navy could count on unlimited operations against *armed* merchantmen if the peace *démarche* failed.[146] This, Bethmann undoubtedly hoped, might prove to be a compromise alternative acceptable to the military authorities. The upshot, apparently, was agreement, reached at a conference among the Emperor, Hindenburg, and Bethmann on December 8, that the Chancellor should make his peace move on December 12, and that all-out operations against armed ships should begin if it miscarried.[147]

Bethmann thus returned to Berlin and handed Germany's peace note to Chargé Grew in the morning of December 12. It was written in French and began by lamenting the war's ravages and its threat to European civilization. Germany and her allies had demonstrated that they were invincible in the test of arms. They did not seek to annihilate their enemies, and they were ready to meet the Allies at the peace table in an effort to restore a lasting peace. If, in spite of this offer, the struggle had to continue, then the Central Powers were determined to fight to a victorious end while solemnly declining all responsibility before humanity and history for prolonging the war. The Imperial

[144] K. E. Birnbaum, *Peace Moves and U-Boat Warfare*, pp. 228-235.
[145] "Notes on the interview of General Field Marshal v. Hindenburg with the Emperor," December 8, 1916, *Official German Documents*, II, 1071-1072.
[146] "Report in the handwriting of Imperial Chancelor [*sic*] v. Bethmann-Hollweg," *ibid.*, pp. 1072-1073.
[147] K. E. Birnbaum, *Peace Moves and U-Boat Warfare*, pp. 241-242; W. Görlitz (ed.), *Regierte der Kaiser*, p. 240, entry for December 9, 1916.

German Government, the note concluded, would be grateful if the American authorities transmitted this communication to the governments of France, Great Britain, Japan, Russia, Rumania, and Serbia.[148]

Bethmann went before an excited Reichstag that same afternoon, read the text of his note, and said amid tumultuous applause:

"Gentlemen, in August, 1914, our enemies challenged the superiority of power in the world war. Today we raise the question of peace, which is a question of humanity. We await the answer of our enemies with that sereneness of mind which is guaranteed to us by our exterior and interior strength, and by our clear conscience. If our enemies decline to end the war, if they wish to take upon themselves the world's heavy burden of all these terrors which hereafter will follow, then even in the least and smallest homes every German heart will burn in sacred wrath against our enemies, who are unwilling to stop human slaughter in order that their plans of conquest and annihilation may continue.

"In the fateful hour we took a fateful decision. It has been saturated with the blood of hundreds of thousands of our sons and brothers who gave their lives for the safety of their home. Human wits and human understanding are unable to reach to the extreme and last questions in this struggle of nations, which has unveiled all the terrors of earthly life, but also the grandeur of human courage and human will in ways never seen before. God will be the judge. We can proceed on our way."[149]

Receipt of this news from Berlin on December 12 at first depressed Wilson,[150] presumably because he thought that it indicated that the Germans had decided to pursue an independent policy. But he was immensely encouraged—and spurred to action—by two messages on December 13. One was a letter from Bernstorff, replying for the Chancellor to Wilson's confidential message of November 29.[151] Bethmann, Bernstorff said, had told Chargé Grew that he was extremely

[148] T. von Bethmann Hollweg to Chargé Grew, December 12, 1916, *Foreign Relations, 1916, Supplement,* p. 90. Bethmann also asked the Spanish and Swiss governments to transmit the note to the Allied powers.

[149] *New York Times,* December 13, 1916. For one recent commentary on Bethmann's larger motives—strengthening of German morale, assuagement of neutral opinion, and diplomatic preparation for a possible ruthless undersea campaign—see F. Fischer, *Griff nach der Weltmacht,* pp. 375-379.

[150] According to Colonel House, who was at the White House at this time. House Diary, December 14, 1916 (a composite entry covering events of December 12-13, 1916).

[151] For Wilson's message, see above, pp. 195-196.

gratified to know that he could count on the President's cooperation in the restoration of peace, as much as Wilson could count on the practical cooperation of German authorities. "The Chancellor," Bernstorff added, "wishes me to inform you that the steps he is taking to-day are intended to meet the wishes of the President, and that he, therefore, hopes for the President's cooperation."[152] The other was a dispatch from Grew, repeating what Bethmann had told him upon delivering his peace note. Part of the Chancellor's statement follows:

"It is known to me how lively an interest is taken by the President of the United States, who is desirous to see peace restored to the world, in anything that might lead to that end. What the world is longing for, peace alone will be able to give it; the possibility of each nation to grow and develop towards a higher civilization in the interest of humanity. However, the further separation of nations by still larger streams of blood will not bring about lasting peace; nothing but the common endeavor of all nations, to the end that mutual respect and the recognition of their several rights shall take the place of sanguinary strife, will accomplish this.

"Germany's aim was just this at the time when she drew her sword to defend her right to exist, just as at the present moment of her armies' successes. As I repeatedly stated in my speeches when I declared that we were ready to make peace, we never aimed at the destruction of our enemies. I believe that mutual respect and good will between the nations is likewise the lofty aim of the President of the United States, whose recent message, in which he asked for the cooperation of the German authorities to bring about a situation enabling him to take early action in this direction, you were kind enough to deliver to me on December 5. It is my sincere hope that this formal and solemn offer to enter immediately into peace negotiations made by Germany and her allies will coincide with the wishes of the President of the United States."[153]

Wilson closeted himself in his study on the mornings of December 13 and 14. He worked on his own peace note, drafted a cordial reply to the Imperial Chancellor, which he did not send—but he was obviously immensely pleased by Bethmann's messages—and, most important, thought about what he should say to the Allied governments

[152] J. von Bernstorff to E. M. House, December 12, 1916, House Papers. I assume that House showed this letter to Wilson when he saw him on December 13.

[153] Chargé Grew to the Secretary of State, December 12, 1916, *Foreign Relations, 1916, Supplement,* p. 87.

when he transmitted the German peace note to them. "Subsequent thought has developed the enclosed," he wrote to Lansing on December 15 (after a conference with the Secretary earlier in the day), sending a draft of instructions to the American envoys who were to deliver the German note. "I think it best to be perfectly frank and explicit. This frees what we intend to do of all possible irritation to the Allies, and prepares the way for what we ought to do in any case unless their immediate action renders it unnecessary."[154] Wilson's instructions follow:

"In bringing this note to the attention of the Foreign Office, as requested, intimate quite explicitly that, while you are submitting it on behalf of the respective Governments only, and in no sense as the representative of the Government of the United States, this Government is deeply interested in the result of these unexpected overtures, and would deeply appreciate a confidential intimation of the character and purpose of the response that will be made, and will itself presently have certain very earnest representations to make on behalf of the manifest interests of neutral nations and of humanity itself to which it will ask that very serious consideration be given. It does not make these representations now because it does not wish to connect them with the proposed overtures or have them construed in any way as an attempt at mediation, notwithstanding the fact that these overtures afford an admirable occasion for their consideration. The Government of the United States had it in mind to make them entirely on its own initiative and before it had any knowledge of the present attitude or suggestions of the Central Governments. It will make the same representations to the Governments of the Central powers and wishes to make them almost immediately, if necessary, but not as associated with the overtures of either group of belligerents. The present overtures have created an unexpected opportunity for looking at the world's case as a whole, but the United States would have itself created the occasion had it fallen out otherwise."[155]

Lansing dispatched the German note, along with the foregoing instructions, at five p.m. on December 16. The big question now was when Wilson should send his own note. Press reports of unfavorable reaction to the German offer in Allied capitals, particularly Petrograd, where the Duma voted on December 15 to reject the German offer

[154] W. W. to R. Lansing, December 15, 1916, Baker Collection.
[155] As printed in *Foreign Relations, 1916, Supplement*, pp. 94-95.

out of hand,[156] and an announcement in London on the following day that Lloyd George would make a statement in the House of Commons on December 19,[157] made it clear that the Allies might slam the door to peace altogether unless Wilson moved at once. As he wrote to Colonel House after sending his note, "Things have moved so fast that I did not have time to get you down here to go over it with you. It was ... written and sent off within a very few hours, for fear the governments of the Entente might in the meantime so have committed themselves against peace as to make the situation even more hopeless than it had been."[158] Or, as he put it again, "We are just now, of course, holding our breath for fear the overtures of the Central Powers with regard to peace will meet with a rebuff instead of an acceptance."[159]

Wilson completed revision of his note on December 17 and sent it to Lansing for a final reading. "Here is the note we promised to send and which I think it highly necessary to send at once before it be too late to inject new elements into the debate now going on among the nations at war," he wrote. "... I would be very much obliged if you would as early as possible make any comments upon the matter or manner of the paper which may occur to you, in order that we may get the message off at the earliest possible moment. Have you any special instructions to suggest to Page in London to make him realize what is expected of him?"[160] Lansing returned the document with only minor stylistic changes and extravagant approval. "I do not think," he went on, "that anything can be added to the instruction to Page in London. It is explicit and shows very clearly what is expected of him. I do not think he will say anything to moderate the effect because I do not see what he can say. He will see, I am sure, that you are in downright earnest."[161]

Lansing put the note on the wire to American diplomatic missions in all belligerent capitals at 9:30 in the evening of December 18. The President, the instructions accompanying the document read, "requests that you present it with the utmost earnestness of support. He wishes the impression clearly conveyed that it would be very hard for the Government of the United States to understand a negative reply."

[156] *New York Times*, December 16, 1916.
[157] *ibid.*, December 17, 1916.
[158] W. W. to E. M. House, December 19, 1916, House Papers.
[159] W. W. to P. A. Stovall, December 19, 1916, Wilson Papers.
[160] W. W. to R. Lansing, December 17, 1916, Baker Collection.
[161] R. Lansing to W. W., December 17, 1916, Wilson Papers.

The note itself began by saying that the President, motivated by friendship for the belligerents and concern for the neutrals, had long contemplated the step he was about to take. It was in no way connected with the recent overture of the Central Powers. The President desired to suggest that an early occasion be sought to call out from all the belligerents an avowal of the terms upon which they would be willing to stop fighting and work for restoration of peace. The note continued: "He takes the liberty of calling attention to the fact that the objects which the statesmen of the belligerents on both sides have in mind in this war are virtually the same, as stated in general terms to their own people and to the world. Each side desires to make the rights and privileges of weak peoples and small states as secure against aggression or denial in the future as the rights and privileges of the great and powerful states now at war. Each wishes itself to be made secure in the future, along with all other nations and peoples, against the recurrence of wars like this and against aggression or selfish interference of any kind. Each would be jealous of the formation of any more rival leagues to preserve an uncertain balance of power amidst multiplying suspicions; but each is ready to consider the formation of a league of nations to insure peace and justice throughout the world. Before that final step can be taken, however, each deems it necessary first to settle the issues of the present war upon terms which will certainly safeguard the independence, the territorial integrity, and the political and commercial freedom of the nations involved."

The people and government of the United States, the message went on, were vitally concerned in the settlement and stood ready, even eager, to cooperate in achieving these objectives. But the war had to be ended first, "lest it should presently be too late to accomplish the greater things which lie beyond its conclusion, lest the situation of neutral nations, now exceedingly hard to endure, be rendered altogether intolerable, and lest, more than all, an injury be done civilization itself which can never be atoned for or repaired." The hope of building a new world community would be idle and vain if the war continued until one side or the other was exhausted. The life of the entire world had been affected by the war. "Every part of the great family of mankind has felt the burden and terror of this unprecedented contest of arms." And yet the concrete objects for which it was being fought had never been definitively stated.

The leaders of the rival alliances had talked very much the same way in stating war objectives in general terms. It might be that they were nearer to agreement than they knew, and that an exchange of terms might prepare the way for a conference. "The President," the note concluded, "is not proposing peace; he is not even offering mediation. He is merely proposing that soundings be taken in order that we may learn, the neutral nations with the belligerent, how near the haven of peace we may be for which all mankind longs with an intense and increasing longing. He believes that the spirit in which he speaks and the objects which he seeks will be understood by all concerned, and he confidently hopes for a response which will bring a new light into the affairs of the world."[162]

It was weaker than the first draft in its omission of a specific call for a peace conference. It was weaker also in its description of the impact of the war on the neutrals, and in its omission of the first draft's warning that future American policy would depend to a large degree upon the response that the belligerents returned. But Wilson had strengthened the note by adding the long paragraph assimilating the public war aims of the rival spokesmen. It not only made his own neutrality indelibly clear but also made it difficult for the belligerents to deny that they were not fighting for the noble aims that they had avowed. Finally, the note was more moving in its appeal to the conscience of Europe than the first draft had been.

The future of mankind would depend upon the replies.

[162] The Secretary of State to Ambassadors and Ministers in belligerent countries, December 18, 1916, *Foreign Relations, 1916, Supplement*, pp. 97-99.

CHAPTER VI

The Quest for a Negotiated Peace

WILSON's peace note, published in the morning newspapers on December 21, 1916, set off discussion across the continent. Senator Lodge observed privately that it proved that the President was working hand in glove with the Germans to save them from deserved punishment by the Allies.[1] Theodore Roosevelt said publicly that the note was full of "preposterous absurdities" and "profoundly immoral" and "wickedly false" statements.[2] A few other ardent friends of the Allies agreed.[3] Secretary Baker sent the President a letter from an Ohio correspondent repeating some of these comments and saying that it was now painfully evident that Wilson had "no real conception of the moral issues involved in this great war."[4] Wilson's comments, the only ones on record showing his reaction to this criticism, were revealing. "I wish every day," he wrote, "that there were more *mere* Americans in this country. Almost all of our fellow citizens this side the Rock Mississippi seem to think in terms set by the thinking or the prepossessions of one side or the other across the water. If Professor Johnson had lived with the English statesmen for the past two years and seen the real inside of their minds I think he would feel differently."[5]

Actually, the overwhelming majority of commentators and leaders who expressed an opinion approved Wilson's note more or less extravagantly. "It is a most timely proffer," Senator Stone said, to cite only one, "and I believe and hope it marks the beginning of the end.

[1] H. C. Lodge to T. Roosevelt, December 21, 1916, Roosevelt Papers.

[2] T. Roosevelt, statement in the *New York Times*, January 4, 1917.

[3] e. g., Anderson Diary, December 22, 1916; *ibid.*, December 24, 1916, recording a conversation with Elihu Root; Frank Jewett Mather, Jr., to the Editor, December 24, 1916, New York *Nation*, CIII (December 28, 1916), 607; statement of certain "Christians of America," in the *New York Times*, January 1, 1917; George Burton Adams to the Editor, December 24, 1916, *New York Times*, December 26, 1916; report of a sermon by the Reverend William T. Manning in Trinity Church, New York City, on December 25, 1916, *ibid.*; and the *Wall Street Journal*, December 28, 1916.

[4] W. H. Johnson to N. D. Baker, December 24, 1916, N. D. Baker Papers.

[5] W. W. to N. D. Baker, December 26, 1916, *ibid.*

It throws the question of continuing the war squarely on the belligerents, and I sincerely hope it will lead to negotiations and peace. . . . The President is to be heartily commended for his courage, and to be congratulated on having seized the logical moment to urge the substitution of discussion for the carnage of the battle field."[6]

This reaction was precisely what Lansing feared the most as he scanned the newspapers in the morning of December 21. It was bad enough that Americans would think that peace was not far away. But it was worse still that the world would interpret the President's move as supporting the German peace offer.[7] He had, somehow, to make it clear to the Allies that the American government would stand behind them even to the point of entering the war on their side.[8] Without consulting the President, Lansing made the following statement to a press conference in the morning of December 21:

[6] *New York Times*, December 21, 1916, also quoting Representative Kitchin, Speaker Clark, and Representative W. W. Bailey. See also the New York *World*, December 21, and 22, 1916; H. Croly to E. M. House, December 26, 1916, House Papers; J. H. Clarke to W. W., December 21, 1916, Wilson Papers; John Sharp Williams to W. W., December 22, 1916, *ibid.*; Ida M. Tarbell to W. W., December 30, 1916, *ibid.*; New York *Nation*, c111 (December 28, 1916), 596; *New Republic*, ix (December 30, 1916), 228-231, 231-232; W. J. Bryan, "The President's Peace Note," *The Commoner*, xvii (January 1917), 3.

[7] See the memorandum printed in R. Lansing, *War Memoirs*, pp. 188-190.

[8] Lansing had set down in his diary, December 3, 1916, his deep conviction that Wilson's whole peace move was wrong and unwise because it would gravely alienate the Allies. It was imperative, he added, that the United States support the Allies, not be in controversy with them. The main problem, Lansing went on, was to get Wilson to agree with this proposition.

The Secretary of State, fearing that Wilson would react adversely to a memorandum, drafted a speech on Americanism saying, among other things, that there was a fundamental antagonism between democracies, which were inherently peace-loving, and autocracies, which were inherently militaristic, oppressive, and aggressive, and that a league of nations could succeed only if it was composed of democracies which would keep their word. R. Lansing, "Americanism," MS. in the Lansing Papers, Princeton. He sent this speech to Wilson on about December 15, saying that he contemplated giving it soon and wondered whether the President would approve. He of course hoped to draw out Wilson's private views. "This," Wilson replied, "is so interesting a paper, and is so *true* that it distresses me to suggest that its utterance at this particular time would be unwise. But I must frankly say that I think that the considerations it urges, and the policy, are what we ought to have *in mind* in the weighty transactions which we are (I hope) approaching, but ought not to make explicit before the event and before the necessity to do so. Perhaps it would be possible for you to maintain the general theory of the first part of the paper without making the very specific application of what follows; though that, too, would be difficult, I see. W. W. to R. Lansing, December 19, 1916, *ibid*. See also R. Lansing to W. W., January 23, 1917, Wilson Papers.

The reasons for the sending of the note were as follows:

It isn't our material interest we had in mind when the note was sent, but more and more our own rights are becoming involved by the belligerents on both sides, so that the situation is becoming increasingly critical.

I mean that we are drawing nearer the verge of war ourselves, and therefore we are entitled to know exactly what each belligerent seeks, in order that we may regulate our conduct in the future. . . .

The sending of this note will indicate the possibility of our being forced into the war. That possibility ought to serve as a restraining and sobering force, safeguarding American rights. It may also serve to force an earlier conclusion of the war. Neither the President nor myself regard this note as a peace note; it is merely an effort to get the belligerents to define the end for which they are fighting.[9]

Tumulty sent a copy of the statement to Wilson probably just before lunch,[10] and the President must have erupted in one of the few rages that he ever indulged himself. Lansing's statement, he surely thought, was either misleading or completely false. Wilson knew that it had already set off a war scare in Wall Street[11] and prompted everyone in Washington to think that the American government contemplated hostilities with Germany in the near future. Wilson could have guessed that this impression would in turn make impossible any effective negotiations with either Germany or the Allies. The President told Colonel House later that he almost decided then and there to demand Lansing's resignation.[12] Wilson typed out the following letter to the Secretary of State as soon as he had brought his temper more or less under control:

"I quite understand that you did not realize the impression of your reference to war in your statement of this morning would make, but I feel so strongly that the whole atmosphere of our present representations may be altered by that reference that I wrote [write] to suggest this:

"Would it not be possible for you to issue another statement, for the papers of to-morrow morning, saying that you found that your utterance of this morning had been radically misinterpreted, and ex-

[9] *New York Times*, December 22, 1916.

[10] J. P. Tumulty to W. W., December 21, 1916, Wilson Papers.

[11] Lansing's statement caused panic on the New York Stock Exchange, which had already been upset by the publication of the President's peace note. United States Steel fell from 123⅝ to 100, Crucible Steel, more than nine points, Baldwin Locomotive, thirteen and a half points. *New York Times*, December 22, 1916.

[12] House Diary, January 11, 1917.

plaining that your intention was merely to suggest the very direct interest the neutral nations have in the question of possible terms of peace and that it was not at all in your mind to intimate any change in the policy of neutrality which the country has so far so consistently pursued in the face of accumulating difficulties. You will know how to phrase it and how to give your unqualified endorsement to the whole tone and purpose of our note.

"I write this because caught in a net of engagements from which it seems impossible to extricate myself on short notice."[13]

Lansing went to the White House in the afternoon at Wilson's request. The President repeated the request made in his letter. Lansing tells us in his memoirs that he agreed to do so only on condition that the second statement should not contradict the first.[14] However that may have been, the Secretary of State returned to his office and gave out a statement that was merely a paraphrase of what Wilson had suggested that he say. It read:

I have learned from several quarters that a wrong impression was made by the statement which I made this morning, and I wish to correct that impression.

My intention was to suggest the very direct and necessary interest which this country, as one of the neutral nations, has in the possible terms which the belligerents may have in mind, and I did not intend to intimate that the Government was considering any change in its policy of neutrality, which it has consistently pursued in the face of constantly increasing difficulties.

I regret that my words were open to any other construction, as I now realize that they were. I think that the whole tone and language of the note to the belligerents show the purpose without further comment on my part. It is needless to say that I am unreservedly in support of that purpose and hope to see it accepted.[15]

Other evidence suggests that Lansing had in fact concluded that the national interest and good of mankind demanded that he do his best to sabotage the President's peace effort altogether, or at least make certain that it culminate in American belligerency on the Allied side. The Secretary of State called the French Ambassador, Jusserand, to his office in the afternoon of December 20 to assure him that the President was not supporting the German peace offer. Wilson, Lansing

[13] W. W. to R. Lansing, December 21, 1916, Baker Collection.
[14] R. Lansing, *War Memoirs*, p. 187.
[15] *New York Times*, December 22, 1916.

said, had launched his own appeal, not to stop hostilities or even to mediate, but to hasten the end of the conflict by making known on what conditions the belligerents would consent to conclude peace. They were free to draw up their most extreme demands as they saw fit. One knew well enough, Lansing went on, that the President's preferences lay with the democracies. He sought nothing that could harm the interests of the Allies. He wished only to know what *they* wanted. Speaking personally, he would think that they might rightfully demand the return of Alsace-Lorraine to France, a considerable indemnity for France, Belgium, and Serbia, and settlement of the Balkan affair by an international commission. They might above all make it clear that they would deal only with a reformed and democratized Reich. He had little faith, Lansing added, in the President's league to maintain peace. Only liberalization of the autocracies could guarantee the future peace of the world. Even Jusserand was somewhat startled. Publication of such sweeping terms might, he said, strengthen the German will to resist. Lansing replied that the Germans were much nearer than the Allies thought to acceptance of such demands.[16]

Lansing, in a conference with the British Ambassador, Spring Rice, on December 22 repeated what he had said to Jusserand almost word for word. He then added the following new terms for the Allies to demand: an autonomous Poland under Russian sovereignty, transfer of the Trentino from Austria to Italy, and expulsion of Turkey from Europe.[17] It is almost superfluous to say that Lansing did not inform the President about these conversations.

Lansing well understood that Wilson intended to move beyond his call for terms to independent, neutral mediation. The Secretary of State also knew that the Allies could obtain such terms as he had suggested only by a crushing military victory, and that publication of them would be tantamount to a new declaration of war and would prolong hostilities, not end them. He knew, furthermore, that the Germans would have to resort to an all-out submarine campaign if the war proceeded much longer, and that this in turn would probably provoke American belligerency. Hence we come to what seems to be

[16] Ambassador Jusserand to the Foreign Ministry, December 20, 1916, and Ambassador Jusserand to A. Briand, December 21, 1916, partially quoted and summarized in E. Hoelzle, "Das Experiment des Friedens im Ersten Weltkrieg," *loc. cit.*, p. 477.

[17] Ambassador Jusserand to the Foreign Ministry, December 22, 1916, noted in *ibid.*, p. 478.

the only possible conclusion—that the Secretary of State was maneuvering to promote American intervention on the Allied side.

That, too, was probably the purpose of the "verge of war" statement. It was intended as a not-so-subtle message to the Allied governments and notice to Germany that the American government would support the Allies if the Germans rejected Allied demands and intensified the war at sea. This is probably what he meant in the following cryptic letter:

"In regard to my statements concerning the note to the belligerents I will one of these days tell you the whole story. The inside facts are most interesting and I believe that you will find my course was justified. Of course I have been generally criticized by the press but I do not blame the editors as on the face of it they are right. Unfortunately I can not make public the real reason now—I do not know as I ever can, although I hope it may be possible to do so someday. For the present, however, I must bear the blame of having made an unpardonable blunder, and I do so with perfect equanimity knowing that my action accomplished what it was intended to accomplish."[18]

Lansing never did reveal the "real reason," but, as we will soon see, he had indeed accomplished his main purpose by the time that he wrote this letter.

Meanwhile, Colonel House was in New York, growing more irritated the more he thought about the President's note. Wilson sent him his own typed copy on December 19. House was shocked and upset by what he thought was the President's unpardonable maladroitness in assimilating Allied and German war aims. House, unlike Lansing, was not now seeking to promote American military intervention. "He no longer seemed to regard American intervention in the war as practical politics," Sir Horace Plunkett wrote in his diary, after having lunch with House on December 20. The Colonel simply did not think that peace was possible. America had nothing to fear from Germany, he told Plunkett. England was the only power that could threaten American interests.[19] As House wrote in his diary on that same day:

"I have seldom seen anything he [Wilson] has written with so many changes. My letter to him tells of my thought on this subject. They [*sic*] do not tell, however, that I deprecate one sentence which will

[18] R. Lansing to E. N. Smith, January 21, 1917, Lansing Papers.
[19] The Diary of Sir Horace Plunkett, December 20, 1916, Plunkett Foundation, London; hereinafter cited as the Plunkett Diary.

give further impetus to the belief that he does not yet understand what the Allies are fighting for. That one sentence will enrage them. I talked to him for ten minutes when I was there and got him to eliminate from the original draft a much more pronounced offense of the same character, but he has put it back in a modified form. He seems obsessed with that thought, and he cannot write or talk on the subject of the war without voicing it. It has done more to make him unpopular in the Allied countries than any one thing he has done, and it will probably keep him from taking the part which he ought to take in peace negotiations.

"I find the President has nearly destroyed all the work I have done in Europe. He knows how I feel about this and how the Allies feel about it, and yet the refrain always appears in some form or other. Lansing, too, is afflicted with the same disease, but in his case it is not so serious as with the President.

"Sir Horace Plunkett . . . , too, confirms everything I have heard about the dislike of the United States among the people of England, and he did not deny there was a possibility of future trouble between Great Britain and this country. I am writing the President about this tonight. I wish I could make him realize the seriousness of the international situation and could open his eyes to the state of mind and their feeling toward us. I do not see how he can figure largely in an international adjustment as long as they feel toward him as they do. It is all so unnecessary. He could have done and said the same things if he had said and done them in a different way."[20]

House wrote to Wilson that same night remarking that he was not afraid of Germany after the war, and that it was conceivable that America might have trouble with England if she was victorious. "In my opinion," he added, "it will not be safe for this country to be as belligerent towards her in the future as we have been in the past. Most of Great Britain is as war mad as Germany when I visited there in 1914 and we can no longer count upon their looking at things from the same viewpoint as heretofore."[21] House was deadly serious in his fear of actual armed conflict with Great Britain. For example, in a conversation with Secretary Daniels at the Cabinet dinner at the White House on December 12, he asked Daniels how well the United States was prepared for war if it came tomorrow. "War with whom?" Daniels asked. "With Great Britain," House replied. Britain and

---

[20] House Diary, December 20, 1916.
[21] E. M. House to W. W., December 20, 1916, Wilson Papers.

Japan, House wrote in his diary two days later, could put the United States out of business as quickly as their armies could march across the American continent.[22]

House's mood did not improve during the next few days. Plunkett made the following tantalizing entry in his diary after talking with him on December 22: "I fear Wilson is much of what his enemies say of him. House is disgusted at many of his recent utterances. But I must not write more here."[23]

First reactions in Great Britain and France seemed fully to bear out House's gloomy predictions. The President's note was delivered at Whitehall and the Quai d'Orsay on December 20 and published in the British press on December 22 and in French newspapers on Christmas Eve.

The *New York Times* correspondent in London reported, after publication of the note, that the British public was reeling in shock, surprise, and consternation.[24] Most people in the British Isles were now mesmerized by war passion only recently intensified by huge losses in the Somme offensive. There was reason to fear, Ambassador Page wrote, that Wilson's note "will for a long time cause a deep, even if silent, resentment because, as the British interpret it, it seems to them to mean that the President fails to understand the motives and high necessities, the aims and the sacrifices of the Allies who regard themselves as fighting, now with good hope, to save the world from a despotic inundation."[25] The novelist, Hall Caine, expressed outraged British reaction even more feelingly:

"President Wilson's note is a blow to the allied nations in general and to Great Britain in particular. It is a staggering blow.

"We do not, for one moment, doubt its sincerity. . . . But the very sincerity of the note, coupled with its apparent insensibility to convictions and emotions which at this moment are as deep as our souls, makes it a surprising, almost a stupefying document. . . .

"It is small comfort to us today that he has intervened after millions of lives have been lost, after thousands of millions of money have been spent, after the welfare of the world has been shaken to its founda-

[22] House Diary, December 14, 1916.
[23] Plunkett Diary, December 22, 1916.
[24] C. H. Grasty in the *New York Times*, December 23, 1916.
[25] Ambassador Page to the Secretary of State, December 22, 1916, *Foreign Relations, 1916, Supplement*, pp. 108-109.

"An Unfriendly Act"
Cesare in the New York *Evening Post*

tion, and at a moment when we are being made the victims of an undisguised and undisguisable plot to put us in the wrong before the neutral nations by making us responsible for the continuance of the war. God grant that President Wilson's note, however worthily intended, may not help that plot. We only too plainly see that it may. . . .

"[We are compelled to conclude that Wilson is insensible to the moral issues of the war.] Then we are forced with grief and reluctance to think that the war has never really entered into his soul, that he has never really understood the inner meaning and full tragedy of it, that our faith in him as a probable arbitrator has gone and that the trust we have so long cherished must be considered at an end."[26]

English press reaction on the whole was equally bitter, in spite of a warning from the Foreign Office that editors had to be discreet and avoid questioning the President's sincerity. The *Times* spoke of "the pain and resentment" aroused in all quarters by Wilson's "amazing" note.[27] "The President," the *Pall Mall Gazette* observed, "is as unlucky as he is highminded. His zeal for humanity has evoked a step that will create the bitterest resentment among all who are fighting, working, and dying for the very principles he has at heart."[28] The *Morning Post* suggested that it would be well for America to get into the fighting on one side or the other, no matter which, or mind her own business.[29] "To the joy of Berlin and the amazement of the Allies," the *Observer* added, "a memorable mistake has been made at the White House." Wilson's words, this journal went on, "disparage our cause, they dishonour our dead, they deny by implication the fundamental facts of the case; in the name of perfect neutrality they render exclusive service to the enemy; they are felt as an insult, however undesigned, by every sound man and woman amongst the Allies; they tend to re-exasperate to the utmost the bitterness of the struggle and to prolong the task of bringing it to a just and safe conclusion."[30] The small group of British radicals working for a negotiated peace were, of course, overjoyed,[31] and their spokesmen, the *Manchester Guardian* and the *Nation*, tried valiantly to stem the anti-Wilson tide.[32] But it was too strong to be turned back or even diverted. Comment in the Paris press, when the note was published, was considerably less frenetic, as the French Foreign Ministry was beginning to think that Wilson's

[26] Hall Caine to the Editor, December 23, 1916, *New York Times*, December 24, 1916; also the report of the sermon by the Right Reverend H. E. Ryle in Westminster Abbey on Christmas Day, *ibid.*, December 26, 1916; and especially J. Bryce to E. M. House, December 27, 1916, House Papers, and H. Plunkett to E. M. House, December 27, 1916, Wilson Papers.

[27] London *Times*, December 22 and 23, 1916.

[28] London *Pall Mall Gazette*, December 22, 1916.

[29] London *Morning Post*, December 22, 1916.

[30] London *Observer*, December 24, 1916.

[31] e. g., E. M. House to W. W., December 29, 1916, Wilson Papers, enclosing an undated memorandum by Josiah Wedgwood; J. H. Whitehouse to E. M. House, December 21 and 22, 1916, Whitehouse Papers; N. Buxton to E. M. House, December 25, 1916, House Papers.

[32] *Manchester Guardian*, December 23, 1916; London *Nation*, xx (January 6, 1917), 485.

démarche might not be fatal after all and had instructed editors to use extreme discretion in public comment.[33]

The note caused great dismay, consternation, and surprise in official circles in London and Paris, in spite of the advance warning Wilson had given while transmitting the German peace invitation. "Bryce," Page reported, "came to see me profoundly depressed. . . . I am told that Mr. Asquith when asked about the note replied sadly, 'Don't talk to me about it. It is most disheartening.' A luncheon guest at the palace yesterday informed me that the King wept while he expressed his surprise and depression."[34] Lord Bertie confided to his diary: ". . . [Wilson] has not the vile excuse of Presidential electoral necessities. We shall be obliged to reply with civility and suppressed anger. Unfortunately, the American people generally back up their President when he is arrogant to a foreign Government."[35] And Paul Cambon added: "This professor, with his dogmatism and inspired airs, is acting like a knave."[36]

The director of the Political Division in the French Foreign Ministry, Paul de Margerie, studied Wilson's note between December 18 and 20 and recorded in a memorandum his suspicions that Germany and America were in fact working together, along with the advice that the French government should discredit Wilson's overture with the other neutrals who were envious of the President's role.[37] The Foreign Ministry at once prepared a brief reply thanking Wilson courteously and saying that the time was not ripe for discussion of terms and, on December 22, sent a copy to the British Foreign Office for its comment. Lloyd George was not disposed to act so quickly. The British nation, he knew, faced one of the darkest hours in its long and glorious history. A recent review of the British food and tonnage situations had shown that grave crises in supply impended.[38] Lloyd George had himself prepared a review of the military outlook that clearly indicated

[33] See, e. g., Paris *Le Matin*, December 24, 1916; Paris *Petit Parisien*; S. Pinchon in Paris *Petit Journal*, December 24, 1916; A. Capus in Paris *Figaro*, December 24, 1916.

[34] Ambassador Page to the Secretary of State, December 22, 1916, *Foreign Relations, 1916, Supplement*, p. 109.

[35] Lady Algernon G. Lennox (ed.), *The Diary of Lord Bertie of Thame*, II, 86; entry for December 20, 1916.

[36] P. Cambon "à son fils," December 21, 1916, H. Cambon (ed.), *Paul Cambon, Correspondance, 1870-1924*, III, 135.

[37] P. de Margerie, memorandum dated December 20, 1916, E. Hoelzle, "Das Experiment des Friedens im Ersten Weltkrieg," *loc. cit.*, p. 476.

[38] *Printed for the use of the Cabinet. November 1916. FOOD PROSPECTS IN 1917*, Cabinet paper in the Asquith Papers.

that the Allies were in danger of losing the war and said frankly that time was on the German, not the Allied, side.[39] "We are going to lose this war," he had told Sir Maurice Hankey, secretary of the Imperial Defence Committee, soon after preparing this memorandum.[40] Thus the Foreign Office, undoubtedly at the Prime Minister's direction, had suggested to the French Foreign Minister that the Allies ask the Germans to state their peace proposals precisely. And Lloyd George, in spite of a curt rebuff from the Quai d'Orsay,[41] had indicated in a speech to the House of Commons on December 19, commenting on the German peace offer, that he was not prepared to slam the door on peace discussions. In fact, this speech could be read, in spite of all its bombast, as a challenge to Germany to state her terms.[42]

Lloyd George and the War Cabinet discussed the President's peace note in the morning of December 21, and the Prime Minister talked to the French Ambassador, Paul Cambon, that afternoon. He personally thought, Lloyd George said, that Wilson's assimilation of Allied and German war aims was an insult. But it would be necessary to send a reply, and that would not be easy. It would not do, the Prime Minister knew, to send an outright refusal, for that would be playing directly into German hands. Spring Rice had already warned that the Allies should not decline to receive definite terms of peace from the Germans. "The German position in the U.S.A.," he had added, "would be much strengthened by such a refusal."[43] The War Cabinet, Lloyd George told Cambon, wanted to think about the matter for a day or so. Meanwhile, the Prime Minister went on, he had instructed his Cabinet Ministers to determine the degree to which Great Britain was dependent upon the United States for supplies. He thought that it might be wise if the French government also gave some thought to

[39] *STATEMENT DRAFTED BY MR. LLOYD GEORGE AS A BASIS FOR THE PRIME MINISTER'S STATEMENT AT THE PARIS CONFERENCE ON NOVEMBER 15, 1916. Printed for the Committee of Imperial Defence. December 1916,* copy in the Papers of Alfred, Lord Milner, New College Library, Oxford; printed in D. Lloyd George, *War Memoirs,* I, 545-555.

[40] Lord Hankey, *The Supreme Command, 1914-1918* (2 vols.), II, 557.

[41] The Allies, the French Foreign Ministry said, should tell Germany that they would negotiate with her one day only by imposing terms on her. The Allies would then have their enemies at their mercy and would "enforce the fulfillment of their pledge whether they wanted it or not." P. de Margerie to P. Cambon, December 19, 1916, E. Hoelzle, "Das Experiment des Friedens im Ersten Weltkrieg," *loc. cit.,* p. 476.

[42] *New York Times,* December 20, 1916.

[43] D. Lloyd George, *War Memoirs,* I, 657.

its dependence upon the United States, and he would like to know the result. Wilson would not be able to push things too far if the three democracies of France, Britain, and Italy stood united and firm. It would be well, Lloyd George concluded, if French leaders came to London soon for discussions.

Receipt of messages from Jusserand and Spring Rice between December 21 and December 24 brought new light and much cheer to London and Paris. About reports sent to London, we know definitely only about the one telling of Lansing's conversation with Spring Rice on December 22. But we know all that Jusserand was reporting to the French Foreign Ministry, and we may be certain that his British colleague relayed the same information, along with other intelligence of his own, to the Foreign Office. Jusserand reported by telegram on December 22 that a friend of the President close to all departments had come to assure him that the American peace note should not be interpreted as a threat to the Allies, that the entire administration was behind the Allied cause, and that in any event the country would not follow the President if he attempted to enforce a policy injurious to France.[44] Jusserand also telegraphed Lansing's two statements of December 21 with the explanation that the "verge of war" statement expressed the American government's real fear, namely, that German submarine frightfulness would soon drive the United States into the war.

It seems a reasonable assumption that the British and French leaders concluded, particularly after reading reports of Jusserand's and Spring Rice's conversations with Lansing about terms, that Wilson and Lansing were probably maneuvering to prepare the American people for participation in the war and wanted an Allied statement of war aims that would seem to coincide with Wilson's own announced broad objectives. It is possible that this is an understatement, and that French and British leaders interpreted Lansing's remarks as meaning that the American government wanted a statement of extreme terms in order to prolong the war and thus hasten American participation on the Allied side. However that may have been, Lord Robert Cecil was notably relaxed when he talked to Ambassador Cambon on December 24. The reply to Wilson, Cecil said, would require much thought. It would be well to defer definitive discussion until French representatives were in London on December 28. Moreover, the new inquiry

---

[44] Ambassador Jusserand to the Foreign Ministry, December 22, 1916, E. Hoelzle, "Das Experiment des Friedens im Ersten Weltkrieg," *loc. cit.*, p. 478.

into British dependence on the United States was apparently canceled, as was the one that the French government had undertaken.

Chargé Grew read the President's note to Foreign Secretary Zimmermann in the late afternoon of December 21, and German newspapers published Associated Press summaries of the note on December 22 and the full text on December 23. Naval, Pan-German, and Conservative spokesmen angrily repudiated Wilson's right to interfere and said that the President was trying both to save the Allies from defeat and the United States from belligerency. "Wilson," a typically bellicose editor declared, "knew how to control his peace proclivities and humanitarian fanaticism long enough to make the world war a splendid business for America. . . . America has earned what there was to be earned out of the world war; there is no longer any profit in it. . . . The danger of the submarine war is the other reason for Wilson's peace efforts."[45] Lansing's "verge of war" statement, Count Ernst von Reventlow said, made the President's deeper motives clear. He meant it as a threat that America would enter the war on the Allied side if Germany unleashed her submarines. "Germany," he went on, "is to be prevented from using anything that would bring catastrophe to the Anglo-American cause."[46] The spokesman of the powerful Centre Party added: "America has put her money in Entente business, and America must therefore try to obtain the best possible conditions for her debtors so that they can later fulfill their financial obligations to the United States. For these reasons the United States is out of the question as an impartial mediator, to say nothing of President Wilson, who at every opportunity has shown his weakness for England by his deeds."[47]

Moderate and liberal editors were either more charitable or else openly approving. "We welcome President Wilson's step," Theodor Wolff declared in the *Berliner Tageblatt*, adding that no responsible statesman had the right to reject peace proposals simply because they came from Washington.[48] "Let us not forget," *Vorwärts*, organ of

---

[45] Berlin *Taeglische Rundschau*, evening edn., December 22, 1916.

[46] Berlin *Deutsche Tageszeitung*, evening edn., December 22, 1916.

[47] *Kölnische Volkszeitung*, evening edn., December 22, 1916. In the same vein, see also Georg Bernhard in the Berlin *Vossische Zeitung*, evening edn., December 22, 1916; Berlin *Kreuz-zeitung*, December 22 and 24, 1916, quoted in the *New York Times*, December 24 and 25; Berlin *Morgenpost*, December 24, 1916, quoted in *ibid.*, December 25, 1916; Berlin *Die Post*, December 24, 1916, cited in *ibid.*

[48] *Berliner Tageblatt*, evening edn., December 22, 1916.

the Social Democratic Party, added, "that the chauvinistic press of England rages against Wilson, just as the Pan-German papers among us do. The Pan-Germans brand the Wilson proposal as an English maneuver; the English jingoes say 'the German attitude toward Wilson is nothing but a feint.' . . . In any event, it is a new and important guarantee that negotiations regarding peace cannot now cease, that the question has begun to assume a more concrete form, and that it must steadily gain in intensity and significance."[49]

Reactions in official German circles, except for Zimmermann's initial personal comments to Grew,[50] were overwhelmingly cool or hostile. Zimmermann sent a copy of the American note to the Emperor on December 22, while a Wolff Agency summary of the note and a copy of Lansing's two statements arrived at Supreme Headquarters on the same day. "The President knows the British Program," William wrote in English at the end of the American note. ". . . They began the war[,] they have been beaten all along the line, they must state their intentions first. We the party attacked, being on our defensive purely, will state our proposals afterwards as victors."[51] At the end of Zimmermann's covering letter he commented: "When the President wants to put an end to the war, he needs only to threaten the English blockade pirates with a munitions embargo and a blocking of the market for loans, and take reprisals against robbing of the mails and the black list. Then the war will soon be ended without notes, conferences, etc. I won't go to any conference! Certainly not under his chairmanship!"[52] Finally, the Emperor wrote on the Wolff telegram: "The note has undoubtedly been prepared in collusion with England, so that the conference which we don't want and would be no good to us comes up again, and so that Lloyd George on the other hand does not need to refuse point blank because he fears the odium and fury of the deceived neutrals. He will blame us for rejecting the conference! The threatening submarine war!"[53]

[49] Berlin *Vorwärts*, December 23, 1916; also Berlin *Lokal-Anzeiger*, evening edn., December 22, 1916; *ibid.*, evening edn., December 23, 1916; Berlin *Vossische Zeitung*, morning edn., December 23, 1916 (the editor was much more favorably inclined after reading the full text of Wilson's note); *Kölnische Zeitung*, December 23, 1916, and *Frankfurter Zeitung*, December 23, 1916, both summarized in Ambassador Gerard to the Secretary of State, December 23, 1916, *Foreign Relations, 1916, Supplement*, p. 113.
[50] Chargé Grew to the Secretary of State, December 21, 1916, *ibid.*, pp. 110-111.
[51] K. E. Birnbaum, *Peace Moves and U-Boat Warfare*, p. 368.
[52] *ibid.*, pp. 368-369. My translation.
[53] *ibid.*, p. 369. My translation.

To Hindenburg, the President's note was only further proof that Germany had to proceed to urgent preparations for an all-out submarine campaign. "The Entente," he wrote to Bethmann on December 23, "is proceeding with the war with the means at its disposal. There is no doubt of this, in view of the fact that we have been so roughly repulsed by every parliament. Even Wilson's efforts can accomplish nothing unless our opponents are willing to give themselves the lie. I believe that Wilson's proposal was evoked by England."[54]

Bethmann, Zimmermann, and other civilian leaders in Berlin were also deeply disappointed, if for other reasons. It was bad enough that Wilson has asked the German government to *publish* its peace terms. Bethmann had preserved internal political unity only by appearing as all things to all parties on this subject, and a forthright avowal of terms might well destroy the party truce and set both the Socialists and liberals and the Pan-Germans and Conservatives against the government. Worse still, Bethmann and the Foreign Office believed, Wilson's note indicated that the President, in spite of his disclaimers, really meant to move directly to his own personal mediation. The Imperial Chancellor had hoped all along to use Wilson only to force the Allies to the peace table. Germany, he believed, could not safely permit him to have any hand or voice in conclusion of actual terms of peace. The President, Bethmann thought, was too committed emotionally to Britain, and the American economy was too dependent upon trade with the Allies, to permit Germany to run what would necessarily be the risks of Wilsonian interference.[55]

Thus Bethmann and Zimmermann prepared their reply "as quickly as possible," as the latter put it, "in order not to risk Wilson's some-

[54] K. von Lersner (representative of the political authorities at Supreme Headquarters) to the Imperial Chancellor, December 23, 1916, *Official German Documents*, II, 1201.

[55] Bethmann had explained his position on the possibilities of American mediation to the Bavarian Minister to the Imperial Government on December 5, as follows: "As for Wilson's mediation, the Chancellor pointed out that the mediation could consist only of an invitation from America to all belligerent powers to discuss the peace settlement *among themselves,* as he had in fact made known to Wilson a year ago. Only after an understanding had been reached among the belligerents could a congress with America participating be considered. In that congress there would be discussion of general international questions, arbitration courts to prevent wars. Wilson at that time had agreed to this point of view. Any other method was inconceivable, indeed." Count Lerchenfeld to the Bavarian Government, December 5, 1916, quoted in Wolfgang Steglich, *Bündnissicherung oder Verständingungsfrieden*, p. 96. For a long and thoughtful analysis of this matter, see K. E. Birnbaum, *Peace Moves and U-Boat Warfare*, pp. 254-266.

how sending his emissaries in a follow-up to his note and through them requesting information about our terms."[56] The German reply, approved by the Emperor, Hindenburg, and the Austro-Hungarian government, and handed to Gerard on December 26,[57] expressed profuse thanks for the President's "noble initiative" and said that a direct exchange of views seemed the most promising way of arriving at the desired result. "It is also the view of the Imperial Government," the note went on, "that the great work for the prevention of future wars can first be taken up only after the ending of the present conflict of exhaustion. The Imperial Government is ready, when this point has been reached, to cooperate with the United States at this sublime task."[58] Zimmermann sent the following message to Bernstorff on the same day:

"I would say, in reply to the American peace note, that a direct exchange of views seems to us most adequate in order to reach the result desired. We suggest therefore the immediate gathering of delegates from the belligerent States at some neutral spot. We share the views of the President that only after the termination of the present war could the work of preventing the occurrence of future wars be taken up.

"For your own strictly personal information: We will only consider some place in neutral Europe as the spot for the eventual gathering of the delegates. Quite aside from the difficulties involved in communicating with the United States, the experiences of Portsmouth teach us that American indiscreetness and intermeddling makes [*sic*] it impossible adequately to conduct negotiations. The interposition of the President, even in the form of a clearing house, would be detrimental to our interests and is therefore to be avoided. The basis for a future conclusion of peace we must settle by direct intercourse with our opponents if we do not wish to run the risk of failing to obtain the results desired because of pressure from the neutral Powers. For this reason we also decline to enter into the conference plan. On the other hand, we will not hesitate to send delegates to an international

[56] Quoted in *ibid.,* p. 263. My translation.

[57] Gerard characterized it to Zimmermann as "a damned good note, a fine note, short and sweet." A. Zimmermann to the Emperor, December 26, 1916, *Official German Documents,* II, 1089.

[58] Ambassador Gerard to the Secretary of State, December 26, 1916, *Foreign Relations, 1916, Supplement,* pp. 117-118.

congress called after the conclusion of peace for the consideration of the problem of assuring the future peace of the world."[59]

The German reply, published in the press on December 27, 1916,[60] was a godsend to the British and French leaders who were at this very moment discussing answers to the German and American peace notes at the Prime Minister's residence in London. The conferees, at their first meeting on December 26, approved a reply to the German note that the French Foreign Ministry had prepared. It accused the Imperial German Government of attempting to throw the onus for prolonging the war on the Allies while seeking to impose a German peace on Europe at the moment when the Germans held a transitory military advantage. The Allies, it said, would not consider any German offer as genuine unless it was accompanied by definite conditions.[61] This was sent to Washington on December 29, after the other Allied governments had approved it, published in Paris on December 31, and sent by the State Department to the Central Powers on January 2, 1917.[62]

Then the conferees turned to the reply to Wilson. Lloyd George said that the War Cabinet were undecided whether it was expedient to state terms. Philippe Berthelot of the Political Division of the French Foreign Ministry, speaking for Premier Briand, observed that it would not be wise to be so explicit. Lansing, he said, had made it clear that the American government already knew the Allies' aims and now wanted to know what German objectives were. "That situation," he added, "should be maintained." Lord Robert Cecil disagreed strongly:

". . . [He] thought that the American demand required very careful handling, or the Americans might say that the Allies did not dare avow what they really wanted, namely, the destruction of Germany. The effect of that would be bad in the United States and worse in Germany. The German Government desired above all to be able to say to their people that they really were fighting for their lives. He also felt that a negative reply to the United States might lead in this country to the question why we did not take the opportunity of stating our case. He had seen the American Ambassador this morning

---

[59] Secretary Zimmermann to Ambassador von Bernstorff, December 26, 1916, *Official German Documents*, ii, 1005.

[60] e. g., *New York Times*, December 27, 1916.

[61] For the text, see *Foreign Relations, 1916, Supplement*, pp. 124-125.

[62] The Secretary of State to various diplomatic officers, January 2, 1917, *ibid.*, p. 139.

and had told him quite frankly that the United States Note appeared to us almost hostile. Mr. Page had . . . urged treating the United States Government in the most open way possible. Lord Robert Cecil feared that the reply advocated by M. Briand might be read as missing a great opportunity."

Balfour commented somewhat discursively on what he said was the dangerous fallacy of Wilson's note, that it would be possible to reconstruct the international order after the war no matter what kind of peace was made to end the war. "A reversion to the *status quo ante bellum*," he went on, "would not be in the interests of the world at large. This point required serious attention, because the United States had it in their power to compel peace. . . . The Allies must make the United States see that if the latter desired any lasting good result to come out of the war, that war must end in the sense that the Allies were striving for."[63]

The German reply had been published, and the Allied answer to Wilson's note seemed much less urgent, when the conferees reassembled at 10 Downing Street on the following day, December 27. Indeed, they spent that entire day on the Greek situation and did not return to the American note until the following morning. Lloyd George then suggested that a committee, including Balfour and Ambassador Cambon, should prepare a draft in the afternoon. It was done and approved, apparently without discussion, that same night,[64] and the conferees also agreed that Balfour should send a separate note setting forth his own personal views.[65] There was some delay in delivery of the joint note because all the other Allied governments had to review the document. Premier Briand handed it, along with a separate reply from the Belgian government, to Ambassador Sharp on January 10, 1917.

It began with a long review of the origins and history of the war and a friendly but emphatic repudiation of President Wilson's implication that the Allies and Central Powers were fighting for the same things.

[63] *ANGLO-FRENCH CONFERENCE, Minutes of a Meeting held at 10, Downing Street, S. W., on December 26, 1916*, copy in the Chamberlain Papers.

[64] *ANGLO-FRENCH CONFERENCE. Minutes of a Meeting held at 10, Downing Street, S. W., on December 28, 1916, ibid.; ANGLO-FRENCH CONFERENCE. Conclusions of Meetings held at 10, Downing Street, S. W., on December 26, 27, and 28, 1916, ibid.*

[65] It was sent to Washington on January 13 and handed to the Secretary of State on January 16, 1917. For the text, see *Papers Relating to the Foreign Relations of the United States, 1917, Supplement 1, the World War*, pp. 17-21; hereinafter cited as *Foreign Relations, 1917, Supplement 1*.

The President had asked for a frank avowal of objectives. The Allies were happy to reply as fully as they could at this stage of hostilities. They were fighting for the restoration of Belgium, Serbia, and Montenegro and the indemnities which were due them, and for the evacuation of France, Russia, and Rumania, with just reparation. They sought the reorganization of Europe to preserve future peace, liberation of provinces or territories wrested from the Allies in the past, liberation of Italians, Rumanians, Slavs, and Czecho-Slovaks from alien domination, enfranchisement of populations subject to the bloody tyranny of the Turks, and expulsion of Turkey from Europe. It went without saying, the note continued, that the Allies had never desired and did not now desire to destroy Germany; they wanted only a peace based upon principles of justice and liberty.[66]

It was probably not entirely coincidental that the Allied terms were an almost exact restatement of the ones that Lansing had suggested. Was it possible that the Allies, as Lansing probably desired, proclaimed aims such as could be achieved only on the battlefield in the expectation that their announcement would compel the Germans to launch unrestricted submarine warfare, because this seemed to be the only way to obtain American belligerency? The available records do not answer this question.[67]

Discussions and events in Germany had meanwhile been heading straight toward resolution of the two-year-old controversy over submarine policy. Hindenburg and Ludendorff had been convinced for some weeks that Germany would have to go all-out in submarine warfare if the Allies refused the German peace offer. It was a conclusion born as much of the desperate conviction that Germany could not maintain her gigantic war effort much longer as of hope of winning a decisive victory. To state the hope briefly, the submarine seemed to be the one, the only, weapon capable of forcing the implacable English foe to parley on terms favorable to Germany.

The final phase of the debate began on December 20. "Since Lloyd George has rejected our peace proposal in the lower house," Ludendorff wrote in a telegram to Bethmann and Zimmermann on that day, "I am of the opinion that, as the result of the impressions I have

---

[66] Ambassador Sharp to the Secretary of State, January 10, 1917, *ibid.*, pp. 5-9. The Allied and Belgian notes were published in the American press on January 12, 1917.

[67] The minutes of the Anglo-French conference that prepared the reply to President Wilson obviously omitted much that was said.

received on the western front, the U-boat war should now be launched with the greatest vigor."[68] Zimmermann replied discouragingly, although he held out the hope of unlimited operations against armed merchantmen.[69] Ludendorff came back two days later, saying that Bethmann had agreed, at the Pless conference of August 31, that the Army High Command should make the decision when to launch the all-out submarine campaign. The Field Marshal, Ludendorff went on, did not think that a campaign against armed merchantmen was enough; he wanted ruthless sinking of *all* merchant shipping in British waters to begin at the end of January. Otherwise, he would not be able to retain responsibility for continued direction of military affairs. He was himself convinced, Ludendorff added, that America would come in the war against Germany sooner or later, and that one might as well be prepared for American hostility in any event.[70] Hindenburg confirmed this virtual ultimatum in a personal telegram to Bethmann and Zimmermann on December 23.[71]

Time, along with power to control or even decisively affect the shaping of policy, was running out for the Imperial Chancellor. He had earlier blunted Falkenhayn's and Holtzendorff's thrusts only because he commanded a majority in the Reichstag, and because Falkenhayn had lost the Emperor's and the public's confidence by his failure at Verdun. Hindenburg and Ludendorff had, in contrast, been popular idols, viewed as saviors of the Fatherland, since the battle of Tannenberg. The Emperor might well conclude that he had no choice but to yield if they threatened to resign. Bethmann, moreover, could no longer be confident of majority support in the Reichstag. That body, mainly because of a change in policy by the Centre Party, had adopted a resolution on October 7 advising that the Imperial Chancellor should bear ultimate responsibility for decision on the submarine question, but that he should be guided in his decision by the views of the Supreme Command.[72]

Bethmann replied to the Field Marshal bravely at first, reminding him that he, Bethmann, had agreed only to be guided by the High

[68] K. von Lersner to the Imperial Chancellor and Foreign Secretary, December 20, 1916, *Official German Documents*, II, 1199.

[69] A. Zimmermann to K. von Lersner, December 21, 1916, *ibid.*, pp. 1199-1200.

[70] K. von Lersner to the Foreign Office, December 22, 1916, *ibid.*, pp. 1200-1201.

[71] K. von Lersner to the Imperial Chancellor and Foreign Secretary, December 23, 1916, *ibid.*, pp. 1201-1202.

[72] For the background and adoption of this resolution, see Klaus Epstein, *Matthias Erzberger and the Dilemma of German Democracy*, pp. 159-160.

Command's views in determining when the time was ripe for *discussion* of an all-out underwater campaign. Since the decision would affect relations with neutral states, it was a political choice reserved constitutionally to the Imperial Chancellor alone. To launch an unrestricted submarine campaign at this time, even against armed merchantmen, would be simply to confirm the Allied accusation that the German peace move was cover for an unlimited submarine campaign. Germany could not slam the door to peace. Having said this, Bethmann then began to show signs of crumbling. He would, he went on, be willing to discuss the unrestricted U-boat campaign provided that the High Command was in position to defend the Danish and Dutch frontiers and he, Bethmann, was convinced "that the advantages of an absolutely ruthless U-boat war are greater than the disadvantages resulting from the United States joining our enemies."[73]

Holtzendorff had taken the formal step, on the day before Bethmann wrote the above message, of appealing to the High Command to join the Admiralty in a united demand to the Emperor. Prolongation of hostilities beyond August 1917 would, Holtzendorff said, be fatal for Germany. An unrestricted submarine campaign was now the only hope of ending the war on terms favorable to the Reich. England depended for her supply of food and raw materials on some eleven million tons of shipping. Severe crop failures in Argentina, Canada, and the United States would force the British to use part of this tonnage for the longer voyages from India and Australia. "I do not hesitate to declare," he wrote, "that as things stand at present, England will be forced to sue for peace within five months as the result of launching an unrestricted U-boat war." But Germany could succeed only by a total campaign. A limited campaign such as was now being carried on, even an unrestricted campaign against armed merchantmen, would hurt England badly but not fatally. Moreover, the effort would fail if neutral shipping was exempted, for neutrals supplied about one third of England's tonnage needs. Submarines set free from all restrictions could sink at least 600,000 tons of shipping a month. Such losses, if they continued for five or six months, would reduce England to starvation. He was certainly eager to avoid war with America, Holtzendorff went on. But fear of war with the United States should not cause Germans to renounce the one means of achieving victory. In fact, American belligerency would not matter during the crucial initial

[73] The Imperial Chancellor to K. von Lersner, December 23, 1916, *Official German Documents*, ii, 1202-1203.

period when submarines would bring England to her knees. "I there-fore reach the conclusion," Holtzendorff continued, "that an unre-stricted U-boat war so correctly timed as to bring about peace before the gathering of the harvest of the summer of 1917, that is to say, before August 1, will have to be at the cost of a break with the United States, for the reason that we are left no other choice. It follows that in spite of the danger of a break with America, an unrestricted U-boat war, promptly launched, is the proper means of winning the war. Moreover, it is the only means to this end."[74]

Holtzendorff accompanied this letter with a long memorandum that he and the Admiralty staff had prepared. It marshaled statistics to prove his affirmations and reiterated his own conviction that a vigor-ous submarine campaign was the only hope of preventing the utter exhaustion and defeat of Germany. Germany, this memorandum con-cluded, had to choose between two evils—a submarine campaign which would bring America into the war, and certain defeat unless the un-restricted submarine campaign went forward. "We are obliged to de-cide, although reluctantly, in favor of the lesser one rather than adopt the alternative of certain destruction. . . . I guarantee that for its part the U-boat war will lead to victory."[75]

Holtzendorff did not give the information for reasons of security, but Germany would soon have forty-six long-range submarines capable of operating in English waters and the western Atlantic, twenty-two small submarines for service in the English channel, twenty-two in the Mediterranean, and nine in the Baltic.[76] Roughly speaking, one third of the submarines in service could be in action at any given moment.

Hindenburg replied to Bethmann's telegram of December 23 so threateningly and rudely on December 28[77] that Bethmann at once concluded that there was nothing left to do but go to Pless. He arrived, accompanied by Zimmermann and Helfferich on December 29. "To describe the reception with the words 'ice cold,' " Helfferich later wrote, "is an understatement."[78] The Emperor was not present, and the three civilian leaders talked briefly with the two generals, after Hindenburg

[74] Admiral von Holtzendorff to Field Marshal von Hindenburg, December 22, 1916, *ibid.*, pp. 1214-1219.

[75] Admiral von Holtzendorff to Field Marshal von Hindenburg, December 22, 1916, *ibid.*, pp. 1219-1277.

[76] A. Spindler, *La Guerre Sous-Marine*, III, 12.

[77] K. von Lersner to the Foreign Office, December 26 [28], 1916, *Official German Documents*, II, 1204-1205.

[78] K. Helfferich, *Der Weltkrieg*, II, 397.

had tried to exclude Helfferich from the conference. Bethmann said that the Emperor would have to decide in the event that the civilian and military leadership could not agree. Helfferich argued that no one could prove whether a submarine *démarche* would succeed. The conferees agreed that an announcement of unlimited warfare against armed merchantmen should be dispatched to Washington as soon as the Allies had returned their reply to the German peace offer, although Hindenburg and Ludendorff were not enthusiastic about this measure and still insisted upon a massive, all-out assault. The conferees also discussed German ambitions in the East and apparently came to agreement on Belgium's fate.[79] The main upshot of this conference seems to have been Bethmann's conclusion that he would have to yield to the generals in order to prevent a fatal division in German leadership.[80]

Bethmann's decision probably would have been necessary in any event once the Allied reply to the German peace note had been published. The Chancellor and Austro-Hungarian leaders were not totally discouraged by this note,[81] but the Emperor reacted violently, saying that there could be no further talk of understanding with France and Belgium, that Albert could not be permitted to return to his throne, and that Germany had to annex the coast of Flanders.[82] Even so staunch a moderate as Admiral von Müller was at once converted into a champion of unrestricted submarine warfare.[83]

Resolution came quickly and dramatically on January 8 and 9. Holtzendorff, spurred by scalding reproaches from officers in the High Seas Fleet, resolved to take matters into his own hands by appealing directly to the Emperor for approval of an order commanding inauguration of the unrestricted submarine campaign.[84] He handed copies of his letter to Hindenburg of December 22 and of the Admiralty staff's memorandum to the Imperial Chancellor on January 5,

[79] *ibid.*, pp. 397-398; T. von Bethmann Hollweg to R. von Valentini, December 31, 1916, Rudolf von Valentini, *Kaiser und Kabinettschef* (Bernhard Schwertfeger, compiler), pp. 241-244.

[80] K. E. Birnbaum, *Peace Moves and U-Boat Warfare*, pp. 285-286.

[81] T. von Bethmann Hollweg to the Emperor, January 2, 1917, *Official German Documents*, II, 1090-1091.

[82] K. von Grünau to the Foreign Office, January 2, 1917, *ibid.*, p. 1091. Bethmann was able after much negotiation to obtain permission to send a fairly nonprovocative commentary on the Allied note to the neutral powers. It attempted to throw responsibility for continuing the war on the Allies. See Ambassador Gerard to the Secretary of State, January 12, 1917, *Foreign Relations, 1917, Supplement 1*, pp. 12-14.

[83] W. Görlitz (ed.), *Regierte der Kaiser*, p. 247, entry for January 8, 1917.

[84] K. E. Birnbaum, *Peace Moves and U-Boat Warfare*, pp. 304-306.

1917. He informed the Field Marshal on the following day of his decision to appeal to the throne. Then he set out for Pless, conferring there with Hindenburg and Ludendorff on January 8. They agreed that Bethmann was still using all devices to delay preparations even for a campaign against armed merchantmen, and that an all-out campaign offered the only hope of averting the ruin of the German nation. As Hindenburg put it, "Things can not be worse than they are now. The war must be brought to an end by the use of all means as soon as possible."[85]

The Admiralty chieftain had an audience with the Emperor that same evening. William, Admiral von Müller recorded in his diary, "had somewhat unexpectedly come suddenly to the conclusion that the unrestricted submarine war was necessary and declared himself very decisively for it, even should the Chancellor reject it. He took in this instance the very remarkable position that the submarine war was a purely military matter with which the Chancellor had nothing to do."[86] Holtzendorff on the following morning submitted a new memorandum to the Emperor. It reviewed the military situation, reiterated familiar arguments in favor of an unrestricted submarine campaign, and made it clear that the Army High Command and Admiralty were united in *demanding* inauguration of the campaign on February 1.[87]

Bethmann, informed by Hindenburg of the demand about to be presented to the Emperor, rushed to Pless, arriving in the morning of January 9 excited and discouraged. Admiral von Müller met him at the station and urged him not to be obstructive.[88] The advice was unnecessary; Bethmann had already concluded that his sole duty now was not to sabotage an inevitable move.[89] In conference with Hindenburg, Ludendorff, and von Müller later in the morning, the Chancellor said that he would try to keep America out of the war if His Majesty

[85] "Protocol of the session of January 8, 1917 . . . ," *Official German Documents*, II, 1317-1319.

[86] W. Görlitz (ed.), *Regierte der Kaiser*, p. 247, entry for January 8, 1917. This is the only record extant of this conference.

[87] The memorandum also said that the Allied reply to the German peace offer emphasized the impossibility of obtaining a favorable peace through negotiation and argued that the United States would not be able to mobilize in time to prevent England from going under. K. E. Birnbaum, *Peace Moves and U-Boat Warfare*, pp. 316-318, prints the text in German, along with the text of Holtzendorff's covering letter.

[88] W. Görlitz (ed.), *Regierte der Kaiser*, p. 248, entry for January 9, 1917.

[89] T. von Bethmann Hollweg, *Considérations sur la Guerre Mondiale*, II, 255.

ordered the launching of an all-out submarine campaign. There simply was no doubt about its necessity, Hindenburg replied. The English, French, and Belgians would launch a new drive in the spring of 1917 that would exceed the force of the recent Somme offensive. Every opportunity to curtail the supply of men and matériel to the enemy must be taken. There was no time to lose. He and Ludendorff, Hindenburg went on, could not take responsibility for the conduct of military operations if the unlimited submarine campaign could not begin on or before February 1. They were prepared to take responsibility for all the military consequences, even for the intervention of America and the European neutrals.[90] It was, Bethmann replied, a very serious decision—"the last card"—but he was not in position to contradict the military authorities if they could guarantee the safety of the Danish and Dutch borders. The army had prepared for all contingencies, even American entry, Ludendorff replied. "Of course," Bethmann said, "if success beckons, we must follow."[91]

"When he returned to me at about one o'clock," a member of the Imperial entourage later wrote about the Chancellor, "he was rather exhausted and told me that he had outlined all the important reasons against the intensified submarine war for more than an hour, but what could he do since the commanding admiral guaranteed that England would be forced to her knees within six months and that no American would set foot on French soil as long as the intensified blockade was in force."[92]

An Imperial Conference met that evening at six to ratify the decision. Bethmann now had a telegram from Helfferich analyzing the Admiralty's most recent memorandum on the U-boat war and pointing trenchantly to its fundamental weaknesses—its assumption that the belligerency of the heretofore neutral maritime powers would have no effect on the submarine campaign, and its bland hypothesis that the United States as a belligerent would not take desperate measures to provision England. "Paradoxical as it sounds," Helfferich's telegram went on, "it is not altogether impossible, therefore, that, compared with the limited U-boat war on commerce, the unrestricted U-board war would not in the last analysis, have a harmful effect

[90] K. Helfferich, *Der Weltkrieg*, II, 409-410, repeating Bethmann's summary of this discussion.

[91] "Report of the conference . . . at Pless, January 9, 1917," *Official German Documents*, II, 1320-1321.

[92] R. von Valentini, *Kaiser und Kabinettschef*, pp. 144-145.

upon the supplying of England with breadstuffs, but would rather operate in favor of such supply."[93]

Helfferich, as it turned out, had named the main reasons why the unrestricted submarine campaign would fail. But Bethmann did not use Helfferich's arguments. The Chancellor had given up the struggle. "I had the feeling," he wrote afterward, "that I was in the presence of men with minds made up, who would not tolerate any opposition to the decisions they had already made."[94] Here follows an account of the proceedings by one of the participants:

"From six to seven fifteen in the evening the Imperial Conference met with the Emperor. . . . We all stood around a big table on which the Emperor, pale and excited, rested his hand. Holtzendorff spoke first. From the Navy's point of view all was well, and he was confident of victory throughout. England would be stretched on the ground in six months at the most, in any case before an American had set foot on the mainland. The American danger did not frighten him. Hindenburg spoke very briefly, emphasizing only that we are entitled to expect a shrinkage of American munitions shipments as a result of this measure. Bethmann as last speaker outlined in obviously excited temper the reasons which had impelled him to a dissenting voice against the submarine war exceeding the limits of cruiser warfare until now, namely, his concern for all the consequences of America's going over suddenly to the camp of our enemy. Now, however, in view of the recent changed position of the Supreme Army Command and the Admiral's categorical declarations concerning the success of the measures, he had decided to abandon his opposition. . . .['Finis Germaniae!' this observer wrote in his notebook.]"[95]

The Emperor, who had followed Bethmann's remarks with obvious impatience and disagreement, now spoke, to quote another participant, "very decisively for the unrestricted submarine war while using statistics about the grain and shipping situations." He then signed the prepared Imperial Order, remarking at the same time that he had thoroughly reckoned on an American declaration of war. "Should it not come to this—and the Chancellor should attempt to prevent such through special concessions to American passenger shipping—so much the better."[96]

[93] Undersecretary of State A. Wandschaffe to the Imperial Chancellor, January 9, 1917, *Official German Documents*, ii, 1206-1208.

[94] T. von Bethmann Hollweg, *Considérations sur la Guerre Mondiale*, ii, 256.

[95] R. von Valentini, *Kaiser und Kabinettschef*, pp. 145-146.

[96] W. Görlitz (ed.), *Regierte der Kaiser*, p. 249, entry for January 9, 1917.

The Imperial Order was short and to the point and read as follows: "I command that unlimited submarine warfare begin on February 1 with all possible vigor. You will please take all necessary measures immediately but in such a way that our intention does not become apparent to the enemy and to neutrals in advance. Basic operational plans are to be laid before me."[97] Holtzendorff sent an Imperial Order to the High Seas Fleet and Navy Corps on January 9 commanding submarines to sink only armed freighters without warning until February 1, and all armed ships after that date.[98] Then the Admiral sent the following orders three days later to implement the Imperial decree of January 9:

> From February 1, 1917, onward every enemy merchantman met within the restricted zone is to be attacked without warning. . . .
>
> Neutral steamers, ships of the Belgian Relief Commission, and un-armed enemy passenger liners are to be treated according to prize rules in the restricted area of the North Sea until midnight of February 6/7 and in the other restricted areas until midnight of February 12/13, and thereafter within the collective restricted areas as *enemy* ships. . . .[99]
>
> Outside the restricted zone unarmed merchant ships are to be treated according to prize orders. Armed merchantmen are to be attacked without warning.
>
> For the intimidation of neutral shipping, an effect as strong as possible at the beginning will be of great significance. An occupation of the restricted area, as uninterrupted as possible, will be more important later. . . .[100]

Bethmann dined with Rudolf von Valentini, chief of the Civil Cabinet, in his room after the Imperial Conference on January 9. They were both enormously depressed because convinced, Valentini wrote in his diary, "that the measures would have as a consequence a declaration of war by America and thereby an endless prolongation of the war. We both thought that a quick defeat of England, such as Holtzendorff had suggested, was utopian." Bethmann talked about his possible resignation. He could not resign at this perilous moment in Germany's history, he said; unity had to be shown to the outside world at such a time as this.[101] Admiral von Müller then joined them, and the three

[97] A. Spindler, *La Guerre Sous-Marine*, III, 494; A. von Tirpitz, *Politische Dokumente*, II, 592.

[98] *ibid.*, p. 593.

[99] The period of grace for neutral ships was later extended to March 1, 1917.

[100] A. von Tirpitz, *Politische Dokumente*, II, 593.

[101] R. von Valentini, *Kaiser und Kabinettschef*, p. 146. For Bethmann's further

men had a glass of champagne from a bottle which the Emperor had sent to the Chancellor. "The Chancellor," von Müller recorded, "spoke out very bitterly about the Emperor who also today had injured him in the discussion by a gesture which seemed to say: 'Good Lord! Does the man still have objections?' He (Bethmann) also said that in the last twenty years the Emperor had ruined the German nation completely and had cultivated vanity and chauvinism. Only the lower levels of the nation had remained truly German. The Emperor had damaged his own and the dynasty's respect, going so far that the Emperor's friend, Herr von Buch (parliamentarian), had stated that he would accept no position under this Emperor. I attempted to encourage the Chancellor regarding the difficult decision of today, whereupon the Chancellor replied: 'Yes, I must accept military considerations, but when I paint for myself the future, so we will through the submarine war make the enemy war-weary and ready for peace, but not until they have gained considerable success in pushing back our lines in France and Belgium as far as the Maas and have taken many weapons and prisoners from us. Then we will be forced to conclude a very, very modest peace.' Valentini, who is always a pessimist, agreed with him."[102]

Hindenburg went to the Emperor on the following day, January 10, and demanded Bethmann's dismissal, saying that the Chancellor had shown such indecision that he could no longer work with him. William refused the demand.[103] He issued a proclamation to the German people three days later, after news of the Allied answer to Wilson's peace note had come to Supreme Headquarters, accusing the Allies of aspiring to crush Germany and enslave Europe. "We are ready for all sacrifices," the statement concluded. "The God who planted His glorious spirit of freedom in the hearts of our brave peoples will also give us and our loyal allies, tested in battle, the full victory over all the enemy lust for power and rage for destruction."[104] It was the only public hint to come out of Germany before January 31 of the decision, made at Pless on January 8 and 9, to intensify and extend hostilities, not merely prolong them.

---

explanation of his decision not to resign, see K. Helfferich, *Der Weltkrieg*, II, 410-412, recounting Helfferich's conversation with Bethmann on January 12, 1917, after his return to Berlin.

[102] W. Görlitz (ed.), *Regierte der Kaiser*, p. 249, entry for January 9, 1917.

[103] R. von Valentini, *Kaiser und Kabinettschef*, pp. 146-147.

[104] *New York Times*, January 14, 1917.

Wilson in the meantime had moved to the second stage of his grand plan—secret negotiations with the British and German governments looking toward his own personal mediation. He was working, it is important to say, in utter ignorance of Lansing's private communications to Paris and London, as well as of the conviction in London that the war would be lost without early American entrance and of the general German conclusion that only an unrestricted submarine assault could save the Fatherland from ruin. The remarkable fact is that he probably could not have done more than he did had he fully known and understood the power at his command. But we are ranging far ahead of our story.

It began on December 27, 1916, when Ambassador von Bernstorff visited House at his apartment in New York City. The Ambassador said that he was disappointed in his government's reply, and that the belligerents should be willing to state their terms confidentially. The trouble was, he went on, that the Foreign Office in Berlin feared leaks in the State Department. House had recovered from the blue funk induced by the President's failure to follow his advice and was now eager to explore all possibilities. Germany, he said, could divulge her terms in absolute confidence to the President and himself, and should do so. But she should also reply that her one great objective was prevention of another such holocaust, and that all territorial questions were subordinate to the central one. Such a reply, House went on, would put Germany in an unassailable position and give the President a working basis with the Allies. Bernstorff agreed, and House promised to consult Wilson and let the Ambassador know his reaction. "I feel sure," House wrote to Wilson after relating this conversation, "if we are persistent and ingenious enough a start can be made, and having once started, final negotiations will follow."[105]

Wilson of course approved at once, and House on the same day, instructed Bernstorff to proceed immediately.[106] The Ambassador, consequently, dispatched a long telegram, No. 192, to the Imperial Chancellor via the Buenos Aires-Stockholm-Berlin route* on December 29. The President and Colonel House, it began, were eager to begin confidential negotiations preliminary to a conference but could not proceed until they knew German terms. There was no danger of any

[105] E. M. House to W. W., December 27, 1916, Wilson Papers; House Diary, December 27, 1916.

[106] W. W. to E. M. House, December 28, 1916, Wilson Papers; E. M. House to W. W., December 28, 1916, *ibid.*

*Described in A. S. Link, *Wilson: Confusions and Crises*, p. 187.

leak, the dispatch continued, as negotiations would be confined to Wilson, House, and Bernstorff, and the two Americans were reliable. He had to know whether the Chancellor wanted to go ahead. Wilson was not much interested in territorial terms, but he was profoundly concerned about guarantees for the future—limited disarmament on land and sea, freedom of the seas, settlement of disputes by arbitration, and a league of nations. "I am ignorant," Bernstorff added, "as to whether or not your Excellency might prefer to have the negotiations come to nothing rather than accept American help. In my opinion, we shall not be obliged to agree that the United States shall take part in all the negotiations."[107]

There was nothing that Wilson, House, or Bernstorff could do but wait for a reply from Berlin. House went to the White House on January 3 for a brief visit. He found Wilson far from discouraged by the German public reply; the President believed, in fact, that an end of the war was in sight.[108] They fell to talking about steps that might be taken soon. "The President wished to know," House wrote in his diary on that day, January 3, "what I thought of his stating in some way what, in his opinion, the general terms of the settlement should be, making the keystone of the settlement arch the future security of the world against wars, and letting territorial adjustments be subordinate to the main purpose." House approved enthusiastically, noting afterward in his diary that this was his own idea. Then they talked briefly about specific things that Wilson should say and how and where he might state them. They agreed that it would be best to obtain an invitation from the Senate for information as to what America would demand in the event that she joined a league of nations. Wilson could then reply with a statement of terms without seeming to be meddling in the affairs of the belligerents.[109]

House saw a number of people on the following day. McAdoo told him that he was terribly depressed and thought that "the President had lost all interest and all 'punch'; that things were drifting in an aimless sort of way." He had a long and interesting talk with Jusserand, concluding by assuring the Ambassador that American sympathies lay with France and England. He found Lansing in great discouragement

[107] Ambassador von Bernstorff to the Imperial Chancellor, December 29, 1916, *Official German Documents*, ii, 1010-1011.

[108] So House told J. Howard Whitehouse on January 6. See "The House Report," Whitehouse Papers, entry for January 6, 1917.

[109] House Diary, January 3, 1917.

because the President failed to discuss foreign policy with him.[110] "He says he seldom sees him and that as far as he is concerned, the State Department is sailing without a chart. He said the President sees no one and that 'his mind is a vacuum during your absences.' . . . Lansing desires the President to press the submarine issue and to send Bernstorff home. He has written the President a note urging him to take a firm stand.[111] He believes the President will not do this as the President told him the other day that he did not believe the people of the United States were willing to go to war because a few Americans had been killed."[112] What neither Lansing nor House remarked upon was the reason for the President's coolness toward his Secretary of State—his obvious suspicion that Lansing was hostile to his peace effort and could not be trusted to cooperate loyally. House saw Wilson briefly before he returned to New York that afternoon. The Colonel said that it was unfortunate that the United States was so poorly prepared for war. "There will be no war," Wilson retorted. "This country does not intend to become involved in this war. We are the only one of the great white nations that is free from war to-day, and it would be a crime against civilization for us to go in."[113]

There were a few nagging domestic diversions and worries at this particular time. Wild charges that Tumulty, McAdoo, and other members of the Wilson circle had leaked advanced information about the President's peace note to favored persons in Wall Street, principally Bernard M. Baruch, had set Congress and the country in a minor uproar. The House of Representatives, on January 3, instructed the rules committee to investigate. The committee soon discovered that the rumors had been started by an unprincipled exhibitionist, Thomas W. Lawson, author of the famous or infamous *Frenzied Finance*, and that there had been no leak at all. But the little tempest boiled merrily in

---

[110] Lansing had in fact suggested earlier (and vainly) to Wilson that it might be well if they conferred briefly every day so long as the delicate international situation continued, in order, as Lansing put it, "that I may be kept fully acquainted with your views and wishes, as to any steps which it would be advisable to take." R. Lansing to W. W., December 24, 1916, Wilson Papers.

[111] Lansing was probably referring to his letter to Wilson of December 21, 1916, *ibid.*, in which he asked Wilson, first, to answer his letter of December 8, 1916, which Wilson had also ignored, and, second, to determine upon a definite course of action (rupture with Germany) in view of the German admission of guilt in the *Marina* and *Arabia* cases.

[112] House Diary, January 4, 1917.

[113] *ibid.*

its teapot for a few days.[114] More troubling personally to the President was Doctor Grayson's request for promotion to the rank of rear admiral. Mrs. Wilson told House that her husband had spent many sleepless nights trying to decide whether to follow the dictates of his conscience or his heart.[115] Affection for Grayson prevailed, and Wilson gave Grayson his coveted rank and named him Medical Director of the Navy, even though he had to jump him over 133 experienced naval medical officers to do so.[116] Finally, the Mexican question was coming to a head at this very time on account of the obvious inability of the Joint High Commission to work out an agreement satisfactory to Carranza.[117]

None of these distractions was really serious, and Wilson found much time during the week following Colonel House's departure on January 4 for hard work on his address to the Senate. He had before him, among other things, a thoughtful editorial from the *New Republic*. "I was interested and encouraged," he wrote afterward to Herbert Croly, "when preparing my recent address to the Senate to find an editorial in the New Republic which was not only written along the same lines but which served to clarify and strengthen my thought not a little. In that, as in many other matters, I am your debtor."[118] His address would, he knew, be the most important state paper that he had ever written, and he worked carefully, beginning with a shorthand outline containing the key points and ending with his own typed transcription of his shorthand draft. Neither the Allied reply to Wilson's peace note nor Balfour's separate commentary had arrived; it did not matter, for Wilson had no intention of echoing anyone else's statement of terms and aims. He completed the address probably on January 10, in time for a conference with Colonel House on the following day. The Houses were coming to Washington to attend the Secretary of State's dinner to the President.

House arrived at the White House in the late afternoon of January 11. His following account of the discussion that ensued is the only one that we have:

[114] *New York Times*, January 4, 5, 6, 7, 9, 10, 11, 14, 16, 17, 18, 19, 22, 24, 25, 26, 29, 30, and 31, February 1, 3, 4, 8, 9, 16, and 28, 1917.

[115] House Diary, January 12, 1917.

[116] New York *World*, January 20, 1917.

[117] For details, see below, pp. 328-335.

[118] W. W. to H. Croly, January 25, 1917, Wilson Papers. Wilson was referring either to "Peace Without Victory," *New Republic*, IX (December 23, 1916), 201-202, or to an untitled lead editorial in *ibid.*, January 6, 1917, pp. 252-253, probably the latter.

"Almost as soon as we arrived, the President and I went into executive session. The President closed his study door so as not to be interrupted and we were at it for about two hours, having more time than usual, since the Lansing dinner to the President was not until eight o'clock, while the White House dinner is always at seven. . . .

"He then read the address which he had prepared in accordance with our understanding last week. It is a noble document and one which I think will live.

"As usual, he struck the wrong note in one instance, which he seems unable to avoid. He said, 'This war was brought on by distrust of one another.' I asked him to strike out this sentence, which he did. In another instance he said, 'Both sides say they have no desire to humiliate or destroy the other.' I asked him to strike out 'humiliate,' which he did.

"I asked him if he had shown the address to Lansing. He replied that he had shown it to no one, but that he intended to read it to the Secretary and Senator Stone, before cabling it. He thought Lansing was not in sympathy with his purpose to keep out of war.

"This discussion came up when I mentioned the difficulty I was having with the Department [of State] in getting their permission to send Bernstorff's messages through to Berlin. I told him that Lansing disliked Bernstorff and Bernstorff disliked Lansing, but that the Secretary's grievance was perhaps more just since he thought he had evidence that Bernstorff was trying to have him removed from the State Department. I instanced the many rumors regarding Lansing's resignation appearing from time to time in papers. The President replied, 'Bernstorff is not nearly so dangerous to Lansing as he is to himself, for I came very near asking for his resignation when he gave out the statement regarding the last note.'

"We decided that his address should be delivered before the Senate, and we discussed how best to get the text of it to the peoples of the belligerent nations. The President is not so much concerned about reaching the Governments as he is about reaching the people. . . . I suggested that it be cabled to London, Paris, Berlin, and Petrograd, letting Gerard give it to the Central Powers and Sharp to the Entente other than Russia and England, where it would be sent direct. That was tentatively agreed upon, although he rather hesitated on account of the cost. It was also agreed that the Ambassadors should see that the address was published in full in the several belligerent countries. This is important, as one can see by reading the text of the address."[119]

[119] House Diary, January 11, 1917.

Colonel and Mrs. House returned to New York the following afternoon, January 12, and Wilson read his message to Lansing a short time later, between 3:45 and 5 o'clock.[120] He then called Senator Stone to the White House at 9:30 that night and read it to him. Following this conference, he wrote to Lansing to say that Stone had generously agreed to cooperate in arranging an invitation from the Senate, and also that he, Wilson, was sending the address with the request that it be put into code at once. Wilson had just read the Allied reply to his appeal for a statement of terms. He was startled if not shocked by the pretentiousness of the Allied demands. They were, he thought, impossible and mainly bluff, and he obviously feared that the Allied note would slam the door to peace hard and fast if he did not move quickly. "I feel," he wrote, "that time is of the essence."[121] "Ike" Hoover, head usher at the White House, delivered Wilson's letter with its precious enclosure to Lansing early the next morning, and Lansing sent the trusted Richard C. Sweet, confidential clerk of the State Department, to Room 215 to put it in code.[122]

"The thing," Wilson reported to House on January 16, "is in course. Neither Lansing nor Stone is very *expressive*, but both have acquiesced very generously (Stone, I thought, a little wonderingly, as if the idea stunned him a bit) and the cable went forward, for distribution as planned, yesterday. Poor Sweet worked all Saturday and Sunday [January 13-14] and all of both nights getting it into code, poor fellow, so that as few should be in the secret as possible. We are now waiting to hear that the cables have reached the several embassies. So soon as we hear, I shall arrange to go before the Senate and telegraph the embassies to release at the same time we do here. Senator Stone generously gave up pressing business at home to stay over and be on hand to serve in the whole matter."[123]

"I am to address Congress on Monday [January 22] (the text of the address could not sooner be got to the several capitals and be decoded), I presume at one or two in the afternoon," Wilson wrote again to House on January 19. "Can't you come down and be present, staying with us, of course? Do, please. I must have the address printed, but no advance copies will be given out, and the Senate itself will not be asked to give me the opportunity to address it until Monday forenoon, the whole

[120] Lansing Desk Diary, January 12, 1917.
[121] W. W. to R. Lansing, January 12, 1917, Baker Collection.
[122] Lansing Desk Diary, January 13, 1917.
[123] W. W. to E. M. House, January 16, 1917, House Papers.

affair being meanwhile locked up in the breasts of Stone, Lansing, and W. W. No 'leak' will in such circumstances, I assume, be possible. I pray most earnestly that the effects will be what we hope for!"[124]

These preparations went forward in an atmosphere of rising excitement and expectation engendered by certain things that Bernstorff said to Colonel House on January 15.

The Ambassador's Telegram No. 192 of December 29, 1916, about Wilson's plans to go forward with confidential mediation and his desire to know German terms, arrived at the Foreign Office in Berlin on January 3, 1917. Bethmann, obviously intrigued and tantalized, and almost certainly influenced by an editorial that had just appeared in *Vorwärts*,[125] drafted a reply on the following day encouraging the President to go ahead. It empowered Bernstorff to communicate German terms in absolute confidence to Wilson and House. They now included, *for Germany*: territorial integrity; annexation of Liège, the Briey region, and strategic districts around Metz, in return for which France might possibly obtain compensation in upper Alsace; political, economic, and military protective arrangements in Belgium, to be worked out in direct negotiations with King Albert; establishment of a Kingdom of Poland (to which would be added Lithuania and Courland) under German domination; and colonial restitution in Africa; *for Austria-Hungary and Germany's other allies*: territorial integrity; "territorial expansion" for Austria-Hungary in Serbia, Montenegro, and Rumania, and for Bulgaria in Serbia and the Dobrudja; *for Russia*: free passage through the Straits. It was interesting that the Chancellor did not mention indemnities. "If a preliminary peace is reached between belligerents on this basis," he concluded, "we will be obligated to come out in a general conference for arbitration treaties and a peace league and in effect to look for ways and means of achieving limited disarmament on land and sea by means of which freedom of the seas might be achieved."[126]

---

[124] W. W. to E. M. House, January 19, 1917, *ibid.*

[125] Berlin *Vorwärts*, January 3, 1917.

[126] Bethmann's draft is summarized in *Official German Documents*, I, 138; analyzed in K. E. Birnbaum, *Peace Moves and U-Boat Warfare*, pp. 294-299; and printed in full in Wolfgang Steglich, *Bündnissicherung oder Verständigungsfrieden*, p. 171. It is perhaps important to add that Bethmann regarded the terms listed above as being the conditions for which Germany should negotiate and believed that Germany's ability to realize them would depend upon many unpredictable factors. See, e. g., T. von Bethmann Hollweg to P. von Hindenburg, January 4, 1917, *Official German Documents*, II, 1095-1097.

Bethmann, as one authority has recently pointed out, was obviously toying with the idea of Wilson's direct mediation, in the hope that it would either lead to a peace favorable to Germany or else result in continued American neutrality in the event of all-out submarine warfare.[127]

Zimmermann and Undersecretary Wilhelm von Stumm worked on the same day on another draft of instructions to Bernstorff, whether independently or by Bethmann's direction, we do not know. Their note was radically, momentously, different from the Chancellor's. It began by announcing that Germany positively did not desire American participation in negotiations for immediate settlement of the war. German leaders believed that they could win a military decision, and Bernstorff should be as dilatory as possible about German terms. However, this draft went on, the German government was prepared to give all the guarantees for the future that Wilson desired. In fact, it was willing to sign a treaty of arbitration and a Bryan "cooling-off" treaty immediately, and the Ambassador should thus inform the President. He should also assure Wilson that German terms were moderate, compared to those of the Entente, and did not include annexation of Belgium. The Foreign Office, the note concluded, would like to have Bernstorff's personal opinion as to how far the President would really go in forcing the Entente powers to make peace. "Only an efficient pressure exerted along these lines could relieve us of the necessity of making use of the instrumentality of unrestricted U-boat warfare. If your Excellency should have any suggestions to make as to how unrestricted U-boat warfare can be undertaken without a break with America, I request immediate information by wire."

Bethmann, for reasons which are still obscure, discarded his own draft and chose Zimmermann's instead, perhaps because he knew that the Emperor and Army High Command would never countenance Wilson's intimate participation. He dispatched it to Pless on January 5 or 6 and to Washington on January 7, after the Emperor and Field Marshal had approved it.[128]

The telegram was apparently delayed in transmission, and Bernstorff did not see House until Monday, January 15. The Ambassador was not only immensely encouraging but also slightly indiscreet. His government, he told House, was willing to submit international disputes to

[127] K. E. Birnbaum, *Peace Moves and U-Boat Warfare*, pp. 297-299.
[128] Secretary Zimmermann to Ambassador von Bernstorff, January 7, 1917, *ibid.*, pp. 1012-1013.

arbitration, join a postwar league of nations and limit armaments, and sign a Bryan treaty at once. German terms, Bernstorff went on, were moderate and did not include annexation of Belgium. Then, exceeding instructions, he hinted broadly at other terms—establishment of an independent Poland and Lithuania, a common border for Austria-Hungary and Bulgaria in the Dobrudja, and unification of Serbia and Montenegro under the Montenegrin dynasty. "Bernstorff said he believed if Lloyd George had stated that there should be *mutual* restoration, reparation and indemnity, his Government would have agreed to enter negotiations on those terms."

"To my mind," House added, after reporting this discussion to the President, "this is the most important communication we have had since the war began and gives a real basis for negotiations and for peace. . . . I made notes of the conversations and read them to Bernstorff and he declared they were accurate."[129] Hope and excitement grew the more House thought about the changed outlook. "It seems to me," he wrote again to Wilson on the following day, January 16, "that with the German communication of yesterday you stand in a position to bring about peace much more quickly than I thought possible. They consent to almost everything that liberal opinion in democratic countries have [*sic*] demanded. I think it is important that no move be made now without the most mature consideration. If a false step is not taken, the end seems in sight. The question is how to use the German communication to the best advantage. I am not clear upon this point. Are you?"[130]

It was all more than Wilson could digest quickly, and he was more puzzled than excited. Were the Germans willing to submit the terms upon which the war was to be concluded to arbitration, he wondered, or were they willing only to sign a Bryan treaty?[131] And would the German government agree not to resort to illegal submarine warfare should a German-American dispute over the submarine issue occur and be submitted, as the Bryan treaty would permit, to international investigation for a year? "I do not want to walk into a trap," he said, "and give them immunity for the next year."[132] The best way, House replied, was to ask Bernstorff for direct answers.[133] Thus he wrote to the Ambassador on January 17, requesting him to confirm what he had

[129] E. M. House to W. W., January 15, 1917, Wilson Papers.
[130] E. M. House to W. W., January 16, 1917, *ibid.*
[131] W. W. to E. M. House, January 16, 1917, House Papers.
[132] W. W. to E. M. House, January 17, 1917, *ibid.*
[133] E. M. House to W. W., January 17, 1917, Wilson Papers.

said two days before, including the all-important point that Germany wanted the President to submit a program for a peace conference and would approve the President's plan.[134]

House was still intoxicated by the hope that peace was in sight. The liberal element, he wrote to Wilson on January 18, was now completely in control in Germany, and the German government was willing to take a stand as advanced as any of the democracies. The President and the Allies should take Germany at her word and conclude peace as speedily as possible. He continued:

"To go on much further is to undertake a great gamble. There can be no question that Germany is badly pinched at present and that her rulers are greatly alarmed. The spring and summer campaign on land, augmented by an unbridled submarine warfare at sea, might change the entire situation leaving the Allies in the same position in which Germany finds herself today.

"Would it not be well for me to send Balfour and Lloyd George a cable covering the points enumerated in this letter? To this [it] might be added that the German Government had proposed an immediate signing of an arbitration treaty with us, and that they had proposed submitting the question of peace to arbitration, or, as an alternative, that you submit proposals for a conference. . . .

"If Bernstorff has stated his Government's proposals correctly, peace is in sight for you would be justified in forcing the Allies to consider it.

"If it is decided to send this cable, and if a receptive answer comes back, I think you should then send me to England to press it in person.

"As soon as I hear from Bernstorff I will send you a code message."[135]

The great danger at this moment, House told J. Howard Whitehouse on the same day that he wrote the above letter, "was that the party in England which did not want a settlement might stand out for a continuance of the war. The aim of the President was to reach an end of the war before the next offensive took place. It would be said in some quarters in England that this was an intervention to save Germany. He could not conceive of any attitude so foolish and so dangerous. To continue the war for another summer would be a great gamble. It might quite well be that the Germans would make some further gains and the position would be worse than ever. The President was acting in the supreme interests of the Allies. He could secure them their just aims, and peace for the future. There was a vital change in Germany. . . . It was a fatal mistake for England to think that a military decision could be secured. It could not. He knew it and England knew it. If it became a war of exhaustion the sub-marine policy would be greatly extended and great preparations were already made for this. Very big and dangerous craft were being built in large quantities.

"The President in attempting to reach peace was wholly friendly to England and everything that was fair in their demands could be secured. He would arrange for Russia to have a warm water port for instance. On the other hand it would be wrong to attempt to cut off Austria from the coast. That would only give rise to new trouble in the future. But he could not only meet the Allies in their present claims. He could secure the future.

"A part of the new plan would be for House to go straight to London and there discuss matters for the President with the English Government. The latter might not wish him to go but he could not believe that they would be so foolish.

"There would, he hoped, be time for two steps to be taken by the President before Parliament met. Germany would if necessary be required to speak more definitely, but this would be the second step from the present. . . .

"What appeared to him to be the immediate danger in England was a general belief that they could get a military decision by another offensive. He agreed that the policy of the Note was already vindicated. It had put a term to the war. Each day it was causing the position to be clearer. The Governments could only control the popular feeling drawn out by the Note by promising success in the coming year. It was a most horrible gamble, particularly when the condition of France was remembered."[136]

Wilson's own excitement was rising rapidly now. He responded at once to House's hopeful letter, just quoted, urging his friend to lose no time in obtaining more definite statements from Bernstorff. "Your letter of yesterday," he went on, "certainly does set forth a very striking and significant change of attitude on the part of the German authorities since the old confident days before the war, and it is worth while to make the recital. It carries great encouragement with it. Yes, I hope that you *will* prepare and code for prompt use a message to Balfour and Lloyd George, making a similar review in summary form and setting forth, as you get them in writing from Bernstorff, the terms and methods the Germans now indicate their willingness to accede to. But

[136] "The House Report," Whitehouse Papers, entry for January 18, 1917.

hold it until I can consult Lansing, and until the address I am about to make to the Congress has had time to sink in a little. You will then know what context to associate with your statement of fact and proposal and can complete the message, to be sent when we finally think it time to send it."[137]

Somewhat discouraging news came on the very day that Wilson began to see light, in a letter from Bernstorff to House. It said that his government reaffirmed its support of Wilson's "guarantees for the future" and would welcome American participation and leadership in a general postwar conference to reconstruct the international order. On the other hand, it added, a conference of the *belligerents* would have to meet and arrange terms to end the war before the general postwar conference could assemble.[138] This, House admitted as he sent a copy to Wilson, was not precisely what he had understood Bernstorff to say. He would (and did) write to Bernstorff again, urging him to divulge German terms to the President and asking what Germany would do about submarine warfare if the United States signed a Bryan treaty with the Berlin government.[139]

The arrival of this new inquiry on January 20 found Bernstorff in deep gloom, for he had received only the day before a long telegram from the Imperial Chancellor informing him in absolute confidence that German submarines would begin unrestricted warfare against all shipping in a broad zone surrounding Britain and France, and instructing him to take certain measures if the United States broke diplomatic relations.[140] The Ambassador was not, therefore, very cheerful in his reply to House. The Entente's answer to the President's peace note had, he said, tipped the balance in Berlin in favor of the extremists, and he was afraid that his government would be forced to take severe measures soon. It would be difficult for this reason to obtain any more peace terms from Berlin. As for the Bryan treaty, Germany would certainly not be willing to discontinue unrestricted submarine warfare during the period of investigation of a German-American dispute if she had to undertake it in retaliation against the illegal British starvation policy.[141] Bernstorff's letter, House wrote as he sent a copy to Wilson,

[137] W. W. to E. M. House, January 19, 1917, House Papers.

[138] J. von Bernstorff to E. M. House, January 18, 1917, *ibid.*

[139] E. M. House to W. W., January 19, 1917, Wilson Papers; E. M. House to J. von Bernstorff, January 19, 1917, House Papers.

[140] T. von Bethmann Hollweg to Ambassador von Bernstorff, Telegram No. 157, January 16, 1917, *Official German Documents*, II, 1017-1019.

[141] J. von Bernstorff to E. M. House, January 20, 1917, House Papers.

showed how slippery the Germans were. They were probably maneuvering for position in order to wage unbridled submarine warfare without retaliation from neutrals. That possibility, House added, made the
calling of a conference all the more desperately urgent. "If we can tie
up Germany in a conference, . . . it will be a great point gained; and
if a conference is once started, it can never break up without peace."[142]

The main question now was whether Wilson would have time
enough to deliver his address to the Senate before both the Allies and
the Germans made his mediation impossible by severe intensification of
the war at sea.

The British were now turning the screws on neutral shipowners in a
desperate effort to force them to continue to provide the tonnage vital
to the provisioning of the United Kingdom. Their principal weapon
was the so-called bunkering agreement by which neutral shipowners
promised, in return for the privilege of purchasing British coal at any
port, not to charter vessels to any person or company not approved by
British authorities, not to do business with any country at war with
Britain, to subject all their dealings with European neutrals to the
supervision of the British government, and, in fact, to provide shipping
facilities upon demand of the British Admiralty.[143] Enforcement of the
agreement in late December 1916 evoked a sharp protest from
Lansing,[144] and he and Polk carried on further negotiations through
Spring Rice and Sir Richard Crawford. But it was evident by mid-
January of 1917 that the British would yield to nothing less than an
ultimatum.[145] Wilson might in certain circumstances use such stern
diplomacy. Meanwhile, however, many American ships would be compelled to sail in British waters and run the perils of submarine attacks.
And destruction of American shipping, if it was indiscriminate and
ruthless, might gravely endanger German-American relations before
Wilson could complete his plans for peace.

The armed ship question posed the gravest immediate threat to
America's unsteady relations with both alliances in mid-January 1917.
The French all along had armed merchantmen sailing to American

[142] E. M. House to W. W., January 20, 1917, Wilson Papers.

[143] There is a copy of the bunkering agreement in the Polk Papers. The last condition was not stipulated in the written contract but was often added informally.

[144] The Secretary of State to Ambassador Page, December 28, 1916, *ibid.*

[145] Polk Confidential Diary, December 20 and 28, January 5 and 6, 1917; F. L.
Polk to W. H. Page, December 28, 1916, and January 11, 1917, Polk Papers; W. H.
Page to F. L. Polk, January 3, 1917, *ibid.*

ports. The British began arming them in substantial numbers in the late summer and early autumn of 1916. Moreover, as we have seen, both British and French merchantmen sailed under orders that were in fact offensive. Lansing had continued to follow the rule of use and to demand a pledge from Allied Ambassadors, in each instance when an armed merchant ship entered an American port, that the armament in question would not be used offensively against submarines. It had been an altogether academic matter so long as German U-boats were inactive during the period of the abandonment of the submarine campaign. But it was difficult to avoid facing the issue squarely once the Germans launched their cruiser-type campaign in October 1916, and particularly after they announced, in early January 1917, that they were taking certain measures against armed merchantmen.

This was the new unrestricted campaign against armed merchantmen, which Bethmann hoped might prove to be an acceptable middle course between a limited cruiser-type campaign and one of all-out, ruthless underwater sinkings. The Foreign Office, after several delays on account of the *Marina* and *Arabia* incidents and Bethmann's unwillingness to jeopardize Wilson's peace effort, finally sent the announcement to Bernstorff on January 4, along with what it said was indisputable proof that Allied armed merchantmen sailed under orders that made them men of war.[146]

Bernstorff handed the memoranda, along with a letter saying that they did not cancel the so-called *Sussex* pledge, to Lansing on January 10.[147] He then returned to the German Embassy to warn his superiors that hasty enforcement of the new armed ship policy would probably cause the American government to break diplomatic relations. It would all depend upon Wilson's decision, he added, and his decision might depend upon developments in his peace negotiations.[148] Lansing sent the German memoranda to the President on January 12 with the warning that they probably were "the groundwork for excuse in beginning a more drastic submarine campaign." The Secretary of State added that he would like to know Wilson's views and policy before discussing the armed ship question with the German Ambassador.[149]

[146] Secretary Zimmermann to Ambassador von Bernstorff, January 4, 1916, *Official German Documents*, II, 1011-1012.

[147] Ambassador von Bernstorff to the Secretary of State, January 10, 1917, *Foreign Relations, 1917, Supplement 1*, pp. 82-87.

[148] Ambassador von Bernstorff to the Foreign Office, January 10, 1917, *Official German Documents*, II, 1017.

[149] R. Lansing to W. W., January 12, 1917, *The Lansing Papers*, I, 579.

Wilson, insofar as we know from existing evidence, simply ignored Lansing's letter. Perhaps he suspected that the Secretary of State was once again trying to manipulate him into making a decision that might make a break with Germany inevitable. This is pure conjecture, but we can be almost absolutely certain that the President was determined to permit nothing, certainly not a controversy over armed ships, to divert him from the great climactic peace moves that he now contemplated.

It was not so easy for Lansing to evade the issue, because he still had to try to enforce the rule of use and to demand the pledge that armament would not be used offensively every time an Allied armed merchantman entered an American harbor. As an additional precaution, he instructed customs officials to ask, when inspecting armed ships, whether the gun crews belonged to the naval forces of the country involved. Actually, Lansing was now simply going through certain necessary forms until the President made a decision on the larger aspects of the armed ship question. Some indication of the troubles that lay ahead in the event that the American government should actually classify armed merchantmen as warships came during a remarkable interview between Lansing and Spring Rice on January 18, 1917. The Ambassador, suspecting that the American government was contemplating exclusion of armed ships from its ports,[150] asked whether the recent instructions to American customs officials had been sent at the Secretary's direction. Lansing replied that they had. He wrote this memorandum of the conversation immediately afterward:

"At my answer he grew fairly livid with rage and exclaimed: 'Very well, sir, very well. I then understand your view and shall know what to expect.'

"He paused evidently expecting me to make some reply, but I sat silently looking straight into his eyes which . . . [were] wild with passion. Then he continued, 'Do I understand you, sir, to mean that though a vessel may carry a gun for defense she may not have competent men to serve it? Do you mean that?'

"He paused again and folding up the letter laid it on my desk. I answered, 'I do not comprehend the purpose of your question, but you must know that all along we have considered one of the indices of offensive intention is the fact that a vessel is operating under the

[150] C. Spring Rice to A. J. Balfour, January 19, 1917, S. Gwynn (ed.), *Letters of Spring Rice*, II, 372-373.

orders of a Government or under direction of its naval authorities, so I think that it is entirely proper to make the inquiry that we did.'

"My answer seemed to excite him all the more. 'And you mean to say then,' he cried in a hoarse voice, 'that, while scores of lives are being taken by those damned submarines, you propose to prevent our guns from being properly served and so deprive us of our only means of protection. . . .' His face twitched, his eyes blazed, and his hands clenched until the knuckles showed white.

"Seeing I did not intend to respond he rose from his chair and I did the same. We stood facing each other about three feet apart. He leaned forward and fairly hissed out: 'If you follow this course, sir, of doing nothing while helpless people are murdered or put in open boats three hundred miles from land, and at the same time of stopping our vessels from defending themselves, you will be held personally responsible, yes, you and the President will be personally responsible.'"

Lansing asked Spring Rice to sit down and think over what he had just said. "His mouth," Lansing continued in his account, "began to tremble; his eyes turned downward and seemed suffused with tears; and his hands kept opening and shutting in a nervous way." He apologized profusely in a voice that shook with emotion.[151]

These and other developments, particularly the growing threat of a submarine gamble, showed that American neutral rights could not survive much further intensification of the war at sea and help to account for Wilson's eagerness to deliver his address to the Senate as quickly as possible. As we have seen, he completed the address on January 10 or 11 and transmitted it, with instructions for its subsequent delivery and publication, to the major American embassies in Europe on January 15. He also arranged with Senator Stone to have the Senate invite him to outline a peace settlement that the United States would be willing to defend as a member of a postwar league of nations. Wilson and Stone changed this plan, probably out of fear that some Republican might prevent unanimous consent to the resolution of invitation.[152] Instead, Wilson simply wrote to Vice President

[151] "Memorandum of an Interview with the British Ambassador, Thursday, January 18, 1917," Lansing Diary.

[152] One little episode revealed the danger of the first plan. Senator Gilbert M. Hitchcock of Nebraska offered a resolution on December 21, 1916, affirming that the Senate strongly endorsed and approved the President's peace note. Senator Borah prevented immediate consideration of the resolution. Then Senators Lodge and Gallinger

Marshall on January 21, informing him that he wished to make a personal communication on foreign affairs to the Senate and asking permission to appear before that body. Marshall read the letter to the Senate at noon on January 22.

Wilson came an hour later and, in a low voice that grew stronger as he proceeded, began by reviewing events of the weeks since dispatch of his peace note. All belligerents, he said, agreed that peace must be followed by some definite concert of power which would make another such catastrophe virtually impossible. It was inconceivable that the people of the United States should play no part in this great enterprise. They had been in training for such service to mankind since their birth as a nation. They would join other nations in defending the peace settlement. But it made a great deal of difference in what way and upon what terms the war was ended; and it was important that the world should know American opinions before the peace was made, not afterwards. "The question upon which the whole future peace and policy of the world depends," he went on, "is this: Is the present war a struggle for a just and secure peace, or only for a new balance of power? If it be only a struggle for a new balance of power, who will guarantee, who can guarantee, the stable equilibrium of the new arrangement? Only a tranquil Europe can be a stable Europe. There must be, not a balance of power, but a community of power; not organized rivalries, but an organized common peace."

Leaders of both alliances, Wilson continued, had said that they did not want to crush their enemies. These statements implied that the peace to be made had to be "a peace without victory." This, Wilson said, was simply hard reality. "Victory would mean peace forced upon the loser, a victor's terms imposed upon the vanquished. It would be accepted in humiliation, under duress, at an intolerable sacrifice, and would leave a sting, a resentment, a bitter memory upon which terms of peace would rest, not permanently, but only as upon quick-

---

both argued for delay when the foreign relations committee discussed the Hitchcock resolution on January 2. Lodge and other Republicans carried the fight to the Senate floor when the resolution came up for debate on January 3, criticizing most especially the commitment in Wilson's note to American membership in a league of nations. The Senate finally approved the resolution by a vote of forty-eight to seventeen on January 5, but only after it had been amended to make its approval apply merely to the President's call for terms. *New York Times*, December 22, 1916, January 3, 4, 5, and 6, 1917. Also W. J. Bryan to C. Kitchin, January 2, 1917, Kitchin Papers; W. E. Borah to T. Roosevelt, January 18, 1917, Roosevelt Papers; H. Croly to W. W., January 23, 1917, Wilson Papers; W. W. to H. Croly, January 25, 1917, *ibid*.

sand. Only a peace between equals can last, only a peace the very principle of which is equality and a common participation in a common benefit."

The peace, Wilson added, had to be built upon the bedrock principles that small nations enjoyed the same right to existence and self-development as great powers, and that governments derived all their just powers from the consent of the governed. Statesmen everywhere seemed to agree that there should be a united, independent Poland, and that henceforth peoples living under alien domination should enjoy inviolable security of life, worship, and economic and social development. So far as practicable, moreover, every great nation should be assured a direct outlet to the sea, either by cession of territory or of rights guaranteed by international covenant. "And the paths of the sea must alike in law and in fact be free. The freedom of the seas is the *sine qua non* of peace, equality, and cooperation." Finally, the nations of the world had to find an effective limitation of armaments.

He had spoken, Wilson went on, without reserve. He was perhaps the only person in high authority who was free to speak without holding something back. He was confident that he had said what was in the minds and hearts of the American people, and he hoped that he had spoken for liberals and friends of humanity in every nation, as well as "for the silent mass of mankind everywhere who have as yet had no place or opportunity to speak their real hearts out concerning the death and ruin they see to have come already upon the persons and the homes they hold most dear." He concluded, giving new meaning to ancient American shibboleths:

"And in holding out the expectation that the people and Government of the United States will join the other civilized nations of the world in guaranteeing the permanence of peace upon such terms as I have named I speak with the greater boldness and confidence because it is clear to every man who can think that there is in this promise no breach in either our traditions or our policy as a nation, but a fulfilment, rather, of all that we have professed or striven for.

"I am proposing, as it were, that the nations should with one accord adopt the doctrine of President Monroe as the doctrine of the world: that no nation should seek to extend its polity over any other nation or people, but that every people should be left free to determine its own polity, its own way of development, unhindered, unthreatened, unafraid, the little along with the great and powerful.

"I am proposing that all nations henceforth avoid entangling al-

The New Doctrine

Donahey in the Cleveland *Plain Dealer*

liances which would draw them into competitions of power, catch them in a net of intrigue and selfish rivalry, and disturb their own affairs with influences intruded from without. There is no entangling alliance in a concert of power. When all unite to act in the same sense and with the same purpose, all act in the common interest and are free to live their own lives under a common protection.

"I am proposing government by the consent of the governed; that freedom of the seas which in international conference after conference representatives of the United States have urged with the eloquence of those who are the convinced disciples of liberty; and that moderation of armaments which makes of armies and navies a power for order merely, not an instrument of aggression or of selfish violence.

"These are American principles, American policies. We could stand for no others. And they are also the principles and policies of forward-looking men and women everywhere, of every modern nation, of every enlightened community. They are the principles of mankind and must prevail."[153]

(Wilson told the French Ambassador on March 7 that he was above all eager to see a "scientific" and just peace, one that would not create any new Alsace-Lorraines to disturb the future peace of the world. He said that he had no illusions about the league of nations to be formed and realized that it would have to develop slowly. It would be necessary to begin with an entente, with obligation to submit international disputes to a conference of countries not directly involved. Perhaps that could create little by little precedents which would break the habit of recourse to arms. It would be an experience to try. Wilson said, finally, that he had not meant to suggest the destruction of the Hapsburg Empire. That would not be desirable in any event. All that he had had in mind was a grant of broad autonomy to the Empire's subject nationalities.)

There was a tremendous burst of applause when Wilson finished. Some senators showed by their comments that they realized that they had just heard one of the great addresses of modern history. "We have just passed through a very important hour in the life of the world," Senator La Follette said. "It was the greatest message of a century," Senator John F. Shafroth of Colorado added. The course of events in the future could also be dimly seen in the remarks of Senator Reed that he would never consent to membership in a league

---

[153] From the text in *Foreign Relations, 1917, Supplement 1*, pp. 24-29.

of nations and of Senator Gallinger that the President's program was utterly impracticable.[154]

Extended senatorial discussion of the address was, in fact, set off when Senator Borah introduced a resolution on January 25 reaffirming faith in the Monroe Doctrine and in Washington's and Jefferson's policy of nonparticipation in European politics.[155] Borah's motion was tabled on January 30, but not before the Idaho Senator and other Republicans had ranged far and wide in criticism of the very idea of American participation in a new concert of power. Senator Lodge, who had earlier supported the league idea, came out against it in a long speech on February 1, explaining that second thought had led him to conclude that membership in a league of nations would require too much sacrifice of national sovereignty, and that he could not approve Wilson's linking of the postwar league with a peace without victory.[156] It was true, as the *New Republic* lamented, that many Republicans were seeking to rally their party to defense of isolation mainly because of partisanship and hostility to the President.[157]

There were a few echoes of Borah's and Lodge's criticism in the country at large, echoes sharpened by accusations that Wilson's call for a negotiated peace was made in Germany.[158] Bryan, while affirming complete endorsement of the President's ideals, warned against membership in any league of nations that would be able to decide when the United States should go to war.[159] Theodore Roosevelt and his editorial spokesman said that there was little hope of attaining the kind of peace settlement that Wilson wanted without complete defeat of German militarism.[160] But these few dissenters were only faintly heard amidst the cacophony of approving voices. Never before, it seemed, had a single speech evoked such overwhelming and almost unanimous praise in the United States. Never before, it seemed, had a single speaker succeeded so well in enunciating the political ideals and principles by which the American people in their better moments

[154] *New York Times*, January 23, 1917.

[155] *ibid.*, January 26, 1917.

[156] *ibid.*, January 31, February 2, 1917; for the text of Lodge's speech, see *Congressional Record*, 64th Cong., 2d sess., pp. 2364-2373.

[157] *New Republic*, x (February 3, 1917), 2.

[158] e. g., *New York Herald, Boston Evening Transcript*, and *Providence Journal*, all dated January 23, 1917.

[159] *New York Times*, January 24, 1917.

[160] T. Roosevelt to J. T. Alling, January 26, 1917, Roosevelt Papers; T. Roosevelt, statement in the *New York Times*, January 29, 1917; *The Outlook*, cxv (January 31, 1917), 183-184.

had tried to live. "This," said the Olympian *New York Times*, "is not merely a guarantee of peace, it is a moral transformation."[161] The *New Republic* added, "It will be something to boast of that we have lived in a time when the world called us into partnership, and we went gladly, went remembering what we had always professed, and pledged ourselves to it in a larger theatre. At least it shall not be said that we were too selfish and too timid to attempt it, or that the sources of American idealism have run dry."[162]

The President was enormously moved by the unmistakable outpouring of support; he was also profoundly disturbed by Republican criticism in the Senate. "The country," he wrote to a New York Democrat, "has responded very nobly to what I said, though the Republicans in the Senate have responded very ignobly. I hope that they will some day awake to find out what the true opinion of the country and of the world is."[163] He wrote on the same day to an intimate friend, "I must admit that I have been a little low in my mind the last forty-eight hours because of the absolute lack of any power to see what I am driving at which has been exhibited by the men who are looked upon as the leading Republican members of the Senate. After all, it is upon the Senate that I have to depend for the kind of support which will make acts possible, and there are sometimes hours of discouragement with trying to lift things into a better air. But discouragement is weakness and I do not succumb to it long. I firmly believe that I

[161] *New York Times*, January 23, 1917.

[162] "America Speaks," *New Republic*, IX (January 27, 1917), 340-342. The quotation is from p. 342.

American expressions of approval were so numerous and varied that we can cite only a few representative samples, as follows: J. W. Wescott to W. W., January 23, 1917, Wilson Papers; H. A. Garfield to W. W., January 23, 1917, *ibid.*; A. Carnegie to W. W., January 23, 1917, *ibid.*; H. Croly to W. W., January 23, 1917, *ibid.*; C. H. Dodge to W. W., January 24, 1917, *ibid.*; J. P. Gavit to W. W., January 26, 1917, *ibid.*; New York *World*, New York *Evening Post*, *Philadelphia Public Ledger*, *Springfield* (Mass.) *Republican*, Baltimore *Sun*, *Baltimore American*, *Chicago Herald*, *St. Louis Globe-Democrat*, *Indianapolis Star*, *New Yorker Staats-Zeitung*, *New Yorker Herold*, St. Louis *Westliche Post*, Chicago *Illinois Staats-Zeitung*, all dated January 23, 1917; *New York Evening Post*, January 25, 1917; and other newspaper editorial opinion cited in *Literary Digest*, LIV (February 3, 1917), 229-232; also the New York *Nation*, CIV (January 25, 1917), 94; Chicago *Public*, XX (January 26, 1917), 75; *Congregationalist and Christian World*, CII (February 1, 1917), 141-142; New York *Christian Advocate*, XCI (February 1, 1917), 98-99; *Presbyterian Banner*, CIII (February 1, 1917), 9; Nashville *Christian Advocate*, LXXVIII (February 2, 1917), 100; Chicago (Baptist) *Standard*, LXIV (February 3, 1917), 643; *The Independent*, LXXXIX (February 5, 1917), 202-203.

[163] W. W. to S. Seabury, January 25, 1917, Wilson Papers.

have said the right thing, and I have an invincible confidence in the prevalence of the right if it is fearlessly set forth."[164]

Wilson's address was of course directed even more immediately to Europe than to America, and with two great and closely related objectives. One was to encourage what he thought was a deep yearning for peace among the masses of common people in the belligerent countries by appealing to them over the heads of their governments. As he put it, "The real people I was speaking to was neither the Senate nor foreign governments, as you will realize, but the *people* of the countries now at war."[165] This was the reason he had been so careful to assure publication of the address in all important European capitals. Wilson's second objective was to lay the groundwork for actual peace negotiations in the near future. This was the second stage in his plans for peace. European governments might resist at first, but he believed that they could not withstand the popular demand for peace if only he could arouse it to formidable proportions. It was the first time in history that an American President had made such a breathtaking thrust into European affairs.

Signs soon showed that the President had indeed stirred what one historian has called the forces of movement—liberals, idealists, and labor leaders—as much in Europe as at home. They were the very groups for whom he would in time become the great spokesman, at least in western Europe and the United States. Pope Benedict, who did not represent the forces of movement though he had been working hard for peace for various reasons, called Wilson's speech "the most courageous document which has appeared since the beginning of the war." The Pontiff added, "It contains many truths and revives the principles of Christian civilization."[166] The small group of British idealists in the Union for Democratic Control rejoiced that Wilson had enunciated their own program almost in its entirety.[167] Wilson's speech was "nobly expressed," a newspaper that represented their point of view exclaimed. "How will it be received?" this journal went on. "By the peoples everywhere we cannot doubt joyfully; by men of

[164] W. W. to C. H. Dodge, January 25, 1917, *ibid.*
[165] W. W. to J. P. Gavit, January 29, 1917, *ibid.*
[166] *New York Times*, January 26, 1917.
[167] e. g., N. Buxton to E. M. House, February 8, 1917, House Papers; the Diary of Beatrice Webb, March 18, 1917, Library of the London School of Economics.

good-will and enlightenment everywhere not less joyfully and with a clear perception that this is no vision of Utopia, but a well thought-out and justly framed scheme of a man in a great position and versed in great affairs."[168] Another liberal British editor said, "This great speech, rich and sane in thought as it is generous in motive, has greatly advanced Mr. Wilson's purpose. . . . The national mind is moving."[169] The annual British trades union conference, meeting at Manchester on January 26, approved a resolution urging that "all the British representatives at the peace conference should work for the formation of an international league to enforce the maintenance of peace on the plan advocated by the President of the United States and approved by the British Foreign Secretary."[170] All Socialist members of the French Chamber of Deputies adopted a resolution on the same day warmly approving Wilson's address and calling upon leaders in all belligerent nations to follow the American President's lead to peace.[171] But the most startling pronouncement came from Petrograd on January 26, in an official statement by the Russian Foreign Office. It endorsed Wilson's program unequivocally and said in effect that the Imperial Russian Government was prepared to cooperate in making a negotiated settlement.[172] These two latter clear calls for a negotiated peace reflected the first important breaks in the massive unity of the wartime coalitions of conservatives, liberals, and social democrats in the Allied countries.

On the other hand, the great majority of editors and publicists in France and Great Britain read Wilson's address with emotions ranging from irritation to extreme hostility. The British Foreign Office and French Foreign Ministry obviously set very definite limits to public criticism. A few editors perhaps stepped beyond bounds in demanding to know why Wilson thought that he had any right to speak at all to Europe.[173] But most commentators paid due and perhaps sincere respects to Wilson's noble ideals and ambitions. As the London *Times* put it, "His project is nothing less ambitious, less splendid than the establishment of a perpetual and universal reign of peace."[174]

[168] *Manchester Guardian*, January 23, 1917.
[169] London *Nation*, xx (January 27, 1917), 574.
[170] *New York Times*, January 27, 1917.
[171] *ibid.*   [172] *ibid.*
[173] e. g., London *Evening Standard*, January 23, 1917; London *Outlook*, xxxix (January 27, 1917), 74.
[174] London *Times*, January 23, 1917.

For one reason or another, however, virtually all these spokesmen of wartime coalitions were dedicated heart and soul to continuing the war to victory. To them the "Peace without Victory" address, with its call for a negotiated settlement, was simply additional proof of Wilson's dangerous naiveté. "The ideals which President Wilson sets before us," another London editor said, "are so remote from Prussian militarism that their realisation necessarily carries with it the extinction of German tyranny. His general idea of the world at peace, with the reign of law established, . . . carries with it the consequence that he can only get what he wants if we at the same time get what we want."[175] Paris editors were particularly trenchant in expressing the point of view that, as one of them said, "The only way to attain peace is to vanquish those who broke it."[176]

The majority Anglo-French reaction was expressed most candidly in letters and diaries that did not have to pass the censor's inspection. The following excerpts give some indication of the range:

Lord Bryce

Meantime I send this to say that W. Wilson puts a rather severe strain upon those of us here who are working for the idea of a "Peace League," or the less ambitious idea of such an Alliance as you have advocated. How can there be a "peace without victory" as a precondition to a Peace League? . . . Of course Wilson . . . doesn't want to offend Germany. But can he really think we could make peace now on a *status quo ante* basis?[177]

Sir George Otto Trevelyan

The feelings of honest, true Americans must be touched by Bonar Law's noble, and perhaps immortal, phrase, "What Mr. Wilson is longing for we are fighting for." The man is surely the quintessence of a prig. What a notion that the nations of Europe, after this terrible effort, will join him in putting down international encroachments by arms, at some future time, if he is afraid to denounce such encroachments even in words now![178]

[175] London *Westminster Gazette*, January 23, 1917.
[176] Jean Herbette in *Echo de Paris*, January 23, 1917. See also A. Capus in Paris *Figaro*, January 23, 1917; Paris *Le Temps*, January 24, 25, and 26, 1917; A. Fitzmaurice in Paris *Figaro*, January 26, 1917; Polybe in *ibid.*, January 27, 1917; G. Hanotaux in *ibid.*, January 28, 1917; and especially the long article, "The Idealism (?) of a President," by G. Clemenceau, in Paris *L'Homme Enchaîné*, January 25, 1917, saying, in short, that Wilson's speech was a beautiful sermon with little if any relevance to the present European situation.
[177] Lord Bryce to C. W. Eliot, January 24, 1917, Bryce Papers.
[178] G. O. Trevelyan to Lord Bryce, January 26, 1917, *ibid.*

Geoffrey Dawson, editor of the London *Times*

We followed the old line of being courteous and restrained, but I fancy that "peace without victory" is destined to live as a phrase side by side with "too proud to fight." . . . Personally, I believe that nothing would be so popular here as a real anti-American outburst and a sacking, let us say, of poor old Page's house.[179]

Anatole France

Peace without victory, would this satisfy? Peace without victory is bread without yeast, jugged hare without wine, brill without capers, mushrooms without garlic, love without quarrels, a camel without humps, night without moon, roof without smoke, town without brothel, pork without salt, a pearl without a hole, a rose without scent, a republic without waste, a leg of mutton without the bone, a cat without fur, a tripe-sausage without mustard—in brief, an insipid thing. . . .

No, not even a lame peace, a peace stumbling and becrutched, but a deformed peace squatting on its haunches, a disgusting peace, fetid, ignominious, obscene, fistulous, hemorrhoidal, in short a peace without victory.[180]

British and French Cabinet leaders had remarkably little to say about President Wilson's address, if the dearth of evidence in archives and private manuscript collections is any indication. Since the message was not a diplomatic communication and did not invite answer or comment, there were no Anglo-French exchanges of views about it. No record of discussion by the British Foreign Office or War Cabinet is available, if, indeed, any occurred. Only two pieces of evidence revealing official Allied reactions and opinions are extant, but perhaps they indicate the trend.

The Italian Foreign Minister, Baron Sidney Sonnino, talked to the French Ambassador in Rome on January 24, 1917, with visible agitation. It was necessary, Sonnino said, to put up a good front in a bad game. The trouble was that Wilson's speech put the spotlight on Allied imperialism. Wilson had already done much damage among the war-weary elements of the Italian population. The Allies, Sonnino went on, should do nothing to encourage either the American President's dangerous polemics or his obvious candidacy for participation in the peace conference. The time had come, Sonnino added on the following day, to put an end to this absolutely dangerous con-

[179] G. Dawson to A. Willert, January 23, 1917, John E. Wrench, *Geoffrey Dawson and Our Times*, p. 147.

[180] A. France to "Cher Ami," dated Antibes, February 1917, copy in the House Papers.

versation with American pacifism; the Allies should hereafter give minimum publicity to anything that emanated from the White House.

The French Minister at The Hague reported to the French Foreign Ministry on January 30 that political circles in the Dutch capital interpreted Wilson's speech as being a cover for a new German peace move. These circles were confident, the Minister added, that the Germans had confidentially endorsed the President's terms.

Actually, there was not a great deal that leaders of the Allied governments could say in the immediate aftermath of the "Peace without Victory" speech. They, like the rest of the world, were waiting for the President's next move. As Ambassador Spring Rice warned:

"It is hardly to be expected that the President's efforts in the cause of peace will cease. A new step is expected. Each step has been distinctly an advance. . . . Now the President has stated his own terms, and has offered, if the terms are satisfactory, to guarantee them by the use of the armed forces of the United States. Presumably as the German Government has not stated its terms but has demanded a conference, the next step taken by the President will be to suggest a conference under his auspices. This at least is what is expected here.

"It is rather important to bear in mind the particular conditions here. The President is a transitory being. His glory is effulgent but brief. The temptation to play a great part before the brief authority is over is overpowering. The Democratic party for many years has not had consecutive terms of office. It is a one-man party. It is President Wilson. Peace under the President's auspices must mean the permanent glory of the Democratic party in the person of its head. A man who was quite recently rejected by a local university, and who becomes the arbiter of the destinies of the world, a partner with Pope and Kaiser, is certainly an object of admiration. The awestruck comments of the press on his epoch-making speech are only an earnest of what may come. The President's great talents and imposing character fit him to play a great part. He feels it and he knows it. He is already a mysterious, a rather Olympian personage, and shrouded in darkness from which issue occasional thunderbolts. He sees nobody who could be remotely suspected of being his equal, should any such exist in point of intellect or character. You will see, therefore, that if he is human and if the Democratic party is human, the temptation to mediate is overwhelming."[181]

[181] C. Spring Rice to A. J. Balfour, January 26, 1917, S. Gwynn (ed.), *Letters of Spring Rice*, II, 374-375.

Leading German commentators were deeply moved by Wilson's obvious effort to be scrupulously impartial and his vision of a new world order in which Germany would obviously play a major role. "The President of the United States," *Vorwärts* declared, "has laid down in his message to the Senate principles for the future European peace which are as acceptable as a basis of discussion to the governments of the Central Powers as the reply of the Entente embodying their war aims was unacceptable."[182] The liberal *Berliner Tageblatt* said that it fully endorsed the general principles of the message.[183] Even Conservative and nationalistic spokesmen paid tribute to the American President while saying that Allied determination to punish and humiliate Germany made it impossible to achieve his humane proposals.[184] And from the courageous Maximilian Harden came the warmest tribute to Wilson written by any European commentator at this time. It follows in part:

"In all human providence, for a hundred years to come, on every calendar, on January 23 will shine the sentence: 'Wilson's peace message to the Senate of the United States.'

"If, after these tremendous human experiences, the sentence ever needs explanation, grandfather will say to grandson: 'On this day, the nine hundred and fifth of the colossal war, the world heard the first voice which, in clear, deep tones throughout the world, not veiled by timid wishes, pointed the way to the possibility of enduring world peace.' . . .

"He who has been decried as an 'unwordly theoretician' has dared what many a 'practical man' had perhaps hesitated to do. To the Germans, too, he has gradually grown to the stature of a man who acts solely according to the dictates of his solemn convictions. He who enjoys this reputation is no longer vulnerable by caricature or comic papers' psychology.

"Germany has no occasion to consider him as a peculiarly tender friend, but it has at last learned to believe in his earnest striving after justice, and thanks him for it, with a sincere wish, even in this fight for the German nation's right to live, to continue to maintain a worthy

[182] Berlin *Vorwärts*, January 24, 1917.

[183] *Berliner Tageblatt*, morning edn., January 24, 1917.

[184] e. g., Berlin *Kreuz-zeitung*, January 24, 1917; *Berliner Lokal-Anzeiger*, morning edn., January 24, 1917. Georg Bernhard, in the Berlin *Vossische Zeitung*, morning edn., January 24, 1917, emphatically denied that the United States had any right to participate in rearranging the map of Europe while affirming general agreement with Wilson's ideals.

friendship with the progressive people of the United States and their highest representative."[185]

Circumstances were such in late January 1917 that the future of mankind depended very largely upon what German military and civilian leaders did, not only in response to Wilson's address, but, more importantly, to the President's actions immediately afterward.

Wilson at first thought of following through by sending a copy of his address to each belligerent government, with the specific request that it tell him what it thought about the message as a basis for early peace discussions.[186] There was not much point in doing this, he concluded, until he knew what the Germans would do. Everything now depended on them; he could and would force the Allies to the peace table if Germany returned a favorable response. As he put it in a letter to Colonel House on January 24:

"I am deeply thankful that the address has been as favourably received as it has and I thank you with all my heart for your letters.

"I shall be deeply interested in the opinions reported by [Sir William] Wiseman [a British representative], but I am even more concerned to find out what Germany is thinking,—I mean what those who have the determination of her course of action in their hands are thinking in their hearts.

"I am enclosing messages from Walter Page and Sharp which I know that you will read with interest.[187] What is to be read between the lines of Sharp's message added to things such as you are learning from [Herbert] Hoover convinces me that if Germany really wants peace she can get it, and get it soon, *if she will but confide in me and let me have a chance.* What Bernstorff said to you the other day as trimmed and qualified by what he wrote afterwards amounts to nothing so far as negotiations between the belligerents are concerned. It

---

[185] Berlin *Die Zukunft*, January 27, 1917.

[186] As House told J. Howard Whitehouse on January 27, 1917, "The House Report," Whitehouse Papers, entry for January 27, 1917.

[187] They were Ambassador Page to the Secretary of State, January 20, 1917, and Ambassador Sharp to the Secretary of State, January 21, 1917. Page urged the President to avoid using the phrase "peace without victory," which, he said, the Allies would interpret as pro-German. Sharp reported on a conversation that he had had with Denys Cochin of the French Foreign Ministry on January 20. Cochin, Sharp said, hoped that the Germans had made a confidential statement of peace terms that could be accepted with honor and bring this terrible war to an end. Cochin also said that neither side could subjugate the other. These views, Sharp added, were representative of a growing sentiment among a thoughtful segment of the French people.

occurs to me that it would be well for you to see Bernstorff again at once (not where your meeting can be noted, as the last one was, but at some place which is not under observation) and tell him that this is the time to accomplish something, if they really and truly want peace; that the indications that come to us are of a sort to lead us to believe that with something reasonable to suggest, as from them, I can bring things about; and that otherwise, with the preparations they are apparently making with regard to unrestrained attacks on merchantmen on the plea that they are armed for offense, there is a terrible likelihood that the relations between the United States and Germany may come to a breaking point and everything assume a different aspect. Feelings, exasperations are neither here nor there. Do they in fact want me to help? I am entitled to know because I genuinely want to help and have now put myself in a position to help without favour to either side."[188]

House consequently summoned Bernstorff to his apartment for a conference on January 26. The Ambassador, still in a blue funk over the prospect of an early German-American break, said that the military leaders had taken complete control in Germany and submarine warfare would begin with renewed vigor and determination as soon as the spring campaigns began.[189] House relayed the President's appeal urgently and accurately, and Bernstorff returned to Washington to dispatch a "most urgent" message to Berlin, begging his superiors to keep German submarines bridled until they had read the report that he would send on the following day. It was cabled to Berlin over the State Department's wire and is printed in full, as follows:

> House asked me of his own accord and on Wilson's behalf to call upon him and gave me the following message from the President, stating it to be official: Wilson offers in the first place, in confidence, peace mediation based on his message to the Senate, that is, without interfering in the matter of the territorial conditions of peace. He said that Wilson did not consider as confidential his request, simultaneously addressed to us, for a disclosure of our peace conditions.
>
> House related to me in detail the following line of reasoning of the President: That our enemies had publicly announced their peace conditions, which were impossible of acceptance; that, in direct opposition to this, the President had thereupon announced his program; that from now on we too were under the moral obligation of disclosing our peace

[188] W. W. to E. M. House, January 24, 1917, House Papers.
[189] E. M. House to W. W., January 26, 1917, Wilson Papers.

conditions, because, otherwise, our intentions with regard to peace would not be looked upon as genuine; that after your Excellency had informed Mr. Wilson that our peace conditions were of a moderate nature and that we were willing to enter upon the second peace conference, the President was of the opinion that his message to the Senate was in accordance with our views; that Wilson hoped that we would disclose peace conditions to him which could be made public both here and in Germany, in order that they could become openly known throughout the entire world; that if we would only trust him, he was convinced that he would be able to bring about both peace conferences; that he would be particularly pleased if at the same time your Excellency would be willing to state that we were prepared to enter upon the conferences on the basis of his message to the Senate; that the reason for our announcement could be explained by the fact that Wilson had now asked us directly for our peace conditions. The President was of the opinion that the Entente note to him was a bluff and, for this reason, need not be taken into consideration; that he hoped with reason to be able to bring about peace conferences and, indeed, at such an early date that unnecessary bloodshed in the spring offensive could be avoided.

To what extent your Excellency is willing or is able to meet Wilson can not be judged from this side. In the meantime, I urgently beg leave to make the following suggestion: If the U-boat war is commenced forthwith, the President will look upon this as a slap in the face, and war with the United States will be unavoidable. The war party on this side will gain the upper hand, and we shall not be able, in my opinion, to tell when the war will end, since the resources of the United States are, in spite of all statements to the contrary, very great. On the other hand, if we meet Wilson's proposition and if, in spite of that fact, these plans are brought to naught by the obstinacy of our opponents, it will be a very difficult thing for the President to undertake a war against us, even if we were then to start the unrestricted U-boat warfare. Thus, at the present, all we need is a brief delay in order to improve our diplomatic position. In any event, my view of the situation is that at this time we can get a better peace by means of conferences than if the United States should join our enemies.

Since cablegrams invariably take more than a few days, I ask to be informed by return wireless if telegraphic dispatch 157 [Bethmann's telegram of January 16 informing Bernstorff that unrestricted submarine warfare would begin on February 1] is not to be carried out on the first of February.[190]

---

[190] Ambassador von Bernstorff to the Foreign Office, Telegram No. 239, January 27, 1917, *Official German Documents*, II, 1047-1048.

This, obviously, was the most important message between Washington and Berlin since the beginning of the war. It offered Wilson's right hand of friendship and loyal cooperation in what could have been an absolutely irresistible move for peace. It could have led to a peace without victory and a new chance for mankind. Now it was up to the Germans to choose.

Important discussions took place in New York and Washington while Wilson and House awaited the German reply. The first occurred in House's apartment on January 26, not long after Bernstorff left, when the Colonel received Sir William Wiseman, head of British Naval Intelligence in the United States. House had recently met Wiseman, probably through Frank L. Polk; he had already formed a warm attachment for the soft-spoken and genteel young Englishman and begun to use him, instead of the volatile British Ambassador, for confidential communication with London. He had told Wiseman on January 20 about the President's forthcoming address and urged him to advise his government to consent to an immediate peace conference.[191] Wiseman had returned on January 26 presumably to deliver his government's reply. As House reported the conversation to Wilson:

"Wiseman came this afternoon. His whole tone had changed. He said the atmosphere had cleared wonderfully since yesterday.

"I told him of Bernstorff's visit and what you had asked him to do. This pleased him and we got down to a discussion of peace terms, and the conference which he seemed to now think could be brought about in the event that Germany returns a favorable reply.

"He told me in the *gravest confidence*, a thing which I had already suspected and that is that he is in direct communication with the Foreign Office, and that the Ambassador and other members of the Embassy are not aware of it.

"I am happy beyond measure over this last conference with him, for I judge he reflects the views of his government.

"He went so far as to discuss with me where the conference should be held, and whether or not there should first be a preliminary conference and afterwards a general one. I take it he has heard directly from his government since yesterday for he seemed to speak with authority.

"I know you will appreciate the difference between any statement coming from the English as against one coming from the Germans."[192]

[191] E. M. House to W. W., January 20, 1917, Wilson Papers.
[192] E. M. House to W. W., January 26, 1917, *ibid.*

This might have been the most important communication between London and Washington since the beginning of the war. It is, un-happily, impossible to know what it signified because it stands starkly alone among the available evidence, and will stand alone until the documents of the British Foreign Office for this period are open to scholarly view. There are two possibilities, among others, namely:

First. British Intelligence had intercepted and decoded Bethmann's Telegram No. 157 of January 16, 1917, and probably knew from other sources that the Germans intended to launch all-out submarine op-erations on February 1. Knowledge of this decision probably accounts for the absence in available documents of any evidence of official Brit-ish concern about the "Peace without Victory" speech—because British leaders thought that America and Germany would soon be at war and belligerency would put an abrupt end to Wilson's peace moves. It is also possible that the Prime Minister and Foreign Secretary, on the same assumption, instructed Wiseman to tell House that Britain would not refuse to go to a peace conference if the President obtained a favorable reply from Germany. It would have been a cheap and safe way to earn badly needed credit with the Washington adminis-tration.

Second. It is also possible that Wiseman was in fact transmitting an authentic message from his superiors in London. It is not altogether inconceivable that they feared German victory on account of the im-pending submarine campaign and the possible defection of Russia, about which they were now gravely worried. While they undoubtedly knew about the German submarine decision, they must have also known that the Germans could reverse this decision and accept Wil-son's mediation as an alternative. Perhaps British leaders had con-cluded that the risks of Wilsonian mediation in a peace conference were less than those of a German victory through an undersea assault. Perhaps they had even concluded that a peace settlement based upon the President's address to the Senate was good enough, especially if it brought American membership in a new world system. No evi-dence now available supports these assumptions. This does not mean that they are necessarily incorrect.

Other important discussions took place in Washington at the end of January because it seemed that some decision had to be made on the armed ship question. It will be recalled that Wilson had refused to answer Lansing's letter of January 12 asking for a definite expres-sion of the President's own views. The Secretary of State came back even more urgently in a letter to the President on January 17. He enclosed a dispatch from Ambassador Page reporting that the British were contemplating putting heavier armament on merchantmen and were very eager to know whether the American government would approve.[193] "I do not think," Lansing added, "that we can long delay determining upon a very definite policy in this matter, particularly in view of the fact that a renewal of submarine activities seems imminent."[194] Wilson apparently also ignored this letter. Then Gerard said in a cablegram on January 21 that he believed that the Germans intended to resume reckless U-boat sinkings under cover of a ruthless campaign against armed merchantmen; he also warned that American failure to protest would be interpreted as acquiescence.[195] This report, Lansing warned Wilson on January 23, as he sent a copy of Gerard's cablegram to the White House, "appears to me to create a very serious situation, if Mr. Gerard is accurate in his presumptions—which sound to me very reasonable."[196] This finally drew a reply from Wilson, albeit not the kind that Lansing wanted. Gerard, the President wrote on January 24, was probably right. "I wonder," he went on, "if you have come to any fixed conclusion in your own mind as to whether the recent practices of the British in regard to the arming of their merchantmen force upon us an alteration of our own position in that matter."[197]

Lansing set furiously to work to divert the President from the policy to which he seemed to be rapidly heading—revision of American rules governing treatment of armed merchantmen, perhaps by forbidding them to enter American ports. The Secretary of State had already asked the Joint State and Navy Neutrality Board for its opinion on how far belligerents should be permitted to go in arming merchantmen. The Board had recommended permitting merchantmen to mount up to four guns no larger than six inches in caliber, to be manned by crews not in the active armed forces of their nation.[198]

Lansing sent a copy of the Joint Neutrality Board's memorandum to

[193] Ambassador Page to the Secretary of State, January 5, 1917, *Foreign Relations, 1917, Supplement 1*, pp. 546-548.

[194] R. Lansing to W. W., January 17, 1917, *The Lansing Papers*, 1, 580.

[195] Ambassador Gerard to the Secretary of State, January 21, 1917, *Foreign Relations, 1917, Supplement 1*, pp. 91-92.

[196] R. Lansing to W. W., January 23, 1917, *The Lansing Papers*, 1, 580.

[197] W. W. to R. Lansing, January 24, 1917, *ibid.*, p. 581.

[198] Joint State and Navy Neutrality Board to the Secretary of State, January 26, 1917, State Department Papers.

the President on January 31, along with a long memorandum of his own affirming the right of armed ships to resist capture or destruction.[199] The American government, Lansing warned in an accompanying letter, simply could not postpone decision any longer in view of the German intention to treat all armed merchantmen as warships. Failure to speak would make the United States *particeps criminis* in the campaign. Ruthless submarine attacks against armed ships would enrage the Allies and wreck all hopes for peace. The safest and wisest policy would be to warn the German government that the United States would break diplomatic relations if it carried out its threats. "You may see, Mr. President, from what I have written," Lansing concluded, "that I am greatly agitated over the present state of affairs. I am indeed more anxious than I have been since the *Sussex* affair. In many ways this is even a greater crisis as so much depends on nothing being done which will prevent the movement toward peace, and that movement will, I am firmly convinced, come to an end if submarine war of a reckless sort is renewed by Germany."[200]

It was somewhat curious logic and not an honest argument, and Wilson was totally unconvinced. Perhaps he suspected that Lansing was up to old tricks. "This is, to my mind," he replied at once, after reading the Secretary's memorandum and letter, "quite the most puzzling and difficult question we have had to deal with. It is becoming pretty clear to me that the British are going beyond the spirit, at any rate, of the principles hitherto settled in regard to this matter and that the method in which their ship captains are instructed to use their guns has in many instances gone beyond what could legitimately be called defense. It appears that they have more than once attacked. The question is more whether their guns have been *used* only for defense than whether they exceed in calibre what would reasonably constitute armament for defense and whether their being mounted in the bow is a presumption that they are to be used for offense. I would be glad to know the progress of your own thought in this matter."[201] Lansing discussed the question with the President that same evening, along with more momentous developments. Wilson said that he still doubted the soundness of Lansing's memorandum.[202]

---

[199] "Memorandum on Armed Merchantmen," dated January 30, 1917, *The Lansing Papers*, I, 584-591.

[200] R. Lansing to W. W., January 31, 1917, *ibid.*, pp. 582-584.

[201] W. W. to R. Lansing, January 31, 1917, *ibid.*, p. 581.

[202] Lansing's memorandum of February 1, 1917, *ibid.*, p. 582.

This exchange made what could have been two monumentally important facts altogether clear. First, Wilson did not regard an unrestricted submarine campaign against armed merchantmen as *ipso facto* a violation of the *Sussex* pledge, even though, as he had indicated earlier, he recognized that destruction of American lives on armed ships might pose grave danger to German-American relations. Second, he still had no intention of permitting Lansing to lead him to the verge of war.

Bernstorff's Telegram No. 239 of January 27, 1917, arrived in Berlin over the State Department's wire on the following day, Sunday, January 28. Bethmann summoned Helfferich to his residence at ten o'clock that same evening. "The Chancellor," Helfferich later wrote, "who saw hope brightened once again that war with America could be avoided and perhaps even peace achieved, was in greater excitement than I had ever seen him. He had decided to define to Wilson through Bernstorff those peace conditions which we would want to submit in the event that the peace negotiations which we had proposed took place. Bernstorff's requested holding back of the submarine note was a difficult matter; the submarines had long since set out for their stations which in part lay far in the west of Ireland and could probably no longer be reached."[203]

Bethmann sent a copy of Bernstorff's telegram to Pless and informed the Emperor that he would leave for Supreme Headquarters at once. Then he and Secretary Zimmermann boarded a special train that same night. Receipt of the message neither moved nor excited William and his chieftains. For them, the die had already been cast; all their thoughts and hopes were focused on the great blow at England and the victory that would follow. William remarked after reading the message from Washington that Wilson wished only to delay the submarine campaign in England's favor because he knew how worried the English were about their food supply.[204] Receipt of news that Bethmann was on his way greatly upset the Emperor. Admiral von Müller noted that he was "beside himself that he is once again being called upon to make a decision."

An Imperial Conference met at noon on January 29 to hear Bethmann's recommendations. He read a draft of a message to Bernstorff that he had prepared the day before. It informed the Ambassador that

[203] K. Helfferich, *Der Weltkrieg*, II, 417-418.
[204] W. Görlitz (ed.), *Regierte der Kaiser*, p. 253, entry for January 28, 1917.

the submarine campaign had to go forward on schedule and instructed him to conciliate Wilson by urging him to continue his efforts at peace and informing him confidentially of German peace terms. "The Chancellor," von Müller's account of the discussion continues, "skillfully defended the instructions, which, without sacrificing the submarine war, might create the possibility that at least America might not enter the war immediately. Perhaps in the meantime the submarine war will have become so effective that America will have completely lost its desire [to participate]. Hindenburg agreed. The Emperor too. . . . He demanded that it must be made clear in the instructions that the Emperor will not have Mr. Wilson as mediator and America as a participant at the peace conference."[205]

This, then, was how one of the most important decisions in modern history was made, revealed for the first time upon the publication of von Müller's diary in 1959. It is obvious from the Admiral's somewhat cryptic account that the Emperor and his military advisers approved Bethmann's last-ditch effort to avert war with America only because they were confident that they could force a military decision within a few months. The thought of grasping Wilson's hand and working with him to end the war along lines of the "Peace without Victory" speech seems never to have occurred to them. On the contrary, they now seemed more determined than ever to prevent the American President's participation in hammering out a peace settlement. We cannot be so certain that Bethmann hoped merely to delay or prevent an American declaration of war in the expectation that submarines could soon force a military decision. All the evidence of his thought indicates that he did not believe that the submarine campaign could or would succeed. It is, therefore, at least possible that he meant precisely what he said in his reply to Wilson, and that he sent this reply in the hope that the Emperor and his military advisers would be ready to follow Wilson's lead once it was evident that the submarine campaign could not end the war.

Bernstorff had already been instructed to present two communications to Secretary Lansing on January 31. One (consisting, actually, of two memoranda) announced that, beginning on February 1, German submarines would sink *all* ships without warning in a broad zone around Great Britain, France, and Italy, and in the eastern Mediterranean. Neutral ships already in the war zones or on their way would be safe against ruthless attacks during a period of grace. It was not,

[205] *ibid.*, p. 254, entry for January 29, 1917.

technically speaking, a declaration of blockade, although the word "blockade" was used to characterize the war zones. In addition, one American passenger ship might sail weekly between New York and Falmouth provided that the United States Government guaranteed that these steamers carried no contraband and they were clearly marked with alternate red and white stripes and appropriate flags.[206] The second, in the form of a letter from Bernstorff to Lansing, affirmed Germany's general adherence to the principles enunciated in the President's address of January 22 and promised German cooperation in all efforts to prevent future war. However, the letter continued, the Allies had made it clear in their reply to Wilson's peace note that they intended to dismember and dishonor Germany and her allies, while England was also determined to continue her illegal and inhumane maritime measures. Germany had therefore been compelled to continue her fight for existence with "the full employment of all the weapons which are at its disposal." The letter concluded, "Sincerely trusting that the people and Government of the United States will understand the motives for this decision and its necessity, the Imperial Government hopes that the United States may view the new situation from the lofty heights of impartiality and assist, on their part, to prevent further misery and avoidable sacrifices of human life."[207]

These were the public notice and appeal to the American government and people for sympathetic understanding and forbearance. The Foreign Office (in response to Bethmann's telegraphic orders dispatched from Pless immediately after the Imperial Conference) sent the Chancellor's reply, in his own name, to Wilson's request for terms to Bernstorff by wireless on January 29. It follows in full:

> Kindly express the thanks of the Imperial Government to the President for his communication. We offer him our full confidence, and ask him to give us his in return. Germany is ready to accept the mediation which he offers in confidence for the purpose of bringing about a direct conference of the belligerents,[208] and will recommend the same to its asso-

[206] This was the memorandum, with an accompanying explanatory memorandum, enclosed in the German Ambassador to the Secretary of State, January 31, 1917, *Foreign Relations, 1917, Supplement 1*, pp. 100-102. Bernstorff announced on February 2, 1917, that his government would permit an unlimited number of American passenger ships to sail to Falmouth, provided they did not carry contraband. *New York Times*, February 3, 1917.

[207] This was the German Ambassador to the Secretary of State, January 31, 1917, *Foreign Relations, 1917, Supplement 1*, pp. 97-100.

[208] This was an interesting way of saying that Germany desired Wilson's coopera-

ciates. We ask that our acceptance be regarded as strictly confidential, as was the proposal.

The public disclosure of our peace conditions is now impossible, since the Entente has publicly announced peace conditions pointing to the degradation and destruction of Germany and its associates, which have been characterized by the President himself as impossible. We can not look upon them as being in the nature of a bluff, since they are in entire accord with the utterances of the enemy authorities, not only before, but after their publication, and fit in exactly with the purposes for which Italy and Roumania entered the war; and, moreover, so far as Turkey is concerned, correspond to the assurances made by England and France to Russia in treaty form. As long as these war aims of our opponents continue to be freely and frankly maintained, the public disclosure of our peace conditions would be inadvisable, inasmuch as it would indicate a weakness which does not exist, and would only lead to a prolongation of the war. In order to give President Wilson a proof of our confidence in him, we inform him herewith, but absolutely for his own personal information, of the conditions under which we *would have been* willing to enter into peace negotiations in case the Entente had accepted our peace proposal of December 12 of last year:

Restitution of that part of upper Alsace now occupied by France.

The obtaining of a boundary which would protect Germany and Poland against Russia, strategically and economically.

The restitution of our colonies in the form of an understanding which would assure to Germany such colonial possessions as are adapted to her population and the importance of her economic interests.

The return of French territory occupied by Germany, under reservations concerning the establishment of strategic and economic boundaries, as well as financial compensation.

The restoration of Belgium under certain guarantees assuring Germany's safety, which would have to be reached by negotiations with the Belgian Government.

An economic and financial adjustment on the basis of an interchange of the territory conquered by both sides which is to be returned on the conclusion of peace.

Indemnification of German undertakings and private persons who have been injured by the war.

The renunciation of all economic agreements and measures which would, after the establishment of peace, interfere with normal trade and commerce. Agreements on this point to be concluded in the form of commercial treaties covering the subject.

---

tion in arranging a peace conference, but did not want him to participate when that conference met!

Guarantee of the freedom of the seas.

The peace conditions of our associates are in due proportion to and in agreement with our views.

We are further prepared to take part in the international conference which President Wilson is seeking to bring about after the termination of the war, on the basis of his message to the Senate.

Your Excellency will deliver this communication to the President at the time that you hand over the note regarding the intensive U-boat warfare, and will accompany this with the following announcement:

If his proposal had only been made a few days earlier, we would have been able to put off the commencement of the new U-boat war; inform him that, at the present time, in spite of the best will in the world, it is, unfortunately, too late on account of technical reasons, since far-reaching military preparations have been decided upon from which we are no longer in a position to recede, and because the U-boats have already left port with new instructions. That the form and contents of the enemy's note answering our peace proposal and the note of the President were so blunt that, in view of the newly-announced fight for life and death, we could no longer delay putting to full account those instrumentalities of warfare best adapted to a rapid termination of the war, nor have been able to answer to our own people for our failure to do so.

As is to be observed in the instructions governing the intensive U-boat warfare, we are always ready to do justice to the necessities of the United States as far as in any way possible. We beg the President, in spite of all, to take up and continue his efforts; and we declare ourselves perfectly ready to discontinue the intensive U-boat warfare as soon as we receive satisfactory assurances that the efforts of the President will lead to a peace which would be acceptable to us.[209]

Bethmann then returned to Berlin to break the news of the new submarine campaign to the Budget Committee of the Reichstag on January 31. "America," he said, "is still aloof. We have done and will continue to do all in our power to keep America out. I do not know whether we will succeed. America is and will be uncertain. I will not speak more optimistically than I think. And I believe that America will enter the war. Wilson has committed himself in his notes. On the other hand, the peace message makes his entrance more difficult. According to his own statements, he wants peace without victory. You know that in the past I have considered America's entrance as very serious. But it does not mean the same now as formerly. If submarine

---

[209] The Imperial Chancellor to Ambassador von Bernstorff, January 29, 1917, *Official German Documents*, II, 1048-1050.

warfare accomplishes the expected results, America will not have time to attack before victory is certain. The outcome no longer depends on silver bullets. . . . When, forced by Russia's mobilization, we took up arms in August, 1914, we said, *'We must, therefore we can!'* Uncounted streams of blood have flowed since then, but we must and we can still win. Our decision is the result of sober and serious consideration. We must save our people from need and ignominy."

All party leaders except Eduard David of the Social Democrats approved. America's participation, he warned, would decide the outcome of the war. "As far as the financial and economic situation is concerned," the Naval Minister, von Capelle, replied, "I have always laid great stress on the importance of America's entrance into the war. But from a military point of view, her entrance means nothing. I repeat: *from a military point of view America is as nothing*. I am convinced that almost no Americans will volunteer for war service. That is shown by the lack of volunteers for the conflict with Mexico. And even if many enlist, they must first be trained. This will take time, for America has neither commissioned nor noncommissioned officers enough to train large bodies of troops. And when the men have been trained, how are they to cross the ocean? . . . And, contrary to all appearances, should America be able to provide the necessary transport ships, our submarines could not wish for a better piece of hunting. I repeat, therefore, once more: from a military standpoint, America's entrance is as nothing."[210]

[210] Hans P. Hanssen, *Diary of a Dying Empire*, trans. by Oscar Winther, pp. 161-170.

CHAPTER VII

The Break with Germany

AMBASSADOR von Bernstorff sent an aide to New York on the morning of January 31, 1917, with a document for Colonel House. It was the Imperial Chancellor's message to the President of the United States cast in the form of a letter from Bernstorff to House.[1] Then the Ambassador called the State Department to request an interview with the Secretary of State. Lansing noticed when Bernstorff arrived at 4:10 that he did not walk with his usual springy step or break into his customary smile. After shaking hands he handed Lansing a copy of his government's announcement of unrestricted submarine warfare to begin the next day, saying as he did that he deeply regretted the necessity for the drastic step and that Lansing knew that he had worked constantly for peace. The Secretary was as cordial as circumstances permitted and noted that he felt deep compassion when the Ambassador's eyes filled with tears as he shook hands and said good-by.[2] Lansing then telephoned the White House and was told that the President was out. He thereupon added a postscript to a letter about the armed ship question that he had just written to Wilson and enclosed the German announcement along with the letter and other papers and sent them all in a large envelope to the President by Sweet. "Since writing the foregoing," the postscript read, "the German Ambassador has been to see me and has left me a communication accompanied by two memoranda (Enclosure E), which shows the prognostications were right, and we are face to face with the gravest crisis presented since the war began. I think that as soon as you have read these papers we should have a conference to determine the course to be taken."[3]

Wilson, after playing golf with Grayson until late in the morning, had apparently learned about the German announcement from an Associated Press dispatch in the early afternoon and closeted himself in his office with instructions that he was not to be disturbed. It was a critical moment, and he had to get his bearings. He read the papers

[1] It is printed in this form in *Foreign Relations, 1917, Supplement 1,* pp. 34-36.
[2] R. Lansing, *War Memoirs,* pp. 210-212.
[3] R. Lansing to W. W., January 31, 1917, State Department Papers.

that Lansing sent just before dinner; then, shortly after eight o'clock, he telephoned to ask the Secretary to come to the White House as soon as possible. They talked from eight forty-five until ten thirty. Lansing pleaded for an immediate severance of relations, arguing that Germany's declaration left no alternative and failure to take at least this step would result in a fatal loss of national prestige. Wilson had been wrestling with his own conscience and was now strongly kicking against the pricks.

"The President [Lansing recorded a few days later], though deeply incensed at Germany's insolent notice, said that he was not sure what course we should pursue and must think it over; that he had been more and more impressed with the idea that 'white civilization' and its domination over the world rested largely on our ability to keep this country intact, as we would have to build up the nations ravaged by the war. He said that as this idea had grown upon him he had come to the feeling that he was willing to go to any lengths rather than to have the nation actually involved in the conflict. . . .

"The President said that . . . if he believed it was for the good of the world for the United States to keep out of the war in the present circumstances, he would be willing to bear all the criticism and abuse which would surely follow our failure to break with Germany; that contempt was nothing unless it impaired future usefulness; and that nothing could induce him to break off relations unless he was convinced that, viewed from every angle, it was the wisest thing to do."

They talked further, and Wilson agreed that Lansing should prepare a note breaking relations, to be used in further discussions. The Secretary, still not knowing what the President would do, went home and wrote a first draft of the note.[4]

Colonel House had meanwhile learned the news from Frank Polk, who telephoned soon after Bernstorff left the State Department to ask the Colonel to come to Washington, presumably to stiffen Wilson's backbone. Bernstorff's letter arrived at six-thirty, and House concluded that it had been sent in the hope that the neutrals would give Germany a free hand in submarine warfare. He left for Washington on the midnight train.[5]

There was vast excitement throughout the country when newspapers blazoned news of the German submarine decree on the following morning, February 1. "Germany's answer to President Wilson's address to the Senate is, in effect, a declaration of war," the New York *World*

---

[4] R. Lansing, *War Memoirs*, pp. 212-213.   [5] House Diary, January 31, 1917.

Nailing It There
Kirby in the New York *World*

exclaimed while demanding severance of diplomatic relations. "... To acquiesce in a resumption of ruthless submarine operations is to subject ourselves to the losses of war while depriving ourselves of the means of self-defense. That is intolerable. No peace is worth the price of abject national humiliation and degradation. No peace is worth the surrender of a nation's sovereign rights."[6] Virtually every editor of English-language newspapers across the continent agreed emphatically.[7] "What,

[6] New York *World*, February 1, 1917.
[7] e. g., *New York Times, New York Tribune, Boston Herald, Boston Post, Pitts-*

if anything, the President will do now, I don't know," Theodore Roosevelt wrote in great alarm. "Of course, if he had a spark of manhood about him, he would take such action that Germany would either have to respect us, or face war."[8]

Big-city editors and interventionists like Roosevelt probably spoke only for themselves and a segment of thoughtful opinion, not for the majority of Americans. They were silent with certain notable exceptions. German-American editors either said that they hoped that President Wilson would maintain peaceful relations with Germany or openly welcomed the new submarine campaign.[9] The American Union Against Militarism, a group consisting mainly of New York pacifists and social justice leaders,[10] sent a telegram to the President begging him to avoid "any ignominious eleventh-hour participation in a struggle for mastery which is not our own" and published it in major New York newspapers on February 2. An Emergency Committee of the Socialist party, meeting in Chicago on that day, dispatched an appeal to the President on behalf of "the common people" to impose a complete embargo on shipments of any kind to belligerent countries as the most effective means of avoiding war.[11]

Excitement was already mounting in Washington by the time that Colonel House arrived in the morning of February 1. He had breakfast alone in the White House; the President appeared soon after he had finished. House gave him Bernstorff's letter, and Wilson read it aloud. He was apparently not impressed, for House noted that he saw at once how "perfectly shallow" it was in light of the proclamation of unlimited submarine warfare. Wilson, House noted, "was sad and depressed, and I did not succeed at any time during the day in lifting him into a better frame of mind. He was deeply disappointed in the sudden and unwarranted action of the German Government. . . . The

burgh Gazette-Times, Philadelphia Inquirer, Baltimore *Sun, Providence Journal, Springfield* (Mass.) *Republican, St. Paul Pioneer-Press, Minneapolis Tribune, Sioux Falls Press, Indianapolis Star, Denver Post,* Little Rock *Arkansas Gazette, St. Louis Globe-Democrat, Richmond Times-Dispatch,* Louisville *Courier-Journal,* Charleston *News and Courier,* and *San Francisco Chronicle,* all dated February 1, 1917.

[8] T. Roosevelt to G. E. Roosevelt, February 1, 1917, Roosevelt Papers.

[9] *New Yorker Staats-Zeitung, Cincinnati Volksblatt, Cincinnati Freie Presse,* Cleveland *Waechter und Anzeiger,* Detroit *Abend Post,* all dated February 1, 1917.

[10] They included Amos Pinchot, Oswald Garrison Villard, George Foster Peabody, Carlton J. H. Hayes, Emily G. Balch, Lillian D. Wald, Paul U. Kellogg, Max Eastman, and John Haynes Holmes.

[11] *New York Times,* February 3, 1917; for a copy of the telegram, see V. L. Berger *et al.* to C. Kitchin, February 2, 1917, Kitchin Papers.

President said he felt as if the world had suddenly reversed itself; that after going from east to west, it had begun to go from west to east, and that he could not get his balance."

They then discussed whether the President should break relations at once or wait until some overt act forced his hand.

"The President [House recorded in his diary] was insistent that he would not allow it to lead to war if it could possibly be avoided. He reiterated his belief that it would be a crime for this Government to involve itself in the war to such an extent as to make it impossible to save Europe afterward. He spoke of Germany as 'a madman that should be curbed.' I asked if he thought it fair to the Allies to ask them to do the curbing without doing our share. He noticeably winced at this, but still held to his determination not to become involved if it were humanly possible to do otherwise.

"We sat listlessly during the morning. . . . The President nervously arranged his books and walked up and down the floor. Mrs. Wilson spoke of golf and asked whether I thought it would look badly if the President went on the links. I thought the American people would feel that he should not do anything so trivial at such a time. . . . We had finished the discussion within a half-hour and there was nothing further to say. The President at last suggested that we play a game of pool."[12]

Lansing came at noon, bringing the note severing relations with Germany. The three men returned to the President's study for further conversation. Lansing argued eloquently that peace and civilization depended on establishment of democratic institutions throughout the world, and that Prussian militarism was the inveterate foe of democracy. "The President said that he was not sure of this as it might mean the disintegration of German power and the destruction of the German nation." Lansing thought that he was arguing mainly in order to bring out all possible sides of the question.[13]

Lansing left at 12:50 p.m., and Wilson and House discussed whether the President should call a special Cabinet meeting or wait until the regular session on February 2 to discuss the note with his advisers. House thought not, and Wilson agreed. Wilson also said that, in any event, he had promised Senator Stone that he would not break relations

[12] House Diary, February 1, 1917.

[13] Lansing's memorandum on February 4, 1917, R. Lansing, *War Memoirs*, p. 214; Lansing Desk Diary, February 1, 1917; *New York Times*, February 2, 1917. House's statement in his diary, February 1, 1917, that the three men agreed in this meeting that "it was best to give . . . [Bernstorff] his passports at once," is obviously incorrect.

without discussing the matter beforehand with him. He had telegraphed to summon the Senator, then in St. Louis, and would have to wait until he had arrived in Washington before taking any final steps. House returned to New York in the afternoon.[14]

House gave further intimations of the President's mood in a conversation with the English pacifist, J. Howard Whitehouse, on the following day. Whitehouse had sent a memorandum on January 31 asserting that it would be a disaster for England, America, and mankind if America was suddenly forced into the war—"It would mean the continuance of the war perhaps for years on a scale of unthinkable horror." He begged the President to continue his efforts for peace.[15] House, Whitehouse recorded, "thanked me for the memorandum. It had reached him shortly before he started for Washington and he took it to the President. They read it together.[16] . . . He expressed to House his pleasure at getting it and his agreement with its proposals. They were wholly on the lines of his own thoughts. House went on to tell me that the President had no intention of being rushed. He was as firm as a rock. There were signs of trouble with the cabinet, but the cabinet would not be able to move him. It was his intention to resist the demand for war. If events compelled him to act, he might sever diplomatic relations but he would still try to avoid being drawn into the war. . . . I discussed with House the probable attitude of Congress. He said he thought the President would be able to manage them. He had a larger majority in this Congress than he would have in the one just elected which did not come into power until next session. He did not think they would attempt to take any action to over-rule the President's views. At the same time it would be a great relief when Congress adjourned. There was some danger so long as it remained sitting."[17]

Wilson played golf with Mrs. Wilson in Virginia in the morning of February 2 and returned to his office at eleven to find two letters from Lansing on his desk. One was a violent indictment of the "merciless and inhuman" submarine warfare that had made Germany "an outcast among the nations."[18] The other was an analysis of what

[14] House Diary, February 1, 1917.

[15] J. H. Whitehouse to E. M. House, January 31, 1917, Wilson Papers.

[16] House does not mention this in his diary, but he did at least give the memorandum to the President, and Wilson lent it to Lansing.

[17] "The House Report," Whitehouse Papers, entry for February 2, 1917.

[18] R. Lansing to W. W., February 2, 1917, enclosing a memorandum dated February 1, 1917, Wilson Papers.

Lansing said were the two choices now open to the American government—a break with Germany, accompanied by an announcement that Germany was an international outlaw and American vessels should keep away from seas infested by piratical craft, *or* a break accompanied by an appeal to Congress for a declaration of war. Lansing strongly preferred the second.[19]

The Cabinet met at two-thirty in the afternoon, and the President began the discussion, Lane reported in a letter to his brother, by saying that the German submarine announcement had been an "astounding surprise." He had received no intimation of such a reversal of policy. "In answer to a question as to which side he wished to see win, the President said that he didn't wish to see either side win,—for both had been equally indifferent to the rights of neutrals—though Germany had been brutal in taking life, and England only in taking property. He would like to see the neutrals unite. . . . We talked the world situation over. I spoke of the likelihood of a German-Russian-Japanese alliance as the natural thing at the end of the war because they all were nearly in the same stage of development. He thought the Russian peasant might save the world this misfortune. The fact that Russia had been, but a short time since, on the verge of an independent peace with Germany was brought out as evidencing the possibility of a break on the Allies' side."[20]

Then Wilson asked, "Shall I break off diplomatic relations with Germany?" One member wrote afterward, "He immediately followed this question with a somewhat startling statement. He would say frankly that, if he felt that, in order to keep the white race or part of it strong to meet the yellow race—Japan, for instance, in alliance with Russia, dominating China—it was wise to do nothing, he would do nothing, and would submit to anything and any imputation of weakness or cowardice. This was a novel and unexpected angle."[21] The impulsive McAdoo was for decisive action. Baker, Daniels, Burleson, and William B. Wilson said that they were much impressed by the President's long view, although the Postmaster General thought that the American government had to make good its warning to Germany. Redfield favored a break. Then Houston made an impassioned plea

[19] R. Lansing to W. W., February 2, 1917, *The Lansing Papers*, I, 591-592.

[20] F. K. Lane to G. W. Lane, February 9, 1917, Anne W. Lane and Louise H. Wall (eds.), *The Letters of Franklin K. Lane*, pp. 233-234; hereinafter cited as Lane and Wall, *Letters of Franklin K. Lane*.

[21] David F. Houston, *Eight Years with Wilson's Cabinet, 1913 to 1920* (2 vols.), I, 229.

for a declaration of war and full support of the Allies. At the close of the session the President read the note that Lansing had drafted.

"I think that the part of the discussion which most deeply shocked some of the members [Lansing wrote soon afterward] was the President's comment on the remark which I made concerning the future of the peace of the world. ... I went on to say that it seemed to me there could be no question but that to bring to an end absolutism the Allies ought to succeed, and that it was for our interest and for the interest of the world that we should join the Allies and aid them if we went into the war at all.

"To this the President replied, 'I am not so sure of that.' He then went on to argue that probably greater justice would be done if the conflict ended in a draw."[22]

"I was glad to hear you say," Josephus Daniels wrote to the President after the meeting, "you could not at this time fully trust anybody's judgment in this crisis, not even your own, for my feeling that we are the trustees of the civilization of our race is so strong that the possibility of becoming involved in the world's struggle makes me unable to sleep. After returning to the Department I had a long talk with Admiral [William S.] Benson. Of course I told him nothing of your views or the cabinet discussion, but found he had the same abhorrence of becoming enlisted with either side of combatants that you expressed. His view is that if we lose our equipose, the world will be in darkness."[23]

The meeting broke up at 4:45, and members of the Cabinet left the White House with grave faces. One of them later broke the rule of silence to say only, "The near future will develop something very, very serious."

Wilson now rushed to Senator Stone's office in the Senate Office Building. The Missourian, who had just arrived from St. Louis, was in the office of the foreign relations committee in the Capitol, and Wilson went there at once and talked privately with the Senator for half an hour. Then Wilson repaired to the President's Room while Stone rounded up as many senators as he could find. Sixteen Democrats came at about five-thirty and sat in a semicircle around the President. Except for Atlee Pomerene of Ohio, they all represented southern and western states and included some of the hitherto most ardent cham-

[22] Lansing Diary, February 4, 1917. This is the part of the text that Lansing omitted from his *War Memoirs*, p. 215.
[23] J. Daniels to W. W., February 2, 1917, Wilson Papers.

pions of neutrality in the upper house. There were no Republicans only because the Senate had adjourned and pages could find none.

Wilson opened the discussion by saying that he had come "seeking light," to hear senatorial opinion on what seemed to be, as he put it, the three choices open to the American government: (1) an immediate break with Germany, (2) postponement of a break until Germany had committed an overt act against *American* rights, and (3) a redefinition of American policy, with a final warning that a German offense would lead to rupture in diplomatic relations. He wanted to know the pulse of the Senate in this gravest crisis in American history, the President went on. He wanted each man to speak his mind frankly, with the welfare of the nation and civilization at heart. Stone and J. Hamilton Lewis of Illinois said that they favored assuming that the Germans did not really intend to sink American ships without warning. They would, they added, meet any such violation of American rights with immediate severance of relations. All other senators who spoke said that it was obvious what the Germans were going to do, and that the President should break relations at once. They argued that this was the only dignified course and said they were sure that their constituents would applaud such action. The conference ended at a little after seven o'clock. Each senator shook Wilson's hand on leaving and assured him that he would be sustained by a unanimous Senate whatever course he followed.[24]

The lines of thought about right policy were converging in Wilson's mind by the time that he returned to the White House. It seems absolutely certain that he would not have considered breaking relations if the Germans had limited their unrestricted submarine operations to armed ships. It seems almost equally certain that he would not have contemplated rupture and its risk of war if the Germans had limited unwarned attacks to belligerent merchantmen, spared passenger ships, and continued cruiser-type operations against neutral merchantmen. This, admittedly, is a big conclusion based entirely on circumstantial evidence. But one can come to no other in light of all that Wilson had said and done since the autumn of 1916. He well knew that the war was entering a new and more desperate stage in which both belligerent alliances would intensify their maritime measures in the hope of victory. He had long known that the Germans would sharpen their submarine campaign if they failed to obtain a peace conference. He believed, moreover, that the war was in its final stages, simply because

[24] *New York Times,* February 3, 1917.

Europe could not endure much further agony and attrition. He had come tortuously but firmly to the view that American national interests, to say nothing of the interests of humanity, demanded a draw and a negotiated peace. He did not want to see a decisive Allied victory any more than a decisive German victory. Most important, he was still confident that he could soon move effectively for an armistice and peace. These conclusions help to explain his extreme reluctance to do anything that might set the nation on the path toward war with Germany. They also seem to justify the belief that he would have accepted unrestricted submarine attacks against belligerent shipping even though they would have been violations of the *Sussex* pledge.

The staggering aspect of the German submarine decree of January 31 was its bald threat against American and other neutral shipping. This was what enraged a segment of public opinion. This, and this alone, was apparently the German policy that prompted all senators but two to recommend an immediate break, while even Stone and Lewis advised a rupture if the Germans should enforce their threat. Wilson had never denied the right of German submarine commanders to sink American ships in certain circumstances. He would not, presumably, have denied the right of the Germans to proclaim and enforce a legal blockade. But the Germans had marked out broad zones of international waters and declared war on peaceful neutral shipping in what was obviously a campaign of terror. The significant and decisive aspect of the German decree was that it left no ground for compromise or gradual accommodation by partial withdrawal. It forced Wilson, and all leaders in the American government, to choose between some form of counteraction and a major surrender of national rights, with all that it would have implied in diminution of national prestige and influence and deterioration of the national fiber.

Wilson obviously had been weighing the possibility of withdrawal and surrender. What the senators said to him in the evening conference was apparently the thing that tipped the scales in his mind toward decision to break relations. But, as we will soon see, he was also determined to give the Germans another opportunity, and a large one, to preserve the German-American peace.

Wilson made his decision at least as soon as he returned to the White House, and he worked far into the night alone in his study on a message to Congress announcing the break and explaining the course that he intended to pursue. He saw Tumulty at ten o'clock the following morning and asked him to arrange for a joint session at two o'clock that afternoon. Then Wilson called Lansing to his study at 10:30 to inform him that he had decided to break relations and ask him to make arrangements to hand Bernstorff his passports at the moment when he, Wilson, began his address to Congress.[25]

Several thousand persons cheered the President when he arrived at the Capitol at two o'clock. The chamber of the House of Representatives was packed with congressmen and senators, and the galleries were crowded with members of the Allied diplomatic corps, the Cabinet, and the Supreme Court, along with reporters and other individuals. Mrs. Wilson and members of the family sat in the executive gallery.

Wilson, dressed smartly in a cutaway, spoke soberly, but his voice was calm, and he gave the appearance of being altogether self-possessed. He began by reviewing the *Sussex* correspondence and saying that the recent German announcement left the American government no alternative in action. "I have, therefore," he went on, "directed the Secretary of State to announce to His Excellency the German Ambassador that all diplomatic relations between the United States and the German Empire are severed, and that the American Ambassador at Berlin will immediately be withdrawn; and, in accordance with this decision, to hand to His Excellency his passports." His listeners leaned forward to hear this sentence and burst into applause before he could finish it, with Senators Tillman and Lodge leading the demonstration.

As soon as the noise subsided Wilson went on to say what he would do. He refused to believe, he said, that German authorities would actually destroy *American* ships and take American lives in prosecution of a ruthless submarine campaign. "Only actual overt acts on their part can make me believe it even now." Congressmen and senators applauded even more loudly than before. If the Germans did destroy *American* ships and American lives in heedless contravention of law and the obvious dictates of humanity, Wilson continued, he would come back to Congress to seek authority to protect "our seamen and our people in the prosecution of their peaceful and legitimate errands on the high seas." He could do nothing less, he said, and he assumed that other neutral governments would take the same action. Wilson concluded:

[25] *ibid.*, February 4, 1917; Lansing Desk Diary, February 3, 1917. The note was the Secretary of State to the German Ambassador, February 3, 1917, *Foreign Relations, 1917, Supplement 1*, pp. 106-108. It was a matter-of-fact review of the *Sussex* correspondence, accompanied by the announcement that the new German submarine policy left the United States Government no alternative but to sever diplomatic relations with the German Empire.

"We do not desire any hostile conflict with the Imperial German Government. We are the sincere friends of the German people and earnestly desire to remain at peace with the Government which speaks for them. We shall not believe that they are hostile to us unless and until we are obliged to believe it; and we purpose nothing more than *the reasonable defense of the undoubted rights of our people.* We wish to serve no selfish ends. We seek merely to stand true alike in thought and in action to the immemorial principles of our people which I sought to express in my address to the Senate only two weeks ago,— seek merely to vindicate our right to liberty and justice and an unmolested life. These are the bases of peace, not war. God grant we may not be challenged to defend them by acts of wilful injustice on the part of the Government of Germany!"[26]

Wilson's voice quavered as he read the last sentence, and the audience rose and applauded warmly at the end.[27]

So there was the President's policy, unveiled for all the world to see. It was that the United States, after breaking diplomatic relations, would in fact accept a vastly sharpened submarine campaign, provided that the Germans did not sink American ships illegally and did not destroy American lives, presumably both on American ships and belligerent passenger ships. Had Wilson been deliberately vague about the safety of Americans among the crews of belligerent merchantmen? Perhaps he had. His failure to mention them or belligerent ships at all would seem to indicate that he did not intend to include attacks on belligerent merchantmen among the "actual overt acts." This fact was confirmed by what Wilson said the American government would do if the Germans carried out their threats. It would simply attempt to defend reasonable American maritime rights by protecting its own seamen and people "in the prosecution of their peaceful and legitimate errands on the high seas." Presumably, working on belligerent ships carrying contraband through war zones was not to be included among peaceful and legitimate pursuits. All of Wilson's actions during the next few weeks indicate that these assumptions are correct.

Thus whether the United States resorted to armed neutrality or possibly accepted full-fledged belligerency now depended entirely upon the German government.

Virtually every editor and publicist in the United States warmly approved the President's address. The small minority of intervention-

[26] *The New Democracy*, II, 422-426; italics added.
[27] *New York Times*, February 4, 1917.

ists were delighted because they thought that the break heralded
inevitable belligerency. But the vast majority, including editors of the
Hearst chain, German-American newspapers, and the religious press,
said that Wilson could have done nothing less without sacrificing
national honor and prestige and that full-fledged belligerency could
still be avoided. "This is no time for singing 'hymns of hate,' " a New
York Methodist spokesman declared, "or for indulging in the thoughts
and tempers from which they spring. The President has himself shown
the way to a sympathy and moderation of tone which will help to
carry the nation through the crisis."[28] The rupture of relations, the
editor of the Milwaukee *Germania Herold* added, did not mean a
declaration of war. The President would bring the country through
the crisis with peace and honor as he had done in the past.[29] This,
certainly, was the hope of many senators when they adopted, by a vote
of seventy-eight to five on February 7, a resolution offered by Senator
Stone formally approving the President's action in severing relations
with Germany.[30] Only Senator Lodge, apparently, had a private carping word. He had voted for the resolution, he wrote to Roosevelt, in
the full knowledge that British success against the submarines might

[28] New York *Christian Advocate*, xci (February 8, 1917), 122.

[29] Milwaukee *Germania Herold*, February 4, 1917. For other comment in the German-American press, virtually all of which said that German Americans loyally supported the President, see the following, dated February 4, 1917: *New Yorker Staats-Zeitung, New Yorker Herold*, Philadelphia *Tageblatt* (critical), Philadelphia *Demokrat*, Cincinnati *Freie Presse*, Cincinnati *Volksblatt*, Chicago *Illinois Staats-Zeitung*, St. Paul *Volkszeitung*, Denver *Colorado Herold*, Los Angeles *Germania*.
For general newspaper editorial opinion on the break, see the following, dated February 4, 1917: *New York Times, New York Tribune*, New York *World, Springfield* (Mass.) *Republican, Boston Herald, Providence Journal, Philadelphia Inquirer, Philadelphia Public Ledger, Cleveland Plain Dealer*, Columbus *Ohio State Journal, Detroit Free Press, Minneapolis Journal, St. Paul Pioneer-Press, St. Louis Globe-Democrat*, Little Rock *Arkansas Gazette, Chicago Tribune, Chicago Herald, Omaha Bee, Fargo Courier News, Cheyenne State Leader, Salt Lake* (City) *Tribune, San Francisco Chronicle, Los Angeles Times*, Baltimore *Sun, Atlanta Constitution, Richmond Times-Dispatch, Savannah News, Chattanooga Daily Times, Houston Post*, and *Dallas Morning News*.
For comment in the periodical and religious press, see Dallas *Baptist Standard*, xxviii (February 8, 1917), 6; *Presbyterian Banner*, ciii (February 8, 1917), 8; New York *Nation*, civ (February 8, 1917), 150-151; *The Presbyterian*, lxxxvii (February 15, 1917), 6; *New Republic*, x (February 10, 1917), 30-31, 36-38; *The Independent*, lxxxix (February 12, 1917), 246; *The Outlook*, cxv (February 14, 1917), 263.

[30] *New York Times*, February 8, 1917. William F. Kirby of Arkansas, James K. Vardaman of Mississippi, Robert M. La Follette of Wisconsin, A. J. Gronna of North Dakota, and John D. Works of California, all agrarian radicals or advanced progressives, voted against the resolution.

give Wilson an excuse for not going to war. "He may escape it," Lodge went on. "I think it is not improbable. His one desire is to avoid war at any cost, simply because he is afraid. He can bully Congressmen, but he flinches in the presence of danger, physical and moral."[31] Roosevelt agreed, "Whether we will really go to war or not, Heaven only knows, and certainly Mr. Wilson doesn't."[32]

Announcement of the rupture set off a fierce nationwide struggle and debate over peace and war between leaders of burgeoning interventionists and organized peace groups that would not end until events had run their course.

The interventionists were still a tiny minority organized in the hitherto ineffectual American Rights Committee. They rallied in response to the encouraging events of January 31—February 3 with an advertisement in the *New York Times* and other newspapers on February 12. It called on Americans to demand an immediate declaration of war. The Committee also dispatched a telegram to the President on February 23 urging him to protect American shipping.[33] President Hibben of Princeton University, a leader of this group, made a stirring plea for immediate participation at the Lafayette Avenue Presbyterian Church of Brooklyn on February 25.[34]

This was pitifully weak cannonade, so to speak. One sign that interventionism might become a national movement if German-American relations deteriorated further was the conversion of the *New Republic* to that cause, signaled by an editorial entitled "Justification" on February 10. It argued that the United States was drifting inevitably into war with Germany, not because of disputes over obsolete international law, but because a benevolent British sea power protected American interests and the United States could not safely tolerate a successful German challenge to British dominion of the seas. The United States, which depended for its very existence upon maritime freedom and order, had been justified in pursuing a benevolent neutrality toward the Allies and harsh (although technically neutral)

[31] H. C. Lodge to T. Roosevelt, February 13, 1917, Roosevelt Papers.
[32] T. Roosevelt to H. Johnson, February 17, 1917, *ibid.*
[33] *New York Times,* February 12 and 24, 1917.
[34] *ibid.,* February 26, 1917. Wilson's earlier comment, made when a Methodist minister in Bernardsville, New Jersey, had written saying that he wanted to form a defense league in his church and would appreciate a letter from the President, might have been applicable to Hibben's speech. "The Church," Wilson wrote to Tumulty (n. d., but c. February 20, 1917, Wilson Papers), "seems to me a very queer unit to build a defense league of any kind (I think our ministers are going crazy)."

policies toward Germany. It was now justified in fighting to prevent a German reign of terror on the seas. Beyond the war there had to be a league of nations powerful enough to guarantee the freedom and safety of the seas against all aggressors, even the British.[35] The editors made the same point more emphatically a week later. Germany's war against the western Allies, they wrote, was war against "the civilization of which we are a part." The United States had accepted the illegal British blockade and defied the submarine, winked at British transgressions and resisted German violations of international law, only because of a national necessity to keep open sea lanes to Great Britain and France. The main task now was to bring Germany back into the western community against which she had revolted. The editorial went on:

"What we must fight for is the common interest of the western world, for the integrity of the Atlantic Powers. We must recognize that we are in fact one great community and act as a member of it. Our entrance into it would weight it immeasurably in favor of liberalism, and make the organization of a league for peace an immediately practical object of statesmanship. By showing that we are ready now, as well as in the theoretical future, to defend the western world, the cornerstone of federation would be laid. We would not and could not fight to exclude Germany from that league. We would not and could not fight for a bad settlement. The real danger to a decent peace has always been that the western nations would become so dependent on Russia and Japan that they must pay any price for their loyalty. That danger is almost certainly obviated by our participation."[36]

The break in relations spurred leaders in the peace movement to almost frenzied activity. Bryan issued an appeal, "To the American People," a few hours after the event. The belligerents, Bryan's message said, thought that they were fighting for their lives. There were various ways that the United States could avoid being drawn into the struggle, and Congress, if it came to the worst, could permit the people to decide in national referendum. It concluded:

"The most important thing is that the officials at Washington shall know that the people at home protest against entering this war on either side, with its frightful expenditure of blood and treasure; that

[35] "Justification," *New Republic*, x (February 10, 1917), 36-38.
[36] "The Defense of the Atlantic World," *ibid.*, February 17, 1917, pp. 59-61. There is an interesting entry in the Lansing Desk Diary, February 15, 1917, saying cryptically that Walter Lippmann, one of the editors of the *New Republic*, had been arguing that war was inevitable.

they are not willing to send American soldiers across the Atlantic to march under the banner of any European monarch or to die on European soil in settlement of European quarrels; and that they are not willing to surrender the opportunity to render a supreme service to the world as a friend of all and peacemaker when peace is possible.

"Wire immediately to the President, your senators and your congressmen. A few cents now may save many dollars in taxation and possibly a son."[37]

"The day after the break with Germany," one reporter wrote to Colonel House, "I traveled from Washington to New York in the same car as Mr. Bryan. . . . On the subject of the break he declared that it never should have taken place, and that it was quite unnecessary. He was, it seemed to me, quite bitter on the subject, and it is here that the interesting part comes in. He went on to insist that if the President should go to Congress for further powers, he would demand a referendum in order to repudiate any such action. . . . He made it quite clear to me . . . that he would thwart the President's policy as far as ever he could."[38]

That was the state of mind and disposition of all leaders of the disparate peace forces—pacifists, agrarian radicals, Socialists, German Americans, and others. The Socialist party, Socialist Labor party, Church Peace Union, Woman's Peace party, and Emergency Peace Federation (formerly the American Neutral Conference Committee) held a mass rally in New York on February 5 and conducted a march on the Capitol in Washington on February 12.[39] A group from the Emergency Peace Federation captured a meeting in New York on February 23, called by the American Peace Society, and adopted a resolution demanding a national referendum before a declaration of war could go into effect.[40]

Antiwar partisans of all stripes rallied in massive demonstrations elsewhere. James H. Maurer, Socialist president of the Pennsylvania State Federation of Labor, in a speech in Philadelphia on February 4 demanded a national general strike to prevent preparation for war.[41] German Americans, in a mass meeting in Toledo on the same day, proposed a referendum on war or peace.[42] The Mayor of Minneapolis,

[37] *New York Times*, February 4, 1916; *The Commoner*, xvii (February 1917), 2.
[38] F. H. Dixon to E. M. House, February 15, 1917, House Papers.
[39] *New York Times*, February 6 and 13, 1917.
[40] *ibid.*, February 24, 1917.
[41] *ibid.*, February 5, 1917.
[42] *ibid.*

Thomas Van Lear, called a mass meeting in his city on February 10 to protest against the rupture with Germany, and the state committee of the Socialist party of Minnesota urged all workers to refuse to fight in the event of war.[43] Some 10,000 persons jammed the Chicago Coliseum on February 18 to hear Representative Oscar Callaway, agrarian radical from Texas, denounce the "munition makers, capitalists, American Admirals, Generals, Captains and so-called metropolitan newspapers . . . leagued together to force the United States into the European war."[44] One Chicagoan reported to Bryan, "I am sure you will be interested in learning that our meeting was a most wonderful success. The Coliseum was jammed with humanity. . . . We estimate that seventeen or eighteen thousand people in one way or another participated in our Peace Demonstration."[45] And all the while the Apostle of Peace was counseling his own followers (Bryan had no connection with any of the radical peace groups) and demanding maintenance of peace and, if the worst happened, a popular referendum on a war resolution.[46] Bryan's friend, Callaway, introduced a resolution calling for such a referendum in the House of Representatives on February 9.[47]

No one, least of all Bryan, really thought that Congress would adopt the war referendum resolution, or that workers would go out on general strike if war occurred. The one constructive suggestion to come out of all this furor was the proposal made by Carlton J. H. Hayes, Professor of History at Columbia University, in an article in *The Survey* on February 10. It seemed to offer a workable alternative to full-fledged belligerency. The United States, Hayes said, echoing some of Wilson's own phrases, had no vital interests in the European war and every reason of national interest to prefer a draw. Germany and Great Britain were in a death struggle, and their depredations were aimed at each other, not at the United States. American belligerency would not and could not in the circumstances vindicate neutral maritime rights; it would result only in the victory of powers that had denied American neutral rights nearly as much as Germany. There was one way, Hayes concluded, to defend neutral rights against all aggressors—organization

[43] *ibid.*, February 11, 1917.
[44] New York *World*, February 19, 1917.
[45] H. J. Friedman to W. J. Bryan, February 23, 1917, Bryan Papers, LC.
[46] e. g., his speech before the District of Columbia Anti-War Society on February 4, 1917, *New York Times*, February 5, 1917.
[47] *ibid.*, February 10, 1917. For general reviews, see "Efforts of American Pacifists to Avert War," *Literary Digest*, LIV (February 24, 1917), 451-454; the superb articles in the New York *World*, March 4, 1917; and the article in the *New York Times*, March 4, 1917, on the financing of the peace groups.

of the neutral maritime nations in a league of armed neutrality to protect all legitimate neutral commerce.[48]

Lillian D. Wald sent a copy of Hayes's article to President Wilson on February 8, along with her own strong endorsement.[49] House also sent a copy on the same day, and Wilson relayed the article to Lansing on February 9.[50] The *New York Evening Post* reprinted it on the following day, saying that it offered the only sensible and responsible alternative to meaningless belligerency.[51] The New York *Nation* and *The Survey* endorsed the plan on February 15 and 17.[52] A newly formed Committee for Democratic Control, a group of New York antiwar intellectuals headed by Amos Pinchot, distributed copies of the plan to members of Congress on February 13,[53] and Representative Irvine L. Lenroot of Wisconsin advocated its adoption in a speech in the House of Representatives on February 17.[54]

These and numerous other manifestations did not necessarily reflect majority sentiment, which was, as always, silent. But they generated much heat along with some light, and they made one overriding fact indisputably clear. There was in mid-February virtually no articulate popular desire for participation in the war. The editor of the *Springfield Republican* was probably not far from the mark when he assessed American public opinion in the aftermath of the break in relations as follows:

What is the Public Sentiment?

First, the overwhelming majority of the American people still desire most earnestly to avoid war and hope that the government will succeed in honorably avoiding war.

Second, the American people with virtual unanimity approve the president's action in severing diplomatic relations with Germany.

Third, the mass of the American people will approve necessary measures for the protection of American rights on the high seas, even by the use of force, if flagrant attacks on this country's sovereignty are made in the lawless sinking of American ships.

[48] C. J. H. Hayes, "Which? War without a Purpose? Or Armed Neutrality with a Purpose?" *The Survey*, xxxvii (February 10, 1917), 535-538.
[49] Lillian D. Wald to W. W., February 8, 1917, Wilson Papers.
[50] W. W. to R. Lansing, February 9, 1917, *The Lansing Papers*, I, 596.
[51] *New York Evening Post*, February 10, 1917.
[52] New York *Nation*, civ (February 15, 1917), 178-179; *The Survey*, xxxvii (February 17, 1917), 572-577. For other comment, see "'Limited-Liability' War," *Literary Digest*, liv (March 3, 1917), 538-539.
[53] *New York Times*, February 14, 1917.
[54] *Congressional Record*, 64th Cong., 2d sess., p. 3529.

Fourth, Congress will be sustained by public opinion if it votes to authorize the president to take such measures as circumstances may require, in his judgment, to vindicate the position the nation has occupied in breaking with Germany.

Fifth, a majority of the people would insist that in upholding American rights on the seas, by force if necessary, this country refrain from joining the entente.

Sixth, nine-tenths of the people would be opposed, as the case appears to-day, to sending American soldiers to fight in Europe.

Seventh, the bulk of the American people would prefer measures "short of war," if possible, no entangling military alliances and the restoration of friendly relations with Germany as soon as Germany would make friendly relations possible.

From such studies of public opinion, east and west, north and south, as we have been able to make, the foregoing conclusions seem to be approximately correct.[55]

The outpouring of peace sentiment during this period only strengthened Wilson's own grim determination to go the second mile with Germany. The administration's only act that might have been at all provocative was seizure of certain German vessels lying in American and Panamanian harbors immediately after Lansing gave Bernstorff his passports.[56] But there was clear legal right for these few seizures, and the President announced on February 5 that all German property in the United States would continue to enjoy full protection of the law. "We will do nothing that we have not a clear legal right to do," he said. "When we act we will act on principles of right and not on expediency. There is no haste or panic anywhere."[57] He reiterated these assurances a few days later, adding that the United States would not seize German private property without clear legal right even should actual hostilities break out.[58] "The President," Lane wrote about a Cabinet meeting on February 6, "said that he was 'passionately' determined not to over-step the slightest punctilio of honor in dealing with Germany, or interned Germans, or the property of Germans. He would not take the interned ships, not even though they were being gutted

[55] *Springfield* (Mass.) *Republican*, February 19, 1917.

[56] The ships seized were the interned auxiliary cruisers, *Kronprinz Wilhelm* and *Prinz Eitel Friedrich*, both in Philadelphia harbor; the liner *Appam* at Newport News; the liner *Kronprinzessin Cecilie* at Boston; and four German ships in Cristobal harbor, Panama. American naval guards were also placed on two German and three Austrian steamers at New Orleans. *New York Times*, February 4, 1917.

[57] *ibid.*, February 6, 1917.

[58] New York *World*, February 9, 1917.

of their machinery. He wished an announcement made that all property of Germans would be held inviolate, and that interned sailors on merchant ships could enter the United States."[59]

Wilson also gave personal instructions that there should be no unusual movement of troops or signs of incipient mobilization. "The President," Baker warned the commander of the Eastern Department, General Wood, "deems it imperative that no troops under Federal control be stationed or used in a manner which will excite apprehension or suggest anticipated trouble, and especially that no basis should be given for opinion abroad that we are mobilizing. The breach of diplomatic relations does not justify such action and if taken it might be gravely misunderstood."[60]

Actually, Baker and Daniels and their bureau chiefs were working night and day to facilitate full-scale mobilization if it had to come.[61] Wilson himself went to Baker's and Daniels's offices on February 5 and 8 to discuss and review these preparations,[62] and he asked all bureau chiefs on February 19 to report to him on the condition of the nation's fighting forces.[63] He also conferred frequently during this period with congressional leaders who were sponsoring the army and navy appropriations bills and a measure to prevent espionage and sabotage; and he asked for special authority to commandeer shipyards and munitions plants in certain circumstances.[64] Finally, he and Baker had several long conferences about a plan for universal military service that the War College had submitted to the Senate military affairs committee on December 19, 1916, and that had been embodied in legislation introduced by Senator Chamberlain on February 10, 1917.[65]

Events in the new submarine campaign were meanwhile forcing the President to clarify and define what he had rather obscurely called "actual overt acts." There was momentary alarm on February 3 at news from London of the unwarned torpedoing of the American steamer *Housatonic* off the Scilly Islands. But the American Consul at Plymouth reported on the following day that a German submarine

[59] F. K. Lane to G. W. Lane, February 9, 1917, Lane and Wall, *Letters of Franklin K. Lane*, p. 235.

[60] N. D. Baker to L. Wood, February 3, 1917, copy in the Wilson Papers.

[61] See, e. g., N. D. Baker to W. W., February 7, 1917, *ibid.*, reviewing the steps that the War Department had taken or was in process of taking.

[62] *New York Times*, February 6 and 9, 1917.

[63] New York *World*, February 20, 1917.

[64] *New York Times*, February 4, 6, 7, 21, and 23, 1917.

[65] New York *World*, December 20, 1916, and February 17, 1917; *New York Times*, February 11 and 22, 1917.

had warned *Housatonic* before sinking her and had towed her crew in lifeboats toward land.[66] Then Ambassador Page reported on February 5 that an American seaman had been killed when a submarine shelled the lifeboats of the British merchantman, *Eavestone*, after sinking her. *Eavestone* had tried to escape after being warned.[67]

A Cabinet discussion of the *Eavestone* incident on February 6 led to the first clear definition of American policy. The administration, an obviously inspired report in the *New York Times* said, expected and would ignore submarine attacks against *belligerent* merchantmen, even when American lives were endangered or lost. It was determined to wait for conclusive evidence that the German government was conducting ruthless submarine warfare without regard to the rights and interests of American citizens. Such evidence would consist of an unwarned torpedoing of an *American* ship.[68]

Wilson adhered stubbornly to this policy during the next two and a half weeks in spite of two rather flagrant submarine incidents involving American citizens. One was the unwarned torpedoing of the British merchantman, *Turino*, on February 4. The one American among the crew was uninjured.[69] Much more provocative was the ruthless torpedoing of the armed British passenger liner *Californian* off Fastnet on February 7, killing forty-one persons. The one American aboard was uninjured.[70] A single submarine attacked seven Dutch merchantmen off Falmouth on February 22.[71] Meanwhile, dozens of Allied merchantmen not carrying Americans had been sunk without warning since the onset of the new campaign.

None of the foregoing incidents excited the American public or aroused any widespread demands for war. The only issue to generate some heat and pressure on the administration was the arming of American ships. All American shipping lines canceled sailings after publication of the German decree on February 1, and P. A. S. Franklin, president of the International Mercantile Marine Company, asked the State Department whether he should permit the *St. Louis* and

[66] *ibid.*, February 4 and 5, 1917; Consul J. J. Stephens to the Secretary of State, February 4, 1917, *Foreign Relations, 1917, Supplement 1*, p. 112.

[67] Ambassador Page to the Secretary of State, February 5, 1917, *ibid.*, pp. 114-115; *New York Times*, February 6, 1917.

[68] *ibid.*, February 7, 1917.

[69] *ibid.*, February 9 and 10, 1917; Consul Wesley Frost to the Secretary of State, February 7, 1917, *Foreign Relations, 1917, Supplement 1*, pp. 122-123.

[70] Consul Frost to the Secretary of State, February 7, 1917, two telegrams, *ibid.*, pp. 122-123; *New York Times*, February 8, 1917.

[71] *ibid.*, February 25, 1917.

St. Paul of the American Line to sail to England. The cabinet talked about the inquiry at its session on February 6.[72] "The main question discussed," one Cabinet member wrote a few days later, "was whether we should convoy, or arm, our merchant ships. Secretary Baker said that unless we did our ships would stay in American ports, and thus Germany would have us effectively locked up by her threat. The *St. Louis*, of the American line, wanted to go out with mail but asked the right to arm and the use of guns and gunners. After a long discussion, the decision of the President was that we should not convoy because that made a double hazard,—this being the report of the Navy,—but that ships should be told that they *might* arm, but that without new power from Congress they should not be furnished with guns and gunners."[73]

The Secretary of State, immediately after the Cabinet meeting, prepared a statement to be communicated to the War, Navy, and Treasury Departments in the form of a confidential memorandum for their guidance and to serve as a basis for replies to letters of inquiry to the State Department. He read this to Wilson over the telephone at 6:45 that evening, and Wilson authorized its confidential use. The statement follows:

"The Government cannot give advice to private persons as to whether or not their merchant vessels should sail on voyages to European ports by which they would be compelled to pass through waters delimited in the declaration issued by the German Government on January 31, 1917.

"It, however, asserts that the rights of American vessels to traverse all parts of the high seas are the same now as they were prior to the issuance of the German declaration, and that a neutral merchant vessel may, if its owners believe that it is liable to be unlawfully attacked, take any necessary measures to prevent or resist such attack."[74]

Franklin called by telephone on the following day, February 7, to inquire if Lansing had anything to tell him about a change in policy. Lansing read the statement to him, and Franklin gave it to the newspapers, which published it verbatim on the following day.[75] He tried vainly to purchase cannon and shells from private manufacturers and

[72] Lansing Desk Diary, February 6, 1917; D. F. Houston, *Eight Years with Wilson's Cabinet*, I, 233; New York *World*, February 7, 1917.

[73] F. K. Lane to G. W. Lane, February 9, 1917, Lane and Wall, *Letters of Franklin K. Lane*, pp. 234-235.

[74] "Memorandum by the Secretary of State . . . ," *The Lansing Papers*, I, 595.

[75] *New York Times*, February 8, 1917.

then turned to the Navy Department for help. Daniels put the matter squarely up to the President on February 10. The American liners, he wrote, had to have six-inch guns, which only the navy could provide, if they were to be adequately armed. Daniels also enclosed a memorandum by the Assistant Secretary, Franklin D. Roosevelt, suggesting that the navy lend guns, mounts, and ammunition for use on liners and other large ships.[76]

Franklin wrote again to Lansing on that same day to give notice that, unless the State Department instructed otherwise, the American Line would order the *Philadelphia* and *Finland*, both unarmed, to leave Liverpool for New York on February 14 and 16. "We feel," he added, "that the Government should arrange for their protection through the war zone."[77] The first three American freighters to leave American ports for the war zone since the beginning of the new submarine campaign sailed from New York harbor and Delaware Bay on that same day, February 10. They were all unarmed.[78]

Wilson and the Cabinet discussed the arming of merchantmen on February 9[79] and again more fully and warmly on February 13. McAdoo, at the second session, was strong for action at once. He would, he said, put naval guns and crews on American ships. Wilson replied that the people did not want precipitate action. Arming merchant vessels, he went on, might lead to war, and he did not want to force the hand of Congress. He thought that something would happen within a few days that would make it necessary for him to go to Congress and ask for additional power. The people, McAdoo retorted, expected the President to protect their rights and would gladly accept the consequences if he did. Houston added that Wilson should go to Congress for authority to arm merchantmen, and go as soon as possible. Wilson agreed but said that he had to defer decision. He wanted to avoid any action, he explained, that Germany might construe as an intentional affront designed to force war.[80] Moreover, he was concerned about the fate of fifty-nine American seamen who had been among the crews of three armed English merchantmen sunk by a German

[76] J. Daniels to W. W., February 10, 1917, Wilson Papers; F. D. Roosevelt, "Memorandum for the Secretary," dated February 10, 1917, *ibid*.

[77] P. A. S. Franklin to R. Lansing, February 10, 1917, copy in *ibid*.

[78] *New York Times*, February 10, 1917.

[79] D. F. Houston, *Eight Years with Wilson's Cabinet*, I, 233-234; *New York Times*, February 10, 1917.

[80] F. K. Lane to G. W. Lane, February 10, 1917, Lane and Wall, *Letters of Franklin K. Lane*, p. 235; D. F. Houston, *Eight Years with Wilson's Cabinet*, I, 234-235; *New York Times*, February 14 and 15, 1917.

surface raider and transported to Germany aboard the prize ship *Yarrowdale*. The German government was holding the seamen as hostages against American seizure of German ships and internment of their crews.[81]

It was obvious following the Cabinet meeting of February 13 that the question now was when, not whether, the administration would take action of some kind. Goods were beginning to pile high on wharves, and, as the *New York Times* reported on February 15, the entire economy would soon feel the disastrous effects unless the government took measures to encourage American ship owners to venture into the war zones with some hope of survival. The Navy Department began assembling guns and ammunition at strategic ports along the Atlantic coast on February 14.[82] But Wilson, as he said over and over during Cabinet discussions, was still determined to seek congressional sanction before arming merchantmen. And he would not go to Congress until some German overt act had aroused public and congressional opinion and he could be certain that Congress would approve his request.

The main reasons for Wilson's extreme reluctance to take any irreversible steps were his deep desire to avoid outright belligerency and profound conviction that he could not lead the nation even into defensive armed neutrality until the majority of Americans were ready and eager to follow in this dangerous course. Moreover, the fact that certain newspapers and individuals were now urging him to adopt stronger measures aroused his deep suspicions. As he wrote to Colonel House: "I feel as you do about the character of the support I am now receiving from certain once hostile quarters. You notice the suggestion is being actively renewed that I call their crowd into consultation and have a coalition cabinet at my elbow. It is the *Junkerthum* trying to creep in under cover of the patriotic feeling of the moment. They will not get in. They have now no examples of happy or successful coalitions to point to. The nominal coalition in England is nothing but a Tory cabinet such as they are eager to get a foothold for here. I know them too well, and will hit them straight between the eyes, if necessary, with plain words."[83]

---

[81] See the documents printed in *Foreign Relations, 1917, Supplement 1*, pp. 208-213. The American seamen were not released until March 12 on account of a quarantine imposed after one of the sailors among the *Yarrowdale* group contracted typhus.

[82] *New York Times*, February 15, 1917.

[83] W. W. to E. M. House, February 12, 1917, House Papers.

314 *The Break with Germany*

There were other reasons for his caution, and they were perhaps equally important. To begin with, he still had high hopes of resuming his drive for peace. They were greatly excited by receipt of an extraordinary message from Count Ottokar Czernin, new Austro-Hungarian Foreign Minister. It was addressed to Lansing and read as follows:

"The Imperial and Royal Ambassador, Count Tarnowski, has conveyed to me the kind words which you were good enough to express to him concerning Austria-Hungary and I hasten to transmit to you on that account my very best thanks. [Lansing, on February 3, had expressed the hope to Count Adam Tarnowski, Austro-Hungarian Ambassador-designate in Washington, that the United States would be able to maintain diplomatic relations with the Hapsburg Empire.[84]]

"I need not say I, too, would be very pleased if the diplomatic relations between us and the United States could be maintained intact. But in order to obtain that result I must above all once again ask the Government of the United States to take into consideration the position in which we are placed.

"We have declared—openly and honestly—that we only wage a war of defense, that is, that we are ready to negotiate honorable conditions of peace, a peace without victory. These proposals we are still determined to maintain. The basis, according to which there should be neither victor nor loser, was suggested by Mr. Wilson himself and it is now up to the Entente to accommodate themselves to that basis as we did. As long as the Entente will not give up the program published in their last note, a program which aims at the dismemberment of Austria-Hungary, it is impossible for us to talk about peace, and we are forced to defend ourselves with every means at our disposal.

"A technical modification of the submarine war is impossible. First of all an exchange of views with our allies would be necessary to that purpose. Moreover—and this is the chief reason—the numerous submarines which have left their ports can not be reached by any orders.

"The point of the question is, it seems to me, that Mr. Wilson who

[84] Wilson, House, and Lansing, in their conference on February 1, had discussed the desirability of maintaining relations with Austria-Hungary, and House had urged Wilson to see whether peace proposals could not be made through the Austrians. House Diary, February 1, 1917. Wilson had not, therefore, broken relations with the Hapsburg government even though it had sent a note to Washington on January 31 announcing the beginning of unrestricted submarine warfare in a memorandum similar to the German decree. See Ambassador Penfield to the Secretary of State, February 1, 1917, *Foreign Relations, 1917, Supplement 1*, pp. 104-105.

proposed a peace without victory should now feel morally obliged to use his influence with the powers of the Entente to make them accept that basis as we accepted it. The President has all the qualities to achieve this—on account of his high position, the personal esteem he enjoys all through Europe and on account of the possibility for the United States, by cutting off the requisites of war, to induce the powers of the Entente to conform themselves to Mr. Wilson's point of view.

"I trust that the President of the United States will continue the work of peace he began in a spirit of impartiality and I sincerely hope that he will induce the powers of the Entente to accept, like us, the American point of view, that there should be neither victor nor loser and that the peace concluded should be an honorable one for both sides—a lasting one for the whole world.

"Should the President follow this line of conduct not only the terror of the submarine war, but war in general would come to a sudden end and Mr. Wilson's name will shine with everlasting letters in the history of mankind.

"I beg to request you kindly to bring the above as well as the answer you might send me to the notice of Ambassador Count Tarnowski."[85]

Ambassador Frederick C. Penfield, after dispatching this message, wired a few hours later that Austria-Hungary was in desperate condition and longed for peace. "Economic life of Austria-Hungary," he went on, "seems paralyzed. Intelligent persons assure me Monarchy has food for but two or three months. Nearly every street in Vienna has bread line and misery and destitution visible everywhere. People all classes praying for peace."[86]

Lansing called the President as soon as these telegrams were deciphered in the early afternoon of February 7, and Wilson went to the Secretary's office at three o'clock to pick up copies. He read Czernin's message with mounting excitement. Here, it seemed, was the first really unequivocal response from Europe to his appeal for a negotiated peace. He worked all that same evening on a note to London that he hoped would break the impasse and get actual peace talks started, and he typed out the final copy on his own typewriter and took it personally to Lansing at four o'clock on February 8. Lansing sent it in code to Page at midnight. It reveals Wilson's deepest hopes and purposes during this period with such wonderful clarity that it is printed in full, as follows:

[85] Ambassador Penfield to the Secretary of State, February 5, 1917, *ibid.*, pp. 38-39.
[86] Ambassador Penfield to the Secretary of State, February 6, 1917, *ibid.*, p. 39.

The President directs that you lay the following before the leading members of the British Government in strictest confidence and begs that you will press the points it contains with all the earnestness and directness you would use were they your own personal views. He speaks of the leading members of the Government rather than of the Foreign Office because he does not intend this as in any sense an official but only as a personal message and wishes you to ascertain informally what he might expect should he make the proposals here foreshadowed officially to the Foreign Office.

The President knows that peace is intensely desired by the Teutonic powers, and much more by Austria than by any of her allies because the situation is becoming for many reasons much graver for her than for the others. He is trying to avoid breaking with Austria in order to keep the channels of official intercourse with her open so that he may use her for peace. The chief if not the only obstacle is the threat apparently contained in the peace terms recently stated by the Entente Allies that in case they succeeded they would insist upon a virtual dismemberment of the Austro-Hungarian Empire. Austria needs only to be reassured on that point, and that chiefly with regard to the older units of the Empire. It is the President's view that the large measure of autonomy already secured to those older units is a sufficient guarantee of peace and stability in that part of Europe so far as national and racial influences are concerned and that what Austria regards as the necessities of her development, opportunity, and security to the south of her can be adequately and satisfactorily secured to her by rights of way to the sea given by the common guaranty of the concert which must in any case be arranged if the future peace of the world is to be assured. He does not doubt that Austria can be satisfied without depriving the several Balkan states of their political autonomy and territorial integrity.

The effort of this Government will be constantly for peace even should it become itself involved, although those efforts would not in the least weaken or slacken its vigorous action in such a case. The President still believes and has reason to believe that, were it possible for him to give the necessary assurances to the Government of Austria, which fears radical dismemberment and which thinks that it is now fighting for its very existence, he could in a very short time force the acceptance of peace upon terms which would follow the general lines of his recent address to the Senate regarding the sort of peace the United States would be willing to join in guaranteeing. He is urgently desirous that the Entente Governments should make it possible for him to present such terms and press them for acceptance. The present enthusiastic support which the people of the United States are giving his foreign policy is being given, it is very evident, because they expect him to use the force and influence of the

United States, if he must use force, not to prolong the war, but to insist upon those rights of his own and other peoples which he regards and they regard as the bases and the only bases of peace.[87]

Page communicated the substance of this telegram to Lloyd George in a long conversation on the afternoon of February 10. The Prime Minister said that he knew that Austria-Hungary was eager for peace. The British and French governments were themselves conducting secret negotiations with the Hapsburg authorities at this time. But the British government and its allies preferred to have Austria-Hungary remain in the war, because she was a heavy liability on Germany as a belligerent, and they would neither receive a formal peace offer from Vienna at this time nor give any pledges against dismemberment. Then Lloyd George went on in an astounding personal message for President Wilson:

"We want him to come into the war not so much for help with the war as for help with peace. My reason is not mainly the military nor naval nor economic nor financial pressure that the American Government and people might exert in their own way against Germany; grateful as this would be [*sic*] I have a far loftier reason. American participation is necessary for the complete expression of the moral judgment of the world on the most important subject ever presented to the civilized nations. For America's sake, for our own sake, for the sake of free government, and for the sake of democracy, military despotism must now be ended forever. The President's presence at the peace conference is necessary for the proper organization of the world which must follow peace. I mean that he himself must be there in person. If he sits in the conference that makes peace he will exert the greatest influence that any man has ever exerted in expressing the moral value of free government. Most of the present belligerents will have suffered so heavily that their judgment also may have suffered and most of those that win will want some concrete gain, old wrongs righted, or boundaries changed. Even Great Britain, who wants nothing for herself, will be prevented from returning the German colonies. South Africa and Australia will not permit the giving back of lands that would make them neighbors to German subjects and give Germany secret submarine bases throughout the whole world. The United States wants nothing but justice and an ordered freedom and

[87] The Secretary of State to Ambassador Page, February 8, 1917, *ibid.*, pp. 40-41. For commentary on the alleged naiveté of this message, see Victor S. Mamatey, *The United States and East Central Europe, 1914-1918*, pp. 58-59.

guaranties of these for the future. Nobody therefore can have so commanding a voice as the President. Convey to him this deep conviction of mine. He must help make peace if the peace made at that conference is to be worth keeping. American participation in the war would enable him to be there and the mere moral effect of this participation would shorten the war, might even end it very quickly."[88]

It would be interesting to know whether Lloyd George really believed what he said! Perhaps he did, for he was capable of lofty sentiments, even though they were usually fleeting. In any event, he surely knew the force of such an appeal to Woodrow Wilson. Wilson unfortunately left no record of his reaction either to the Prime Minister's refusal to negotiate or his call for American belligerency. Perhaps the former offset any attraction that the latter might have had for the President. However that may have been, there was nothing that he could have done from Washington.

Another reason for Wilson's caution were certain recent indications that the German government was eager to come to some agreement for protection of American shipping in the war zones. Bernstorff telephoned Doctor Paul Ritter, Swiss Minister in Washington, on February 5[89] to say that George Kirchwey, former dean of the Columbia University Law School and president of the American Peace Society, would come to see him with a message to the *Kölnische Zeitung* from its Washington correspondent, Georg Barthelme. It was, also, a message from Bernstorff to the German Foreign Office. Bernstorff said that the communication had already been sent by wireless[90] and asked Ritter to transmit it to the Foreign Office in Berlin by way of the Swiss diplomatic cable. Ritter, who must have realized the true character of the message, agreed—reluctantly, he said later—to send Barthelme's dispatch to Berlin.[91] He added the suggestion, "in

[88] Ambassador Page to the Secretary of State, February 11, 1917, *Foreign Relations, 1917, Supplement 1*, pp. 41-44.

[89] Bernstorff and other members of the German Embassy staff did not leave Washington until February 14. They sailed to Rotterdam aboard the Danish liner *Friedrich VIII* on that same day.

[90] Kirchwey had taken the dispatch to Secretary Daniels to ask him to expedite its transmission, as the Navy Department operated the two German-owned transatlantic wireless stations in the United States. Daniels went through the message, deleting parts of it, and, after obtaining approval from the State Department, agreed to its transmission by the wireless at Sayville, Long Island. See the *New York Times*, February 14, 1917, and Kirchwey's statement in *ibid.*, February 15, 1917.

[91] R. Lansing, "Memorandum of Conversation with the Swiss Minister, February 21, 1917," Wilson Papers.

agreement with Count Bernstorff," that negotiations along the lines suggested by Barthelme might prove fruitful.[92]

Barthelme's dispatch follows:

From high sources whose identity cannot be disclosed I am urged, almost implored, to convey to German people and if possible to Government the idea that [President's] message [breaking diplomatic relations with Germany] should not be construed as indicating any desire on the part of the Government or the people for war with Germany.

Attention is called to following passage: "I refuse to believe is intention German authorities to do in fact what they warned us they will feel at liberty to do," and so forth; "only actual overt acts can make me believe it even now."

Further attention called following sentence: "If this inveterate confidence should unhappily prove unfounded, I shall take liberty coming again before Congress to ask authority to use any means necessary for protection our seamen and people."

These passages widely construed: First, an expression of confidence some way out might be found; second, not containing any threat of war. Widely shared opinion is President could do nothing else but sever relations to make good former note; now up to Germany to provide an opening. First thing necessary, avoid everything which makes maintenance friendly relations impossible.

Particularly refrain from destruction American ships not carrying contraband, thus inducing a delay of perhaps one month to make permissible limit of submarine activities object of negotiations; such delay offered as special token of ancient friendship two countries. Then consider possibilities provided in Hensley resolution for calling conference of powers. These possibilities closed by hasty action.

Some explanation about sailing of only four especially marked American ships would remove very bitter impression created by this wholly incomprehensible proviso, hurting the national pride as nothing else. My informants assure in most emphatic manner country is not for war, and will be for war only when forced into it. Only certain small circles clamoring for hostilities, but huge majority praying for peace with honor.

Feel it my solemn duty to inform you about these sentiments and opinions entertained by men of highest standing, noblest character, responsible position, and loftiest ideals and thoroughly good-will. Should you deem advisable to exert influence of our great paper, do so, to find way out of situation not yet unavoidably pregnant with gravest possibilities. I honestly believe country just anxiously waiting for one more good word.[93]

[92] Minister Romberg, from Berne, to the Foreign Office, quoted in Secretary Zimmermann to K. von Grünau, February 8, 1917, *Official German Documents*, II, 1326.

[93] As published in the *New York Times*, February 13, 1917.

Barthelme's message and Ritter's confirming telegram arrived in Berlin on February 8, at a time when Zimmermann was apparently in sole command at the Foreign Office. The Foreign Secretary had neither the ordinary good sense to see what opportunities beckoned, nor the desire to seek accord with the United States; nor did he have sufficient prestige to be willing to risk a battle with the navy for modification of the submarine campaign. Like the military and naval leaders, he simply did not care profoundly whether the United States entered the war, especially since it was now evident that the European maritime neutrals would not break relations with Germany on account of the submarine decree.

The telegrams from Washington arrived in Berlin, moreover, at a time when Zimmermann was upset about Czernin's recent overture to Wilson. Czernin had given a copy of his message to the American President to the German Ambassador in Vienna, Count Botho von Wedel, on the same day that he handed it to Ambassador Penfield.[94] The Austrian Foreign Minister had, in addition, suggested that it might be wise for Austria-Hungary to avoid a break with the United States so that she could be in position further to encourage Wilson's peace efforts.[95]

Zimmermann had replied somewhat brusquely to Vienna on February 6. Czernin's note to Wilson, he said, considerably misrepresented the German position. The German government had promised to abandon the submarine campaign only if Wilson's peace moves led to a peace acceptable to Germany, not if Wilson guaranteed a peace conference. Nor had the German government said that it would accept a peace without victory. On the contrary, the German government believed that it could obtain even its moderate demands only through decisive victory. It was perfectly obvious, Zimmermann went on, that the President was trying to drive a wedge between the two governments, and Czernin should be careful not to show too friendly an attitude. "Wilson's present attitude," Zimmermann concluded, ". . . shows him in his true light, that of an adherent of the Entente at all costs. His purpose to throw military obstacles in our way is apparent. As a mediator, he would exert all his influence against us."[96]

---

[94] Ambassador von Wedel to the Foreign Office, February 5, 1917, *Official German Documents*, II, 1322-1324.

[95] Ambassador von Wedel to the Foreign Office, February 6, 1917, *ibid.*, p. 1324.

[96] Secretary Zimmermann to Ambassador von Wedel, February 6, 1917, *ibid.*, pp. 1324-1325.

Thus Zimmermann knew that more than a possible understanding with the United States might hang upon his reply to Ritter. A too encouraging reply might also encourage Wilson to continue his peace efforts and tempt Czernin to follow Washington's lead in demanding serious peace talks.

The Foreign Secretary discussed the telegrams from Washington with Admiral von Holtzendorff on February 8 and sent a proposed reply with the Admiralty head's approval to Supreme Headquarters on the same day. "Germany, as before," it read, "ready for negotiations with America provided that the blockade against our enemies' commerce shall not be interrupted." Such an answer, Zimmermann explained, would not make any concessions on the unrestricted submarine campaign. But it was now obvious that the United States wanted to avoid war, and his reply might make negotiations possible and at least delay hostilities with America.[97]

It was perhaps well for Zimmermann that he did not counsel a positive overture, for the Emperor was in a black mood over Wilson's rupture of relations and particularly the President's appeal to other neutrals to follow America's example. He would approve Zimmermann's reply, he said, but only provided that Zimmermann laid down the condition that the United States had to resume diplomatic relations *before* negotiations could take place. As von Grünau reported on February 8:

"The Emperor argues as follows: Wilson's *démarche* has been carried out in order that England may be protected against the U-boat war and to force us to give in as the result of pressure exerted by him and the European neutrals—that he did not desire war or, if he did, only in case the remaining neutrals would join him and could be brought into line. After it has been seen that the neutrals will become reconciled to the U-boat war, and will not declare themselves on the side of England, then we will find the inclination to pull in the reins in order to avoid the danger in some other way. That we should make use of the disadvantageous position into which the United States has brought itself, by demanding satisfaction for the affront which it has offered us by relying on our alleged bad faith and therefore breaking off diplomatic relations prematurely. That, if the United States now wants to take up the question of negotiating once more, she will have to do so by immediately allowing the normal media of international intercourse to resume their functions.

[97] A. Zimmermann to K. von Grünau, February 8, 1917, *ibid.*, p. 1326.

"The Supreme High Command of the Army agrees to the instructions."[98]

Zimmermann now sent his original telegram to Berne for transmission to Washington, along with a new paragraph that read: "It is ... scarcely necessary to say that Germany could not enter into negotiations of this character before diplomatic relations had been reestablished between Germany and the United States. Moreover, the object of these *pourparlers* must be limited exclusively to certain concessions regarding the transportation of American passengers in order that the stoppage of importations from abroad, established against our enemies by means of unrestricted submarine warfare, be not weakened in any way whatsoever, even if diplomatic relations should be reestablished."[99] Two days later, on February 11, Zimmermann sent a telegram to Ambassador von Wedel instructing him to make it clear that, as far as Germany was concerned, Wilson's role as mediator was finished. "If the President," Zimmermann added, "were to come to us with renewed proposals of this nature, we would reject them unqualifiedly."[100]

This was the background of what seemed to be Ritter's important action on February 10. He called Counselor Polk at the State Department and read him only that part of Zimmermann's telegram saying that Germany was willing to negotiate on any point with the United States except the submarine blockade against England.[101] Polk at once informed Lansing, and the Secretary of State immediately discussed the matter over the telephone with the President. Lansing instructed Polk on the following day to ascertain whether Ritter was speaking officially for the German government. Polk went to Ritter's home at 12:45 p.m. (it was a Sunday), and Ritter said that he was now representing the German government. Polk said that the State Department would like to have Ritter's message in writing, and Ritter set it down in a memorandum for Polk that night.[102]

[98] K. von Grünau to the Foreign Office, February 8, 1917, *ibid.*, pp. 1327-1328.

[99] As paraphrased in Minister P. A. Stovall, Berne, to the Secretary of State, February 19, 1917, *Foreign Relations, 1917, Supplement 1*, p. 137.

[100] Secretary Zimmermann to Ambassador von Wedel, February 11, 1917, *Official German Documents*, II, 1328. "Regrettable as is a break with America," Zimmermann told the Budget Committee on February 21, 1917, "it is well that now, once and for all, we are free from Wilson as a peace mediator." H. P. Hanssen, *Diary of a Dying Empire*, p. 171.

[101] Polk Confidential Diary, February 10, 1917.

[102] *ibid.*, February 11, 1917; the Swiss Minister to the Secretary of State, February 11, 1917, *Foreign Relations, 1917, Supplement 1*, p. 126; *New York Times*, February 13, 1917.

Wilson and Lansing discussed what they thought was the *German* overture on Monday, February 12, and Lansing, at Wilson's direction, sent the following reply to Ritter:

"I am requested by the President to say to you, in acknowledging the memorandum which you were kind enough to send me on the 11th instant, that the Government of the United States would gladly discuss with the German Government any questions it might propose for discussion were it to withdraw its proclamation of the 31st of January, in which, suddenly and without previous intimation of any kind, it canceled the assurances which it had given this government on the 4th of May last, but that it does not feel that it can enter into any discussion with the German Government concerning the policy of submarine warfare against neutrals which it is now pursuing unless and until the German Government renews its assurances of the 4th of May and acts upon those assurances."[103]

This was, at least in its first sentences, a straightforward reply. Wilson seemed to be saying that the United States would not negotiate unless Germany withdrew its submarine decree and reaffirmed its pledge, made in the *Sussex* note, to follow the rules of cruiser warfare in attacking all merchantmen, belligerent and neutral. Then, however, followed the startling statement that the United States could not negotiate with Germany "concerning the policy of submarine warfare against neutrals which it is now pursuing unless and until. . . ." Had Wilson forgotten the precise terms of the *Sussex* pledge, and did he now think that its guarantees covered only *neutral* shipping? (The reader will remember that he had told Colonel House not long before that the *Sussex* pledge applied only to passenger ships![104]) And was the President saying in fact that the Washington government would not negotiate until Germany reaffirmed its pledges concerning neutral shipping?

An obviously inspired report in the *New York Times* on February 13 seemed to indicate positive answers to these questions. It said that Wilson had directed Lansing to notify the Swiss Minister that Germany's informal proposal could not be accepted "until the blockade order was withdrawn and the German Government renewed its broken pledges to sink no neutral merchant vessels without warning and without provision for the safety of passengers and crews." This report

---

[103] The Secretary of State to Minister Ritter, February 12, 1917, *Foreign Relations, 1917, Supplement 1*, p. 129.
[104] See above, p. 187.

also made it plain that the President would not compromise on this fundamental point.[105] As Wilson wrote to Colonel House on February 12: "Give yourself no uneasiness about the Swiss-German move; it will not work. They must renew and carry out the pledge of last April [*sic*] if they want to talk to us now,—or else propose peace on terms they know we can act upon."[106]

The German government had numerous other evidences at this time that Wilson was concerned, fundamentally, only about the safety of American shipping (and, presumably, American lives on passenger ships generally), that he might very well be willing to conduct negotiations if the Germans were prepared to give specific guarantees, and that such guarantees in turn might suffice to avert serious conflict with the United States. William Randolph Hearst, conducting his own private diplomacy, informed his correspondent in Berlin, William Bayard Hale, that "a big peace statement" from the Emperor or Bethmann Hollweg might "solve the whole situation," and that the country and President continued to hope for peace.[107] The German Minister in The Hague reported to Berlin on February 14 that he had been confidentially informed that President Wilson had sent various friends to certain neutral Ministers in Washington to ask if their governments could suggest some means of reaching agreement for mitigation of the submarine campaign. These same informants, this dispatch went on, made it plain that Wilson was "seeking for some escape from his position."[108] Finally, the Foreign Office, on February 15, received the following telegram from Bernstorff in Washington, sent, undoubtedly by the Swiss Minister, on February 10:

> In view of the fact that since the 1st of February no *contretemps* has arisen of which an American [ship?] has been the victim, the war feeling has greatly diminished; the country desires no war. In case an accident does occur, Wilson's plan will be primarily only to adopt steps which will protect American ships and to wait and see what we do; we should be able to postpone actual war for quite a while yet if we do not actually attack the United States of America ourselves. If necessary, negotiations can always be carried on by the Austrian Embassy or by the Swiss Minister; Wilson will in no event enter into an alliance with our enemies.[109]

[105] *New York Times*, February 13, 1917. This same issue published the text of Lansing's note to Ritter.
[106] W. W. to E. M. House, February 12, 1917, House Papers.
[107] New York *American* to W. B. Hale, February 8, 1917, received at the Foreign Office on February 13, 1917, *Official German Documents*, II, 1330.
[108] Minister Rosen to the Foreign Office, February 14, 1917, *ibid.*
[109] Ambassador von Bernstorff to the Foreign Office, February 10, 1917, *ibid.*, p. 1331.

Zimmermann's only action in response to the furor created by the publicity given to Lansing's note to Ritter was to tell reporters on February 13 that Germany had not made any overtures whatsoever to the United States,[110] and to add in an official notice on the following afternoon: "From abroad reports have latterly come, according to which it is believed that the sea barrier of submarines and mines against England had been weakened, or is to be relaxed, out of consideration for America or for other reasons. Regard for neutrals prompts the clearest declaration that unrestricted war against all sea traffic in the announced barred zones is now in full swing and will under no circumstances be restricted."[111] "So far as Mr. Lansing is concerned," the *Berliner Lokal-Anzeiger* added, "he has again gone to considerable expense for nothing. Germany has nothing to retract, and will take back nothing, and should new negotiations take place with America, America must first restore diplomatic relations with us. All honor to the Swiss Minister for his trouble, but from our present charted course no power on earth can turn us aside now."[112]

These were incredibly busy days for Wilson, not merely on account of the break with Germany and all the problems that it brought. Midwinter was the height of the social season in Washington, and the President and Mrs. Wilson could not escape the whirl. They were out frequently during January and February—to the Lansings' dinner on January 11, for example, the Attorney General's dinner on January 22, the Postmaster General's on January 29, the Secretary of the Navy's on February 5, the Gridiron Dinner on February 17, the Secretary of War's dinner on February 19, and so on. There were also grand and festive affairs at the White House—diplomatic dinners on January 9 and 16, a congressional reception on January 23, with 1,758 guests, a dinner for the Supreme Court on January 30, and a dinner for the Speaker of the House on February 13, with covers for sixty-six persons. The White House, moreover, was full of relatives and friends all through these weeks.

More seriously distracting was the unsatisfactory state of affairs in Congress. Wilson had gone to the Capitol on January 19, 22, 24, and 29 for long conferences with Democratic leaders in both houses to plead

---

[110] *New York Times*, February 14, 1917.

[111] New York *World*, February 15, 1917; *New York Times*, February 15, 1917. See also Zimmermann's remarks to the Budget Committee on February 21, 1917, quoted in H. P. Hanssen, *Diary of a Dying Empire*, pp. 171-172.

[112] *Berliner Lokal-Anzeiger*, evening edn., February 14, 1917.

for action on his legislative program—the essential appropriations bills, the river and harbor bill, conservation legislation, a new revenue bill, railroad labor legislation, a bill to permit American manufacturers to combine for export business, a federal corrupt practices bill, a measure to enlarge Puerto Rican self-government, provision for federal assistance to vocational education, and the measure being sponsored by Senator Overman of North Carolina to deal with espionage and sabotage.[118]

Congress had made virtually no progress on major legislation by the end of January. Bills to encourage wise exploitation of natural resources in the public domain and establish a system of licensing water power projects on navigable rivers or on streams in the public domain were once again being done to death in the crossfire between Westerners and conservationists, as they had been ever since 1913.[114] The indispensable appropriations bills would presumably pass at the last moment, as no one thought at this time that Congress would want the President to have to call a special session to adopt them. But the foreign trade and corrupt practices bills were dead, and so was the measure for which the President had worked hardest—a bill to prevent strikes and lockouts on railroads during federal investigation of labor disputes. It had drawn the bitter opposition of the brotherhoods and organized labor generally,[115] and the Senate interstate commerce committee killed it on January 24.[116] Wilson admitted defeat when Secretary William B. Wilson, in mid-February, submitted the draft of a new bill to create a commission on industrial arbitration. "I have been in constant touch with the committees of the House on this subject," the President wrote to his Secretary of Labor, "and feel that it would be fruitless to propose a new measure at this session. I fear that no action of any kind will be taken and that fear is associated with very great anxiety as to what may be the result."[117]

There was some evidence of improvement in February. Senator Hoke Smith finally pushed his vocational education bill through, and Wilson signed it on February 23. The Puerto Rican bill passed miracu-

---

[118] *New York Times*, January 20, 23, 25, and 30, 1917.

[114] See A. S. Link, *Wilson: The New Freedom*, pp. 128-135, for an account of this controversy.

[115] S. Gompers, statement in the *New York Times*, December 6, 1916; S. Gompers, "Freedom Must Not Be Surrendered," *American Federationist*, xxiv (January 1917), 45-46; W. S. Stone *et al.* (for the brotherhoods) to W. W., January 24, 1917, Wilson Papers.

[116] *New York Times*, January 25, 1917.

[117] W. W. to W. B. Wilson, February 20, 1917, Wilson Papers.

lously at the very end of the month and received the President's signature on March 2.[118] The Overman bill won the Senate's approval on February 20 after some forensic pyrotechnics, only to die in the House of Representatives. Most encouraging was the steady progress on an emergency revenue bill. Representative Kitchin rammed a measure, designed to raise an additional $200,000,000 annually by a 50 per cent increase in the estate tax and a new excess profits tax, through the Democratic caucus on January 26 and the House of Representatives on February 1. The Senate approved it without amendment on February 28.[119]

Congressional leaders worked hardest, ironically, on the one measure that Wilson was loath to see adopted. It was the immigration bill sponsored by Representative John L. Burnett of Alabama with the support of the American Federation of Labor and many social workers, barring adult immigrants who could not pass a simple literacy test. It was aimed quite frankly at the southern and eastern Europeans who had poured through the gates at Ellis Island since the late 1890's. Wilson, following the examples of Presidents Cleveland and Taft, had successfully vetoed the Burnett bill in 1915 in a ringing defense of unrestricted immigration.[120] But a bipartisan coalition was determined to close the doors as much as was politically possible against people whom they for various reasons thought to be undesirable. The House re-enacted the Burnett bill by the huge majority of 308 to eighty-seven on March 30, 1916, and Wilson was able to block approval by the Senate later in the summer only by using all his power as party leader.[121] The Senate adopted an amended Burnett bill on December 14, 1916, and the measure went to the President on January 16, 1917, after both houses had approved the conference committee's report.

Wilson still felt bound by pledges that he had given to certain representatives of foreign-born groups in 1912, although he had no profound convictions for or against moderate restriction. He returned the Burnett bill to the House of Representatives on January 29 with his veto, saying that he could not rid himself of the conviction that the literacy test was a radical change in national policy not justified in principle. "It is not a test of character, of quality, or of personal fitness,"

---

[118] For a brief history and analysis, see A. S. Link, *Wilson: Confusions and Crises*, p. 356.

[119] *New York Times*, January 27, February 2, and March 1, 1917; *Congressional Record*, 64th Cong., 2d sess., pp. 2441-2442, 4524.

[120] See A. S. Link, *Wilson: The New Freedom*, pp. 274-276, for an account of the struggle over the first Burnett bill and Wilson's veto.

[121] *New York Times*, March 31, August 1, 22, and 23, 1916.

he added, "but would operate in most cases merely as a penalty for lack of opportunity in the country from which the alien seeking admission came. . . . Tests of quality and of purpose cannot be objected to on principle, but tests of opportunity surely may be." He also disliked a clause permitting the Secretary of Labor to authorize entrance of illiterate immigrants who were victims of religious persecution, on the ground that such action might reflect on foreign governments and cause diplomatic embarrassments.[122] This provision had, ironically, been inserted to meet objections that Wilson had raised in his veto of the first Burnett bill.

Wilson's arguments were neither impressive nor convincing, and the House overrode the veto by a nonpartisan vote of 287 to 106 on February 1, the Senate, by a vote of sixty-two to nineteen four days later.[123] Thus the open door to America—long the gateway of opportunity for countless millions—was partially closed for the first time in general legislation.

Meanwhile, events had compelled Wilson to make certain decisions affecting the future of Mexican-American relations, and it is necessary to pick up the threads of this story where we left them in an earlier chapter. The reader will recall that the American members of the Mexican-American Joint High Commission, on September 22, 1916, asked their Mexican colleagues to join them in discussing protection of foreign life and property and religion and other matters; that the Mexicans replied that they could not participate in such discussions without specific instructions from the First Chief, Carranza; and that the Commission adjourned to meet later in Atlantic City once instructions had arrived.[124]

The Mexican commissioners finally received definite instructions,[125] and the Joint High Commission reconvened in the Hotel Traymore in Atlantic City on October 2. The *de facto* government, its commissioners said, insisted that the Commission discuss and prepare definite plans for withdrawal of the Punitive Expedition and a joint border patrol before any other subject was discussed. Moreover, they presented a plan for border patrol and close cooperation between Mexican and American military forces, along with an agreement giving the forces of either

[122] *The New Democracy*, II, 420-421.
[123] *New York Times*, February 2 and 6, 1917; *Congressional Record*, 64th Cong., 2d sess., pp. 2456-2457, 2629.
[124] See above, p. 123.
[125] V. Carranza to L. Cabrera, September 27, 1916, *Mexican White Paper*, p. 279.

country the right to cross the border on a hot trail within a specified zone one hundred miles wide.[126] They would be glad to discuss other questions of an *international* character, the Mexicans added, but only after agreement had been reached on the first two subjects.[127]

The Commission was at a dead end, Lane advised the President on October 6, and the American representatives needed to know how to proceed.[128] Lane apparently discussed the matter with Wilson at "Shadow Lawn" on about October 8. We have no record of their conversation, but it seems probable that the American commissioners followed lines laid down by the President in their subsequent negotiations. In brief, they temporarily waived discussion of Mexican internal problems and concentrated, as the Mexicans desired, on a protocol for withdrawal of the Punitive Expedition and defense of the border. They and the Mexican commissioners tentatively approved an agreement for withdrawal on November 14. It provided that the United States would begin evacuating its troops from Mexican soil within forty days after ratification of the agreement on condition that adequate Mexican forces occupied the evacuated territory and no *Villista* forces threatened the safety of the border. In the latter event, Pershing's retirement would "not be delayed beyond the period strictly necessary to overcome such activities."[129] The Joint High Commission then turned to a plan for border patrol. But such irreconcilable differences developed over details that the Americans withdrew their draft protocol for Pershing's evacuation.[130]

Wilson, Lane, Lansing, and Baker met at the White House from 8:15 p.m. to 11:30 p.m. on November 18 to discuss the dreadful mess both in Atlantic City and Mexico.[131] Villa, now stronger than at any time since the Columbus raid, had just captured Parral,[132] while large parts of the states of Chihuahua, Durango, and Torreón were being ravaged by bandits, disease, and starvation.[133] The British and French governments were both on the verge of a break in diplomatic relations

[126] New York *World*, October 3, 1916.
[127] L. Cabrera *et al.* to F. K. Lane *et al.*, October 6, 1916, quoted in F. K. Lane to W. W., October 6, 1916, Wilson Papers.
[128] F. K. Lane to W. W., October 6, 1916, *ibid*.
[129] F. K. Lane to the Secretary of State, November 14, 1916, enclosing a copy of the draft agreement, State Department Papers.
[130] F. K. Lane to the Secretary of State, November 15, 16, and 17, 1916, *ibid*.
[131] Lansing Desk Diary, November 18, 1916; *New York Times*, November 19, 1916.
[132] *ibid*., November 3, 1916; G. C. Carothers to the Secretary of State, November 3, 1916, State Department Papers.
[133] Consul H. C. Coen to the Secretary of State, November 17, 1916, *ibid*.

with the *de facto* regime on account of its recent punitive action against French- and British-owned banks in Mexico City, and the French Ambassador had gone personally to Wilson to warn that his government intended to use force to obtain redress once it was in position to do so. The American election was now over, and Wilson once again had a more or less free hand in Mexican policy. His patience was nearly at an end, and he sent Lane back to Atlantic City with comprehensive instructions and an ominous warning.

The Secretary of the Interior transmitted this message to the Mexican delegates at a meeting of the Joint High Commission on November 21. First, however, he presented what he said was the final American proposal. It was the earlier draft protocol for withdrawal, with the addition of a new provision stipulating simply that each government would guard its side of the boundary, along with what Lane said was an informal statement of the American government's position on pursuit of marauders, as follows: "It is essential, as a matter of governmental policy, that the United States reserve the right to deal with any serious hostile incursion from Mexico into American territory as may be deemed advisable at the time, including the right to pursue marauders into Mexican territory when such pursuit is necessary to our own protection. Duly mindful of the obligations imposed upon us by international law, such pursuit will not be intended, and should not be considered an act hostile to the Constitutionalist Government of Mexico."

The American government, Lane continued, also insisted that the Joint High Commission should proceed, after approving the protocol, to serious discussion of Mexico's internal troubles. Moreover, Lane went on, the President of the United States had instructed him to request assurance from Carranza that he would agree, once the protocol had been ratified, that his delegates should discuss "with the American Commissioners those questions deemed by the American Government of vital importance, such as protection of life and property of foreigners in Mexico, the establishment of an international claims commission, and such other questions as may be submitted by the American or Mexican Commissioners affecting the continuance and strengthening of the friendly relations between the two countries, *with a view to arriving at definite conclusions to be submitted to the two governments for their approval.*" (italics added)

Lane then conveyed Wilson's warning (which the President must have set down on paper), putting it in his own words, as follows:

"The desire of the President to see the *de facto* government strengthened and placed in a position to restore order in Mexico has in no way diminished. In this respect the views of the members of the American Commission are entirely in harmony with those of the President, and it was probably for this reason that they were selected to fulfill this mission. With the President, we are anxious to see a Mexico strong, independent, sovereign, and completely fulfilling her domestic as well as her international obligations. The President's purpose and our purpose in coming into this conference was to draft with you a constructive program which would strengthen the Carranza Government, and would assist in the restoration of order and prosperity in Mexico. This was our hope, and it is still our expectation.

"I must inform you, in all solemnity, that the President's patience is at an end, and that he regards present conditions in Mexico as intolerable.

"The plan of withdrawal of troops and border control which we are proposing to you this morning is but a step toward that larger constructive program which we confidently expect you to draw up with us in the same spirit of helpfulness and cooperation in which we approach these questions. Nothing short of this will satisfy either the Government or the people of the United States, and it is well for you to know this clearly and definitely at the present moment. We do not wish to do anything that will either hurt your pride or diminish your sovereignty. We have no designs on the integrity of your territory or your freedom of action in the determination of your national policy, but we are deeply and vitally interested in the fulfillment of your obligations to protect the lives and property of foreigners who have cast their lot with you, and in the satisfactory adjustment of every question which affects the cordial relations between the United States and your country. This can only be done through a policy characterized by frankness, cordiality, mutual trust and cooperation. If, however, you have reached the conclusion that you do not desire the cooperation of the United States, if you feel that you want to cut yourselves off completely, it is well for us to know this as soon as possible, as it will vitally affect our policy with reference to Mexico."

Cabrera observed that it was evident that Mexico had to follow the road indicated by the United States. Lane hastened to add: "There is no desire on the part of the United States to dictate to Mexico the policy that she should pursue. We have assured you time and again that we desire to respect your sovereignty and independence, but it is

evident that many of the problems confronting you cannot be satisfactorily solved unless you have the friendship and cooperation of the
United States. It is up to you three gentlemen to determine whether
Mexico is to have the benefit of such cooperation, or whether she desires
to pursue a policy of isolation. This latter policy can lead to but one
result, namely the downfall of the Carranza Government, with all the
consequences that this will involve."[134]

It was a virtual ultimatum, and the shocked Mexicans begged the
American commissioners to withdraw the demand for explicit assurance from Carranza that the Joint High Commission should discuss
internal Mexican problems. "It," they said, "would raise a doubt in
Carranza's mind as to whether the United States intended to withdraw
the troops unless satisfactory agreements were reached on the other
vital questions."[135] But the Americans would not relent, and the Mexican commissioners signed the protocol at 3:40 in the afternoon of
November 24. One of them, Alberto J. Pani, left on the following day
accompanied by the American correspondent, David Lawrence, to
take the protocol (along with copies of Lane's oral statement reserving
American right to pursue marauders into Mexican territory and Lane's
letter demanding Carranza's approval of a subsequent broad inquiry)
to the First Chief, who was then in Querétaro.

It seemed for a brief moment that Villa might succeed in forcing
Wilson to take violent action even before the First Chief had had
opportunity to reply. Pancho attacked Chihuahua City once again on
November 23, capturing it after several days of fierce fighting.[136] General Funston in San Antonio and General Bell in El Paso were
certain that Pancho would now race northward to attack Juárez, the
defenseless port city opposite El Paso.[137] They made hasty preparations
for Bell to move southward and Pershing to move northeastward from
Colonia Dublan to catch Villa in a gigantic trap and destroy him.[138]

[134] The above narrative of the session of November 21 is based upon F. K. Lane to
the Secretary of State, telegram, November 21, 1916, *ibid.*, and F. K. Lane to R.
Lansing, letter with enclosures, November 21, 1916, *ibid.* Lansing sent Lane's letter
to Wilson on November 23.

[135] F. K. Lane to the Secretary of State, November 22, 1916, *ibid.*

[136] Consul T. D. Edwards to the Secretary of State, November 24 and 25, December
1, 1916, *ibid.*; General Funston to the Adjutant General (sending reports from General
Bell), December 1 (two telegrams), 5, and 9, 1916, *ibid.; New York Times*, November 28, 1916.

[137] General Funston to the Adjutant General, transmitting a report from General
Bell, November 30, 1916, Wilson Papers.

[138] N. D. Baker to W. W., November 29, 1916, *ibid.*

It was a tantalizing opportunity, but Secretary Baker instructed Funston to take no action without explicit instructions from the War Department.[139] Then General Francisco Murguia, new *Carrancista* commander in the State of Chihuahua, struck Villa hard about thirty miles south of Chihuahua City on December 2, and the threat to Juárez, along with the opportunity to destroy Villa, passed.[140] Wilson had been briefly tempted, but news of Murguia's victory caused him to draw back. As he wrote to Secretary Baker on December 3:

"Would it not be safer to instruct Pershing, with an inevitable hint of what was in mind, not to disturb the movement of Villista forces northwards toward Juarez until it was pretty clear that all had got north of him that there was any immediate purpose of sending? He might by his own scouting and other movements frighten them back or arouse their suspicions.

"The news in this morning's papers makes it look as if our plan would not have to [be] acted upon in the near future at least, but perhaps it would be wise to let Pershing have as much of our mind as is safe at once."[141]

That suggestion, as it turned out, only encouraged Funston and Pershing to contemplate more ambitious plans. They came back on December 9, after Villa had fled southward, with a new proposal that Pershing be permitted to open a major offensive and advance as far south as the State of Durango in pursuit of the bandit chieftain.[142] Wilson ignored this advice, even though Villa captured Torreón on December 22 and 23 and was again threatening to move northward with a greatly augmented force of some 10,000 men.[143]

Villa's revival and Carranza's apparent inability to subdue him greatly compounded the difficulty of the decisions that events were forcing upon Wilson. The Mexican-American Joint High Commission reconvened at the Bellevue-Stratford Hotel in Philadelphia on December 18 to hear Carranza's comments on the protocol. The First Chief, Pani reported, was worried by the provision for withdrawal of the Punitive Expedition, because it stipulated no definite date for the

[139] N. D. Baker to F. Funston, November 28, 1916, quoted in *ibid.*

[140] *New York Times*, December 3, 1916.

[141] W. W. to N. D. Baker, December 3, 1916, N. D. Baker Papers.

[142] General Funston to the Adjutant General, December 9, 1916, Wilson Papers, and *Foreign Relations, 1916*, p. 623.

[143] G. C. Carothers to the Secretary of State, December 22 and 24, 1916, State Department Papers; Z. L. Cobb to the Secretary of State, December 23, 1916, *ibid.*; New York *World*, December 27, 1916.

evacuation, while Mexican approval of the agreement might be interpreted as sanctioning occupation of Mexican soil by American troops if anything occurred to delay Pershing's movement northward. Carranza, Pani went on, was also disturbed because the proposed protocol did not make adequate provision for Mexican-American cooperation in safeguarding the border. Pani then submitted a new protocol on behalf of the *de facto* government. It provided for Pershing's withdrawal immediately after ratification of the agreement and close military cooperation between Mexican and American forces along the border. What, Secretary Lane now asked, had the First Chief said about the letter from the American commissioners requesting his personal approval of discussion of certain internal Mexican problems? Pani replied that Carranza believed that it would be best to have Mexican soil entirely free of American troops before discussing any other questions. The two countries would then be dealing on a plane of equality and able to cope effectively with the other *international* matters in dispute.[144]

The American commissioners replied on the following day, December 19, that the new arrangements proposed by the *de facto* government were neither practical nor wise; they added that they reflected on the good faith of the United States and that Mexican rejection of the protocol would end "the function of this Commission."[145] Cabrera sent a long report of this discussion to Carranza on December 21, requesting instructions and adding that he and his fellow-commissioners believed that the American government really wanted to withdraw the Punitive Expedition and would do so as soon as the *de facto* government was able to send adequate forces into the evacuated area.[146]

Carranza did not reply until December 26,[147] and Cabrera conveyed his message to Lane in Washington on December 28. It said that the Mexican commissioners were still confident that agreement was possible but would leave the decision about the fate of the Joint High Commission to the Americans. The Mexican members, it went on,

[144] F. K. Lane to the Secretary of State, December 18, 1916, enclosing copies of the protocol signed on November 24, 1916, and the new protocol submitted by the Mexican government, along with L. Cabrera *et al.* to F. K. Lane *et al.*, December 18, 1916, State Department Papers.

[145] F. K. Lane *et al.* to L. Cabrera *et al.*, December 19, 1916, quoted in F. K. Lane to R. Lansing, December 19, 1916, *ibid.* Lansing sent this report to the President on December 20, 1916.

[146] L. Cabrera to V. Carranza, December 21, 1916, *Mexican White Paper*, pp. 322-324.

[147] V. Carranza to L. Cabrera, December 26, 1916, *ibid.*, p. 324.

had ironclad instructions to discuss no other questions until American troops had been withdrawn from Mexican soil. This did not imply lack of confidence in the good faith of the United States but was dictated by "a proper regard for the dignity of our country."[148]

Lane discussed this communication with the President at the White House during the evening of December 29.[149] The Secretary of the Interior returned with his fellow-commissioners to the White House on January 3, 1917, to submit a report reviewing the work of the Joint High Commission and urging the President both to begin withdrawal of the Punitive Expedition as soon as possible and undertake direct negotiations with the Mexican government. Such negotiations, the report concluded, were now all the more urgent because "the proceedings of the Constitutional Convention now in session at Queretaro indicate a fixed and settled purpose to place in the organic law of the republic provisions which tend to make the position of foreigners in Mexico intolerable, which open the door to confiscation of legally acquired property and which carry with them the germs of international friction."[150]

Washington correspondents indicated as early as January 2 that the President had also come to the same conclusions.[151] Perhaps he had said as much to Lane on December 29, and Lane and his colleagues simply repeated the President's own recommendations in their report of January 3. In any event, Wilson had apparently made a firm decision by January 12 to recall Pershing's command. It was greatly facilitated by news on January 6 that General Murguia had just inflicted a smashing defeat on Villa at Jiminez, north of Torreón.[152] Lansing later said that the controlling reason for the President's decision was his determination not to run any risks of military involvement so long as there was any serious possibility of war with Germany.[153] This may have been more or less true. But it also seems probable that Wilson would have made the same decision had German-American relations been altogether serene.

Events now raced toward conclusion of the unhappiest chapter in the history of Mexican-American relations since the war of 1846-1848.

---

[148] The Mexican Commissioners to the American Commissioners, December 27, 1916, Polk Papers; *New York Times*, December 29, 1916.

[149] *ibid.*, December 30, 1916.

[150] F. K. Lane *et al.* to W. W., January 3, 1917, Wilson Papers.

[151] *New York Times*, January 3, 1917.

[152] *ibid.*, January 6, 1917.

[153] R. Lansing to E. N. Smith, March 3, 1917, Lansing Papers, LC.

The Joint High Commission met once again at the Hotel Biltmore in New York City on January 15 and adjourned *sine die*.[154] Secretary Baker instructed General Funston three days later to inform Pershing that the government intended to withdraw his command from Mexico at an early date and he should begin to plan accordingly.[155] "General Pershing," Baker told reporters on January 28, "has been ordered to bring his troops out of Mexico. The movement is to be an immediate one, and is probably already under way."[156] It was completed when the last American troops in Mexico crossed the border at three p.m. on February 5.[157] Murguia had meanwhile been pressing his offensive so vigorously that American consular officials could now report that the *Villistas* had really been decimated and conditions in northern Mexico were returning to normal.[158]

Wilson's next decision—whether to enter into full diplomatic intercourse with the new constitutional Mexican government then in process of being formed—was as crucial and almost as perplexing as the decision to recall Pershing. A constitutional convention, elected on October 22, 1916, had met in Querétaro between November 21, 1916, and January 31, 1917, and adopted a new Constitution with bold provisions for social and economic reform. One of them, Article 27, vesting ownership of all subsoil minerals, oils, and gases in the Mexican nation, aroused the fears of Americans with large mining and oil interests as soon as it was introduced. They organized a committee for protection of American and other foreign interests in Mexico on November 15 and employed the well-connected Chandler P. Anderson to put appropriate pressure on the American members of the Joint High Commission and the State Department.[159]

One result was the dispatch of a telegram, prepared by Counselor Polk, to Querétaro on January 22, 1917, protesting strongly against

[154] *New York Times*, January 16, 1917; F. K. Lane to W. W., January 16, 1917, Polk Papers.

[155] The Adjutant General to General Funston, January 18, 1917, Wilson Papers.

[156] *New York Times*, January 29, 1917.

[157] General Funston to the Adjutant General, February 6, 1917, *Foreign Relations, 1917*, p. 908.

[158] Consul General P. C. Hanna to the Secretary of State, January 25, 1917, State Department Papers; Consul T. D. Edwards to the Secretary of State, January 25 and February 5, 1917, *ibid.*; Consul W. P. Blocker to the Secretary of State, February 8, 1917, *ibid.* For subsequent reports, all of which indicated steady progress toward complete pacification of northern Mexico, see Consul Edwards to the Secretary of State, February 25 and 28, March 4, 1917, *ibid.*, and Consul General Hanna to the Secretary of State, February 27 and March 2, 1917, *ibid.*

[159] Anderson Diary, November 15, 1916.

Article 27 and other provisions that threatened the rights of foreigners.[160] This, Anderson and his employers thought, was totally useless. The State Department, Anderson said, should make recognition dependent upon conclusion of a treaty protecting American rights and property against retroactive application of Article 27 and other discriminatory provisions of the new Mexican Constitution.[161] Anderson discussed his plan with Lansing and then with Polk on March 10. They both agreed that Anderson's suggestion was excellent. The trouble, they said in some despair, was that the President was determined to deal with Carranza more cordially in the future and to grant full recognition without asking any price. Polk said that Wilson believed that this was the only way to prevent the First Chief from surrendering to German influences.[162]

Lansing and Polk were surely right about Wilson's plans. He had no intention of imperiling Mexican-American relations merely in order to protect foreign property owners in Mexico. He refused to see Edward L. Doheny, who had large oil interests around Tampico, and Judge Delbert J. Haff, who represented certain large miners and smelterers, when they asked for an interview.[163] Lansing sent two letters from the French Ambassador relative to certain Mexican moves against foreign-owned banks in Mexico City to the White House on January 18.[164] Wilson replied in a letter written on his own typewriter, as follows:

"I have no doubt that there is here a real ground of grave complaint; and I think that it is probably our duty to make a very grave protest to the *de facto* government.

"May I make this suggestion? Our difficulties in getting the attention of the authorities in Mexico in matters of this kind has [*sic*] been due very often to their feeling that our protests were curt and peremptory. I think it will be entirely worth our while to study in dealing with them the fullest forms of courtesy. I believe it will have a real effect on the results. It is a mere matter of phrases, but it has proved of the essence."[165]

[160] The Secretary of State to C. B. Parker, January 22, 1917, *Foreign Relations, 1917*, pp. 947-949.

[161] Anderson Diary, March 8, 1917.   [162] *ibid.*, March 10, 1917.

[163] E. L. Doheny to F. K. Lane, January 5, 1917; F. K. Lane to E. L. Doheny, January 6, 1917, both in the State Department Papers.

[164] R. Lansing to W. W., January 18, 1917, enclosing copies of J. J. Jusserand to R. Lansing, December 9 and 28, 1916, and the Foreign Minister to the Mexican Minister in Paris, October 18, 1916, *ibid.*

[165] W. W. to R. Lansing, January 24, 1917, *ibid.*

There is also some reason to believe that Polk described Wilson's motives incompletely, if he did not misrepresent them altogether. He would not put a price tag on recognition and friendship, if we may believe what he told the reporter, George Creel, at this time, precisely because he still believed passionately that Mexicans had the right to settle internal problems in their own way. "No peace will be imposed upon Mexico," he said, "that will suppress permanently a people's struggle to freedom and self-government. No aid will be given to the restoration of a dictatorship. The safety of the border must be secured, and no activity will be spared to protect American lives and property, but this course is in no wise incompatible with the firm conviction that Mexico can never become a peaceful, law-abiding neighbor until she has been permitted to achieve a permanent and basic settlement of her troubles without outside interference. Lack of appreciation of the patience and forbearance of the United States may irritate and anger, but in no wise does it change the fundamental issues."[166]

There was not much point in pursuing further the project of a special treaty, and Anderson came up next with the suggestion that the American government make its recognition conditional upon the willingness of the Mexican authorities not to apply the retroactive provisions of the new Constitution. Lansing and Polk both concurred and asked Anderson to talk to Lane, presumably in the hope that he might be willing to pass the suggestion on to the President.[167] Lane opposed the whole scheme somewhat vehemently,[168] and Wilson apparently never heard of it.

Actually, it was too late to stop machinery of recognition now in motion. Henry P. Fletcher had already presented his credentials as Ambassador Extraordinary and Plenipotentiary to Carranza as head of the *de facto* government on March 3, 1917. Carranza was named President of Mexico in the first election under the new Constitution on March 11. President Wilson then received Ygnacio Bonillas as Ambassador of the *de facto* government of Mexico on April 21, after Carranza had formally announced his accession to the presidency.

Withdrawal of the Punitive Expedition and resumption of normal diplomatic relations between the two countries were the outward and visible signs of Carranza's victory, not only over the wild forces of

[166] G. Creel, "The Next Four Years, An Interview with the President," *Everybody's Magazine*, xxxvi (February 1917), 137-138.

[167] Anderson Diary, March 29, 1917.

[168] *ibid.*, March 30, 1917.

the Revolution at home, but also over a man in the White House with a well-known tendency to stubbornness. Carranza had never wavered since the first days of the Constitutionalist movement in his determination to preserve the independence and integrity of the Mexican Revolution. As a result, Mexico was now more or less free to undertake its great experiment and its long and difficult progress toward democratic institutions under constitutional forms.

Woodrow Wilson in considerable measure had made this opportunity possible. He believed in the Mexican Revolution, and believed in it all the more passionately the more he learned about its causes and objectives. Almost alone, he had stood off Europe during the days of the *Huertista* dictatorship, resisted powerful forces in his own country and administration that sought defeat of the Revolution, and refused to permit complications arising from the dispatch of the Punitive Expedition to lead to war. The tragedy was that in trying to help guide the Mexican people toward constitutional government he interfered so much that relations were embittered for many years to come. But no one ever does great things without making mistakes, and Wilson's mistakes were not to be compared to his accomplishments in Mexican policy.

CHAPTER VIII

The Decision for Armed Neutrality

WILSON discussed arming of merchantmen with the Cabinet on February 16, 1917, without, however, disclosing his intentions.[1] He had apparently decided to go to Congress as soon as circumstances permitted to request power to meet the German threat head on—not by war, but by armed neutrality. This, he probably concluded, especially after reading Professor Hayes's memorandum, might suffice. Indeed, it seemed to be the only alternative to full-fledged belligerency. The American people, he must have thought, would tolerate neither supine submission to the German so-called blockade nor indiscriminate destruction of helpless American ships. Perhaps they would accept armed neutrality as a middle course.

The single question was when to act. Wilson discussed congressional reactions with Burleson and Lansing, along with what the Secretary of State called a plan of intermediate presentation of the case to Congress before the overt act, immediately after the Cabinet meeting on February 16.[2] The President disclosed his intentions to a number of Democratic senators in conferences at the Capitol on the following day. He was, he said, eager to avoid an extra session, and he planned to ask Congress to empower him to arm merchant ships defensively and take such other steps as were necessary to protect American rights and lives. He would call an extra session only if unforeseen German action required a formal declaration of war.[3]

Wilson disclosed some of his thoughts on February 19 in a conversation with Henri Bergson, the French philosopher, who had come to sound out official American opinion for the French Foreign Ministry. Americans, Wilson said, were still badly divided, and many Westerners were for peace at any price. He had to move cautiously, even if armed neutrality led to actual fighting. England, Wilson went on, was fighting solely for commercial supremacy, and he had no desire to abet her

---

[1] *New York Times*, February 17, 1917; D. F. Houston, *Eight Years with Wilson's Cabinet*, I, 235.

[2] Lansing Desk Diary, February 16, 1917.

[3] *New York Times*, February 18, 1917.

struggle. The Germans were weary of Prussian militarism and perhaps even of the Imperial regime. Bergson reported that he did not succeed in changing Wilson's mind on the latter point.

The Cabinet met on February 20 for what seemed to be another useless discussion. "No light yet on what our policy will be as to Germany," Lane wrote immediately afterward. "We evidently are waiting for the 'overt act,' which I think Germany will not commit. We are all, with the exception of one or two pro-Germans, feeling humiliated by the situation, but nothing can be done."[4] Wilson, actually, was preparing to do a great deal more than he was willing to tell the Cabinet. He asked Lansing immediately after the discussion for a memorandum on defensive armament for merchant ships. The Secretary of State sent it to the White House on the following day. It was a calm exposition of the right of merchantmen to arm for defense and of a government to install and man defensive armament on merchant vessels, accompanied by clear warning that the United States would run very grave risks of war if it enforced a policy of armed neutrality in the somewhat peculiar circumstances created by the German submarine campaign.[5] Wilson then closeted himself in his study in the late afternoon and worked far into the night on a message to Congress. He summoned Lansing at 2:30 on the following afternoon, February 22, read the address to him, and said that he would deliver it on Monday, February 26.[6]

The Cabinet met in the afternoon of February 23 for what was, in light of the President's recent decision, a somewhat irrelevant discussion. Lane set it off by asking whether it was true that the wives of American consuls had been subjected to certain indignities on leaving Germany. Lansing replied that it was true. "This led," Lane wrote two days later, "to a discussion of the great problem which we all had been afraid to raise—why shouldn't we send our ships out with guns or convoys? Daniels said we must not convoy—that would be dangerous. (Think of a Secretary of the Navy talking of danger!) The President said that the country was not willing that we should take any risks of war. I said that I got no such sentiment out of the country, but if the country knew that our Consuls' wives had been treated so outrageously

[4] F. K. Lane to G. W. Lane, February 20, 1917, Lane and Wall, *Letters of Franklin K. Lane*, p. 238.

[5] R. Lansing to W. W., February 21, 1917, enclosing "Memorandum by the Secretary of State on the Arming of Merchant Vessels," dated February 20, 1917, *The Lansing Papers*, I, 609-612.

[6] Lansing Desk Diary, February 22, 1917.

that there would be no question as to the sentiment. This, the President took as a suggestion that we should work up a propaganda of hatred against Germany. Of course, I said I had no such idea, but that I felt that in a Democracy the people were entitled to know the facts. McAdoo, Houston, and Redfield joined me. The President turned on them bitterly, especially on McAdoo, and reproached all of us with appealing to the spirit of the *Code Duello*. We couldn't get the idea out of his head that we were bent on pushing the country into war. Houston talked of resigning after the meeting."[7]

Republican senators met in caucus on that same day and agreed unanimously to filibuster against the vital appropriations bills in order to force the President to call a special session of Congress soon after the expiration of the Sixty-fourth Congress on March 4. Interventionists like Lodge did not trust Wilson to act decisively enough; antiwar senators like La Follette were afraid that he would act provocatively. Both groups, and the majority of Republican moderates as well, thought that Congress should be in Washington during the critical days ahead. As Lodge put it, "I have also come to the conclusion that we must force an extra session. Although I have not much faith in Congress we should be safer with Congress here than we should be with Wilson alone for nine months."[8] Senator Lawrence Y. Sherman of Illinois began the filibuster that afternoon with a long speech on the revenue bill. Wilson on the same day called the Senate to meet in extraordinary session on March 5.[9] What he had in mind, although no one in Congress knew it, was to ask the Senate once again to give its consent to ratification of the Colombian treaty of 1914.[10]

An urgent secret message from Page in London, labeled "For the President and Secretary of State," began to come in over the wire in the State Department at 8:30 on Saturday evening, February 24. Balfour, Page wrote, had just handed him the text of a cipher telegram that Foreign Secretary Zimmermann had sent to the German Minister

[7] F. K. Lane to G. W. Lane, February 25, 1917, Lane and Wall, *Letters of Franklin K. Lane*, pp. 239-240.

[8] H. C. Lodge to T. Roosevelt, February 27, 1917, Roosevelt Papers.

[9] *New York Times*, February 24, 1917.

[10] This was the Treaty of Bogotá, signed on April 6, 1914, in which the United States made reparation for Theodore Roosevelt's alleged complicity in the Panamanian revolution of 1903. The foreign relations committee had reported the treaty with certain amendments early in 1916, but the Senate had refused to vote on it. See A. S. Link, *Wilson: The New Freedom*, pp. 320-323.

in Mexico, Heinrich von Eckhardt, by way of the German Embassy in Washington on January 19, 1917. Its text follows:

Telegram No. 1.
Absolutely confidential.
To be personally deciphered.

It is our purpose on the 1st of February to commence the unrestricted U-boat war. The attempt will be made to keep America neutral in spite of it all.

In case we should not be successful in this, we propose Mexico an alliance upon the following terms: Joint conduct of the war. Joint conclusion of peace. Ample financial support and an agreement on our part that Mexico shall gain back by conquest the territory lost by her at a prior period in Texas, New Mexico, and Arizona. Arrangement as to details is entrusted to your Excellency.

Your Excellency will make the above known to the President [Carranza] in strict confidence at the moment that war breaks out with the United States, and you will add the suggestion that Japan be requested to take part at once and that he simultaneously mediate between ourselves and Japan.

Please inform the President that the unrestricted use of our U-boats now offers the prospect of forcing England to sue for peace in the course of a few months.

Confirm receipt.

Zimmermann[11]

British officials, Page went on, had lost no time in communicating the message to him. The British government, he explained, had obtained a copy of the German diplomatic code early in the war; copies of Zimmermann's and other telegrams had not been obtained in Washington but had been bought in Mexico. "I have thanked Balfour for the service his Government has rendered us," Page concluded, "and suggest that a private official message of thanks from our Government to him would be beneficial."[12]

[11] As printed in *Official German Documents*, II, 1337. Zimmermann dispatched a second message to von Eckhardt on February 5, authorizing him to raise the question of an alliance with Carranza at once, provided that there was no risk of the secret being betrayed to the United States. The conclusion of the alliance, Zimmermann went on, would depend on the outbreak of war between Germany and the United States. "If the President [Carranza]," the Foreign Secretary concluded, "were to reject our proposal through fear of later American vengeance, you are empowered to offer a defensive alliance after peace is concluded, provided that Mexico succeeds in including Japan in the alliance." Foreign Secretary Zimmermann to Minister von Eckhardt, February 5, 1917, *ibid.*, p. 1338.

[12] Ambassador Page to the Secretary of State, February 24, 1917, *Foreign Relations, 1917, Supplement 1*, pp. 147-148.

We know virtually nothing about the origins of the Zimmermann telegram or the discussions, if any, which preceded its dispatch. Available German documents shed no light.* German leaders all seem to have joined a conspiracy of silence about the subject in their memoirs. Bethmann, for example, did not mention the telegram in his reflections on the World War, and we do not know what part he played, if any, in its dispatch. The Reichstag Commission of Inquiry of 1919 carefully avoided any questions about the telegram when Zimmermann was on the stand.

There was some discussion in the Reichstag Budget Committee on March 5, 1917, after the telegram had been published, when certain members criticized the Foreign Secretary for what they said was an unbelievable blunder that had made German diplomacy the laughing-stock of the world. Zimmermann admitted that he had not made the offer of alliance to Mexico in good faith. He certainly did not believe, he said, that Mexico could win American territory. "But," he went on, "I was looking towards a definite objective. *I would set new enemies on America's neck*—enemies which give them plenty to take care of over there. By holding up these American States as bait, I would urge Mexico to invade the United States as quickly as possible and so keep the American army busy.[13] Besides—I must emphasize the fact that all we have done is to make an offer which imposes no obligation on us. The offer was, however, essential in order to induce Mexico to take immediate steps."

Mexico and Japan, Zimmermann further explained, had cordial relations. The Japanese Ambassador in Stockholm had repeatedly told the German Ambassador that Germany and Japan should come to agreement. Zimmermann then read a message from Carranza dated November 3, 1916, saying that Mexico was strongly pro-German in sympathy and sought intimate relations with the Reich. Carranza, Zimmermann went on, had told Minister von Eckhardt that Mexico would provide permanent bases for German submarines. Hence his telegram and proposal of an alliance, Zimmermann concluded, even

[13] Zimmermann later informed an American correspondent that he told his colleagues in the government that Germany "should make Mexico . . . [its] friend and that would keep the American soldiers busy fighting Mexico so they could not come and fight us." He added, "I knew Mexico was not a strong military country, but I was sure it would take a very large army to conquer her. . . . Then I thought if Mexico was at war with the United States, maybe America would hesitate about going into the war in Europe." David W. Hazen, *Giants and Ghosts of Central Europe*, pp. 37-38.   * For new evidence, see Appendix, p. 433.

though he had no idea that Mexico could win a war against the United States.[14]

We know a great deal more about the Zimmermann telegram after it left its author's hands. The Foreign Office, as it often did in dispatching important messages to Bernstorff, sent the telegram both by wireless, hoping that it would slip past the American censor, and by the Berlin-Stockholm-Buenos Aires-Washington route. Then, to make absolutely certain that the telegram would get through, Zimmermann attached it to the end of Bethmann's Telegram No. 157 of January 16, 1917,[15] which was going to Bernstorff over the State Department's wire. Bernstorff transmitted Zimmermann's message to von Eckhardt in the German diplomatic code by Western Union.

The British intercepted all three messages. Their own radio receivers picked up the wireless dispatch. They obtained the two telegrams by taps on the Berlin-Stockholm wire in Copenhagen and the State Department wire in London. A British agent also obtained a copy in Mexico City. Balfour did not give the telegram to Page until the copy had come from Mexico, because British Intelligence wanted neither the American nor the German government to know that it was tapping their private wires. Balfour could honestly say that the British had obtained the copy in Mexico, and the Germans would think, if the telegram was published, that the American government had somehow intercepted the message between Washington and Mexico City.[16]

Lansing was at White Sulphur Springs for a brief vacation when Page's message arrived on Saturday night, and Polk, who was Acting Secretary of State, apparently did not decipher it until the following afternoon, February 25. He took it to the President at six o'clock that evening. Wilson was shocked and angry. It was almost incredible, he must have thought, that any government could be so evil and intriguing. It had been conniving to entice bankrupt and war-ravaged Mexico to attack the United States at the very time that he, Wilson, had been negotiating with German leaders for peace and reconstruction of the international community! And that lure of the southwestern states! It was ridiculous, Wilson knew, but it proved that the Germans would stop at nothing, not even respect for the territorial in-

[14] H. P. Hanssen, *Diary of a Dying Empire*, pp. 175-179.
[15] For which, see above, p. 260.
[16] The above account is based largely on B. J. Hendrick, *The Life and Letters of Walter H. Page*, III, 331-343, along with Samuel R. Spencer, Jr., *Decision for War, 1917*, pp. 55-69 and Barbara Tuchman, *The Zimmermann Telegram*, pp. 144-147.

tegrity of a friendly power, to advance their plans for world domination.

We have only two pieces of evidence of Wilson's immediate reaction, but they suffice. Polk, on telling Lansing about this conference, said that the President "had shown much indignation and was disposed to make the text public without delay." Polk advised him to await Lansing's return, and he agreed to do this.[17] Wilson received some of the leaders of the Emergency Peace Federation at the White House on February 28.[18] "As for our informal discussion with President Wilson after the formal presentation of our points of view," one of the visitors, William I. Hull, afterward remembered, "I recall that he enumerated with great emphasis our various grievances against the Hohenzollern government . . . and stressed repeatedly his conviction that it was impossible to deal further in peaceful method with that government. When I ventured to press upon him the possibility of making a successful appeal to the German people, over the heads of their government, he said that he considered that attempt impracticable. Finally, I recall with great vividness his tone and manner—a mixture of great indignation and determination—when he said: 'Dr. Hull, if you knew what I know at this present moment, . . . you would not ask me to attempt further peaceful dealings with the Germans.' "[19]

The Zimmermann telegram did not convert Wilson to war or even prompt him to decide to ask Congress for authority to arm American ships. He had already made that decision. It simply caused him to lose all faith in the German government. That was no unimportant change of mind for a man who believed, perhaps hopefully, that nations as much as individuals are subject to and should live by the moral law. Wilson's reaction to the Zimmermann telegram alone justifies the conclusion that it was one of the most maladroit as well as monstrous blunders in modern diplomatic history. As we will see, it had other consequences equally momentous.

Wilson went grimly forward with his plan to go to Congress on Monday, February 26, to ask for emergency powers. Senator Stone and Representative Flood came to the White House at Wilson's request at 9:30 and 10:00 respectively, that morning. The President must

[17] R. Lansing, *War Memoirs*, p. 227; Lansing Desk Diary, February 27, 1917.
[18] *New York Times*, March 1, 1917.
[19] W. I. Hull to R. S. Baker, October 10, 1928, Baker Collection.

have read his message to them,[20] but he did not tell them about the Zimmermann telegram. Someone from the White House—it was probably Tumulty—called the Capitol at ten o'clock to say that the President would like to address a joint session of Congress at one o'clock that afternoon. The news spread rapidly, and the Capitol was crowded with people when Wilson arrived. He waited in Speaker Clark's office until the committee came to escort him to the House chamber. He entered the chamber at 1:02 and began:

"I have again asked the privilege of addressing you because we are moving through critical times during which it seems to me to be my duty to keep in close touch with the Houses of Congress, so that neither counsel nor action shall run at cross purposes between us."

Someone came into the chamber at this point bringing news that a German submarine had sunk a Cunard liner, *Laconia*, with Americans aboard. Word was passed from mouth to mouth through the chamber.

The new German submarine policy, Wilson went on, had been in force now for nearly four weeks. *Neutral* commerce was suffering, but not much more severely than before February 1. American commerce was suffering "rather in apprehension than in fact, rather because so many of our ships are timidly keeping to their home ports than because American ships have been sunk." In fact, Wilson went on, only two American ships—*Housatonic* and *Lyman M. Law*[21]— had been destroyed in the war zones, both after warning. Thus, although American shipping had been largely paralyzed and the Germans were accomplishing one of the objectives of their new campaign, no overt act against American rights, happily, had occurred.[22] Even so, it would be foolish to deny that the situation was fraught with the gravest dangers and, moreover, most unprudent to be unprepared to defend elementary neutral rights. Since the present session of Congress was about to expire and the assembling and organization of the new Congress would require an unusual length of time, Wilson

[20] The White House Diary, MS. in the Wilson Papers, indicates that Stone and Flood came separately. There was apparently no significance in this fact.

[21] *Housatonic's* sinking has been noted above, pp. 309-310. *Lyman M. Law*, an American schooner, was sunk by a submarine, after warning and evacuation of crew, not far off the coast of Sardinia on February 12. The Consul General at Rome to the Secretary of State, February 13, 1917, *Foreign Relations, 1917, Supplement 1*, p. 131; Ambassador T. N. Page to the Secretary of State, February 20, 1917, *ibid.*, p. 139.

[22] This was true, it is perhaps important to add, only because the German Admiralty had instructed submarines to observe the rules of cruiser warfare in attacking neutral ships during a period of grace that extended from February 1 to February 28, 1917.

went on, he thought that he should ask for full and immediate assurance of authority for action that he might be compelled to take at any time. He had abundant constitutional authority to defend American rights, but, he continued, he wanted the authority and power of Congress behind him if he had to act.

"No one doubts," he said, "what it is our duty to do. We must defend our commerce and the lives of our people in the midst of the present trying circumstances, with discretion but with clear and steadfast purpose. Only the method and the extent remain to be chosen, upon the occasion, if occasion should indeed arise. Since it has unhappily proved impossible to safeguard our neutral rights by diplomatic means against the unwarranted infringements they are suffering at the hands of Germany, there may be no recourse but to *armed* neutrality, which we shall know how to maintain and for which there is abundant American precedent."

He devoutly hoped, Wilson added quickly, that force would not have to be used. The American people did not want conflict any more than he wanted it. "I am not now," he continued, "proposing or contemplating war or any steps that need lead to it. I merely request that you will accord me by your own vote and definite bestowal the means and the authority to safeguard in practice the right of a great people who are at peace and who are desirous of exercising none but the rights of peace to follow the pursuits of peace in quietness and good will—rights recognized time out of mind by all the civilized nations of the world. No course of my choosing or of theirs will lead to war. War can come only by the wilful acts and aggressions of others." He believed, he continued, that the people trusted him to act cautiously. In this belief he was requesting specific authority from Congress "to supply our merchant ships with defensive arms, should that become necessary, and with the means of using them, and to employ any other instrumentalities or methods that may be necessary and adequate to protect our ships and our people in their legitimate and peaceful pursuits on the seas. I request also that you will grant me at the same time, along with the powers I ask, a sufficient credit to enable me to provide adequate means of protection where they are lacking, including adequate insurance against the present war risks."

He was not thinking, Wilson concluded, merely of material interests. He was thinking about more fundamental things—the right to life, the rights of humanity, and the righteous passion for justice that was the foundation of all law and liberty and America's existence as a nation.

"I cannot imagine any man with American principles at his heart hesitating to defend these things."[23]

Congressmen and senators sat silently while Wilson spoke, straining to catch every word. La Follette threw up both hands in despair when the President asked for authority to arm ships; Lodge "unclasped his fingers and gently tapped the points of them together, not, apparently, in applause, but as one would say, a little cynically, 'Well, well!' "[24] Wilson completed his reading at 1:15. There were rebel yells and warm applause on the Democratic side, but most Republicans stood silently while the President departed.

Representative Flood and other Democratic leaders in the House straightway drafted an armed ship bill, using a memorandum that Wilson had prepared and McAdoo had brought to the Capitol, and Flood introduced it in the House of Representatives in the late afternoon. It authorized the President to arm merchant ships and "employ such other instrumentalities and methods as may in his judgment and discretion seem necessary and adequate to protect such ships and the citizens of the United States in their lawful pursuits on the high seas." It also empowered the President to spend up to $100,000,000 for these purposes, to be raised by a bond issue. Senator Stone presented a similar measure to the foreign relations committee at six o'clock. Both antiwar and nationalistic Republicans in the two houses had meanwhile made it plain that they believed that the President already had ample authority to arm merchantmen, and that they had no intention of granting him authority to employ "other instrumentalities and methods," that is, wage undeclared war, without the sanction of a formal declaration.[25]

There was no lack of furor following Wilson's address. Editors who now wanted war said that Wilson would not use emergency authority if he possessed it and that Congress should be in session to compel him to defend American rights.[26] The Hearst newspapers said that Congress should meet in special session on its own initiative in order to prevent the Chief Executive from dragging the country into war.[27] But the vast, overwhelming majority of big-city editors from

[23] *The New Democracy*, II, 428-432.

[24] From R. S. Baker's notes made at the time, R. S. Baker, *Woodrow Wilson*, VI, 476-477.

[25] *New York Times*, February 27, 1917.

[26] e. g., New York *Sun, New York Tribune, Boston Herald, Boston Advertiser*, and *Pittsburgh Gazette-Times*, all dated February 27, 1917.

[27] e. g., New York *American*, February 27, 1917.

coast to coast warmly approved the message and its request. "The President is right," the *New York Times* declared, for example. ". . . The Time and the occasion for action have come. We must defend our people and our seamen in the exercise of their rights or make a cowardly surrender to the power that has forbidden us to exercise them."[28]

The newspapers also reported on February 27 that the armed liner *Laconia*, carrying six Americans among her passengers and fourteen in her crew had been torpedoed twice without warning near the end of her voyage from New York and sunk off the Irish coast during the night of February 25. Two American passengers, Mrs. Elizabeth Hoy of Chicago and her daughter, Elizabeth, among others, died from exposure.[29] This news was blazoned on the front pages of newspapers alongside reports of the President's address to Congress.

Secretary Lansing returned to Washington that same morning, February 27, and went to the White House at 11:30. He and the President talked first about the Zimmermann telegram, and Wilson said that he had been wondering how the German Foreign Office got the message through to Bernstorff and whether the telegram could be authentic after all. Lansing then remembered that an exceptionally long dispatch of 1,000 groups had come from Berlin over the State Department's wire on January 17. This message had been delivered to Bernstorff on January 18, and the Ambassador had sent the telegram to Mexico City on the following day. "The President," Lansing recorded, "two or three times during the recital of the foregoing exclaimed 'Good Lord!' and when I had finished said he believed that the deduction as to how Bernstorff received his orders was correct. He showed much resentment at the German Government for having imposed upon our kindness in this way and for having made us the innocent agents to advance a conspiracy against this country." They agreed that it would not be wise to publish the Zimmermann telegram

[28] *New York Times*, February 27, 1917. See also, e. g., the New York *World*, *Washington Post*, *Providence Journal*, *Charlotte Daily Observer*, *Richmond Times-Dispatch*, *Nashville Tennesseean*, *Dallas Morning News*, *Kansas City Star*, *Chicago Herald*, *St. Paul Pioneer-Press*, Lincoln *Nebraska State Journal*, *Salt Lake* (City) *Tribune*, *Bismarck Tribune*, *Seattle Post-Intelligencer*, and *San Francisco Chronicle*, all dated February 27, 1917.

[29] *New York Times*, February 27, 1917; Consul Frost to the Secretary of State, February 26, 1917, *Foreign Relations, 1917, Supplement 1*, p. 149; Consul H. L. Washington to the Secretary of State, February 27, 1917, *ibid.*, p. 151.

immediately and to wait, in any event, until the State Department had completed its efforts to confirm its authenticity.[30]

Wilson and Lansing also discussed the *Laconia* incident and its implications, and they, or perhaps Wilson alone, decided to exploit it in the fight now just beginning in Congress for the armed ship bill. The French Ambassador reported to the Foreign Ministry in Paris that Wilson was keenly affected by the destruction of the ship, and that Mrs. Wilson, who had known Mrs. Hoy and her daughter, was even more upset. This was probably true. But Wilson's decision to capitalize on the incident was apparently part of his strategy for focusing public pressure on Congress. It was now abundantly plain that the armed ship bill was in grave danger. He was determined that it should pass. As he wrote on that same day, "I dare say, as I see things now, that it perhaps would have been well to go to Congress earlier, but you may be sure that I shall use every legitimate influence I can exercise to bring about a 'show down' now."[31] Hence either Wilson or Lansing told reporters following their conference that the President and Secretary of State both regarded the sinking of the *Laconia* as a clearcut act of war and the overt act which the President had indicated would compel a more vigorous policy toward Germany. The President, this report went on, would take no action until Congress had approved the armed ship bill. Action now depended on Congress. Its reactions would determine the measure of the administration's resentment against Germany's paralysis of American commerce and killing of American citizens.[32]

This report probably reached Capitol Hill by the grapevine in the early afternoon of February 27. In any event, we know that Burleson conveyed its gist to both the Senate foreign relations committee and the House foreign affairs committee. They met in the afternoon to consider armed ship bills while the Cabinet was in session, and Burleson acted as Wilson's spokesman in telephonic conversations with Stone and Flood. The foreign relations committee, under Lodge's spur, approved a bill giving the President actually more power than he had requested.[33] Only four members—Stone, James A. O'Gorman of New

[30] R. Lansing, *War Memoirs*, pp. 227-228.

[31] W. W. to J. Shouse, February 27, 1917, Wilson Papers.

[32] *New York Times*, February 28, 1917; New York *World*, February 28, 1917.

[33] Lodge disclosed his strategy in a letter to Theodore Roosevelt on February 27, 1917, Roosevelt Papers, as follows: "I am going to try to stiffen the language [of the bill] and give him [Wilson] the authority so that there will be no possibility of his evading responsibility on that point."

York, Hitchcock of Nebraska, and William Alden Smith of Michigan—voted against the amended bill.[34]

It was a different story in the foreign affairs committee. Flood called Burleson to say that various members were proposing amendments to forbid arming of merchantmen carrying munitions or any contraband and to omit the provision authorizing the President to use "other instrumentalities and methods." "I hope very much," Wilson wrote in a penciled note after Burleson had transmitted this report, "that none of these amendments will be adopted. The original language was most carefully studied."[35] It did no good, and the committee took no action.[36] Wilson or some White House spokesman called in reporters during the evening and told them that the President was ready to use to the utmost the authority he had requested to resist German attacks on *American* ships as soon as Congress acted.[37]

Much of the reaction to the startling news that the President considered the *Laconia* incident to be the overt act, which Wilson expected and obviously desired, did in fact occur. Newspapers heralded the announcement in large headlines on February 28, and editors said that destruction of the liner emphasized the necessity for adoption of the armed ship bill.[38] The *New York Times* correspondent in Washington noted the impact at once. Members of Congress, he reported on February 28, began that morning to receive telegrams from constituents demanding vigorous action.[39] There was, however, virtually no demand for war, aside from the few editors who had already come out for intervention.[40] It was difficult for the average observer to understand the administration's excitement over the *Laconia* in light of its failure to condemn the destruction of the *Californian* on February 7 with much heavier loss of life. As *The New Republic* correctly remarked, the sinking of the *Laconia* simply proved that the Germans meant to press their submarine campaign. "The Laconia sinking," this journal went on, "is not an act that will unite the country in support of a declaration of war. It does not loom sufficiently large among the atrocities of the

[34] *New York Times*, February 28, 1917.

[35] A. S. Burleson to W. W. [February 27, 1917], Burleson Papers; W. W. to A. S. Burleson [February 27, 1917], *ibid.*

[36] *New York Times*, February 28, 1917.

[37] *ibid.*

[38] e. g., New York *World*, February 28, 1917.

[39] *New York Times*, March 1, 1917.

[40] See the editorials from the *New York Tribune* and Louisville *Courier-Journal*, cited in "Imminence of War with Germany," *Literary Digest*, LIV (March 10, 1917), 605.

war. On every hand it will be urged that the fact that American lives were lost was more or less an accident. Accordingly we can only say that we are nearer than before to the irreconcilable conflict of national wills that presages war."[41]

The foreign affairs committee, reacting to the excitement on February 28, reported a compromise bill that authorized the President to arm merchant ships while omitting reference to "other instrumentalities and methods" and prohibiting the War Risk Insurance Bureau[42] from insuring ships carrying munitions. Democratic leaders in Congress, along with the President, were confident that the House would eventually approve the stronger Senate version.[43]

Wilson decided on this same day, February 28, to arrange for publication of the Zimmermann telegram. It was an important decision, and it is necessary to say something about his motives because they have often been misunderstood. He did not authorize publication of the telegram because he thought that the armed ship bill was in danger and wanted to stampede Congress. On the contrary, as we have just seen, the road now seemed clear for passage of some version of the bill. Nor did he fear a Senate filibuster against the measure. Republicans had begun a filibuster, to be sure, but only in order to assure a special session, not to prevent adoption of the armed ship bill. Wilson arranged for publication of the Zimmermann telegram (at least so this writer has concluded), in the first place, because he thought that the American people had a right to know the facts. He also *wanted* them to know the facts because he was sure that they, and Congress as well, would then support him in the risky course of armed neutrality once it was put into force.

Polk had meanwhile obtained a copy of the Zimmermann telegram in code from Western Union. Wilson called Lansing in the morning of February 28 to suggest that he and Lansing have a private conference with McAdoo and Burleson about the matter. Both men were at the Capitol, out of reach, and Wilson called Lansing again at four in the afternoon to say that he thought it would be wise to give the telegram to reporters at once. Wilson also suggested that the Secretary of State show the message to Senator Hitchcock, who had charge

[41] *New Republic*, x (March 3, 1917), 117.
[42] For a description of the work of this agency, established in 1914, see A. S. Link, *Wilson: The Struggle for Neutrality*, pp. 83-84.
[43] *New York Times*, March 1, 1917.

of the armed ship bill in the upper house. Lansing thought that it would be better to publish the telegram indirectly through the Associated Press. "Then," Lansing went on, "when we were asked about it we could say that we knew of it and knew that it was authentic." Wilson agreed, and Lansing read the telegram soon afterward to Hitchcock and asked him to tell Stone about the message. The Secretary then gave a copy to the Associated Press correspondent at six o'clock, with strict instructions that he should not disclose his source or put the story on the wires before ten o'clock.[44]

Newspapers published the Zimmermann telegram on the following morning, March 1, and it was as if a gigantic bolt had struck from the blue across the American continent. No other event of the war to this point, not even the German invasion of Belgium or the sinking of the *Lusitania*, so stunned the American people. They were speechless, a bit incredulous, and generally voiceless (insofar as printed expressions of opinion were concerned), for newspapers had received the Associated Press story too late for editorial comment.

Excitement approaching panic raged all day in Washington. The House of Representatives approved the amended armed ship bill by a vote of 403 to thirteen, after a long session in which members vied with one another in expressions of patriotism and denunciations of Germany. Even Representative Kitchin voted for the measure, saying that he did so only because he knew that the President sincerely wanted to avoid war.[45] Lodge, as soon as the Senate convened, introduced a resolution asking the President whether the telegram was genuine. "As soon as I saw it," he wrote to Roosevelt on the following day, "I felt sure it came from the Administration. I felt that it would arouse the country more than anything that has happened, and that it would widen the breach with Germany and drive us toward the Allies. The one thing lacking was a declaration from the President as to its authenticity, and with his endorsement on it I knew

[44] R. Lansing, *War Memoirs*, pp. 228-229; Lansing Desk Diary, February 28, 1917.

[45] *New York Times*, March 2, 1917. There was one clearcut division on the bill just before the House took its final vote. Representative Henry A. Cooper, Republican of Wisconsin, moved that the bill be recommitted to the foreign affairs committee with instructions that it add an amendment forbidding armed American ships from carrying munitions or belligerent nationals to a belligerent country. One hundred and twenty-five representatives, including 46.9 per cent of the members from the Middle West and 63.6 per cent of the members from the Far West, voted for the amendment. Two hundred and ninety-three members voted against it. *Congressional Record*, 64th Cong., 2d sess., p. 4691. For an excellent analysis, see "How Congress Divided," *New Republic*, x (March 24, 1917), 218-219.

Exploding in His Hand
Kirby in the New York *World*

the country would be bound to accept it and that he would be tied
up. It seemed to me of almost unlimited use in forcing the situation."[46]

Indeed, German-American spokesmen were already saying that the
telegram was a brazen forgery. It was, the *New Yorker Staats-Zeitung*
declared, simply another effort by pro-Allied propagandists to stir up
hatred of Germany.[47] "An unpardonable crime it would be if German
diplomacy really wove the plan which the Associated Press claims to
have discovered . . . ," a St. Louis editor added. "We have no hesitation in declaring the supposed note of Zimmermann a forgery. Even
the assertion of President Wilson that the note is authentic in its main

[46] H. C. Lodge to T. Roosevelt, March 2, 1917, Roosevelt Papers.
[47] *New Yorker Staats-Zeitung*, evening edn., March 1, 1917.

features will not cause us to change our belief."[48] Or, as George Sylvester Viereck put it in a telegram to the Postmaster General on March 1:

> The alleged letter of Alfred [*sic*] Zimmermann published today is obviously faked; it is impossible to believe that the German Foreign Secretary would place his name under such a preposterous document. The letter is unquestionably a brazen forgery planted by British agents to stampede us into an alliance and to justify violations of the Monroe Doctrine by Great Britain. This impudent hoax is made public simultaneously with frantic appeals of allied premiers enjoining the United States to enter the war. If Germany were plotting against us she would hardly adopt so clumsy a method. The real politiker of the Wilhelmstrasse would never offer an alliance based on such ludicrous positions as the conquest by Mexico of American territory. The creaking of the machinery of the British propaganda is clearly perceptible; the intention is of course to arouse the war spirit of the peace loving West and to overwhelm the pacifists in every part of the country. The entire story reads like a dime novel concocted by our guest Sir Gilbert Parker, Great Britain's chief propagandist, in [co]operation with E. Phillips Oppenheim. Despite the insidious work of various imaginary artists in the pay of Great Britain we have still retained our common sense. We can still differentiate between fiction and fact. The American people are willing to be thrilled but refuse to be humbugged.[49]

This "final" commentary was also published in the newspapers.[50]

Senator Claude A. Swanson of Virginia called the White House as soon as Lodge introduced his resolution. He came back to tell the Massachusetts Senator that the President had said that the telegram was authentic and he would be glad to answer an inquiry from the Senate. That body later adopted a substitute resolution offered by Hoke Smith simply asking the President to furnish information about the German plot. Lodge insisted throughout the debate that the Senate should accept the President's reply at face value without inquiring about his source. "It goes against my grain to be as civil to him as I am obliged to be," Lodge explained to Roosevelt, "but I know you will understand the necessity of it."[51] Wilson replied that same evening by sending a statement prepared by Lansing with his approval. It said that the government had evidence, obtained during the present

[48] St. Louis *Amerika*, March 2, 1917.
[49] G. S. Viereck to A. S. Burleson, March 1, 1917, Burleson Papers.
[50] e. g., *New York Times*, March 2, 1917.
[51] H. C. Lodge to T. Roosevelt, March 2, 1917, Roosevelt Papers.

week, establishing the authenticity of the telegram, and that it was incompatible with the public interest to say anything more.[52]

Editors, commenting for the first time in the afternoon newspapers on March 1 and morning newspapers on the following day, reflected the overwhelming national feeling of outrage and fury. That, surely, was not remarkable given the circumstances. What was momentously significant was the fact that a large number of editors in all sections said that the Zimmermann telegram proved that Germany was an implacable foe and called for war for the first time. One wonders whether Wilson had foreseen this result. As Frank Cobb, editor of the New York *World*, put it in a typical editorial:

"Germany has been making war upon the United States for more than two years. It has not been an open and honorable war but a sneaking and despicable war. . . . In all the history of nations there is no other record of such a lying friendship as that which Germany has professed for the United States or of such a lying peace as that which has been maintained during the last two years. . . .

"It is unthinkable that the American people should be so heedless of the future welfare and safety of their country as to hold longer to their attitude of non-resistance. Germany under a desperate and criminal autocracy has made itself the enemy of mankind, and in such circumstances there is only one course for a Nation to take which is strong enough to assert its own rights and which retains sufficient moral courage to appreciate its responsibility toward its own civilization."[53]

A dénouement that further embittered American sentiment soon followed. Zimmermann, in response to repeated inquiries from reporters, gave out a statement on March 3 blandly admitting that he had sent the telegram to von Eckhardt and claiming, correctly, that his proposal to Mexico had been conditioned on an American declara-

[52] W. W. to the Senate, March 1, 1917, enclosing R. Lansing to W. W., [March 1, 1917], *New York Times*, March 2, 1917.

[53] New York *World*, March 2, 1917. See also, more or less in the same vein, the New York *Sun*, *New York Herald*, *New York Times*, *New York Tribune*, New York *American*, *Springfield* (Mass.) *Republican*, *Boston Globe*, Little Rock *Arkansas Democrat*, *New Orleans Times-Picayune*, *Detroit Free Press*, *Cleveland Plain Dealer*, and *Chicago Herald*, all dated March 2, 1917; Louisville *Courier-Journal*, *Dallas Morning News*, *El Paso Times*, and *San Antonio Light*, all cited in "Imminence of War with Germany," *Literary Digest*, LIV (March 10, 1917), 605-607; New York *Nation*, CIV (March 8, 1917), 255, 258; *New Republic*, X (March 10, 1917), 151-153; *The Outlook*, CXV (March 7, 1917), 402-403.

tion of war against Germany. He very discreetly said nothing about the bait that he had used.[54]

It was too much for some German-American editors. The Zimmermann telegram, Bernhard Ridder wrote in the *New Yorker Staats-Zeitung*, was "a mistake so grave that it renders the situation almost hopeless." Even Viereck, the most virulent German apologist in the country, had to say that America and Germany had reached the parting of the ways if Germany really sought alliances with enemies of the United States.[55] Moderate German editors could only comment ruefully while excoriating the Foreign Secretary's folly. "The thought of bringing about the partition of America during the war, *Vorwärts* said, "and the thought of enticing Japan to the side of the Central Powers through Mexican mediation is dumbfounding."[56] "After we have puffed ourselves up with righteousness," Theodor Wolff added, "we can quietly say that no jewel of statesmanship was lost between Berlin and Mexico."[57] Count Ernst von Reventlow, ardent U-boat champion and nationalist, saw the significance of the episode as clearly as anyone on either side of the Atlantic. He wrote:

"As a result of the publication of the German offer to Mexico, and all that will be said in addition and lied about it, the previously divided public opinion in the United States has now stepped with near unanimity behind the President. We see in this fact and all its possible consequences nothing which could fill us with pessimism. But all those who placed great hope for the preservation of the peace on the divided opinion in the United States will not be able to do otherwise than to regret deeply, and to condemn as unwise, that at just this moment a policy should have been followed which can only be called a fuse on a powder keg.

"The offer of such an alliance would seem to stem largely from a lack of intimate knowledge of Mexican affairs and relations with America. Those desiring a policy permitting a return of the United

---

[54] *New York Times*, March 4, 1917. Zimmermann's statement of course ended the argument over the authenticity of his instructions to von Eckhardt. Lansing, however, had sent a copy of the telegram in code to Ambassador Page, and Edward Bell, a member of the American Embassy in London, had decoded the message, using the code in possession of British Naval Intelligence. See the Secretary of State to Ambassador Page, March 1, 1917, *Foreign Relations, 1917, Supplement 1*, p. 155, and Ambassador Page to the Secretary of State, March 1 and 2, 1917, B. J. Hendrick, *The Life and Letters of Walter H. Page*, III, 344-346.

[55] Both quoted in *New York Times*, March 4, 1917.

[56] Berlin *Vorwärts*, March 3, 1917.

[57] *Berliner Tageblatt*, morning edn., March 5, 1917.

States to normal relations after the war cannot help deploring the German alliance plan from this point of view alone. Mexico is a frontier neighbor of the United States, and the German offer will not be soon forgotten."[58]

Meanwhile, the Japanese Embassy in Washington had condemned the "monstrous" and "outrageous" German plot and reaffirmed Japan's loyalty to her allies and friendship for the United States.[59] "It is preposterous to imagine that Mexico could induce Japan to follow such a course," the Japanese Foreign Minister said a few days later.[60] Carranza, after the Mexican Foreign Office had indicated some interest in Zimmermann's proposal, later told Minister von Eckhardt that it had been stultified by premature publication.[61]

Publication of the Zimmermann telegram seemed momentarily to break the log jam in the Senate, as Wilson undoubtedly had hoped it would. Senators agreed on March 1 to ballot on the naval appropriations bill on the following day, and Democratic leaders were confident that they could obtain a vote on the armed ship bill immediately afterward.[62] Stone moved that the Senate consider the foreign relations committee's armed ship bill as soon as the naval appropriations bill was approved on March 2. Senators then discussed the legal aspects of armed neutrality for eight hours without any sign of a filibuster, until Senator Hitchcock asked unanimous consent to table the foreign relations committee's bill and take up the measure already adopted by the House of Representatives. Senator La Follette objected, and the Senate recessed at 12:45 in the morning of March 3.[63]

The situation clarified starkly when the Senate resumed debate later in the day on March 3 and senators all agreed that adoption of armed neutrality was bound in the circumstances to lead to hostilities on the seas and then to full-fledged belligerency. The vast majority of senators who spoke were willing to assume the risks, and Albert B. Fall of New Mexico and Frank Brandegee of Connecticut said that they

[58] Berlin *Deutsche Tageszeitung*, evening edn., March 3, 1917.

[59] *New York Times*, March 1, 1917.

[60] Ambassador G. W. Guthrie to the Secretary of State, March 3, 1917, *Foreign Relations, 1917, Supplement 1*, pp. 160-161.

[61] Minister von Eckhardt to A. Zimmermann, April 14, 1917, B. J. Hendrick, *The Life and Letters of Walter H. Page*, III, 354.

[62] *New York Times*, March 2, 1917. The naval appropriations bill went through on schedule, and the two houses approved a conference report during the evening of March 3.

[63] *ibid.*, March 3, 1917; *Congressional Record*, 64th Cong., 2d sess., pp. 4744-4781.

would welcome war with Germany at the earliest possible moment. Stone, in one of the greatest and most painful forensic efforts of his life, spoke for four hours against the foreign relations committee's bill. Saying that it delegated the decision for belligerency to the President, he offered an amendment to prohibit the arming or convoying of ships carrying munitions. But the Missourian did nothing more to block action. He had no hand whatsoever in further efforts to prevent a vote.[64]

Events in the late afternoon and evening, following Stone's speech, revealed that four Midwesterners—La Follette, George W. Norris of Nebraska, Albert B. Cummins of Iowa, and A. J. Gronna of North Dakota—had now resolved to prevent any action on any armed ship bill. They blocked every motion for unanimous consent to limit debate and vote, and speakers droned on through the night and into the morning of Sunday, March 4. Republican leaders, both progressive and conservative, now certain that the President would have to call a special session on account of the failure of most major appropriations bills to pass,[65] pleaded to no avail with the four rebels. Then Lodge, Borah, and Brandegee, eager to show the country that their party was not responsible for the fiasco, drafted a statement declaring that its signatories would have voted for the armed ship bill if they had had opportunity to do so. It was presented to the Senate in the morning of March 4 with seventy-five signatures. Ten other senators were either ill or out of town and had no chance to add their names. Eleven senators—La Follette, Norris, Gronna, Stone, O'Gorman, Moses E. Clapp of Minnesota, John D. Works of California, James K. Vardaman of Mississippi, William F. Kirby of Arkansas, and Harry Lane of Oregon—refused to sign.[66] Their refusal did not, of course, signify that they had participated in efforts to prevent a vote.

The scene in the Senate chamber during the final hours of the session was, reporters said, one of the most dramatic in the history of the Congress. Most senators had sat through the night and were dishevelled and unshaven. The floor was littered with paper, half chewed

---

[64] See his statement in the New York *World*, March 5, 1917.

[65] Among them were the army appropriations, sundry civil, general deficiency, and rivers and harbors bills, along with other major parts of the administration's program—a bill to enlarge the membership of the Interstate Commerce Commission, railroad labor legislation, the bill to permit combinations for foreign trade, conservation legislation, the Overman espionage bill, and an amendment to the Shipping Act of 1916 to permit the President to commandeer shipping in certain circumstances.

[66] *New York Times*, March 4 and 5, 1917.

cigar stumps, bits of sandwiches, and other debris. Senators were angry, petulant, and ill-mannered. La Follette entered the chamber at ten o'clock, refreshed after a nap and carefully groomed, to deliver a carefully prepared final speech on the armed ship bill before the packed galleries. Willard Saulsbury of Delaware was in the chair and refused by a prearranged plan to recognize La Follette. He appealed to the floor, but the Senate upheld the chair, much to the Wisconsin Senator's disgust.[67] Hitchcock was speaking when Vice President Marshall declared the Senate adjourned *sine die* at noon.[68]

Wilson had been watching and waiting with mounting frustration and irritation. Colonel and Mrs. House arrived at the White House on March 3, and Wilson and House sat up until midnight following reports from the Capitol. Wilson, accompanied by Mrs. Wilson, Tumulty, and other members of the White House staff, went to the President's Room at 10:45 on the following morning. He threw his overcoat on a chair and immediately began signing bills. The Chief Justice, some members of the Cabinet, and friends came in at a little before noon for private inaugural ceremonies. The formal ceremonies had been set for the following day because this March 4 fell on Sunday. The Chief Justice administered the oath at 12:04 p.m., and Wilson kissed the Bible at the passage of the forty-sixth Psalm that reads:

> God is our refuge and strength, a very present help in trouble.
> Therefore will not we fear, though the earth be removed, and though the mountains be carried into the midst of the sea;
> Though the waters thereof roar and be troubled, though the mountains shake with the swelling thereof.

Chief Justice White shook Wilson's hand fervently, saying, "Mr. President, I am very, very happy." Wilson sat down quickly at his desk and completed his work; then he and his party returned to the White House.[69]

Wilson, House wrote in his diary about events of the afternoon, "showed much excitement and was bitter in his denunciation of the small band of Senators who undertook to use the arbitrary rules of the Senate to defeat the wishes of the majority regarding the arming

[67] He published his speech as "The Armed Ship Bill Meant War," *La Follette's Magazine*, IX (March 1917), 1-4.

[68] New York *World*, March 5, 1917; *New York Times*, March 5, 1917; *Congressional Record*, 64th Cong., 2d sess., pp. 4859-4919, 4977-5020.

[69] *New York Times*, March 5, 1917.

of merchantmen."[70] I suggested that he say to the public what he was saying to me, and to say it immediately. His answer was that he could not put it in his Inaugural Address, because it would spoil the texture of it, but he would put it out in a few days. I urged him to do it now, giving it to the newspapers [for] to-morrow morning, in order to strike while the iron was hot. He wondered whether he could do it so quickly, but said he would try."[71]

Wilson worked alone in his study most of the afternoon. He had completed his statement by dinner, and he called in McAdoo, Burleson, Tumulty, House, and Vance McCormick, who was also visiting at the White House, after dinner and read the statement to them. They all thought that he should give it to reporters at once, and this was done as soon as mimeographed copies could be run off.

"The termination of the last session of the Sixty-fourth Congress by constitutional limitation," it began, "disclosed a situation unparalleled in the history of the country, perhaps unparalleled in the history of any modern Government." Congress, in the midst of the gravest international crisis in the nation's history, had been unable to act either to safeguard the country or to vindicate the elementary rights of its citizens. A little group of eleven senators had determined that it should not act. They had prevented adoption, not merely of the armed ship bill, but also of other measures vital to the country's welfare.

It would not cure the difficulty, the statement went on, to call the Sixty-fifth Congress in extraordinary session. The paralysis of the Senate would remain, even though Congress was more united in purpose and spirit than it had been within the memory of living man. But the Senate could not act unless its leaders could obtain unanimous consent. Its majority was powerless, helpless. "In the midst of a crisis of extraordinary peril, when only definite and decided action can make the nation safe or shield it from war itself by the aggression of others, action is impossible." And the worst of it was that governments abroad would conclude that they could act as they pleased because the American government could do nothing. "A little group of willful men, representing no opinion but their own, have rendered the great Government of the United States helpless and contemptible." There was,

[70] He told Tumulty, for example, that he was "through with Stone" and would never shake hands with him again. Actually, he *did* shake hands with the Missourian later. The Diary of Thomas W. Brahany, March 4, 1917; copy in the Papers of Woodrow Wilson, Princeton University, hereinafter cited as the Brahany Diary.

[71] House Diary, March 4, 1917.

the statement concluded, only one remedy—change in the rules so that the Senate could act. "The country can be relied upon to draw the moral. I believe that the Senate can be relied on to supply the means of action and save the country from disaster."[72]

Later that same night Wilson issued what he called a "Supplementary Statement from the White House." It read as follows:

> At the same time the President authorized the further statement that what rendered the situation even more grave than it had been supposed that it was, was the discovery that, while the President under his general constitutional powers could do much of what he had asked the Congress to empower him to do, it had been found that there were certain old statutes as yet unrepealed which may raise insuperable practical obstacles and may nullify his power.[73]

These were, assuredly, two of the three most unfortunate public statements that Woodrow Wilson made during his entire political career, the other being his call for a Democratic Congress in October 1918. The main statement was conceived in frustration and written in anger, hastily, and without much regard either for facts or consequences. It ignored the fact that Wilson's own delay in asking Congress for special authority had been partially responsible for the débâcle. This had been a mistake sheerly in timing, to be sure—there is no good evidence that Wilson waited until the last days of the session in order to coerce Congress into granting the power that he requested—but it was fatal none the less. Leaders in the Senate might well have put the armed ship bill through if they had had an additional week in which to wear out the three or four men bent on preventing a vote. The statement was, moreover, inaccurate in saying that the armed ship filibusterers had been responsible for failure of other legislation. Republican leaders would have maintained the filibuster that they had already begun, in order to force Wilson to call a special session, if La Follette and his friends had not done their work for them.

Wilson's main statement also cruelly impugned the patriotism of all opponents of the armed ship bill. Senators had all agreed that armed neutrality would lead to war. This was not necessarily true, but it was the thoughtful opinion of both advocates and opponents of the measure. Senators who opposed the bill thought that they were being true to their country's traditions in refusing to permit the President

---

[72] *The New Democracy*, ii, 433-435.
[73] *New York Times*, March 5, 1917.

to wage undeclared war without the express knowledge and consent of Congress; they were, moreover, sincere in saying that a vote for the armed ship bill was a vote for war, and that they could not in conscience vote for war. Worse still, the statement inaccurately and unfairly indicted most of the eleven senators who had refused to sign the manifesto saying they would have voted for the armed ship bill. Only four of them, insofar as we know, had actually blocked a vote; the other seven opposed the bill but did not try to prevent action.[74] Yet Wilson's blow fell as heavily on them as on the four obstructionists. Stone, who had been the President's most loyal lieutenant in the Senate, particularly did not deserve such rough treatment.

Wilson's statement was inaccurate in other respects because he cited failure of the armed ship bill as justification for refusing to call a special session. The truth was that Wilson did not want Congress in Washington during the coming months. He wanted a free hand to try armed neutrality, and he thought that he had a better chance of avoiding belligerency if Congress was not in session. But he said that there was no point in calling a special session to consider the armed ship bill because any senator could prevent its approval by refusing to give unanimous consent. This was not accurate. Unanimous consent was necessary only for suspension of the rules and special rules such as a rule to limit debate or to vote on a bill ahead of its place on the calendar. It was not necessary for a vote in ordinary course. To be sure, senators enjoyed the right of unlimited debate, but four obstructionists could not have sustained a filibuster very long. The Senate could have stayed in continuous session and worn them out with reasonable dispatch.

Finally, the supplementary statement was not much less unfortunate than the main one. Wilson was referring to a statute of 1819 which permitted arming of merchantmen against pirates but stipulated that the armament should not be used against a public armed vessel of a nation with which the United States was "in amity." The foreign relations committee had discovered the statute, and Senator Lodge had informed the Senate on March 2 that the President did not in fact have power

[74] Stone's role is explained above. Vardaman, O'Gorman, Cummins, and Lane all later declared that they would have voted for the bill with the Stone amendment to prohibit armed ships from carrying munitions. Vardaman said that he had spoken against the armed ship bill for sixteen minutes and never objected to a vote; O'Gorman, that he had spoken against the bill for no more than five minutes and never objected to a vote; Lane, that he had not spoken or objected at all. *New York Times*, March 7, 1917.

to arm merchantmen in the present circumstances. Neither Wilson, the Secretary of State, nor the Attorney General had studied the statute closely; as we will see, they later concluded that it did not stand in the way. It would obviously have been more prudent for Wilson to have been certain of the facts before saying publicly that he probably did not have power to arm merchantmen.

Wilson's excoriation of the "willful men" spurred editors across the country to compose even more savage condemnations. "As for those wretches in the Senate," Frank Cobb exploded, "envious, pusillanimous or abandoned, who with doubts and quibbles have denied their country's conscience and courage in order to make a Prussian holiday, they may well be left to the judgment that good men and true never fail to pass upon delinquents and dastards."[75] A Memphis editor exclaimed: "The American Republic was betrayed in the Senate of the United States yesterday. . . . The liberty of the American Republic was jeopardized by a small group of men. . . . Our kaiserbund is already formed. The charter members have seats in the Senate of the United States."[76] Epithets like "poltroons," "traitors," "pro-German contingent," and "weaklings" crowded editorial pages.[77] It did the eleven senators no good when the *Frankfurter Zeitung* referred to them as "fine Americans who remained uncontaminated by Wilson's blind devotion to England,"[78] and this remark was reprinted in American newspapers.[79]

The legislatures of Ohio, Washington, and Arkansas and the Assembly of Idaho adopted resolutions on March 5 strongly denouncing the alleged filibusterers and pledging their support to the President. The Kentucky Senate on March 6 adopted a resolution the preamble of which said that "certain un-American, disloyal, unpatriotic, traitorous, and cowardly Senators" had refused to permit the armed ship bill to pass, "knowing full well that upon the passage of said measure depended the lives of hundreds of brave American seamen." The Oklahoma legislature and the Tennessee House, ratifying a resolution already approved by the state Senate, condemned the "willful" sena-

[75] New York *World*, March 5, 1917.
[76] *Memphis Commercial Appeal*, March 5, 1917.
[77] See, e. g., *Richmond Times-Dispatch*, *Providence Journal*, *New York Herald*, *Philadelphia Record*, Baltimore *Sun*, *Raleigh News and Observer*, *Montgomery Advertiser*, *Houston Post*, *Des Moines Register*, and *Seattle Post-Intelligencer*, all dated March 5, 1917.
[78] *Frankfurter Zeitung*, evening edn., March 6, 1917.
[79] e. g., *New York Times*, March 7, 1917.

The Only Adequate Reward

Kirby in the New York *World*

tors on the same day.[80] Students at the University of Illinois hanged
La Follette in effigy on March 5, while the trustees of Columbia University announced that they had appointed a committee to ascertain
whether any of the university's faculty were teaching subversive or
unpatriotic doctrines.[81] Wilson did not help to stem the hysteria when

[80] *ibid.*, March 6 and 7, 1917. The Wisconsin Senate, Nebraska Senate, Colorado
Senate, and Iowa House of Representatives on March 7 all defeated resolutions censur-
ing the "willful" senators, the latter going so far as to expunge the resolution from its
record. *ibid.*, March 8, 1917.

[81] *ibid.*, March 6, 1917.

he told members of the Democratic National Committee on March 6 that he was still thoroughly "mad" over defeat of the armed ship bill.[82]

Washington was wet and cold on Monday, March 5. The driving rain that had drenched the city on Saturday and Sunday had ended, but the sky was overcast, and a raw wind blew from the Northwest. The President and Mrs. Wilson, accompanied by the Vice President and a committee from the two houses of Congress, rode in an open carriage drawn by four horses from the White House to the Capitol for the inaugural ceremonies. A hollow square of Secret Service men surrounded the carriage, while troopers of the Second Calvary rode in front and behind, and Pennsylvania Avenue was lined with soldiers from the 69th and 12th Regiments of the New York National Guard.

The ceremonies began in the Senate chamber at 11:45, when Senator Saulsbury, President Pro Tempore, administered the oath to Thomas R. Marshall, first Vice President to succeed himself since John C. Calhoun. New senators were sworn in following Marshall's inaugural address, and then the assemblage marched out through the Rotunda to a platform on the east front of the Capitol. Chief Justice White administered the oath, and Wilson turned to the throng of some 40,000 persons in front of the stands.

He began by briefly reviewing the domestic accomplishments of the past four years and remarking that developments abroad had drawn Americans more and more irresistibly into their own current and influence. It had been, he went on, impossible to avoid the impact of a war that had affected the life of the whole world, "and yet all the while we have been conscious that we were not part of it." Americans had grown more and more certain that their great objective was peace. "We have," Wilson continued, "been obliged to arm ourselves to make good our claim to a certain minimum of right and of freedom of action. We stand firm in armed neutrality since it seems that in no other way can we demonstrate what it is we insist upon and cannot forego.[83] We may even be drawn on, by circumstances, not by our own purpose or desire, to a more active assertion of our rights as we see them and a more immediate association with the great struggle itself. But nothing will alter our thought or our purpose. They are too clear to be obscured. They are too deeply rooted in the principles of our national life to be altered."

---

[82] *ibid.*, March 7, 1917.

[83] It is interesting that Wilson, after completing his address on about March 1, did not change these sentences to avoid this inaccuracy.

Americans, Wilson went on, were no longer provincials. The tragic events of the past thirty months had made them citizens of the world. Americans would remain true to themselves if they but remained true to the principles of a liberated mankind on which they had been bred. "These, therefore," he went on, "are the things we shall stand for, whether in war or in peace:

"That all nations are equally interested in the peace of the world and in the political stability of free peoples, and equally responsible for their maintenance;

"That the essential principle of peace is the actual equality of nations in all matters of right or privilege;

"That peace cannot securely or justly rest upon an armed balance of power;

"That governments derive all their just powers from the consent of the governed and that no other powers should be supported by the common thought, purpose, or power of the family of nations.

"That the seas should be equally free and safe for the use of all peoples, under rules set up by common agreement and consent, and that, so far as practicable, they should be accessible to all upon equal terms;

"That national armaments should be limited to the necessities of national order and domestic safety;

"That the community of interest and of power upon which peace must henceforth depend imposes upon each nation the duty of seeing to it that all influences proceeding from its own citizens meant to encourage or assist revolution in other states should be sternly and effectually suppressed and prevented."

Americans, Wilson concluded, could and would stand together upon such a platform. He was the servant of the American people united in purpose and in vision of duty, opportunity, and service. "For myself I beg your tolerance, your countenance, and your united aid. The shadows that now lie dark upon our path will soon be dispelled and we shall walk with the light all about us if we be but true to ourselves,—to ourselves as we have wished to be known in the counsels of the world and in the thought of all those who love liberty and justice and the right exalted."[84]

The wind was so strong that only Mrs. Wilson and the Chief Justice, who stood by the President's side, could hear him clearly. There was

[84] R. S. Baker and W. E. Dodd (eds.), *The Public Papers of Woodrow Wilson, War and Peace* (2 vols.), I, 1-5; hereinafter cited as *War and Peace*.

virtually no applause at the end.[85] It was not one of Wilson's great public papers. It lacked the beauty of style, emotional warmth, and tone of his first inaugural address. Its enunciation of the right principles of international life was decidedly inferior to the statement in his "Peace without Victory" speech. Only its affirmation of determination to stand firm in armed neutrality, while accepting the risks of war that accompanied such policy, was unequivocal. But that, actually, was somewhat premature, since armed neutrality was not yet a fact.

The ceremony was over at 1:03, and the President and Mrs. Wilson rode up Pennsylvania Avenue to the White House, arriving at the mansion at 1:45. They had lunch alone in the small dining room—the state dining room was full of relatives and friends—and went at 2:10 p.m. to a stand outside the White House to review the inaugural parade. It was over at 5:20, and they returned to their private apartments until dinner. "We had a quiet dinner," Colonel House recorded, "and went upstairs to the oval sitting room to witness the fireworks. The family generally were at the main windows. The President and Mrs. Wilson sat by a side window, curtained off, and asked me to join them. The President was holding Mrs. Wilson's hand and leaning with his face against her's. We talked quietly of the happenings of the day and I spoke of my joy that we three, rather than the Hughes family, were looking at the fireworks from the White House windows.

"Shortly after nine, the President suggested that we drive through the streets to see the illuminations. This turned out to be rather a risky adventure. There was no secret service man on the box, although a car with them followed. We had gone no distance before we were in a jam and the people, thronging the sidewalks and streets, recognized the President and sent up cheer after cheer. It was a dangerous moment, far more than anything we had gone through during the day. I sat with my automatic in my hand ready to act if the occasion arose."[86]

They returned to the White House at 9:55. Wilson went to his study, and Mrs. Wilson and Colonel House talked until eleven o'clock. She suggested that House accept the post as Ambassador to Great Britain. Wilson had said on January 3, and again on January 12, that he intended to accept Page's resignation as soon as he could find a suitable replacement, and Mrs. Wilson had shown some eagerness to arrange

[85] *New York Times*, March 6, 1917.
[86] House Diary, March 5, 1917.

House's departure. House declined the honor quickly, as he had done earlier.[87]

The most immediate result of the President's denunciation of the "willful men" was the Senate's adoption, by a vote of seventy-six to three, sixteen not voting, of a cloture rule on March 8. It provided that the Senate, two days after notice in writing from sixteen members, should vote without debate on the question of ending discussion of the bill named in the petition. If two thirds of the senators voted affirmatively, then members would be limited to one hour of debate on the measure before the house. The rule also provided that no amendment could be offered without unanimous consent once cloture was in effect.[88]

The road was rougher for Wilson in achieving the objective for which he had called the Senate into special session—approval of the Treaty of Bogotá. The Colombian Minister in Washington had appealed to Wilson on January 24 to expedite action by the upper house.[89] "Your feeling," the President replied, "that one of the best ways we could prove the sincerity of the doctrines I uttered the other day before the Senate would be to ratify the recently signed [*sic*!] treaty between Colombia and the United States I frankly share, and I beg to assure you that I shall do everything in my power to bring about a ratification of that treaty at as early a date as possible."[90]

Wilson had been as good as his word, writing to Senator Stone on February 17 to urge the foreign relations committee to report the Treaty favorably.[91] But Republican members, principally Lodge, had

[87] House Diary, January 3 and 12, March 5, 1917. Wilson, on February 6, asked his intimate friend, Cleveland H. Dodge, whether he would be interested in going to London. W. W. to C. H. Dodge, February 6, 1917, Wilson Papers. Dodge replied that he was unfit to hold the post and that his health would not permit acceptance in any event. C. H. Dodge to W. W., February 8, 1917, *ibid*.

House later suggested to Wilson that he send Newton D. Baker to London. "He thought Baker would do admirably," House wrote in his diary on March 28, 1917, "but said that recently, in a misguided moment, he had told Page he could continue and he supposed 'we would be compelled to have a British-American representing the United States at the Court of St. James.' One reason he gave for having Page was that he could not find a suitable man to take his place."

[88] Congressional Record, 65th Cong., Special Session of the Senate, p. 45; *New York Times*, March 9, 1917.

[89] J. Betancourt to W. W., January 24, 1917, Wilson Papers.

[90] W. W. to J. Betancourt, January 25, 1917, *ibid*.

[91] W. W. to W. J. Stone, February 17, 1917, *ibid*., also published in the *New York Times*, February 22, 1917.

announced that they would fight the Treaty to the bitter end, and Stone had to tell the President that there was no point trying to get the Treaty through the short session, and that the only hope was Senate action in a special session.[92]

Lansing opened the administration's campaign anew on March 1, even before the lame-duck session had expired, addressing a confidential letter to the foreign relations committee to warn that the German government was intriguing in Colombia as much as in Mexico, and to urge approval of the Treaty of Bogotá on the high ground of national security.[93] Lodge was unmoved, even when his friend, Henry White, pleaded with him on March 8 to support ratification.[94] Then Wilson called Thomas S. Martin, Senate majority leader, on March 12 to say that the Colombian Treaty simply had to go through.[95] As Lodge reported on that same day:

"Wilson has informed his people this morning that they must put through the Colombian Treaty. I need hardly say to you that I and practically all the Republicans are against it anyway but to put it through at this time would be simply infamous. The argument which he is using with the Foreign Relations Committee is that unless we give this money to Colombia she will help Germany and give her submarine bases. I need not go into his other arguments. They are all of the same kind; that we must buy Colombia off, and he plans to have the Republicans reject it unless he can carry it through by the patriotic plea, and then denounce us for treason. I will do everything I can to help him in war and will vote to give him all the powers he wants but I will not pay blackmail or tribute."[96]

The President's appeal did at least jolt the foreign relations committee into reporting the Treaty favorably on March 13.[97] The British Ambassador, Sir Cecil Spring Rice, called on Lodge on that day to urge him to support ratification.[98] But Lodge and other Republicans were adamant, and Stone and Martin agreed on March 16, only one day after debate on the Treaty had begun, that they could not find a

[92] H. C. Lodge to T. Roosevelt, February 22, 1917, Roosevelt Papers; *New York Times*, February 22, 1917.

[93] H. C. Lodge to T. Roosevelt, March 2, 1917, Roosevelt Papers.

[94] Lansing Desk Diary, March 8, 1917.

[95] *New York Times*, March 13, 1917.

[96] H. C. Lodge to T. Roosevelt, March 12, 1917, Roosevelt Papers.

[97] With amendments mutualizing the expression of regret in Article I and adding a new article in which Colombia acknowledged unreservedly the American title to the Panama Canal Zone. *New York Times*, March 14, 1917.

[98] Lansing Desk Diary, March 13, 1917.

two-thirds majority. Thus Stone moved that the Treaty be sent back
to the foreign relations committee, and the Senate adjourned at three
o'clock that afternoon.[99]

Wilson, meanwhile, following adjournment of the Sixty-fourth
Congress, had given virtually all his thought to the problem of arming American merchantmen. There seemed to be no doubt that Congress and the vast majority of Americans wanted action. Even many
of the antiwar leaders had said and were saying that armed neutrality
was the proper response to the German submarine threat. More important, there was now no doubt whatsoever that armed neutrality
offered the only hope of maintaining and defending American commerce on the high seas. The German Admiralty announced on March
2 that the period of grace for neutral ships in the Atlantic had expired, and that submarines would hereafter sink *all* ships, armed and
unarmed, belligerent and neutral, without warning.[100]

Wilson on March 5 asked Attorney General Gregory to examine
the statutes, particularly the piracy statute of 1819, to determine whether
there were legal impediments, and to report within twenty-four
hours.[101] The Attorney General replied, apparently orally, the following morning that he did not think that the piracy statute applied to
the present situation.[102] Wilson went to the State Department at 3:15
in the afternoon and discussed the legal issues with Lansing. The Secretary of State argued emphatically that the statute of 1819 did not
limit the President's power in present circumstances. He asserted with
equal forcefulness that the government should place armed guards
on merchantmen so long as the German government menaced American lives by refusing to obey elementary international law.[103] Wilson
next visited Daniels in his office to inquire about plans to speed naval
construction and ask him to prepare a memorandum on arming merchant ships.

Lansing came to the White House on the following morning,

[99] *ibid.*, March 16, 1917; *New York Times*, March 16 and 17, 1917; H. C. Lodge to
T. Roosevelt, March 16, 1917, Roosevelt Papers.
[100] *New York Times*, March 3, 1917.
[101] *ibid.*, March 6, 1917.
[102] Lansing Desk Diary, March 6, 1917. Newspapers reported that Gregory prepared
a memorandum for the President on the legal aspects involved in arming merchantmen. New York *World*, March 7 and 9, 1917. The present writer has been unable to
find a copy of this document.
[103] Lansing put these arguments on paper as soon as Wilson left, in R. Lansing to
W. W., March 6, 1917, *The Lansing Papers*, I, 613-616.

March 7, for an hour's conference presumably about armament for merchantmen.[104] Doctor Grayson put the President to bed that afternoon with a heavy cold that he had caught standing in the wind on inaugural day. The memorandum from Daniels, explaining three policies that might be followed in armed neutrality, arrived on the following day, March 8, and Wilson had the head usher call the Secretary to the White House. He had decided to arm American ships, Wilson told Daniels, but he did not like certain features of the regulations that the Navy Department had proposed.[105] Daniels returned to his office for further conferences. He sent a revised memorandum and a long letter to the White House on the following morning, March 9.

Daniels began his letter by reporting that Admiral William S. Benson, Chief of Naval Operations, had conferred with P. A. S. Franklin of the American Line and others in New York City on the preceding night. The important question, Daniels went on, was the best policy to follow in executing armed neutrality. His memorandum of March 8, the Secretary added, had outlined three possible policies as follows:

First, to reply to the German threat by permitting armed American merchantmen to shoot on sight at German submarines encountered anywhere, on the assumption that submarines would attack all American ships without warning.

Second, to permit armed American merchantmen to shoot on sight at German submarines only in the war zones, and to require armed American merchant ships to grant German submarines the right of visit and search in all other areas of the high seas.

Third, to require armed American merchantmen to submit to visit and search by German submarines everywhere, but to permit merchantmen to resist certain unlawful acts of submarines.[106]

He was, Daniels continued, enclosing a new draft of the memorandum, recommending adoption of the second policy. It had the disadvantages, Daniels warned, of making the United States a party to

---

[104] Lansing Desk Diary, March 7, 1917. We have no record of this conversation. Lansing wrote to Wilson on the following day to urge him to accept the hypothesis that the United States would soon be at war with Germany, and to arm merchantmen forthwith as the first step in a more vigorous policy. This, he said, would crystallize public opinion and unite the people behind the government. R. Lansing to W. W., March 8, 1917, *The Lansing Papers*, I, pp. 616-618.

[105] The Diary of Josephus Daniels, March 8, 1917, E. David Cronon (ed.), *The Cabinet Diaries of Josephus Daniels, 1913-1921*, pp. 109-110.

[106] Daniels, in enumerating these three choices, was following a memorandum entitled "RULES FOR THE CONDUCT OF AMERICAN MERCHANT VESSELS," no date, no author, the Papers of Josephus Daniels, Library of Congress; hereinafter cited as the Daniels Papers.

transportation of contraband, which was an act of war, and of being difficult to enforce because merchant vessels would tend to use their armament outside proscribed zones.[107] Germany, Daniels went on in his letter, might say that the United States was denying her the belligerent right to visit and search ships anywhere on the high seas. The American government could reply that Germany's notice of intention to sink all ships without warning in certain areas fully justified such action.

Admiral Benson, Daniels continued, strongly believed that the American government should forthwith notify Germany that it intended to arm its ships for protection on account of the German declaration of ruthless undersea warfare. Benson thought that it was barely possible that such warning might prevent execution of the German threat. "If we deny the right of visit," the Secretary went on, "Germany would declare that to be a warlike act, and that we were responsible for bringing on war. It is entirely probable that the next step would be war. If we must enter it to protect our rights and the lives of our people, I have felt we ought to do nothing to put the responsibility for this step upon our government." He had conferred last night, Daniels continued, with Rear Admiral Leigh C. Palmer of the Bureau of Navigation about crews to man the guns. Palmer had just written to make it clear that Germany would probably regard the presence of American armed forces on merchant ships as an act of war, that German submarines would probably attack American armed merchantmen without warning, and that armed merchantmen would necessarily fire at submarines on sight.[108]

"The question arises, too," Daniels added, "whether it would not be wisest to state that you had reached the conclusion that you had a

---

[107] J. Daniels to W. W., March 9, 1917, original in *ibid*. Daniels in this memorandum was summarizing some of the points made in F. H. Schofield, memorandum for the Secretary of the Navy, March 9, 1917, *ibid*. Schofield also argued that arming merchantmen would only invite unwarned attack, and that American ships would be safer without armament. The American government, he went on, should realize that armed vessels would carry contraband to the enemies of Germany. "The United States," he added, "by guarding those vessels does an act of war. Resistance to the armed vessels of Germany is war. *We have therefore to choose between not arming vessels and making war.*" Schofield recommended that the United States Government arm no ships until it had decided to accept war with Germany in preference to acquiescence in her present submarine campaign, and that vessels when armed should be permitted to shoot on sight at submarines wherever encountered. Daniels apparently did not send a copy of Schofield's memorandum to the President.

[108] Daniels quoted the entire text of Palmer's letter (L. C. Palmer to Operations, March 9, 1917), which said much the same as Schofield's memorandum.

right to arm the ships and would do so, making no statement as to the time or the method. I cannot resist the feeling that this would be the best course and meet public approval. If Germany wants war, she will try to sink in any event. If she wishes to avert war with us, there would be time to modify her orders to Naval commanders so they would not commit the overt act. . . . The protection of our ships and their reaching ports in safety raises so many difficult questions, and the consequences are so grave, that I am trying to present them to you before the final order to arm is given, though, of course, they have been present in your mind during the whole controversy."[109]

Wilson sent Daniels's letter and revised memorandum to Lansing for his comment in the late morning (of March 9), asking him to reply as quickly as possible since he, Wilson, wanted to issue orders that day.[110] The Secretary of State replied that afternoon, saying emphatically that he preferred the second policy, but with addition of instructions permitting armed guards to resist illegal attack outside the war zones. A confidential message from Page arrived at the State Department at this very time. It read:

"For the President and the Secretary only. In reporting on the general feeling here I find that continued delay in sending out American ships, especially American liners, is producing an increasingly unfavorable impression. In spite of all explanations, which are imperfectly understood here, delay is taken to mean the submission of our Government to the German blockade. This is the view of the public and of most of the press. There is a tendency even in high government circles to regard the reasons for delay which are published here as technicalities which a national crisis should sweep aside. British opinion couples the delay of our ships with the sinking of the *Laconia* and the Z[immermann] telegram and seems to be reaching the conclusion that our Government will not be able to take positive action under any provocation. The feeling which the newspaper despatches from the United States produce on the British mind is that our Government is holding back our people until the blockade of our ships, the Z telegram, and the *Laconia* shall be forgotten and until the British Navy shall overcome the German submarines. There is danger that this feeling harden into a conviction and interfere with any influence that we might otherwise have when peace comes.

"So friendly a man as Viscount Grey of Fallodon writes me pri-

[109] J. Daniels to W. W., March 9, 1917, printed in *The Lansing Papers*, i, 618-621.
[110] Edith B. Wilson to R. Lansing, March 9, 1917, *ibid.*, p. 618.

vately from his retirement: 'I do not see how the United States can sit still while neutral shipping is swept off the sea. If no action is taken, it will be like a great blot in history or a failure that must grievously depress the future history of America.' "[111]

The President probably saw this message soon after it arrived, but it is not likely that it had any decisive effect. Wilson had decided as early as February 16 to arm merchantmen as soon as it was apparent that the Germans meant what they said about attacking neutral ships without warning. He had waited for clear proof both of German intention and congressional and public opinion. There was no longer any doubt on either score. He also knew that armed neutrality carried heavy risks of war. Germany might well declare war if armed American merchantmen began shooting at submarines on sight, and it might be impossible to restrain congressional and public demands for a declaration of war if fighting on the seas went on very long. Wilson was surely aware of these hazards.

There simply did not seem to be any alternative but complete withdrawal and submission to the German threat. Wilson had earlier said that he would submit if that was necessary to avoid American belligerency and it was right to avoid war. Had the rising, overwhelming demand for armed neutrality caused his change of mind? Perhaps it had had its effect without Wilson's knowing it fully. The Zimmermann telegram and the sinking of the *Laconia* had also made their important contributions. Wilson had decided to go to armed neutrality *if the Germans committed overt acts against American shipping* before public opinion at home was aroused, the Zimmermann dispatch was disclosed, and the *Laconia* went to the bottom of the Irish Sea. But he had apparently made this decision without full realization of the risks of war that it involved. We can conclude, therefore, that these developments confirmed in Wilson's mind the necessity and wisdom of the decision for armed neutrality even though the Germans had not yet committed an overt act against American commerce and he now realized that armed neutrality would probably lead to hostilities and a declaration of war.

Wilson announced from his sick bed in the late afternoon of March 9 that he was instructing the navy to put guns and gun crews on liners and merchantmen. He also issued a proclamation calling Congress into special session on April 16 and a special statement to the

[111] Ambassador Page to the Secretary of State, March 9, 1917, *Foreign Relations, 1917, Supplement 1*, p. 170.

country, as follows: "Secretary Tumulty stated in connection with the President's call for an extra session of Congress that the President is convinced that he has the power to arm American merchant ships and is free to exercise it at once. But so much necessary legislation is pressing for consideration that he is convinced that it is for the best interests of the country to have an early session of the Sixty-fifth Congress, whose support he will also need in all matters collateral to the defense of our merchant marine."[112]

Work on orders to ship captains and gun crews went forward in the State and Navy Departments while senators in Washington and editors throughout the country were applauding the President's announcement. Daniels discussed the proposed regulations with Wilson on March 10 and Lansing on March 10,[113] and the Secretary of the Navy sent a draft to the Secretary of State on the following day.[114] Lansing must have gone over this paper with the President when he visited him in his bedroom between 9:45 and 10:25 on March 11.[115] Lansing then prepared a memorandum to serve as a basis for revision of these orders and handed it to Daniels in the afternoon of March 12. The Secretary of State on the same day sent formal notices to foreign governments that the United States Government had decided to place armed guards on all American merchant vessels entering the war zones delimited in the German decree of January 31, 1917.[116] Daniels issued the final orders on March 13. They permitted ship captains and naval officers commanding gun crews to shoot on sight at submarines if they came within torpedo range in the war zones. But the orders forbade American ships to pursue or search out submarines or to engage in any aggressive warfare against them anywhere. They also forbade offensive action against submarines outside the proscribed zones unless the U-boat was submerged or guilty of unlawful acts that jeopardized the safety of the ship.[117]

One important side effect of the break with Germany and decision for armed neutrality was lessening of tension on the official level be-

---

[112] *New York Times*, March 10, 1917.

[113] E. D. Cronon (ed.), *Cabinet Diaries of Josephus Daniels*, p. 110; Lansing Desk Diary, March 10, 1917.

[114] J. Daniels to R. Lansing, March 11, 1917, *The Lansing Papers*, I, 622-623.

[115] Lansing Desk Diary, March 11, 1917.

[116] *Foreign Relations, 1917, Supplement 1*, p. 171; *New York Times*, March 13, 1917.

[117] *The Lansing Papers*, I, 623-626; E. D. Cronon (ed.), *Cabinet Diaries of Josephus Daniels*, pp. 112-113.

tween the United States and Britain and France. The change was subtle and gradual, but it was actually a rather massive *détente* that led the American government to put into practice nothing less than a benevolent neutrality toward the Allies.

The State Department, for one thing, simply abandoned all efforts to protect American neutral trading rights against ever-increasing British encroachments. Bunkering agreements, the blacklist, mail seizures, and other measures that had drawn sharp protests from Washington only a few months before now went unchallenged by former guardians of American rights.[118] The British government on February 21 promulgated a new Order in Council stipulating that any ship encountered on her way to or from any neutral country with access to enemy territory without first calling at British or Allied ports would be deemed to be carrying enemy goods and subject to seizure and confiscation.[119] This measure had been the subject of much correspondence between the British Foreign Office and the French Foreign Ministry, mainly because Ambassador Jusserand had protested passionately against its adoption, saying that it made a scrap of paper out of the Declaration of Paris of 1856 and was liable to inflame American sentiment. Sir Eyre Crowe, Undersecretary of State for Foreign Affairs, had replied that Britain was simply obeying the law of necessity in tightening the blockade. Jusserand's fears were groundless; not a word of protest went from Washington.

Wilson's decision to arm American merchantmen also ended once for all Lansing's vigilance over Allied armed merchant ships in American ports. The first sign that the Washington government had no intention of harrying the Allies further on this matter came on February 21. The armed French ship *Guyane* arrived in New York harbor on that day after having apparently sunk a German submarine in offensive action. The British Ambassador, at the request of the Admiralty in London, asked Jusserand to instruct the captain of the *Guyane* to refuse to give any details about his encounter with the submarine to American port authorities and to say only that he had used his cannon defensively. Jusserand informed Counselor Polk about the instructions that he was sending to New York, explaining that

[118] Lansing did carry on some correspondence at this time about continued Allied seizure of American mails, but only with the objectives of persuading the French to adopt the practice followed by the British and of reserving legal claims to be presented at a later date. See *Foreign Relations, 1917, Supplement 1*, pp. 520-523.

[119] Consul General R. P. Skinner to the Secretary of State, February 22, 1917, *ibid.*, p. 493.

reasons of security prevented disclosure of details. Polk replied that he thought that the Ambassador's action was perfectly legitimate. Then the French liner *Rochambeau* arrived at New York on March 8 with guns mounted both fore and aft. She was the first Allied ship to come so heavily armed since the late summer of 1914, when the British ships *Adriatic* and *Merion* had docked at New York and Philadelphia carrying four and six guns, respectively. These had been removed at the request of the State Department before the ships sailed. Jusserand took the precaution of inquiring whether the State Department objected to *Rochambeau's* armament. He was told that she would be granted immediate clearance. As he reported to the Quai d'Orsay, this little fact disclosed a change of policy that was interesting to contemplate.

The Federal Reserve Board gave the help that counted most with the Allies. Their financial situation was now racing toward crisis if not disaster in April or May, when virtually all their dollar resources would be exhausted. The outlook was particularly black at the beginning of the year, because the House of Morgan had just informed the British and French Financial Missions that it could not float a large unsecured Anglo-French loan in January, as it had hoped to do. Anglo-French needs could be met in the near future, J. P. Morgan told the French agents, only by short-term loans against collateral.

The Chancellor of the Exchequer, Andrew Bonar Law, described the British financial plight to the Imperial War Cabinet on April 3, 1917, as follows:

"We had [on April 1] American securities unrealised of 490,000,000 dollars, we had an overdraft of 358,000,000, leaving a balance of 132,000,000 dollars; we had gold in America to the extent of 87,000,000 dollars, making a total of 219,000,000 dollars now actually available in New York, but our expenditure was at the rate of 75,000,000 dollars a week, so that would only last three weeks. We had on the way assets which represent 244,000,000 dollars, which would have carried us on for another three or perhaps four weeks; beyond that, the only assets visible were gold in the Bank of England and the Joint Stock Banks to the extent of 114,000,000 £. sterling. Russia and France had about 107,000,000 £. and 130,000,000 £. of gold respectively, but neither of them could be induced to part with it unless some actual necessity arises. In both these countries Finance Ministers told us that the shortage of gold was accountable for the loss of the exchange. Mr. Bonar

Law said that he did not think we could count on receiving any serious support in the way of gold from either of these two countries.

"As regards our other Allies, the number of American securities which were now saleable on the New York market which were in our hands was very small, and this in spite of the fact that we were now requisitioning all securities. The Cabinet would therefore see that on the face of it our position was a very black one indeed. The British Government had been deliberately going ahead with the knowledge that danger in this direction was in front of them which we might be unable to face. We had felt that the use of our gold and all our other resources would carry us on as long as possible."[120]

There was a remarkable change in the disposition of the Federal Reserve Board in February and early March 1917. As late as January 5, 1917, Governor Harding and Frederic A. Delano, another member of the Board, were emphasizing the danger to officials of the Federal Reserve Bank of New York of bank investment in unliquid securities, and Harding said that it was inadvisable even for private investors to "load up" with foreign securities at a time when peace seemed somewhat near.[121] Henry P. Davison conferred with Harding and Secretary McAdoo on February 14 and again brought up his plan to finance Allied purchases by unsecured Treasury notes. Harding replied, and McAdoo agreed, that the Board's views might change if conditions changed, and that war with Germany would be such a change.[122] Davison on the next day presented a plan for an issue of $250,000,000 of British Treasury notes to run two years, with a gold reserve of 20 per cent to be held in Ottawa to pay these notes before their expiration if purchasers so demanded.[123] McAdoo and Harding indicated that they would not object to purchase of these notes by American banks. Charles S. Hamlin, another member of the Board, said that he would not object to private investors purchasing the securities.[124]

[120] *Printed for the Imperial War Cabinet. April 1917. MR. BONAR LAW'S STATE-MENT ON FINANCE AT THE SEVENTH MEETING OF THE IMPERIAL WAR CABINET HELD AT 10, DOWNING STREET, S.W., ON THE 3RD APRIL, 1917,* Chamberlain Papers. The British Treasury, Bonar Law explained further, had been working on other schemes to find dollars, for example, conversion of Canadian Pacific Railway bonds into dollar securities so that they could be used as collateral against loans in the United States.

[121] The Diary of Charles S. Hamlin, January 5, 1917, Senate Special Committee, *Munitions Industry*, Pt. 5, p. 208.

[122] The Diary of Charles S. Hamlin, February 14, 1917, *ibid.*, pp. 208-209.

[123] The Diary of Charles S. Hamlin, February 15, 1917, *ibid.*, p. 209.

[124] The Diary of Charles S. Hamlin, February 19 and 20, 1917, *ibid.*

The British Treasury apparently decided not to issue the notes immediately, most probably because it believed that America's rupture with Germany had created a situation favorable to a large unsecured loan, which it very desperately wanted to float. There were plenty of signs from Washington that the Federal Reserve Board would not be shocked by such a suggestion now. Henri Bergson reported to the French Foreign Ministry on March 3 that Adolph C. Miller, a member of the Board, had told him confidentially that certain measures would be taken to encourage the American public to lend money to the Allies without security. W. P. G. Harding, in a conversation with a French financial agent on March 4, added the cheering news that the Board would take an important step as soon as Secretary McAdoo approved, and that McAdoo himself strongly favored an unsecured Anglo-French loan. Harding was apparently hinting at a statement that the Federal Reserve Board had already prepared and submitted to McAdoo for his and the President's approval.[125]

An urgent dispatch from Ambassador Page arrived at the State Department at the very moment that Harding, McAdoo, and others were discussing the proposed statement. Page warned, without giving details, that British gold resources were nearly exhausted and paralysis of Anglo-American trade would ensue unless some way was found to solve the exchange problem. "France and England," he went on, "must have a large enough credit in the United States to prevent the collapse of world trade and of the whole of European finance."[126] Lansing undoubtedly discussed this telegram with McAdoo, for the two men went together to Wilson's sickroom in the morning of March 8. We have no direct evidence of their conversation, but they surely talked about Page's telegram, the exchange crisis, and the statement that the Board proposed to issue. Wilson, in addition, must have approved publication of the statement.

The Federal Reserve Board met that same afternoon. One member recorded their discussions in his diary, as follows:

"Sec. M. said Ambassador Page had cabled President that Board's warning had scared investors and injured British credit; that neither Great Britain nor France could continue shipping gold to U. S.; that, if something not done, Great Britain would suspend specie payments.

---

[125] This statement must have been prepared on March 3 or 4, 1917.

[126] Ambassador Page to the Secretary of State, March 5, 1917, *Papers Relating to the Foreign Relations of the United States, 1917, Supplement 2, The World War* (2 vols.), I, 516-518.

"Board prepared new draft and with Sec. M.'s consent voted to publish it tomorrow."[127]

The statement said that there was much misunderstanding about the Board's attitude toward investments in foreign loans in the United States. "So far from objecting to the placing of foreign loans in the American market," it went on, "it regards them as a very important, natural, and proper means of settling the balances created in our favor by our large export trade. There are times when such loans should be encouraged as an essential means of maintaining and protecting our foreign trade." The Board's warning of November 28, 1916, against overpurchase by American banks of Allied short-term notes, the statement continued, had not been meant to reflect on any country's credit. It had simply been aimed at what the Board still thought was an unsound practice. But the country's gold reserves had been so greatly augmented since November, the statement added, that there was now no reason why banks should not invest to a reasonable degree in foreign securities. The statement concluded:

"The board did not, of course, undertake to give advice concerning any particular loan. It desires, however, to make clear that it did not seek to create an unfavorable attitude on the part of the American investors toward desirable foreign securities, and to emphasize the point that American funds available for investment may, with advantage to the country's foreign trade and the domestic economic situation, be employed in the purchase of such securities."[128]

It is not surprising that Ambassador Jusserand reported to the Quai d'Orsay that all Allied representatives were satisfied. The Board's statement did open the door again to bank purchases of short-term Allied Treasury notes, and it meant that a new Anglo-French unsecured loan would at least have Washington's sanction. But it would be easy to exaggerate the statement's significance. It did not remedy what was still the fatal weakness in the Allied financial situation—the aversion of most Americans to invest in European war loans unsecured by good collateral. As Page pointed out in the cablegram cited above, the problem was simply getting too large for solution by private agencies. They might postpone the crisis now that the American government had withdrawn its objection to unsecured loans, but they could not avert it forever.

[127] The Diary of Charles S. Hamlin, March 8, 1917, Senate Special Committee, *Munitions Industry*, Pt. 5, p. 210.
[128] *New York Times*, March 9, 1917.

These indications that the American government was finally abandoning its strict neutrality and moving toward outright if limited support of the Entente Allies were of course soon followed by other signs in late February and early March that the United States might indeed be drawn into the fighting on the seas, if not into full-fledged belligerency. To the embattled Allies, these were the first really heartening signs of better days ahead since the outbreak of hostilities in 1914. All responsible Allied leaders now desperately desired American participation in any form and to any degree. Some of them, particularly Lloyd George, believed that only American belligerency could avert a German victory.

But Allied leaders also knew that American participation would bring new hazards to their collective cause and plans. The great danger was Wilson himself. Leaders in western Europe saw the President largely through the eyes of their governments' envoys in Washington. The image of early 1917 was that of a man who was indecisive, eager to avoid trouble with Germany, given to substituting rhetoric for action, insensitive to the moral issues of the war, yet dangerous because he was a naïve idealist stubbornly determined to have his own way. It might be positively disastrous if he played any important part in the peace settlement.

An interesting discussion was set off by a report from the French Minister in Holland to the Quai d'Orsay on February 10, 1917, saying that he had learned from a good source that the English had little desire to promote American belligerency because of the difficulties that Wilson's participation in peace negotiations would create.[129] The Foreign Ministry repeated this telegram to the French Ambassadors in Rome and Washington. The former reported that the Italian Foreign Office and Allied diplomats were preoccupied with the consequences of American participation in the peace conference in the event of American belligerency. Wilson, they all agreed, would not be an easy ally.[130] Jusserand replied that he had heard the same reports in Washington, and that it was not impossible that the British Embassy had

---

[129] The report was certainly incorrect or at least reflected only the opinion of the British Minister in The Hague. Leaders in the British government had many grave misgivings about Wilson, as I have tried to show in *President Wilson and His English Critics*; but they were now desperately eager for an American declaration of war, as Lloyd George's message to Wilson of February 10, 1917, made altogether clear. For this message, see above, pp. 317-318.

[130] The French Ambassador in Rome added that he personally believed that it would be a very great mistake to do anything to deflect Wilson from a war course.

been spreading them. He could hardly believe, Jusserand added, that any intelligent person could hold such a view.

It was enough, at any rate, to prompt someone in the French Foreign Ministry—it was probably de Margerie—to put down some thoughts in a memorandum soon afterward. The "Peace without Victory" speech made it obvious, it began, that the President wanted a negotiated peace based on law and justice. The United States if neutral would not be able to participate in the peace conference; but the United States if a belligerent might perhaps be able to impose its policy. American public opinion was rallying behind the President. Now that the American diplomatic rupture with Germany seemed to promise early American entry into the war, the British government manifested little enthusiasm for Wilson's views. Should France endorse American policy or resist it? Was France strong enough to defy the United States by insisting upon conquests and indemnities? The sincerity and loyalty of French friendship for the United States as much as for England demanded that these questions be rigorously examined and frankly answered.

We do not know what discussions ensued, but the French government decided to do what it could discreetly and quietly to encourage American participation and so informed Ambassador Jusserand on March 8. Two days later Louis Aubert of the Foreign Ministry, after discussions with the Premier and other leaders in Paris, set down what might have been the settled views of the French government on the question of American entry. The United States, this memorandum began, would want to take first place in a peace conference even though she intended to make only a minor military contribution and to come into the war, not as an ally, but as a lukewarm collaborator. American interest lay in Europe's return to the prewar political and economic equilibrium, in short, peace without victory. The French government would perforce have to work to promote full-scale American participation. The United States might then extend large financial and material assistance and even send an army to France. But the more America participated, the more she would demand guarantees for her kind of peace settlement and other things like recognition of the Monroe Doctrine and Anglo-French support against Japan. Indeed, it seemed likely that Wilson would insist upon Allied acceptance of his peace program as the price of American belligerency, and the Allies might soon be engaged in a great negotiation that would in fact be the prelude to the peace conference. Since the Allies had to have American assistance they would have to answer American demands. The great task of French diplomacy now was reconciliation of American material and moral force to the cause and plans of the Allies.

There was one greater threat to French hopes than Wilsonian interference in the peace settlement after adoption of an American declaration of war. It was the danger that Germany would, even yet, offer guarantees for American shipping, and that Wilson would then resume his campaign for mediation and an immediate armistice.

The initiative for what was to be the President's last peace *démarche* before American belligerency came, significantly, from England. Lloyd George informed Ambassador Page on February 20 that the British government would now be glad to receive a formal peace offer from Austria-Hungary, provided only that President Wilson should conduct negotiations in absolute secrecy.[131] We do not know whether this was simply an additional British move to detach Austria-Hungary from her major ally or part of a larger scheme.[132] Page noted in his diary soon afterward that Bonar Law had talked about the possibility of making peace at Russia's expense, by offering to give Germany a free hand in the East in return for evacuation of Belgium and northern France and perhaps the cession of Lorraine to France.[133] Lloyd George certainly knew, as Wilson did, that the shortest route to peace talks with Germany now ran through Vienna. Perhaps he was contemplating negotiations that would begin with the Hapsburg authorities and then involve the German government. The truth of this matter will remain hidden until the essential British documents are opened to investigation.

Wilson conferred at once with Lansing and then dispatched the

[131] Ambassador Page to the Secretary of State, February 20, 1917, *Foreign Relations, 1917, Supplement 1*, pp. 55-56.

[132] It is certainly possible that Lloyd George's change of policy reflected the advice of Alfred Lord Milner, a member of the Cabinet who was at this very time preparing, at the Prime Minister's request, a memorandum on British and Dominion peace objectives for an Imperial Conference that was to meet in April. Milner said very strongly that the breakup of Austria-Hungary by the creation of Czechoslovakia and Yugoslavia and the enlargement of Rumania was neither practical nor desirable, although he favored trying to make arrangements for the autonomy of the subject peoples of the Hapsburg Empire. See Milner's interview of late March 1917 with Sidney Low, in *The History of the Times, the 150th Anniversary and Beyond, 1912-1948* (2 Parts), Part 1, pp. 328-330. There is a copy of Milner's memorandum in the Chamberlain Papers.

[133] Page Diary, entry dated March 1917.

following telegram, drafted for the most part by the Secretary of State, to Ambassador Penfield in Vienna:

> When there is opportunity for you to see the Minister of Foreign Affairs alone you may say to him, provided the occasion seems suitable, that you have received information from the highest authority which convinces you that in arranging terms of peace the Allied Governments have no desire or purpose to disrupt the Austro-Hungarian Empire by the separation of Hungary and Bohemia from Austria unless a continuation of the war causes a change of conditions; that undoubtedly a definite assurance of this might be obtained through this Government if the Austrian Government, indicating a desire for an early peace, wished that you should act secretly to that end; and that you would be pleased to convey to this Government any comments, suggestions or proposals in regard to this subject which the Austrian Government may be pleased to make, it being understood that whatever exchanges may take place will be treated in the strictest confidence.
>
> You should make it perfectly clear to the Minister of Foreign Affairs before making the foregoing statement that you are about to give him information of the most confidential character and that you rely upon him to prevent it from becoming known for if it should through mischance become public or reach any other government you would be compelled to repudiate it.
>
> In view of the secrecy which should be preserved in this matter you will in no circumstances commit anything you may say to writing or permit any notes to be made in your presence. You may however, if you wish, show this telegram to Grew [now Counselor of Embassy in Vienna] impressing upon him the importance of absolute secrecy.
>
> The President relies upon you to use the greatest discretion in this delicate negotiation and hopes that you may soon be able to report in strict confidence the result of your interview.[134]

Penfield saw Foreign Minister Czernin on February 26-27 and again on March 13, after Czernin had discussed the President's offer with Emperor Charles. The Foreign Minister on both occasions reiterated his government's sincere desire for peace but just as emphatically said that it would not consider a separate peace.[135] Wilson dropped the matter momentarily, for he obviously had no intention of making another peace overture to Germany at this particular moment.

This interchange only intensified Czernin's desire to maintain re-

[134] The Secretary of State to Ambassador Penfield, February 22, 1917, *Foreign Relations, 1917, Supplement 1*, pp. 57-58.

[135] Ambassador Penfield to the Secretary of State, February 27 and March 13, 1917, *ibid.*, pp. 62-63, 65-66.

lations with the United States and, above all, to avert the German-American war that would almost inevitably snap his link with Washington. He was at this very time trying to convince the Washington government that Austria-Hungary's feeble participation in the unrestricted submarine campaign did not justify American rupture of relations. Czernin, following his conversation with Penfield on March 13, moved somewhat boldly, and perhaps desperately, to deflect Germany from the path of war with the United States. He called in the German Ambassador, Count von Wedel, and told him nothing about Wilson's most recent peace feeler. Czernin said instead that his conversations with Penfield had convinced him that Wilson wanted to avoid war and thought that war might be averted if armed American merchantmen were "fortuitously" spared.[136] Then Czernin sent the following memorandum to the Austro-Hungarian Embassy in Berlin:

"On the 13th instant, the American Ambassador in Vienna expressed the wish to Count Czernin, quite spontaneously, that the next American ships which were *en route* for England might be 'overlooked' and not torpedoed. That this would satisfy President Wilson in the light of the public opinion of the United States; that thereafter it was certain that no more ships would proceed; that, as things stood, the United States must determine whether it was to be war or peace; that in case of the former America would not henceforth be able to export appreciable amounts of ammunition; and in case of the latter—which President Wilson hoped for—complications would be avoided.

"Although Count Czernin fully appreciates the weak side of this argument, he has nevertheless instructed the Imperial and Royal Embassy to bring his conversation which he has had with Mr. Penfield to the knowledge of the foreign office, since he has gotten the impression that the American Ambassador, in addressing him, was following instructions."[137]

It was a most remarkable bit of intelligence, and it was almost certainly fabricated, as it does not seem possible that Penfield could have talked this way without instructions, which, it can be said emphatically, he did not have. But to the Germans the memorandum did appear to convey an authentic, formal overture, and it seemed to show

[136] Ambassador von Wedel to Imperial Chancellor von Bethmann Hollweg, March 14, 1917, *Official German Documents*, II, 1333-1334.
[137] Memorandum of the Austro-Hungarian Embassy, March 14, 1917, *ibid.*, pp. 1334-1335.

that there was even yet one way to prevent war with the United States.

The Foreign Office sent the memorandum to Holtzendorff, then in Pless, and the Admiralty chieftain prepared a commentary for the Emperor on March 18. It simply was not possible, it said, to instruct submarine commanders to refrain from attacking American ships already on the high seas. U-boats were already at their stations with orders to sink all ships on sight, and wireless communication with them was unreliable. It would take at least six weeks to get new orders to all submarines. Holtzendorff's commentary continued:

"But, moreover, this would mean a possible taking up of negotiations which would make impossible demands upon us, both from the military and political standpoints. To allow American ships to proceed to the ports of the enemy, and at the same time to prevent with all means at our command the shipping traffic of the small neutral States to do the same, would have a very damaging effect from every point of view; in fact, probably the opposite of the effect which President Wilson presumably desires in connection with his wish to promote peace. But, leaving this circumstance to one side, it would mean that we would operate in direct opposition to the end and aim of the U-boat war if we were to make exceptions by allowing American imports the special privilege of passing through our commerce blockade at the present critical period.

"Your Majesty's diplomatists will know how to deal with the formal request which consists of the attempt to conduct further negotiations under the guise of a certain incognito and by devious paths, after diplomatic relations have been broken off.

"But I consider it my duty to point out the flippant and rascally game which is being played with the destinies of great States and peoples, which is revealed by President Wilson's course of action. He wants the question of war and peace to depend upon our winking at the passing through of a few American steamers which were sent into the war zone; in other words, that *we* are to avoid the danger which *he* is obviously, and in the sight of all the world conspiring to bring about. In fact, the danger of war lies in the utter lack of conscience of a national government which operates with farcical means, and, according to my judgment and feeling, we should most positively avoid even the mere semblance of allowing German politics or warfare to be ridden by the American desire, which would lead our national policy into a U-boat trap, or have America retreat from her stand by means of Germany's humiliation. For this reason, it seems to me to be of the utmost importance that neither the German people nor the neutral Powers be longer left in the dark with regard to President Wilson's attitude touching the question of war with Germany, and not to allow ourselves to be put in a wrong position in the eyes of the world by added procrastination and fumbling around with questions of negotiation. Our entire press should be well informed on this point, and should express this thought firmly and clearly—if possible, before the first encounter in the restricted area."[138]

That, the Emperor thought, was said in good German language. "Agreed, reject," he wrote on the margin. Then, sending the documents back to the Foreign Office, he added: "Now, once and for all, an *end* to negotiations with America. If Wilson wants war, let him make it, and let him then have it."[139]

The Foreign Office gave a paraphrase of Holtzendorff's memorandum and the Emperor's remarks to the newspapers on about March 21, and they repeated them editorially on March 22. As the *Berliner Lokal-Anzeiger*, after saying that Germany would make no concession to American shipping, put it, for example: "If Wilson wantonly wants war, let him bring it on, and he can then have it, too. For our part there remains only to give the assurance that we have once for all put an end to negotiations regarding the submarine war. The colossal guilt for a German-American war, if it comes, would fall wholly and exclusively on President Wilson and his government."[140] Bethmann said the same thing more politely in a speech to the Reichstag on March 29. Germany, he said, did not desire war with the United States. But the submarine campaign had to go forward, and "If the American nation considers this a cause for which to declare war against the German nation with which it has lived in peace for more than one hundred years, if this action warrants an increase of bloodshed, we shall not have to bear the responsibility for it. The German Nation, which feels neither hatred nor hostility against the United States of America, shall also bear and overcome this."[141]

[138] H. von Holtzendorff to the Emperor, March 18, 1917, *ibid.*, pp. 1335-1336.
[139] William II to the Foreign Office, March 18, 1917, *ibid.*, p. 1336.
[140] *Berliner Lokal-Anzeiger*, evening edn., March 22, 1917.
[141] *New York Times*, March 30, 1917.

CHAPTER IX

The Decision for War

NAVAL crews installed guns on the *Manchuria*, a cargo liner of the Atlantic Transport Line, on March 13, and work proceeded on other vessels immediately afterward. Wilson, still recovering from his cold, stayed in his private apartment on March 13 and 14 and saw only intimate members of his family. One of the documents that he read most intently was a memorandum that Walter Lippmann had prepared after a conversation with Colonel House and left at the White House on March 12. It argued that the American government was resisting German assaults on American neutral rights mainly because it believed that the Reich was "fighting for a victory subversive of the world system in which America lives." The memorandum went on:

"The only victory in this war that could compensate mankind for its horrors is the victory of international order over national aggression. Whatever measures America takes will always be adapted to that end. It has no designs on Germany's life or her legitimate national development. It does not seek to humiliate the German people. It does not even propose to return upon them the grievous injuries inflicted by their government upon us.

"But it does propose to resist the aggression which is touching America. It will not commit itself to any aggression upon Germany or her allies. It will reserve freedom of action for itself, and whenever Germany is ready to abandon aggression and enter a league of nations, America will be ready to discuss the matter through open diplomacy.[1]

Lippmann added in a covering letter that Herbert Croly and he believed that the Germans were making much impression in the United States with their plea that the American government was enforcing its rights against Germany and ignoring British infringements. The President, Lippmann went on, needed to educate Americans to the truth that the fundamental issue with Germany was not legal or commercial but one arising out of America's vital interest in a just and lasting peace. Wilson, by reviving his proposal for a league of nations,

---

[1] W. Lippmann, "Memorandum," Wilson Papers. Lippmann said very much the same thing in the *New Republic*, x (March 10, 1917), 147-148.

would capture liberal sentiment in Allied countries, encourage German radicals to force a statement of German terms, and warn American jingoes that American belligerency would remain subordinate to liberal policy and objectives.[2]

Wilson did not comment or reply, probably because he saw at once that Lippmann was seeking to lead him to commitment to belligerency. Events soon afterward, on March 14, revealed that he was still far from ready to admit that war was inevitable. There was a report at noon that day from the American Consul in Plymouth, England, that a German submarine had sunk the American steamer *Algonquin* by shell fire without warning and without loss of life on March 12.[3] It was the first case of unwarned sinking of an American ship since the German announcement of January 31, 1917. Nothing in the incident, said a report that could only have been inspired by the White House, changed the situation between the United States and Germany. The American government, this report added, had already done everything short of war to meet German assaults on American shipping.[4] Wilson saw Ambassador Gerard—the first person outside the White House circle he had seen since March 12—on the following day, March 15. "He was in a most serious mood," Gerard afterward wrote. "He said that he had done everything to preserve peace and even yet he hoped that the Germans would abandon the ruthless submarine war."[5]

Public opinion, even after the sinking of the *Algonquin*, was more quiescent than it had been at any time since the armed ship fight in Congress. Theodore Roosevelt's editorial spokesman, *The Outlook*, called for a declaration of war in its issue of March 14.[6] The American Rights Committee was working to stimulate other such demands, and an overwhelming majority of the members of the New York Federation of Churches indicated in a poll completed on March 11 that they favored extreme measures for protection of American lives and commerce.[7] The paucity of such expressions only emphasized that enthusiasm for full-fledged involvement had considerably diminished since the excitement engendered by the Zimmermann telegram, the sinking of the *Laconia*, and the armed ship fight.

[2] W. Lippmann to W. W., March 11, 1917, Wilson Papers.
[3] Consul J. J. Stephens to the Secretary of State, March 14, 1917, *Foreign Relations, 1917, Supplement 1*, p. 174; *New York Times*, March 15, 1917.
[4] *ibid.*
[5] J. W. Gerard, memorandum quoted in R. S. Baker, *Woodrow Wilson*, vi, 488.
[6] *The Outlook*, cxv (March 14, 1917), 452.
[7] *New York Times*, March 12, 1917.

"More than a month and a half has passed since we broke relations with Germany," Elihu Root lamented, "and we have done nothing but talk, and print interviews, and fill the papers with headlines, while we have carefully avoided doing one single thing to prepare to fight."[8] Roosevelt agreed, writing: "I regard Wilson as far more blameworthy than the 'willful' Senators. I am as yet holding in; but if he does not go to war with Germany I shall skin him alive. To think of Hughes' folly, and the folly of those who nominated Hughes, having cursed the country with the really hideous misfortune of four years more of Wilson in this great and terrible world crisis!"[9] And Page wrote in his diary about Wilson: "He shut himself up . . . and engaged in what he called 'thought.' The air currents of the world never ventilated his mind. . . . He has not breathed a spirit into the people: he has encouraged them to supineness. He is *not* a leader, but rather a stubborn phrasemaker. His chief counsel is with—House, as timid a dependent-in-thought as one man ever found in another."[10]

News of two momentous events came to Wilson in his seclusion on March 15 and 16. The first was a report from the Hotel Biltmore in New York City that the National Conference Committee of the Railways and the brotherhood chieftains, who had been discussing the demand of the brotherhoods that the railroads put the eight-hour day into effect forthwith, even before the Supreme Court ruled on the Adamson Act, had come to total impasse, and that railroad workers would begin a progressive strike at seven p.m. on March 17. Wilson, a White House correspondent said, was amazed at the news.[11] "If a strike should start at this time," Tumulty warned the President on the following morning, "God only knows how it might spread."[12]

The crisis brought the President from his sick room, prematurely, Grayson said, at noon on March 16. He held a brief Cabinet meeting at two-thirty. Then he dispatched a telegram to the Conference Committee and the brotherhood presidents, urging them to accept the mediation of a special committee of the Council of National Defense. "A general interruption of the railway traffic of the country at this

[8] E. Root to R. G. Monroe, March 17, 1917, the Papers of Elihu Root, Library of Congress.

[9] T. Roosevelt to H. C. Lodge, March 13, 1917, E. E. Morison *et al.* (eds.), *Letters of Theodore Roosevelt*, VIII, 1162.

[10] Page Diary, April 1, 1917.

[11] *New York Times*, March 16, 1917.

[12] J. P. Tumulty to W. W., March 16, 1917, Wilson Papers.

time," he added, "would entail a danger to the nation against which I have the right to enter my most solemn and earnest protest. It is now the duty of every patriotic man to bring matters of this sort to immediate accommodation. The safety of the country against manifest perils affecting its own peace and the peace of the whole world makes accommodation absolutely imperative and seems to me to render any other choice or action inconceivable."[13]

The brotherhood presidents responded by postponing the strike for forty-eight hours and warning that this was absolutely their last concession. "I am exceedingly glad," Wilson wrote in a telegram to the conferees in New York on March 17, "that the conferences have been reopened and that the prospect of a settlement looks brighter. I hope most earnestly for the sake of all concerned and most of all for the sake of the nation, that the two parties will continue to draw closer together and that a little further conference will lead to the result the whole country hopes for and expects."[14] The mediators from the Council of National Defense—Secretary Lane, Secretary William B. Wilson, Samuel Gompers, and Daniel Willard, president of the Baltimore & Ohio Railroad—worked with both sides in the Hotel Biltmore all through March 18, but to no avail. Lane telephoned the discouraging news to the White House at about midnight, and Wilson responded with a dire warning that he was determined to prevent a strike at all costs. The railroad managers caved in thirty minutes later and authorized the mediators to grant whatever demands were necessary to prevent the walkout.[15] The brotherhood presidents revoked the strike order a short time later.[16]

Both sides signed an agreement early in the morning of March 19 giving brotherhood members ten hours' pay for eight hours' work and overtime pro rata, regardless of the Supreme Court's verdict on the Adamson Act.[17] Chief Justice White, speaking for a bare majority of the Court a few hours later, upheld the Adamson Act in sweeping language.[18]

The second report on March 15, much amplified and clarified during the following two days, thrilled the President and country as much

[13] W. W. to E. Lee *et al.*, March 16, 1917, *ibid.*, also published in the *New York Times*, March 17, 1917.
[14] W. W. to E. Lee *et al.*, March 17, 1917, Wilson Papers.
[15] E. Lee to F. K. Lane *et al.*, March 19, 1917, *New York Times*, March 19, 1917.
[16] *ibid.*
[17] *ibid.*, March 20, 1917.
[18] Wilson *v.* New, 243 *United States Reports*, 332.

as news of the impending railroad strike frightened them. It was word from Petrograd, confirmed definitively on March 17, that a liberal group representing a majority in the Russian parliament had deposed the Czar, formed a provisional government, and promised to establish a new constitutional order and carry on the war for democratic aims.[19] The liberation of the Russian people from Romanov despotism seemed also to herald the end of Prussian autocracy. Bethmann Hollweg, speaking as Minister President in the Prussian House of Lords on March 15, announced a "new orientation" in German political history—a movement after the war to democratize Prussian political institutions. "Woe to the statesman," he said with great emotion, "who does not recognize the signs of the times and who, after this castastrophe, the like of which the world has never seen, believes that he can take up his work at the same point at which it was interrupted."[20]

It seemed incontrovertible that autocracy was doomed everywhere in Europe. "What the Russians have done," exclaimed the New York *World*, "the Germans and the Austrians and Hungarians can do if they will. They at last are masters of their own destiny so far as the character of their Government is concerned."[21] Added the *New York Evening Post*: "Not since August 1, 1914, has anything come out of Europe to stir the pulse and fire imagination like the news from Russia."[22] Americans who believed that the Allies on the whole represented the cause of European democracy were particularly heartened. As the New York *Nation* put it in the most incisive contemporary comment:

"With a single gesture the Russian people has won its own freedom and lifted a heavy burden from the shoulders of the Entente. The democratic nations of Western Europe have been emancipated from the handicap of Czarism and have won a new ally—democratic Russia. To the nations engaged in the defence of public law against the power of the mailed fist, and of the right of the little peoples against the ambitions of *Weltmacht*, it has been from the beginning a pain and a drag that their necessary partner should be the Russia of Polish oppression and Kishineff massacres, the Russia of corrupt and stupid

[19] Ambassador D. R. Francis to the Secretary of State, March 14 and 17 (two telegrams), 1917, *Papers Relating to the Foreign Relations of the United States, 1918, Russia* (3 vols.), I, 1-2, 3-4; the Russian Ambassador to the Secretary of State, March 18, 1917, *ibid.*, pp. 4-5.

[20] New York *World*, March 16, 1917.

[21] *ibid.*, March 17, 1917.

[22] *New York Evening Post*, March 16, 1917.

bureaucrats, of witch-doctors and bribe-takers and Black Hundreds. . . .
The revolution at Petrograd has enormously enriched the issues for
which the Allies are contending, to such an extent as almost to make
one forget the original objects of the war. . . . The preservation and

The Scepter
Cesare in the *New York Evening Post*

extension of the liberties so rapidly won in Russia are now inextricably
bound up with the success of the Allies. A German victory now would
mean the collapse of free Russia.[23]

Wilson left no evidence of his first reactions. It seems reasonable

[23] New York *Nation*, civ (March 22, 1917), 330.

to assume that he shared the general American enthusiasm for what seemed to be a momentous triumph for human liberty, and, more important, that he interpreted the Russian Revolution and German reactions as further evidence that the war was entering its final apocalyptic stage of death grapple between despotism and democracy. It must be said with some emphasis that there is no evidence that events in Petrograd had any direct influence on his later decision for war with Germany. The most that can be said is that the Russian Revolution might possibly have facilitated his final decision.

Lansing sent to the President on March 16 a long telegram from Samuel N. Harper, the leading American authority on Russia, saying that Harper was convinced that the liberal element was in control and Russia would henceforth be better able to prosecute her war effort.[24] Colonel House urged the President on March 17 to recognize the new Russian government, adding, "I am not too sure that the present outcome in Russia is not due largely to your influence."[25]

Wilson needed no prodding. He had decided to recognize the provisional Russian government, he told the French Ambassador on about March 19, in order to encourage the effort of this great democracy. Everyone could see that the men now in power in Petrograd were honorable; and the fact that the new government's position was precarious was all the more reason for giving it diplomatic support. The old order of things, Wilson added, has no chance of being reestablished. Therefore, let us recognize the new immediately. Lansing sent instructions to Ambassador David R. Francis in Petrograd on March 20; he granted formal recognition to Foreign Minister Paul Milyukov at eleven a.m. on March 22.[26]

Washington was rocked on Sunday, March 18, by news that German submarines had just destroyed three American ships—*City of Memphis*, sunk with no casualties off the Irish coast on March 17 after warning and evacuation of crew; *Illinois*, sent to the bottom by gunfire without warning off Alderney on March 18, one member of the crew being wounded; and *Vigilancia*, torpedoed without warn-

[24] R. Lansing to W. W., March 16, 1917, Wilson Papers.
[25] E. M. House to W. W., March 17, 1917, *ibid.*
[26] The Secretary of State to Ambassador Francis, March 20, 1917, and Ambassador Francis to the Secretary of State, March 22, 1917, *Papers Relating to the Foreign Relations of the United States, 1918, Russia*, I, 12-13; *New York Times*, March 23, 1917.

ing west of Bishop on March 16, with fifteen members of the crew being drowned while launching the lifeboats.[27]

The President and Mrs. Wilson stayed in their private quarters all morning and then had lunch with Wilson's cousin, James Woodrow. Wilson received the Attorney General at 2:15 for a brief conference and then went motoring with Mrs. Wilson for the balance of the afternoon. Excitement, stimulated by newspaper reports and editorials and a statement by Theodore Roosevelt demanding an immediate declaration of war,[28] was spreading over the country by the time that Lansing, responding to the President's summons, went to the White House at a little after eleven o'clock on Monday morning, March 19. "For an hour," Lansing noted in his diary, "the President and I sat in his study and debated the course of action which should be followed. The President said that he did not see that we could do more than we were doing in the way of protecting our vessels as already three of the American Line steamships had sailed for Europe with armed guards, each carrying four guns and forty men. I argued that war was inevitable, that I had felt so for months, and that the sooner we openly admitted the fact so much stronger our position would be with our own people and before the world. I left the President without a definite impression as to what his decision would be."[29]

"I have just returned from a conference with the President," Lansing wrote to Colonel House as soon as he returned to his office. "He is disposed not to summon Congress as a result of the sinking of these vessels. He feels that all he could ask would be powers to do what he is already doing. I suggested that he might call them to consider declaring war, and urged the present was the psychological moment in view of the Russian revolution and the anti-Prussian spirit in Germany, and that to throw our moral influence in the scale at this time would aid the Russian liberals and might even cause revolution in Germany. He indicated to me the fear he had of the queries and investigations of a Congress which could not be depended upon because of the out-and-out pacifists and the other group of men like Senator Stone. If

[27] *New York Times*, March 19, 1917; Consul W. Frost to the Secretary of State, received March 18, 1917, *Foreign Relations, 1917, Supplement I*, p. 180; Consul J. N. McCunn to the Secretary of State, received March 20, 1917, *ibid.*, pp. 181-182; Consul A. W. Swalm to the Secretary of State, received March 23, 1917, *ibid.*, p. 184; Consul Stephens to the Secretary of State, March 21, 1917, *ibid.*, p. 182; New York *World*, March 20, 1917.

[28] *New York Times*, March 20, 1917.

[29] R. Lansing, *War Memoirs*, p. 233.

you agree with me that we should act now, will you not please put your shoulder to the wheel?"[30] Lansing also talked to Polk, and he called House twice to urge him to come to Washington and stir the President from his inertia.[31]

Wilson was going through considerably greater agony of spirit than he revealed to his Secretary of State. The only alternative to armed neutrality was war, and he was not yet prepared to drink that cup. He had lunch alone with Mrs. Wilson and then walked over to the Navy Department to talk to Secretary Daniels. "Wished everything possible done in addition to Armed Guards to protect American shipping, hoping this would meet the ends we have in view," Daniels wrote in his diary. "He had been urged to call Congress and to declare war. He still hoped to avoid it and wished no cost & no effort spared to protect shipping."[32] He returned to the White House and received Frank Cobb, editor of the New York *World*, at three-thirty. Cobb's recollection of their conversation follows in part:

"He said he couldn't see any alternative, that he had tried every way he knew to avoid war. 'I think I know what war means,' he said, and he added that if there were any possibility of avoiding war he wanted to try it. 'What else can I do?' he asked. 'Is there anything else I can do?'

"I told him his hand had been forced by Germany, that so far as I could see we couldn't keep out.

" 'Yes,' he said, 'but do you know what that means?' He said that war would overturn the world we had known; that so long as we remained out there was a preponderance of neutrality, but that if we joined with the Allies the world would be off the peace basis and onto a war basis.

"It would mean that we should lose our heads along with the rest and stop weighing right and wrong. It would mean that a majority of people in this hemisphere would go war-mad, quit thinking and devote their energies to destruction. The President said a declaration of war would mean that Germany would be beaten and so badly beaten that there would be a dictated peace, a victorious peace.

" 'It means,' he said, 'an attempt to reconstruct a peace-time civilization with war standards, and at the end of the war there will be no bystanders with sufficient power to influence the terms. There won't

[30] R. Lansing to E. M. House, March 19, 1917, House Papers.
[31] House Diary, March 19, 1917.
[32] E. D. Cronon (ed.), *Cabinet Diaries of Josephus Daniels*, pp. 116-117.

be any peace standards left to work with. There will be only war standards.'

"The President said that such a basis was what the Allies thought they wanted, and that they would have their way in the very thing America had hoped against and struggled against. . . . He had the whole panorama in his mind. He went on to say that so far as he knew he had considered every loophole of escape and as fast as they were discovered Germany deliberately blocked them with some new outrage.

"Then he began to talk about the consequences to the United States. He had no illusions about the fashion in which we were likely to fight the war.

"He said that when a war got going it was just war and there weren't two kinds of it. It required illiberalism at home to reinforce the men at the front. We couldn't fight Germany and maintain the ideals of Government that all thinking men shared. He said we would try it but it would be too much for us.

" 'Once lead this people into war,' he said, 'and they'll forget there ever was such a thing as tolerance. To fight you must be brutal and ruthless, and the spirit of ruthless brutality will enter into the very fibre of our national life, infecting Congress, the courts, the policeman on the beat, the man in the street.' Conformity would be the only virtue, said the President, and every man who refused to conform would have to pay the penalty.

"He thought the Constitution would not survive it; that free speech and the right of assembly would go. He said a nation couldn't put its strength into a war and keep its head level; it had never been done.

" 'If there is any alternative, for God's sake, let's take it,' he exclaimed. Well I couldn't see any, and I told him so."[33]

Representative William C. Adamson, who talked with Wilson several times during this period, later testified that these were indeed some of Wilson's fundamental concerns. As Adamson remembered these conversations:

"He stressed elaborately and most earnestly his aversion to being drawn into the war, urging many reasons therefor. . . . Time and again

[33] John L. Heaton, *Cobb of "The World,"* pp. 268-270. Cobb later remembered having this conversation with Wilson at one o'clock in the morning of April 2, just before Wilson delivered his war message to Congress. There is no evidence whatsoever that Cobb went to the White House at this time. The White House diary shows that he went on March 19, and what Wilson told him assumes all the greater meaning because he said it at the very time that he was still deliberating the decision for war.

he told the writer that in addition to the disorganization of business and expenditure of treasure and the possible loss of life in the field, he dreaded the general disorganization consequent upon war and conditions inevitably connected therewith and produced thereby. He said that a state of war suspended the law, and legal and moral restraints being relaxed, there not only ensues an era of recklessness and crime, but also the disregard of commercial integrity and a saturnalia of exploitation, profiteering and robbery. Men who in time of peace deport themselves decently, in times of war regard it as no robbery to extort anything obtainable from fellow citizens, friend or foe. Industry would be so demoralized, profiteering run rampant, robbery would become the order of the hour and prices would soar so high that even after peace should be restored, it would require a generation to restore normal conditions."[34]

Cobb left in the late afternoon, and Wilson had dinner with Mrs. Wilson and members of the Bolling family and saw no other persons during the evening. Lansing went to the Japanese Embassy for dinner and returned home at eleven o'clock. Between eleven and one in the morning he put down in a letter to the President all the conclusions that had taken form in his mind since their conversation of the preceding morning. He now agreed, Lansing began, that the sinking of the three ships was no good reason for a declaration of war. But war would come soon, just as soon as there was fighting between an armed American merchantman and a German submarine. The advantage of waiting to recognize that a state of war existed would seem to be that Germany might herself declare war after an encounter on the high seas. Still, Lansing went on, he was convinced that the German government would not declare war in any circumstances. It would prefer to profit from the submarine blockade without adding the United States to its enemies.

If war *was* inevitable, Lansing went on, then there were certainly many reasons for immediate American participation. It would greatly encourage the new Russian government and put heart into the democratic element in Germany. It would give great moral support to the Allies, already encouraged by recent military successes, and tend to shorten the conflict. It would gratify the American people, who were bitterly critical of the administration's failure to act. Finally, America's future influence in world affairs would be greatly enhanced by action in favor of democracy and against absolutism. "This would be first

[34] W. C. Adamson, undated memorandum in the Baker Collection.

shown in the peace negotiations and in the general readjustment of international relations. It is my belief that the longer we delay in declaring against the military absolutism which menaces the rule of liberty and justice in the world, so much the less will be our influence in the days when Germany will need a merciful and unselfish foe."

"I have written my views with great frankness," Lansing concluded, "as I am sure you would wish me to do, and I trust that you will understand my views are in no way influenced by any bitterness of feeling toward Germany or by any conscious emotion awakened by recent events. I have tried to view the situation coldly, dispassionately and justly."[35]

Lansing's lofty sentiments were no doubt genuine. None the less, he had not been entirely artless in making the case for a war declaration on the only grounds that Wilson could approve.

Wilson played golf with Grayson from nine until ten forty-five on the following morning, March 20. He then went to his office where he found, among other things, Lansing's letter. We may be sure that he read it carefully. He had lunch with Mrs. Wilson and then went to the Cabinet meeting. The following memorandum from the Lansing diary tells the story in a moving narrative:

> The Cabinet Meeting of today I consider the most momentous and, therefore, the most historic of any of those which have been held since I became Secretary of State, since it involved, unless a miracle occurs, the question of war with Germany. . . .
>
> [Here Lansing describes events of Sunday, March 18, to Tuesday, March 20, and recounts his conversation with Wilson on the morning of March 19.]
>
> From Sunday noon until Tuesday noon there was intense public excitement. Many of the newspapers clamored for war and inveighed bitterly at the President's failure to act. There was a general feeling that, if war did not come at once, it would come shortly, and that there was no valid reason for waiting for another outrage. I myself shared this feeling and was prepared to urge immediate action at the meeting of the Cabinet.
>
> The corridors of the State Department and the Executive Office swarmed with press correspondents seeking to get some inkling of what would be done from passing officials. It was through these eager crowds of news-gatherers that I forced my way at half past two Tuesday afternoon under a bombardment of questions, to which I made no reply, and entered the Cabinet room where all the other members had arrived.

[35] R. Lansing to W. W., March 19, 1917, *The Lansing Papers*, I, 626-628.

Three minutes later the President came in and passed to his place at the head of the table shaking hands with each member and smiling as genially and composedly as if nothing of importance was to be considered. Composure is a marked characteristic of the President. Nothing ruffles the calmness of his manner or address. It has a sobering effect on all who sit with him in council. Excitement would seem very much out of place at the Cabinet table with Woodrow Wilson presiding.

After felicitating Secretaries Lane and Wilson on the success of their efforts at mediation between the railroad managers and the "Four Brotherhoods," the President said that he desired advice from the Cabinet on our relations with Germany and the course which should be pursued. He began with a review of his actions up to the present time pointing out that he had said to Congress on February 3rd that, while the announced policy had compelled the severance of diplomatic relations, he could not bring himself to believe that the German Government would carry it out against American vessels, but that, if an "overt act" occurred, he would come before them again and ask means to protect Americans on the high seas even though he thought he possessed the constitutional power to act without Congress. He said that the situation compelled him to do this on February 23rd and Congress had desired to adopt the measures which he sought, but had been prevented, and that he had then acted on his own authority and placed armed guards on American vessels intending to proceed to the German barred zone.

He went on to say that he did not see from a practical point of view what else could be done to safeguard American vessels more than had already been done unless we declared war or declared that a state of war existed, which was the same thing; and that the power to do this lay with Congress.

He said that the two questions as to which he wished to be advised were—

Should he summon Congress to meet at an earlier date than April 16th, for which he had already issued a call?

Second. What should he lay before Congress when it did assemble?

He then spoke in general terms of the political situations in the belligerent countries, particularly in Russia where the revolution against the autocracy had been successful, and in Germany where the liberal element in the Prussian Diet was grumbling loudly against their rulers. He also spoke of the situation in this country, of the indignation and bitterness in the East and the apparent apathy of the Middle West.

After the President had finished McAdoo was the first to speak. He said that war seemed to him a certainty and he could see no reason for delay in saying so and acting accordingly; that we might just as well face the issue and come out squarely in opposition to Germany, whose Government represented every evil in history; that, if we did not do so at once, the American people would compel action and we would be in the position of being pushed forward instead of leading, which would be humiliating and unwise. He further said that he believed that we could best aid the Allies against Germany by standing back of their credit, by underwriting their loans, and that they were sorely in need of such aid. He felt, however, that we could do little else, and doubted whether we could furnish men.

McAdoo spoke with great positiveness in advocating an immediate call of Congress. His voice was low and his utterance deliberate, but he gave the impression of great earnestness.

Houston, who followed, said that he agreed with McAdoo that it would create a most unfortunate, if not disasterous [*sic*], impression on the American public as well as in Europe if we waited any longer to take a firm stand now that Germany had shown her hand. He said that he doubted whether we should plan to do more than to use our navy and to give financial aid to the Allies; that to equip an army of any size would divert the production of our industrial plants and so cut off from the Allies much needed supplies; and he thought that we ought to be very careful about interfering with their efficiency. He concluded by urging the President to summon Congress at once because he felt that a state of war already existed and should be declared.

Redfield followed Houston with his usual certainty of manner and vigor of expression. He was for declaring war and doing everything possible to aid in bringing the Kaiser to his knees. He made no points which particularly impressed me; and, as he had so often shown his strong pro-ally sentiments, I was sure his words made little impression upon the President.

Baker was the next to express an opinion and he did so with the wonderful clearness of diction of which he is master. He said that he considered the state of affairs called for drastic action with as little delay as possible, and that he believed Congress should meet before April 16th. He said that the recent German outrages showed that the Germans did not intend to modify in the least degree their policy of inhumanity and lawlessness, and that such act could mean only one thing, and that was war.

Since we were now forced into the struggle he favored entering into it with all our vigor. He advocated preparing an army at once to be sent to Europe in case the Allies became straightened [*sic*] in the number of their men. He said that he believed the very knowledge of our preparations would force the Central Powers to realize that their cause was hopeless. He went on to discuss the details of raising, equipping and training a large force.

I followed Baker and can very naturally remember what I said better and more fully than I can the remarks of others.

I began with the statement that in my opinion an actual state of war existed today between this country and Germany, but that, as the acknowledgement of such a state officially amounted to a declaration of war, I doubted the wisdom as well as the constitutional power of the President to announce such fact or to act upon it; that I thought that the facts should be laid before Congress and that they should be asked to declare the existence of a state of war and to enact the laws necessary to meet the exigencies of the case. I pointed out that many things could be done under our present statutes which seriously menaced our national safety and that the Executive was powerless to prevent their being done. I referred in some detail to the exodus of Germans from this country to Mexico and Cuba since we severed diplomatic relations, to the activities of German agents here, to the transference of funds by Germans to Latin American countries, to the uncensored use of the telegraph and the mails, etc.

For the foregoing reasons I said that I felt that there should be no delay in calling Congress together and securing these necessary powers.

In addition to these reasons which so vitally affected our domestic situation I said that the revolution in Russia, which appeared to be successful, had removed the one objection to affirming that the European war was a war between Democracy and Absolutism; that the only hope of a permanent peace between all nations depended upon the establishment of democratic institutions throughout the world; that no League of Peace would be of value if a powerful autocracy was a member, and that no League of Peace would be necessary if all nations were democratic; and that in going into the war at this time we could do more to advance the cause of Democracy than if we failed to show sympathy with the democratic powers in their struggle against the autocratic government of Germany.

I said that the present time seemed to me especially propitious for action by us because it would have a great moral influence in Russia, because it would encourage the democratic movement in Germany, because it would put new spirit in the Allies already flushed with recent military successes, and because it would put an end to the charges of vacillation and hesitation, which were becoming general, and bring the people solidly behind the President.

"The time for delay and inaction," I said, "has passed. Only a definite, vigorous and uncompromising policy will satisfy or ought to satisfy the American people. Of this I am convinced. We are at war now. Why not say so without faltering? Silence will be interpreted abroad as weakness, at home as indecision. I believe that the people long for a strong and sure leadership. They are ready to go through to the very end. If we enter this war, and there is not the slightest doubt but that we will enter[,] if not today then tomorrow, the Government will lose ground which it can never regain by acting as if it was uncertain of its duty or afraid to perform that duty, a duty which seems to me very plain."

I said a good deal more in the same vein and urged the propriety of taking the advantage of the aroused sentiment of the people since it would have a tremendous influence in keeping Congress in line. I said that I would not permit my judgment to be swayed by this sentiment but that as a matter of expediency in affecting congressional action it ought to be used. I must have spoken with vehemence because the President asked me to lower my voice so that no one in the corridor could hear.

The President said that he did not see how he could speak of a war for Democracy or of Russia's revolution in addressing Congress. I replied that I did not perceive any objection but in any event I was sure that he could do so indirectly by attacking the character of the autocratic government of Germany as manifested by its deeds of inhumanity, by its broken promises, and by its plots and conspiracies against this country.

To this the President only answered "Possibly."

[Another Cabinet member wrote in his diary: "The President said that the principal things which had occurred since he had last addressed Congress which differed, except in degree, from what had been discussed, were the Russian Revolution, the talk of more liberal institutions in Germany, and the continued reluctance of our ships to sail. If our entering the war would hasten and fix the movements in Russia and Germany, it would be a marked gain to the world and would tend to give additional justification for the whole struggle, but he could not assign these things as reasons for calling Congress at an earlier date. The justification would have to rest on the conduct of Germany, the clear need of protecting our rights, of getting ready, and of safeguarding civilization against the domination of Prussian militarism."[36]]

Whether the President was impressed with the idea of a general indictment of the German Government I do not know. I felt strongly that to go to war solely because American ships had been sunk and Americans killed would cause debate, and that the sounder basis was the duty of this and every other democratic nation to suppress an autocratic government like the German because of its atrocious character and because it was a menace to the national safety of this country and of all other countries with liberal systems of government. Such an arraignment would appeal to every liberty-loving man the world over. This I said during the discussion, but just when I do not remember.

When I had finished, Secretary Wilson in his usual slow but emphatic way said: "Mr. President, I think we must recognize the fact that Germany has made war upon this country and, therefore, I am for calling Congress together as soon as possible. I have reached this conviction with

[36] D. F. Houston, *Eight Years with Wilson's Cabinet*, I, 244.

very great reluctance, but having reached it I feel that we should enter the war with the determination to employ all our resources to put an end to Prussian rule over Germany which menaces human liberty and peace all over the world. I do not believe we should employ half-measures or do it half-heartedly."

In view of the fact that Wilson had on previous occasions shown a disposition to temporize with the German Government and had opposed war because of submarine attacks, I was surprised at his frank assertion in favor of radical measures. There is this to be said of Secretary Wilson, he never speaks at hap-hazard; he is slow to express an opinion but very firm in it when it is once declared. When I have disagreed with him I have always had to acknowledge the soundness of his reasoning unless the subject was Labor, as to that he is biased. I consider him a valuable adviser because he is equipped with an abundance of common sense.

Gregory, who had been listening with much attention although on account of his deafness I am sure only heard his neighbors at the table, gave it as his opinion that it was useless to delay longer, that the possibility of peace with Germany was a thing of the past, and that he was in favor of assembling Congress as soon as possible, of enacting all necessary legislation, and of pursuing as aggressive action toward Germany as we were able. He went on to speak of German intrigues here, of the departure of German reservists and of the helplessness of his Department under existing laws. He said that every day's delay increased the danger and Congress ought to be called on to act at once.

After Gregory had given his views the President said, "We have not yet heard from Burleson and Daniels."

Burleson spoke up immediately and said: "Mr. President, I am in favor of calling Congress together and declaring war; and when we do that I want it to be understood that we are in the war to the end, that we will do everything we can to aid the Allies and weaken Germany with money, munitions, ships and men, so that those Prussians will realize that, when they made war on this country, they woke up a giant which will surely defeat them. I would authorize the issue of five billions in bonds and go the limit." He stopped a moment and then added, "There are many personal reasons why I regret this step, but there is no other way. It must be carried through to the bitter end."

The President then turned his head towards Daniels who sat opposite Burleson and said: "Well, Daniels?" Daniels hesitated a moment as if weighing his words and then spoke in a voice which was low and trembled with emotion. His eyes were suffused with tears. He said that he saw no other course than to enter the war, that do what we would it seemed bound to come, and that, therefore, he was in favor of summoning Congress as soon as possible and getting their support for active measures against Germany.

Burleson had at previous meetings resisted an aggressive policy toward Germany, and he had, as late as the Cabinet meeting on Friday, the 16th, advocated very earnestly taking a radical stand against Great Britain on account of detention of the mails. Whenever I had called attention to the illegal acts of Germany he would speak of British wrong-doings. I felt sure that he did this to cause a diversion of attention from the German violations of law. Possibly I misjudged him, and there was no such motive. His words at this meeting indicated hostility to Germany and a desire for drastic action, so I may have been mistaken.

As for Daniels his pacifist tendencies and personal devotion to Mr. Bryan and his ideas were well known. It was, therefore, a surprise to us all when he announced himself to be in favor of war. I could not but wonder whether he spoke from conviction or because he lacked strength of mind to stand out against the united opinion of his colleagues. I prefer to believe the former reason, though I am not sure.

The President said, as Daniels ceased speaking: "Everybody has spoken but you, Lane."

Lane answered that he had nothing to add to what had been said by the other members of the Cabinet, with whom he entirely agreed as to the necessity of summoning Congress, declaring war and obtaining powers. He reviewed some of the things which had been said but contributed no new thought. He emphasized particularly the intensity of public indignation against the Germans and said that he felt that the people would force us to act even if we were unwilling to do so.

Knowing the President's mental attitude as to the idea of being forced to do *anything* by popular opinion, these remarks of Lane seemed to me unwise and dangerous to the policy which he advocated. I could almost feel the President stiffen as if to resist and see his powerful jaw set as Lane spoke. Fortunately before the President had time to comment Lane kept on in his cool and placid way drifting into another phase of the subject which was more to the President's taste since it appealed to his conception that he must be guided by the principle of right and by his duty to this country and to all mankind. Thus what might have been a dangerous incident was avoided.

The foregoing is a brief outline of the debate which occupied over two hours and which frequently was diverted into other channels such as the effectiveness of armed guards on merchant ships, the use of patrol boats, German plots in Latin America, the danger of riots and vandalism in this country, the moving of interned vessels, the need of censors, etc., etc.

When at last every Cabinet officer had spoken and all had expressed the opinion that war was inevitable and that Congress ought to be called in extraordinary session as soon as possible, the President [said] in his cool, unemotional way: "Well, gentlemen, I think that there is no doubt as to what your advice is. I thank you." . . .

Thus ended a Cabinet meeting the influence of which may change the course of history and determine the destinies of the United States and possibly of the world. The possible results are almost inconceivably great. I am sure that every member of the Cabinet felt the vital importance of the occasion and spoke with a full realization of the grave responsibility which rested upon him as he advised the President to adopt a course which if followed can only mean open and vigorous war against the Kaiser and his Government. The solemnity of the occasion as one after another spoke was increasingly impressive and showed in every man's face as he rose from the council table and prepared to leave the room. Lane, Houston and Redfield, however, did not hide their gratification, and I believe we all felt a deep sense of relief that not a dissenting voice had been raised to break the unanimity of opinion that there should be no further parley or delay. The ten councillors of the President had spoken as one, and he—well, no one could be sure that he would echo the same opinion and act accordingly.[37]

Wilson asked Lansing and Burleson, after the other Cabinet members had left, how long it would take to prepare the necessary legislation for submission to Congress in the event that a state of war was declared. They agreed that more than a week would be required, and that it would not be wise to call Congress to meet before April 2.[38] Wilson issued the call on March 21, requesting Congress to meet in special session on April 2 "to receive a communication concerning grave matters of national policy."[39]

This meant, as the Washington correspondents noted at the time, that Wilson made the decision for war either during or immediately following the Cabinet meeting of March 20. It was apparently a firm decision, even though he disclosed it to no one for a week. White House correspondents reported on March 22 that the President was assembling materials for his war message on that date.[40] He asked Daniels after the Cabinet meeting on March 20 to discuss the submarine menace with the General Board. And when Daniels reported

[37] "Memorandum of the Cabinet Meeting, 2:30-5 P.M. Tuesday, March 20, 1917," Lansing Diary; for another brief account, see E. D. Cronon (ed.), *Cabinet Diaries of Josephus Daniels*, pp. 117-118.

[38] R. Lansing, *War Memoirs*, pp. 236-237.

[39] *New York Times*, March 22, 1917.

[40] *ibid.*, March 23, 1917.

that the General Board had said that there was no effective defense against submarines,[41] Wilson instructed the Secretary to establish confidential liaison immediately, "until the Congress has acted," with the British Admiralty and work out some plan of cooperation. "As yet," he added, "sufficient attention has not been given, it seems to me, by the authorities on the other side of the water to the routes to be followed or to plans by which the safest possible approach may be made to the British ports. As few ports as possible should be used, for one thing, and every possible precaution thought out. Can we not set this afoot at once and save all the time possible?" Daniels, on March 26, instructed Rear Admiral William S. Sims, soon to be appointed commander of American naval operations in European waters, to come to Washington, preparatory to going to London to establish liaison with British naval authorities.[42]

Other actions left no doubt about Wilson's intentions. He called the Council of National Defense to meet on March 23; ordered Brand Whitlock, Minister to Belgium, and American members of the Belgian Relief Commission on March 24 to withdraw from Belgian territory; increased the enlisted strength of the Navy and Marine Corps and mobilized certain units of National Guard on March 25 and 26; and suspended the mustering out of National Guard units still on the Mexican border on March 27. The Cabinet discussed these and more far-reaching plans on March 23 and 27. Baker, consequently, submitted a new army bill on March 29. It increased the Regular Army to war strength, called the entire National Guard into federal service, and authorized the raising of a "first unit," 500,000 men strong, of a new national army "exclusively by selective draft."[43] The idea of laying down terms to the Allies for American participation never seemed to have occurred to Wilson at this time.

The abundant evidence of Wilson's reactions and thought does not leave much doubt, as we have already seen, why he decided to break relations with Germany and adopt a policy of armed neutrality. The only troubling question at this later point is why he decided to abandon armed neutrality without really giving it a try and accept the

[41] J. Daniels to W. W., March 20, 1917, Wilson Papers.

[42] W. W. to J. Daniels, March 24, 1917, Daniels Papers, commenting on C. J. Badger to J. Daniels [March 23, 1917], *ibid.*, concerning arrangements for routing American merchant ships and cooperating with the British Admiralty and French Naval Ministry; E. D. Cronon (ed.), *Cabinet Diaries of Josephus Daniels*, p. 122.

[43] N. D. Baker to W. W., March 29, 1917, Wilson Papers; *New York Times*, March 30, 1917; New York *World*, April 1, 1917.

decision for full-fledged belligerency that his Cabinet advisers pressed upon him on March 20. The evidence on this crucial point is neither definitive nor absolutely revealing.

We can be more confident of our ground in saying why he did not make the fateful decision. For one thing, he did not accept belligerency because he thought that the Allies were in danger of losing the war and a German victory would imperil American national interests. We now know that the Allies were in desperate straits if not in danger of defeat. The French had begun to draw upon their last manpower and were already in the midst of what they called their "crisis of reserves." The submarine campaign was succeeding, actually beyond the expectations of the German Admiralty. Nearly 600,000 tons of Allied and neutral shipping were sunk during March, and the toll would reach the staggering figure of nearly 900,000 tons in April. The British and French faced an exchange problem that seemed insoluble.

But Wilson and his advisers knew virtually none of these facts. The French guarded the secret of their "crisis of reserves" so carefully that the American Embassy in Paris did not discover it until about March 23,[44] and officials in Washington did not learn the frightening news until after the United States was in the war. There had been some recent Allied successes on the western front, and American leaders thought, as the Cabinet discussions of March 20 revealed, that they heralded a great Allied offensive in the spring, as, indeed, they did. Few persons in America (or Europe, either, for that matter) thought that the Russian Revolution would soon lead to Russian withdrawal from the war.[45] On the contrary, virtually everyone assumed that the new Russian government would wage war more efficiently and enthusiastically than the old, as, indeed, it tried to do. American officials could have been only vaguely aware of the staggering effect

[44] A. H. Frazier to E. M. House, March 23, 1917, House Papers. The French Foreign Ministry did not inform Ambassador Jusserand of the "crisis of reserves" until March 26, 1917.

[45] Except President Wilson "He next discussed the question of Russia," J. Howard Whitehouse recorded after an interview with the President on April 14. "He said the position of Russia was very uncertain. It might be that in setting up their new form of Government and working out domestic reforms they would find the war an intolerable evil and would desire to get to an end of it on any reasonable terms. It would be a serious blow to the Allies if that took place. He was being asked to advance loans to Russia and he was making a stipulation that the money lent should be spent upon the war. He was not prepared to finance Russia at this point in order that she might get out of the war." "The House Report," Whitehouse Papers, entry for April 14, 1917.

of the submarine campaign on the British economy. Wilson and other leaders in Washington did know, as we have seen, something about the dimensions of the exchange crisis, but no one thought that a solution depended upon American belligerency.

All the evidence of Wilson's thinking since the summer of 1916 about long-range American national interests in the outcome in Europe leads to the conclusion that he believed that American interests, to say nothing of the interests of mankind, would be best served by a draw in Europe. He not only thought that a peace without victory offered the best hope for the right reconstruction of the world order, but he also now feared destruction of German power and an absolute Anglo-French-Russian military hegemony in Europe.

We can say with some assurance, in the second place, that Wilson did not accept the decision for war because he thought that the Allies were fighting altogether for worthy objectives and the Germans altogether for unworthy ones. There is no need to review the evidence in this volume and the preceding two on Wilson's thinking about the issues of the European war. It must suffice to say that his views had become increasingly sophisticated and detached once the shock of the war's outbreak wore off in the autumn of 1914. He certainly had no illusions about Allied objectives by the end of 1916; if anything, he tended to give the British less credit for idealism and generous motives than they deserved. His suspicion accounts in large part for his decision, once the United States had entered the war, not to join the Allies in any political commitments but to maintain a free hand to conclude peace once American objectives were attained.

It is equally clear that Wilson was not pushed into war by an aroused public opinion. There was an authentic demand for a declaration of war, reflected largely in the big-city newspapers and the Senate, from the moment that the Zimmermann telegram was published. It grew louder after news on March 18 of the sinking of the three American ships. But it was still far from being obviously a great, overwhelming, and irresistible national demand when Wilson made his own decision for belligerency on March 20 or 21. One is entitled to doubt that Wilson in any event would have chosen belligerency only because public opinion demanded it.

It is almost abundantly clear that Wilson simply concluded that there was no alternative to full-fledged belligerency. The United States was a great power. It could not submit to Germany's flagrant—so it seemed to Wilson and his contemporaries—assault on American sovereignty without yielding its honor and destroying its influence for constructive work in the world. Wilson's first response was of course armed neutrality. But he soon concluded that armed neutrality was neither a feasible nor a sufficient response. He fortunately explained, at least partially, why he came to this conclusion in an exchange of letters before he went to Congress on April 2. John P. Gavit of the *New York Evening Post*, Senator Joseph I. France of Maryland, Matthew Hale, and Senator Hitchcock wrote between March 25 and March 29 urging Wilson to stand firm in armed neutrality and saying, further, that this was the most sensible way to protect maritime rights and the great majority of Americans did not want full-fledged participation.[46] Wilson replied most explicitly to Hale, as follows:

"I value your letter of March twenty-eighth and find that it has stirred many sympathetic thoughts in me.

"I would be inclined to adopt the third course you mention [continuance of armed neutrality, at least until Germany declared war], indeed, as you know, I had already adopted it, but this is the difficulty: To defend our rights upon the seas, we must fight submarines. From the point of view of international law, they are when used as Germany has used them against merchantmen in effect outlaws to begin with. Merchantmen cannot defend themselves against them in the way which international law has regarded as consistent with neutrality. They must be attacked on sight and to attack them is practically to commit an act of war if they are attacked before showing an intention themselves to attack. Germany has intimated that she would regard the only sort of warfare that is possible against her submarines as an act of war and would treat any persons who fell into her hands from the ships that attacked her submarines as beyond the pale of law.[47] Apparently, to make even the measures of defense legitimate we must obtain the status of belligerents, and if we do that, we have taken the second of the three courses that you mention.[48]

Wilson was not altogether using a technicality to mask a deeper

[46] J. P. Gavit to W. W., March 25, 1917; J. I. France to W. W., March 28, 1917; M. Hale to W. W., March 28, 1917; G. M. Hitchcock to W. W., March 29, 1917, all in the Wilson Papers.

[47] Wilson was referring here to a *note verbale* that the German Foreign Office gave to Ambassador Gerard on January 20, 1917. It warned that neutral armed ships that used their armament against German submarines would be treated as pirates by German naval forces. Ambassador Gerard to the Secretary of State, January 21, 1917, *Foreign Relations, 1917, Supplement 1*, pp. 91-92.

[48] W. W. to M. Hale, March 31, 1917, Wilson Papers.

motive. The problem he described was a serious one, given the assumption that well-defined international law should govern the relations of nations. Naval advisers, as we have seen, had already warned that, legally speaking, armed neutrality was war in the circumstances created by use of submarines as commerce destroyers. Therefore, war between the United States and Germany would most probably ensue. Once he accepted this conclusion, Wilson must have been very greatly moved by the argument of some Cabinet members that it would be difficult to fight even a limited war on the seas unless the government enjoyed the advantages and privileges that accompanied formal belligerency.

Even so, Wilson knew, as Lansing had been frank enough to say in his letter of March 19, that there was a good chance that Germany would prefer American armed neutrality to belligerency and refrain both from declaring war in the event of hostilities between an armed ship and a submarine and mistreating American seamen if a submarine captured any after such an engagement. We now have good evidence that Wilson thought that the "piracy talk" was absurd, that is, that it was nonsense to believe that the Germans would deal with the captured crews of armed American merchantmen as if they were pirates.[49] Wilson, in any event, did not wait and see what the Germans would do. Thus it has to be said that to some degree he chose war, even though the issue had obviously been forced upon him.

He chose war over a risky and ambiguous armed neutrality in part, certainly, because he had lost all confidence in the Imperial German Government on account of its assault upon American shipping and the Zimmermann telegram. He was not indiscriminate in his indictment, but events had convinced him that militarists and extreme nationalists were now in the saddle in Berlin, and that he simply could not do business with them or hope for any lasting peace so long as they were in control of German policy. It is also difficult to see how Wilson could have failed to be impressed by the fact that his Cabinet advisers, to say nothing of many others in the second rank of officialdom, were now united in the belief that circumstances left no alternative to belligerency. Wilson would almost surely have stood his ground, as he did in the later struggle over ratification of the Versailles Treaty, if duty had spoken unmistakably. But duty did not speak so clearly in 1917. Wilson said over and over that he was struggling

[49] E. D. Cronon (ed.), *Cabinet Diaries of Josephus Daniels*, p. 123; entry for March 28, 1917.

for right policy and unsure of his ground. In such a situation the united advice of counselors must have weighed heavily in his thinking.

It is this writer's opinion that the most important reason for Wilson's decision was his conviction that American belligerency now offered the surest hope for early peace and the reconstruction of the international community. Wilson, we may be reasonably confident, believed that the European conflict was in its final stages. Perhaps he thought that it would end after Germany had shot her submarine bolt and the Allies had tried one last offensive in the spring and summer of 1917. In any event, he certainly believed that American participation, as decisive as possible, would hasten the end of the ghastly carnage, if not end it quickly. American entry would spell Germany's inevitable defeat, or at least frustration of German plans. The German people, or their leaders in the Reichstag, might take control as liberals had done in Russia and refuse to fight for imperialistic ends.

Then there was a final tempting thought. It was that American belligerency would enhance his own ability to force an early settlement. He would continue as a neutral to be frustrated by both sides in his efforts for peace. He would have more influence with the Allies as a belligerent and, finally, some bargaining power with Germany. American belligerency would assure American guarantee of the peace settlement and membership in a postwar league of nations. This knowledge might make the English and French willing to negotiate a reasonable settlement. And when the great day did come he would have a seat at the peace table, not a stool outside the conference room. Jane Addams, who visited the White House with other members of the Emergency Peace Federation on February 28, later remembered that Wilson said that "as head of a nation participating in the war, the President of the United States would have a seat at the Peace Table, but that if he remained the representative of a neutral country he could at best only 'call through a crack in the door.' "[50]

Colonel House almost certainly spoke accurately for the President when he told Whitehouse on March 30 and April 5:

"The President was going into this war to fight against Junkerism in every country. We had it in England but in England it would disappear after the war. He was convinced that no real peace was possible so long as the Prussian ideals remained. But the President was not going into the war for the obscure reasons that might actuate the Allies, nor was he going to be bound by an[y] treaty with them, and

---

[50] Jane Addams, *Peace and Bread in Time of War*, p. 64.

he was going to reach the end of it at the earliest possible moment. . . .

"House wished me specially to tell the members of the House of Commons who took a moderate view on the war that the President was entirely democratic in his sympathies, and his aim was to bring the war to an end at the earliest possible moment. He would certainly not sign the Allies agreement about a separate peace and would preserve his freedom to act as a mediating influence still. He had a profound disbelief in secret diplomacy and in the way it had been practiced in Europe by all countries including England. He was going to try to set another example. . . .

"The question of peace terms would now take a new form with America in the war. England would now have the guaranties for the future which she desired as America would be a party to whatever settlement was arrived at. The objections to England going into a conference in the future would be removed."[51]

All this has been said with no intention of suggesting that Wilson ever wanted war. He had continued to hope to the very end that the Germans would yield the single thing that he demanded, observance of the rules of cruiser warfare in dealing with American merchantmen, and presumably safeguarding of human life on passenger liners. His agony was great as he passed through the dark valley of his doubts. He saw the dangers of intervention, to both his own people and the world, with wonderful clarity. But he could see no alternative, and he set aside his doubts in the hope that acting as a belligerent he could erect and achieve objectives to justify the decision he had made.

It would surely be superfluous to discourse on the significance of the decision, except perhaps to recall Winston Churchill's words: "Writing with every sense of respect, it seems no exaggeration to pronounce that the action of the United States with its repercussions on the history of the world depended, during the awful period of Armageddon, upon the workings of this man's mind and spirit to the exclusion of almost every other factor; and that he played a part in the fate of nations incomparably more direct and personal than any other man."[52]

The popular demand for war, set off on a large scale by the sinking of the three ships and Theodore Roosevelt's demand for immediate entry, was beginning to burgeon just at the time that Wilson was

[51] "The House Report," Whitehouse Papers, entries for March 30 and April 5, 1917.
[52] W. S. Churchill, *The World Crisis* (6 vols.), III, 234.

making his own decision. It was in fact greatly stimulated by accurate brief accounts in the newspapers of the Cabinet's discussion of March 20[53] and by the report of the President's proclamation calling Congress into special session on April 2. This call was widely interpreted as heralding a request for a declaration of war.[54] So also were reports of various preparations for hostilities that filled front pages of newspapers during the following week. Excitement was further fired by news on March 22 that the American tanker *Healdton* had been torpedoed without warning in the North Sea on the preceding day with the loss of twenty-one lives.[55]

Newspapers and periodicals, joined now by some religious journals, took the lead in whipping up enthusiasm for war,[56] but other spokesmen were not far behind. Six hundred eastern leaders of the Republican party, including Roosevelt, Root, and Hughes, met at the Union League Club in New York City on March 20 and adopted resolutions declaring among other things that "war now exists by the act of Germany."[57] Twelve thousand persons in Madison Square Garden on March 22 cheered wildly for war at a mass meeting called by the American Rights Committee.[58] William English Walling, Charles Edward Russell, Upton Sinclair, and virtually all other intellectual leaders in the Socialist party came out for hostilities on the following day.[59] These demands had their echo on the Plains, as Governor Arthur Capper of Kansas, heretofore an ardent opponent of preparedness and war, declared on March 24 that the United States had to fight to defend itself against Germany's "criminal" and "murderous assaults."[60] Many ministers in New York City seconded Capper's demand in sermons on March 25.[61] President John Grier Hibben of Princeton University refused to permit the pacifist, David Starr Jordan, former president of Stanford University, to speak on the Princeton campus.

[53] *New York Times,* March 21, 1917.
[54] *ibid.,* March 22, 1917.
[55] *ibid.,* March 23, 1917; Consul F. W. Mahin to the Secretary of State, March 22 and 23, 1917, *Foreign Relations, 1917, Supplement 1,* pp. 183, 185.
[56] See the review of press opinion in "A 'State of War' with Germany," *Literary Digest,* LIV (March 31, 1917), 881-882; also *Congregationalist and Christian World,* CII (March 22, 1917), 371-372; New York *World,* March 21, 1917; *New York Times,* March 22, 1917; *New Republic,* x (March 24, 1917), 210-211; Chicago *Standard,* LXIV (March 31, 1917), 899.
[57] *New York Times,* March 21, 1917.
[58] *ibid.,* March 23, 1917.
[59] New York *World,* March 24, 1917.
[60] *New York Times,* March 25, 1917.
[61] *ibid.,* March 26, 1917.

Jordan spoke instead in the First Presbyterian Church on March 26 but was heckled and booed by undergraduates when he criticized President Wilson.[62] Former Secretary of War Henry L. Stimson and Frederic R. Coudert, a New York lawyer, set out on April 1 on a two-week speaking tour of the Middle West and Far West to stir support for universal military training.[63] Irate citizens in Thermopolis, Wyoming, hanged a stranger on April 2 when he shouted "Hoch der Kaiser!" in a saloon. He was cut down before dead, forced to kiss the flag, and run out of town.[64] "The prospect for our country is gloomy," one southern agrarian radical commented. "The advocates of preparedness have won their fight. The metropolitan newspapers have created a sentiment that seems to be sweeping the White House like a cyclone. God alone knows what will be the outcome."[65]

The most impressive evidences of spreading popular determination to get on with war came on March 31. Thousands of persons paraded and demonstrated in Independence Square in Philadelphia, and the Progressive, Senator Hiram Johnson of California, spoke from the same platform with the Old Guard leader, Senator Boies Penrose of Pennsylvania, in demanding vindication of national rights. Another parade in Chicago was followed by a mass meeting at which Governor Frank O. Lowden and others spoke. And mass meetings in Boston, Denver, and Manchester, New Hampshire, echoed sentiments that seemed to be coursing over the continent.[66]

It was also the moment of direst crisis for leaders in the peace movement, and they rallied in one final effort to halt the inexorable course of events. Eugene V. Debs, speaking for the majority of the Socialist party at Cooper Union in New York City on March 7, said that he would rather be shot as a traitor than "go to war for Wall Street."[67] Benjamin C. Marsh said two days later at Carnegie Hall that workers, if armed, would march on Washington and restore the government to the people.[68] Bryan sent a more moderate appeal to members of the House and Senate and published it in the newspapers on March 30.[69]

[62] New York *World*, March 26, 1917; *New York Times*, March 27, 1917.
[63] *ibid.*, April 2, 1917.
[64] *ibid.*, April 3, 1917.
[65] J. K. Vardaman to W. J. Bryan, March 31, 1917, Bryan Papers, LC.
[66] *New York Times*, April 1 and 2, 1917.
[67] *ibid.*, March 8, 1917.
[68] *ibid.*, March 10, 1917.
[69] W. J. Bryan to members of the Senate and House of Representatives, March 28, 1917, copy in the Walsh Papers; *New York Times*, March 30, 1917.

Leaders in the Emergency Peace Federation carried the heaviest burdens in this desperate campaign. They sent out "Twelve Apostles of Peace" on March 9 to hold mass meetings, in spite of heckling and harassment by police, in many cities.[70] They devised a new peace plan—submission of German-American disputes to a joint high commission or a conference of neutrals—and publicized it in full-page advertisements in the *New York Times* and other newspapers on March 29.[71] Finally, they deluged Wilson with letters, petitions, proposals, and requests for interviews.[72] As David Starr Jordan, one of the new Apostles of Peace, reported:

"We have been doing the best we knew to make known to the President and Congressmen alternatives to war. There would be no difficulty in the matter if the people concerned really wanted peace. Meanwhile, it is very evident that the Wall St. people are running this thing in their own interest, and that the thousands of conscientious men who think we . . . [should] do something for France or England are mere flies on the wheel by the side of the great prospects of having Uncle Sam endorse billions of European bonds and throw his money with Morgan & Company into the bottomless pit of war. . . . The Germans have behaved like sin, for such is the nature of war,—but the intolerance and tyranny with which we are being pushed into war far eclipses [*sic*] the riotous methods which threw the Kaiser off his feet and brought on the crash in 1914."[73]

Other pacifists rushed to the ramparts with new appeals. Amos Pinchot and Owen R. Lovejoy formed an American Committee on War Finance on March 30 to agitate for higher income taxes and confiscation of all net incomes exceeding $100,000 a year if war came, but in the conviction, as Pinchot said, that rich men would stop demanding war if they knew they would have to pay for it.[74] The American Union Against Militarism published a full-page statement in the *New York Times* on March 29 demanding continuance of armed neutrality and further efforts to end the war, and warning that partici-

---

[70] *ibid.*, March 10, 24, 25, and 30, 1917.

[71] *ibid.*, March 29, 1917.

[72] Lella Faye Secor to J. P. Tumulty, March 16, 1917, Wilson Papers; D. S. Jordan to W. W., March 17, 1917, *ibid.*; D. S. Jordan *et al.* to W. W., March 23, 1917, *ibid.*; J. F. Moors and D. S. Jordan to W. W., March 24, 1917, *ibid.*; L. P. Lochner to W. W., March 27, 1917, *ibid.*; J. E. Milholland to W. W., March 25, 1917, *ibid.*

[73] D. S. Jordan to W. Kent, April 1, 1917, the Papers of William Kent, Yale University Library.

[74] New York *World*, March 31, 1917; *New York Times*, April 1 and 2, 1917.

pation would mean the end of democracy at home. German-American editors and leaders were generally discreetly silent.

We can only guess what the great masses of people, who said nothing in print and left no records of their sentiments, felt and thought. One reporter, Edward G. Lowry, who made a two-week trip through Kansas and Missouri in the latter half of March, told Colonel House that the people of those states did not want war but would follow the President. Most Missourians, he said, did not seem to know what the war was all about.[75] We can be confident in making only one very crude generalization—that articulate Americans were profoundly divided up to the very end of American neutrality, and that organized peace activity and visible signs of peace sentiment were nearly as strong, if not fully as strong, as organized war activity and signs of war sentiment. As Oswald Garrison Villard wisely wrote to the president of the American Rights Committee: "Must we not recognize the fact that the nation as well as the city [New York] is hopelessly divided on this issue? If we do not go to war, your friends will be bitterly unhappy and think we are disgraced; and if we go to war, my friends will be bitterly unhappy and feel that we are disgraced; and between them there will be a great body of pro-Germans who will be still unhappier."[76]

Wilson had meanwhile been gathering materials and his thoughts for his message to Congress. Colonel House, who came on his own initiative to Washington on March 27, found the President thinking about little else. Wilson, House wrote in his diary, "had just finished with the Cabinet meeting, which he now holds in the afternoon. He was not well and complained of a headache. We went to his study and discussed matters, particularly his forthcoming message.

"The President asked whether I thought he should ask Congress to declare war, or whether he should say that a state of war exists and ask them for the necessary means to carry it on. I advised the latter. I was afraid of an acrimonious debate if he puts it up to Congress to declare war. . . .

"I said it was not as difficult a situation as many he had already successfully met, but that it was one for which he was not well fitted. He admitted this and said he did not believe he was fitted for the Presidency under such conditions. I thought he was too refined, too

[75] House Diary, March 31, 1917.
[76] O. G. Villard to G. H. Putnam, March 26, 1917, Villard Papers.

civilized, too intellectual, too cultivated not to see the incongruity and absurdity of war. It needs a man of coarser fibre and one less a philosopher than the President, to conduct a brutal, vigorous, and successful war.

"I made him feel, as Mrs. Wilson told me later, that he was not up against so difficult a proposition as he had imagined. . . . I thought, however, he ought to change Daniels and Baker; that they were good men in peace time but did not fit in with war. That even if they were fit, the country did not believe them to be, and the mistakes that were sure to be made would be laid upon his shoulders because of them. I felt that he had taken a gamble that there would be no war and had lost, and the country would hold it to his discredit unless he prosecuted the war successfully, and he could not do this unless he had better timber than was generally thought to be in the War and Navy Departments. . . . He listened with a kindly and sympathetic attention and while he argued with me upon many of the points, he did it dispassionately."[77]

The President and Colonel House went to Keith's Theater that evening. They resumed their conversation at about noon on the following day, March 28, after Wilson had returned from golf with Mrs. Wilson and worked briefly in his office. "We talked further of his message," House wrote in his diary. "Since last night he had made a memorandum of the subjects he thought proper to incorporate and which I approved, for most of them were suggestions I have made from time to time both verbally and through letters. . . . My purpose was, and is, to break down the German Government by 'building a fire' back of it within Germany. The President agreed to incorporate the thought that the United States would not be willing to join a league of peace with an autocracy as a member. That is the main note I have urged him to strike, that is, this is a war for democracy and it is a war for the German people as well as for other nations."[78] House returned to New York that afternoon. "It's all right," he said when Polk called him by telephone on the following day.[79]

Wilson worked on his message when he could find the time during the busy days between March 29 and April 1. Only twice, during the morning of March 30 and the afternoon of the following day, was he able to find any considerable stretch of free time. The Chief Clerk

[77] House Diary, March 27, 1917.
[78] *ibid.*, March 28, 1917.
[79] Lansing Desk Diary, March 29, 1917.

of the White House Executive Office has left an intimate glimpse of the President on March 31, as follows:

"The President and Mrs. Wilson played golf this morning. When Hoover came over to the office this afternoon he said, 'If the President is writing as he feels Germany is going to get Hell in the address to Congress. I never knew him to be more peevish. He's out of sorts, doesn't feel well, and has a headache. Soon after lunch he went to the study, leaving word that he desired quiet and didn't want to be disturbed. Mrs. Wilson left the house to call on some friends. I thought some noise downstairs might annoy the President, so I sent one of the ushers upstairs to close the study door. 'Who told you to close the door,' asked the President in a sharp tone. 'Mr. Hoover, Sir,' replied the usher. 'Tell Hoover,' said the President, 'that I don't want it closed—all I want is quiet.' He's certainly getting all the quiet he wants now—all of us are walking tiptoe and speaking in whispers.' "

"As usual, the President is sitting before his own little typewriting machine, and slowly but accurately and neatly, typing a message which will probably be his greatest State paper."[80]

Wilson attended divine services at Central Presbyterian Church on Sunday, April 1, and took a long drive with Mrs. Wilson in the afternoon. He worked in his study after dinner and apparently completed the address at about ten o'clock, for he called the Secretary of State then to check on a passage relating to armed neutrality and to ask him to prepare a war resolution along the lines of the request in his message.[81] He repeated this request in a letter immediately afterward.[82]

The President sent his message to the Public Printer for a reading copy before breakfast on the following morning, April 2. He had typed it on his Hammond portable as he had his other important state papers. He played golf with Mrs. Wilson in Virginia after breakfast until a little after eleven. Lansing came to the White House at 11:30 bringing a copy of the war resolution that he had drafted. Wilson approved it and asked the Secretary to show it to leaders on the Hill.

About 1,500 demonstrators from the Emergency Peace Federation had descended on the Capitol, and groups of them were in the corridors to plead with congressmen and senators when they arrived that same morning. One of the pacifists exchanged blows with Senator Lodge and was badly beaten by Capitol police afterward. "At my age there is

[80] Brahany Diary, March 31, 1917.
[81] R. Lansing, *War Memoirs*, p. 238.
[82] W. W., to R. Lansing, April 1, 1917, *The Lansing Papers*, I, 634.

a certain aspect of folly about the whole thing," Lodge wrote, "and yet I am glad that I hit him. The Senators all appeared to be perfectly delighted with my having done so."[83] The Sixty-fifth Congress met at noon, and the Democrats, even though they were a minority, elected Champ Clark Speaker again by a vote of 217 to 205, because six of the eight assorted independent members voted for Clark and five Republicans refused to vote for their leader, James R. Mann, an outspoken pro-German from Chicago.[84]

Wilson had lunch with his cousins, Edward T. Brown and John A. Wilson. He had planned to go before Congress at two in the afternoon, but Mann delayed organization of the House by insisting on roll call votes to elect committee chairmen in the hope of capturing a few for his party. Wilson spent most of the afternoon with Colonel House, who had arrived that morning, waiting for word that Congress was ready to receive him. "The President," House recorded, "was apparently calm during the day, but, as a matter of fact, I could see signs of nervousness." Wilson read his war message, and House suggested deleting a phrase which went something like "until the German people have a government we can trust." It looked too much as if Wilson were inciting revolution, House said, and Wilson agreed. "I asked him why he had not shown the Cabinet his address," House continued in this diary account of the conversation. "He replied that, if he had, every man in it would have had some suggestion to make and it would have been picked to pieces if he had heeded their criticism. He said he preferred to keep it to himself and take the responsibility. I feel that he does his Cabinet an injustice. He should not humiliate them to such an extent. I have noticed recently that he holds a tighter rein over his Cabinet and that he is impatient of any initiative on their part."[85] House did not note the additional fact that Wilson had also not invited him to the White House and sought his counsel while making the decision for war and preparing the message.

The afternoon hours passed slowly. Word finally came that the House would complete its organization at about five o'clock, and Wilson replied that he would come at eight-thirty that night. Then, at 4:40 p.m., he walked to the Navy Department and, a few minutes later, to Lansing's office. Lansing by this time had discussed the war resolu-

[83] H. C. Lodge to T. Roosevelt, April 4, 1917, Roosevelt Papers.

[84] *Congressional Record*, 65th Cong., 1st sess., pp. 107-108; New York *World*, April 3, 1917.

[85] House Diary, April 2, 1917.

tion with Senator Swanson, Senator P. C. Knox of Pennsylvania, and Representative Flood. They had suggested a few minor changes, and Wilson said that they were all right.[86] The Secretary of State, moreover, insisted that the President should not go to the Capitol without an armed guard. Wilson scoffed at the suggestion and made light of the danger of violence, but Lansing made arrangements for a cavalry escort with Baker.[87]

Wilson had dinner with members of the family and Colonel House at six-thirty. "We talked," House wrote, "of everything excepting the matter in hand." Mrs. Wilson, Colonel House, and members of the family left for the Capitol at 8:10. Wilson, accompanied by Tumulty, Grayson, and an army aide, left at 8:20 escorted by a troop of cavalry. The President entered the packed and cheering chamber of the House of Representatives at 8:32 p.m.

He began, speaking in a conversational tone, without gestures, with a matter-of-fact review of events since the rupture of relations with Germany. It had become all too evident since then, he went on, that the German submarine war against commerce was warfare against all mankind. He had earlier thought that armed neutrality would suffice to protect American lives and shipping. But armed neutrality, it now appeared, was not feasible. Here Wilson repeated the explanation that he had made in his letter of March 31 to Matthew Hale. Armed neutrality, he went on, was ineffectual at best. In the present circumstances and in the face of German pretensions it was worse than ineffectual: It was likely to cause the fighting that it was meant to prevent, and it was practically certain to draw the country into war without either the privileges or effectiveness that went with belligerency. "There is," Wilson continued, "one choice we cannot make, we are incapable of making: we will not choose the path of submission and suffer the most sacred rights of our Nation and our people to be ignored or violated." Chief Justice White, who sat in front of the Speaker's stand with other members of the Supreme Court, dropped his hat at the word "submission" and led applause that roared through the chamber like a storm.

"With a profound sense of the solemn and even tragical character of the step I am taking," Wilson continued, "and of the grave responsibilities which it involves, but in unhesitating obedience to what I deem my constitutional duty, I advise that the Congress declare the recent

---

[86] See Lansing's comments on the draft printed in *The Lansing Papers*, I, 635.
[87] R. Lansing, *War Memoirs*, pp. 238-239.

course of the Imperial German Government to be in fact nothing less than war against the government and people of the United States; that it formally accept the status of belligerent which has thus been thrust upon it; and that it take immediate steps not only to put the country in a more thorough state of defense but also to exert all its power and employ all its resources to bring the Government of the German Empire to terms and end the war." The Chief Justice began cheering mid-way in this paragraph, and virtually the entire body were on their feet yelling wildly by the time Wilson had completed it.

Belligerency, Wilson went on, would mean intimate cooperation with and financial support of other governments at war with Germany. It would require mobilization of resources at home and expansion of the armed forces, preferably through universal liability to service— Wilson's first public endorsement of universal military training. It would demand heavier taxes. He would make specific recommendations on all these matters.

Wilson then turned to the larger issues of the war, saying "let us be very clear, and make very clear to all the world what our motives and our objects are." He had, he said, exactly the same things in mind as when he addressed the Senate on January 22 and the two houses on February 3 and 23. America's object now, as then, was to vindicate the principles of peace and justice and establish a concert of power among the really free peoples of the world to defend them. Americans had no quarrel with the German people, Wilson said, echoing House's words. They had only feelings of sympathy and friendship toward them. The German people were not responsible for this war. It was caused by little groups of ambitious men accustomed to using their fellow-men as pawns and tools. Wilson was careful at this point not to say that these ambitious men were all Germans and Austrians.

"A steadfast concert for peace," the President added, again echoing House's and Lansing's sentiments, "can never be maintained except by a partnership of democratic nations. No autocratic government could be trusted to keep faith within it or observe its covenants." Hence the assurance for the future peace of the world that had come with the recent wonderful news from Petrograd. The Russian people, democratic at heart and in all their intimate relationships, had thrown off an aristocracy that was not Russian in origin, character, or purpose. The "great, generous Russian people have been added in all their naïve majesty and might to the forces that are fighting for freedom in the world, for justice, and for peace. Here is a fit partner for a League of Honor."

The Prussian autocracy, Wilson continued, abruptly changing the subject, had given ample evidence of its hostility to the United States by filling unsuspecting communities and even offices of the government with spies and saboteurs. "That it means to stir up enemies against us at our very doors the intercepted note to the German Minister at Mexico City is eloquent evidence." Americans accepted this challenge of hostile purpose because they finally knew that the German government was a natural foe of liberty. "We are glad," Wilson went on, ". . . to fight thus for the ultimate peace of the world and for the liberation of its peoples, the German peoples included: for the rights of nations great and small and the privilege of men everywhere to choose their way of life and of obedience. The world must be made safe for democracy." Senator John Sharp Williams broke the momentum of this passage by applauding loudly, alone at first. The whole body joined the Mississippian as soon as they understood the significance of the phrase. "Its peace must be planted upon the tested foundations of political liberty," Wilson then continued. "We have no selfish ends to serve. We desire no conquest, no dominion. We seek no indemnities for ourselves, no material compensation for the sacrifices we shall freely make. We are but one of the champions of the rights of mankind. We shall be satisfied when those rights have been made as secure as the faith and the freedom of nations can make them."

Americans, Wilson reiterated, had no enmity against the German people. They were the sincere friends of the German people and desired nothing so much as the early re-establishment of cordial relations with them. Americans could prove that friendship in their actions toward the millions of men and women of German birth and sympathy in their midst, and they would prove it toward all who were loyal to America in its hour of testing. Disloyalty would be suppressed with a stern hand; but it would not have the support of the overwhelming majority of German Americans. Wilson concluded:

"It is a distressing and oppressive duty, Gentlemen of the Congress, which I have performed in thus addressing you. There are, it may be, many months of fiery trial and sacrifice ahead of us. It is a fearful thing to lead this great peaceful people into war, into the most terrible and disastrous of all wars, civilization itself seeming to be in the balance. But the right is more precious than peace, and we shall fight for the things which we have always carried nearest our hearts,—for democracy, for the right of those who submit to authority to have a voice in their own Governments, for the rights and liberties of small nations, for a universal dominion of right by such a concert of free peoples as shall bring peace and safety to all nations and make the world itself at last free. To such a task we can dedicate our lives and our fortunes, everything that we are and everything that we have, with the pride of those who know that the day has come when America is privileged to spend her blood and her might for the principles that gave her birth and happiness and the peace which she has treasured. God helping her, she can do no other."[88]

Wilson ended at 9:11, having spoken thirty-six minutes. The great crowd, overcome by the peroration, was on its feet, cheering and waving flags. Senator Lodge shook Wilson's hand warmly, saying, "Mr. President, you have expressed in the loftiest manner possible the sentiments of the American people." Senator La Follette, chewing gum and smiling sardonically, stood motionless with arms folded tight and high on his chest.[89]

Few persons in the chamber ever forgot the electrical drama of that evening or the President's dignity, solemnity, and rhetorical power. "From the moment that he entered the auditorium up to the time that he passed out into the corridors of the Capitol," Lansing wrote afterward, "he was the master of the situation. . . . One who heard that impressive address and saw the dignity and sternness of the leader as he stood on the rostrum, recognized him as a leader of men than whom there was no greater within the boundaries of the United States."[90]

One poet put these feelings into verse, as follows:

> This is the man they deemed of languid blood,
>   A schoolman versed in books, who, Hamlet-like,
>   Showed but heat-flashes powerless to strike—
> His resolution blighted in the bud.
>
> They knew him not—nor we, who trusted him.
>   See! how his brooding purpose, taking form,
>   Falls like swift lightning from long-gathered storm,
> While fateful thunder shakes the round world's rim.
>
> .   .   .   .   .
>
> Beleaguered Liberty takes heart again,
>   Hearing afar the rescuing bugles blow;
>   And even in the strongholds of the foe
> His name becomes the whispered hope of men.[91]

---

[88] *War and Peace*, I, 6-16.
[89] *New York Times*, April 3, 1917.
[90] R. Lansing, *War Memoirs*, p. 243.
[91] Robert Underwood Johnson, "The Leader," *New York Times*, April 7, 1917.

Wilson returned at once to the White House. "The President, Mrs. Wilson, Margaret [Wilson], and I foregathered in the Oval Room and talked it over as families are prone to do after some eventful occasion," Colonel House wrote in his diary. House remarked that Wilson had "taken a position as to policies which no other statesman had yet assumed." Wilson, House wrote, seemed surprised by this remark and said that he thought that perhaps Webster, Lincoln, and Gladstone had announced the same principles. "I could see," House added, "the President was relieved that the tension was over and the die cast."[92]

Tumulty, in a much-quoted passage in his book, later wrote that Wilson went with him to the Cabinet room after their return from the White House. "Think what it was they were applauding," Tumulty remembered the President saying. "My message to-day was a message of death for our young men. How strange it seems to applaud that." Then Wilson allegedly went on in a long monologue, saying that he had realized the futility of neutrality from the beginning but had not been able to move faster than public opinion would permit. He had, Wilson allegedly added, been cruelly misunderstood and maligned. Then he read a letter from an admiring friend. "That man," the President allegedly said, "understood me and sympathized." As he said this, Tumulty tells us, he wiped away great tears; laying his head on the table, he sobbed as if he was a child.[93]

It is a good story, but it should not be repeated without the admonition that it is too preposterous to be true. Tumulty did return with the President's party to the White House, but there is no evidence that he remained, and it seems most improbable that Wilson left family and guests for a private conversation with Tumulty. Wilson was not in the habit of wallowing in self-pity, and he was not emotionally a child who burst into tears at the thought of being misunderstood. He surely did not utter the words that Tumulty put in his mouth, except, perhaps, the remark about the irony of the applause.

All public reactions indicated that the President had voiced the deepest thoughts and convictions and highest resolves of a united people. "In the solemn words uttered by Woodrow Wilson last night," Frank Cobb said, "rests the hope of democracy and the hope of man-

[92] House Diary, April 2, 1917.
[93] J. P. Tumulty, *Woodrow Wilson As I Know Him*, pp. 256-259.

kind."[94] An editor who had excoriated Wilson more than once agreed, saying, "No praise can be too high for the words and the purposes of the President. Never in all the long period in which he has directed American policy has he seemed to come nearer to the ideal of the American people, the ideal of a President who should lead."[95] "How vastly more impressive and conclusive this arraignment of German aggression becomes," a midwestern editor added, "from the fact that the President has so steadfastly held to a patient and forbearing course! How incomparably fewer will be the voices of protest than if he had been among the raging, vituperative ones from the first!"[96] The paean of praise continued in private letters that poured into the White House[97] and in newspapers in England and France. As the stately *Times* of London said: "The cause in which America draws the sword and the grounds on which the President justifies the momentous step he has taken are auguries that the final outcome will be for the happiness and welfare of mankind. We doubt if in all history a great community has ever been summoned to war on grounds so largely ideal."[98] News of the President's message evoked a storm of applause in Tauride Palace in Petrograd.[99] Only German editors and publicists had bitter, carping, and sad words to say.[100]

[94] New York *World*, April 3, 1917.   [95] *New York Tribune*, April 3, 1917.

[96] *Indianapolis Star*, April 3, 1917. For other significant editorial comment, see, e. g., the *New York Times, Springfield* (Mass.) *Republican, Providence Journal, Boston Post, Philadelphia Public Ledger*, Baltimore *Sun*, and *Chicago Herald*, all dated April 3, 1917; New York *Nation*, CIV (April 5, 1917), 388; *Congregationalist and Christian World*, CII (April 12, 1917), 465-466; *The Independent*, XC (April 14, 1917), 98; and "Who Willed American Participation," *New Republic*, X (April 14, 1917), 308-310.

[97] e. g., N. D. Baker to W. W., April 3, 1917, Wilson Papers; W. G. McAdoo to W. W., April 3, 1917, *ibid.*; John Sharp Williams to W. W., April 3, 1917, *ibid.*; W. Lippmann to W. W., April 3, 1917, *ibid.*; and especially H. Hoover to W. W., April 4, 1917, *ibid.*

[98] London *Times*, April 4, 1917; also London *Westminster Gazette*, April 3, 1917; London *Evening Star*, April 3, 1917; *Manchester Guardian*, April 4, 1917; London *Daily Express*, April 4, 1917; London *Daily Telegraph*, April 4, 1917; London *Spectator*, CXVIII (April 7, 1917), 401; G. Clemenceau in *L'Homme Enchaîné* of Paris, April 5, 1917; A. Capus in Paris *Figaro*, April 4, 1917; Paris *Le Temps*, April 4 and 5, 1917.

[99] *New York Times*, April 5, 1917.

[100] e. g., *Berliner Tageblatt*, morning edn., April 3, 1917, morning edn., April 4, 1917; *Berliner Lokal-Anzeiger*, morning edn., April 4, 1917; *Frankfurter Zeitung*, evening edn., April 4, 1917; Berlin *Deutsche Tageszeitung*, morning edn., April 4, 1917; Berlin *Vorwärts*, April 4, 1917; Berlin *Vossische Zeitung*, morning edn., April 4, 1917; *Kölnische Zeitung*, noon edn., April 3, 1917; *Kölnische Volkszeitung*, morning edn., April 4, 1917.

At home there were deep currents of opposition underneath the façade of unity. A straw ballot conducted in Sheboygan, Wisconsin, allegedly one of the most Germanic cities in the United States, yielded 4,112 votes against and seventeen in favor of war. Another straw ballot in Manitowoc, Wisconsin, returned 1,460 votes against and fifteen in favor of a war resolution. These were as fair samplings of German-American opinion as we are likely to find.[101] Socialists in Carnegie Hall during the evening of April 2 hissed and hooted when the chairman announced that Wilson had asked for a declaration of war. One of the speakers, Winter Russell, brought half the audience to its feet by declaring, "Whether there is a revolution in Germany or not, we need one here."[102] Antiwar congressmen and senators were deluged with appeals from persons in all walks of life begging them to vote against a war resolution.[103]

There never was any doubt, however, what Congress would do, especially after receipt of news on April 2 and 5 that the armed American merchantman *Aztec* and unarmed American steamer *Missourian* had been sunk, both without warning and with loss of twelve American lives in the first instance.[104] Senator La Follette objected to immediate consideration when Martin of Virginia introduced the war resolution on April 3. Martin warned that the Senate would not be permitted to do any other business until the resolution had been adopted, and the body adjourned to wait out the day that the rules permitted a senator to postpone discussion of a war resolution.[105]

The Senate began debate on the measure at ten o'clock on the follow-

[101] Both straw ballots were reported in the New York *World*, April 4, 1917.

[102] *New York Times*, April 3, 1917.

[103] The Kitchin Papers at the University of North Carolina deserve special study for the light that they shed on public opinion on the war resolution in a state that had virtually no German Americans. Telegrams and letters in this collection show on their face an overwhelming sentiment in North Carolina against war. Opponents of war were obviously more active in writing to Kitchin than advocates of intervention, but it was certainly not without some significance that hundreds of North Carolinians, many of whom were leaders in their communities, wrote to Kitchin after he voted against the war resolution, and that nine out of ten of these correspondents approved his action. Senator La Follette, in his speech against the war resolution, analyzed the letters and telegrams that he had received, along with numerous straw ballots taken in various parts of the country. They all showed opinion about ten to one against war. Belle C. and Fola M. La Follette, *Robert M. La Follette* (2 vols.), I, 658-659. This and other evidence does not by any means prove that a majority of Americans opposed the war resolution—or approved it. It simply shows that opposition to war was still very wide and deep.

[104] *New York Times*, April 3 and 6, 1917.

[105] *ibid.*, April 4, 1917.

ing morning, April 4. It proceeded all day long and into the night, not because there was a filibuster but because most senators wanted to affirm their support of the resolution. La Follette spoke for four hours criticizing Wilson's policies as unneutral and declaring once again that the vast majority of Americans did not want to go to war. George W. Norris of Nebraska made the bitterest speech, saying, "We are going into war upon the command of gold. . . . I feel that we are about to put the dollar sign upon the American flag."[106] Senator Reed of Missouri broke in to say that this was near to treason. Senator Stone, nearly overcome with grief, cried out at the end of his speech, "I shall vote against this mistake, to prevent which, God helping me, I would gladly lay down my life." These words were later graven on his tombstone. Only Vardaman and Gronna also spoke against the resolution. It carried by a vote of eighty-two to six at eleven minutes past eleven o'clock that night.[107]

The House of Representatives had been biding its time until the Senate acted. The foreign affairs committee reported the war resolution, in the form in which the foreign relations committee had approved it, to the House on April 4, and debate began at 10:35 on the following morning. It proceeded all through the day under a rule limiting speeches to twenty minutes each, because about one hundred members wanted to record their sentiments for the sake of posterity and constituents. Some twenty congressmen, led by Majority Leader Kitchin, spoke against the resolution. The House finally approved it at 3:12 in the morning of April 6, Good Friday, by a vote of 373 to fifty. Nine out of Wisconsin's eleven representatives were among the minority.[108]

Speaker Clark signed the resolution at once, the Vice President, at 12:14 p.m. the following afternoon. Wilson was at lunch with Mrs. Wilson and his cousin, Helen Woodrow Bones, when a messenger brought the document to the White House. He signed it in the lobby at 1:18. Rudolph Forster, an usher, rushed to the Executive Offices and announced the news to reporters. A naval officer ran out of the Executive Offices to signal the news to another naval officer standing at a window in the Navy Department. Formal notice that the United

[106] For an important answer, see "Who Willed American Participation," *New Republic*, x (April 14, 1917), 308-310.

[107] Lane of Oregon joined the five senators who had spoken against the war resolution in voting against it. The eight absent senators all favored the measure. *New York Times*, April 5, 1917; *Congressional Record*, 65th Cong., 1st sess., pp. 200-261.

[108] *ibid.*, pp. 306-413; New York *World*, April 6, 1917; *New York Times*, April 6, 1917.

States was at war went by telegraph and wireless a few minutes later to war vessels, naval stations, army posts, and American diplomatic missions. The President signed a proclamation announcing the state of war shortly afterward and then went to Cabinet meeting at 2:30 to discuss measures to get the war effort under way.[109]

"For all time," Frank Cobb wrote, "April 6 will remain a mighty day in the annals of the United States, a day on which was consummated the most far-reaching policy to which democracy has ever consecrated itself. The old isolation is finished. We are no longer aloof from Europe, we are no longer aloof from the rest of the world. For weal or woe, whatever happens now concerns us, and from none of it can be withheld the force of our influence."[110]

[109] *ibid.*, April 7, 1917.
[110] New York *World*, April 7, 1917.

APPENDIX

New Light on the Zimmermann Telegram

FRIEDRICH KATZ, *Deutschland, Diaz und die mexikanische Revolution, die deutsche Politik in Mexiko 1870-1920* (Berlin: Deutscher Verlag der Wissenschaften, 1964), pp. 337-473, has recently shed much important new light on the Zimmermann telegram.

Katz, of the Institute for General History of the Humboldt University in Berlin, shows that the author of the idea of a German-Mexican alliance was one von Kemnitz, Latin-American specialist in the Foreign Office. Carranza, in November 1916, had made a formal suggestion that Mexico and Germany cooperate, going so far as to offer submarine bases to the Germans. This feeler had been politely declined, but von Kemnitz pressed for its acceptance once the decision for an all-out submarine campaign had been made. Von Kemnitz then drafted what would soon be called the Zimmermann telegram and, against the opposition of some of his colleagues, persuaded the Foreign Secretary to send it.

The Mexican government neither rejected the German offer out of hand nor considered it to be wholly chimerical. Carranza still feared the return of American troops and hoped to be able to make trouble in the southwestern United States if renewed American intervention did occur. Thus Carranza cautiously rejected the German proposal once it had been published. It was renewed in May 1917 by an agent of the German General Staff, and Carranza then replied that Mexico would observe a strict neutrality. Katz discounts contemporary American charges that Carranza had been paid by German agents, but he produces evidence that some of the First Chief's generals cooperated closely with German intelligence agents and warned that they would turn Carranza out if he cooperated with the United States in her war against the Reich.

Dr. Katz, in a letter to the present writer on March 22, 1965, made the following additional comments, which are quoted with his kind permission:

"I believe you are right when you speak of a German conspiracy of silence about the Zimmermann Telegram. Of the three questions you have raised in your letter: Who thought the Zimmermann Telegram up? Did Bethmann-Hollweg know about it? Was it ever discussed (in 1917) at Supreme Headquarters? I would say that the first question can be answered, the second cannot, while the third can be inferred.

"The man who thought up the telegram was the 'Ostasienreferent' of the German Foreign Office, v. Kemnitz. This fact is confirmed by at least three different sources: A report by the representative of the German Foreign Office at Supreme Headquarters, an investigation carried out by the German Foreign Office in November 1918 and the reports of the Austrian Ambassador in Berlin. But this fact is of less interest than the answer to the question of who else, besides Zimmermann, participated in drafting the Telegram, or at least approved it before it was sent. The first thing I sought to establish was whether Bethmann-Hollweg was in any way involved. After finding nothing about this either in the files of the German Foreign Office in Bonn or in those located in Potsdam I had pinned great hopes on the files of the Reichs Chancellery which are in Potsdam. I went through them very carefully and found absolutely nothing. The only mention of Bethmann-Hollweg in relation to the Zimmermann Telegram I have ever seen is a very unreliable piece of evidence which I located after my book was already in print. It is an anonymous article in the Nürnberger Nachrichten of the 25th of October 1918. It states that the real author of the Telegram was Kemnitz, who suggested the whole thing to Zimmermann. The latter sent the telegram without consulting Bethmann-Hollweg who was only informed later. Such newspaper reports, written at a time when everyone who was or had been in power in Germany was trying to escape responsibility for having contributed to the entrance of the United States into the war, are highly unreliable. Still, the anonymous author obviously had some knowledge of the real story of the Telegram since up to that time Kemnitz's role was completely unknown to the public.

"Was the Supreme Command consulted before the Telegram was sent? This question cannot be answered on the basis of the evidence which I have seen up to now.

"What can be assumed is that from March 1917 on, the Supreme Command had a positive attitude towards Zimmermann's Mexican plan. This can be inferred from two facts. One is a message from the 'Sektion Politik des Grossen Generalstabs' to the Foreign Office dated March 8, 1917, in which the Supreme Command 'nach Rücksprache mit Chef des Generalstabes des Feldheeres und nach Benehmen mit Admiralstab der Marine' declared itself ready to allot 30,000 rifles etc. to Mexico. I consider of even greater importance for determining the attitude of the Supreme Command towards Zimmermann's plans the fact that his second proposal of alliance was brought to Mexico and presented to Carranza by the representative of the Supreme Command, Delmar. If, in spite of the fiasco of the original Zimmermann Telegram the Supreme Command was ready to participate in a renewed effort of this type it must have been a warm supporter of Zimmermann's projects.

"All these facts show the attitude of Supreme Headquarters after the publication of the Zimmermann Telegram. They do not answer the question of whether the Supreme Command was consulted before the Telegram was sent or not.

"Zimmermann does not seem to have asked the Kaiser's opinion, either, before sending the dispatch, but Wilhelm seems to have had something to do with it. That is what I gather from Zimmermann's remark to the Kaiser during the discussion of the affair. 'Der Staatssekretär betonte,' the Austrian Ambassador in Berlin reported, 'es sei selbstverständliche Pflicht gewesen zu trachten, sich für den Kriegsfall die mexikanische Hilfe zu sichern, was ihm ja der Kaiser selbst seinerzeit nahegelegt habe.' This implies that Zimmermann and Wilhelm talked the problem over in a general way, probably some time before the Telegram was conceived. Since Wilhelm had shown a lively interest in Mexico from 1898 onward and seems to have had great illusions concerning Japanese-Mexican relations this is not surprising.

"Is it conceivable at all that Zimmermann should have sent his proposal without consulting either Bethmann-Hollweg or the Supreme Command? I believe it possible for two reasons:

"1.) In Zimmermann's eyes his proposal was much less than what its contents imply. It was not, as I have tried to show, a real, definitive proposal of alliance as it was generally made out later. . . . [Here Dr. Katz quotes Zimmermann's testimony before the Reichstag Budget Committee on March 5, 1917.] Kemnitz later stated that the alliance would have been ratified only if Japan had participated.

"It is conceivable that Zimmermann would only have consulted Bethmann-Hollweg or Supreme Headquarters in the unlikely case that his proposal would have come up for ratification.

"2.) The fact that he had spoken of the project of a Mexican-German alliance with the Kaiser may have influenced Zimmermann not to consult either Bethmann-Hollweg or the Supreme Command."

In view of Dr. Katz's exhaustive research, not only in all extant German sources but also in Mexican archives, it would seem that he has said the final word about the Zimmermann telegram.

Bibliography of Sources and Works Cited[1]

The author wishes to acknowledge his indebtedness to the Yale University Library for permission to quote from the letters and Diary of Edward M. House; Miss Nancy Lane, for permission to quote from *The Letters of Franklin K. Lane*; E. P. Dutton & Co., Inc., for permission to quote from John L. Heaton, *Cobb of "The World"*; and Constable and Co., Ltd., for permission to quote from Stephen Gwynn (ed.), *The Letters and Friendships of Sir Cecil Spring Rice*.

MANUSCRIPTS

The Diary and Papers of Chandler P. Anderson, Library of Congress.

The Papers of Herbert Asquith, Bodleian Library, Oxford.

The Papers of Warren Worth Bailey, Princeton University Library.

The Papers of Newton D. Baker, Library of Congress.

The Ray Stannard Baker Collection of Wilsonia, Library of Congress.

"Bernstorff Wireless Despatches—1916," the Papers of Walter H. Page, Harvard University Library.

The Papers of Albert J. Beveridge, Library of Congress.

The Papers of Sir Robert L. Borden, Canadian Public Archives, Ottawa.

The Diary of Thomas W. Brahany, photographic copy in the Papers of Woodrow Wilson, Princeton University Library.

The Papers of Louis D. Brandeis, Law Library of the University of Louisville.

The Papers of William Jennings Bryan, Library of Congress.

The Papers of James, Viscount Bryce, Bodleian Library, Oxford.

The Papers of Arthur Bullard, Princeton University Library.

The Papers of Albert S. Burleson, Library of Congress.

The Papers of Austen Chamberlain, University of Birmingham Library.

The Papers of Josephus Daniels, Library of Congress.

The Papers of the Department of State, National Archives.

The Papers of John Grier Hibben, Princeton University Library.

The Diary and Papers of Edward M. House, Yale University Library.

The Papers of David F. Houston, Harvard University Library.

The Papers of William Kent, Yale University Library.

The Papers of John Maynard Keynes, Economics Library, Cambridge University.

The Papers of Claude Kitchin, University of North Carolina Library.

The Diary, Desk Diary, and Papers of Robert Lansing, Library of Congress.

---

[1] This bibliography includes *only* works and sources cited in the footnotes in this volume. For a survey of literature and sources dealing with the period 1916-1917, see Arthur S. Link, *Woodrow Wilson and the Progressive Era* (New York: Harper Torchbooks, 1963), pp. 283-314.

The Papers of Robert Lansing, Princeton University Library.

The Papers of William G. McAdoo, Library of Congress.

The Papers of Alfred, Lord Milner, New College Library, Oxford.

The Diary and Papers of Walter H. Page, Harvard University Library.

The Diary and Papers of Sir Horace Plunkett, Plunkett Foundation, London.

The Diary, Confidential Diary, and Papers of Frank L. Polk, Yale University Library.

The Papers of Theodore Roosevelt, Library of Congress.

The Papers of Elihu Root, Library of Congress.

The Charles L. Swem Collection of Wilsoniana, Princeton University Library.

The Papers of William Howard Taft, Library of Congress.

The Papers of Oswald Garrison Villard, Harvard University Library.

The Papers of Thomas J. Walsh, Library of Congress.

The Diary of Beatrice Webb, London School of Economics Library.

The Papers of J. Howard Whitehouse, the Bembridge School, Bembridge, Isle of Wight.

The Papers of William B. Wilson, Pennsylvania Historical Society, Philadelphia.

The Papers of Woodrow Wilson, Library of Congress.

The Lawrence C. Woods-Samuel J. Graham Correspondence, Princeton University Library.

The Papers of Lester H. Woolsey, Library of Congress.

PUBLIC DOCUMENTS

PUBLICATIONS OF THE UNITED STATES GOVERNMENT

Congressional Record, 64th Cong., 1st sess. through 65th Cong., 1st sess. Washington, 1916-1917.

Department of State. *Papers Relating to the Foreign Relations of the United States, 1916*. Washington, 1925.

Department of State. *Papers Relating to the Foreign Relations of the United States, 1916, Supplement, the World War*. Washington, 1929.

Department of State. *Papers Relating to the Foreign Relations of the United States, 1917*. Washington, 1926.

Department of State. *Papers Relating to the Foreign Relations of the United States, 1917, Supplement 1, the World War*. Washington, 1931.

Department of State. *Papers Relating to the Foreign Relations of the United States, 1917, Supplement 2, the World War*. 2 v., Washington, 1932.

Department of State. *Papers Relating to the Foreign Relations of the United States, The Lansing Papers, 1914-1920*. 2 v., Washington, 1939-1940.

Department of State. *Papers Relating to the Foreign Relations of the United States, 1918, Russia*. 3 v., Washington, 1931.

United States Senate. Special Committee on Investigation of the Munitions Industry. *Munitions Industry.* 74th Cong., 2d sess., Senate Report No. 944, Parts 5 and 6. Washington, 1936.

PUBLICATIONS OF FOREIGN GOVERNMENTS

[Germany] Reichstag Commission of Inquiry. *Official German Documents Relating to the World War.* 2 v., New York: Oxford University Press, 1923.

Mexican Foreign Office. *Diplomatic Dealings of the Constitutionalist Revolution in Mexico.* Mexico City: Imprenta Nacional, n. d.

[United Kingdom] *Parliamentary Debates*, Fifth Series, Vol. XXIII. London: H. M. Stationery Office, 1917.

CORRESPONDENCE, COLLECTED WORKS, AND DIARIES

Baker, Ray Stannard, and William E. Dodd (eds.). *The Public Papers of Woodrow Wilson, The New Democracy.* 2 v., New York: Harper & Brothers, 1926.

Baker, Ray Stannard, and William E. Dodd (eds.). *The Public Papers of Woodrow Wilson, War and Peace*, 2 v., New York: Harper & Brothers, 1927.

Baker, Ray Stannard. *Woodrow Wilson: Life and Letters.* 8 v., Garden City: Doubleday, Page, and Doubleday, Doran, 1927-1939.

Cambon, Henri (ed.). *Paul Cambon, Correspondance, 1870-1924.* 3 v., Paris: Editions Bernard Grasset, 1940-1946.

Cronon, E. David (ed.). *The Cabinet Diaries of Josephus Daniels, 1913-1921.* Lincoln: University of Nebraska Press, 1963.

Görlitz, Walter (ed.). *Regierte der Kaiser? Kriegstagebücher, Aufzeichnungen und Briefe des Chefs des Marine-Kabinetts Admiral Georg Alexander von Müller, 1914-1918.* Göttingen: Musterschmidt Verlag, 1959.

Gwynn, Stephen (ed.). *The Letters and Friendships of Sir Cecil Spring Rice.* 2 v., London: Constable, 1929.

Hanssen, Hans Peter. *Diary of a Dying Empire,* translated by Oscar O. Winther. Bloomington, Ind.: Indiana University Press, 1955.

Hendrick, Burton J. *The Life and Letters of Walter H. Page.* 3 v., Garden City: Doubleday, Page, 1924-1926.

Lane, Anne W., and Louise H. Wall (eds.). *The Letters of Franklin K. Lane.* Boston: Houghton Mifflin, 1922.

Lennox, Lady Algernon G. (ed.). *The Diary of Lord Bertie of Thame, 1914-1918.* 2 v., London: Hodder and Stoughton, 1924.

Morison, Elting E., *et al.* (eds.). *The Letters of Theodore Roosevelt.* 8 v., Cambridge, Mass.: Harvard University Press, 1951-1954.

Porter, Kirk H., and D. B. Johnson (eds.). *National Party Platforms, 1840-1956.* Urbana: University of Illinois Press, 1956.

Seymour, Charles (ed.). *The Intimate Papers of Colonel House.* 4 v., Boston: Houghton Mifflin, 1926-1928.

Tirpitz, Alfred von. *Politische Dokumente von A. von Tirpitiz.* 2 v., Stuttgart and Berlin: Cotta, 1924-1926.

Valentini, Rudolf von. *Kaiser und Kabinettschef,* compiled by Bernard Schwertfeger. Oldenburg i. Oder: Gerhard Stalling, 1931.

MEMOIRS

Addams, Jane. *Peace and Bread in Time of War.* New York: Macmillan, 1922.

Bernstorff, Johann H. von. *My Three Years in America.* New York: Scribner's, 1920.

Bethmann Hollweg, Theobald von. *Considérations sur la Guerre Mondiale.* 2 v., Paris: Charles-Lavauzelle & Cie., 1924.

Gerard, James W. *My Four Years in Germany.* New York: George H. Doran Co., 1917.

Grey, Edward (Viscount Grey of Fallodon). *Twenty-Five Years, 1892-1916.* 2 v., New York: Frederick A. Stokes, 1925.

Hankey, Lord Maurice. *The Supreme Command, 1914-1918.* 2 v., London: George Allen and Unwin, 1961.

Helfferich, Karl. *Der Weltkrieg.* 2 v., Berlin: Ullstein and Co., 1919.

Houston, David F. *Eight Years with Wilson's Cabinet, 1913 to 1920.* 2 v., Garden City: Doubleday, Page, 1926.

Lansing, Robert. *War Memoirs of Robert Lansing.* Indianapolis: Bobbs-Merrill, 1935.

Lloyd George, David. *War Memoirs of David Lloyd George.* 2 v., London: Oldhams Press, n.d.

Tumulty, Joseph P. *Woodrow Wilson As I Know Him.* Garden City: Doubleday, Page, 1921.

Wilson, Edith Bolling. *My Memoir.* Indianapolis: Bobbs-Merrill, 1939.

MISCELLANEOUS CONTEMPORARY WORKS

American Truth Society. *A Statement issued by the American Truth Society in defense of its President against an unjust attack made upon him by the President of the United States.* New York: American Truth Society, 1916.

Democratic National Committee. New York, 1916:
 Charles "E-vasion" Hughes.
 Children's Emancipation Day.
 "Complete Accord with Roosevelt."

Cornelius A. Hughes Discusses Wilson and Why Colored Men Should Favor His Re-election.

The Democratic Text Book.

How Wilson Has Kept Faith with the Farmer.

Independents Are for Wilson. WHY?

Labor's Charter of Freedom. Labor Legislation Passed by Congress and Approved by President Wilson.

Mexico. Woodrow Wilson Fights for the Just Rights and Liberty of an Oppressed and Helpless People—Against Billions of Money.

President Wilson a True Progressive.

Prosperity Under the Democratic Tariff.

Record of Hughes as an Enemy of Labor.

The Schoolmaster in the White House.

Sixteen Million Voters Appeal for Light!

The So-Called American Truth Society.

Ten Reasons for Voting for Wilson, by Dr. Irving Fisher.

The Whole Truth About the Eight-hour Law.

Why Justice Hughes Should Not Be a Candidate, by Justice Charles E. Hughes, Judge William H. Taft, Concurring.

Wilson and Labor.

Woodrow Wilson and Social Justice.

"Yes" or "No!" Mr. Hughes?

Hazen, David W. *Giants and Ghosts of Central Europe.* Portland, Oregon: Metropolitan Press, 1933.

Kremer, J. Bruce (comp.). *Official Report of the Proceedings of the Democratic National Convention . . . 1916.* n. p., n. d.

Neutral Conference for Continuous Mediation. *President Wilson and the Peace of Europe.* Stockholm: Neutral Conference, 1916.

O'Leary, Jeremiah A. *Why Woodrow Wilson Should Be Defeated and a Republican Congress Elected.* New York: American Truth Society, 1916.

Publicity Bureau for the Exposure of Political Romanism. *Stupendous Issues, The Case Stated and Evidence Presented.* New York: Masonic Hall, 1916.

NEWSPAPERS

AMERICAN

Albany (N.Y.) *Knickerbocker Press*, 1916.

Atlanta Constitution, 1917.

Baltimore *American*, 1917.

Baltimore *Sun*, 1916-1917.

Bismarck Tribune, 1917.

Boston Advertiser, 1917.

Boston *American*, 1917.

Boston Evening Transcript, 1916-1917.
Boston Globe, 1917.
Boston Herald, 1916-1917.
Boston Post, 1916-1917.
Brooklyn Eagle, 1916.
Charleston (S.C.) *News and Courier,* 1917.
Charlotte Daily Observer, 1917.
Chattanooga Daily Times, 1917.
Cheyenne State Leader, 1917.
Chicago Herald, 1916-1917.
Chicago *Illinois Staats-Zeitung,* 1917.
Chicago Tribune, 1917.
Cincinnati *Freie Presse,* 1917.
Cincinnati Volksblatt, 1917.
Cleveland Plain Dealer, 1917.
Cleveland *Waechter und Anzeiger,* 1917.
Columbus *Ohio State Journal,* 1917.
Dallas Morning News, 1917.
Denver *Colorado Herold,* 1917.
Denver Post, 1916-1917.
Des Moines Register, 1916-1917.
Detroit *Abend Post,* 1917.
Detroit Free Press, 1917.
Fargo *Courier-News,* 1917.
Houston Post, 1917.
Indianapolis News, 1916.
Indianapolis Star, 1916-1917.
Johnstown (Pa.) *Democrat,* 1916-1917.
Kansas City Star, 1917.
Lincoln *Nebraska State Journal,* 1917.
Little Rock *Arkansas Gazette,* 1917.
Los Angeles *Germania,* 1917.
Los Angeles Times, 1917.
Louisville *Courier-Journal,* 1917.
Memphis Commercial Appeal, 1917.
Milwaukee *Germania Herold,* 1917.
Milwaukee Sentinel, 1916.
Minneapolis Journal, 1917.
Minneapolis Tribune, 1917.
Montgomery Advertiser, 1917.
Nashville Tennessean, 1917.
New Orleans States, 1916.
New Orleans Times-Picayune, 1917.

New York *American*, 1917.
New York Evening Post, 1916-1917.
New York Herald, 1917.
New Yorker Herold, 1916-1917.
New Yorker Staats-Zeitung, 1916-1917.
New York *Sun*, 1916-1917.
New York Times, 1916-1917.
New York Tribune, 1916-1917.
New York *World*, 1916-1917.
Omaha Bee, 1917.
Philadelphia *Demokrat*, 1917.
Philadelphia Inquirer, 1917.
Philadelphia Public Ledger, 1916-1917.
Philadelphia Record, 1917.
Philadelphia *Tageblatt*, 1917.
Pittsburgh Gazette-Times, 1916-1917.
Pittsburgh *Volksblatt und Freiheitsfreund*, 1916.
Providence Journal, 1917.
Raleigh News and Observer, 1917.
Richmond Times-Dispatch, 1917.
St. Louis *Amerika*, 1917.
St. Louis Globe-Democrat, 1917.
St. Louis Republic, 1916.
St. Louis *Westliche Post*, 1917.
St. Paul Pioneer-Press, 1917.
St. Paul Volkszeitung, 1917.
Salt Lake (City) *Tribune*, 1917.
San Francisco Chronicle, 1917.
Savannah News, 1917.
Seattle Post-Intelligencer, 1917.
Sioux Falls Press, 1917.
Springfield (Mass.) *Republican*, 1916-1917.
Wall Street Journal, 1916.
Washington *Catholic News Bulletin*, 1916.
Washington Post, 1917.

FOREIGN
Berlin *Deutsche Tageszeitung*, 1916-1917.
Berlin *Kreuz-zeitung*, 1916-1917.
Berliner Lokal-Anzeiger, 1916-1917.
Berlin *Taegliche Rundschau*, 1916.
Berliner Tageblatt, 1916-1917.
Berlin *Vorwärts*, 1916-1917.
Berlin *Vossische Zeitung*, 1916-1917.

Berlin *Die Zukunft*, 1917.
Frankfurter Zeitung, 1916-1917.
Kölnische Volkszeitung, 1916-1917.
Kölnische Zeitung, 1916-1917.
London *Daily Mail*, 1916.
London *Daily Express*, 1917.
London *Evening Standard*, 1917.
London *Morning Post*, 1916.
London *Observer*, 1916.
London *Pall Mall Gazette*, 1916.
London *Daily Telegraph*, 1917.
London *Times*, 1916-1917.
London *Westminster Gazette*, 1916-1917.
Manchester Guardian, 1916-1917.
Paris *Echo de Paris*, 1917.
Paris *Figaro*, 1916-1917.
Paris *L'Homme Enchainé*, 1916-1917.
Paris *Journal des Débats*, 1916.
Paris *Le Matin*, 1916.
Paris *Petit Journal*, 1916.
Paris *Petit Parisien*, 1916.
Paris *Le Temps*, 1916-1917.

PERIODICALS

America, 1916.
American Federationist, 1916.
Baptist Standard (Dallas), 1916-1917.
The Christian Advocate (Nashville), 1916-1917.
The Christian Advocate (New York), 1917.
Collier's, 1916.
The Commoner, 1915-1917.
The Congregationalist and Christian World, 1916-1917.
Farmer's Open Forum, 1916.
The Independent, 1916-1917.
La Follette's Magazine, 1916.
Literary Digest, 1916-1917.
The Living Church, 1916.
The *Nation* (London), 1916-1917.
The *Nation* (New York), 1916-1917.
The New Republic, 1916-1917.
The Outlook (London), 1917.
The Outlook (New York), 1916-1917.

The Presbyterian, 1916-1917.
Presbyterian Banner, 1917.
The Public (Chicago), 1916-1917.
The Spectator (London), 1917.
The Standard, A Baptist Newspaper (Chicago), 1916-1917.
The Survey, 1916-1917.

SIGNED CONTEMPORARY ARTICLES

Baker, Ray Stannard, "Wilson," *Collier's*, LVIII (October 7, 1916), 5-6.
Bryan, William J., "President's Message Analyzed," *The Commoner*, xv (December 1915), 1.
Bryan, W. J., "The President's Opportunity," *The Commoner*, xvi (May 1916), 1.
Bryan, W. J., "The President's Peace Note," *The Commoner*, xvii (January 1917), 3.
Clemenceau, Georges, "The Idealism (?) of a President," Paris *L'Homme Enchaîné*, January 25, 1917.
Creel, George, "The Next Four Years, An Interview with the President," *Everybody's Magazine*, xxxvi (February 1917), 137-138.
Croly, Herbert, "The Two Parties in 1916," *New Republic*, viii (October 21, 1916), 286.
Gompers, Samuel, "Freedom Must Not Be Surrendered," *American Federationist*, xxiv (January 1917), 45-46.
Gompers, Samuel, "On Which Side Are You?" *American Federationist*, xxiii (November 1916), 1067-1068.
Hayes, Carlton J. H., "Which? War without a Purpose? Or Armed Neutrality with a Purpose?" *The Survey*, xxxvii (February 10, 1917), 535-538.
La Follette, Robert M., "Another Step toward Industrial Justice," *La Follette's Magazine*, viii (September 1916), 1-2.
La Follette, R. M., "The Armed Ship Bill Meant War," *La Follette's Magazine*, ix (March 1917), 1-4.
Lippmann, Walter, "The Case for Wilson," *New Republic*, viii (October 14, 1916), 263.
Post, Louis F., "A Campaign Talk to Old Friends," *The Public*, xix (October 20 and 27, 1916), 992-994, 1016-1019.
Tarbell, Ida M., "A Talk with the President of the United States," *Collier's*, LVIII (October 28, 1916), 5-6, 40.
White, William Allen, "Who Killed Cock Robin?" *Collier's*, LVIII (December 16, 1916), 5-6, 26-27.

UNSIGNED CONTEMPORARY ARTICLES

"America Speaks," *New Republic*, IX (January 27, 1917), 340-342.

"Bringing the War to Our Doors," *Literary Digest*, LIII (October 21, 1916), 1015-1017.

"Britain's Black List of Firms in America," *Literary Digest*, LIII (July 29, 1916), 235-236.

"The Defense of the Atlantic World," *New Republic*, X (February 17, 1917), 59-61.

"The Democrats as Legislators," *New Republic*, VIII (September 2, 1916), 103-104.

"Efforts of American Pacifists to Avert War," *Literary Digest*, LIV (February 24, 1917), 451-454.

"How Congress Divided," *New Republic*, X (March 24, 1917), 218-219.

"Imminence of War with Germany," *Literary Digest*, LIV (March 10, 1917), 605-607.

"Justification," *New Republic*, X (February 10, 1917), 36-38.

" 'Limited-Liability' War," *Literary Digest*, LIV (March 3, 1917), 538-539.

"Mr. Wilson's Great Utterance," *New Republic*, VII (June 3, 1916), 102-104.

"The New Irish Revolt," *Literary Digest*, LII (May 6, 1916), 1263-1265.

"Peace Without Victory," *New Republic*, IX (December 23, 1916), 201-202.

"The President and the Hyphen," *Literary Digest*, LIII (October 14, 1916), 935.

"President Wilson's Peace-Plan," *Literary Digest*, LII (June 10, 1916), 1683-1685.

"A Presidential 'Straw Vote' of Union Labor," *Literary Digest*, LIII (October 7, 1916), 871-874.

"Promises and Performances," *American Federationist*, XXIII (July 1916), 539-542.

"A 'State of War' with Germany," *Literary Digest*, LIV (March 31, 1917), 881-882.

"The Two Mr. Wilsons," *New Republic*, VIII (September 9, 1916), 129.

"Who Willed American Participation," *New Republic*, X (April 14, 1917), 308-310.

SECONDARY WORKS AND ARTICLES

Birnbaum, Karl E. *Peace Moves and U-Boat Warfare*. Stockholm: Almquist & Wiksell, 1958.

Blum, John M. *Joe Tumulty and the Wilson Era*. Boston: Houghton Mifflin, 1956.

Child, Clifton J. *The German-Americans in Politics, 1914-1917*. Madison: University of Wisconsin Press, 1939.

Churchill, Winston S. *The World Crisis.* 6 v., New York: Scribner's, 1927.

Epstein, Klaus. *Matthias Erzberger and the Dilemma of German Democracy.* Princeton: Princeton University Press, 1959.

Fischer, Fritz. *Griff nach der Weltmacht: Die Kriegszielpolitik des Kaiserlichen Deutschland, 1914-1918.* Düsseldorf: Droste Verlag, 1961.

Garraty, John A. *Henry Cabot Lodge, a Biography.* New York: Alfred A. Knopf, 1953.

Garraty, J. A. *Right-Hand Man: The Life of George W. Perkins.* New York: Harper, 1960.

Gatzke, Hans W. *Germany's Drive to the West.* Baltimore: Johns Hopkins Press, 1950.

Gibson R. H., and M. Prendergast. *The German Submarine War, 1914-1918.* New York: R. R. Smith, 1931.

Harbaugh, William H. *Power and Responsibility, The Life and Times of Theodore Roosevelt.* New York: Farrar, Straus, and Cudahy, 1961.

Heaton, John L. *Cobb of "The World."* New York: Dutton, 1924.

Hoelzle, Erwin, "Das Experiment des Friedens im Ersten Weltkrieg, 1914-1917," *Geschichte in Wissenschaft und Unterricht,* 13th Year (August 1962), 465-522.

La Follette, Belle C. and Fola M. *Robert M. La Follette.* 2 v., New York: Macmillan, 1953.

Link, Arthur S. *President Wilson and His English Critics.* Oxford: Clarendon Press, 1959.

Link, A. S., "President Wilson's Plan to Resign in 1916," *The Princeton University Library Chronicle,* xxiii (Summer 1962), 167-172.

Link, A. S. *Wilson: Confusions and Crises, 1915-1916.* Princeton: Princeton University Press, 1964.

Link, A. S. *Wilson: The New Freedom.* Princeton: Princeton University Press, 1956.

Link, A. S. *Wilson: The Road to the White House.* Princeton: Princeton University Press, 1947.

Link, A. S. *Woodrow Wilson and the Progressive Era.* New York: Harper, 1954 and 1963.

Mamatey, Victor S. *The United States and East Central Europe, 1914-1918.* Princeton: Princeton University Press, 1957.

Mowry, George E. *Theodore Roosevelt and the Progressive Movement.* Madison: University of Wisconsin Press, 1946.

Pusey, Merlo J. *Charles Evans Hughes.* 2 v., New York: Macmillan, 1951.

Spencer, Samuel R., Jr. *Decision for War, 1917.* Rindge, N. H.: R. R. Smith, 1953.

Spindler, Arno. *La Guerre Sous-Marine,* translated by René Jouan. 3 v., Paris: Payot, 1933-1935.

Steglich, Wolfgang. *Bündnissicherung oder Verständigungsfrieden*. Göttingen: Musterschmidt Verlag, 1958.

Tansill, Charles C. *The Purchase of the Danish West Indies*. Baltimore: Johns Hopkins Press, 1932.

The Times. *The History of the Times, the 150th Anniversary and Beyond, 1912-1948*. 2 Parts, London: The Times, 1952.

Tuchman, Barbara. *The Zimmermann Telegram*. New York: Viking, 1958.

Wittke, Carl. *The Irish in America*. Baton Rouge: Louisiana State University Press, 1956.

Wrench, John E. *Geoffrey Dawson and Our Times*. London: Hutchinson, 1955.

Index

Textual material in footnotes is indexed by reference to the page or pages on which the footnote occurs, but without indication that the item appears in a note. Titles, manuscript collections, authors of letters, etc., in footnotes are not indexed when they have merely been cited as references.